MW01275278

Peer Relationships in Cultural Context

This edited volume responds to the absence of a comprehensive consideration of the implications of culture for children's peer relationships. Although research in this field has burgeoned in recent years, cultural issues have often been overlooked. The chapters in this book tap such issues as the impact of social circumstances and cultural values on peer relationships, culturally prescribed socialization patterns and processes, emotional experience and regulation in peer interactions, children's social behaviors, cultural aspects of friendships, and peer influences on social and school adjustment in cultural context. The role of culture and development is particularly emphasized in the chapters. The authors incorporate into their discussions findings from research programs using multiple methodologies, including both qualitative (e.g., interviewing, ethnographic, and observational) and quantitative (e.g., large-scale survey, standardized questionnaire) approaches, based on a wide range of ages (from early childhood to youth) of children in cultures from East to West and from South to North (Asia, South America, the Mid East, Southern Europe, and ethnic groups in the United States).

Xinyin Chen is Professor of Psychology at the University of Western Ontario, Canada. He has received a William T. Grant Scholars Award and several other academic awards. He has published a number of articles in major developmental journals and book chapters concerning culture, children's social behaviors and peer relationships, and parental socialization practices.

Doran C. French is Professor of Psychology and Department Chair at Illinois Wesleyan University. He has published articles and book chapters on various aspects of child and adolescent peer relationships including cross-age interaction, sociometric status, developmental psychopathology, school adjustment, aggression, and friendship.

Barry H. Schneider is Professor of Psychology at the University of Ottawa, Canada. He has received several professional awards, including the Bea Wickett Award for an outstanding contribution to mental health in education, and Fellow status with the Canadian Psychological Association. In addition to his research in Canada, he has worked in Costa Rica, Cuba, France, Hungary, and Italy.

Cambridge Studies in Social and Emotional Development

Recent books in the series:

Conflict in Child and Adolescent Development
Edited by Carolyn Uhlinger Shantz and Willard W. Hartup

Children in Time and Place
Edited by Glen H. Elder, Jr., John Modell, and Ross D. Parke

Disclosure Processes in Children and Adolescents
Edited by Ken J. Rotenberg

Morality in Everyday Life
Edited by Melanie Killen and Daniel Hart

The Company They Keep
Edited by William M. Bukowski, Andrew F. Newcomb, and Willard W. Hartup

Developmental Science
Edited by Robert B. Cairns, Glen H. Elder, and Jane E. Costello

Social Motivation
Edited by Jaana Juvonen and Kathryn R. Wentzel

Emotional Development
By L. Alan Sroufe

Comparisons in Human Development
Edited by Jonathan Tudge, Michael J. Shanahan, and Jaan Valsiner

Development Course and Marital Dysfunction
Edited by Thomas Bradbury

Mothers at Work
By Lois Hoffman and Lise Youngblade

The Development of Romantic Relationships in Adolescence
Edited by Wyndol Furman, B. Bradford Brown, and Candice Feiring

Emotion, Development, and Self-Organization
Edited by Marc D. Lewis and Isabela Granic

Developmental Psychology and Social Change
Edited by David S. Pillemer and Sheldon H. White

Peer Relationships in Cultural Context

Edited by

XINYIN CHEN
University of Western Ontario

DORAN C. FRENCH
Illinois Wesleyan University

BARRY H. SCHNEIDER
University of Ottawa

CAMBRIDGE UNIVERSITY PRESS
Cambridge, New York, Melbourne, Madrid, Cape Town, Singapore, São Paulo

Cambridge University Press
40 West 20th Street, New York, NY 10011-4211, USA

www.cambridge.org
Information on this title: www.cambridge.org/9780521842075

First published 2006

Printed in the United States of America

A catalog record for this publication is available from the British Library.

Library of Congress Cataloging in Publication Data

Peer relationships in cultural context / edited by Xinyin Chen, Doran C. French, Barry H. Schneider.
p. cm. – (Cambridge studies in social and emotional development)
Includes bibliographical references and index.
ISBN-13: 978-0-521-84207-5 (hardback)
ISBN-10: 0-521-84207-7 (hardback)
1. Interpersonal relations in children. 2. Social interaction in children.
3. Culture–Psychological aspects. I. Chen, Xinyin.
II. French, Doran C. III. Schneider, Barry H. IV. Title. V. Series.
BF723.I646P444 2006
302.3′4083 – dc22 2005028729

ISBN-13 978-0-521-84207-5 hardback
ISBN-10 0-521-84207-7 hardback

Contents

Commentary II

Contributors

Ryan Adams
Concordia University
Montreal, Quebec, Canada

Margarita Azmitia
University of California at Santa Cruz
Santa Cruz, California, USA

Seth Bernstein
York University
Downsview, Ontario, Canada

Charlotte Brenk
Free University
Berlin, Germany

Jill Brown
University of Nebraska – Lincoln
Lincoln, Nebraska, USA

William M. Bukowski
Concordia University
Montreal, Quebec, Canada

Noel A. Card
University of Kansas
Lawrence, Kansas, USA

Consuelo Cervino
Universidad de Valencia
Valencia, Spain

Claire Champion
Arizona State University
Tempe, Arizona, USA

Lei Chang
The Chinese University of Hong Kong
Hong Kong, P.R. China

Xinyin Chen
University of Western Ontario
London, Ontario, Canada

Pamela M. Cole
Pennsylvania State University
University Park, Pennsylvania, USA

William A. Corsaro
Indiana University
Bloomington, Indiana, USA

Maria Rosario Tretasco de Guzman
University of Nebraska – Lincoln
Lincoln, Nebraska, USA

Amanda DeSouza
University of Western Ontario
London, Ontario, Canada

Maria del Pilar Soteras de Toro
Universidad de Oriente
Santiago de Cuba, Cuba

Carolyn Pope Edwards
University of Nebraska – Lincoln
Lincoln, Nebraska, USA

Nancy Eisenberg
Arizona State University
Tempe, Arizona, USA

Jo Ann M. Farver
University of Southern California
Los Angeles, California, USA

Doran C. French
Illinois Wesleyan University
Bloomington, Illinois, USA

Marta Fulop
Hungarian Academy of Sciences
Budapest, Hungary

Suzanne Gaskins
Northeastern Illinois University
Chicago, Illinois, USA

Paul P. Goudena
Utrecht University
Utrecht, The Netherlands

Craig H. Hart
Brigham Young University
Provo, Utah, USA

Angela Ittel
Free University
Berlin, Germany

Shenghua Jin
Beijing Normal University
Beijing, P.R. China

Asiye Kumru
Abant Izzet Baysal Universitesi
Bolu, Turkey

Mukta Singh Lama-Tamang
Cornell University
Ithaca, New York, USA

Okhwa Lee
Chungbuk National University
Heungdukku Cheongju City
Chungbuk, Korea

Jeffrey Liew
Arizona State University
Tempe, Arizona, USA

Todd D. Little
University of Kansas
Lawrence, Kansas, USA

David A. Nelson
Brigham Young University
Provo, Utah, USA

Larry J. Nelson
Brigham Young University
Provo, Utah, USA

Sri Untari Pidada
Padjadjaran University
Bandung, Indonesia

Kenneth H. Rubin
University of Maryland
College Park, Maryland, USA

Monica Sandor
Hungarian Academy of Sciences
Budapest, Hungary

Barry H. Schneider
University of Ottawa
Ottawa, Ontario, Canada

Ruth Sharabany
University of Haifa
Haifa, Israel

Joan Stevenson-Hinde
Cambridge University
High St., Madingley
Cambridge, U.K.

Anne Marie Tietjen
Western Washington University
Bellingham, Washington, USA

Maykel Verkuyten
Utrecht University
Utrecht, The Netherlands

Alisha R. Walker
Sacred Heart University
Fairfield, Connecticut
USA

Li Wang
Peking University
Beijing, P.R. China

Niobe Way
New York University
New York, New York, USA

Sharon Woodburn
Universidad Nacional
Heredia, Costa Rica

Yiyuan Xu
University of Hawaii at Manoa
Honolulu, Hawaii, USA

Chongming Yang
Duke University
Durham, North Carolina, USA

Lidong Yu
Jiangsu University of Science and Technology
Zhenjiang, P.R. China

Zengxiu Zhang
East China Normal University
Shanghai, P.R. China

Qing Zhou
Arizona State University
Tempe, Arizona, USA

Introduction

1 Culture and Peer Relationships

Xinyin Chen, Doran C. French, and Barry H. Schneider

Cultural context plays an important role in the development of individual social and behavioral characteristics and peer relationships (e.g., Hinde, 1987). As a result, children in different cultures may engage in different types of social interactions and develop different types of relationships. Moreover, cultural values and beliefs, particularly those pertaining to developmental goals and socialization practices, may affect the function and organization of peer relationships. Specifically, cultural norms and values may serve as a basis for the interpretation of particular behaviors (e.g., aggression, sociability, shyness–inhibition) and for the judgment about the appropriateness of these behaviors. The interpretation and evaluation of social behaviors in turn may have pervasive implications for the processes of peer interactions and the formation of dyadic and group relationships. Finally, the cultural aspects of children's peer experiences are reflected in how they affect developmental pathways and outcomes. For example, the extent to which children's interactions with each other do or do not include responsibility for younger children in a culture (see Gaskins, this volume) may be associated with the later display of nurturance and prosocial behavior.

Despite the importance of cultural context for individual social functioning and peer interactions, the research on peer relationships has traditionally focused on Western, particularly North American, cultures. In the past decade, researchers have expanded their work considerably in non-Western regions of the world (e.g., Brown, Larson, & Saraswathi, 2002). There has been a steady increase in the number of studies focused on peer relationships in different cultures, and the findings have illustrated the variations of child and adolescent peer experiences across cultures. We initiated this volume to bring this work together. In the sections that follow, we discuss some general issues involved in the study of peer relationships in cultural context. We then provide an overview of the sections of this book.

Cultural Involvement in Individual Functioning and Social Relationships: Theoretical Perspectives

Developmental theorists have explored the role of culture in human social and cognitive development from two major perspectives. The first perspective, represented by Bronfenbrenner's ecological theory (1979), focuses on culture as a context or a component of the socioecological environment. Within this contextualist perspective, it is assumed that social interactions and relationships are affected by the beliefs, values, and practices that are typically but often not universally endorsed within a cultural group. Peer relationships may be more directly influenced by these cultural beliefs and values than individual characteristics because peer activities are often based on social norms and norm-related interpersonal perceptions, evaluations, and reactions (Hinde, 1987). Because peer relationships constitute a social setting that exerts immediate and proximal influence on the child, cultural beliefs and values that guide peer activities are likely to be reflected in individual functioning.

In addition to its direct effects, culture may affect peer interactions and individual development through the organization of various social settings, such as community services, school, and day-care arrangements (Tietjen, this volume). Cultural beliefs about socialization goals and practices may guide governments and socialization agents to set up institutions, distribute resources, and coordinate events in the society so that they influence the development of children and adolescents in a systematic and meaningful manner (Super & Harkness, 1986). In many contemporary societies, schools provide children with the primary context for peer involvement because they congregate large numbers of non-kin same-age children under the care of relatively few non-kin adults. The school setting may be a precondition for establishing large same-age peer groups.

One of the cultural dimensions that has been extensively explored is collectivism versus individualism or interdependent versus independent orientations (Hofstede, 1980; Markus & Kitayama, 1991; Triandis, 1990). In individualistic societies, individual needs and characteristics, personal freedom and independence, and self-realization are highly emphasized. People are encouraged to become autonomous, self-reliant, and emotionally detached from their groups and form only loose social associations (e.g., Triandis, 1995). In collectivistic societies, however, the interests of the individual are considered subordinated to those of the collective. The expression of individuals' needs or striving for personal autonomy, especially when it threatens the group functioning, is often viewed as unacceptable (Greenfield & Suzuki, 1998). Cultures with collectivistic values typically emphasize interdependent ties among individuals, group loyalty, limited personal privacy, conformity to collective standards, and respect for authority (Triandis, 1995). These values are of considerable relevance to social interactions and relationships in the peer context.

The broad framework of collectivism versus individualism has been criticized on both theoretical and methodological grounds. Theoretically, there are concerns regarding its oversimplistic categorization of complex cultural systems (e.g., Miller, 2002), as well as the inadequacy of these dimensions to explain the substantial heterogeneity within cultures and massive differences between cultures that are assumed to be collectivist or individualist. Methodologically, there are questions about what the defining features of individualistic and collectivist cultures are and how one can assess them. Many of the problems have arisen from researchers' attempts to use the individualism and collectivism constructs to understand and compare individual personality traits across and within cultures (e.g., Triandis, 1990). This may not be consistent with Hofstede's initial notions of culture at the national level because collectivism and individualism are mainly "sociological" rather than "psychological" constructs (Hofstede, 1994) and are mainly defined by political, social, and economic organizations (e.g., socialist vs. capitalist economic systems) and general ideological orientations. These macro- or context-level organization styles and orientations may not be measured using attitudinal scales at the individual level (see Oyserman, Coon, & Kemmelmeier, 2002). The influence of social and cultural contexts on personal value systems, relationships, and behaviors at the individual level is not straightforward (e.g., Oyserman et al., 2002), and the manner in which societal or group-level cultural orientations are reflected in individual beliefs and behaviors needs rigorous scientific investigation.

Many researchers, nevertheless, continue to rely on the collectivism–individualism value dimension to explain cross-cultural differences in individual attitudes and behaviors. Two reasons may account for this reality. First, there is a paucity of theories that can be employed to explain similarities and differences among various cultural systems, and researchers have necessarily used the theories that are available. Second, the constructs of collectivism and individualism appear to be useful in characterizing some of the main differences between cultures that differ in extreme form on these dimensions (e.g., the United States and many Asian countries). The utility of these constructs, however, appears to break down when one attempts to compare different collectivist (e.g., South Korean and Indonesian) or individualistic (Swedish vs. United States) cultures or to describe cultures that display a clear mix of individualistic and collectivist features.

The second major perspective on cultural influence, represented by the Russian sociocultural and activity theories (Leontiev, 1981; Luria, 1928; Vygotsky, 1978), focuses mainly on the process of the transmission or internalization of cultural values from the interpersonal or social level to intrapersonal or psychological level. According to this perspective, the development of human mental processes is mediated by psychological "tools" (e.g., language, concepts, signs, and symbols) that are products of human culture. During development, children master these tools through internalization of the external signs, along with their cultural meanings, so that they can rely on them to perform various mental processes, such as remembering and recalling (Karpov, 2005). A major mechanism of internalization is collaborative or guided learning in which more experienced peers or adults, as skilled tutors and representatives of the culture, assist the child to understand and solve the task. Peer interactions among same-age children have received relatively little attention, as these are not considered as important for cultural internalization as activities under the guidance or "tutoring" of adults, older siblings, or more knowledgeable peers. Nevertheless, the descriptions of cultural mechanisms and processes in the sociocultural and activities theories, such as the "zone of proximal development," participation in cultural practices, and interpersonal cooperation, are useful for understanding peer interactions, especially with more competent peers who may serve as co-constructivists (e.g., Rogoff, 2003).

Researchers from the sociocultural perspective have typically been interested in uncovering the processes by which activities in a particular cultural setting affect the development of competencies. For example, Luria (1976) explored in the 1930s how cultural change from traditional pastoralism to participation in collective activities and schooling led to cognitive development (e.g., from context-specific reasoning to more abstract thinking) (Cole, 2005). Similar studies have been conducted in recent years in other societies to investigate how participation in different cultural activities affects individual development (e.g., Cole, 1996; Rogoff, 2003).

Theorists and researchers from both the contextualist and sociocultural backgrounds have become increasingly aware of the active role of the child in cultural activities. There is evidence that child disposition, behaviors, and experiences may interact with socialization practices, such as parenting (e.g., Collins et al., 2000; Schafer, 2000). Moreover, children are not passive recipients of cultural influence, but instead, are active participants in adopting and modifying existing conventions and values, and more importantly, in constructing their own norms and cultures in peer interactions (Corsaro & Nelson, 2003; Edwards et al., this volume). The active role of the child in socialization requires that scholars and researchers theorize and investigate the mutual influences among the child, peer relationships, and culture from a contextualized, dynamic, and developmental perspective.

Cultural Imprint on Peer Relationships

Cultural beliefs and values are likely reflected at each level of children's peer relationships, including interactions, friendships, social networks, and acceptance and rejection within the larger peer group. At the *interactional* level, cultural norms and values may affect how sociable or active children are with peers. DeSouza and Chen (2005), for example, recently found that Canadian preschool-age children were more active in participating in peer interactions than their Chinese counterparts. In contrast, Chinese children engaged in more nonsocial behaviors, such as passive solitary and parallel play activities, than Canadian children. The differences found in this study between Chinese and Canadian children on the overall engagement of peer interactions may indicate the different cultural expectations concerning the development of sociability, as this is less valued and encouraged in Chinese culture than in North American cultures (Chen et al., 2000; Liang, 1987; Yang, 1986).

Distinct cultural features may also be found in how children display specific behaviors in initiating and responding to social contact. Consistent with the argument on collectivism–individualism (e.g., Greenfield & Suzuki, 1998; Triandis, 1990), children in European American societies are socialized to behave in assertive, self-directive, and autonomous ways in social interactions. Moreover, within Western individualistic cultures, individuals are often encouraged to follow their interests (self-determination and self-governance; (e.g., Deci & Ryan, 1985; Hodgins, Koestner, & Duncan, 1996) and personally choose whether or not to enter into social relationships and assume the social responsibilities (Greenfield & Suzuki, 1998). Children are expected and encouraged to maintain personal autonomy and freedom during peer interactions (Larson, 1999; Triandis, 1995), and peer interactions are considered important largely as a social context for the achievement of individual competencies (Oyserman et al., 2002).

In many Asian and Latino group-oriented societies, however, peer interactions are characterized by more affiliative and cooperative activities and greater self-control (Chen, 2000; Domino, 1992; Orlick, Zhou, & Partington, 1990), which may indicate cultural endorsement of interpersonal harmony and individual responsibility for the group. As a major socialization goal, children are encouraged to learn skills and behaviors that are conducive to interpersonal cooperation and group functioning (Chen, 2000; Greenfield & Suzuki, 1998). As a result, children in these societies may display relatively lower autonomy and competitiveness and higher mutual sensitivity and compliance in social interactions (Liu et al., in press; Schneider et al., 2005).

Considerable variation across cultures is also seen in the extent to which conflicts are openly expressed and in the preferred methods for addressing interpersonal conflicts (Markus & Lin, 1999). In the United States, conflict is often viewed as inevitable and reflective of ongoing struggles between desires for integration and autonomy (Rothbaum et al., 2000). In many other cultures, conflict is minimized, particularly when it threatens relationships (Markus & Lin, 1999). For example, in Indonesia, individuals are expected to maintain interpersonal harmony and to avoid conflict by staying away from some individuals and refraining from focusing on problematic topics. When conflicts arise, they are often dealt with by disengagement, in contrast to the preference of U.S. children to display assertiveness and negotiation (French, Pidada, Denoma et al., in press).

Cultural values may be reflected in the structural and functional characteristics of friendship and group relationships. French, Bae et al. (in press) found that Korean adolescents tended to form smaller exclusive friendship networks than their counterparts in Indonesia and the United States. Moreover, the friendships of Korean and U.S. college students lasted longer in duration than those of Indonesian students. The results seem to suggest that the Korean culture, with a strong Confucian tradition that emphasizes intensive support and interdependence among friends, may influence the organization of friendships (French, Bae et al., in press).

Cross-cultural differences on the functional roles that children's friendships and peer group networks fulfill have been reported in several studies (e.g., Chen et al., 2004; French Setiono, & Eddy, 1999; French et al., 2003; Tietjen, 1989). For example, whereas the enhancement of self-esteem is regarded as significant among friends in Western cultures, it is not particularly salient in Chinese and Indonesian children (e.g., Chen et al., 2004; French, Pidada, Victor et al., in press). Similarly, whereas group affiliation is viewed in Western cultures as fulfilling individual psychological needs, such as the development of self-identity and enhancement of feelings about self-worth (e.g., Rubin, Bukowski, & Parker, 1998; Sullivan, 1953), some Asian cultures place greater emphasis on socializing members to develop cooperative and compliant behavior with others rather than to stand out as individuals (Chen et al., 2004). Accordingly, "good" friendships and groups are those that encourage socially valued goals and norms, whereas "bad" relationships are those that reinforce and facilitate defiant and irresponsible behaviors. Although good and bad relationships may both provide children with emotional closeness, the emotional functions are valued only when they are directed by, and serve, the "right" social goals (Chen et al., 2004; Luo, 1996).

Instrumental aid is an additional provision of friendships that may be appreciated differently across cultures. According to Smart (1999), friendships in Asian cultures, at least in the Chinese culture, are likely to be instrumental, rather than expressive or emotional. This argument has been recently challenged by Chen et al. (2004). In their cross-cultural studies, Chen et al. (2004) found that, although Chinese children were more likely than Canadian children to appreciate the instrumental value of their friendships, both Chinese and Canadian children reported that companionship and intimate disclosure were more important than instrumental assistance in their friendships. French, Bae et al. (in press) similarly found that, although instrumental aid was more salient among Indonesian than U.S. youth, similar to the findings of Chen et al. (2004), this aspect of friendships was rated as being less important than other provisions of the relationship.

Finally, at the *overall peer acceptance* level, cultural values play a major role in establishing standards for the acceptance and rejection of children with different social and nonsocial profiles. Culture may define appropriate or inappropriate behaviors by providing a frame of reference for the social evaluation of the behaviors (Bornstein, 1995; Chen, 2000; Kleinman, 1988). The social evaluation may, in turn, affect how children interpret and react to each other's behaviors in social interactions and eventually determine whether a child is accepted or rejected by peers. Empirical findings have indicated cultural differences in the acceptance of children who are prototypically assertive–sociable (Chen et al., 2000), aggressive (Casiglia, Lo Coco, & Zapulla, 1998; Krispin, Sternberg, & Lamb, 1992; Tomada & Schneider, 1997), or shy–anxious (Chen, Rubin, & Sun, 1992; Valdivia et al., in press) among their peers. For example, Chen et al. found that, whereas shy–anxious children are likely to be rejected or isolated in Canada, their counterparts in China were accepted by peers and well adjusted to the social environment (e.g., Chen et al., 1992; Chen, Rubin, & Li, 1995). The different experiences of shy–anxious children in peer acceptance in China and Canada may be related to different cultural values on shy, wary, and sensitive behaviors. In Western cultures, shy and sensitive behavior is taken to reflect internal anxiety and fearfulness and a lack of self-confidence in social-evaluative situations (Asendorpf, 1990). Because of the emphasis on assertiveness, expressiveness, and competitiveness, children who display shy behavior are often regarded as socially immature and deviant (Rubin, Burgess, & Coplan, 2002). In traditional Chinese culture, however, shy, sensitive, and restrained behaviors are considered an indication of social accomplishment and maturity; shy children are perceived as well behaved and understanding (Liang, 1987; Yang, 1986). The cultural endorsement may help shy children obtain social approval and support in peer interactions.

Taking a different perspective, in the peer relationship literature (Hymel & Rubin, 1985), peer acceptance is often considered an index of social competence and used as an operational definition of success in social settings. This opens up the possibility of examining various competent and incompetent behaviors within a particular culture by linking them to peer acceptance. This strategy was applied by Eisenberg et al. (this volume) in their attempts to study relations between various aspects of emotional control and peer acceptance. Similarly, French, Pidada, Denoma et al. (in press) examined how disengagement from conflict was associated with social competence for Indonesian but not U.S. children. The approach is consistent with the notion that social competence must be considered in reference to cultural context. According to Ogbu (1995), individuals within a culture typically share assumptions about the attributes and competencies that individuals require to be successful. The assumptions are often developed in relation to the subsistence requirements and thus vary between societies as well as different subgroup members within the society. Within-culture links between individual attributes and peer acceptance indicate how children construe social competence in a specific context from an insider's perspective.

The Regulatory Role of Culturally Organized Peer Relationships in Human Development

According to Sullivan (1953), being accepted by peers and establishing close relationships or "chumships" with peers are intrinsic needs of children during the period of childhood and preadolescence. Although Sullivan emphasizes peer relationships mainly in terms of their functions in the development of a sense of well-being or self-validation, the needs for peer affiliation and belongingness may motivate children to modify their behavior to conform to peer norms. This regulatory function may be facilitated by the social learning processes in children's peer interactions (e.g., Hartup, 1992). In a study of children's group entry behavior, Borja-Alvarez, Zarbatany, and Pepper (1991) found that, whereas the behavior of the entering child affected the group functioning, the attitude of the group (e.g., positive initiation, ignoring, overt rejection) in turn influenced the response styles and entry strategies of the entering child and his or her group entry outcomes.

The regulatory function of peer relationships may depend on specific peer activities (e.g., display of autonomous versus cooperative behaviors), types of relationships (e.g., affective vs. instrumental), and group norms and standards (e.g., encouraging assertiveness vs. social inhibition). Thus, particular patterns of peer interactions and relationships in a culture determine, to a large extent, how they regulate individual behaviors and developmental processes. At a more general level, however, the regulatory function of peer relationships may be affected by such cultural beliefs and values as collectivistic versus individualistic orientations. In societies with a strong individualistic orientation, children are often encouraged to maintain personal identity and autonomy in peer interactions and group activities (e.g., Triandis, 1995). Thus, the self-oriented cultural context may constrain or attenuate the role of peer relationships in regulating individual behaviors. This argument seems to be consistent with the findings from empirical research that, although peer support and communications are associated with self-worth and self-feelings, the effects of peer relationships such as friendships are generally modest on children's social and cognitive performance (e.g., Berndt, 1996; Ladd, Kochenderfer, & Coleman, 1996; Parker & Asher, 1993; Tremblay et al., 1995).

In contrast, peers may exert extensive influence on individual behaviors in collectivistic or group-oriented cultures because of the emphasis on interdependence among individuals, group loyalty, and conformity to group norms (Oyserman et al., 2002; Triandis, 1990). At the same time, children in these cultures may be highly *sensitive* to peers' evaluations and *responsive* to peer group pressure. Thus, it seems reasonable to argue that collectivistic cultural values may reinforce and facilitate the regulatory effect of peer context on children's behaviors and development in various domains (e.g., Chen, Chang, & He, 2003; Azmitia & Cooper, 2004).

The regulation of peer relationships indicates that children may play an active role in socialization and cultural transmission through participating peer group activities. During these activities, children may adopt some components of the existing culture passed on from previous generations, and they may also construct their own cultural norms according to their circumstances (Corsaro & Nelson, 2003; Harris, 1995). Researchers have found substantial between-group variations and within-group homogeneity in social norms that direct group organization. For example, Brown et al. (1993) found that peer groups developed norms consistent with their group identities, such as "jocks," "brains," "populars," "partyers," "nerds," and "burnouts." Similarly, Chen et al. (2003) found that peer groups among Chinese children differed systematically in their academic achievement and prosocial–antisocial dimensions. The peer culture formed on the basis of group activities may have a significant effect, not only on group organization but also on individual attitudes and behaviors, including how they react to other socialization influences, such as parenting attempts (Chen et al., 2005; Lansford et al., 2003; Schwartz et al., 2000).

The production of new peer culture norms and their role in regulating individual behaviors may be particularly evident in social interactions of immigrant children and children of immigrants. Children from immigrant families differ from others in many aspects of social and school adjustment, such as friendship and peer networks (e.g., Azmitia & Cooper, 2004; Way & Pahl, 2001). The experience of diverse cultural values during socialization may be one of the major factors responsible for the differences. Whereas the different, or even conflictual, cultural experiences in the home and the school may lead to confusion, frustration, and distress, mixed cultural backgrounds may also be a resource for the development of social competence. In their interactions with family members and individuals in the school, children with different backgrounds may develop coherent and sophisticated peer cultures that incorporate diverse, and perhaps complementary, values and behavioral norms, such as responsibility, achievement, independent skills, and individual autonomy (Conzen et al., 1992; Fuligi, 1998; Zhou, 1997). The integrated cultural beliefs and values may play a unique role in guiding children's peer interactions, friendship formation, and group organization (e.g., Way & Pahl, 2001). From a different perspective, it is possible that the peer group culture that children from immigrant families form, either among themselves or with peers of different backgrounds, may be a buffering factor that protects these children in their adjustment to the challenging social environment outside the family. From this perspective, it is also possible that, in many societies that are undergoing dramatic social and economic transitions, peer cultures may buffer the stressful experience of children and adolescents.

The Organization of the Book

There are five sections in this book. The focus of the first section is on theoretical and methodological issues in the study of peer relationships. The chapter "Children's Social Behaviors and Peer Interactions in Diverse Cultures" by Edwards et al. presents recent views on cultural involvement in children's peer interactions, with a particular emphasis on the active role of the child through self-guided participation in socialization. This chapter also analyzes the relations among the child's characteristics, peer interactions, and cultural context from a developmental perspective. The chapter "Cultural Influences on Peer

Relations: An Ecological Perspective" by Tietjen focuses on cultural influences from the socioecological perspective. In this chapter, the author indicates that culture may exist at various levels of the socioecological settings beyond the macrosystem and demonstrates how cultural factors at each level may affect children's peer relationships in the United States, Sweden, and the Maisin of Papua New Guinea. The next two chapters, by Card and Little and by Corsaro, address qualitative and quantitative methods in the study of peer relationships in cultural context. The authors demonstrate the usefulness of these methods in cultural and cross-cultural research through their own research programs and at the same time point out issues that are involved in the application of the methods.

In the section "Temperamental and Emotional Influences on Peer Relationships," Chen, Wang, and DeSouza propose a conceptual model concerning how cultural values and two fundamental temperamental dimensions, social initiative and self-control, may interact in affecting socioemotional functioning. Based on the model, the authors discuss the role of culturally directed socialization patterns in the development of shyness–inhibition and different functional meanings of shyness–inhibition in children's peer interactions and relationships in Chinese and North American contexts. In the chapter "Emotional Aspects of Peer Relations Among Children in Rural Nepal," Cole, Walker, and Lama-Tamang argue that cultural values and socioecological circumstances may play an important role in socializing children in emotion expression and regulation and in organizing children's emotions in peer interactions. This argument has been supported by their findings in two culturally distinct Nepali villages concerning the expression of anger and shame and reasons for the display and suppression of the emotions in social situations. The findings are consistent with the model described in the chapter by Eisenberg et al. As indicated by these authors, cultures likely differ in their attitudes toward the experience and expression of emotion, as reflected in cultural display rules, which in turn may affect individual appraisals of emotion-eliciting situations and motivation in these situations. As a result, relations between emotion and emotion regulation and peer competence may vary across cultures. Eisenberg et al. indicate that, despite cultural influences on emotion and temperament, cross-cultural similarities may be observed, especially on the significance of such characteristics as effortful control for peer relationships.

The section "Peers and Parents" focuses on the effect of parenting styles and strategies on children's social behaviors and peer relationships. Nelson, Nelson, Hart, Yang, and Jin review the cross-cultural research on some major parenting styles in the Western literature, such as parental control and warmth and their relations with children's adaptive and maladaptive behaviors. The findings from various programs seem to suggest that these major parenting styles may serve similar functions in the development of social competence in diverse societies. These authors describe how they have explored culturally specific parenting constructs, such as shaming and encouragement of modesty in Chinese parents. From a different perspective, Xu et al., have investigated how parental endorsement of Chinese values, such as filial piety, may be related to children's strategies, including the indigenous Chinese strategy of *ren*, in coping with stress and distress in peer interactions. The results reported in the chapter indicate a coherent system among broad cultural orientations, parental socialization beliefs, and children's behavioral styles. Goudena's chapter further elaborates different pathways in which children are socialized in collectivistic and individualistic contexts. The author believes that different social behaviors in peer interactions and conflict resolution, such as those between Andalusian and Dutch children, are likely the result of differences in cultural encouragement of the "vertical versus horizontal qualities" during parent–child interactions.

Cultural influences on social behaviors in peer interactions are discussed extensively in the section on "Peer Interactions and Social Behaviors." In the chapter "The Cultural Organization of Yucatec Mayan Children's Social Interactions," Gaskins raises several important questions about how to compare children in a peasant culture like the Yucatec Maya with European American children in social development, given the dramatically different social experiences early in life. For example, do different social and cultural conditions prepare children differently for interactions with peers? Are same-age peer interactions important for later social, emotional, and cognitive development in all cultures? If so, how do children living in an environment that does not provide opportunities to interact with peers develop social skills and become competent adults? The findings from her research may constitute a serious challenge to the major peer relation theories in the Western literature. Unlike Gaskins's chapter, which focuses on an intensive analysis of social interactions in a single culture, Schneider et al.'s chapter and Verkuyten's chapter tap two important social behaviors in peer interactions, competition and ethnic peer victimization, from a broader perspective. The authors discuss various issues involved in the constructs, assessments, and practical implications in the study of these behaviors. These discussions may be helpful for us to understand other social behaviors in the peer context, such as prosocial–cooperative behavior, disruptive behavior, dominance versus submissiveness, gossip, and social problem solving.

The final section concerns cultural context and friendship. The four chapters in this section cover the cultural effect on the structural as well as functional aspects of dyadic relationships among friends in childhood and adolescence. Whereas Sharabany argues, based on her findings with Arab and kibbutz children, that some major cultural characteristics such as collectivism may lead to group-level variations in friendship quality such as intimacy, French, Lee, and Pidada demonstrate that dramatic differences in friendship may result from more specific social, historical, and cultural conditions, such as those in the collectivistic societies of Indonesia and South Korea. Similar to French et al., Way emphasizes the role of particular features of the community and cultural traditions in understanding the common as well as unique experiences and practices of friendship among African American, Latin American, and Asian American youth. Azmitia, Ittel, and Brenk further discuss within-community differences among Latin American adolescents on friendship patterns, which may be the result of such situational factors as the generation of immigration, family socioeconomic status, and geographical location. Together, the chapters in this section provide comprehensive views on how different aspects of the social and cultural context are involved in the development of friendship.

There are three commentaries in addition to the chapters. The main purposes of the commentaries are to: (1) integrate the ideas and findings of the chapters to provide some coherent themes in the area, (2) comment on the chapters in terms of major strengths and weaknesses, and (3) provide suggestions for future directions. As indicated earlier, research on peer relationships has expanded rapidly in many different non-Western regions of the world, as reflected in the contributions to the book. It is now common knowledge that children's social functioning and peer relationships cannot be understood accurately and completely without taking into account cultural factors. Our goal in putting together this volume is to provide a forum for systematic and in-depth discussions of the importance of cultural context for peer relationships, research findings, theoretical and methodological issues in the research, and strategies to solve the problems in this area. We hope these discussions will be conducive to further exploration of cultural issues in peer relationships in the future.

References

Asendorpf, J. (1990). Beyond social withdrawal: Shyness, unsociability and peer avoidance. *Human Development, 33*, 250–259.

Azmitia, M., & Cooper, C. R. (2004). Good or bad? Peer influences on Latino and European American adolescents' pathways through school. *Journal of Education for Students Placed at Risk, 6*, 45–71.

Berndt, T. J. (1996). Friendship quality affects adolescents' self esteem and social behavior. In W. M. Bukowski, A. F. Newcomb, & W. W. Hartup (Eds.), *The company they keep: Friendship during childhood and adolescence*. New York: Cambridge University Press.

Borja-Alvarez, T., Zarbatany, L., Pepper, S. (1991). Contributions of male and female guests and hosts to peer group entry. *Child Development, 62*, 1079–1090.

Bornstein, M. H. (1995). Form and function: Implications for studies of culture and human development. *Culture and Psychology, 1*(1), 123–138.

Bronfenbrenner, U. (1979). *The ecology of human development: Experiments by nature and design*. Cambridge, MA: Harvard University Press.

Brown, B. B., Larson, R. W., & Saraswathi, T. S. (2002). *The worlds' youth: Adolescence in eight regions of the globe*. New York: Cambridge University Press.

Brown, B. B., Mounts, N., Lamborn, S., & Steinberg, L. (1993). Parenting practices and peer group affiliation in adolescence. *Child Development, 64*, 467–482.

Casiglia, A. C., Lo Coco, A., & Zappulla, C. (1998). Aspects of social reputation and peer relationships in Italian children: A cross-cultural perspective. *Developmental Psychology, 34*, 723–730.

Chen, X. (2000). Social and emotional development in Chinese children and adolescents: A contextual cross-cultural perspective. In F. Columbus (Ed.), *Advances in psychology research* (Vol. I, pp. 229–251). Huntington, NY: Nova Science Publishers.

Chen, X., Chang, L., & He, Y. (2003). The peer group as a context: Mediating and moderating effects on the relations between academic achievement and social functioning in Chinese children. *Child Development, 74*, 710–727.

Chen, X., Chang, L., He, Y., & Liu, H. (2005). The peer group as a context: Moderating effects on relations between maternal parenting and social and school adjustment in Chinese children. *Child Development, 76*, 417–434.

Chen, X., Kaspar, V., Zhang, Y., Wang. L., & Zheng, S. (2004). Peer relationships among Chinese and North American boys: A cross-cultural perspective. In N. Way & J. Chu (Eds.), *Adolescent boys in context* (pp. 197–218). New York: New York University Press.

Chen, X., Li, D., Li, Z., Li, B., & Liu, M. (2000). Sociable and prosocial dimensions of social competence in Chinese children: Common and unique contributions to social, academic and psychological adjustment. *Developmental Psychology, 36*, 302–314.

Chen, X., Rubin, K. H., & Li, Z. (1995). Social functioning and adjustment in Chinese children: A longitudinal study. *Developmental Psychology, 31*, 531–539.

Chen, X., Rubin, K. H., & Sun, Y. (1992). Social reputation and peer relationships in Chinese and Canadian children: A cross-cultural study. *Child Development, 63*, 1336–1343.

Cole, M. (1996). *Cultural psychology*. Cambridge, MA: Harvard University Press.

Cole, M. (2005). Cultural-historical activity theory in the family of socio-cultural approaches. *International Society for the Study of Behavioural Development Newsletter, 47*, 1–4.

Collins, W. A., Maccoby, E. E., Steinberg, L., Hetherington, E. M., & Bornstein, M. H. (2000). Contemporary research on parenting. *American Psychologist, 55*, 218–232.

Conzen, K. N., Gerber, D. A., Morawska, E., Pozzetta, G. E., & Vecoli, R. J. (1992). The invention of ethnicity: A perspective from the U.S.A. *Journal of American Ethnic History, 11*, 3–41.

Cooley, C. H. (1902). *Human nature and the social order*. New York: Scribner.

Corsaro, W. A., & Nelson, E. (2003). Children's collective activities and peer culture in early literacy in American and Italian preschools. *Sociology of Education, 76*, 209–227.

Deci, E. L., & Ryan, R. M. (1985). The General Causality Orientations Scale: Self-determination in personality. *Journal of Research in Personality, 19*, 109–134.

DeSouza, A., & Chen, X. (2005). *Behavioral inhibition and peer experiences in Chinese and Canadian children*. Unpublished manuscript.

Domino, G. (1992). Cooperation and competition in Chinese and American children. *Journal of Cross-Cultural Psychology, 23*, 456–467.

Edwards, C. P., de Guzman, M. R. T., Brown, J., & Kumru, A. (this volume). Children's social behaviors and peer interactions in diverse cultures. In X. Chen, D. French, & B. Schneider (Eds.), *Peer relationships in cultural context*. New York: Cambridge University Press.

Eisenberg, N., Zhou, Q., Liew, J., Champion, C., & Pidada, S. (this volume). Emotion, emotion-related regulation, and social functioning. In X. Chen, D. French, & B. Schneider (Eds.), *Peer relationships in cultural context*. New York: Cambridge University Press.

French, D. C., Bae, A., Pidada, S., & Lee, O. (in press). Friendships of Indonesian, S. Korean and U. S. College Students. *Personal Relationships*.

French, D. C., Jansen, E. A., Riansari, M., & Setiono, K. (2003). Friendships of Indonesian children: Adjustment of children who differ in friendship presence and similarity between mutual friends. *Social Development, 12*, 605–621.

French, D. C., Pidada, S., Denoma, J., McDonald, K., & Lawton, A. (in press). Reported Peer Conflicts of Children in the United States and Indonesia. *Social Development*.

French, D. C., Pidada, S., Victor, A., & Lee (in press). Friendships of Indonesian and United States youth. *International Journal for Behavioral Development*.

French, D. C., Setiono, K., & Eddy, J. M. (1999). Bootstrapping through the cultural comparison minefield: Childhood social status and friendships in the United States and Indonesia. In W. A. Collins & B. Laursen (Eds.), *Relationships as developmental contexts: Minnesota Symposium of Child Psychology* (Vol. 30, pp. 109–131). Hillsdale, NJ: Lawrence Erlbaum Associates.

Fuligni, A. J. (2001). A comparative longitudinal approach to acculturation among children from immigrant families. *Harvard Educational Review, 71*, 566–578.

Gaskins, S. (this volume). The cultural organization of Yucatec Mayan children's social interactions. In X. Chen, D. French, & B. Schneider (Eds.), *Peer relationships in cultural context*. New York: Cambridge University Press.

Greenfield, P. M., & Suzuki, L. K. (1998). Culture and human development: Implications for parenting, education, pediatrics, and mental health. In W. Damon (Ed.), & I. E. Eigel & K. A. Renninger (Vol. Eds.), *Handbook of Child Psychology* (Vol. 4, Child Psychology in practice, 5th ed., pp. 1059–1109).

Harris, J. R. (1995). Where is the child's environment? A group socialization theory of development. *Psychological Review, 102*, 458–489.

Hartup, W. W. (1992). Social relationships and their developmental significance. *American Psychologist, 44*, 120–126.

Hinde, R. A. (1987). *Individuals, relationships and culture*. Cambridge, England: Cambridge University Press.

Hodgins, H. S., Koestner, R., & Duncan, N. (1996). On the compatibility of autonomy and relatedness. *Personality and Social Psychology Bulletin, 22*, 227–237.

Hofstede, G. (1980). *Culture's consequences: International differences in work-related values*. Beverly Hills, CA: Sage.

Hofstede, G. (1994). Foreward. In U. Kim, H. C. Triandis, C. Kagitcibasi, S. C. Choi, & G. Yoon, *Individualism and collectivism: Theory, method, and applications*. (pp. ix–xiii). Thousand Oaks, CA: Sage.

Hymel, S., & Rubin, K. H. (1985). Children with peer relationship and social skills problems: Conceptual, methodological, and developmental issues. In G. J. Whitehurst (Ed.), *Annals of child development* (Vol. 2, pp. 254–297). Greenwich, CT: JAI Press.

Karpov, Y. V. (2005). Psychological tools, internalization, and mediation: The Neo-Vygotskian elaboration of Vygotsky's notions. *The International Society for the Study of Behavioral Development (ISSBD) Newsletter, 47, 4–7.*

Kleinman, A. (1988). *Rethinking psychiatry: From cultural category to personal experience*. New York: The Free Press.

Krispin, O., Sternberg, K. J., & Lamb, M. E. (1992). The dimensions of peer evaluation in Israel: A cross-cultural perspective. *International Journal of Behavioral Development, 15*, 299–314.

Ladd, G. W., Kochenderfer, B. J., & Coleman, C. C. (1996). Friendship quality as a predictor of young children's early school adjustment. *Child Development, 67*, 1103–1118.

Lansford, J. E., Criss, M. M., Pettit, G. S., Dodge, K. A., & Bates, J. E. (2003). Friendship quality, peer group affiliation, and peer antisocial behavior as moderators of the link between negative parenting and adolescent externalizing behavior. *Journal of Research on Adolescence, 13*, 161–184.

Larson, R. W. (1999). The uses of loneliness in adolescence. In K. J. Rotenberg & S. Hymel (Eds.), *Loneliness in childhood and adolescence* (pp. 244–262). New York: Cambridge University Press.

Leontiev, A. N. (1981). The problem of activity in psychology. In J. V. Wertsch (Ed.), *The concept of activity in Soviet psychology*. Armonk, NY: M. E. Sharpe.

Liang, S. (1987). *The outline of Chinese culture*. Shanghai Teachers' University Press, Shanghai, China: Xue Lin.

Liu, M., Chen, X., Rubin, K. H., Zheng, S., Cui, L., Li, D., Chen, H., et al. (in press). Autonomy- vs. connectedness-oriented parenting behaviors in Chinese and Canadian mothers. *International Journal of Behavioral Development*.

Luo, G. (1996). *Chinese traditional social and moral ideas and rules*. Beijing, China: University of Chinese People Press.

Luria, A. R. (1928). The problem of the cultural development of the child. *Journal of Genetic Psychology, 35*, 493–506.

Luria. A. R. (1976). *Cognitive development*. Cambridge, MA: Harvard University Press.

Markus, H. R., & Kitayama, S. (1991). Culture and the self: Implications for cognition, emotion, and motivation. *Psychological Review, 98*, 224–253.

Markus, H. R., & Lin, L. R.(1999). Conflictways: Cultural diversity in the meanings and practices of conflict. In D. A. Prentice & D. T. Miller (Eds.), *Cultural divides: Understanding and overcoming group conflict* (pp. 302–333). New York: Russell Sage Foundation.

Miller, J. G. (2002). Bring culture to basic psychological theory – Beyond individualism and collectivism: Comment on Oyserman et al. (2002). *Psychological Bulletin, 128*, 97–109.

Ogbu, J. U. (1995). Origins of human competence: A cultural-ecological perspective. In N. R. Goldberger & J. B. Veroff (Eds.), *The culture and psychology reader* (pp. 245–275). New York: New York University Press.

Orlick, T., Zhou, Q. Y., & Partington, J. (1990). Co-operation and conflict within Chinese and Canadian kindergarten settings. *Canadian Journal of Behavioral Science, 22*, 20–25.

Oyserman, D., Coon, H. M., & Kemmelmeier, M. (2002). Rethinking individualism and collectivism: Evaluation of theoretical assumptions and meta-analyses. *Psychological Bulletin, 128*(1), 3–72.

Parker, J. G., & Asher, S. R. (1993). Friendship and friendship quality in middle childhood: Links with peer group acceptance and feelings of loneliness and social dissatisfaction. *Developmental Psychology, 29*, 611–621.

Rogoff, B. (2003). *The cultural nature of human development*. New York: Oxford University Press.

Rothbaum, F., Pott, M., Azuma, H. Miyake, K., & Weisz, J. (2000). The development of close relationships in Japan and the United States. Paths of symbiotic harmony and generative tension. *Child Development, 71*, 1121–1142.

Rubin, K. H., Bukowski, W., & Parker, J. (1998). Peer interactions, relationships, and groups. In W. Damon (Ed.) N. Eisenberg (Vol. Ed.), *Handbook of child psychology: Vol. 3. Social, Emotional, and Personality Development* (5th ed., pp. 619–700). New York: Wiley.

Rubin, K. H., Burgess, K. B., & Coplan, R. J. (2002). Social withdrawal and shyness. In P. K., Smith & C. H. Hart, (Eds.), *Blackwell handbook of childhood social development* (pp. 330–352), Malden, MA: Blackwell.

Schaffer, H. R. (2000). The early experience assumption: Past, present and future. *International Journal of Behavioral Development, 24*, 5–14.

Schneider, B. H., Woodburn, S., Soteras-de Toro, M., & Udvari, S. (2005). Cultural and gender differences in the implications of competition for early adolescent friendship, *Merrill-Palmer Quarterly, 51*, 163–191.

Schwartz, D., Dodge, K. A., Pettit, G. S., & Bates, J. E. (2000). Friendship as a moderating factor in the pathway between early harsh home environment and later victimization in the peer group. *Developmental Psychology, 36*, 646–662.

Smart, A. (1999). Expressions of interest: Friendship and *guanxi* in Chinese societies. In S. Bell & S. Coleman (Eds.), *The anthropology of friendship* (pp. 119–136). Oxford, England: Berg.

Sullivan, H. S. (1953). *The interpersonal theory of psychiatry*. New York: Norton.

Super, C. M., & Harkness, S. (1986). The development niche: A conceptualization at the interface of child and culture. *International Journal of Behavioral Development, 9*, 545–569.

Tietjen, A. M. (1989). The ecology of children's social support networks. In D. Belle (Ed.), *Children's social support networks and social supports* (pp. 37–69). New York: Wiley.

Tietjen, A. M. (this volume). Cultural influences on peer relations: An ecological perspective. In X. Chen, D. French, & B. Schneider (Eds.), *Peer relationships in cultural context*. New York: Cambridge University Press.

Tomada, G., & Schneider, B. H. (1997). Relational aggression, gender, and peer acceptance: Invariance across culture, stability over time, and concordance among informants. *Developmental Psychology, 33*, 601–609.

Tremblay, R., Masse, L. C., Vitaro, F., & Dobkin, P. L. (1995). The impact of friends' deviant behavior on early onset of delinquency: Longitudinal data from 6 to 13 years of age. *Development and Psychopathology, 7*, 649–668.

Triandis, H. C. (1990). Cross-cultural studies of individualism and collectivism. In J. J. Berman, (Ed.), *Nebraska Symposium on Motivation, 1989: Cross-cultural perspectives* (pp. 41–133). Lincoln: University of Nebraska Press.

Triandis, H. C. (1995). *Individualism and collectivism.* Boulder, CO: Westview Press.

Valdivia, I. A., Schneider, B. H., Chavez, K. L., & Chen, X. (in press). Social withdrawal and maladjustment in a very group-oriented society. *International Journal of Behavioral Development.*

Vygotsky, L. S. (1978). M. Cole, V. John-Steiner, S. Scribner, & E. Souberman (Eds.), *Mind in society: The development of higher psychological processes.* Cambridge, MA: Harvard University Press.

Way, N., & Pahl, K. (2001). The predictors of friendship quality among ethnic minority, low-income adolescents. *Journal of Research on Adolescence, 11*, 325–349.

Yang, K. S. (1986). Chinese personality and its change. In M. H. Bond (Ed.), *The psychology of the Chinese people* (pp. 106–170). New York: Oxford University Press.

Zhou, M. (1997). Growing up American: The challenge confronting immigrant children and children of immigrants. *Annual Review of Sociology, 23*, 63–95.

PART I

Culture and Peer Relationships: Theoretical and Methodological Issues

2 Children's Social Behaviors and Peer Interactions in Diverse Cultures

Carolyn Pope Edwards, Maria Rosario Tretasco de Guzman, Jill Brown, and Asiye Kumru

Cultural socialization has long interested behavioral and social scientists, but recent advances in theory and methodology have allowed researchers to construct new and more powerful theoretical frameworks for conceptualizing the complex ways in which children interact with their environments during the course of development. Studies of childhood socialization in the classic tradition of cross-cultural research were static in their approach to analyzing underlying processes because of limitations in the theories and methods available at the time they were conducted. Many studies, for example, involved straightforward associations or comparisons of levels of parental socialization pressure (the antecedent condition) with children's social or cognitive behavior (the consequent condition). In contrast, using new theoretical and methodological tools, researchers today can go beyond testing predictions about how differences in childhood environments may predict group differences in some kind of child characteristic and instead consider dynamic and transactional child–environment relations. For instance, current researchers have employed theoretical frameworks from social–cognitive development, Vygotskian psychology, and cultural psychology to characterize the children and their contexts in reframed ways and to highlight such themes as *self-socialization* and *guided participation* in cultural socialization.

In this chapter, we address the topic of *peer relations in cultural context* to elaborate how classic and recent approaches to research can be brought together to construct a set of guiding principles for thinking about the cultural dimensions of children's socialization by peers. We define peers as nonfamily children who are similar to one another in age and competence level. The discussion allows for a close analysis of children's self-initiated and self-directed behavior within peer relationships and provides ways to understand how participation in activity settings containing peers gradually channels children toward higher levels of expertise with respect to culturally valued skills and competencies. Throughout the chapter, we argue that one of the most important remaining challenges for the field is to find ways to integrate this more sophisticated understanding of self-socialization, activity settings, and guided participation with an equally complex understanding of the role of *biodevelopmental processes* in cultural socialization within the peer context.

To begin with some definitions, *self-socialization* is the process whereby children influence the directions and outcomes of their development through selective observation, imitation, and choosing to engage in particular activities and modalities of interaction that reinforce some rather than other child development outcomes. In many or most cultures, peers relative to adults play ever more prominent roles in socialization as children leave behind early childhood and move into middle childhood and adolescence.

Activity settings are the routine everyday experiences that provide children with opportunities to learn and develop through modeling and interacting with others. They are the instantiation of the ecological and cultural systems surrounding the child and family, and the means by which institutions and prevailing cultural norms make themselves felt in the lives of children and influence their development.

Guided participation can be defined as the process by which children become actively involved in progressively more advanced activities and skills, for example, engaging with peers more competent than themselves who structure their tasks, actions, and experiences, and thereby shape the direction and outcomes of learning and development.

These concepts of self-socialization, activity settings, and guided participation readily lend themselves to a consideration of how cultural socialization may reflect not only purely social processes but also biodevelopmental processes. Scarr and McCartney (1983) have proposed a theory of genotype–environment interaction that can be applied to this kind of analysis. In their theory, there are three types of genotype–environment interactions. As we will discuss, these apply to cultural socialization within peer contexts because opportunities for peer interaction are differentially constituted and available for children across cultures.

The first type of genotype–environment interaction, *passive*, involves children being exposed to socializing environments that reflect both the children's and the parents' genetic predispositions. Parents provide their children with their genes, and at the same time, parents frame child-rearing environments for their offspring that are generally correlated with these genotypes. Children passively receive both. For example, parents who are genetically predisposed to be physically active and coordinated may create childhood environments that encourage athletic interests with peers in whatever way is culturally appropriate (e.g., through contact with the culturally preferred sports and through training and practice in physical skills). Thus, just by being born into a certain type of family, children become passive recipients of socialization experiences that may reinforce their participation in certain directions rather than others with respect to peer interaction.

Second, the *evocative* type of genotype–environment interaction involves children receiving enhanced opportunities for socialization that are influenced by the children's own genotypes, which may evoke or elicit particular patterns of reactions from others. For example, social companions often respond differently (within the frameworks of their cultural values) to physically active, coordinated children than they do to low-active, uncoordinated ones. Most likely, people will engage the active children in high-arousal games of some kind, for example, play with bouts of laughter, tickling, rough and tumble, running, chasing, or throwing – according to the norms of what is age, gender, and culture appropriate. Such reactions to children (and their genetically influenced attributes) by adults and peers are environmental influences that interact to exert modifying influence on children's developmental outcomes.

Third, the *active* type of gene–environment interaction involves children coming to manage and direct aspects of their own learning and development by choosing (from within the choices culturally available) those kinds of companions and activities that are most compatible with their genetic endowments and developing predispositions. For example, as children grow older, they direct selective attention to certain kinds of peer companions in preference to others, and they seek out particular activities with peers that they have found favorable to them and that further enhance their distinguishing characteristics. Athletically inclined children, for instance, may join sports teams, practice and refine skills, and increase their exposure to physical challenge. As children select environmental niches for themselves, they self-socialize, that is, organize their own learning and development in particular ways.

In sum, children, both through genetic order and environment, create individual meaning out of their experiences. Passive and evocative interaction may predominate during infancy and early childhood stages, but active interaction comes on line during middle childhood and adolescence, when individuals gain more and more control of their daily activities, settings, and companions. From the beginning of life, children construct cognitive and emotional sense of the events and people that are the form and content of their guided participation. At the same time, as they grow older, they exert more and more of their own influence on their environments through the choices they make; they accept, resist, or transform their interactions and activities and become co-creators of their socialization and self-socialization. As White (1996) has put it:

> A child lives in a complex ecology of homes, schools, farms, stores, roads, and factories. Part of the growing child's task is to learn how to act in these behavior settings; part of the child's task is to learn how to move among them, selecting some and rejecting others; part of a child's task is to learn how to build them and redesign them. (p. 28)

The full picture of cultural socialization, then, must be understood within this framework of activity settings, complex guided participation, self-socialization, and gene–environment interactions. Culture is implicated in all of children's socialization experiences. Because culture is embedded inside everyday life, normative routines, and patterns of social interaction, cultural influences on socialization cannot be studied as a source of statistical variance separate from social class, ethnicity, or religion. Culture must be identified inside developmental contexts, for example, inside peer relationships, the subject of this volume, rather than being modeled as a source of influence on human development with its own independent pathways.

In this chapter, we seek to move toward such an updated understanding by laying out five significant implications, or guiding principles for research, about children's peer relationships in cultural context, deriving from classic and recent views of cultural socialization. Drawing from our own research studies as well as those by other researchers, we provide examples of empirical findings supporting each of the five principles; in addition, we note where we believe there are important questions and gaps in the literature.

Early Parental Scripts for Children's Peer Relationships

The first principle is that *cultural scripts for socialization in peer relationships are evident in early childhood.* This principle carries a strong line of continuity with the great body of classic research on cultural socialization where cultural differences have been convincingly established in every area, from gender socialization to training for responsibility and aggression (Gardiner & Kosmitzki, 2004; Munroe & Munroe, 1975). We define cultural scripts for socialization as shared childrearing routines that guide a community's behavior toward children, for example, the normative patterns of discipline (for boys and girls, different ages, etc.), formal instruction, task assignment, and moral socialization. LeVine and his colleagues consider these scripts to be part of the "cultural software" of human parental care (LeVine et al., 1994, pp. 18–19). They derive from the traditions and ideologies but shift over time as communities adapt and respond to changing conditions and as the scripts are communicated from generation to generation.

The major point to be made here is that cultural scripts for interaction with young children are evident not only in adult–child but also child–peer relationships. Certainly, cultural differences have been extensively documented in organization and physical/verbal styles of adult caregiving (e.g., Bornstein, 1991; Field et al., 1981; LeVine et al., 1994; Morelli & Tronick, 1992; Munroe & Munroe, 1992; Nugent, Lester, & Brazelton, 1989; Whiting & Edwards, 1988). Cultures vary significantly primarily along two dimensions. The first is *who* provides different elements of nurturance throughout the day (for example, whether fathers, grandparents, older siblings, or nonfamilial child care supplement maternal care), but usually one or a few individuals play the role of significant attachment figures. The second dimension is the *how*, or stylistic mode, in which care and stimulation are provided, for example, whether it is more proximal and kinesthetic or instead more distal and vocal in orientation. However, underlying these variations in interactions with infants are certain commonalities: The vast majority of social interactions with infants and toddlers can be coded as nurturance or sociability (Whiting & Edwards, 1988).

Likewise, because young children have limited social competence, their social interaction with peers necessarily follows simple scripts, such as watching, physical play, simple play with objects, and beginning constructive and symbolic play. Observational data from the Six Culture study suggest that physical practice play and simple play with objects are culturally universal, but that specific norms and cultural opportunities predict the degree to which symbolic and constructive play with peers are encouraged, depending on whether adults consider play to be a good use of children's time or just an annoyance, whether adults prefer to preserve conservative tradition or instead encourage innovation, and whether the environment provides easy access to models and materials for creative and constructive play (Edwards, 2000).

Cultural communities vary significantly along one dimension of early peer relationships: *age of access*. Three societal-level factors influence children's opportunities for interaction with peers, defined as nonfamily age-mates: (1) settlement pattern (the density and clustering of families in space), (2) reproductive strategies (number and spacing of children), and (3) educational goals and institutions (affecting age at which children first attend school or preschool). In places where children have more autonomy to explore the neighborhood or where communal play areas or preschool bring together large groups of children, young children have more and earlier contact with peers and more opportunity to divide themselves into sex- and age-segregated play groups. Thus, in most of the world's (traditional) communities until recent times, infants have only rare or occasional interaction with nonfamily peers. Toddlers likewise have little peer experience and make most contact with peers as a result of their mothers' patterns of movement and sociability. They receive most opportunity to observe and make contact with peers when they live in settlements with a greater density of people and where women have more freedom of movement (for shopping, visiting, etc.). Children aged four or five years are the first age-grade to have independent access to their entire house and yard or homestead area, and cultural differences in children's autonomy and access to peer relations become more salient. In communities with clustered housing and public areas, young children typically have greater opportunity for peer interaction.

As children gain access to activity settings outside the family, they become subject for the first time to cultural scripts about appropriate interaction with peers. Observational evidence suggests that children similar to the self (in size, age, and gender) elicit a high proportion of both affiliation (sociability) and conflict and challenge behavior (Edwards, 1992; Whiting & Edwards, 1988). In a twelve-culture comparison, girls aged two to twelve, in all but one community, most frequently engaged in sociability (defined as behavior – such as chatting, greeting, singing together – whose judged intent is friendly interaction) with same-sex peers. The behavior that ranked second varied by cultural community: Nurturance was most frequent in the three communities where girls were most involved in child-caretaking, whereas miscellaneous aggression or dominance was more frequent in the others. For boys, sociability ranked first in four of the communities, whereas various forms of testing behavior (egoistic dominance, rough and tumble play, or miscellaneous aggression) ranked first in the others. For boys in particular, peer interaction was characterized by frequent tussling, social comparison, and jockeying for dominance, sometimes in the context of competitive games, sometimes not. Boys' peer interaction was especially high in a set of behaviors called "challenging." This included verbal challenges (insulting, threatening, boasting, taunting, warning, comparing the self, and inciting to competition) and physical challenges (all sorts of physical testing and rough and tumble play). True assaulting (attempts to physically hurt another) was rare. Constant moments of comparison and challenge seemed to arise in peer interaction because of the children's relative equality in size, strength, and verbal ability. Peers have similar cognitive and social agendas that make competition and comparison particularly interesting and motivating to all concerned. In sum, peer relations provide opportunities for learning about the self (the gendered self) through reciprocal interaction and social testing and comparison.

Community goals about when and where children should interact in organized settings create the major source of cross-cultural contrast in the scripts for children's early peer relations. Rogoff (2003) notes that the growth of emphasis in many societies on age-graded institutions has created conditions in which associations with similar-age people have taken precedence over intergenerational family and community relations. Whereas in the past, primary schools were the institutions that usually first introduced children to the age-graded society of peers, today the growth of preprimary care and education are creating a further massive shift in children's expected age of access to peer relationships (Edwards, Gandini, & Giovannini, 1996; Tobin, Wu, & Davidson, 1989).

Preprimary settings (preschools, child care) have certain common features (hired teachers or caregivers, child-oriented environments, toys and play resources). However, parents come to them with ideas about what they want their children to gain from their preschool experience. These ideas are studied as examples of parental ethnotheories, or cultural belief systems (Harkness & Super, 1996).

Hess and colleagues initiated a productive line of research on parents' and teachers' belief systems about young children's development (Hess et al., 1980; Hess et al., 1981). They developed an instrument that compares parents or teachers in terms of their developmental timetables: how early they expect young children to master skills of emotional maturity (such as not crying easily) and independence (such as taking care of one's clothes and doing regular household chores). Three comparative studies, using the same methodology, have shown that mothers in certain groups expect early mastery of verbal assertiveness and social skills with peers, whereas mothers in other groups look equally (or more) toward development of competencies for family harmony and group cohesion. For instance, in the original study by Hess and colleagues (1980), Japanese mothers from Tokyo and Sapporo, relative to American mothers from the San Francisco Bay area, showed earlier expectations for emotional self-control, compliance with adult authority, and courtesy in interaction with adults. The San Francisco Bay mothers, in contrast, had earlier expectations for social skills with peers (e.g., showing sympathy, taking initiative, negotiating, standing up for their rights) and verbal skills (seeking information, stating own needs, explaining ideas) – all clearly related to getting along and getting ahead with peers and teachers at preschool. Goodnow et al. (1984) used 32 items of the same instrument with 81 native-born (Anglo) and Lebanese-immigrant mothers from Sydney, Australia. The Anglo Australian mothers had significantly earlier expectations than the Lebanese immigrants, and the domains of sharpest difference related to the social skills with peers and verbal assertiveness. Finally, Edwards et al. (1996) used the instrument to study parents and teachers of preschool children in two small cities in the United States and Italy that have extensive early childhood programs. The Amherst, Massachusetts (United States), mothers showed significantly earlier expectations than did the Pistoia, Tuscany (Italy) mothers on most items. The Pistoia, Italy, mothers actually had quite early expectations for social skills with peers and verbal assertiveness; their mean scores were comparable with the San Francisco Bay and Anglo Australian samples. But the Amherst, Massachusetts, sample was simply even farther out on these dimensions and had the earliest social and verbal expectations of any group tested so far.

Besides their developmental timetables, parents have many other cultural beliefs about young children's peer relationships that relate to the types of child care and preschool they favor. For example, a study of parents of preschool and child care children in four communities found strong group differences in parental descriptions of their own child's early friendships and in their ethnotheories about the importance of young children developing intimate and long-term ties with peer friends (Aukrust et al., 2003). Oslo (Norway) parents favored the value of close, long-term (multiyear) continuity with peers and teachers. Lincoln, Nebraska (United States), parents had a more academic than relational focus on school and wanted their children to deal successfully with (new) teachers and children from year to year. Ankara (Turkey) parents (an upwardly mobile sample) were low in reporting their child's friendships at preschool but valued parent–teacher and child–child relationships there. Seoul (Korea) parents were oriented to education as a means to economic success and favored their children having quality learning experiences while getting along in a large classroom peer group. They rated the importance of their child developing an attachment to the teacher as low.

In sum, beginning in early childhood, cultural differences are already emerging in caregivers' conceptions and expectations for children's peer relationships. These cultural differences are also reflected in children's experiences – both in availability of companions and access to peer contexts. Likely, there are also differences in the nature of peer interactions (Tietjen, 1989) as the contexts in which early peer contact occur also differ; for instance, whether they occur in nonorganized peer play without adult supervision or in structured preschool or child care settings where trained adults are readily present to guide children's play and help mediate disputes. Although the role of self-socialization might not be as important in early peer relationships as in later childhood and adolescence (as discussed previously), nonetheless, cultural scripts for peer socialization are already evident during early childhood.

Children's Increasingly Active Role in the Socialization Process

The second principle about peer relationships in cultural context is that *both across and within cultural communities, children's active role in the socialization process becomes increasingly evident as they grow older*. Children's own characteristics, based on their gender, age, and unique characteristics such as their temperaments, personalities, and interests, become ever more important in determining their behavior, response patterns, and choices of preferred playmates, settings, and activities. Children are active protagonists in their own development in ways that become ever more influential as their personal characteristics become more elaborated and their scope of control increases. This principle is based directly on the theory about gene–environment effects, which states that active and evocative forms of gene–environment interactions become more prominent as children grow older, whereas the passive form becomes secondary. The very environments in which children participate are both influenced by and reflective of their genetic predispositions; indeed, children become actively more able to choose their contexts and manage their experiences.

Studies examining how children become engaged in their own activities show how children play an agentic role in their own socialization experiences. For instance, Tudge and Hogan (2005) have developed an observational methodology that includes recording not only the types of activities children engage in, but also the extent to which they are engaged, *how* they became involved, and their role in initiating others' participation. They provide empirical data suggesting that children are active agents in their participation in various contexts and activities and are by no means passively experiencing settings and events structured and chosen by adult figures. Children are indeed able to choose to participate in various activities, initiate new ones, and encourage the participation of others, including adult caregivers (Tudge et al., 2000; Tudge et al., 1999). Moreover, active engagement in activities appears to be related to perceived competence over the years and varies within cultures along the lines of social class.

This ability to engage in one's own choices and to play an active role in one's experiences also increases with age. As such, children's own preferences and individual proclivities in peer interaction become more evident. This is reflected in the increasing variability in children's choice of companions. For instance, in studies of U.S. children, where most of this research has been conducted, friendships evolve dramatically between early and middle childhood (Rubin, Bukowski, & Parker, 1998), likely reflecting both societal experiences at those ages, as well as developmental changes that they are undergoing.

Older children spend more time with peers (Feiring & Lewis, 1989) and attribute more importance to peer relationships than do younger children (Berndt & Hoyle, 1985; Buhrmester & Furman, 1987; Pitcher & Schultz, 1983). Older children's friendships also tend to be more stable (Berndt & Hoyle, 1985), and, at least for girls, more intimate (Buhrmester & Furman, 1987). Lastly, children's conceptions of friendship evolve to focus on more affective, motivational, and prosocial intentions and less on external characteristics (Furman & Bierman, 1983). Thus, with age, children's friendships become more delineated and stable, and conceptions of friendship become more sophisticated.

With age, children are more able to choose with whom to interact and, as such, children's own preferences become emergent. One of the most substantiated and cross-culturally robust patterns in peer relationships is the tendency to spend time with same-gender companions (e.g., Belle, 1989; Feiring & Lewis, 1987; Pitcher & Schultz, 1983). In fact, researchers have found the same-gender friendship pattern in studies using several methodologies, including observations of children's interactions (e.g., Boyatzis, Mallis, & Leon, 1999; Harkness & Super, 1985; La Freniere, Strayer, & Gauthier, 1984; Whiting & Edwards, 1988), nominations of friends (e.g., Graham et al., 1998), and sociometric ratings of peers (Lockheed, 1986). Children as young as 33 months display the same-gender friendship pattern (Jacklin & Maccoby, 1978). This pattern appears to increase in intensity with age until middle childhood (Belle, 1989; Benenson, Apostoleris, & Parnass, 1998; Maccoby, 1988, 1990).

Although children show same-gender preference across cultures, it is likely that contextual factors affect these patterns. For example, children in different communities develop preferences for same-gender peers at different ages (de Guzman et al., 2004). In forming this preference, availability of companions is clearly important. Harkness and Super (1985) found that same-gender friendship preferences among children in Kokwet, Kenya, emerged later than in the United States. The relatively late emergence of same-gender friendship preference in Kokwet coincided with parental and social expectations at that age, including the greater freedom that older children experienced as they moved around the neighborhood either to socialize or to do assigned chores, such as running errands, gathering wood and water, and herding. As such, gender segregation emerged when children had greater autonomy to seek out their own companions.

The ways by which children spend their time around the world and the contexts in which they choose to participate are also reflective of these evolving capabilities of children to become agents of their own socialization. Older children have a greater array of settings that they can frequent and a steadily broadening social network with whom to interact. Consequently, children's time use and activities show greater variability with age – both across and within cultures (Larson & Verma, 1999). There is increased variability in the relative amounts of time spent with family and peers and engagement in structured and unstructured activities, as well as in other various types of endeavors. Certainly, cultural scripts limit children's choices. For example, there are large differences in the amounts of unstructured leisure time allowed to children and adolescents, depending on whether they live in East Asian or Western postindustrial societies (Larson & Verma, 1999). Children in different cultural communities also have different amounts of freedom to leave their house and yard for the wider neighborhood (Whiting & Edwards, 1988). However, children work within the allowable constraints to put their own individual imprint on the quality and quantity of their peer interaction (de Guzman, Edwards, & Carlo, 2005).

Children, therefore, become increasingly active in their own socialization with respect to peer relationships. Although the nature and frequency of their interactions are somewhat limited and shaped by the sociocultural milieu in which they live, as well as availability of companions and contexts with and in which they can participate, children have increasing capabilities to pick and choose their interactions. With age, their choices become more apparent, and variability in individual preferences becomes emergent; their active role in their own socialization thus becomes even more evident with age.

Socialization Process

The third principle is that *because children are active agents in their own socialization, they can not only make choices but can also negotiate, deflect, and resist socializing attempts by others*. Traditionally, child compliance has been a central focus of developmental research because compliance to parental requests and demands is considered such a good indicator of socioemotional competence and the development of conscience, whereas noncompliance is seen as evidence of immaturity or behavioral disorder (Abe & Izard, 1999). However, noncompliant behavior may not necessarily reflect immaturity or disordered behavior. It can also indicate resistance to socialization pressure and evidence of children thinking for themselves and participating actively (perhaps unpredictably) in the socialization process.

In the Children of Different Worlds study, children's "total compliance" (immediate or delayed) to mothers' prosocial commands and reprimands was examined for children aged three to ten years in twelve cultural communities.

Even in those communities where mothers strongly valued child cooperation and obedience, total compliance rates were only 67 and 58 percent across sex and age groups – meaning that one-third or more of mothers' commands were not obeyed (Whiting & Edwards, 1988, p. 151). In our recent re-analysis of the Ngecha, Kenya, observational data on children aged two to ten years (Whiting, 2004b), children's responses to mothers' prosocial demands were closely examined (de Guzman et al., 2003). Prosocial task demands included tending to younger siblings and infants, performing household chores, garden and animal labor, and the like. We found that, although there was a high incidence of immediate compliance (80 percent) to mothers' demands, children also showed noncompliance (9 percent), and often negotiated with their mothers rather than simply complying (11 percent). Further, children's rates of compliance differed somewhat, depending on the type of task – with the highest rate of compliance to baby-tending demands, followed by various household chores and labor demands. The lowest rate of compliance was to demands with regard to self-care and propriety (e.g., to act appropriately). These findings suggest that Ngecha children complied most readily to commands that seem really important to them – concerning welfare of other children – and most slowly to commands about hygiene and proper behavior.

An even more striking example of children's systematic resistance to socialization pressure can be seen in Munroe's (2004) findings on sex-role choices among children aged three to nine years in four cultures (Logoli of Kenya, Newars of Nepal, Black Carib of Belize, and American Samoans). The first two of these cultures are structured patricentrically, with virilocal residence patterns, patrilineal descent systems, initiation rites for boys but not girls, and lower frequency of child labor for boys than for girls. The latter two are not structured patricentrically. As an initial hypothesis, Munroe had predicted that because of salient gender differentiation at the societal level, the Logoli and Newar children would be more sex-differentiated than the Black Carib and Samoan children on two structured tasks: (1) choosing same-sex *kinship roles* (when asked, for instance, whether they would prefer to be a mother or father, son or daughter); and (2) choosing same-sex *tasks* (when asked, for instance, if they would rather herd cows or wash clothes, chop firewood or carry water). The tasks included for each group of children were established according to the results of interviews with community adults about what tasks were masculine and feminine, and Munroe expected that children's behavior would reflect, or mirror, adult culture. However, to his surprise, Munroe found that the results were opposite to the predicted outcomes in thirty-one of thirty-two instances. Children in the more differentiated cultural settings were significantly *less* sex-differentiated on both kinds of tasks at all four ages. These perplexing findings in a large-scale and rigorously conducted study cannot be interpreted without discussing the ways that children in gender-differentiated societies use fantasy to try out opposite-gender roles, or how children in less-gender-differentiated societies maintain appropriate self-definitions by selecting same-gender choices. Whatever the correct explanation, clearly, the children were not passively internalizing the surrounding culture and unthinkingly accepting cultural norms but instead responding to the experimenter's tasks as an opportunity to "think aloud" about gender socialization in their communities.

Children's Active Role in their Long-Term Developmental Outcomes

The fourth principle is that *children's choices and preferences (self-socialization) during middle childhood have measurable and lasting effects on their developmental outcomes during adolescence*. Less evidence exists to establish this principle than any of the others, and little of this evidence comes from non-Western cultures, but some tentative findings can be brought forward. The major point is that, as children enter the school years, they increasingly try to control and plan their lives so that they can acquire particular skills and competencies, cultivate particular forms of knowledge and expertise, and gain selected material possessions and resources. Middle childhood forecasts adolescence, and children look ahead to the teenage years and construct their own systems of meaning about what resources and opportunities will be available to them in the next few years, as well as what kinds of behaviors and demeanors they may want to learn, practice, and avoid, not only for now, but also for the long term.

Middle childhood is a period that is important in itself because of the significant developments in cognitive, neurological, physical, and socioemotional domains that occur at this age. It is also an important time because, in many ways, it serves as a transitional period between childhood and adolescence – a time in which children gain the necessary skills and competencies to compete as productive members of their society later on. In many places around the world, formal schooling begins at middle childhood, and there are dramatic changes in the expectations for children and the social experiences that are available to them (Sameroff & Haith, 1996). Worldwide, children receive an increased number of assigned tasks, chores, and responsibilities (Weisner, 1996), likely reflecting both their increasing capabilities as well as higher societal expectations that come with age. However, these patterns are somewhat different for children in preindustrialized and postindustrialized societies – with children from the latter spending less time doing chores at the onset of formal schooling (Larson & Verma, 1999). Altogether, the skills and competencies gained and learned during middle childhood become important building blocks for further training during adolescence and beyond.

Evidence suggests that children display increasingly differentiated skills during this time – again in ways consistent with future societal expectations. Children's skills and competencies differ both across and within countries, such as between boys and girls. For instance, Maynard's (2004) study on Zinacantec Mayan children showed that skills become differentiated and more specialized along the lines of future gender roles. With age, both boys and girls increasingly performed gender-stereotyped tasks, though girls performed more gender-stereotyped tasks at an earlier age. Maynard (2004) proposed that older siblings played an integral role both in the acquisition of gender-stereotyped skills and the disjunction in the age at which they appear. In particular, older siblings provided both younger sisters and brothers with opportunities to participate in feminine tasks. Younger brothers were not necessarily exposed to masculine tasks and instead learned masculine roles through play (e.g., playing soccer). Taken together, this suggests that, at the later stages of childhood, social expectations and future social roles become increasingly reflected in children's experiences, choice of activities, and training – a sort of specialization of skills toward those that are expected for each individual's future social roles.

At the same time that children gain practical skills and competencies, they consider peer relationships to be extremely important to the pleasure and interest they find in everyday activities, including school, play, and work. Adolescence is a time in which peer relations and friendships become linked to identity development (Howes & Aikins, 2002) as teenagers move slowly from reliance and interdependence on family and test the limits of their autonomy in the context of their peer relations. Middle childhood is the time of transition to the adolescent focus on peer relationships, during which they are eager to learn the rules and roles associated with success in the peer world (Feiring & Lewis, 1991). During middle childhood, they have greater access than before to choose and create the peer contexts in which to forge their social identity. Studies (conducted in Western societies) suggest age-related patterns in children's peer relations; middle childhood marks the time when many patterns such as gender segregation become evident (Maccoby, 1998). Middle childhood is also the time at which "true" friendships and peer groups emerge – with friendships and cliques becoming clearly defined and stable relative to the more transient and superficial friendships at earlier ages. Although parents continue to hold significant roles in children's lives, children also have an increased amount of time spent with peers and decreased amount of time with parents relative to when they were younger (Collins & Russell, 1991).

Within peer relationships, children are able to develop mutual trust and high levels of self-disclosure that will provide critical support during the early adolescent periods for youths who experienced a kind of piling up of changes, such as early maturation, starting to date, and changes in schools. Adolescents, as they mature or change goals or orientations, have some degrees of freedom to actively shift alliances within the network (Emirbayer & Goodwin, 1994; Giordano, Cernkovich, & Holland, 2003). Children cooperatively co-construct their reality in a unique and selective manner through their peer interactions. This unique selection process is more likely to create novel and independent cultural worlds (Corsaro & Eder, 1990). Peer group interactions provide extensive opportunities for children and adolescents to learn from others (Hartup, 1992). They play an increasingly active role in shaping their own identities and social niches across cultures.

Conflict, disagreement, and change are an integral part of the peer relationship dynamics (Degirmencioglu et al., 1998). Children and adolescents also learn a great deal about themselves, their social worth/identity, and the broader cultural world they live in through experiences beyond close friendships. Brown, Mory, and Kinney (1994) reported that crowds play an important channeling role, providing opportunities for interaction with friends or the opposite sex and setting rules for approval or disapproval of particular choices. Crowds create tougher audiences for developing adolescents by putting more weight on the adolescent's apparent social worth/identity and causing feelings of awkwardness and insecurity. Peer relationships thus become an important venue through which children learn social rules surrounding interactions with others, which become increasingly important during adolescence, and these varied social relationships and social contexts leave long-term marks in their normative development (Howes & Aikins, 2002).

It should be noted that peer relationships, or at least the amount of time spent with peers, vary greatly across societies. These differences become more pronounced during early adolescence and middle childhood, when children from industrialized (and non-Asian) societies experience a decline in time spent with family (Larson & Verma, 1999). Thus, just as competency and skill development diverge in important ways during this period to forecast later social roles and expectations, middle childhood is also a time in which social experiences begin to differ dramatically. It is during this time that group differences in social relationships become very pronounced – with girls and boys diverging in their favorite companions, the size of their social networks, their preferred activities with peers, the amount of time they spend with parents

(Collins & Russell, 1991), and the general amount of time they spend with various members of their social networks (Larson & Verma, 1999).

Thus, middle childhood is an important period in many areas of development – including both in the development of skills and varied competencies as well as in learning rules and roles integral to social development. Peer relationships begin to emerge as an integral component of socialization, allowing children to learn the social rules that will likely be of paramount importance as they enter into the world of adolescence.

Social Change as a Source of Stress and Opportunity for Childhood Peers

The fifth and final principle is that *periods of rapid social change create exceptional stresses as well as opportunities for childhood peers.* Large-scale societal transformations must be considered when studying childhood socialization, because such forces as education, technology, family support, division of labor, and exposure to crime and violence have enormous impacts on the quality of children's lives. Pinquart and Silbereisen (2004) have recently noted the lack of research on the impact of social change on individual development. They discuss the lack of specific theories on psychological consequences of either gradual or abrupt social change, but suggest that Bronfenbrenner's ecological paradigm and life-span theories of stress and coping have obvious utility for studying the effects of social change.

When societies undergo large-scale transformations, the implications for the daily life and practices of children and families are remarkable and not predictable in advance (e.g., Weisner, Bradley, & Kilbride, 1997). Coping with social change is an active process, with age variation in individual and social resources and vulnerabilities. Children's own personal and developmental agendas and their meaning systems about new events and experiences must be taken into account when analyzing how children are affected by these societal forces.

Educational anthropologists have provided many studies of differences between formal and informal educational processes and the ways in which schooling changes the lives of children in developing societies. The introduction of schools and preschools into developing societies poses issues and challenges to children, but in general these challenges seem to be ones to which children have readily adapted.

For example, the process of changing values and goals for children is portrayed for Ngecha, a Gikuyu village in Kenya studied during a five-year period of rapid social change, 1968–1973, soon after national independence

(Edwards & Whiting, 2004). Village women in their roles as mothers acted as the mediators of social change for their children by accepting values related to success in a market economy and a national political and educational system. Parents tried hard to find the cash to pay their children's school fees so that all of their children, including daughters, could receive at least a primary and sometimes even a secondary education. For the first time in Kenyan history, the majority of parents sent their children to spend their days outside the family compound and away from the multiage kin groups of playmates. The mothers were thereby sacrificing the valuable assistance of their school-aged children as child nurses and household helpers to give the children access to new kinds of skills. In school, learning symbolic skills was more valued than learning pragmatic skills. The most modernized of the Ngecha mothers were found to have altered their conceptions of what constituted praiseworthy attributes for a "good" child (Whiting, 2004a); they considered the constellation of "clever, inquisitive, confident, brave" more praiseworthy than the traditional Gikuyu values of "respectful, obedient, generous, and good-hearted."

Ngecha school children faced at least four major kinds of changing value systems, and all of them involve peer relationships (Whiting & Edwards, 1988). First, the children had to learn to accept the constant monitoring and evaluation of their behavior – their level of individual academic achievement, leadership, and athletic skill – by nonrelatives (teachers and coaches) in the presence of peers. Even in the Ngecha Nursery School, individuals received attention for coming to the front of 60 or more classmates to recite a story (Whiting et al., 2004). Second, school children had to learn to manage competition within a large peer group of children who were not kin-related, who had not been their constant companions since early childhood, and whose relative age was not their most striking ordering characteristic. Both schools and nucleated settlements provided more interaction with peers, and children in these communities scored relatively lower in nurturance and prosocial responsibility (Whiting & Whiting, 1975). Third, in societies with social classes or mixed ethnic groups, school children had to learn to interact with children whose families had different conventions and lifestyles. When Gikuyu children went off to secondary school and the university with others of mixed language and tribal heritage, they began to develop moral values that were acceptable to the mixed group and oriented toward larger reference groups (Edwards, 1978, 1982, 2004). Finally, school children had to learn new motives for good performance that involved the acceptance of remote goals, such as future income, status, or power, where the reference group for success was not a kinship unit such as extended family, lineage, or clan, but instead where they engaged with others as citizens of mixed ethnicity coming together in a new nation.

The peers they encountered in primary, secondary, and postsecondary settings were the kinds of strangers who acquainted the school children with this larger reference group for future success. Ngecha children in the late 1960s were receiving what amounted to a crash course in individualistic and material values, according to Ciarunji's (2004) comparative analysis of themes in traditional Gikuyu folktales and proverbs and in their primary school reading texts.

Another well-studied type of social change with implications for children's peer relationships involves the immigration experience. Immigrant families often experience abrupt changes in their lives as they move from one country to another and tackle the arduous task adjusting to and thriving in a new and foreign place (McDermott, 2001). In such cases, family members sometimes undergo role change and an increased need for interdependence as parents and children rely on each other to successfully cope with the new pressures they experience. Possibly because of these new challenges and the increased pressures, immigrant children may be at risk for negative developmental outcomes, such as school dropout and risky behaviors. However, the challenges faced by immigrant families can also provide opportunities for growth and skill development, as parents often rely more on their children to contribute to family needs. Children are sometimes called on to participate responsibly in family tasks, care for their siblings, and in some cases, help their parents adjust to the new country – as children are often more readily able to learn the new language and ways in their new home. In fact, research suggests that role flexibility within families and the reliance on extended family members can be an integral component of immigrants' successful survival in their new country (Garcia Coll, Meyer, & Brillon, 2002; Harrison et al., 1990; Julian, McKenry, & McKelvey, 1994; Padilla, 2002). These experiences can provide valuable opportunities for families not only to be closer, but for children to acquire skills and capabilities that will benefit them in the future. This ability of immigrant families to be flexible in their roles has been found to help promote positive outcomes in children (de Guzman & Carlo, 2004).

Although there might be an increased need for members of immigrant families to rely on each other for support during the transitional period, peers can also play a prominent role in the successful adjustment of children to a new society. Children's interactions with peers can serve as adaptive means by which children can adjust to their new community in multiple ways. For example, Long (1997) notes that many studies reveal immigrant children learn language from native-speaking peers. Further, she reflects on her own experience of migrating to Iceland from the United States and suggests that her own seven-year-old child's language learning of Icelandic was supported by peer interactions. Most important was her daughter's motivation to interact with peers and that those interactions occurred in the context of activities that were mutually comprehensible, purposeful, and enjoyable. Time for play was accompanied by material resources, such as games and toys, available as needed to support and extend the play.

In considering the effects of social change, however, it is evident that not all events and experiences represent growth-enhancing opportunities. Indeed, economic and technological transformations may mean that situations that once were positive and conducive to learning may be potentially harmful or even exploitative. To make such evaluations, we need clear definitions of "growth-enhancing" versus "harmful." We would define a growth-enhancing environment as one where children have one of three kinds of opportunities: (1) children acquire knowledge and skills that, from their own and other people's perspectives, will be of long-term use to them; (2) children encounter cognitive challenges of sufficient merit to promote their learning and development; and (3) children's level of peer interaction is sufficiently rich and complex that they can stretch themselves socially and emotionally. In contrast, we would consider an environment to be exploitative or harmful if it does not take into account the developmental needs of the child and denies them opportunities for guided participation to a higher level of social, cognitive, or emotional functioning.

Childhood labor is one important situation that may be either growth-enhancing or harmful, depending on the specific conditions. Youth employment has been extensively studied, at least in Western societies, but outcomes for younger children are less well understood. In their review, Greenberger and Steinberg (1986) concluded that adolescent employment is generally harmful – even part-time youth employment for full-time students – because it interferes with academic learning. Frone (1999), in contrast, looked at the developmental consequences of youth employment and found many positive outcomes in terms of self-esteem, responsibility, and maturity.

However, the outcomes of labor by younger children have received considerably less attention (Hobbs & Cornwell, 1986), perhaps because most psychologists and educators in Western Europe and North America assume that child employment is an exploitative situation. Throughout most of the 1800s, of course, American children were used as cheap labor in textile factories and other manufacturing jobs under conditions that were often extreme, unhealthy, and dangerous. Today, children in many societies still work in industrial, handcraft, and agricultural jobs under harsh conditions for little pay (Kielburger & Major, 2000). In 2000, the International Labor Organization estimated that 186 million children between the ages of five and fourteeen years (roughly one in six) were illegal laborers, mostly in the developing world. Of these, 111 million did hazardous work, such as hard farm labor and mining. Some 8 million were slave laborers, child soldiers, and prostitutes. In the face of data like these, the consensus of psychologists, educators, and child advocates is that childhood is supposed to be a time spent primarily in play ("the work of children"), family time, and schoolwork. A moderate amount of organized work or chores is desirable for teaching prosocial responsibility and time management, as long as it does not unduly restrict time for play and schoolwork.

Anthropological studies, however, have documented the important contribution of children to household economies in traditional communities, without making the assumption that such work is harmful for children (Porter, 1999). Rogoff (2003) argues that excluding children from family labor keeps them from having the experience of pitching in as a member of a productive unit in conjunction with people whose lives they share. In family work, they see the direct products of their work and how their role fits in the overall process. Whiting and Whiting (1971, 1975) and Weisner (1987) argue that observations of children's participation in household and agricultural work and sibling care offer empirical evidence of the development of social skills, including nurturance (offering care), responsibility, and prosocial dominance, which will be useful to children as they grow into maturity and need to manage their own complex households. Greenfield and colleagues (Greenfield, 2004; Greenfield, Maynard, & Childs, 2003) discuss how, through apprenticeship in weaving, children use processes of observation and imitation to acquire an array of cognitive skills that integrate them gradually into the adult society.

A close analysis of the quality of children's daily experiences in traditional, informal family work contexts of sibling care and household work suggests why anthropologists have responded differently to it than to organized child employment. Not only does industrial and agricultural child employment expose children to conditions that are often unhealthy and dangerous, but also it involves them in tasks that are repetitive, dull, confining, and extremely limited socially, particularly with respect to opportunities for child–child interaction.

Bloch and Adler's (1994) observations of children's developing work skills in a Senegalese village suggest a useful way to evaluate whether child labor has growth-enhancing potential. Instead of looking simply at the social and cognitive skills gained through children's apprenticeship, they consider how work is integrated with play. They define work as activity that is assigned, expected, or structured into children's days by adults, in contrast to object play and peer play, which are spontaneous, child-directed, and unstructured by adults. In Senegal, Bloch and Adler (1994) found children "learning to labor" through processes of play they label as "play-work." The concept of play-work became necessary because toddlers' first forays into work were hard to distinguish as either pure work or pure play. For example, they tried to pull out weeds as their parents and siblings gardened, but their attempts were not particularly persistent or successful. They tried to soothe or entertain babies, but whether they did this for fun or to be useful was not always evident. Adults did not criticize their results and allowed the children to role-play work as they picked up skills of handling tools and made an imperceptible transition to real work.

Descriptions of children at work in family contexts reveal how often peer and sibling play is integrated into ongoing work (Whiting & Edwards, 1988). Child nurses in Ngecha, Kenya, were observed playing with their peers while carrying a baby on their back. Herd boys gathered in the fields and incorporated games of dam-building and hunting of insects and small animals into their duties (Edwards, 2000). Likewise, traditional work contexts are often rich in peer and sibling interaction. Weisner (1989) and Edwards and Whiting (1993) have argued that a close analysis of the stream of interaction in rural Kenyan households shows young children are involved in a rich social life that contains a continuous blend of counterposed intentions, including behaviors that can be interpreted as nurturant, sociable, teasing, provocative, dominant, and aggressive. Weisner (1989) speaks of a distinct Abaluyia cultural style that confronts children with cognitive and emotional challenge that guides them to learn culturally valued modes of skillful social interaction and many different techniques of persuasion. Crying and whining may get an adult to intervene, for example, but on those occasions when the adult is not present, the child must learn to fight back, outwit, or better yet, deflect the other child's behavior into playfulness. The young child thereby is stimulated to cognitively discriminate between different kinds of social situations and to develop a rich repertory of behavioral responses.

In conclusion, we argue that it is important to look carefully at children's activity settings and see how much scope they contain for self-paced learning, playful and rich interaction with other children, and initiative or problem solving. Insofar as activity settings are lacking in these possibilities, they become exploitative rather than development-enhancing. In extreme cases of child labor, normal gene–environment interactions are inhibited. Although children may still be receiving messages and socializing responses from others that are influenced by the child's genotype (evocative), children are not choosing socializing settings or self-selecting into environments they find favorable.

The flexibility of moving between the imaginary and the real is absent. Play is divorced from work and schoolwork, which subsequently divorces the child's own environment from his developmental agenda.

Conclusions

In this chapter, we have laid out five principles to guide research on peer relationships in cultural context that reflect both current and earlier bodies of research literature. According to recent views of socialization, children are seen as active agents in their own development – with the degree of their self-socialization constrained by their contexts, available companions and choice of activities, and parental cultural belief systems about child development and child-rearing. The parental ethnotheories surrounding peer relationships are evident from children's earliest infancy and continue to influence the company that children keep, the settings they occupy, and the activities that take up their time throughout middle childhood – a period that forecasts and prepares the child for future social roles. With increasing age, however, children's abilities to self-select become increasingly evident as their own preferences, proclivities, and scope for choice and control become emergent. Furthermore, their abilities to negotiate with socializing agents and even to resist socialization pressure also increase. The increasing importance of self-socialization processes is reflected not only in their noncompliance to adults but also in their interaction and relationships with peers. Clearly, *who*, *how*, and *how much* children interact with different social partners is influenced by the dynamics of individual characteristics and by contextual factors.

Finally, continuing the theme of children as active agents, the chapter concludes by urging the need for more studies to examine peer relationships under current conditions of social change. Research in child development has traditionally been dominated by studies of normative development, and very little is known regarding the role that either abrupt or gradual societal change, with its incumbent stresses and risks, may potentially bring about for child development. Periods of social change can be experienced as difficult and challenging, but they can also bring about promising experiences that provide the child with significant developmental opportunities. Distinctions need to be made, however, regarding which opportunities are harmful and which are enriching.

Although newer models and methods of examining cross-cultural socialization are emerging, many gaps in research continue to exist. The greatest body of literature describes cross-cultural (and within-cultural) differences in children's settings, activities, and companions, and adults' cultural belief systems around child development and child-rearing. However, much less research can be found on the interplay between children and their environments across developmental (and historical) time. We know more about what is done *to* children than about how children interpret and respond to their socializing agents and settings and, in general, how they actively contribute to their own socialization. We need a better understanding of how children's biodevelopmental dispositions, constructed meaning systems, and interests, preferences, and choices relate to their peer interactions and relationships across cultures and how their self-guided participation in peer settings influence their long-term development. For example, although issues of same-gender preference, gender differences, and the like are well documented in U.S. samples, much less is known regarding the extent to which these are also found among non-U.S. children and how important they are to developmental outcomes. Children in all societies seek out particular kinds of companions for play and learning, but how much of what kinds of peer experiences are required for healthy development is still not known. Likewise, the peer issues faced by children around the world as they cross over into adolescence need to be further explored. Among U.S. adolescents, several important issues have been identified with regard to peer relationships, such as the increasing importance of these relationships for identity development. However, it is not clear to what extent these phenomena are unique to North American populations. Moreover, if adolescent experiences differ across societies, and middle childhood forecasts and prepares the individual for that period, then individual, cultural, and contextual influences on preadolescent experiences need to be better understood. Although it is now widely recognized that children actively shape their own experience, researchers still seem to assume that children's behavior passively reflects, or mirrors, adult values and beliefs. They continue to ignore or underestimate children's evident capacities to ignore adults, noncomply, resist, and improvize their own meanings. Indeed, if the older generations in the world's societies are to support and take full advantage of children's immense creative potential to navigate complex and rapidly changing environments, then we all need to learn much more about children's growth, development, and adaptation in the context of the ambiguities, risks, and multiple pathways encountered in contemporary life worldwide.

References

Abe, J. A., & Izard, C. E. (1999). Compliance, noncompliance strategies, and the correlates of compliance in 5-year-old Japanese and American children. *Social Development, 8*(1), 1–20.

Aukrust, V., Edwards, C. P., Kumru, A., Knoche, L., & Kim, M. (2003). Young children's extended relationships in school: Parental ethnotheories in four communities, in Norway, United States, Turkey, and Korea. *International Journal of Behavioral Development, 27*(6), 481–494.

Belle, D. (1989). Gender differences in children's social networks and supports. In D. Belle (Ed.), *Children's social networks and social supports* (pp. 173–188). New York: Wiley.

Benenson, J., Apostoleris, N., & Parnass, J. (1998). The organization of children's same-sex peer relationships. In W. M. Bukowski & A. H. Cillessen (Eds.), *Sociometry then and now: Building on six decades of measuring children's experience with the peer group* (pp. 5–23). San Francisco: Jossey-Bass.

Berndt, T. J., & Hoyle, S. G. (1985). Stability and change in childhood and adolescent friendships. *Developmental Psychology, 21*, 1007–1015.

Bloch, M. N., & Adler, S. M. (1994). African children's play and the emergence of the sexual division of labor. In J. Roopnarine, J. Johnson, & F. Hooper (Eds.), *Children's play in diverse cultures*, (pp. 148–178). Albany: State University of New York Press.

Bornstein, M. H. (Ed.). (1991). *Cultural approaches to parenting*. Hillsdale, NJ: Lawrence Erlbaum Associates.

Boyatzis, C. J., Mallis, M., & Leon, I. (1999). Effects of game type on children's gender-based peer preferences: A naturalistic observational study. *Sex Roles, 40*, 93–105.

Brown, B. B., Mory, M. S., & Kinney, D. (1994). Casting adolescent crowds in a relational perspective: Caricature, channel, and context. In R. Montemayor, G. R. Adams, & T. P. Gullotta, (Eds.), *Personal relationships during adolescence*. (pp.123–167). London: Sage.

Buhrmester, D., & Furman, W. (1987). The development of companionship and intimacy. *Child Development, 58*, 1101–1113.

Ciarunji, C. (2004). The teaching of values old and new. In C. P. Edwards & B. B. Whiting (Eds.), *Ngecha: A Kenyan village in a time of rapid social change* (pp. 153–178). Lincoln: University of Nebraska Press.

Collins, W. A., & Russell, G. (1991). Mother-child and father-child relationships in middle childhood and adolescence: A developmental analysis. *Developmental Review, 11*, 99–136.

Corsaro, W. A., & Eder, D. J. (1990). Children's peer cultures. *Annual Review of Sociology, 16*, 197–220.

Degirmencioglu, S. M., Urberg, K. A., Tolson, J. M., & Richard, P. (1998). Adolescent friendship networks: Continuity and change over the school year. *Merrill-Palmer Quarterly, 44*, 313–337.

de Guzman, M. R. T., Brown, J., Kirkland, T., Edwards, C. P., & Carlo, G. (2003, April). *"Do as you're told": Examining the contexts and consequences of Gikuyu mothers' prosocial demands on their children.* Poster presented at the annual meeting of the Nebraska Symposium on Motivation, Lincoln, NE.

de Guzman, M. R. T., & Carlo, G. (2004). Family, peer, and acculturative correlates of prosocial development among Latino youth in Nebraska. *Great Plains Research, 14*, 182–202.

de Guzman, M. R. T., Carlo, G., Ontai, L. L., Koller, S. H., & Knight, G. P. (2004). Gender and age differences in Brazilian children's friendship nominations and peer sociometric ratings. *Sex Roles, 51*, 217–255.

de Guzman, M. R. T., Edwards, C. P., & Carlo, G. (2005). Prosocial behaviors in context: A study of the Gikuyu children of Ngecha, Kenya. *Journal of Applied Developmental Psychology, 26* (2005), 542–558).

Edwards, C. P. (1978). Social experience and moral judgment in East African young adults. *Journal of Genetic Psychology, 133*, 19–29.

Edwards, C. P. (1982). Moral development in comparative cultural perspective. In D. Wagner & H. W. Stevenson (Eds.), *Cultural perspectives on child development* (pp. 258–279). San Francisco: Freeman.

Edwards, C. P. (1992). Cross-cultural perspectives on family-peer relations. In R. D. Parke & G. W. Ladd (Eds.), *Family-peer relationships: Modes of linkage* (pp. 285–316). Hillsdale, NJ: Lawrence Erlbaum Associates.

Edwards, C. P. (2000). Children's play in cross-cultural perspective: A new look at the Six Culture Study. *Cross Cultural Research, 34*(4), 318–338.

Edwards, C. (2004). The university as gateway to a complex world. In C. P. Edwards & B. B. Whiting (Eds.), *Ngecha: A Kenyan village in a time of rapid social change* (pp. 215–244). Lincoln: University of Nebraska Press.

Edwards, C. P., Gandini, L., & Giovannini, D. (1996). The contrasting developmental expectations of parents and early childhood teachers in two cultural communities. In S. Harkness & C. Super (Eds.), *Parents' cultural belief systems* (pp. 270–288). New York: Guilford.

Edwards, C. P., & Whiting, B. B. (1993). "Mother, older sibling, and me": The overlapping roles of caregivers and companions in the social world of two- to three-year-olds in Ngecha, Kenya. In K. MacDonald (Ed.), *Parent-child play: Descriptions and implications* (pp. 305–328). Albany: State University of New York Press.

Edwards, C. P., & Whiting, B. B. (Eds.) (2004). *Ngecha: A Kenyan village in a time of rapid social change*. Lincoln: University of Nebraska Press.

Emirbayer, M., & Goodwin, J. (1994). Network analysis, culture, and the problem of agency. *American Journal of Sociology, 99*, 1411–1454.

Feiring, C., & Lewis, M. (1987). The child's social network: Sex differences from three to six years. *Sex Roles, 17*, 621–636.

Feiring, C., & Lewis, M. (1989). The social networks of girls and boys from early through middle childhood. In D. Belle (Ed.), *Children's social networks and social supports* (pp. 119–172). New York: Wiley.

Feiring, C., & Lewis, M. (1991). The development of social networks from early to middle childhood: Gender differences and the relation to school competence. *Sex Roles: A Journal of Research, 25*, 237–53.

Field, T. M., Sostek, A. M., Vietze, P., & Leiderman, P. H. (Eds.). (1981). *Culture and early interactions*. Hillsdale, NJ: Lawrence Erlbaum Associates.

Frone, M. R. (1999). Developmental consequences of youth employment. In J. Barling & E. K. Kelloway (Eds.), *Young workers: Varieties of experience*. Washington DC: American Psychological Association.

Furman, W., & Bierman, K. L. (1983). Developmental changes in young children's conceptions of friendship. *Child Development, 54*, 549–556.

Garcia Coll, C. T., Meyer, E. C., & Brillon, L. (2002). Ethnic and minority parenting. In M. H. Bornstein (Ed.), *Handbook of parenting, Vol. 2: Biology and ecology of parenting* (pp. 189–209). Mahwah, NJ: Lawrence Erlbaum Associates.

Gardiner, H. W., & Kosmitzki, C. (2004). *Lives across cultures: Cross-cultural human development*. Boston, MA: Allyn & Bacon.

Giordano, P. C., Cernkovich, S. A., & Holland, D. D. (2003). Changes in friendship relations over the life course: Implications for desistance from crime. *Criminology, 41*, 293–328.

Goodnow, J. J., Cashmore, J., Cotton, S., & Knight, R. (1984). Mothers' developmental timetables in two cultural groups. *International Journal of Psychology, 19*, 193–205.

Graham, J. A., Cohen, R., Zbikowski, S. M., & Secrist, M. E. (1998). A longitudinal investigation of race and sex as factors in children's classroom friendship choices. *Child Study Journal, 28*, 245–27.

Greenberger, E., & Steinberg, L. D. (1986). *When teenagers work: The psychological and social costs of adolescent employment*. New York: Basic Books.

Greenfield, P. M. (2004). *Weaving generations together: Evolving creativity in the Maya of Chiapas*. Santa Fe, NM: SAR Press.

Greenfield, P. M., Maynard, A. E., & Childs, C. P. (2003). Historical change, cultural learning, and cognitive representation in Zinacantec Maya children. *Cognitive Development, 18*, 455–487.

Harkness, S., & Super, C. M. (1985). The cultural context of gender segregation in children's peer groups. *Child Development, 56*, 219–224.

Harkness, S., & Super, C. (Eds.). (1996). *Parents' cultural belief systems* (pp. 270–288). New York: Guilford.

Harrison, A. O., Wilson, M. N., Pine, C. J., Chan, S. Q., & Buriel, R. (1990). Family Ecologies of ethnic minority children. *Child Development, 61*, 347–362.

Hartup, W. W. (1992). Social relationships and their developmental significance. *American Psychologist, 44*, 120–126.

Hess, R. D., Kashiwagi, K., Azuma, H., Price, G. G., & Dickson, W. P. (1980). Maternal expectations for mastery of developmental tasks in Japan and the United States. *International Journal of Psychology, 15*, 259–271.

Hess, R. D., Price, G. G., Dickson, W. P., & Conroy, M. (1981). Different roles for mothers and teachers: Contrasting styles of child care. In S. Kilmer (Ed.), *Advances in early education and day care* (Vol. 2, pp. 1–28). Greenwich, CT: JAI Press.

Hobbs, S., & Cornwell, D. (1986). Child labor: An underdeveloped topic in psychology, *International Journal of Psychology, 21*, 225–234.

Howes, C. & Aikins, J. W. (2002). Peer relations in the transition to adolescence. *Advances in Child Development and Behavior, 29*, 195–230.

Jacklin, C. N., & Maccoby, E. E. (1978). Social behavior at thirty-three months in same-sex and mixed-sex dyads. *Child Development, 49*, 557–569.

Julian, T. W., McKenry, P. C., & McKelvey, M. W. (1994). Cultural variations in parenting: Perceptions of Caucasian, African-American, Hispanic, and Asian-American parents. *Family Relations: Interdisciplinary Journal of Applied Family Studies, 43*, 30–37.

Kielburger, C., & Major, K. (2000). *Free the children: A young man fights against child labor and proves that children can change the world*. New York: Harper Collins.

La Freniere, P., Strayer, F. F., & Gauthier, R. (1984). The emergence of same-sex affiliative preferences among preschool peers: A developmental/ethological perspective. *Child Development, 55*, 1958–1965.

Larson, R., & Verma, S. (1999). How children and adolescents around the world spend time: Work, play, and developmental opportunities. *Psychological Bulletin, 125*, 701–736.

LeVine, R. A., Dixon, S., LeVine, S., Richman, A., Leiderman, P. H., Keefer, C. H., & Brazelton, T. B. (1994). *Child care and culture: Lessons from Africa*. New York: Cambridge University Press.

Lockheed, M. E. (1986). Reshaping the social order: The case of gender segregation. *Sex Roles, 14*, 617–628.

Long, S. (1997). Friends as teachers: The impact of peer interaction on the acquisition of a new language. In E. Gregory (Ed.), *One child, many worlds: Early learning in multicultural communities* (pp. 123–136). New York: Teachers College Press.

Maccoby, E. E. (1988). Gender as a social category. *Developmental Psychology, 24*, 755–765.

Maccoby, E. E. (1990). Gender and relationships. *American Psychologist, 45*, 513–520.

Maccoby, E. E. (1998). *The two sexes: Growing up apart, coming together*. Cambridge, MA: Bellknap Press.

Maynard, A. E. (2004, February). *Baby boys can make tortillas, but men can't: Gender and development in Zinacantec Maya sibling interactions*. Paper session presented at the 33rd Annual Meeting of the Society for Cross Cultural Research, San Jose, CA.

McDermott, D. (2001). Parenting and ethnicity. In M. J. Fine & S. W. Lee (Eds.), *Handbook of diversity in parent education: The changing faces of parenting and parent education*. San Diego, CA: Academic Press.

Morelli, G., & Tronick, E. Z. (1992). Male care among Efe foragers and Lese farmers. In B. S. Hewlett (Ed.), *Father-child relations: Cultural and biosocial contexts* (pp. 231–261). Hawthorne, NY: Aldine de Gruyter.

Munroe, R. L. (2004). Social structure and sex-role choices. *Cross-Cultural Research, 38*(4), 387–406.

Munroe, R. L., & Munroe, R. H. (1975). *Cross-cultural human development*. Prospect Heights, IL: Waveland Press.

Munroe, R. L., & Munroe, R. H. (1992). Fathers in children's environments: A four culture study. In B. S. Hewlett (Ed.), *Father-child relations: Cultural and biosocial contexts* (pp. 213–239). Hawthorne, NY: Aldine de Gruyter.

Nugent, J. K., Lester, B. M., & Brazelton, T. B. (1989). *The cultural context of infancy*. Norwood, NJ: Ablex.

Padilla, Y. C. (2002). The social ecology of child development in the Mexican American population: Current theoretical and empirical perspectives. *Journal of Human Behavior in the Social Environment, 5*, 9–29.

Pinquart, M., & Silbereisen, R. K. (2004). Human development in times of social change: Theoretical considerations and research needs. *International Journal of Behavioral Development, 28*(4), 289–298.

Pitcher, E. G., & Schultz, L. H. (1983). *Boys and girls at play: The development of sex roles*. New York: Bergin & Garvey.

Porter, K. (1999, November 19). An anthropological defense of child labor. *The Chronicle of Higher Education*.

Rogoff, B. (2003). *The cultural nature of human development.* New York: Oxford University Press.

Rubin, K. H., Bukowski, W., & Parker, J. G. (1998). Peer interactions, relationships, and groups. In N. Eisenberg (Vol. Ed.), *Handbook of child psychology: Social and personality development* (Vol. 3, pp. 619–700). New York: Wiley.

Sameroff, A. J., & Haith, M. M. (Eds.). (1996). *The five to seven year shift: The age of reason and responsibility.* Chicago: University of Chicago Press.

Scarr, S., & McCartney, K. (1983). How people make their own environments: A theory of genotype-environment effects. *Child Development, 54*, 424–435.

Tietjen, A. M. (1989). The ecology of children's social support networks. In D. Belle (Ed.), *Children's social networks and social supports* (pp. 37–69). New York: Wiley.

Tobin, J. J., Wu, D. Y. H., & Davidson, D. H. (1989). *Preschool in three cultures: Japan, China, and the United States.* New Haven, CT: Yale University Press.

Tudge, J., Hayes, S., Doucet, F., Odero, D. Kulakova, N., Tammeveski, P., et al. (2000). Parents' participation in cultural practices with their preschoolers. *Psicologia: Teoria e Pesquisa, 16*, 1–10.

Tudge, J. & Hogan, D. (2005). An ecological approach to naturalistic observation. In S. M. Greene & D. M. Hogan (Eds.), *Researching children's experiences: Approaches and methods* (pp. 102–121). London: Sage.

Tudge, J. R. H., Hogan, D. M., Lee, S., Meltsas, M., Tammeveski, P., Kulakova, N. N., et al. (1999). Cultural heterogeneity: Parental values and beliefs and their preschoolers' activities in the United States, South Korea, Russia, and Estonia. In A. Goncu (Ed.), *Children's engagement in the world*, (pp. 62–96). New York: Cambridge University Press.

Weisner, T. S. (1987). Socialization for parenthood in sibling caretaking societies. In J. Lancaster, A. Rossi, J. Altmann, & L. Sherrod (Eds.). *Parenting across the lifespan* (pp. 237–270). New York: Aldine Press.

Weisner, T. S. (1989). Cultural and universal aspects of social support for children: Evidence from the Abaluyia of Kenya. In D. Belle (Ed.), *Children's social networks and social supports* (pp. 70–90). New York: Wiley.

Weisner, T. S. (1996). The 5 to 7 transition as an ecocultural project. In A. J. Sameroff & M. M. Haith (Eds.), *The five to seven year shift: The age of reason and responsibility* (pp. 295–328). Chicago: University of Chicago Press.

Weisner, T. S., Bradley, C., & Kilbride, P. L. (Eds.). (1997). *African families and the crisis of social change.* Westport, CT: Bergin & Garvey.

White, S. H. (1996). The child's entry into the "age of reason." In A. J. Sameroff & M. M. Haith (Eds.), *The five to seven year shift: The age of reason and responsibility* (pp. 17–32). Chicago: University of Chicago Press.

Whiting, B. (2004a). Changing concepts of the good child and good mothering. In C. P. Edwards & B. B. Whiting (Eds.), *Ngecha: A Kenyan village in a time of rapid social change* (pp. 119–152). Lincoln: University of Nebraska Press.

Whiting, B. B. (2004b). *Ngecha, Kenya, behavior observations. Collected by Beatrice Whiting and research collaborators in 1968–1972* [CD ROM]. C. P. Edwards (Ed.) & M. R. T. de Guzman (compiled). New Haven, CT: Human Relations Area Files Press.

Whiting, B. B. & Edwards, C. P. (1988). *Children of different worlds: The formation of social behavior.* Cambridge, MA: Harvard University Press.

Whiting, B., Whiting, J., Herzog, J., & Edwards, C. (2004). The historical stage. In C. P. Edwards & B. B. Whiting (Eds.), *Ngecha: A Kenyan village in a time of rapid social change* (pp. 53–90). Lincoln: University of Nebraska Press.

Whiting, B. B., & Whiting, J. W. M. (1971). Task assignment and personality: A consideration of the effect of herding on boys. In W. W. Lambert & R. Weisbrod (Eds.), *Comparative perspectives on social psychology* (pp. 33–44). Boston, MA: Little, Brown.

Whiting, B. B., & Whiting, J. W. M. (1975). *Children of six cultures: A psychocultural analysis*. Cambridge, MA: Harvard University Press.

3 Cultural Influences on Peer Relations: An Ecological Perspective

Anne Marie Tietjen

Bronfenbrenner's ecological perspective (e.g., Bronfenbrenner, 1979; Bronfenbrenner & Morris, 1998) has had a deep and far-reaching effect on the study of human development during the past three decades. It has led researchers to investigate many influences on development beyond those that are immediate to the individual in space and time. The results of these investigations have greatly expanded and enriched our knowledge of the ways in which developing individuals are influenced by cultural beliefs, social policies and institutions, and experiences in interpersonal processes.

In the study of children's peer relations in cultural context, one of the enduring challenges has been to find ways to demonstrate the processes by which particular characteristics of cultures are linked to particular dimensions or patterns of peer relationships (Schneider, 2000). The ecological perspective offers a response to this challenge. The goal of this chapter is to show that cultural beliefs and values are manifest in children's peer relations through events and circumstances at intermediate levels of the environment. This ecological conceptualization allows researchers to identify and investigate mediating factors in the links between culture and peer relations.

Following a brief summary of Bronfenbrenner's ecological perspective, three cultures with contrasting positions on the continuum of collectivism–individualism will be introduced. These contrasting positions and their manifestations in the United States, Sweden, and the Maisin of Papua New Guinea will be traced through the layers of the ecological environment to the peer relations of children by means of a review of research findings. This will be followed by a discussion of the concept of time in the ecology of children's peer relations and a summary of the conclusions generated by the literature review.

The Ecological Perspective: A Brief Summary

In the ecological model, the sociocultural environment is seen as "a set of nested structures, each inside the other like a set of Russian dolls" (Bronfenbrenner, 1979, p. 3). The outermost layer (*macrosystem*) is comprised of the ideological or cultural blueprints for society and its institutions. These cultural blueprints, or beliefs and values, are embodied at the *exosystem* level in policies, institutions, and settings in which the child does not participate directly, but in which events and activities take place that influence the child's development indirectly. *Mesosystems*, which are the linkages among the immediate settings containing the child, and *microsystems*, which are the immediate settings in which children live their daily lives, are shaped by events and circumstances at the macro- and exosystem levels. The most current summary of the model (Bronfenbrenner & Morris, 1998) elaborates on characteristics of the developing person and on the dimension of time as significant forces in shaping development. It also expands and refines the concept of proximal processes and their role in development.

From an ecological perspective, processes take center stage in development. The proximal processes that take place between children and others in their various microsystems are viewed as more powerful influences on development than the environmental contexts in which they occur. Characteristics of the environment and the nature of links among the individual's immediate settings play a role in determining the strength of the effects of the processes by either fostering or interfering with proximal processes. The full model involves a view of human development as influenced by specific interpersonal processes, which in turn are influenced by characteristics of the developing person, the sociocultural environment, and the historical context. Bronfenbrenner and Morris (1998) refer to this as a *person-process-environment-time* model.

Issues in Examining Culture and Peer Relations From an Ecological Perspective

Most existing studies of the ecology of peer relations have examined the influence of factors at only one or two levels of the environment, leaving much to be learned about the relationships among the various layers. Demonstrating that cultural beliefs and values are manifest in the peer relationships of children through circumstances and events at the exo-, meso-, and microsystem levels of the environment requires drawing together findings that empirically support segments of the model and making the connections among them.

In the ecological model, the individual is viewed as both product and producer of his or her own development. Thus, peer relationships are important as both a product of, and an influence on development. They may be seen as a manifestation of social competence as defined by a culture and also as a context in which important aspects of development occur, such as the acquisition of culturally appropriate social and instrumental skills (Tietjen, 1989) or academic achievement (Chen, 2003). The focus in this chapter is on peer relations as the product of cultural and other environmental influences.

Among the dimensions of peer relationships that have been studied from an ecological perspective are social skills, aggression, rejection, empathy, prosocial behavior toward peers, popularity, amount of time spent with peers, number of friends reported, choice of deviant or conventional peers, and participation in groups. Findings concerning these dimensions and others will be reported in the analysis presented here, but the primary focus is on understanding what the ecological perspective can reveal about the cultural contexts of peer relations rather than on expanding knowledge of any particular dimension or set of dimensions.

Cultural Assumptions and Beliefs: Three Contrasting Macrosystems

One of the most important and most studied differences among the cultures of the world is the contrast between collectivistic and individualistic cultures (Hofstede, 1980; Triandis, 1990). In individualistic cultures, individuals are viewed as autonomous entities, abstracted from their social roles. Individuation and separation are salient values and processes in these cultures. In collectivistic cultures, the individual is viewed as embedded in a social context, such as family or clan. Relatedness and orientation to the needs of the group are primary values in collectivistic societies. Complex industrial societies tend to be individualistic in orientation, with the United States generally regarded as the most individualistic culture of all. Small-scale traditional cultures, particularly those that are subsistence-based and homogeneous, tend to be collectivistic. Most cultures combine elements of both collectivistic and individualistic orientations.

Within each of these broad, overarching orientations are systems of values and beliefs about particular aspects of social relations. In the analysis presented here, cultural beliefs about access to economic resources and about the closely related issue of provision of child care as a public versus a private or individual concern are explored from an ecological perspective. Cultural responses to these issues at the macrosystem level are traced through the exo-, meso-, and microsystem layers of the ecological environment to children's peer relations in an individualistic culture (the United States), a collectivistic culture (the Maisin of Papua New Guinea), and a culture that combines elements of both (Sweden).

The United States

In highly individualistic cultures, gaining access to economic resources is believed to be the responsibility of the individual. Differences among individuals in the amount of resources they control are seen as a function of characteristics of the individual – intelligence, willingness to work hard and make sacrifices, or luck. Although in principle, individuals have equal opportunities for economic success in the United States, market forces, in concert with historical, economic, and political circumstances, tend to produce an uneven distribution of resources, leaving some families struggling to meet basic needs. The United States has no coherent social policy directed toward supporting the functions of families and is the only major industrialized nation without a national policy supporting the care of children through subsidized child care or paid parental leave (Silverstein, 1991). Middle- and upper-income families pay for services in the private sector, whereas those with constrained access to economic resources are supported by meager and disparate government programs. Child care is considered to be the responsibility of parents and not of the state.

Sweden

In Sweden, a different set of historical, economic, and political circumstances, together with the homogeneity of the society in terms of ethnicity, religion, and political ideology (Lamb et al., 1992), has produced a culture in which economic resources are more evenly distributed. The Swedish government is heavily involved in the provision of public services designed to protect the economic well-being of individuals of all ages and social groups. These services include pension plans, health insurance, housing subsidies, support for education, a universal child allowance, generous parental leave policies, and subsidized child care in high-quality neighborhood facilities (Larner, 1990). The care of young children is treated as the joint responsibility of parents and the state.

The Maisin of Papua New Guinea

The Maisin culture of Papua New Guinea is a small-scale, homogeneous, traditional society with a total membership of about 2,500, about 500 of whom lived in the two villages studied by this author. The Maisin are subsistence gardeners who also hunt and fish. Any cash income they have comes in the form of remittances from relatives employed in the towns (Barker, 1991; Tietjen 1985a; 1989). Despite early contact and relatively good education compared with other parts of the country, the Maisin villages have remained relatively isolated in an area without roads or regular sea transportation. The Maisin maintain many of their traditional beliefs and practices, although they have a local government that combines elements of traditional and colonial forms, and are practicing Anglican Christians. The national government of Papua New Guinea provides no economic supports to families and children, but traditional values and practices make this largely irrelevant for the Maisin.

The Maisin have strong egalitarian beliefs and practices concerning access to resources (Barker, 1991; Tietjen, 1986, 1989; Tietjen & Walker, 1985). A central concept in traditional Maisin culture is *marawa wawe*, which refers to a state of harmony with others, achieved when reciprocal obligations have been met and the community is in balance. Cooperation and helpfulness are as important to Maisin physical and social survival today as they have always been. Placing oneself or one's needs above those of another person or the community is regarded as antisocial and grounds for the use of sorcery.

Daily food exchanges among families related by blood or marriage are a primary traditional means of distributing resources equitably. Toddlers are often called on to deliver the food, ensuring that they will learn the practice early in life. Maisin children are taught to be aware of the needs of others and to help anyone who needs help, whether help is requested or not. The needs of others are easily noticed, as much of life is lived outdoors, and Maisin houses are close to each other and made of bush materials with no soundproofing. Mature Maisin prosocial reasoning focuses on empathic concern with the needs of others (Tietjen, 1986).

The Maisin live within a second, nationally based macrosystem as well as their own traditional one. This new macrosystem is the product of a colonial history, various Western religious influences, the combination of many disparate traditional tribal cultures into the young nation of Papua New Guinea, and modern multinational industries. For the most part, Western influences have entered the Maisin culture gradually, and some have been successfully integrated into the culture. The new macrosystem allows for individual achievement through education and employment beyond the village, but those who achieve are expected to maintain obligations to family and clan. To neglect those obligations is to break one's ties to the village and the culture, ties that are useful in the towns as well as in the villages. The Maisin consider child care to be primarily the responsibility of parents, but others provide care as well (Tietjen, 1985a).

Exosystems in Three Cultures

In these three contrasting macrosystems, cultural blueprints are embodied in very different ways in policies, institutions, and settings containing parents and other adults.

Parents' Workplaces

In the absence of widespread societal support, working parents with young children in the United States often find themselves caught between societal expectations that they will care for their children with little or no government assistance and that they will at the same time meet the demands of employers (Hewlett & West, 1998). In addition, parents' workplaces are often the source of decisions that require geographic moves for families, disrupting children's peer relations as well as adults' support networks.

The supports, stresses, and demands of the parental workplace play a role in determining how effective parents can be in their child-rearing roles at home and the degree to which they can engage in the proximal processes that influence the development of children's peer relations. U.S. studies of parents' work and children's socioemotional development indicate that work stressors tend to erode family and child functioning, whereas work support and satisfaction tend to enhance them (Daniels & Moos, 1988). Stressful workplace conditions have been found to be associated with high family conflict and poorer socioemotional functioning among children in the family (Billings & Moos, 1983; Holahan & Moos, 1987.)

When workplace stresses are manageable, employment can enhance the socioemotional functioning of parents and children. For mothers in the United States, being employed outside the home is associated with having more socially skilled children, mediated by mothers' parenting style (Hoffman & Youngblade 1999). The workplace can be an important context for network building among parents, as well as providing the financial means for sustaining relationships with network members (Cochran et al., 1990). In circumstances of economic hardship, the absence of job security undermines this potential, increasing competition and social distancing among workmates.

Evidence from two studies suggests that, in some circumstances, mothers' work involvement may be at cross-purposes with their children's development of peer relationships. Tietjen (1985b) reported that for Swedish mothers and their preadolescent children, the number of hours mothers worked outside the home was inversely related to the number of friends their children reported. Zelkowitz and Jacobs (1985) reported a similar finding among American families. Fathers' working hours, however, were reported by Zelkowitz and Jacobs to be positively associated with their children having larger networks including more relatives.

In the United States, Sweden, and many other Western societies, children are segregated from adult work and spend most of their time in child-focused nonwork activities with peers and adults (Morelli, Rogoff, & Angelillo, 2003). In Maisin society, adults' workplaces (home and garden) include children as active participants and apprentices (Tietjen, 1989). The participation of children in their parents' and others' work may influence children's peer relations by fostering mutual reliance as the basis for relations among community members of all ages.

Parents' Networks

The pathways by which parents' networks influence their children's peer relationships in the United States appear to be similar to those by which parents' workplace and employment variables operate. Parents' networks can help parents deal with stressors that undermine their parenting and may also provide them with role models and sanctions for parenting (Cochran & Brassard, 1979). Parents' social support systems are linked to greater parental satisfaction and parental warmth, and reduced use of punitive discipline strategies (e.g., Crnic et al., 1984; Taylor & Roberts, 1995; Weinraub & Wolf, 1983). Responsive, supportive parenting, as reported below, is associated with better social skills and peer relations among children.

Parents' peer relations may also influence children's peer relations directly. Significant similarities between the self-reports of social networks of mothers and their preadolescent children were found in a Swedish urban setting (Tietjen, 1985c). Processes by which mothers' network involvement may influence their children's networks include modeling, teaching, sanctioning, providing opportunities for social interactions, and providing a secure emotional base. The same processes were identified in a U.S. study by Simpkins and Parke (2001), who found that children's perceptions of their own friendships, as well as their observed behavior while interacting with a friend, were positively related to characteristics of both mothers' and fathers' friendships. Other U.S. studies have reported that parents' involvement with friends and formal organizations is associated with children's participation in friendships (Homel, Burns, & Goodnow, 1987) and that the quality of the mother's closest friendship predicts children's popularity and the quality of their friendships (Doyle, Markiewicz, & Hardy, 1994).

Cochran et al. (1990) reported that, in all four of the cultures they studied (Germany, Sweden, the United States, and Wales), the educational attainment level of the parents was found to be the single best predictor of the size and richness of their personal social networks. Educational attainment led to more economically rewarding jobs, which in turn fostered the building of personal relationships through the workplace and allowed parents to purchase homes in neighborhoods safe enough to facilitate the creation and maintenance of neighborhood-based relationships for adults and children. Particularly in the United States, educational attainment is largely determined by one's access to economic resources.

In the United States, the supportive function of parents' networks varies as a function of families' access to economic resources. The networks of economically secure families are more likely to provide companionship and emotional support than material assistance (Cochran, 1990). For parents living in poverty-stricken communities, the benefits of social support from personal network members are compromised by the demands made by these same individuals, who are themselves, likely to be living in poverty (Belle, 1982a, 1982b). Brodsky (1999) reported that single, African American mothers in poor neighborhoods regarded their relationships with friends and kin as sources of stress in their lives, rather than support, and valued their independence from these relationships. Ceballo and McLoyd (2002) found that among economically disadvantaged single mothers, those who experienced high levels of support from their network members were more nurturing toward their children and used punishment less frequently. In poorer, high-crime neighborhoods, however, social support was less effective in enhancing parenting behavior.

Cochran et al. (1990) demonstrated that neighborhoods are directly affected by the policies and institutions that determine economic resource distribution patterns in a given society and that the resulting characteristics of neighborhoods shape the pool of potential network members available to parents and children. Residents of U.S. neighborhoods with adequate resources had social networks that facilitated child-rearing by providing support for parents and protection and nurturance for their children. In neighborhoods with limited resources, residents were often afraid to initiate and maintain social contact with other residents. Mobility was high among the residents of these areas.

Among the Swedish families who moved during the three-year period of the study by Cochran et al. (1990) only 10 percent moved to escape negative residential circumstances, whereas almost half of American families did so. In contrast to U.S. single mothers, Swedish single mothers were no more likely to make a geographic move during the three-year period of the study than were married Swedish mothers, reflecting a cultural difference in access to economic resources for single mothers.

Social policies intended to reduce the economic strain of single parenthood through the provision of rent subsidies, good day care, and job training demonstrate Sweden's cultural commitment to income redistribution. Evidence of the success of the policy is seen in Larner's (1990) finding that Swedish single mothers were less dependent on relatives and lived farther from them than American single mothers, who tended to have low incomes and limited opportunities to develop marketable skills. Tietjen (1985c) reported that Swedish single mothers received more instrumental and emotional support from their network members than married mothers did, but were only slightly more indebted to their network members for support than married mothers were, and this indebtedness was primarily to their own parents for child care. Children of single mothers, however, had more limited social networks than children from two parent families (Tietjen, 1982). Even when economic stress is reduced, growing up in a single-parent family presents challenges for children's peer relations.

Exosystems and Maisin Culture

In traditional Maisin society, there were no exosystems or specialized institutions making social policy decisions. Clan elders met, as they still do today, to make decisions about social issues (Tietjen & Walker, 1985). There are no public settings in which children do not participate, at least as observers. Parents' networks and children's networks contain the same individuals, although roles and patterns of interaction among them differ. The integration of children into the multiage social fabric of the community is considered to be essential for their survival and the survival of the culture.

As Western influence has spread and nations have formed, members of small-scale societies worldwide are increasingly influenced by decisions, events, and institutions at the exosystem level. For the Maisin and other Melanesian groups, governments and businesses have affected traditional cultures with varying consequences. For example, the Maisin successfully used legal means in 2002 to avoid having their forest lands sold to a foreign timber company, which would have destroyed their way of life, as oil palm plantations and mining operations have done to other tribal groups in Papua New Guinea (Barker, 2004).

Mesosystems: Links Among Children's Behavior Settings in Three Cultures

An important contribution of the ecological model is its focus on the interactive and synergistic nature of links between the family and other settings in which children spend their time. Strong, supportive links among a child's various settings can reinforce the values of each and make transitions between microsystems easier for children. Processes occurring in one microsystem can mediate or moderate those occurring in another. This function is illustrated in connections between families and neighborhoods.

Families and Neighborhoods

In the United States, the nature of the relationship between families and neighborhoods and the means by which they influence children's peer relationships changes over the course of development (Leventhal & Brooks-Gunn, 2000). For young children, neighborhood influences may be primarily indirect, mediated by parents' behavior. Adolescents may participate directly in the neighborhood as a microsystem, and schools and peers may play a larger role than families in mediating neighborhood effects at this stage.

Access to economic resources appears to have a significant effect on family–neighborhood connections in the United States. Among rural, single-parent African American families, mothers who had greater financial resources were more likely to be involved in their children's elementary school activities, strengthening the mesosystem of home–school connections (Brody & Flor, 1998). For poor children in the United States who live in neighborhoods with high rates of crime, street violence, and residential turnover, links between family and neighborhood are likely to be weak and unsupportive. Parents who live in dangerous neighborhoods tend to be more controlling and restrictive than parents in safer areas (Furstenberg et al., 1999), and children who live in physically unsafe neighborhoods have fewer friends than those who live in safer neighborhoods (Medrich et al., 1982).

For older children and adolescents, living in a poor neighborhood may increase the likelihood of associating with deviant peers, depending on the nature of the mesosystems in operation. In a study of ten- to twelve-year-old African American children Brody et al. (2001) found that children who lived in disadvantaged communities were more likely to affiliate with deviant peers than children who lived in neighborhoods with more social advantages, but these effects were moderated by parental behavior and neighborhood processes. Children whose parents were nurturant and involved, or who lived in neighborhoods where collective socialization processes were operating, were less likely to affiliate with deviant peers. These effects were strongest for children living in the most economically disadvantaged neighborhoods.

Home and Child Care

In the past two decades, Sweden has developed the "open preschool" model, in which a preschool teacher and premises are provided by the city. Parents who bring their children to the preschool must remain with them while they are there. This arrangement provides opportunities for parents to meet other parents, to consult with staff about child development issues, and to provide preschoolers with opportunities to interact with other children (Cochran, 1990). The open preschool model may be an example of how social policy, through the community, can facilitate both parental caregiving and shared caregiving, and through them, children's peer relations.

Mesosystems in Maisin Culture

Maisin children's microsystems are home (including gardens), school, and neighborhood, or clan area. Links between home and clan area are generally very strong, as both are firmly rooted in tradition, and clan areas are comprised of the homes of close kin. Maisin traditional social structure emphasized the multiage clan as the child's main social group. Western-style schooling introduced the idea of cross-clan peer groups, although classrooms usually contain children whose ages span several years. Because the school includes children from all Maisin clans, children are more likely to have school friends based on choice, rather than clan membership, than they were before the school was introduced. Outside school, however, there is little visiting between children belonging to different clans (Tietjen, 1989). Links between home and school can be strong or weak for Maisin children. Somewhat ironically, teachers tend to assert that they are educating their students for village life, whereas most parents hope that some of their children will go on to further schooling and jobs in towns so that they can help their parents and others financially. In the 1980s many Maisin parents were unable to help their children with schoolwork because their English was limited, weakening the link between home and school, but this is less of a problem today.

Proximal Processes and Peer Relations: Microsystem Influences

Parenting and Peer Relations

Perhaps the most studied of proximal processes involving young children in their families in both individualistic and collectivistic cultures are those such as warmth and responsiveness, associated with attachment between infants and caregivers (Bowlby, 1969/1982, 1988). Attachment security is associated with having more positive peer relationships early in life (Park & Waters, 1989; Sroufe, 1983). Kindergartners with a secure representation of attachment to mothers and fathers are more popular, better accepted by their peers, and show more prosocial behavior toward their peers (Verschueren & Marcoen, 1999). During middle childhood, they are more likely to form lasting peer relationships and to function well in both a group context and a friendship (Sroufe, Egeland, & Carlson, 1999). During adolescence, securely attached children are more effective socially and more able to tolerate vulnerability and intimacy in relationships (Englund et al., 2000). Research on attachment processes has shown that they are evident in many cultural contexts and that variation in the prevalence of the various patterns of attachment in different cultures reflects historical circumstances and cultural values regarding families' roles in caregiving.

Parenting styles (e.g., Baumrind, 1975) have also been found to influence peer relations in the United States. Hoffman and Youngblade (1999) reported that, across social class, mothers who used an authoritative parenting style had children who displayed less shy behavior (as rated by peers and teachers), more positive assertive behaviors, and a higher sense of self-efficacy. The authoritarian style of control was associated with having children who were less well-liked by peers and had less adequate social skills. Parents who are warm and supportive and express more positive emotions in the presence of their children are more likely to have children who are rated by their mothers and teachers as more empathic and more socially competent with peers (Zhou et al., 2002). In the context of parent–child relationships, children learn social behaviors that they employ in their peer relationships (Putallaz, 1987; Putallaz & Heflin, 1990).

Parents' spousal relationships may also influence children's peer relations. Divorce and marital conflict are associated with a lack of competence in children's relationships with peers (e.g., Gottman & Katz, 1989; Hetherington, Cox, & Cox, 1979). United States children in two-parent families reported more companionship, help and support, and closeness in their friendships than children in single-parent families (Doyle et al., 1994). Children of single parents in Sweden had fewer friends with whom they played at home, were less likely to belong to activity groups, and were more likely to report that they spent more time with siblings than with friends (Tietjen, 1982), compared with children in two-parent families.

Recent studies in the United States have found a strong link between parental economic resources and children's peer relations, mediated by parenting behavior. Parents under economic stress are more likely to experience high rates of negative life events and chronic negative conditions than non-poor adults and to use harsh and inconsistent discipline with their children, leading to socioemotional problems in the children. The longer children live in poverty, the more likely they are to develop behavior problems (McLoyd, 1998). Mistry et al. (2002) reported that African American and Hispanic parents experiencing economic hardship felt less effective in disciplining their children and were less affectionate in interacting with them. These parenting difficulties predicted lower teacher ratings of children's positive social behavior and higher teacher ratings of behavior problems. In a sample of rural, single-parent African American families with elementary school children, mothers with adequate financial resources were more likely to use a style of parenting characterized by firm parental control and warmth and to have warm and harmonious relationships with their children. These parenting variables were indirectly related to children's social competence with peers through the children's ability to self-regulate (Brody & Flor, 1998; Brody, Flor, & Gibson, 1999).

In Maisin society, mothers take primary responsibility for the care of children. Many others, including fathers, grandparents, aunts, uncles, siblings, and cousins are active participants in child care as well (Barker, 1991; Tietjen, 1985a). According to the Maisin kinship system, each child has several related adults classified as mothers, fathers, siblings, and grandparents, in addition to members of their biological family. Children are taught to use the appropriate kin terms for the people in their lives during infancy and toddlerhood. The system integrates children into society and ensures that they will be cared for if biological parents should die.

Child Care and Peer Relations

Two recent studies provide evidence that proximal processes occurring in high-quality child care play a role in shaping children's peer relationships in the United States context. The NICHD Network for Early Child Care Research (2001) reported that children with more experience in child-care settings were more positive and skilled in their play with peers in child care at twenty-four and thirty-six months of age. Sensitive, responsive caregiver behavior was the feature of child care most consistently associated with more positive play with other children. Peisner-Feinberg et al. (2001) reported that children who experienced higher quality preschool child-care settings demonstrated better socioemotional skills during kindergarten. The closeness of the child's relationship with the preschool teacher was the strongest predictor of social skills in the kindergarten classroom.

Poor children in the United States who experience high-quality infant and preschool care show more social competence in later years than do poor children without child-care experience or with experience in lower quality care (Field, 1991; Ramey & Ramey, 1992). For poor children, high-quality child care may offer learning opportunities and social and emotional supports that many would not experience at home. Children from middle- and upper-income families appear to be less affected by the quality of nonparental care in the long term as long as it is safe.

In Sweden, uniformly high-quality child care centers are provided and viewed as a right for all families with children. Andersson (1989) reported that children with early experiences of either center day care or family day care were rated by their teachers as more socially competent in interactions with peers at age seven than children who had been cared for exclusively at home. Broberg, Hwang, & Chace (1993) found no long-term effects of differences in Swedish child-care environments on children's social adjustment at eight or nine years of age, as the quality of care is uniformly high in Swedish child-care facilities of various types.

Maisin children spend much of their time when not in school caring for their younger siblings and are thus in a position to provide them with important socialization experiences (Tietjen, 1989). These caregiving relationships also serve as opportunities for older siblings to learn empathy, patience, and other qualities that are beneficial in forming and maintaining relationships with others (Weisner, 1984; Whiting & Edwards, 1989).

Neighborhoods and Peer Relations

Bryant (1985) reported that the availability of informal meeting places in a child's neighborhood in the United States was associated with greater acceptance of peers. United States elementary school children living in poor neighborhoods have higher rates of aggressive behavior toward peers (Duncan, Brooks-Gunn, & Klebanov, 1994; Kupersmidt et al., 1995) over and above the variance accounted for by family characteristics. Guerra, Huesmann, and Spindler (2003) found that witnessing violence in one's neighborhood significantly increased children's aggressive behavior toward peers. In a Swedish city, no differences in peer relationships were found between preadolescent children living in neighborhoods with commercial and social services and children living in neighborhoods with less access to these public venues (Tietjen 1982).

Maisin children spend most of their time away from school in the open spaces around the homes of clan members. These clan areas function as neighborhoods for Maisin children. Maisin children included more adults and more children younger and older than themselves in their networks than did Swedish children of the same age (Tietjen, 1989). They were also more likely to spend time in the company of several other children, as opposed to alone or with one friend. These findings reflect the neighborhood functions of clan areas as well as Maisin social structure and collectivistic orientation.

In an observational study of Maisin children's social interactions in their clan areas, Tietjen (1994) reported that, for children between the ages of five and eleven, peers (defined as children whose age was within two years of that of the observed child) were the primary interactional partners and providers of support. Nine- to eleven-year-old boys and girls were spending much of their time caring for younger siblings, often in the company of peers who were doing the same thing. Consistent with cultural values, Maisin children gave and received little or no praise in their interactions with peers or adults. To praise another person is to elevate that person above others, which can put the individual at risk for sorcery in this fiercely egalitarian society.

Summaries: The Ecology of Peer Relations for U.S., Swedish, and Maisin Children

The foregoing analysis reveals three very different ecologies of peer relations in the three contrasting cultures. A brief summary of some of the important features of each follows.

In the United States, economic circumstances stemming from individualistic cultural values play a major role in determining children's social connections. Social and economic policies lead to wide disparities in income levels among families, which lead to further disparities in the quality of neighborhoods, parents' personal social networks, and stability of parental employment. The stresses created by economic hardship increase the likelihood that parents will use harsh and authoritarian parenting styles. Parents with adequate economic resources are more likely to employ parenting practices that contribute to the development of positive peer relationships.

In Sweden, where there is a commitment at the macrosystem level to provide economic supports to families with children, neighborhoods are generally safe, have relatively low mobility, and provide a variety of social services. Child care is of uniformly high quality. Connections among family, child care, and neighborhood are facilitated by government policies. Variations in children's peer relationships in Sweden may be influenced more by personal characteristics and family circumstances, including living in a single-parent family, than by the social structural factors salient in the United States.

The Maisin, whose traditional macrosystem values include equality, cooperation, and shared responsibility, are also living within a macrosystem created by the influence of Western cultures. In traditional life, there were no exosystems, but today, Maisin social life is affected by government agencies, economic conditions in urban areas, religious groups, and other entities and events that have brought change to village life. Traditional Maisin social structure and village structure built in connections among children's behavior settings, and this is still largely the case today. Maisin children's peer relationships still appear to be influenced primarily by traditional values and structures directly, but this is changing as global influences increase.

Time in the Ecology of Children's Peer Relations

The ecological model provides a framework for studying the functions of stability and instability in children's relationships. Bronfenbrenner and Morris (1998) assert that "proximal processes cannot function effectively in environments that are unstable and unpredictable across space and time" (p. 1019).

Elder's longitudinal studies of the Great Depression (Elder, 1974) and the Iowa farm crisis (Conger & Elder, 1994; Elder, King, & Conger, 1996) provide examples of the effects of macrosystem changes on the development of individuals. Children's responses to the event were influenced by changes in their parents' emotional functioning and parenting behavior and by the timing of the event in the children's lives. Elder's work also demonstrated that the effects of processes occurring in one setting may not be observable until the person enters another setting later in life (Bronfenbrenner & Morris, 1998). Another example of a study of individuals' responses to change at the macrosystem level is the work of Silbereisen and colleagues in the former East Germany (Silbereisen, Juang, & Reitzle, 2000), who found that the cultural and institutional changes that occurred in the process of reunification affected individual lives, mediated by such factors as family relationships and personal attributes.

The work of Pulkkinen (1983; Pulkkinen & Saastamoinen, 1986) in Finland illustrates the effect of contextual instability on children's socioemotional development and peer relationships within a stable society. With a sample of children followed from age eight into adulthood, Pulkkinen used a global measure of family stability that included measures of the frequency of such events as number of family moves, changes in day care or school arrangements, incidence of divorce and remarriage, and changes in conditions of maternal employment. Higher levels of family instability were associated with greater submissiveness, aggressiveness, anxiety, and social problems among older children and adolescents.

Recent economic changes in the urban areas of Papua New Guinea have resulted in some Maisin families returning to the villages after a decade or more of city life. The transition to village life that the children in these families must make, and the adaptation of village children to their new peers, could be a fruitful topic for research.

Children whose lives are disrupted by war, displacement, and emigration as refugees may experience significant change in all levels of their environment at once. Almqvist and Broberg (1999) studied the mental health and social adjustment of a group of Iranian refugee children twelve months and again two and a half years after arriving in Sweden. Current positive peer relationships and length of time in Sweden predicted positive social adjustment. Negative peer relations, including exposure to bullying, predicted low self-worth and poor social adjustment.

Studies of contextual change suggest that the developmental timing of the event in the life of the individual can play a significant role in determining the significance of the event. Elder's (1974) study indicated that the effects of the Depression were more deleterious for children who experienced it early in their lives than for those who were older when it occurred. McLoyd's (1998) review of the effects of poverty on development reported similar findings and also raises the question of the effects of chronic versus temporary exposure to challenging contextual conditions or environmental changes.

Conclusions

The findings presented here concerning the links between cultural beliefs about access to resources at the macrosystem level and characteristics of children's peer relations support several general conclusions: (1) in large-scale industrial societies, cultural values and social policies concerning children and families are reflected in settings such as parents' workplaces and neighborhoods; (2) the conditions, events, and interpersonal processes that occur in these culturally defined settings affect the well-being of parents, the manner in which they interact with their children, and the ways in which they mediate the connections among children's behavior settings; (3) children's relationships with their peers reflect, in addition to personal characteristics and family circumstances, experiences in interpersonal processes with parents, caregivers, teachers, and others, all of whom are embedded in the cultural environment; (4) peer relationships in small-scale, subsistence-based cultures, in which traditional values and beliefs are still enacted directly in everyday activities and relationships, are increasingly affected by events, policies, and institutions at the macro- and exosystem levels; (5) instability or change at one or more levels of the environment can have significant effects on interpersonal processes and relationships over time.

Although the ecological perspective is acknowledged as useful and influential by many cultural psychologists (e.g., LeVine et al., 1994; Rogoff, 2003), it has not often been used systematically as a set of guidelines for cultural research. Some researchers find the concept of nested structures too constraining. In the analysis presented here, it has emerged that some structures, such as the neighborhood and parents' networks, may function at more than one level. Moreover, structures at the same ecological level, for example, neighborhoods, social networks, and parental workplaces, appear to influence each other laterally. Viewing the various levels of the environment as fluid increases the usefulness of the model.

Other cultural researchers see the framework as relevant to large-scale industrial societies but not to small-scale traditional cultures, which lack the structures that mediate between culture and behavior. Examples from the Maisin situation indicate that even relatively isolated small-scale societies are increasingly influenced by events, ideologies, and policies at levels of the environment in which they do not participate directly. Studying the nature and implications of this influence could expand our understanding of the processes of cultural change and suggest points of intervention in these processes that might not be considered without the broad perspective provided by the ecological framework.

Employing the ecological model in cultural research presents new methodological challenges in addition to those already familiar to cultural researchers. Research based on the ecological model requires systematic information regarding the structure and substance of the environments in which the reported behavior takes place, as well as documentation of characteristics of the persons studied and of the interactional processes that link environment and outcome. The ecological model calls for research designs that incorporate process, person, environment, and time (Bronfenbrenner & Morris, 1998).

The ecological model has always been associated with the goal of understanding and promoting environmental conditions that optimize development for all children (Bronfenbrenner, 1979). Findings generated by the model suggest that interventions at the level of the individual or the microsystem are unlikely to be effective if the structures in which they are embedded do not support the intervention. Cochran et al. (1990) suggest that the Swedish preference for intervention at the level of social policies designed to support families and children is likely to be more effective for enhancing personal relationships than interventions at the level of the individual or the family. Improving access to good-quality education, stable employment, safe neighborhoods, and high-quality child care may support the development of peer relations more effectively than social skills training. Research generated by the ecological model could be used to contribute to the development of social policies that are culturally appropriate and supportive to families and children. Using the ecological framework in the study of culture and peer relations could further our understanding of the processes by which cultures produce new generations competent to function effectively in their own culture and enable us to identify the levels at which cultures succeed or fail in providing the ecological supports necessary for this to occur.

References

Almqvist, K., & Broberg, A. G. (1999). Mental health and social adjustment in young refugee children 3 1/2 years after their arrival in Sweden. *Journal of the American Academy of Child & Adolescent Psychiatry, 38*(6), 723–730.

Andersson, B. (1989). Effects of public day care – A longitudinal study. *Child Development, 60*, 857–867.

Barker, J. (1991). Maisin. In Hays, T. E. (Eds.), *Oceania. Encyclopedia of world cultures* (Vol. II). New Haven, CT: Human Relations Area Files.

Barker, J. (2004). Between heaven and earth: Missionaries, environmentalists, and the Maisin. In V. Lockwood (Eds.), *Globalization and culture change in the Pacific Islands*. Upper Saddle River, NJ: Pearson Education.

Baumrind, D. (1975). The contribution of the family to the development of competence in children. *Schizophrenia Bulletin, 14*, 12–37.

Belle, D. (1982a). The impact of poverty on social networks and supports. *Marriage and Family Review, 5*(4), 89–103.

Belle, D. (1982b). Social ties and social support. In D. Belle (Ed.), *Lives in stress: Women and depression*. Beverly Hills, CA: Sage.

Billings, A. G., & Moos, R. H. (1983). Comparisons of children of depressed and nondepressed parents: A social-environmental perspective. *Journal of Abnormal Child Psychology, 11*, 463–485.

Bowlby, J. (1982). *Attachment and loss: Vol. 1. Attachment*. New York: Basic Books. (Original work published 1969)

Bowlby, J. (1988). *A secure base: Parent-child attachment and healthy human development*. New York: Basic Books.

Broberg, A. G., Hwang, C. P., & Chace, S. V. (April, 1993). *Effects of day care on elementary school performance and adjustment*. Paper presented at the Society for Research in Child Development, New Orleans, LA.

Brodsky, A. E. (1999). Making it: The components and process of resilience among urban, African-American, single mothers. *American Journal of Orthopsychiatry, 69*, 148–160.

Brody, G., & Flor, D. (1998). Maternal resources, parenting practices, and child competence in rural, single-parent African American families. *Child Development, 69*(3), 803–816.

Brody, G., Flor, D., & Gibson, N. M. (1999). Linking maternal efficacy beliefs, developmental goals, parenting practices, and child competence in rural single-parent African American families. *Child Development, 70*(5), 1197–1208.

Brody, G., Ge, X., Conger, R., Gibbons, F., Murry, V., Gerrard, M., et al. (2001). The influence of neighborhood disadvantage, collective socialization, and parenting on African American children's affiliation with deviant peers. *Child Development, 72*(4), 1231–1246.

Bronfenbrenner, U. (1979). *The ecology of human development: Experiments by nature and design*. Cambridge, MA: Harvard University Press.

Bronfenbrenner, U., & Morris, P. A. (1998). The ecology of developmental processes. In W. Damon & R. M. Lerner (Eds.), *Handbook of child psychology: Theoretical models of human development* (5th ed., Vol. 1, pp. 993–1028). New York: Wiley.

Bryant, B. (1985). *The neighborhood walk: Sources of support in middle childhood. Monographs of the Society for Research in Child Development, 50, 210*(3).

Ceballo, R., & McLoyd, V. (2002). Social support and parenting in poor, dangerous neighborhoods. *Child Development, 73*(4), 1310–1321.

Chen, X. (2003). The peer group as a context: Mediating and moderating effects on relations between academic achievement and social functioning in Chinese children. *Child Development, 74*(3), 710–727.

Cochran, M. (1990). Environmental factors constraining network development. In M. Cochran, M. Larner, D. Riley, L. Gunnarson, & Henderson, C. R., Jr., *Extending families: The social networks of parents and their children*. New York: Cambridge University Press, pp. 277–296.

Cochran, M., & Brassard, J. (1979). Child development and personal social networks. *Child Development, 50*, 601–616.

Cochran, M., Larner, M., Riley, D., Gunnarsson, L., & Henderson, C. R., Jr. (1990). *Extending families: The social networks of parents and their children*. New York: Cambridge University Press.

Conger, R., & Elder, G. H. J. (1994). *Families in troubled times: Adapting to change in rural America*. Chicago: Aldine-de Gruyter.

Crnic, K., Greenberg, M., Robinson, N. M., & Ragozin, A. S. (1984). Maternal stress and social support: Effects on the mother-infant relationship from birth to 18 months. *American Journal of Orthopsychiatry, 54*, 224–235.

Daniels, D., & Moos, R. H. (1988). Exosystem influences on family and child functioning. *Journal of Social and Personal Relationships, 3*(4), 113–133.

Doyle, A. B., Markiewicz, D., & Hardy, C. (1994). Mothers' and children's friendships: Intergenerational associations. *Journal of Social and Personal Relationships*, pp. 363–377.

Duncan, G., Brooks-Gunn, J., & Klebanov, P. (1994). Economic deprivation and early childhood development. *Child Development, 65*, 296–318.

Elder, G. H., Jr. (1974). *Children of the great depression*. Chicago: University of Chicago Press.

Elder, G. H., Jr., King, V., & Conger, R. (1996). Intergenerational continuity and changes in rural lives: Historical and develomental insights. *International Journal of Behavioral Development, 10*, 439–466.

Englund, M., Levy, A., Hyson, D., & Sroufe, L. A. (2000). Adolescent social competence: Effectiveness in a group setting. *Child Development, 71*, 1049–1060.

Field, T. (1991). Quality infant day-care and grade school behavior and performance. *Child Development, 62*, 863–870.

Furstenberg, F. F., Jr., Cook, T. D., Eccles, J., Elder, G. H. Jr., & Sameroff, A. (1999). *Managing to make it: Urban families and adolescent success*. Chicago: University of Chicago Press.

Gottman, J. M., & Katz, L. F. (1989). Effects of marital discord on young children's peer interaction and health. *Developmental Psychology, 25*, 373–381.

Guerra, N. G., Huesmann, L. R., & Spindler, A. (2003). Community violence exposure, social cognition, and aggression among urban elementary school children. *Child Development, 74*(5), 1561–1576.

Hetherington, E. M., Cox, M., & Cox, R. (1979). Play and social interaction in children following divorce. *Journal of Social Issues, 35*, 26–49.

Hewlett, S. A., & West, C. (1998). *The war against parents*. Boston: Houghton Mifflin Company.

Hoffman, L. W., & Youngblade, L. (1999). *Mothers at work*. New York: Cambridge University Press.

Hofstede, G. (1980). *Culture's consequences: International differences in work-related values*. Beverly Hills: Sage.

Holahan, C. J., & Moos, R. H. (1987). Risk, resistance, and psychological distress: A longitudinal analysis with adults and children. *Journal of Abnormal Psychology, 96*, 3–13.

Homel, R., Burns, A., & Goodnow, J. (1987). Parental social networks and child development. *Journal of Social and Personal Relationships, 4*, 159–177.

Kupersmidt, J., Griesler, P., DeRosier, M., Patterson, C., & Davis, P. (1995). Childhood aggression and peer relations in the context of family and neighborhood. *Child Development, 66*, 360–375.

Lamb, M. S., K., Hwang, C.-P., & Broberg, A. (Eds.). (1992). *Child care in context*. Hillsdale, NJ: Lawrence Erlbaum Associates.

Larner, M. (1990). Local residential mobility and its effects on social networks: A cross-cultural comparison. In M. Cochran, M. Larner, D. Riley, L. Gunnarsson, & C. R. Henderson, Jr. (Eds.), *Extending families: The social networks of parents and their children*. New York: Cambridge University Press, pp. 205–229.

Leventhal, T., & Brooks-Gunn, J. (2000). The neighborhoods they live in: The effects of neighborhood residence on child and adolescent outcomes. *Psychological Bulletin, 126*(2), 309–337.

LeVine, R. D., Dixon, S., LeVine, S., Richman, A., Leiderman, P. H., Keefer, C. H., & Brazelton, B. (1994). *Child care and culture*. New York: Cambridge University Press.

McLoyd, V. (1998). Socioeconomic disadvantage and child development. *American Psychologist, 53*(2), 185–204.

Medrich, E. A., Roizen, J. A., Rubin, V., & Buckley, S. (1982). *The serious business of growing up: A study of children's lives outside school*. Berkeley: University of California Press.

Mistry, R., Vandewater, E., Huston, A., & McLoyd, V. (2002). Economic well-being and children's social adjustment: The role of family process in an ethnically diverse low-income sample. *Child Development, 73*(3), 935–951.

Morelli, G., Rogoff, B., & Angellilo, C. (2003). Cultural variation in young children's access to work or involvement in specialised child-focused activities. *International Journal of Behavioral Development, 27*, 264–274.

NICHD Network for Early Child Care Research. (2001). Child care and children's peer interaction at 24 and 36 Months: The NICHD study of early child care. *Child Development, 72*(5), 1478–1500.

Park, K., & Waters, E. (1989). Security of attachment and preschool friendships. *Child Development, 60*, 1076–1081.

Peisner-Feinberg, E. S., Burchinal, M. R., Clifford, R. M., Culkin, M. L., Howes, C., Kagan, S. L., et al. (2001). The relation of preschool child-care quality to children's cognitive and social developmental trajectories through second grade. *Child Development, 72*(5), 1534–1553.

Pulkkinen, L. (1983). Finland: The search for alternatives to aggression. In A. P. Goldstein & M. Segall (Eds.), *Aggression in global perspective*. (pp. 104–144). New York: Pergamon.

Pulkkinen, L., & Saastamoinen, M. (1986). Cross-cultural perspectives on youth violence. In S. J. Apter & A. P. Goldstein (Eds.), *Youth violence: Programs and prospects*. (pp. 262–281). New York: Pergamon Press.

Putallaz, M. (1987). Maternal behavior and children's sociometric status. *Child Development, 58*, 324–340.

Putallaz, M., & Heflin, A. H. (1990). Parent-child interaction. In S. R. Asher & J. Coie (Eds.), *Peer rejection in childhood*. New York: Cambridge University Press.

Ramey, C., & Ramey, S. (1992). Early educational intervention with disadvantaged children – To what effect? *Applied and Preventive Psychology, 1*, 131–140.

Rogoff, B. (2003). *The cultural nature of human development*. Oxford, England: Oxford University Press.

Schneider, B. (2000). *Friends and enemies*. New York: Oxford University Press.

Silbereisen, R., Juang, L., & Reitzle, M. (2000). The transition to adulthood in the context of a changed Germany. *International Journal of Behavioral Development Newsletter, 37*(2), 1–4.

Silverstein, L. B. (1991). Transforming the data about child care and maternal employment. *American Psychologist, 46*, 1025–1032.

Simpkins, S., & Parke, R. D. (2001). The relations between parental friendships and children's friendships: Self-report and observational analysis. *Child Development, 72*(2), 569–582.

Sroufe, L. A. (1983). Infant-caregiver attachment and patterns of adaptation in preschool: The roots of maladaptation and competence. In M. Perlmutter (Ed.),

Minnesota symposium in child psychology (Vol. 16). Hillsdale, NJ: Lawrence Erlbaum Associates.

Sroufe, L. A., Egeland, B., & Carlson, E. (1999). One social world: The integrated development of parent-child and peer relationships. In A. Collins & B. Laursen (Eds.), *Relationships as developmental contexts* (pp. 241–261). Mahwah, NJ: Lawrence Erlbaum Associates.

Taylor, R. D., & Roberts, D. (1995). Kinship support and maternal and adolescent well-being in economically disadvantaged African American families. *Child Development, 66*, 1585–1597.

Tietjen, A. (1982). The social networks of preadolescent children in Sweden. *International Journal of Behavioral Development, 5*, 111–130.

Tietjen, A. (1985a). Infant care and feeding practices and the beginnings of socialization among the Maisin of Papua New Guinea. In L. Marshall (Ed.), *Infant care and feeding in the South Pacific*. New York: Gordon and Breach Science Publishers.

Tietjen, A. (1985b). Relationships between the social networks of mothers and their children. *International Journal of Behavioral Development, 8*, 195–216.

Tietjen, A. (1985c, May). The social networks and social support of married and single mothers in Sweden. *Journal of Marriage and the Family*, 489–496.

Tietjen, A. (1986). Prosocial reasoning among children and adults in a Papua New Guinea society. *Developmental Psychology, 22*(6), 861–868.

Tietjen, A. (1989). The ecology of children's social support networks. In D. Belle (Ed.), *Children's social networks and social supports*. New York: Wiley.

Tietjen, A. (June, 1994). *Receiving and giving social support: The development of cultural competence in a Papua New Guinea Society*. Paper presented at the International Society for the Study of Behavioral Development, Amsterdam, Netherlands.

Tietjen, A., & Walker, L. (1985). Moral reasoning and leadership among men in a Papua New Guinea village. *Developmental Psychology, 21*, 982–992.

Triandis, H. C. (1990). *Cross-cultural studies of individualism and collectivism*. Lincoln: University of Nebraska Press.

Verschueren, K., & Marcoen, A. (1999). Representation of self and socioemotional competence in kindergartners: Differential and combined effects of attachment to mother and to father. *Child Development, 70*(1), 183–201.

Weinraub, M., & Wolf, B. M. (1983). Effects of stress and social support on mother-child interations in single- and two-parent families. *Child Development, 54*, 647–656.

Weisner, T. (1984). Ecocultural niches of middle childhood: A cross-cultural perspective. In W. A. Collins (Ed.), *Development during middle childhood*. Washington, DC: National Academy Press.

Whiting, B. B., & Edwards, C. P. (1988). *Children of different worlds*. Cambridge, MA: Harvard University Press.

Zelkowitz, P., & Jacobs, E. (April, 1985). *The composition of the social networks of preschool-age children*. Paper presented at the Society for Research in Child Development, Toronto.

Zhou, Q., Eisenberg, N., Losoya, S. H., Fabes, R., Reiser, M., Guthrie, I. K., et al. (2002). The relations of parental warmth and positive expressiveness to children's empathy-related responding and social functioning: A longitudinal study. *Child Development, 73*(3), 893–915.

4 Analytic Considerations in Cross-Cultural Research on Peer Relations

Noel A. Card and Todd D. Little

In this chapter, we review analytic strategies for examining various aspects of peer relations across cultures. Specifically, we review techniques of comparing measures across cultural contexts, with an emphasis on means and covariance structures (MACS) analysis. We then describe the comparisons of mean levels, variances, and covariances across cultures using this approach. Next, we describe techniques of examining intercultural perception and interaction using the social relations model, an underutilized approach in studying youths' peer relations. Finally, we briefly discuss some other analytic approaches and offer our view of the state of the art and future directions for analyzing cross-cultural peer relations data.

Comparing Cultures – Measurement

Given that there is little consensus regarding the measurement of group-level status (e.g., peer acceptance and rejection, perceived popularity and rejection, victimization), dyadic relationships of liking (e.g., friendships, romantic relationships) and disliking (e.g., enemies, mutual antipathies), and interpersonal behaviors (e.g., aggression, prosocial behaviors, interpersonal withdrawal) even within cultures predominantly studied by peer relations researchers (i.e., primarily White, English-speaking youths), it is little wonder that measuring these constructs across cultures poses significant challenges. Although it is beyond the scope of this chapter to attempt to define these constructs or to offer specific suggestions for how these may be assessed in specific cultures, we wish to remind readers of the importance of this process. No amount of analytic sophistication can remedy problematic operationalization of a construct (though the methods we describe next can evaluate the success of cross-cultural measurement of a construct). Therefore, it is of critical importance that the researcher is familiar with both the constructs and the cultures being investigated. Moreover, although procedures for translating instruments across languages are well known, we also recommend that the translators are familiar with the underlying constructs that are being assessed by individual items. This familiarity will avoid many of the ambiguities of items that may arise if they are translated across languages without a clear understanding of the construct that the items are meant to capture. Although good examples of this process are presented in the other chapters of this book, we emphasize that the expression "garbage in, garbage out" is especially relevant in poorly conceived cross-cultural research. After careful attention to these issues, the researcher can evaluate the success of the operationalizations and, if successful, can begin to compare cultures in terms of the underlying constructs of interest. We present in this section an analytic approach to evaluating the comparability of assessment of constructs across cultures.

MACS analysis represents a useful analytic tool for assessing construct comparability across cultures (see Little, 1997). Like confirmatory factor analysis, a MACS analysis models the latent commonalities among a series of indicators (items or parcels of a scale, different scales assessing the same construct) designed to assess the same construct. In addition to providing estimates of the loadings of each indicator onto the construct, overall fit of the modeled relations among indicators and constructs are provided (i.e., fit indices). MACS analysis differs from traditional confirmatory factor analysis, however, in that it also analyzes the intercepts of the indicators (and, with multiple groups, allows for comparison of latent variable means across groups, a topic described in the next section; see Little, 1997; Little & Slegers, in press).

As an example, imagine that a researcher is interested in studying peer victimization in two cultures (more than two could be examined), perhaps among children in the United States and China (for an example of assessing victimization among Chinese children, see Schwartz, Chang, & Farver, 2001). After taking appropriate efforts to identify indicators adequately assessing different aspects of victimization (e.g., physical, verbal, and social) in both cultures and following recommended procedures regarding translation of items (see e.g., Novy et al., 2001), these scales are administered to samples of children in each country. The researcher might then model the hypothesized measurement structure of these scales within the two cultures as depicted in Figure 4.1.

Measurement equivalence across cultures can be defined as equivalence in both loadings and intercepts of indicators (known as strong factorial invariance; see Meredith, 1993). In the victimization example displayed in Figure 4.1, this would mean that the loadings of each indicator onto the victimization construct (λ_1, λ_2, and λ_3) would be equal in the United States and Chinese populations represented by the samples, as would the intercepts of each indicator (τ_1, τ_2, and τ_3) . Although some might argue that the residual variance terms of the indicators (θ_1, θ_2, and θ_3) should also be equated across cultures (known as strict factorial invariance), we do not recommend this approach, as it could bias other parameters in the model by forcing culturally unique aspects of the indicators and random error into the structural portion of the model (see Little, 1997; Little & Slegers, in press; Meredith, 1993).

To assess (strong) measurement invariance across cultures, one first fits an unrestricted model in which the indicator loadings (λ_1, λ_2, and λ_3) and intercepts (τ_1, τ_2, and τ_3) are separately estimated within each culture (note that to identify the parameters and set the scale for the latent victimization constructs, the variances, ψ_{11}, in each culture are initially set to 1, and to identify the mean structure, the latent intercepts, αs, are initially set to 0; see Little, Slegers, & Card, in press, for details on alternative methods of identification that can also be used in these kinds of comparisons). In a second model, one restricts the indicator loadings (λ_1, λ_2, and λ_3) and intercepts (τ_1, τ_2, and τ_3) to be equal across the (two or more) cultural contexts (and frees the construct variance, ψ_{11}, in the other cultures to avoid introducing unnecessary restrictions in the model). The unrestricted and restricted models are then compared in one of two ways. From a statistical rationale, one could perform nested-model comparisons between the unrestricted and restricted models,

$$\Delta\chi^2 = \chi^2_{\text{restricted}} - \chi^2_{\text{unrestricted}} \text{ with } \Delta df = df_{\text{restricted}} - df_{\text{unrestricted}}.$$

However, especially with large sample sizes or when numerous restrictions are imposed, this approach is likely to indicate measurement inequalities across cultures, even in the presence of substantively trivial differences. Alternatively, and as the approach we recommend, a modeling rationale would suggest that if the restricted model exhibits adequate fit as indexed by common fit indexes, then equality of measurement (i.e., measurement invariance) across the cultures can be concluded to reasonably approximate the data. Such fit indices include the non-normed fit index (NNFI), which is considered acceptable if greater than 0.90 (Bentler & Bonett, 1980) and the root mean square error of approximation (RMSES), which is considered adequate if below 0.08 (Steiger, 1990; see Browne & Cudek, 1993; Cheung & Rensvold, 2002; Hu & Bentler, 1995).

If measurement invariance across cultures can reasonably be concluded, then one can begin examining differences across cultures in the latent constructs, because constructs can be presumed to represent fundamentally similar phenomena in the cultures under investigation. If measurement invariance is not tenable, then several options must be considered (see Little & Slegers, in press). One must first determine which indicators most contribute to poor model fit and consider the size of this misfit (usually determined by examining modification indices and residuals of the restricted model described earlier). If it seems that the differences between the indicators are small enough that they are substantively equitable, one could argue that it is appropriate to proceed with cross-cultural equality constraints in place.

If there is a reasonable post-hoc explanation for why some indicators do not assess the underlying construct equally across cultures, then it is defensible to remove those specific indicators and model the latent construct only with those indicators that are invariant across cultures (if this is done, it should be fully reported to provide others with valuable information on assessing such constructs). Alternatively, one could relax the cross-cultural equality constraints on the offending indicators and proceed with latent variable analysis of this partially invariant model; the researcher then should cautiously interpret latent similarities and differences in this construct across cultures (see Millsap & Kwok, 2004). Finally, it might be necessary to conclude that measurement invariance cannot be established using the indicators selected, and the researcher must reconsider how to better evaluate the constructs of interest across cultures in the next study (this, we hope, adds emphasis to our previous advice to place great attention to the initial operationalization across cultures).

Comparing Cultures – Differences in Mean Levels and Variances

Once measurement invariance or a reasonable approximation of it (e.g., partial invariance) is established, it is then possible to begin evaluating similarities and differences across cultures in the latent constructs. In this section, we describe techniques to compare cultures in terms of mean levels and variances of constructs.

In evaluating mean-level differences in the latent construct across cultures, one begins by freeing the implied restriction of 0 on the paths between the unit constant (i.e., the triangle in Figure 4.1) and the latent constructs of each culture; in other words, paths are added from the constant to the latent construct in each culture. Note that the mean structure of the model that includes estimated latent means (αs) can now be identified because of the equating of the manifest intercepts (τs) across cultures, as this equating also gains back degrees of freedom.

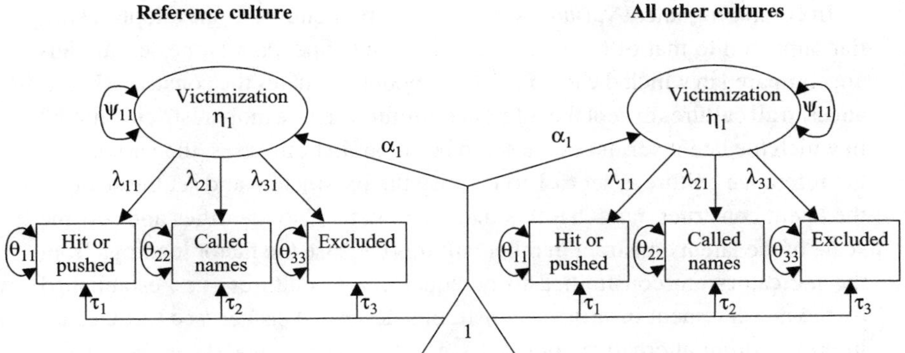

Figure 4.1. Evaluating measurement equivalence and latent means and variances across cultures.

To examine differences between means in the latent construct across cultures, one can simply compare nested models in which the less restricted model estimates construct means (αs, the paths from the constant to the latent construct in Figure 4.1) in all cultures except the reference culture (which is set to 0 to provide a reference mean, but see Little et al., in press, for an alternative approach) versus a more restricted model in which the latent means (αs) are set to be equal. The test of significance in the difference between the two models ($\Delta\chi^2 = \chi^2{}_{\text{restricted}} - \chi^2{}_{\text{unrestricted}}$ with $\Delta df = df_{\text{restricted}} - df_{\text{unrestricted}}$) indicates whether the means of the construct can be considered reliably different across cultures.

We would like to note that, in contrast to our view on using a modeling rationale for evaluating measurement invariance across cultures, we support the use of nested-model significance testing in evaluating cross-cultural differences in latent construct parameters (i.e., means, variances, and covariances). A modeling rationale is appropriate for cross-cultural comparison at the measurement level because we want to make conclusions regarding the reasonableness of the assumption of measurement equality across cultures. A statistical rationale is appropriate for comparisons at the latent level because we want to make probabilistic statements about differences between cultures (i.e., perform significance tests; see Little, 1997). Of course, one should also evaluate the mean-level differences in terms of effect sizes to make conclusions regarding the importance of any statistically significant mean-level differences (e.g., Cohen's d for the difference between a culture's and the reference group's latent means, $d = \alpha_{\text{Culture1}}/\sqrt{[1/2(\psi_{11\text{Culture1}} + \psi_{11\text{ReferenceCulture}})]}$, could be computed as one effect size measure).

In comparing latent variances (i.e., ψ_{11}) across cultures, one adopts a similar approach to that of comparing latent means. Specifically, nested models are compared in which the less restricted model estimates the constructs' variances in all cultures except the reference culture versus a more restricted model in which the latent variances are set to be equal. In both cases, the variance of the reference culture is set to 1 to identify the parameters and set the scale of the latent construct; note that this fixed parameter also identifies and sets the scale of the latent construct in other cultures because the factor loadings from the indicators are constrained to be equal across cultures (i.e., established by the measurement invariance constraints described earlier; see Little et al., in press, for an alternative approach). The two nested models are compared using $\Delta\chi^2 = \chi^2_{\text{restricted}} - \chi^2_{\text{unrestricted}}$ with $\Delta df = df_{\text{restricted}} - df_{\text{unrestricted}}$ to evaluate differences in variances of the latent constructs across cultures. We note that comparisons of variances across cultures are uncommon in peer relations (and other) research, yet MACS analysis makes the decision to evaluate differences in latent variances explicit. Such comparisons, if more widely undertaken, have the potential to provide valuable information about the range of children's peer experiences across cultures.

Considering again the victimization example shown in Figure 4.1, one begins by evaluating measurement invariance as described in the previous section. If substantive measurement invariance could reasonably be assumed (i.e., if the restricted model, with factor loadings λ_1, λ_2, and λ_3 and intercepts τ_1, τ_2, and τ_3 equated across cultures, fits the data adequately), then one could evaluate differences in the latent means and variances across cultures (in this example, children in the United States and China). The unrestricted model would equate the factor loading and intercepts of the manifest indicators across cultures and would set the latent variance in victimization to 1.0 and latent mean to 0 in the reference culture (in this example, the United States because the scales are more commonly used within this population), but would freely estimate the latent variances and means in the Chinese sample. The researcher then would fit two restricted models, one in which the latent victimization construct mean (α_1) was restricted to be equal across the cultures and one in which the latent victimization variance (ψ_{11}) was restricted to be equal. Comparison of each of these restricted models to the unrestricted model in terms of increase in $\Delta\chi^2$ (with $\Delta df = df_{\text{restricted}} - df_{\text{unrestricted}}$) would indicate differences in the latent victimization means and variances, respectively, between United States and Chinese children. Note that more than two cultures could be compared, and the tests would represent omnibus tests of differences across the cultures investigated, which could be followed up by a series of more specific comparisons.

Comparing Cultures – Differences in Processes

In this section, we describe a technique to compare cultures in terms of processes, or associations between constructs. Before beginning, however, we would like to emphasize the difference between comparing cultures in terms of mean levels (or variances) and comparing cultures in terms of processes. Comparison of mean levels, described in the previous section, answers the question, "Does culture A have higher or lower levels of X than culture B?" Independent of the similarities or differences in mean levels between cultures are questions of differences in processes. Comparisons of processes answers the question, "Is X differentially related to Y in cultures A and B?" Following the example in the previous section, one might evaluate whether rates of victimization among children differ between two cultures as a mean-level comparison, but also consider whether victimization is more strongly related to social status in one culture relative to another as a process comparison. As mentioned, the answer to one question is completely independent of the answer to the other (the former can be considered a main effect and the latter an interaction, or moderated, effect).

MACS analyses can address differences in latent correlations across cultures simply by an elaboration of the approach described in the prior section. This approach, using associations between victimization and social status as an example, is depicted in Figure 4.2. Here, we have rearranged the locations of the different cultures (now on the top and bottom of the figure) only to simplify the figure. Notice that there are now two latent variables representing each construct in each culture. If we had represented the victimization and social status constructs with one latent variable each, the path connecting the two constructs would have been in covariance terms. This would be inadequate to test differences in association across cultures, as any differences in covariance would be the product of both differences in correlations and differences in variances across cultures.

To address this problem, we recommend an alternative approach (see Little, 1997; Little, Card, Slegers, & Ledford, in press) involving the creation of a second-order latent construct (e.g., η_2 in Figure 4.2) for each first-order construct (e.g., η_1). The variance of the first-order latent construct (η_1) is fixed at zero, and the variance of the second-order latent construct (η_2) is fixed at 1.0 in both cultures. Information regarding variances is not lost, however, as this information is now contained in the regression coefficient between the two latent variables (e.g., β_{12} in Figure 4.2). Note that the variance is still restricted in the reference cultural group, here at 1.0, but estimated in the other groups; thus, the latent variance of this group is equal to the square of this coefficient

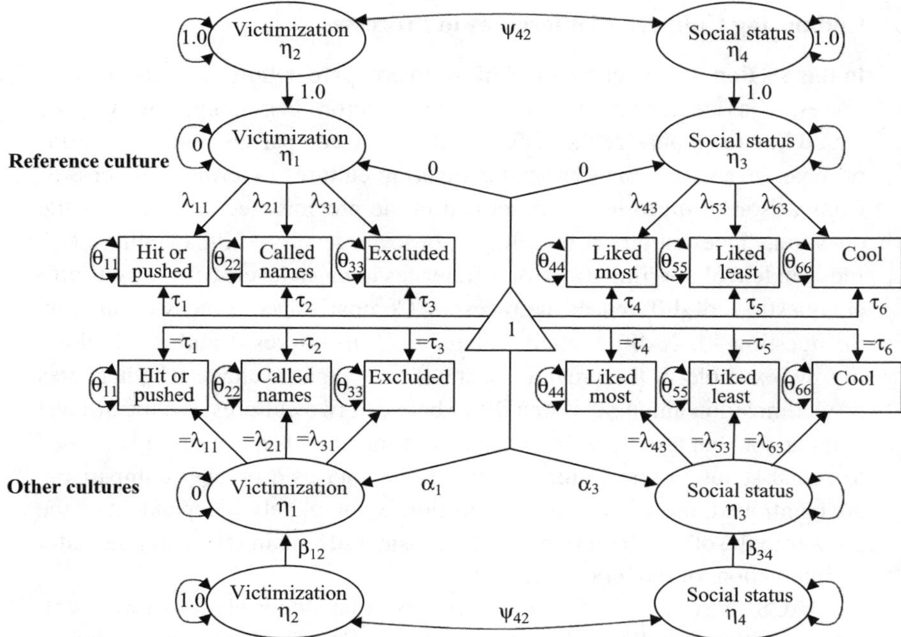

Figure 4.2. Comparing processes (latent correlations) across cultures.

(e.g., $\beta_{12}{}^2$). With this approach, however, we are now able to interpret the paths between the second-order latent variables of the two constructs (ψ_{42} in Figure 4.2) as latent (i.e., disattenuated) correlation coefficients (an identical approach could be applied to directional effects between η_2 and η_4).

From here, comparison of latent associations (i.e., correlations) proceeds as described for latent means and variances. Specifically, nested model comparison between an unrestricted model, in which the latent correlations (ψ_{42}) are separately estimated in each culture, and a restricted model, in which these latent correlations are constrained to be equal, reveals differences in these associations across cultures. Using the example described, this test would examine whether the latent correlation between victimization and social status reliably differs between children in the United States and China (i.e., examine whether the latent correlation, ψ_{42}, is equal among children in the two cultures).

Analyzing Interculture Interaction – The Social Relations Model

The reality of the modern world is that cultures do not exist in discrete, nonoverlapping contexts; instead, youths of different cultures often interact.

Modeling these interactions requires special techniques of analyzing data (i.e., dyadic, triadic, and other *n*-adic approaches). Here, we will describe the social relations model as a flexible tool for analyzing interpersonal perception, affect, and behavior, and suggest a method of using this approach for studying intercultural interaction.

Given that the social relations model has received little application in child and adolescent peer relations research (for exceptions, see Coie et al., 1999; Hubbard et al., 2001; Malloy et al., 1995; Malloy et al., 1996; Ross & Lollis, 1989; Scarpati, Malloy, & Fleming, 1996), we first describe this model in brief detail. The social relations model is a conceptual, methodological, and analytic approach that captures the interpersonal nature of perception, affect (i.e., liking and disliking), and behavior (see Kenny, 1994; Kenny & La Voie, 1984; Malloy & Kenny, 1986). Conceptually, it offers insight into the consideration of the dyadic nature of interpersonal interaction. Methodologically, it requires data to be collected so that dyadic measures (i.e., ratings, nominations, or behavioral observations of one individual toward another) from a set of youths are specifically directed toward another set of youths. Specific designs include half-block (one set of youths completes measures of a second, distinct set of youths), block (two sets of youths complete measures of youths in the other set, but not in their own set), round robin (youths complete measures of all peers), and block-round robin (youths in two sets complete measures of all peers, both those in their own set and those in the other set) designs (see Figure 4.3). Analytically, it provides a sophisticated method of managing the interdependency among these data (whereas traditional analytic approaches make assumptions regarding independence of observations that are clearly violated).

In its basic form, the social relations model provides information on three aspects of interpersonal perceptions, affect, or behavior: group means, variance partitioning, and reciprocity. First, it provides unbiased estimates of mean levels of variables within the entire groups. It also partitions the variance among these scores into that which is due to individual differences among those from whom the measure originates (i.e., perceivers, likers/dislikers, or those enacting the behavior), termed actor variance[1] and into that which is due to individual differences among those toward whom the measure originates (i.e., those perceived, liked/disliked, or receiving the behavior), termed partner variance; and, if the dyadic construct of interest is assessed using multiple items or at multiple time points, it is also possible to distinguish the uniqueness of scores (perception, affect, or behavior) between two individuals, after accounting for the actor's tendency to have these scores toward others and the partner's tendency to receive these scores from others, into that due to stable relationship effects and that due to random error. Finally, the social relations

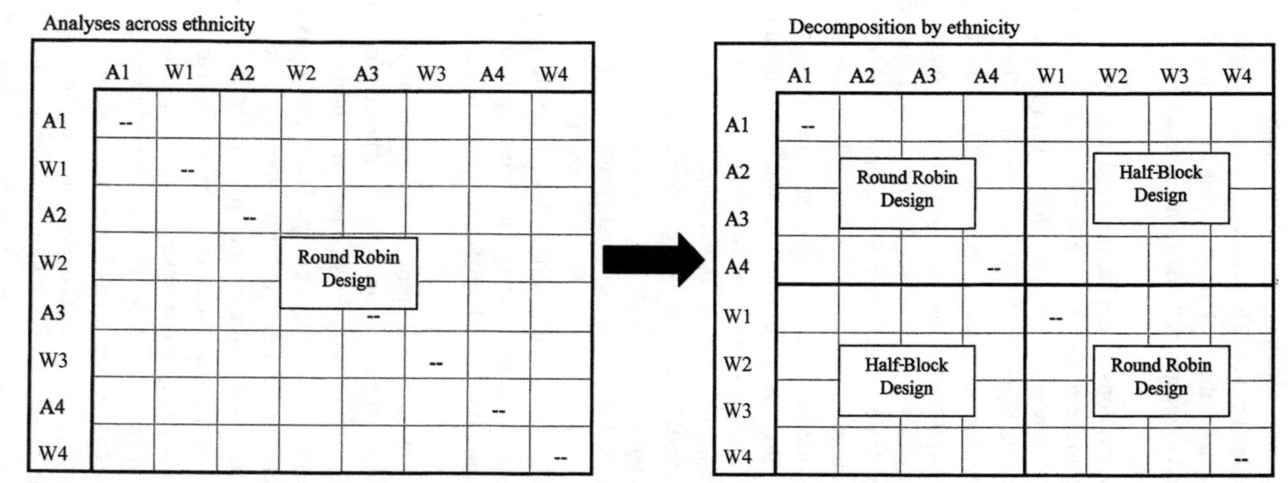

Figure 4.3. Decomposition of round robin matrix to facilitate examination of intra- and intergroup perceptions. *Note:* A1, A2, etc., represent the first, second, etc., African American students in the class, and W1, W2, etc., represent the first, second, etc., White students in the class.

model allows the computation of two indexes of reciprocity. Generalized reciprocity refers to tendencies of individuals who perceive, like/dislike, or behave toward others in a certain way to also be perceived, liked/disliked, or behaved toward by others at a high or low rate. Dyadic reciprocity refers to the correlation between one individual's perception, affect, or behavior toward a particular peer and that particular peer's perception, affect, or behavior toward the individual.

To illustrate these concepts, consider a situation in which a researcher observes aggression within children's artificial play groups (for an example of this type of study, see Coie et al., 1999). The researcher might observe occurrences of aggression of all children with all possible peers (i.e., a round robin design). The overall frequency of aggression within that play group would be indexed by the group mean. It might be expected that some children, irrespective of the particular peer with whom they interact, would tend to more frequently behave aggressively (i.e., have a high actor effect), whereas other children would tend to rarely enact aggression (i.e., have a low actor effect). Individual differences in these tendencies to enact aggression toward peers would be indexed by the degree of actor variance. It is also likely that some youths would frequently be the targets of their peers' aggression (i.e., have a high partner effect), whereas others would rarely be targeted (i.e., have a low partner effect); individual differences in these tendencies would be indexed by partner variance.

Now, imagine that the researcher observed that Adam very frequently hits Billy, even more than would be expected given Adam's general tendency to hit others and Billy's general tendency to be hit by others. If the researcher had other measures of aggression (e.g., how often Adam calls Billy names, how often Adam tries to exclude Billy from the group) or had observations at several time points (e.g., in play groups on subsequent days), and Adam was found to be especially aggressive toward Billy on these other indicators as well, then one might be able to conclude that there is a relationship effect of high aggression from Adam to Billy (beyond Adam's general aggressiveness and Billy's general victimization). The degree of differences among the dyads of this group, after controlling for the actor and partner effects of the individuals in the dyads, are indexed by the amount of relationship variance. The researcher might also examine whether children who are highly aggressive toward others are also frequently the targets of others' aggression, which would be indicated by a positive generalized reciprocity correlation (alternatively, a researcher might find that children who are highly aggressive toward others are rarely the targets of others' aggression, indicated by a negative generalized reciprocity correlation). Finally, the researcher might examine whether there is, across all dyads in the group, a positive or negative relation between a child's aggression toward a particular peer (e.g., Adam's aggression toward Billy) and that particular peer's aggression toward the child (e.g., Billy's aggression toward Adam); this is indexed by the dyadic reciprocity correlation. Description of the computation of these parameters is beyond the scope of this chapter, but is described in detail in several other sources (e.g., Kenny, 1994; Lashley & Bond, 1997).

Although several methods of computing standard errors (for significance testing or computation of confidence intervals) of each estimate exist (see Lashley & Bond, 1997), we will briefly describe one of the more common approaches. If estimates of each of the previously mentioned parameters (group means; actor, partner, and relationship variances; generalized and dyadic reciprocities) are obtained from several independent groups (e.g., separate play groups or classrooms), standard errors of estimates of each parameter can be obtained by assessing the dispersion of these estimates among the groups (with estimates from each group weighted by number in group minus 1, if group sizes differ); specifically, the standard error equals the square root of the variance of parameter estimates across groups divided by the number of groups minus 1.

Although we have provided only a brief description of the social relations model, we hope that this will serve as a foundation of basic understanding. More detailed overviews can be found in Kenny (1994), Kenny and La Voie (1984), and Malloy and Kenny (1986); further information on the statistical details, including significance testing, can be found in Kenny (1994), Lashley and Bond (1997), and Lashley and Kenny (1998). We next describe an approach of decomposing social relations model designs to gain a better understanding of dyadic variables within and across cultures (for similar approaches applied to adults' cross-cultural perceptions, see Albright et al., 1997).

Consider another example in which interpersonal perceptions of a construct (e.g., perceived popularity) are obtained via peer reports within multiethnic classrooms. If all children are asked to report on all peers, then this could be represented as a round robin design. However, if we then decompose this round robin matrix according to the ethnicities of nominators and targets, then we can conceptualize these data as fitting a block-round robin design. For simplicity, we will imagine that our classrooms consist only of White and African American students (though multiple ethnicities could be considered[2]), which would yield a 2 × 2 decomposition of the round robin matrix (see Figure 4.3; for a similar example considering children's perceptions within and across sexes, see Card et al., 2005).

The researcher can then analyze these submatrices as a series of round robin or half-block designs. Returning to our example on perceived popularity, mean ratings of popularity (group means[3]), individual differences in perceiving others as popular (actor variances), individual differences in being perceived as popular (partner variances), and differences among dyads in reliable unique perceptions of popularity (relationship variances) could be computed within each submatrix: African American students' ratings of other African American students, African American students' ratings of White students, White students' ratings of African American students, and White students' ratings of other White students. With estimates from multiple classrooms, ethnic differences in perceiving others, being perceived by others, and interperceptual/intraperceptual difference would be indicated by the two main effects and the interaction effect, respectively, of a 2 (perceiver ethnicity) × 2 (target ethnicity) repeated-measures analysis of variances (ANOVA) across classrooms. Generalized reciprocities could also be computed for the four ethnicity-rating groups, though the reciprocities of cross-ethnicity perceptions would consist of the correlations between the actor effects (i.e., row means) of one half-block with the partner effects (i.e., column means) of the other half-block (paralleling analysis of block designs); for example, the correlation between African American students' perceptions of White students (the row means of the upper right submatrix of Figure 4.3) with White students' perceptions of the African American students (the column means of the lower left submatrix of Figure 4.3). Tests of ethnic differences by perceiver, target, and their interaction could then also be performed through a 2 × 2 ANOVA. A special case is made for dyadic reciprocity; given that the correlation between African American students' perceptions of particular White students and those particular White students' perceptions of African American students represent all cross-ethnic perceptions, a one-way three-level (African American, cross-ethnic, and White) repeated-measures ANOVA is used to assess ethnic differences.

Having discussed methods of computing group means, actor, partner, and relationship variances, and generalized and dyadic reciprocities in intra- and interethnic perceptions (similar approaches could be used for measures of affect or dyadic behaviors), we now discuss the interpretation of these effects.

Differences in group means indicate differences in mean levels of perceptions; nominator ethnic differences would indicate that one ethnic group perceives peers in general in a certain way more so than another ethnic group (e.g., African American or White students may differ in perceiving others as popular); target ethnic differences would indicate that one ethnic group is seen differently (e.g., as more popular) than another; and nominator × target interactions would indicate that there is an intra- or interethnic bias (e.g., perceiving one's own ethnicity as more popular), after controlling for the main effects of nominator and target ethnicity.

Differences in variance partitioning also offer interesting insight into interpersonal perception within and across groups. Ethnic differences in actor variances would indicate ethnic differences in the degree of individual differences in general perceptions of others. Nominator differences would indicate that there exists more variability within one group than another in generalized views of peers, whereas target differences would indicate that there exists greater variability of peers' generalized perceptions of one group than another. Perhaps most interesting are nominator × target interactions, which can address questions regarding the degree of variability in same- and cross-ethnic perceptions. Differences in partner variances would indicate ethnic differences in consensus, or agreement among peers regarding who is high or low on a characteristic. Nominator differences would indicate that one group has greater consensus in their views of peers, whereas target differences would indicate that there is more consensus in the characteristics of one group relative to another. Nominator × target interactions would be indicative of greater within- or between-group consensus. Relationship variance indexes the uniqueness of interpersonal perception and can be interpreted in a variety of ways, including unique behaviors enacted within the dyadic context (i.e., unique perceptions are the result of witnessing different behaviors of the target than those observed by others) and differences in meaning systems assigned to similar behaviors (i.e., unique perceptions are the result of viewing characteristics of the target differently than others). Either interpretation is substantively interesting in exploring the role of culture in peer relationships. Relationship variance is the variability in these unique effects, after removing measurement error, and can also be interpreted in terms of ethnic differences among nominators, targets, and nominator × target interactions.

Group differences in reciprocity also have promise in understanding the role of culture in peer relations. Generalized reciprocity can be interpreted as the result of children's self-perceptions influencing how they perceive peers (assuming that others' perceptions correspond to self-perceptions), children's perceptions of peers leading them to adopt behaviors that influence how they are perceived by others, or children's behaviors influencing both peers' views of the child and the child's perception of peers (possibly by eliciting certain behaviors from peers). Similar interpretations can be made for dyadic reciprocity, with the qualification that each of these processes are occurring within a dyadic (rather than group) context. Examination of group differences for generalized reciprocity (nominator, target, and nominator × target group differences) and dyadic reciprocity (differences among two intragroup reciprocity estimates and one intragroup reciprocity estimate) has the potential to reveal the extent to which these processes occur depending on the ethnicity (or other cultural factor) of the children or their peers.

We view potential group differences in (a) means; (b) variance partitioning among actor, partner, and relationship effects; and (c) generalized and dyadic reciprocities as potentially useful approaches to understand the role of culture in interpersonal perception, liking/disliking, and behaviors. However, the social relations model has not been widely used in peer relations research to date. One reason for this may be a lack of familiarity with the social relations model and the apparent complexity of the analyses. Furthermore, conceptualizing potential effects of culture is difficult if researchers are already unfamiliar with the social relations model. Despite these obstacles, we believe that the social relations model represents a valuable and highly flexible tool for studying processes within and across cultures in multicultural settings. Fortunately, there exist several accessible introductions to the social relations model that can give researchers a useful start in using this approach (e.g., Kenny, 1994; Kenny & La Voie, 1984; Malloy & Kenny, 1986); moreover, Kenny (http://davidakenny.net/kenny.htm) is developing user-friendly interfaces for the analysis programs (*BLOCKO*, *SOREMO*) commonly used.

Other advances include the translation of social relations model principles into more traditional approaches, such as structural equation modeling. For example, one study (Branje, van Acken, & van Lieshout, 2002; see also Cook, 1994) examined the amount of support given among fathers, mothers, older children, and younger children using a round robin design within families. By modeling support between each combination of individuals (e.g., father to mother, father to older, father to younger, mother to father, mother to older, etc.), it was possible to model latent actor variances (e.g., the between-family differences in father's support to other family members) and partner variances (e.g., the between-family differences in support received by younger children from other family members) for each role (i.e., father, mother, older, and younger). Relationship effects can also be modeled as the latent variance (i.e., that in common among multiple indicators of each dyad after controlling for latent actor and partner variances). Furthermore, this structural equation modeling approach to roles also allows estimation of both covariances (i.e., generalized and dyadic). Thus, social-relations designs that include distinct roles for individuals have been accurately represented as structural equation models. Although we are not aware of prior research including mean values, it would also be possible to represent social relations models as MACS analyses; such an approach would provide all of the variance and covariance estimates of traditional social relations models plus allow mean-level comparisons (e.g., do fathers or mothers provide more support within families). Although we have discussed a study involving family functioning, there is no reason that this approach could not be adapted to the study of peer relations.[4]

Other Analytic Approaches

We have focused primarily on two general analytic approaches in this chapter, MACS analyses and the social relations model. Although this might seem quite limited, we would like to note that these are extraordinarily flexible approaches that can address a multitude of research questions besides those discussed in this chapter. Here, we briefly mention some of these extensions, referring interested readers to more detailed descriptions.

Peer relations researchers, like most developmental scientists, often rely on longitudinal studies and analytic techniques (e.g., growth curve modeling). MACS analyses, like other structural models, can be easily adapted to address questions regarding longitudinal growth trajectories (see, e.g., McArdle & Epstein, 1987). Alternative person-centered approaches to studying trajectories of growth over time, such as Nagin's group-based approach (1999; Nagin & Tremblay, 2001) and Muthén's growth mixture modeling can also be modeled using MACS analyses (see Muthén, 2001). An advantage of representing growth-curve models (and other multilevel models) and person-centered trajectories as MACS analyses is that it allows one to evaluate cross-cultural equivalence of the measurement structures (advances in MACS analyses now allow for evaluation of cross-level interactions, so we view latent variable modeling as the generalized approach to these previously discrete techniques). We also note that in longitudinal research, it is important to assess measurement invariance across time as well as across cultures.

There also exist several variations of social relations modeling, such as the weighted-average model of perception (WAM; see Kenny, 1991), extensions to examine similarity in perceptions among friends (e.g., Kenny & Kashy, 1994), and the actor-partner interdependence model (APIM; e.g., Kenny, 1996), which allow researchers to examine other dyadic phenomenon of cross-cultural interactions. Also, triadic (and higher order) extensions of the social relations model (Bond, Horn, & Kenny, 1997; Bond et al., 2000) allow for more analysis of more complex social interactions, which can also be recast to answer questions of cultural similarities and differences (e.g., do youths provide more protection against victimization toward their friends if the aggressor is of the same or different ethnicity?). Finally, the more general approach of social network analysis (see Knoke & Kuklinski, 1982;

Wasserman & Faust, 1994) represents an extensive collection of strategies that can be used to answer many other questions involving peer relations of children of different cultures.

Conclusions and Future Directions

We believe that cross-cultural peer relations research is limited less by the availability of appropriate analytic techniques than by researchers' efforts to study the wide range of unexplored issues (such as those described in other chapters of this volume) – this is not to say that sophisticated analysis is simple (as many readers of this chapter may agree), but we do believe that these techniques are accessible to those who wish to perform this research.

In this chapter, we have described two analytic approaches that can answer many of the questions posed by cross-cultural peer relations research. With MACS analyses, the evaluation of the cross-cultural measurement equivalence of constructs is made explicit. This measurement equivalence is important, because constructs such as aggression and victimization, group-level status such as popularity and social preference, and dyadic relationships such as friendships and mutual antipathies are likely to vary considerably in their manifestations across cultures (see e.g., Krappmann, 1996; Smith et al., 2002; and the chapters throughout this book). If it can be reasonably concluded that the constructs of interest are being similarly measured in different cultures (i.e., there is strong factorial invariance), then MACS analyses can examine all of the same aspects of more traditional analytic approaches – comparisons of means across groups (traditionally performed with analysis of variance), comparisons of correlations and directional paths among constructs (traditionally performed within a correlation or regression framework), growth curve analyses (traditionally performed as multilevel models), and person-centered approaches – all within a latent variable framework in which the constructs are equated across cultures. We therefore view MACS analysis as an extremely general approach that can be readily adapted to various research questions.

The other analytic strategy that we have presented, the social relations model, is a more specialized technique. We have chosen to highlight it based on our view that the interdependencies among children lie at the heart of peer relations research; they are not simply violations of traditional analytic assumptions to be avoided. Research has demonstrated the interdependent nature of aggressive behavior both in artificial play groups (Coie et al., 1999; Hubbard et al., 2001) and in school settings (Card, 2001; Card, Isaacs, & Hodges, 2000). Similarly, examination of friendships and other dyadic relationships (e.g., mutual antipathies, parent–child relationships) necessarily involves consideration of interdependency, the degree of which is, again, of substantive interest rather than a nuisance to be overcome. We believe that the social relations model and the related analytic approaches (e.g., APIM, WAM, triadic data analysis, social network analysis) represent an important set of analytic tools to help peer relations researchers conceptualize, study, and analyze the interdependencies that are inherent in this research. Consideration of the interdependencies within and between cultures, as we have demonstrated in our hypothetical example of perceptions of popularity among African American and White students, stands as an equally important future direction.

Although we have tried to be general with our presentation, we expect that as new research questions arise, it will be necessary to adapt these strategies to best answer these questions. Fortunately, the techniques we have described in this chapter are quite flexible, as we hopefully have demonstrated here. We believe that analytic techniques have evolved to the point that most questions of interest to peer relations researchers are answerable through available approaches. Thus, future research of cross-cultural similarities and differences now lies with researchers' creative asking of questions and their creative adaptation of analytic techniques.

Acknowledgments

We thank Fang Fang Chen and Thomas E. Malloy for commenting on a draft of this chapter. This work was supported in part by grants from the National Institutes of Health to the University of Kansas through the Mental Retardation and Developmental Disabilities Research Center (5 P30 HD002528), the Center for Biobehavioral Neurosciences in Communication Disorders (5 P30 DC005803), and an NRSA fellowship to the first author (1 F32 MH072005).

Notes

1 An important additional aspect of actor variance is that there is within-person consistency. For example, if child A gives high ratings of all peers and child B gives low ratings of all peers, actor variance is maximized to the extent that there is high between-actor variability but low within-actor variability. Similarly, partner variance is maximized when there is a high degree of individual differences but low within-person variability in ratings received.

2 To compute all components of the social relations model, the minimum number of individuals in any subgroup is four. If generalized reciprocities for the round robin of that subgroup are not estimated (i.e., they are fixed at zero), then the minimum number in a subgroup is three.

3 This method of evaluating ethnic differences in means is actually an unnecessarily low power test, as one could perform these analyses at the individual level using children's estimated actor or partner effects (with identical results using either). We present this conservative method of computing group means at the subgroup level only because the researcher may wish to compare group means using this approach to parallel analyses on other social relations model parameters.

4 Currently, modeling social relations models such as structural equation models (with or without means) requires that individuals within each group can be meaningfully assigned to specific roles. The reason for this is that dyadic measures (i.e., perceptions, liking/disliking, or behaviors) must be able to be nonarbitrarily assigned to load on specific latent variables consistently across groups. Although we are not aware of current techniques that do not require specific roles, it seems possible that this limitation could be overcome with further development (e.g., through extension of current exchangeable case procedures for dyads; see Griffin & Gonzalez, 1995). Nevertheless, there exist numerous role classifications within the peer relations literature (e.g., sociometric classifications) that could meaningfully be used through existing approaches.

References

Albright, L., Malloy, T. E., Dong, Q., Kenny, D. A., Fang, X., Winquist, L., et al. (1997). Cross-cultural consensus in personality judgments. *Journal of Personality and Social Psychology, 72*, 558–569.

Bentler, P. M., & Bonett, D. G. (1980). Significance tests and goodness of fit in the analysis of covariance structures. *Psychological Bulletin, 88*, 588–606.

Bond, C. F., Jr., Horn, E. M., & Kenny, D. A. (1997). A model for triadic relations. *Psychological Methods, 2*, 79–94.

Bond, C. F., Jr., Kenny, D. A., Broome, E. H., Stokes-Zoota, J. J., & Richard, F. D. (2000). Multivariate analysis of triadic relations. *Multivariate Behavioral Research, 35*, 397–426.

Branje, S. J. T., van Acken, M. A. G., & van Lieshout, C. F. M. (2002). Relational support in families with adolescents. *Journal of Family Psychology, 16*, 351–362.

Browne, M. W., & Cudek, R. (1993). Alternative ways of assessing model fit. In K. A. Bollen & J. S. Long (Eds.), *Testing structural equation models* (pp. 136–162). Newbury Park, CA: Sage.

Card, N. A. (2001). *Who aggresses against whom? An examination of aggressors and victims in a school setting*. Unpublished master's thesis. St. John's University, Jamaica, NY.

Card, N. A., Hodges, E. V. E., Little, T. D., & Hawley, P. H. (2005). Gender effects in peer nominations for aggression and social status. *International Journal of Behavioral Development, 29*, 146–155.

Card, N. A., Isaacs, J., & Hodges, E. V. E. (2000, March). Dynamics of interpersonal aggression in the school context: Who aggresses against whom? Poster presented at the 8th biennial meeting of the Society for Research on Adolescence, Chicago, IL.

Cheung, G. W., & Rensvold, R. B. (2002). Evaluating goodness-of-fit indexes for testing measurement invariance. *Structural Equation Modeling, 9*, 233–255.

Coie, J. D., Cillessen, A. H. N., Dodge, K. A., Hubbard, J. A., Schwartz, D., Lemerise, E. A., et al. (1999). It takes two to fight: A test of relational factors and a method of assessing aggressive dyads. *Developmental Psychology, 35*, 1179–1188.

Cook, W. L. (1994). A structural equation model of dyadic relationships within the family system. *Journal of Consulting and Clinical Psychology, 62*, 500–509.

Griffen, D., & Gonzalez, R. (1995). Correlational analysis of dyad-level data in the exchangeable case. *Psychological Bulletin, 118*, 430–439.

Hu, L.-T., & Bentler, P. M. (1995). Evaluating model fit. In R. H. Hoyle (Ed.), *Structural equation modeling: Concepts, issues, and applications*. Thousand Oaks, CA: Sage.

Hubbard, J. A., Dodge, K. A., Cillessen, A. H. N., Coie, J. D., & Schwartz, D. (2001). The dyadic nature of social information processing in boys' reactive and proactive aggression. *Journal of Personality and Social Psychology, 80*, 268–280.

Kenny, D. A. (1991). A general model of consensus and accuracy in interpersonal perception. *Psychological Review, 98*, 155–163.

Kenny, D. A. (1994). *Interpersonal perception: A social relations analysis*. New York: Guilford.

Kenny, D. A. (1996). Models of nonindependence in dyadic research. *Journal of Social and Personal Relationships, 13*, 279–294.

Kenny, D. A., & Kashy, D. A. (1994). Enhanced co-orientation among friends: A social relations analysis. *Journal of Personality and Social Psychology, 67*, 1024–1033.

Kenny, D. A., & La Voie, L. J. (1984). The social relations model. In L. Berkowitz (Ed.), *Advances in experimental social psychology* (Vol. 18, pp. 142–182). San Diego, CA: Academic Press.

Knoke, D., & Kuklinski, J. H. (1982). *Network analysis*. Sage university paper series on quantitative applications in the social sciences, 07–028. Beverly Hills, CA: Sage.

Krappmann, L. (1996). Amicitia, drujba, shin-yu, philia, freundschaft, friendship: On the cultural diversity of a human relationship. In W. M. Bukowski, A. F. Newcomb, & W. W. Hartup (Eds.), *The company they keep: Friendship in childhood and adolescence* (pp. 19–40). New York: Cambridge University Press.

Lashley, B. R., & Bond, C. F., Jr. (1997). Significance testing for round robin data. *Psychological Methods, 2*, 278–291.

Lashley, B. R., & Kenny, D. A. (1998). Power estimation in social relations analyses. *Psychological Methods, 3*, 328–338.

Little, T. D. (1997). Mean and covariance structures (MACS) analyses of cross-cultural data: Practical and theoretical issues. *Multivariate Behavioral Research, 32*, 53–76.

Little, T. D., Card, N. A., Slegers, D. W., & Ledford, E. C. (in press). Testing direct, mediated, and moderated effects in multiple-groups MACS models. In T. D. Little, J. A. Bovaird, & N. A. Card (Eds.), *Modeling ecological and contextual effects in longitudinal analyses of human development*. Mahwah, NJ: Lawrence Erlbaum Associates.

Little, T. D., & Slegers, D. W. (in press). Factor Analysis: Multiple groups with means. In D. Rindskopf (Section Ed.), *Encyclopedia of statistic in behavioral sciences*. West Sussex, England: Wiley.

Little, T. D., & Slegers, D. W., & Card, N. A. (in press). *An alternative method of identifying and scaling latent variables in SEM and MACS models. Structural Equation Modeling: A Multidisciplinary Journal*. Manuscript submitted for publication.

Malloy, T. E., & Kenny, D. A. (1986). The social relations model: An integrative method for personality research. *Journal of Personality, 54*, 199–225.
Malloy, T. E., Sugarman, D. B., Montvilo, R. K., & Ben-Zeev, T. (1995). Children's interpersonal perceptions: A social relations analysis of perceiver and target effects. *Journal of Personality and Social Psychology, 68*, 418–426.
Malloy, T. E., Yarlas, A., Montvilo, R. K., & Sugarman, D. B. (1996). Agreement and accuracy in children's interpersonal perceptions: A social relations analysis. *Journal of Personality and Social Psychology, 71*, 692–702.
McArdle, J. J., & Epstein, D. (1987). Latent growth curves within developmental structural equation models. *Child Development, 58*, 110–133.
Meredith, W. (1993). Measurement invariance, factor analysis and factorial invariance. *Psychometrika, 58*, 525–543.
Millsap, R. E., & Kwok, O. M. (2004). Evaluating the impact of partial factorial invariance on selection in two populations. *Psychological Methods, 9*, 93–115.
Muthén, B. O. (2001). Latent variable mixture modeling. In G. A. Marcoulides & R. E. Shumacker (Eds.), *New developments and techniques in structural equation modeling* (pp. 1–33). Mahwah, NJ: Lawrence Erlbaum Associates.
Nagin, D. S. (1999). Analyzing developmental trajectories: A semiparametric, group-based approach. *Psychological Methods, 4*, 139–157.
Nagin, D. S., & Tremblay, R. E. (2001). Analyzing developmental trajectories of distinct but related behaviors: A group-based method. *Psychological Methods, 6*, 18–34
Novy, D. M., Stanley, M. A., Averill, P., & Daza, P. (2001). Psychometric comparability of English- and Spanish-language measures of anxiety and related affective symptoms. *Psychological Assessment, 13*, 347–355.
Ross, H. S., & Lollis, S. P. (1989). A social relations analysis of toddler peer relations. *Child Development, 60*, 1082–1091.
Scarpati, S., Malloy, T. E., & Fleming, R. (1996). Interpersonal perception of skill efficacy and behavioral control of adolescents with learning disabilities: A social relations approach. *Learning Disability Quarterly, 19*, 15–22.
Schwartz, D., Chang, L., & Farver, J. M. (2001). Correlates of victimization in Chinese children's peer groups. *Developmental Psychology, 37*, 520–532.
Smith, P. K., Cowie, H., Olafsson, R. F., Liefooghe, A. P. D., Almeida, A., Araki, H., et al. (2002). Definitions of bullying: A comparison of terms used, and age and gender differences, in a fourteen-country international comparison. *Child Development, 73*, 1119–1133.
Steiger, J. H. (1990). Structural model evaluation and modification: An interval estimation approach. *Multivariate Behavioral Research, 25*, 173–180.
Wasserman, S., & Faust, K. (1994). *Social network analysis: Methods and applications.* New York: Cambridge University Press.

5 Qualitative Research on Children's Peer Relations in Cultural Context

William A. Corsaro

Recently, we have seen important changes in the conceptualization of human development in psychology, sociology, and anthropology. In general, these changes involve a greater focus on children's agency, more concern for the importance of social and cultural context, and agreement that children's experiences beyond their early years in the family (especially their interactions and experiences with peers) are in need of more careful theoretical consideration and empirical research. Also, at least in sociology and anthropology, there is recognition that children both affect and are affected by society and culture. This recognition has increased the appreciation of the creativity and autonomy of children's peer cultures and the awareness that the nature and quality of children's lives, even in their first years, is enriched or constrained by power relations and social policies in the cultures in which they live (Corsaro & Fingerson, 2003).

Although some aspects of children's peer relations and cultures may be universal, the way these aspects are developed and manifested, and other features of children's cultures, are clearly affected by the larger cultural context in which they develop (Corsaro, 1988, 1994, 2005; Corsaro, Molinari, & Rosier, 2002). Therefore, in studying children's peer relations, it is necessary to take a comparative perspective and to attempt to identify how key processes in children's peer cultures both affect and are affected by the larger cultural structures and processes within which they are embedded.

In sociology and anthropology, a substantial amount of empirical research that focuses on peer relations in cultural context has been qualitative and comparative. Much of this work has involved ethnography, with researchers entering into and becoming part of children's worlds in different cultural contexts by way of acceptance as an adult friend. Other researchers have relied on individual and group interviews, whereas some have devised innovative methods relying on historical records, children's drawings and art, and having children take an active role in data collection and analysis.

In this chapter, I first generally describe and evaluate various qualitative methods used to study children's worlds and their social development within cultural context. I then examine research on children's everyday experiences in their peer cultures, looking at children's friendships, play routines, fantasy play, and experiences related to gender as these processes are situated in cultural context. I conclude with a general evaluation of qualitative studies of children's peer relations related to their social development and evolving membership in their cultures from a comparative perspective.

Types of Qualitative Methods in Researching Peer Interactions and Relationships

What are some of the special issues in doing qualitative research with children? Some researchers argue that children themselves are not unique compared with adults; instead, qualitative methods for studying any group should include a rigorous application of techniques applied to that group with careful attention to the group's specific needs and particularities (Christensen & James, 2000a). Children are a diverse group, and any method should be examined in the context of that diversity, not only by age.

A central methodological issue is conducting research *with* children, rather than *on* them (Christensen & James, 2000a). This position stresses the importance of hearing children's own voices, attempting to experience the world from their physical and emotional perspectives, and recognizing that they are the most knowledgeable and most experienced in their own lives. A variety of types of qualitative method are well suited to meet these goals.

Ethnography

Ethnography is an excellent method for studying young children because many features of their interactions and peer cultures are produced and shared in the present and cannot easily be obtained by way of interviews, surveys, or experiments. Three central features of ethnography with children are that it be sustained and engaged, microscopic and holistic, and flexible and self-corrective (Gaskins, Miller, & Corsaro, 1992). Ethnography usually involves prolonged fieldwork in which the researcher gains access to a group, develops a participant status, and carries out intensive observations for a period of months or years. The value of prolonged observation is that the ethnographer discovers what daily life is like for members of the group – their physical and social settings; their everyday routines and rituals; their beliefs, values, and concerns; and the linguistic and communicative systems that mediate all these contexts and activities.

Sustained and Engaged Research. In my own work on children's peer culture, I have conducted six intensive and comparative studies, in preschool settings in the United States and Italy, of peer interaction and culture over the course of an academic year. In several of these projects, I returned for shorter periods to observe some members of the children's groups who spent successive years in the preschool, and in others, I continued ethnographic observation as children made the transition from preschool to elementary school and then through elementary school (Corsaro, 1985, 1994, 2003; Corsaro & Molinari, 2000a, 2000b; Corsaro, Molinari, & Rosier, 2002). The sustained nature of these and other comparative ethnographic studies of young children (Evaldsson, 1993; Goodwin, 1998) documents crucial changes and transitions in children's lives, which are essential for understanding socialization as a process of what I term "interpretive reproduction" (Corsaro, 1992, 2005).

To gain access to children's worlds and acquire the status of friend is especially challenging, given that adults are physically larger than children, are more powerful, and are often seen as having control over children's behavior. Several ethnographers have discussed strategies for overcoming these obstacles, being accepted, and participating in children's worlds to varying degrees (Corsaro, 1985, 2003; Corsaro & Molinari, 2000a; Fine & Sandstrom, 1988).

In my ethnographic work in preschools and elementary schools, my goal has always been to discover the children's perspectives, to see what it is like to be a child in the school, and to document the children's peer cultures. To do this, I have to overcome the children's tendency to see me as a typical adult. A significant problem is physical size; I am much bigger than the children. In my early work in an American preschool, I found that a "reactive" method of field entry into children's worlds worked best (Corsaro, 1985). After observing the children from a concealed observation for several weeks and learning a lot about them and their daily routines, I moved into the school. In using the reactive method, I enter free play areas, sit down on the floor, and wait for the kids to react to me. (I should point out that this is pretty much the opposite of what most adults do in such settings. Teachers, parents, and other adults normally do not sit down in play areas, and when they enter, it is usually to ask questions, give advice, or settle disputes. In short, they are more active in their dealings with children.) I find that the reactive method does work, but in American schools, it normally takes some time. After a while, the children begin to ask me questions, and they are always surprised and pleased when I know their names because they do not know me. Soon they draw me into their activities and gradually define me as an atypical adult. Size is still a factor, however, and the children come to see me as a big kid, often referring to me as "Big Bill."

When I have used the reactive method in Italian preschool, things have gone somewhat differently. To the Italian children, as soon as I spoke in my fractured Italian, I was peculiar, funny, and fascinating. I was not just an atypical adult but also an incompetent one – not just a big kid but sort of big, dumb kid (Corsaro, 2003). From these experiences, I began to see what it was like for children when those around you assume you are incompetent, incomplete, and in need of training. For example, long after my Italian improved, I was still teased about my grammatical errors, accent, and failure to understand something someone had said. The youngest kids especially enjoyed this teasing, often saying: "*Bill, lui capisce niente!*" ("Bill, he doesn't understand anything!"). Of course, the children knew this was untrue, but they loved turning the tables on an adult. The issue runs deeper than this, however. The children often extended my incompetence in language to other areas of social knowledge. Once, on a field trip to a zoo that had scale models of dinosaurs, I pointed out to a small group of kids in very good Italian that the dinosaur we were looking at had lived in the same place where I now lived in the United States (I was certain I was right about this because the map in the exhibit clearly indicated as much). The kids roared with laughter, and one, Romano, said, "Bill, he's crazy! He says the dinosaur lived in the United States." Then, pointing to the dinosaur, he added, "But you can see it lived right here!"

It was a new experience for me to be on the receiving end of the power differential between kids and adults. Adults, of course, are often quick to dismiss children's insights, knowledge, and contributions to the wider adult culture. We usually do not do this in a mean way; it is more that we take children's perspectives for granted and our own views as the correct ones. Gaining acceptance into children's worlds requires that ethnographers overcome these tendencies and put themselves in a position to document children's peer cultures.

Microscopic and Holistic Ethnography. To ensure that ethnographic interpretations are culturally valid, they must be grounded in an accumulation of the specifics of everyday life. However, describing what is seen and heard is not enough, as ethnographers must engage in a process of "thick description" (Geertz, 1973). This mode of interpretation goes beyond the microscopic examination of actions to their contextualization in a more holistic sense, to capture actions and events as they are understood by the actors themselves.

For example, through observation and audiovisual records, I documented that preschoolers often resist the access of peers into established play routines (Corsaro, 1985, 2003). At the level of thin description (and from an adult perspective), this behavior is viewed as a refusal to share. Given features of preschool settings, however, I interpreted such behavior as the "protection of interactive space" and argued that it was not that children did not want to share. Instead, they wanted to keep sharing the fragile play activities they were already sharing. They knew from experience that their activities were often disrupted by the entry of others who were not aware of the nature of play. In fact, through careful observation, I found that children who used more indirect access strategies, like watching from a distance and discovering the nature of play and then entering and contributing to the play verbally or nonverbally, were readily accepted – because they showed they could play. On the other hand, more direct strategies, like asking to play or demanding that others share their play, were frequently met with resistance (Corsaro, 2003). Further, in exploring this aspect of children's peer relations from a comparative perspective, I found that Italian children were more likely to inform children of their peer activities and even invite them into their play, but only if they agreed to follow rules and directions set down by the original participants. I tied this difference in more openness among Italian compared with American children in their peer relations and play to the nature of "relations in public" among Italian adults. Among Italian adults, brief visits and short exchanges and greetings with a wide range of acquaintances were often interwoven within more intense and involved discussion with a smaller subset of friends. Often, several conversations occur at once, but there were no apparent problems in maintaining order (Corsaro, 1988, p. 12).

Flexibility and Self-Correction. An important feature of ethnography is that it provides continual feedback in which initial questions may change during the course of inquiry. This flexibility in inquiry is accompanied by self-correction when the ethnographer searches for additional support for emerging hypotheses, including negative cases, which can lead to refinements and expansions of initial interpretations. It is this feature of ethnography that fits with our earlier discussion of research *with* rather than *on* children. Over the course of research, children, like adult ethnographic informants, come to reflect on the nature of ethnography and its place in their lives. For example, in my work with Italian preschoolers (Corsaro & Molinari, 2000a), the children often wanted to display their art and literacy skills by drawing and printing in my notebook. In a sense, given my interest in developing literacy, children were inscribing field notes directly into my notebook (Corsaro & Nelson, 2003). Over time, however, it went further than this as the children became co-researchers, even suggesting things I need to record about them in my notes. Consider the following example:

> *A Letter for Luciano's Little Sister*
>
> I am sitting at a worktable with Luciano, Stefania, and several other children. Luciano is printing a letter to his sister. Stefania tells me to write what Luciano is doing in my notebook. I do so in Italian and show it to her. Luciano then suggests that Stefania also write a letter to his sister, which she does with Luciano's help. It reads:
>
> *CARA LUISA,*
> *TANTI BACIONI DA STEFANIA LUCIANO E DA BILL.* (MANY BIG KISSES FROM STEFANIA LUCIANO AND FROM BILL.)

This example nicely captures how literacy activities (like printing one's name or a short letter), first presented in teacher-directed tasks, are appropriated and used by the children in the peer activities. The process is much in line with Vygotsky's (1978) notion of the zone of proximal development. Furthermore, the children document these learning activities directly into my notebook. We see here an excellent example of research *with* children. Finally, this documentation by children of data directly relevant to my research interests demonstrates the value of comparative, longitudinal ethnography. It was the result of my acceptance, participation, and evolving membership in the school and peer cultures (Corsaro & Molinari, 2000a).

Individual and Group Interviewing

Ethnography explores how children act: their everyday play and talk. Interviews allow researchers access to how children perceive their actions and their worlds. Given the reflective demands of interviews, they are thus more appropriate for school-age compared with preschool children. Eder and Fingerson (2002) contend that using individual and group interviews with children is one of the strongest methods of exploring children's own interpretations of their lives. Using interviews, Eder and Fingerson further argue that researchers can study topics that are highly salient for children, yet may be seldom discussed in everyday interactions, such as divorce, family relationships, violence, or other sensitive issues. However, as with ethnography, there remains the power imbalance between the researcher and respondent. Ways of reducing this power difference include group interviews (as children feel more comfortable in groups compared with the adult interviewer–child respondent dyad); creating a natural context; carrying out interviews over time, thus establishing a history of rapport; and engaging in reciprocity.

For example, Mayall (2002) uses the "research conversation" to learn about children's health and health care. She engaged small groups of five- to nine-year-old children in conversations during their everyday school activities. The children felt secure in this familiar setting and engaged in discussions similar to their own "natural" conversations that Mayall heard in the school's classrooms and corridors during observations she made prior to the interviews. The children chose topics for discussion and controlled the pace and direction of the conversation. In this way, Mayall was able to capture issues related to health that were important to the children, rather than having the children respond to specific questions she prepared in advance. Mayall also had the opportunities in these conversations to probe in directions in line with her research interests, but in ways that did not disrupt the children's group discussions.

In Davies's (1989) research on children's understandings of gender, she held "study groups" of fifth- and sixth-graders. The groups met once per week for ninety minutes for more than a year. Activities included having discussions, sharing photos of family, taking pictures with disposable cameras, making collages, reading traditional and feminist stories, and writing stories and autobiographies. Through this wide variety of literacy activities, Davies learned how children communicated about their lives, what their reflective and empathy skills were, and how they expressed discourses of gender from multiple angles.

Nontraditional Methods of Studying Children. Although researchers can gather rich data on children's peer interactions and relationships using traditional qualitative methods like ethnography and interviews, there is a need for new ways of using these methods and other innovative techniques to encourage children to present their own images and representations of their lives (Williams & Bendelow, 1998).

A number of researchers, including Williams and Bendelow, use drawings to elicit stories and understanding of children's everyday lives. For example, Holmes (1995) asked kindergartners to draw self-portraits while telling her about what they were drawing, so as to understand how they construct race and ethnicity. Christensen and James (2000b) use drawings to document similarities and differences in ten-year-olds' daily activities and organization of their time in their families and communities. The children were given a sheet of paper inscribed with a large circle titled, "My Week." They were then asked to divide the circle to represent their weekly activities and how much time they spent in each activity. The children had complete freedom to fill in the circle in any way they felt best represented their experiences. During the activity, which was completed in small groups, the researchers were present and had a tape recorder running.

Children can also serve as research assistants and informants, helping adult investigators with interviews and with understanding children's local cultures and analyzing data (Alderson, 2000). In his study of street children in Brazil, Hecht (1998) used children as interviewers. He found that they asked questions that he, as an adult and outsider, would not have been able to elicit. Through the use of child interviewers, Hecht was able to capture the details of begging and street crime among the children and how it gave them a feeling of independence and small economic rewards in an oppressive system driven by global economic forces in large cities like Recife in Brazil.

Although not all these examples involved comparative analyses, they clearly display the strengths of a variety of qualitative methods for identifying children's agency in their peer relations as well as in their interactions with adults. These various types of qualitative methods can be used both comparatively and longitudinally to capture how children's peer relations are embedded in the wider cultural contexts. We now turn to some specific examples that capture the use of qualitative methods for this purpose.

Children's Peer Relationships in Cultural Context

Much of the traditional work on peer culture in sociology and anthropology has focused on adolescents and the effects (positive and negative) of experiences with peers on individual development. Most of this work has a functionalist view of culture, that is, culture is viewed as consisting of internalized shared values and norms that guide behavior. More recent work on childhood socialization takes an interpretive view, which maintains that children creatively appropriate information from the adult world to produce their own unique peer cultures (Corsaro, 2003, 2005; James, Jenks, & Prout, 1998). From the interpretive perspective, children's individual development is part of more general collective processes in which children become active members of the adult culture through processes of interpretive reproduction.

In my own work, I see culture as public, collective, and performative, and I define children's peer culture as *a stable set of activities or routines, artifacts, values, and concerns that children produce and share in interaction with each other* (Corsaro, 2003, 2005; Corsaro & Eder, 1990). Although a wide range of features of children's peer cultures have been identified, two central themes consistently appear: Children make a persistent attempt to *gain control* of their lives and to *share* that control with each other. In the preschool years, children have an overriding concern with social participation and with challenging adult authority. In elementary school, such challenging of adult authority persists, but there is also a gradual movement toward social differentiation within the peer culture. This differentiation is marked by negotiations and conflicts as children attempt to gain control over the attitudes and behaviors of peers.

In exploring children's peer relations and cultures, I and other qualitative researchers have used comparative methods, which help to place general and specific features of children's peer relations in cultural context.

Children's Friendships

As Winterhoff (1997) argues, two metatheoretical assumptions underlie most of the research on children's friendship. The first assumption, "friendship as outcome," sees relationships as if they were static entities and often strives to identify a universal definition of friendship. The second assumption, "friendship as process," sees friendships as socially constructed and seeks to identify patterns and variations in their collective construction over time and across sociocultural settings.

The outcome assumption fits well with traditional, individualistic models of human development, which stress the child's movement from immaturity to adult competence. In this approach, "a rigid or entified definition of friendship *as an outcome*" is adopted before the actual research, and children's approximation to this adult definition is examined by age (Winterhoff, 1997, p. 226; author's emphasis). In the process approach, friendship formation "involves recognizing its developmental fluidity *along with* its genesis as a sociocultural promoted construction and explaining its temporal flow within the main current (system) of socioculturally promoted activities and skills" (Winterhoff, 1997, p. 227; author's emphasis). Especially important is the theoretical assumption that knowledge, skills, and behaviors pertaining to friendship are not simply internalized and reproduced by children, but rather are transformed constructively within activities in local cultures (family, school, and peer group) that make up their everyday lives.

Although the outcome approach dominated most of the theory and early research on children's friendships in developmental psychology (Selman, 1980), many developmental psychologists have begun to question this perspective and to argue for the potential of the process approach (Tesson &

Youniss, 1995). However, it is recent theory and research on children's friendships and peer relations in sociology and anthropology that have fully developed the importance of the process approach. Most of this research has been ethnographic and conducted in educational settings with a focus on friendship processes in classrooms and on playgrounds in a variety of cultural contexts (Corsaro, 1985, 2003, 2005; Evaldsson, 1993; Rizzo, 1989). However, there have also been ethnographic studies of children's friendship processes in homes, neighborhoods, and community organizations (Adler & Adler, 1998; Fine, 1987; Goodwin, 1990; 1998).

Many recent studies have been comparative in that they examine children's friendships across age, gender, class, race and ethnicity, and cultural groups. All of the studies are longitudinal in that children are observed or interviewed over several months or years. Surprisingly, a good deal of work on children's friendships documents the importance of discussion, debate, and conflict (Corsaro, 2003, 2004; Rizzo, 1992; Shantz, 1987). For example, I found that Italian and African American preschool children often forge and develop friendship ties through debates and teasing. Neither these children nor their teachers were overly sensitive to conflict and disagreements. In fact, it was clear that disagreements, debates, and teasing were valued in peer relations and were often the basis of friendship and group bonds, whereas White middle-class American preschool children were highly sensitive to conflict and quickly became upset when it occurred, often going to teachers for aid in settling their disputes. Still, the middle-class American children are quick to use the denial of friendship ("I won't be your Buddy" or "You can't come to my birthday party" if you do not play with me or play the way I like). Overall, conflict among the Italian and African American children increased solidarity in the group (the children cooperated in friendly competition with each other), whereas the White middle-class American children took conflict much more seriously and personally (Corsaro, 1994).

These findings in turn can be linked to patterns of social relations and beliefs about conflict in the children's wider social communities. Discussion and debate is a common feature of adult relations in public in Italy, and the preschool teachers encouraged debate in group meetings and expected children to settle their own disputes. The oppositional and teasing style of the African American children is also a reflection of the children's experiences with their teachers and adults in their community. Among African Americans, opposition and conflict "tend to be viewed as constant contrarieties, antagonisms that cannot be eliminated and in fact may be used to effect a larger sense of cultural affirmation of community through a dramatization of opposing forces" (Abrahams, 1975, p. 63). In contrast to the Italian and

African American teachers, the teachers in the White middle-class preschool saw conflict as threatening to peer relations and were quick to intervene in children's disputes, urging them to "talk about" their problems. The teachers' stance was no doubt related to the wishes of parents in this private preschool who in teacher–parent meetings espoused that children "talk over" problems and often lamented the fact that their children sometimes complained about conflict in friendship relations.

These findings regarding White middle-class American preschool children are similar to Rizzo's in his study of middle-class first-grade American children. Rizzo (1989) found that when the children noticed problems in their friends' behaviors, they insisted that their friends change their behavior. Such challenges often led to emotional disputes. Rizzo argued that such disputes not only helped the children obtain a better understanding of what they could expect from each other as friends, but also brought about personal reflection, resulting in the children's development of unique insight into their own actions and roles as friends.

Just as it is important to study and understand children's friendship processes in a variety of children's social and cultural spaces, it is also important to investigate friendship processes over time. Most research of children's friendship processes conducted in child-care settings, preschools, and elementary schools is longitudinal in that groups of children are observed and interviewed over several months or the entire school term. As a result, it is possible to trace how particular friendships are cultivated, nourished, and in some cases, ended. It is also possible to document the nature of differentiation in the groups studied by identifying the development of clique structures.

However we know much less about how children make and keep friends over key transition points in their lives. Transition points often reflect children moving from one educational institution to another, for example, from preschool to elementary school, elementary school to middle school, and so on. Most research has been on children's transition to kindergarten in the United States, and this work primarily focuses on children's overall adjustment to formal schooling and seldom considers friendship processes.

In work on Italian children, Corsaro et al. (2003) carried out a longitudinal ethnographic study of a group of preschoolers' transition to elementary school. In most Italian preschools, children stay together in the same group with the same teachers for the entire three years of preschool. This fact was important in the children's and teachers' production of a highly integrated community. This community was evident in the lack of status differentiation in the peer culture: Most of the children played with a wide range of peers. Although there was some gender separation in the children's play contacts in preschool, this division was developed much less fully than those described in studies of kindergarten-age in the United States. Italian elementary schools are structured like preschools, with children joining a group with two teachers and remaining in that group usually with the same teachers for all five years of elementary school. The preschool children studied by Corsaro et al. (2003) joined one of four first-grade classes, and the research involved observations and interviews over the entire period of elementary school.

In the four first-grade classrooms and in the peer culture in general, we saw similarities, extensions, and divergences in friendship processes in relation to the preschool. For the most part, the individual classroom and peer cultures were differentiated more strongly by gender and status as the children went about keeping old friends and making new ones. Yet, this differentiation was buffered in at least three of the classes by elements of the Italian early education system. The practice of keeping children together in the same group with the same teachers, as well as the emphasis placed on discussion and negotiation, worked against rigid boundaries and exclusive friendship groups (Corsaro et al., 2003, p. 288; also see Corsaro & Molinari, 2005). Over time in elementary school, differentiation in friendship groups increased somewhat in all classes in second to fourth grade, with stronger friendships within individual classes. However, by fifth grade, friendship groups were less differentiated by gender and status, and there were many more friendships across the four classes. These results differ from research on elementary school children in the United States, which found more differentiation in friendship groups over time in the schools (Adler & Adler, 1998).

Overall, we see the value of comparative, longitudinal ethnography for capturing key processes in children's friendship relations in various organizational settings and how friendship and peer relations are affected by more general beliefs, values, and educational policies in the wider cultural community.

Children's Bodies and Nonverbal and Verbal Play Routines

Children's bodies are absent in much of the adult-oriented sociological work on the body, and the work that has been done is directed at children rather than based in children's own knowledge and experience (Williams & Bendelow, 1998). Childhood and the body are each topics that have experienced recent growth in sociological interest, but there has been little contact between these two fields (Prout, 2000).

Children experience and understand their bodies in ways significantly different from adults. Bodily change in childhood is a salient marker not only of a childhood identity itself, but also a marker of different ages in the structural placement in childhood (James, 2000). James argues that the body, in particular, represents the passage of time for children as the body grows and develops at a much more accelerated pace than the adult body. For example, James finds in her ethnographic fieldwork among children aged four through nine that height is a significant marker of age and status. The children use height to mark their social rank within the larger group and their progress towards being an adult, a position of power and maturity. Additionally, James finds that the children are involved in "body work," as they constantly negotiate the presentation of their bodies, their bodies' actions, and their bodies' appearances.

Orchestrated and repeated body movements – often seen as just running around – are accepted routines in the peer cultures of young children. Several studies of children from different cultures identify such routines among toddlers and preschool children (Corsaro, 2004; Corsaro & Molinari, 1990; Løkken, 2000; Mussati & Panni, 1981). One example, "the little chairs routine," captures the flavor of primarily nonverbal play among toddlers (Corsaro & Molinari, 1990). The routine took place regularly in large room in an Italian *asilo nido* (preschool for two- and three-year-olds). In the routine, the children appropriate the small chairs they sit on for snacks and other activities to create their own play routine. The children begin by pushing the little chairs to the center of the room to make a long line from one wall to a small platform sitting against the opposite wall. Once the line is finished, the children are careful to make sure the chairs are together and the line is straight. Then the children walk across the room from chair to chair – sometimes swaying and saying "I'm falling! I'm falling," but always keeping their balance – until they reach the platform and jump down. They then run back to the other side of the room to take another turn. During the routine, the teachers want the children to be careful, but they rarely intervene. An important feature of toddler routines like the "little chairs" is their simple and primarily nonverbal participant structure, which consists of a series of orchestrated bodily actions. The structure also incorporates the option of frequent recycling, which allows the children to begin and end participation (with some entering and others leaving) and to embellish certain features of the routine like the swaying and pretending to lose their balance.

These studies are important not only because of what they tell us about children's use of their bodies in peer relations and their ability to establish shared routines at an early age, but also because of the nature of social institutions in which these peer relations are established. Child-care institutions in European countries are often subsidized by the government and are seen as promoting social and emotional skills in children, even in the second year of life. In the United States, there is, in contrast, a tendency to see child care for very young children as an unfortunate necessity for families and that spending time in such settings may actually have negative effects on children's social and emotional development (Maccoby & Lewis, 2003; National Institute of Child Health and Human Development Early Child Care Research Network, 2003). Thus, where some cultures see opportunity for developing social skills and emotional bonds at an early age, others see a social problem. These differing stances not only affect the nature of peer relations at an early age, but also influence the types of research funding and studies, which view children in peer relations in very different perspectives.

Children's Fantasy Play, Language Play, and Sharing Rituals

Numerous studies document the complexity of children's fantasy play. I identified the complex language and paralinguistic skills children exhibit in fantasy play events. I also documented three underlying themes in their play (lost-found, danger-rescue, and death-rebirth), which enable children to address important emotional concerns in their lives (Corsaro, 1985, 2003). Sawyer (1997) and Goldman (1998) offer detailed sociolinguistic studies of pretend play in which they reveal its poetic qualities. Sawyer, relying on work in metapragmatics, impressively identifies the improvisational nature of a group of American children's play, comparing it with improvisational jazz and theater. Goldman studied Huli children of Papua New Guinea and, by viewing the children's play as oral poetry, demonstrates how pretense is socially mediated and linguistically constructed. In her work in "doing reality with play," Strandell (1997) argues that children's play should not be seen only as a competence or a means of reaching adult competence by practicing play. Rather, she argues that play is a resource used by children in everyday life activities. Strandell presents numerous examples of Finnish children's play, in which she demonstrates how children use play to create and control social space, to reinforce group identity, and to challenge and even control adults to some degree. These studies and other work on children's fantasy and language play leads to the argument that such play demonstrates improvisational skills that surpass those of most older children and adults. We also see in this range of studies across cultures that fantasy play may indeed be a universal feature of children's peer cultures.

Although children's cultures are composed of a wide range of language and behavioral routines, none are perhaps more symbolic of childhood ethos than sharing rituals. These collective activities involve patterned, repetitive, and cooperative expressions of the shared values and concerns of childhood. They often involve stylized performances and "constitute ritualized moments which are distinctive to the childhood world in which they are embedded and which punctuate the flow of social exchanges in that world" (Katriel, 1987, p. 306). Sometimes, such stylized performances are embedded in more general peer activities, as seen in Goodwin's (1985) study of African American girls' negotiations during the game of jump rope and Mishler's (1979) analysis of "trading and bargaining" among middle-class American six-year-olds at lunchtime. A fascinating example of the power of Taiwanese children's language play routines can be seen in the work of Hadley (2003). Hadley found that through word play (such as manipulating teachers' and classmates' names), Taiwanese kindergartners "both resisted and accommodated the Confucian values that the teachers aimed to instill in them" (2003, p. 205).

Again, the previously mentioned studies capture the importance of the comparative nature of qualitative studies of children's peer relations across cultural groups. In these studies, the nature of children's negotiations and cooperative play reflected both the agency of children in their peer cultures and their awareness of wider cultural values and beliefs regarding cooperation, sharing, and respect for peers and adults.

Children's Experience of Gender

The first sign of social differentiation in children's peer relations is increasing gender separation, with children as young as age three showing preference for play with other children of the same sex. Gender separation becomes so dramatic in elementary school that "it is meaningful to speak of separate girls' and boys' worlds" (Thorne, 1986, p. 167). In one of the first ethnographies of preschool children, Berentzen (1984) observed peer interaction among five- to seven-year-old children in a Norwegian preschool in 1967. Berentzen found that both boys and girls followed the self-imposed rule that "girls/boys don't play with boys/girls," with few exceptions (1984, p. 158). Girls and boys also organized their activities around different concerns: Boys valued competition and toughness, whereas girls were concerned mostly with affiliation.

Later studies in American, British, and Australian preschools and elementary schools, as well as on children's sports team, reported similar findings (Best, 1983; Davies, 1989; Messner, 2000; Thorne, 1993; Walkerdine, 1990). Is gender differentiation among young children always so dramatic? Is it universal? As Thorne (1993) notes, much of the work has a tendency to exaggerate gender differences and ignore similarities. Boys and girls do play and work together in educational settings, especially in more structured and group projects. Also, although instances of boys and girls playing together in free play are rare, they do occur and merit careful analysis. Features of group composition, setting, culture, and ethnicity are important.

Recent comparative research shows that children of various cultures differ in the construction of gender concepts and behaviors. Goodwin (1990, 2003) found that African American boys and girls often engaged in playful, cross-sex debates and teasing. Goodwin (1998) also found that African American and Latina girls were much more likely to tease each other and debate the enforcement of rules in their play of games than were White middle-class American girls. Kyratzis and Guo (2001) found cross-cultural differences in the gendered speech patterns of preschoolers in the United States and China. They found that, among American children, boys tend to be more assertive than girls in same-sex interactions, but in China, girls are more assertive with one another than boys are. Both Chinese girls and American boys used bold, directive speech when they disagreed with their classmates, whereas American girls used mitigated requests (e.g., the use of "please" and the conditional tense) during disputes.

In my research in the United States and Italy, I have found, in line with the general findings previously noted, much more gender segregation among older children (five- to six-year-olds) compared with younger children (three- to five-year-olds). However, gender segregation and different activity preferences by gender were greater for American upper-middle-class children than for African American or Italian children, regardless of age.

The differences regarding gender behavior and concepts in the different preschools I studied were complex and fascinating (Aydt & Corsaro, 2003; Corsaro, 2005). In the American preschools, there was a high degree of gender differences in play groups once the children reached the age of five. However, the kids often spoke and joked about gender in same- and mixed-sex groups during structured play activities and meals and snacks. When the children spoke about gender, they often did so in the context of discussions about adult relationships, such as marriage.

Once, at morning snack time, a girl named Veronica said that she and Martin were going to get married. Martin agreed and said they were going to be doctors. "And live in New York," added Veronica. "Are you going to kiss and do sex?" asked Mark. The others laugh at this, and then meeting time was announced.

Although the children enjoy joking about subjects they find titillating, it becomes apparent from this example that marriage is considered important, if not inevitable, by the kids. The "marriage talk" is significant in that it provides a script for what a close relationship between a male and female entails. This script changes the way kids look at the opposite-sex peers, and it encourages kids to think about relationships between people of the opposite sex as fundamentally different from the relationships between people of the same sex. Because there is no well-defined model of what a close platonic friendship between a boy and a girl might look like, cross-sex relations are likely to be coded by the children as romantic and emotionally charged. Consider the following example of some five-year-olds in an American preschool.

> Anita, Ruth, and Sarah are chasing Sean and David who come over to a big rock where I [the researcher] am sitting and claim it as home base. Once when Anita and Sarah chase Sean and David they start to pull up their shirts and say, "You want to see my bra?" Anita says, "I have a bra for my belly button" and holds up her shirt to show her belly button. (Aydt & Corsaro, 2003, p. 1316)

Although the girls are far too young to actually have breasts, they are aware that women develop breasts and wear bras. Furthermore, they seem to grasp that displaying breasts intimidates the boys, and they use this knowledge to enhance their run-and-chase play.

In my research in a Head Start center, I found that there was a good bit of gender separation among the predominately African American children, but there was more cross-gender play than in the private upper-middle-class preschools I studied. Boys and girls mixed more, and boys often engaged in family role-play, cleaning house, fixing meals, sweeping the floor, and so on, with girls and each other (Corsaro, 2005). Also, the African American girls were more assertive in the play with other girls and boys compared with the White middle-class children. One girl, Delia, frequently stood up to boys and delighted in taking them on in verbal disputes. She was particularly assertive in her relationship with Ramone, who had a crush on her. He told several of the other children and me that Delia was his girlfriend and that he visited her house. Delia denied both claims. Still, Ramone did not give up and continued to pursue her attention.

One day, Delia and another girl were sitting at a table putting together a puzzle. Ramone came over and asked to play. Delia said, "If you play with girls, then you are a tomgirl!" Ramone took this as a rejection and moved away briefly, but then returned and picked up a piece of the puzzle. Delia took it away and said that when she plays with boys she is called a tomboy, so if Ramone plays with them, he is a tomgirl. She also said they did not want Ramone to play anyway. With this retort, Ramone gave up and moved to another area of the classroom. Overall, from these examples, we can see the complexity of the Head Start children's construction and use of gender in their play (Corsaro, 2003, 2005).

Earlier, I noted observing more cross-gender play in Italian preschools than in American upper-middle-class schools. One factor that contributed to the lack of differentiation by gender in the peer culture was the popularity of certain play routines. Although mainly girls engaged in domestic role play, both girls and boys often participated in types of role-play that blurred and stretched gender stereotypes.

The most common was animal family role-play, where both boys and girls pretended to be wild dogs, lions, or tigers. In most instances, the mother of this pack of wild animals was a girl who was very rough in disciplining her charges (both boys and girls), who went around growling and scratching each other and other children in the school (Corsaro, 2005; Evaldsson & Corsaro, 1998).

What do these diverse findings on gender segregation and integration suggest regarding the formation of gender identity among young children? Traditional developmental theories – with their emphasis on biological factors, reinforcement contingencies, or stages of cognitive development – fall short in that they all focus on gender development as a process of individual change or adjustment to social roles. The focus is on outcome, rather than on children's active construction and involvement in their social worlds and in their particular cultural group. In the past twenty years or so, a number of theorists have linked gender identity directly to social action and collective practices in cultural context (Connell, 1987; Davies, 1989; Thorne, 1993).

Perhaps the best example of this theoretical approach applied to preschool children and gender can be seen in the work of Davies (1989; also see Fernie et al., 1993). Davies argues that masculinity and femininity are not inherent properties of individuals, but rather they are structural properties of society. Social actors are constrained but not determined by these properties. Through our use of discursive practices (how we speak and act), we contribute to reproduction and change in society. Therefore, "as children learn the discursive practices of their society, they learn to position themselves correctly as male or female, since that is what is required of them to have a recognizable identity within the existing social order" Davies, 1989, p. 13). The rigidity of such positioning, however, can often be problematic and constraining, and children soon realize that minor refinements and even genuinely different positionings are possible and desirable.

Davies and colleagues provide examples that demonstrate the creativity and flexibility of preschool children "in their invention and maintenance of the rigid structure" of traditional gender roles (Fernie et al., 1993, p. 103). They present the positioning strategies of a young girl, Lisa, as an example of the breaking of traditional gender frames. Over the course of the year, Lisa aligned herself with a high-status, core group of five boys in her preschool, boys who frequently engaged in superhero play. Lisa embraced the male superhero role of Batman rather than the female alternative, Batgirl. Furthermore, it was clear that Lisa did not take the role just to gain entry to the boys' core group: She assumed the role even when the boys were not present. In one instance, Lisa persuaded one of the youngest girls in the class to come to her Batman house, wear a cape, and hold a stick for a gun. Happy with her new recruit, Lisa put her hands on her hips and announced, "We're bad. Stay out. This is our house" (Fernie et al., 1993, p. 102).

Overall, we see in these studies that children's gender play and the development of gender identity varies across cultural and subcultural groups. The findings indicate that children's gender development and gender relations are best studied comparatively and within cultural context. Theories that maintain basic essential differences between boys' and girls' play and the nature of their social relations and identities are often based on studies of White middle-class American children (Gilligan, 1982; Lever, 1976). Following an interpretive and cultural perspective, Thorne (1993) and Goodwin (2003) advocate taking a nongendered, contextual approach, where researchers look for patterns and themes among all the children and then see if any parse out by gender or by other differences. They believe that when researchers enter the field expecting gender differences, they will significantly limit their ability to see similarities among girls and boys. This approach also argues for comparative research, like the studies reviewed earlier, in a wide variety of social and cultural contexts.

Conclusion

In this review I have described the different types of qualitative methods researchers use in studying children's peer relations in cultural context. I noted a general trend toward methods that focus on research *with* compared with research *on* children. I then went on to review and discuss a number of qualitative studies on children's peer relations, including children's friendship, play routines and rituals, fantasy play, and their experiences related to gender knowledge and cross-gender relations. In this review, I highlighted comparative research in which the importance of cultural context is more transparent. Given space limitations, the reviews of these topics were far from complete, and there were many other topics that I did not consider in which excellent qualitative research has been done (see Corsaro, 2005 for a more detailed review).

Qualitative research with children, when conducted in a rigorous way, gives us insight into children's lives, perspectives, agency, and social and emotional development within cultural context. Most of this research is guided by an interpretive approach to human development, which views children as active agents who are influenced by and influence others. Although most of the research discussed has been carried out by sociologists and anthropologists, it is in line with the increasing recognition of the importance of context (physical, societal, and sociocultural) for human development in psychology. For example, in psychology, context at different levels is central to systems theories (Thelen & Smith, 1998), sociocultural theory (Rogoff, 2003), and new conceptualizations of Piagetian theory (Tesson and Youniss, 1995; Youniss & Damon, 1994). These theories call for a movement away from searching for underlying competencies or causes for human development and stress the importance of direct studies of developmental processes over time and space to identify how developmental processes are constructed by their own history and systemwide activity.

In this review, I have highlighted qualitative studies that contribute to a comparative perspective of children's peer relations in cultural context. Some of these studies have found important differences in styles of play, interaction, and friendship processes across subcultural groups in the United States (Goodwin, 1998). Others have compared peer relations across cultural groups and note important differences in interactive style, friendship relations, and cross-gender relations among children from Italy, African American children, and White middle-class American children (Aydt & Corsaro, 2003; Corsaro, 1988; 1994; 2003; Corsaro et al., 2002). These differences are related to different styles of interaction, value systems and beliefs, and social and educational policies in different cultures. The studies show the value of fine-grained comparative ethnography in identifying important variations in peer relations and friendship process, and then placing these differences in broader cultural context to interpret their meaning and significance.

In sociology, there has long been an emphasis on the effects of social structure and historical context on developmental outcomes, as seen in the work on social structure and personality and life course theory. Interpretive theory refines these views by arguing that children live their lives and contribute to social reproduction in the present, while at the same time acquiring cultural knowledge and skills that prepare them for the future.

References

Abrahams, R. (1975). Negotiating respect: Patterns of presentation among Black women. In C. R. Farrer (Ed.), *Women and folklore* (pp. 58–80). Austin: University of Texas Press.

Adler, P. A., & Adler, P. (1998). *Peer power: Preadolescent culture and identity*. New Brunswick, NJ: Rutgers University Press.

Alderson, P. (2000). Children as researchers: The effects of participation rights on research methodology. In P. Christensen & A. James (Eds.), *Research with children: Perspectives and practices* (pp. 241–257). London: Falmer Press.

Aydt, H., & Corsaro, W. A. (2003). Differences in children's construction of gender across culture: An interpretive approach. American Behavioral Scientist, *46*, 1306–1325.

Berentzen, S. (1984). *Children constructing their social world*. University of Bergen: Bergen, Norway.

Best, R. (1983). *We've all got scars: What boys and girls learn in elementary school*. Bloomington: Indiana University Press.

Christensen, P. & James. A. (2000a). Introduction: Researching children and childhood: Cultures of communication. In P. Christensen & A. James (Eds.), *Research with children: Perspectives and practices* (pp. 1–8). London: Falmer Press.

Christensen, P. & James, A. (2000b). Childhood diversity and commonality: Some methodological insights. In P. Christensen & A. James (Eds), *Research with children: Perspectives and practices* (pp. 160–178). London: Falmer Press.

Connell, R. (1987). *Gender and power: Society, the person and sexual politics*. Stanford, CA: Stanford University Press.

Corsaro, W. A. (1985). *Friendship and peer culture in the early years*. Norwood, NJ: Ablex.

Corsaro, W. A. (1988). Routines in the peer culture of American and Italian nursery school children. *Sociology of Education, 61*, 1–14.

Corsaro, W. A. (1992). Interpretive reproduction in children's peer cultures. *Social Psychology Quarterly*, *55*, 160–177.

Corsaro, W. A. (1994). Discussion, debate, and friendship: Peer discourse in nursery schools in the US and Italy. *Sociology of Education, 67*, 1–26.

Corsaro, W. A. (2003). *"We're friends, right?": Inside kids' culture*. Washington, DC: Joseph Henry Press.

Corsaro, W. A. (2005). *The sociology of childhood* (2nd ed.). Thousand Oaks, CA: Pine Forge Press.

Corsaro, W. A., & Eder, D. (1990). Children's peer cultures. *Annual Review of Sociology, 16*, 197–220.

Corsaro, W. A., & Fingerson, L. (2003). Development and socialization in childhood. In J. Delamater (Ed.), *Handbook of social psychology* (pp. 125–155). New York: Kluwer/Plenum

Corsaro, W., & Molinari, L. (1990). From *seggiolini* to *discussione*: The generation and extension of peer culture among Italian preschool children. *International Journal of Qualitative Studies in Education, 3*, 213–230.

Corsaro, W. A., & Molinari, L. (2000a). Entering and observing in children's worlds: A reflection on a longitudinal ethnography of early education in Italy. In P. Christensen

& A. James (Eds.), *Research with children: Perspectives and practices* (pp. 179–200). London: Falmer Press.

Corsaro, W. A., & Molinari, L. (2000b). Priming events and Italian children's transition from preschool to elementary school: Representations and actions. *Social Psychology Quarterly, 63*, 16–33.

Corsaro, W. A., & Molinari, L. (2005). *I compagni: Understanding children's transition from preschool to elementary school*. New York: Teachers College Press.

Corsaro, W. A., Molinari, L., Hadley, K., & Sugioka, H. (2003). Keeping and making friends in Italian children's transition from preschool to elementary school. *Social Psychology Quarterly*, *66*, 272–292.

Corsaro, W., Molinari, L., & Rosier, K. (2002). Zena and Carlotta: Transition narratives and early education in the United States and Italy. *Human Development*, *45*, 323–348.

Corsaro, W. A., & Nelson, E. (2003). Children's collective activities and peer culture in early literacy in American and Italian preschools. *Sociology of Education*, *76*, 209–227.

Davies, B. (1989). *Frogs and snails and feminist tales: Preschool children and gender*. Boston: Allen & Unwin.

Eder, D., & Fingerson, L. (2002). Interviewing children and adolescents. In J. F. Gubrium & J. A. Holstein (Eds.), *Handbook of interview research* (pp. 181–201). Thousand Oaks, CA: Sage.

Evaldsson, A. (1993). *Play, disputes and social order: Everyday life in two Swedish after-school centers*. Linköping, Sweden: Linköping University.

Evaldsson, A., & Corsaro, W. A. (1998). Play and games in the peer culture of preschool and preadolescent children: An interpretive approach. *Childhood*, *5*, 377–402.

Fernie, D., Davies, B, Kantor, R. & McMurray. P. (1993). Becoming a person in the preschool: Creating integrated gender, school culture, and peer culture positionings. *Qualitative Studies in Education, 6*, 95–110.

Fine, G. (1987). *With the boys: Little league baseball and preadolescent culture*. Chicago: University of Chicago Press

Fine, G., & Sandstrom, K. (1988). *Knowing children: Participant observation with minors*. Newbury Park, CA: Sage.

Gaskins, S., Miller, P. J., & Corsaro. W. A. (1992). Theoretical and methodological perspectives in the interpretive study of children. In W. A. Corsaro & P. J. Miller (Eds.), *Interpretive approaches to children's socialization*, (pp. 5–23). San Francisco: Jossey-Bass.

Geertz, C. (1973). *The interpretation of cultures*. New York: Basic Books.

Gilligan, C. (1982). *In a different voice: Psychological theory and women's development*. Cambridge, MA: Harvard University Press.

Goldman, L. R. (1998). *Child's play: Myth, mimesis and make-believe*. New York: Oxford.

Goodwin, M. H. (1985). The serious side of jump rope: Conversational practices and social organization in the frame of play. *Folklore, 98*, 315–330.

Goodwin, M. H. (1990). *He-said-she-said: Talk as social organization among Black children*. Bloomington: Indiana University Press.

Goodwin, M. H. (1998). Games of stance: Conflict and footing in hopscotch. In S. Hoyle & C. T. Adger (Eds.), *Kids' talk: Strategic language use in later childhood* (pp. 23–46). New York: Oxford.

Goodwin, M. H. (2003) The relevance of ethnicity, class, and gender in children's peer negotiations. In J. Holmes & M. Meyerhoff (Eds.), *Handbook of language and gender* (pp. 229–251). New York: Blackwell.

Hadley, K. (2003). Children's word play: Resisting and accommodating Confucian values in a Taiwanese kindergarten classroom. *Sociology of Education, 76*, 193–208.

Hecht, T. (1998). *At home in the street: Street children of northeast Brazil*. Cambridge, England: Cambridge University Press.

Holmes, R. (1995). *How children perceive race*. Thousand Oaks, CA: Sage.

James, A. (2000). Embodied beings: Understanding the self and the body in childhood. In A. Prout (Ed.), *The body, childhood and society* (pp. 19–37). New York: St. Martin's Press.

James, A., Jenks, C., & Prout, A. (1998). *Theorizing childhood*. New York: Teachers College Press.

Katriel, T. (1987). "*Bexibùdim!*": Ritualized sharing among Israeli children's conflicts. *Language in Society, 16*, 305–320.

Kyratzis, A., & Guo, J. (2001). Preschool girls' and boys' verbal conflict strategies in the United States and China. *Research on Language and Social Interaction, 34*, 45–74.

Lever, J. (1976). Sex differences in the games children play. *Social Problems, 23*, 478–487.

Løkken, G. (2000). The playful quality of the toddling "style." *International Journal of Qualitative Studies in Education, 13*, 531–542.

Maccoby, E. E., & Lewis, C. (2003). Less day care or different day care? *Child Development, 74*, 1069–1075.

Mayall, B. (2002). *Towards a sociology for childhood: Thinking from children's lives*. Philadelphia: Open University Press.

Messner, M. A. (2000). Barbie girls versus sea monsters: Children constructing gender. *Gender & Society, 14*, 765–784.

Mishler, E. (1979). "Won't you trade cookies with the popcorn?": The talk of trades among six year olds. In O. Garnica & M. King (Eds.), *Language, children, and society: The effects of social factors on children's learning to communicate* (pp. 21–36). Elmsford, NY: Pergamon.

Mussati, T., & Panni., S. (1981). Social behavior and interaction among day care center toddlers. *Early Child Development and Care, 7*, 5–27.

National Institute of Child Health and Human Development Early Child Care Research Network. (2003). Does amount of time spent in child care predict socio-emotional adjustment during the transition to kindergarten? *Child Development, 74*, 976–1005.

Prout, A. (2000). Childhood bodies: Construction, agency and hybridity. In A. Prout (Ed.), *The body, childhood and society*, (pp. 1–18). New York: St. Martin's Press.

Rizzo, T, A. (1989). *Friendship development among children in school*. Norwood, NJ: Ablex.

Rizzo, T. A. (1992). The role of conflict in children's friendship development. In W. A. Corsaro & P. J. Miller (Eds.), *Interpretive approaches to children's socialization* (pp. 93–111). San Francisco: Jossey-Bass.

Rogoff, B. (2003). *The cultural nature of human development*. New York: Oxford University Press.

Sawyer, R. K. (1997). *Pretend play as improvisation*. Mahwah, NJ: Lawrence Erlbaum Associates.

Selman, R. (1980). *The growth of personal understanding*. New York: Academic Press.

Shantz, C. (1987). Conflicts between children. *Child Development, 58*, 283–305.

Strandell, H. (1997). Doing reality with play: Play as a children's resource in organizing everyday life in daycare centres. *Childhood,* 4, 445–464.

Tesson G., & Youniss, J. (1995). Micro-sociology and psychological development: A sociological interpretation of Piaget's theory. In A. Ambert (Ed.), *Sociological studies of children (vol. 7* pp. 101–126). Greenwich, CT: JAI Press.

Thelen E., & Smith, L. (1998). Dynamic systems theories. In R. Lerner (Ed.), *Handbook of child psychology* (pp. 563–634). New York: Wiley.

Thorne, B. (1986). Girls and boys together . . . but mostly apart: Gender arrangements in elementary schools. In W. Hartrup & Z. Rubin (Eds.), *Relationships and development* (pp. 167–184). Hillsdale, NJ: Lawrence Erlbaum Associates.

Thorne, B. (1993). *Gender play: Girls and boys in school.* New Brunswick, NJ: Rutgers University Press.

Vygotsky, L. V. (1978). *Mind in society*. Cambridge, MA: Harvard University Press.

Walkerdine, V. (1990). *Schoolgirl fictions*. New York: Verso Press.

Williams, S. J., & Bendelow, G. A. (1998). Malignant bodies: Children's beliefs about health, cancer and risk. In S. Nettleton & J. Watson (Eds.), *The body in everyday life*. (pp. 103–123). London: Routledge.

Winterhoff, P. A. (1997.) Sociocultural promotions constraining children's social activity: Comparisons and variability in the development of friendships. In J. Tudge, M. Shanahan, & J. Valsiner (Eds.), *Comparisons in human development: Understanding time and context* (pp. 222–251). New York: Cambridge University Press.

Youniss, J., & Damon, W. (1994). Social construction and Piaget's theory. In B. Puka (Ed.), *Moral Development: Vol. 5, New research in moral development* (pp. 407–426). New York: Garland.

PART II

Temperamental and Emotional Influences on Peer Relationships

6 Temperament, Socioemotional Functioning, and Peer Relationships in Chinese and North American Children

Xinyin Chen, Li Wang, and Amanda DeSouza

Temperamental characteristics may play a significant role in the development of social competence and adjustment. Support for this belief comes from a number of studies in North America and Western Europe (see Kagan, 1989, and Rothbart & Bates, 1998 for comprehensive reviews). Nevertheless, the impact of temperamental factors on development takes place in cultural context. Culture may influence the display of personal traits and the way in which they contribute to adaptive and maladaptive functioning. During development, temperament and culture interact, which may lead to different developmental patterns and outcomes of certain dispositional characteristics, such as sociability and shyness, across cultural contexts. The mechanism for the temperament–culture interaction mainly involves the socialization process, such as culturally directed social interpretations and responses in children's relationships with adults and peers (Chen, 2000). Social judgments, evaluations, and responses determine, to a large extent, the functional "meanings" of the characteristics and their effect on individual behavior and adjustment status. Children may actively engage in the processes through their participation in endorsing, transforming, and constructing cultural norms and values in social interactions.

In this chapter, we focus on the relations between temperament and peer interactions and relationships in Chinese and North American children. We first describe a conceptual model concerning some basic dimensions of temperament, social functioning, and cultural context. We then discuss major socioemotional characteristics, particularly shyness–inhibition, in Chinese and Western cultures. Our discussion focuses on how shyness–inhibition is interpreted and responded to by others in socialization and social interactions and consequently makes distinct contributions to peer relationships and general social adjustment in Chinese and North American children. We also discuss how the significance of dispositional factors for social relationships and adjustment may be affected by macrolevel changes in the society. These discussions are based mostly on the findings of a series of ongoing cross-cultural projects our research team has been conducting in China and Canada for the past 15 years. Finally, some suggestions are offered about future directions in the cross-cultural study of child temperament and peer relationships.

Social Initiative and Self-Control in Cultural Context: A Conceptual Model

Chen (2000) proposed a preliminary two-dimensional model concerning socioemotional characteristics and cultural context. According to this model, social initiative and self-control, as manifestations of the fundamental temperamental dimensions of reactivity and regulation (Rothbart & Bates, 1998) in social domains, are two distinct systems that may account for individual differences in social functioning and interactional styles. *Social initiative* represents the tendency to initiate and maintain social interactions, which is often indicated by children's reactions to challenging social situations. For example, whereas some children are confident and display high interest in social activities, others may be more timid, reticent, and inactive in interacting with others (Kagan, 1998; Kochanska & Radke-Yarrow, 1992). High social initiative may be driven by the child's approach motive in social situations. In contrast, internal anxiety or approach–avoidance conflict may impede spontaneous engagement in social participation, leading to a low level of social initiative (Asendorpf, 1990). *Self-control*, on the other hand, represents the ability to modulate behavioral and emotional reactivity and promote the appropriateness of children's behaviors during social interactions. A variety of psychological processes, including attention, language, memory, communicative skills, and sense of self, are involved in the development of self-control (e.g., Kochanska & Aksan, 1995; Kopp, 1982). In early childhood, self-control is often reflected in compliant and cooperative behaviors, such as initiating, modifying, or restraining certain behaviors in response to adults' requests and demands (Kopp, 1982). Parents help their children exercise control and restraint through the issuance of frequent directions (Kuczynski & Kochanska, 1990). With age, control shifts to the child himself or herself, and adults increasingly assume the role of distal monitors. As a result, children may "internalize" social standards and regulate their behaviors without intervention from adults (Kochanska & Aksan, 1995). The significance of self-control is reflected mainly in its role in regulating individual behaviors to maintain and promote interpersonal harmony and group well-being. Thus, the broad construct of self-control contains the components

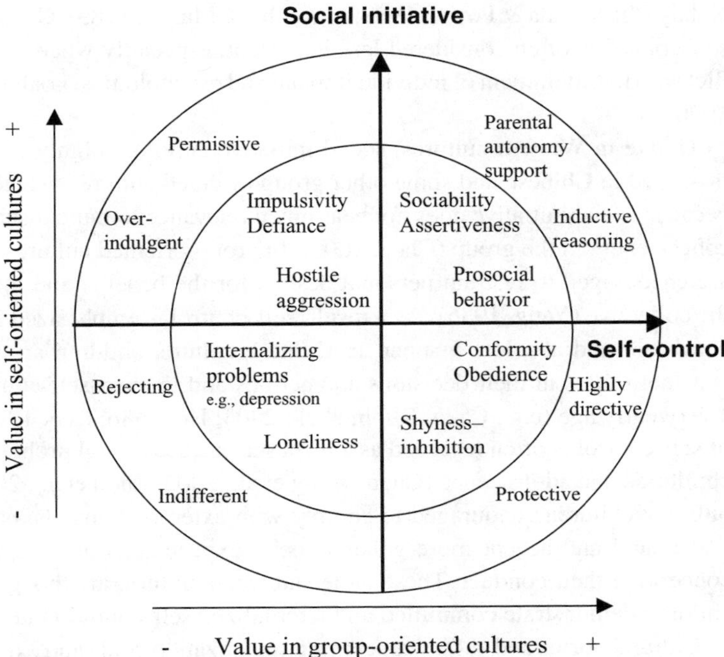

Figure 6.1. A contextual model: Parenting styles (outer circle) and socio-emotional characteristics (inner circle) in relation to social initiative and self-control and their value in self-oriented vs. group-oriented cultures.

of other-orientation, social responsibility, and responsiveness to socialization pressure, especially during the school years.

An important aspect of the contextual model is about the linkage between the temperamental dimensions and cultural values. As shown in Figure 6.1, whereas social initiative is relatively more emphasized in Western individualistic societies, self-control may be more valued in the group-oriented societies, such as Chinese society. In Western cultures, because acquiring individual autonomy, competitiveness, and self-expressive skills are important socialization goals (Maccoby & Martin, 1983), social initiative is viewed as a major index of social competence; the lack of active social participation and assertiveness is considered maladaptive (Rubin & Asendorpf, 1993). On the other hand, although self-control is encouraged (Chamberlain & Patterson, 1995; Maccoby & Martin, 1983), the cultural emphasis on individual decision-making and freedom requires socialization agents to help children learn to balance the needs of the self with those of others (Edwards, 1995;

Kobayashi-Winata & Power, 1989; Maccoby & Martin, 1983). Consequently, self-control is often considered less important, especially when it is in conflict with the attainment of individual social and psychological goals (Triandis, 1990).

Unlike in Western cultures, social initiative is not so highly appreciated or valued in Chinese and some other group-oriented cultures, which may be because social initiative does not bear much relevance to mutual support and cohesiveness in the group (Chen, 2000). In group-oriented cultures, children are encouraged to restrain personal desires for the benefits and interests of the collective (Yang, 1986). As a result, self-control is emphasized in a more consistent and absolute manner. In Chinese culture, children are taught to consider others in their decisions and actions and to exert self-control from a very early age (e.g., Chen, Rubin et al., 2003; Ho, 1986; Luo, 1996). Lack of self-control is often regarded as a most serious behavioral problem during childhood and adolescence (Chen, Wang et al., 2002; Zhou et al., 2004). Not only are children encouraged to comply with external demands, but also to understand and accept more general social expectations and requirements concerning their conduct. These understandings, in turn, are thought to help children demonstrate committed and internalized self-control (Luo, 1996).

Cultural norms and values concerning socialization goals and expectations may be reflected in parental child-rearing beliefs, attitudes, and behaviors (e.g., Super & Harkness, 1986; Whiting & Edwards, 1988). In traditional Chinese culture, for example, parents are responsible for "governing" (i.e., teaching, disciplining) their children and are held accountable for their children's failures. In turn, children are required to pledge obedience and reverence to parents as indicated in the Confucian doctrine of "filial piety" (e.g., Ho, 1986). Consistently, it has been reported that, compared with Western parents, Chinese parents are more controlling and protective in child-rearing (Chao, 1994; Kriger & Kroes, 1972; Lin & Fu, 1990). The directive parenting style and high parental involvement may "fit" the cultural values on the socialization of self-control (Chao, 1995; Ho, 1986). Relative to Chinese parents, Western parents are more likely to support the child's autonomy and exploration (e.g., Liu et al., in press). Further, they are encouraged to be sensitive to their children's needs and to interact with children in a low-power, "child-centered" manner (Rubin, Stewart, & Chen, 1995). These parenting beliefs and practices may be conducive to the development of social assertiveness and initiative in the self-oriented cultural context.

Different cultural values on social initiative and self-control and the corresponding socialization beliefs and practices are directly related to the meanings of specific socioemotional characteristics, such as aggression-disruption (based on high social initiative and low self-control), shyness–social inhibition (relatively low initiative and high control), and aspects of social competence, such as sociability and prosocial orientation in Chinese and North American children. Parental beliefs and attitudes may serve as a basis for parents' interpretations of, and responses to, the display of a socioemotional characteristic in children, which in turn constitute important socialization conditions for their development. Moreover, through the socialization process, children may learn the cultural values and eventually use them to direct their own attitudes and behaviors in their interactions with others. In the past decade, our research team has investigated cultural meanings of compliance (Chen, Rubin et al., 2003), shyness (e.g., Chen et al., 1998), and sociable and prosocial behaviors (e.g., Chen et al., 2000) in Chinese and North American children. Based on these studies, we have found that the significance of individual characteristics for peer interactions and relationships may be moderated by cultural context. As a result, adaptive and maladaptive behaviors may be defined similarly or differently across cultures (Benedict, 1934; Bornstein, 1995; Chen, 2000). In the sections that follow, we focus on shyness–inhibition and discuss its meaning and developmental consequences in Chinese and North American cultures.

Shyness–Inhibition and Peer Relationships in Chinese and North American Children

Shyness–inhibition, often manifested in wary, vigilant, and sensitive behaviors, is taken to reflect internal insecurity and anxiety in social-evaluative situations (Asendorpf, 1990; Stevenson-Hinde & Shouldice, 1993). In the Western literature, children who display shy, wary, and inhibited behaviors are believed to be socially incompetent and immature because these behaviors indicate a low level of social initiative and assertiveness (e.g., Asendorpf, 1991; Larson, 1999, Rubin, Bukowski, & Parker, 1998; Triandis, 1990). Consistently, it has been found that shy–inhibited children are likely to experience difficulties in peer acceptance and social adjustment, especially in the school years when peer interactions become an important part of social lives (e.g., Rubin, Burgess, & Coplan, 2002). When shy children recognize their social difficulties, they tend to develop negative self-perceptions and self-feelings, such as depression (e.g., Boivin, Hymel, & Bukowski, 1995; Rubin, Chen et al., 1995).

Some researchers have argued that the occurrence of shy–inhibited behavior may involve the *psychological* process of dysregulation (e.g., Asendorpf, 1991; Rubin, Coplan et al., 1995). This is because shy, wary, and sensitive behavior in social situations is associated with feelings of anxiety and lack of self-confidence (e.g., Rubin et al., 2002). However, to direct and maintain emotional reactions toward the self, rather than others, and to display constrained behaviors, adequate self-control is required. Moreover, regardless of the underlying psychoemotional process, shy–inhibited behavior usually does not threaten the welfare of others and the functioning of the group. Thus, at the *behavioral* or *social* level, self-control is an important attribute of shyness–inhibition, as indicated in Figure 6.1. Shy–inhibited children are perceived as well-behaved and understanding, which are indications of internalized self-control in traditional Chinese culture (Chen, 2000; Liang, 1987, Lou, 1996; Yang, 1986). The cultural endorsement may help shy children obtain social support and approval in peer interactions and develop self-confidence in social performance. Given this background, we have been interested in shyness–inhibition and its implications for social interactions and relationships in Chinese and North American children.

According to Hinde (1987, 1995), children's social and psychological functioning may be analyzed at multiple levels according to its social complexity. At the *intrapersonal* level, children carry with them somewhat stable, personal characteristics, such as temperament, that dispose them to display particular reactions to social stimuli. At the *interaction* level, children engage in dyadic behaviors with others, involving the process of social initiation and response. Most interactions are embedded in long-term *relationships* and *group networks*, which represent a higher level of social experience (Hinde, 1987; Rubin et al., 1998). Social relationships and groups often develop based on shared expectations and norms and serve to regulate individual behaviors and activities. Finally, Hinde (1987) emphasizes that the different levels of individual and social experiences are embedded within an all-reaching "umbrella" of the cultural macrosystem. Following Hinde's paradigm, we will discuss how cultural context is involved in organizing the developmental setting for shy–inhibited children and directing the role of shy–inhibited behavior in social interactions and relationships and general social and psychological adjustment.

Shyness–Inhibition in Toddlerhood: Cross-Cultural Differences in Prevalence and Parental Attitudes

Cross-cultural differences in shyness–inhibition between Chinese and North American children were reported in several studies (Chan & Eysenck, 1981; Freedman & Freedman, 1969; Kagan, Kearsley, & Zelazo, 1978). In general, Chinese children displayed more shy and wary behaviors in novel situations

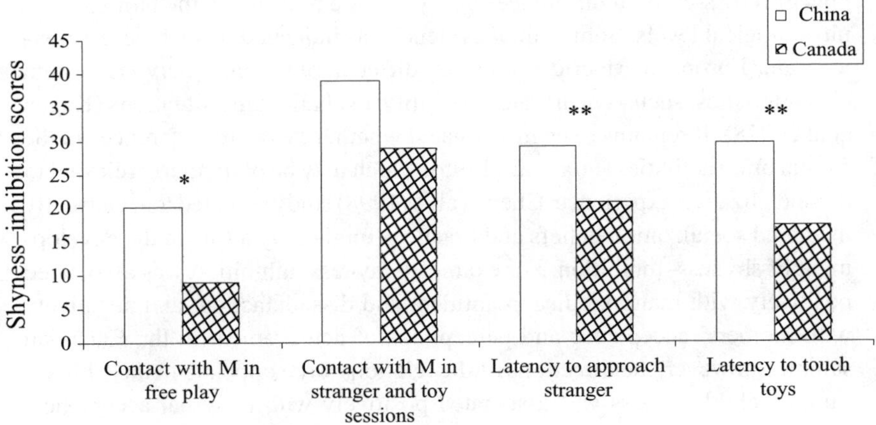

Figure 6.2. Shyness–inhibition scores of Chinese and Canadian toddlers. * = $p < .01$, ** = $p < .001$.

than their North American counterparts. In a recent cross-cultural study conducted by Chen et al. (1998), for example, a sample of Chinese and Canadian toddlers were observed in a variety of activities, including free play, interacting with a stranger, and other typical episodes of the inhibition paradigm (e.g., a stranger quietly played with a toy truck and robot) in the laboratory situation (e.g., Kagan, 1989). Compared with the Canadian counterparts, Chinese toddlers were clearly more shy and inhibited in the stressful situation. As shown in Figure 6.2, Chinese toddlers stayed closer to the mother and were less likely to explore in free play sessions. Moreover, they displayed more anxious and fearful behaviors in interacting with the stranger, as indicated by their higher scores on the latency to approach the stranger and to touch the toys. The percentages of toddlers who made contact with their mothers in the free play and truck and robot episodes in the Chinese sample (41 percent and 61 percent, respectively) were almost double those in the Canadian sample (21 percent and 37 percent, respectively). There were significantly more children in the Chinese sample (21 percent and 43 percent, respectively) than in the Canadian sample (6 percent and 12 percent, respectively) who did not approach the stranger or touch the robot. Similar cross-cultural differences have been reported in the attachment literature (e.g., Miyake, Chen, & Campos, 1985; Mizuta et al., 1996). In these studies, Asian infants have been found to be more fearful and insecure, and more likely to seek close physical contact with the caregiver and display ambivalent behaviors in the strange situation than Western infants. Shyness–inhibition is a characteristic that may be biologically rooted (Asendorpf, 1991; Kagan, 1989). It is unclear at this time how the cross-cultural differences in shyness are reflected at the biological or physiological levels. Some initial evidence has indicated that Chinese American and European American children differ in autonomic nervous system characteristics, such as heart rate variability, in challenging situations (Kagan et al., 1978). It remains to be investigated whether there are differences in the frontal brain activities (Fox et al., 1995), which may be particularly relevant to the socialization experience. Chen et al.'s (1998) study revealed that culturally mediated socialization beliefs and practices might play a role in the development of shyness–inhibition. For example, shyness–inhibition was associated positively with maternal disappointment and dissatisfaction, and negatively with mothers' acceptance and perceptions of achievement in the Canadian sample. However, the directions of the relations were opposite in the Chinese sample; child shyness was associated positively with maternal acceptance, approval, and encouragement of achievement, and negatively with maternal negative attitudes.

The different relations between parental attitudes and children's shy–inhibited behavior indicate parental culturally distinct perceptions of shy–inhibited behavior in Chinese and Canadian children. At the same time, the attitudes and reactions of Chinese and Canadian parents toward shy–inhibited behavior in early childhood constitute different social environments that shy–inhibited children may experience in the early years in China and North America, which is likely to affect their interactions and relationships with peers outside of the family and the general "internal working model" concerning the self and others in the future.

Shyness–Inhibition and Peer Interactions in Early Childhood

Peer interactions occur through the process involving the elicitation of social contact and the response of others. Whereas social initiations represent a necessary condition for the establishment of social interactions, responses from the target child may determine whether the social interactions continue. Findings from various research programs have indicated that the ability to establish and maintain positive peer interactions is important for the development of social relationships and adjustment in other areas (Black & Logan, 1995; Dodge et al., 1986; Putallaz & Gottman, 1981).

In studies of Western children (e.g., Dodge et al., 1983; Rubin et al., 2002), shyness–inhibition is often associated with "incompetent" interaction styles. When shy–inhibited children initiate a social interaction, their initiations are often passive, as indicated by hovering, waiting, and nonverbal behaviors (Dodge et al., 1983; Schmidt & Fox, 1998). Moreover, because shy children are viewed as incompetent and deviant by their peers, social initiations made by shy children may be negatively responded to by peers, with overt rejection or intentional ignoring (Rubin et al., 2002).

It is largely unknown how shy–inhibited children are involved in social interactions in different cultural contexts. Because of their internal anxiety and wariness, shy–inhibited children typically participate in fewer interactions than others in social situations. But when shy–inhibited children engage in social interactions, are there cross-cultural differences in their interaction patterns? For example, do shy–inhibited children in China and North America differ in the strategies that they use to make social initiations because of their different experiences during socialization? Do peers respond differently when shy–inhibited children make initiations? When shy–inhibited children do not make active initiations, do peers voluntarily initiate social interactions toward them, and if so, are there differences in peer voluntary initiations in Chinese and North American children? To examine these issues, we recently conducted a study in Chinese and Canadian children to explore the processes in which shy–inhibited children engaged in peer interactions (DeSouza & Chen, 2002).

Participants in the study were four-year-old Chinese and Canadian children ($N = 200$ and 180, respectively). Children who were the same sex and within six months of each other in age were invited to the laboratory in quartets, and their interactions were observed in two fifteen-minute free play sessions. Shyness–inhibition was coded using the Play Observation Scale (Rubin, 1989). Children's onlooker (watching the activities of others but not entering the activity) and unoccupied (an absence of focus or intent, wandering aimlessly, or staring blankly into space) behaviors were included as indexes of shyness–inhibition. Following the procedure used by other researchers (e.g., Asendorpf, 1990, 1991), 50 (24 boys and 26 girls) and 45 (23 boys and 22 girls) shy children were identified, and 100 (48 boys and 52 girls) and 90 (46 boys and 44 girls) non-shy children were identified in the Chinese and Canadian samples, respectively.

Shy–inhibited Chinese and Canadian children were less likely than their non-shy counterparts to make active initiations. Initiations made by shy–inhibited children were largely nonverbal and passive (e.g., approaching the target and starting to engage in the same play behavior as the target child within a close proximity). Thus, regardless of culture, shy–inhibited children's internal anxiety, vigilance, and wariness may prevent them from initiating social contact in an assertive manner (e.g., Asendorpf, 1991; Rubin et al., 2002).

There were significant cultural differences in the responses that shy children received from peers and the initiations that peers made voluntarily to shy children. As indicated in Figure 6.3, in general, when shy Canadian children

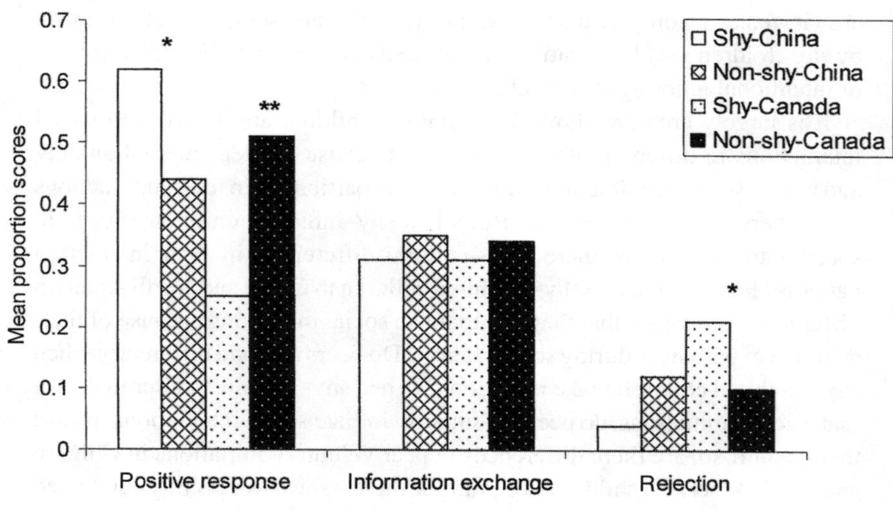

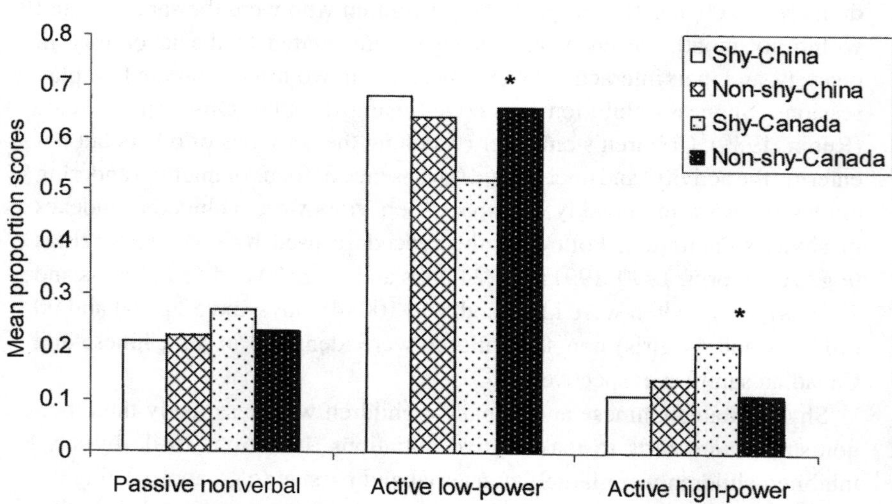

Figure 6.3. Social responses and initiations shy and non-shy children received in China and Canada. * = $p < 0.5$, ** = $p < .01$.

made social initiations, peers were less likely to make positive responses, such as approval, cooperation, and support (e.g., "I really like your drawing!"), and were more likely to make negative responses, such as overt refusal, disagreement, and intentional ignoring of an initiation (e.g., "No!" or "I won't do it"). However, peers responded in a more positive manner in China. Further analyses indicated that the cross-cultural differences in peer responses emerged mainly when shy children made nonverbal passive initiations (e.g., the child put building blocks into a truck with the target child or played with a toy car in the same manner as the target child) and active low power initiations (the child's tendency to influence the target's behavior in a polite and positive manner, e.g., "Can I play with you?" and offering or sharing toys). However, peers tended to respond negatively in both samples when shy children used high-power strategies in initiations (direct demands, prohibitions, and verbal and nonverbal aggression and disruption, e.g., "Don't throw blocks!" or child grabs toy out of target's hands).

There were also differences between the samples in peer voluntary initiations to shy children. When peers voluntarily made initiations, the initiations were more likely to be coercive (e.g., a direct demand, such as "Gimme that," or verbal teasing) and less likely to be cooperative (e.g., "Can I play with you?") in Canada. This was not the case in China; there were nonsignificant differences in peer voluntary initiations to shy and non-shy children. In addition, when peers made active low-power initiations, shy children in Canada were more likely to respond negatively than non-shy children; there was a nonsignificant difference in the Chinese sample.

Taken together, the results suggest that, although shy children in both Canada and China were generally inactive in making initiations and responses in peer interactions, Canadian shy children appeared to be relatively more defensive and incompetent in responding to peers' voluntary active initiations. This may be because shy children in Canada tend to experience difficulties and frustration in their daily peer interactions (e.g., Rubin et al., 1998). The negative experiences that Canadian inhibited children have may, in turn, impede the formation of positive attitudes toward others and facilitate the development of destructive behavioral styles in social responses. The differences between Chinese and Canadian children were more salient in peer responses to shy children's initiations and peer voluntary initiations to shy children. Whereas peers were generally antagonistic, forceful, or nonresponsive in their interactions with shy–inhibited children in Canada, peers appeared more supportive and cooperative toward them in China.

These results indicate that cultural norms and values may play an important role in peer interactions. As indicated earlier, North American cultures endorse self-confidence and assertiveness in social interactions (Larson, 1999; Oyserman, Coon, & Kemmelmeier, 2002; Triandis, 1990). Shy–inhibited behaviors are often viewed as incompetent and deviant by peers and adults (Rubin & Asendorpf, 1993; Rubin et al., 1998). These cultural values may affect the attitudes and reactions of peers in their interactions with shy children through various means during the socialization processes. Unlike Western cultures, shyness and social wariness are considered acceptable or even desirable in social situations in Chinese culture (e.g., Chen, 2000; Chen, Rubin, & Sun, 1992; Yang, 1986). Thus, anxious and restrained behaviors that shy children display in social situations may be perceived as normal by peers. Consequently, when shy children make cautious social overtures, peers are likely to react in the same manner as to non-shy children or attempt to maintain the interactions by controlling their negative responses. The results of the present study suggest that cultural context may be involved in the microsystem process (e.g., Bronfenbrenner, 1988), which may help us better understand peer relationships and the general adjustment status of shy–inhibited children in Chinese and North American societies.

Shyness–Inhibition in Middle and Late Childhood: Relations With Peer Relationships and Social and Psychological Adjustment

Peer relationships are an important social context for learning social and cognitive skills and achieving personal and social success (e.g., Hartup, 1992; Piaget, 1932; Rubin et al., 1998). Children who maintain positive relationships in the peer group may have more opportunities than others to obtain instrumental and informational assistance and guidance from peers, which may be helpful for the development of socially appropriate behaviors and the acquisition of social status. Moreover, children who are accepted by peers and engage in positive social interactions may become increasingly skillful and competent, through social learning process, in solving interpersonal problems (Rubin & Krasnor, 1986). Peer relationships may also be a source of social and emotional support for children in coping with adjustment difficulties and thus may help children develop confidence and feelings of security in the exploration of social and nonsocial worlds. It has been argued that, as a basic social need, being associated with, and accepted by, peers may provide a sense of belongingness and self-validation (Furman & Robbins, 1985; Sullivan, 1953). Consistent with the arguments about the significance of peer relationships for children's social and psychological adjustment, findings from empirical research programs have indicated that children who have difficulties in peer acceptance may develop problems, such as academic failure, juvenile delinquency, and psychopathological symptoms (e.g., Coie et al., 1992; DeRosier, Kupersmidt, & Patterson 1994; Ollendick et al., 1990).

Given this background, it is not surprising that researchers have been interested in factors that may predict the quality of peer relationships. Among various antecedents and correlates of peer relationship difficulties, shy–inhibited behavior has received substantial attention in the West. It has been found that shyness and social wariness are associated with, and predictive of, low social status in the peer group; shy children are likely to be neglected or rejected by peers in the school (Cillessen et al., 1992; Coie & Kupersmidt, 1983). Moreover, teachers often rate shy children as socially incompetent and immature (Hymel et al., 1990). Finally, in late childhood and adolescence, shy–inhibited children may develop negative self-perceptions of social competence and feelings of loneliness when they come to understand their difficulties with peers (Boivin et al., 1995; Rubin, Chen et al., 1995).

Our research team has systematically examined relations between shyness and peer acceptance and other indexes of social and psychological adjustment in Chinese and Canadian children. We believe that different cultural views on shy, wary, and sensitive behavior may have direct influences on how shy children are accepted by peers, which in turn may affect children's performance in social, school, and psychological areas.

In the Shanghai Longitudinal Project (e.g., Chen et al., 1992; Chen et al., 1999), for example, we selected a random sample of children, initially at ages eight and ten years, in China and a comparison group in Canada. In a group session, the children were administered a peer assessment measure of social functioning, including shyness-sensitivity and a sociometric nomination measure. Teachers completed a measure for all participants concerning their social competence. We also obtained information about children's leadership, distinguished studentship, and academic achievement from the school records in the Chinese sample. In addition, we collected data concerning socioemotional adjustment, such as self-perceptions, loneliness and depression. The data were re-collected roughly every two years for fourteen years.

In general, the results indicated that, consistent with the Western literature (e.g., Rubin et al., 2002), shyness was positively associated with peer rejection and negatively associated with teacher-rated social competence in Canadian children. However, shyness was positively associated with peer acceptance, teacher-rated social competence, leadership, distinguished studentship, and academic achievement in Chinese children. The results, based on the original study, are presented in Table 6.1. The concurrent associations were consistent across different age groups in childhood and adolescence, although the

Table 6.1. *Concurrent Correlations Between Shyness and Adjustment in Chinese and Canadian Children*

	China	Canada
Positive sociometric nominations	$.27^b$	$-.21^b$
Negative sociometric nominations	.05	.01
Teacher-rated competence	$.17^b$	$-.30^b$
Leadership	$.29^b$	
Distinguished studentship	$.29^b$	
Academic achievement	$.12^a$	

Note: $N = 612$ and 304 in Chinese and Canadian samples, respectively.
$^a\ p < .01$, $^b\ p < .001$.

magnitude of the associations tended to become weaker in higher grades. Shy–inhibited children in China appeared to have more difficulties than others in establishing positive peer relationships during the transitional period, such as the first grade in high school (e.g., Chen, Rubin, & Li, 1995b). However, they continued to adjust well when the social environment became stable. The results concerning the relations at different ages in the Chinese sample are presented in Table 6.2.

Longitudinal data from the Chinese sample indicated that shyness in early childhood significantly predicted later sociometric status and social and school competence (Chen et al., 1999). Moreover, shyness positively contributed to the development of psychological well-being, such as self-perceptions of social competence and general self-worth, and negatively contributed to the development of psychological problems, including feelings of loneliness and depression (Chen, Rubin, & Li, 1995a; Chen et al., 1999). It

Table 6.2. *Concurrent Correlations Between Shyness and Adjustment in Chinese Children and Adolescents*

Adjustment Variables	8 years $N = 300$	10 years $N = 555$	12 years $N = 540$	14 years $N = 526$
Positive sociometric nominations	$.39^b$	$.15^b$	$.09^a$	$.16^b$
Negative sociometric nominations	.09	−.02	.08	.06
Teacher-rated competence	$.17^a$	$.21^b$	$.09^a$	$.10^a$
Leadership	$.30^b$	$.23^b$	$.12^a$	$.17^b$
Distinguished studentship	$.24^b$	$.20^b$	$.18^b$	$.12^a$
Academic achievement	$.13^a$	$.15^b$	.05	$.19^b$

$^a\ p < .01$, $^b\ p < .001$.

should be noted that these results have been replicated in several other studies conducted with different samples of Chinese children (e.g., Chen, Chang, & He, 2003; Chen, Chen, & Kaspar, 2001; Chen, Dong, & Zhou, 1997).

The findings from our research program clearly indicate that whereas their counterparts experience various difficulties in peer relationships and social adjustment in North America, shy–sensitive children are liked by peers and regarded by adults as socially competent in China. Shy Chinese children feel positively about their social competence and develop few internalizing psychological problems as reported in the Western literature (e.g., Rubin et al., 2002). These findings suggest that the significance of shyness for social adaptation, including peer interactions and relationships, varies across cultures. As indicated earlier, shy and inhibited behaviors are viewed as incompetent and maladaptive, particularly in school-aged children, in most North American and Western European cultures, where social initiative and assertiveness are endorsed (Asendorpf, 1991; Larson, 1999, Rubin et al., 2002). In contrast, shyness–social inhibition is considered an indication of social accomplishment and maturity in traditional Chinese culture; shy–inhibited children are often perceived as well behaved (Liang, 1987). The cultural values provide important standards for individual judgments and evaluations of shy behaviors, serve as a basis for the formation of different attitudes toward shy children among peers, and eventually lead to different relationships that shy children establish with others. Thus, whereas their North American counterparts have extensive difficulties in social and psychological adjustment, shy children in China live in a relatively desirable social environment that may help them attain achievement in various areas, including school performance and socioemotional well-being. The different social experiences of shy children in China and North America are likely to determine culturally distinct patterns and outcomes of their development.

The Impact of Social Change on Individual Functioning and Peer Relationships

Our cross-cultural research has indicated the importance of social and cultural background for understanding individual functioning and peer relationships. However, social and cultural conditions for individual development are not static, but rather constantly change (Crockett & Silbereisen, 2000). According to social ecological theory (e.g., Bronfenbrenner & Morris, 1998; Elder, 1998), human lives carry the imprint of their particular social worlds that are subject to historical change. Thus, it is important to understand cultural influences on individual behaviors in a historical context. Chinese society has changed dramatically since the early 1980s, particularly in the last decade. During this period, China has carried out a full-scale reform toward a market economy that allows for the adoption of many aspects of capitalism. The rapid expansion of the market systems to all different sectors has led to major changes in economic and social structures. As a result, there is increased variation in individual and family income, massive movement of the population, decline in the government control of social welfare and protection, and rapid rise in unemployment rate and competition (e.g., Zhang, 2000). The dramatic changes in social structure and organization and the introduction of individualistic values and ideologies, such as liberty and individual freedom from North America and Western Europe (Cai & Wu, 1999; Huang, 1999), may have a significant effect on children's social functioning and interactions.

In a recent study using a cohort design, we investigated relations between shyness–inhibition and social, school, and psychological adjustment in Chinese children at different times of the societal transition (Chen et al., 2005). We collected data on shyness and adjustment in three cohorts (1990, 1998, and 2002), which represented different phases of the social transition in the Chinese society. China implemented the "internal vitalization" policy in rural areas and the "open-door" policy in some Southern regions in the early 1980s. The rise of the township and village enterprises and foreign investment represented the main features of the economic reform in the 1980s and early 1990s. The full-scale social and economic reform was expanded to cities and other parts of the country in the early 1990s. Since then, the reform has been significantly accelerated, and its influence has rapidly spread to various aspects of the society and individual daily lives.

Multigroup invariance tests through LISREL revealed overall significant cross-cohort differences in the relations between shyness–inhibition and all adjustment variables. Further invariance analyses indicated that there was a significant cross-cohort difference in the relation between shyness and each adjustment variable, with $X^2(df = 2)$ ranging from 9.52 to 25.88, $ps < .01$. The results concerning the effects of shyness in predicting specific adjustment variables are presented in Table 6.3. The relations between shyness and the adjustment variables were all different between the 1990 cohort and the 2002 cohort. The relations between shyness and negative sociometric nominations and teacher-rated competence were significantly different between the 1990 cohort and the 1998 cohort. Finally, the relations between shyness and all adjustment variables were different between the 1998 cohort and the 2002 cohort, except for negative sociometric nominations. In general, shyness was positively associated with peer acceptance, leadership, and academic achievement in the 1990 cohort. However, shyness was negatively associated

Table 6.3. *Effects of Shyness in Predicting Adjustment Variables in Different Cohorts*

Adjustment Variable	1990 Cohort	1998 Cohort	2002 Cohort
Positive sociometric nominations	.16[b]	.12[a]	−.13[a]
Negative sociometric nominations	.06	.28[c]	.27[c]
Teacher-rated Competence	.16[c]	−.05	−.20[c]
Leadership	.19[c]	.11[a]	−.10
Academic achievement	.15[b]	.09	−.08
Depression	−.03	.01	.19[c]

Note: $N = 429$, 390, and 266 in the 1990, 1998, and 2002 cohorts, respectively. The effect of sex was controlled in the analyses.
[a] $= p < .05$, [b] $= p < .01$, [c] $= p < .001$.

with peer acceptance and school adjustment and positively associated with peer rejection and depression in the 2002 cohort. The patterns of the relations between shyness and peer relationships and adjustment variables were nonsignificant or mixed in the 1998 cohort.

As indicated earlier, shy, wary, and sensitive behavior has been traditionally valued and encouraged in Chinese children (Feng, 1962; Yang, 1986). However, the extensive changes toward the capitalistic system in the economic reform and the introduction of Western ideologies may have led to the decline in the adaptive value of shy–inhibited behavior. In the new, competitive environment, behavioral characteristics that facilitate the achievement of personal goals, such as social assertiveness and initiative, may be appreciated and encouraged. In contrast, shy, anxious, and inhibited behavior that may impede self-expression, active social communication, and exploration, particularly in stressful situations, may no longer be regarded as adaptive and competent. In other words, shy–inhibited behavior may become increasingly unsuitable for the demands of the changing society. As a result, shy children may be at a disadvantage in obtaining social acceptance and approval and maintaining social status. Moreover, like their Western counterparts (e.g., Rubin & Asendorpf, 1993), when they realize their social difficulties, they may develop negative attitudes toward others and themselves. Thus, shyness–inhibition becomes an undesirable behavioral characteristic in social and psychological adjustment.

The influence of the social and historical transition on individual attitudes and behaviors and social relationships may be an ongoing process that occurs gradually and cumulatively through a variety of means (Silbereisen, 2000). Whereas children in the 1990 cohort experienced relatively limited influence of the comprehensive reform and children in the 2002 cohort were socialized in an increased self-oriented cultural context, the 1998 cohort represented an intermediate phase in which children might have mixed socialization experiences in the family and the peer group. An interesting finding was that shyness was positively associated with both peer acceptance and peer rejection in the 1998 cohort. The analysis of the sociometric classification (Coie, Dodge, & Coppotelli, 1982) indicated that, whereas shy children were more popular in the 1990 cohort and more rejected in the 2002 cohort than others, shy children in the 1998 cohort were controversial; they were liked and disliked by peers at the same time. These results indicate mixed attitudes of peers toward shy–inhibited children, which, to some extent, may reflect the cultural conflict between imported Western values on social initiative and individual autonomy and traditional Chinese values on self-control.

In summary, the results of our recent studies suggest that the dramatic transition in Chinese society in the last decade may have led to changes in the values on the basic dimensions of socioemotional functioning, such as social initiative and self-control. These changes have considerable implications for children's social interactions and adjustment. Historical context is an important aspect of socioecological and cultural conditions for human development, which should be considered seriously in the study of individual disposition and social relationships.

Conclusions and Future Directions

Temperament may make substantial contributions to the development of social functioning and peer relationships. However, temperamental influence on individual behaviors and relationships is likely to be constrained by the social and cultural context. For example, group- and self-oriented cultures may place different values on the fundamental dimensions of socioemotional functioning, such as social initiative and self-control. The cultural values may affect parental socialization goals and beliefs, and regulate parental attitudes toward, and reactions to, specific child behaviors (e.g., shy–inhibited behavior) in parent–child interactions. Moreover, the early socialization experience of children in the family may in turn have a pervasive effect on how they behave and how they respond to others' behaviors in peer interactions. Consequently, the linkage between a temperamental trait and the pattern of peer interactions and relationships may vary across cultures. In this chapter, we discussed shyness–inhibition and its relations with peer interactions and relationships in Chinese and North American children from a developmental and contextual perspective. Based on the discussion, it may be reasonable to conclude that social and cultural circumstances play an important role in defining the functional "meanings" of individual socioemotional characteristics in peer relationships.

Our research program represents a first step toward the understanding of cultural involvement in individual socioemotional characteristics and peer relationships. Several major issues remain to be examined. First, we proposed a conceptual model concerning fundamental temperamental dimensions, social functioning, and cultural context. This model has guided our research effort and helped us understand the findings from a broader contextual perspective. However, the model is largely speculative; supporting evidence is needed for the general framework as well as specific components. Our research has focused mostly on shyness–inhibition, and to a lesser extent, on compliance (e.g., Chen, Rubin et al., 2003), sociable and prosocial behaviors (e.g., Chen et al., 2000; Chen et al., 2002), and parenting (e.g., Chen et al., 2001). Many other aspects of socioemotional functioning, such as aggression–disruption and internalizing problems, need to be investigated in Chinese and other cultures.

Second, parenting beliefs and practices have been considered a major "mediator" of cultural influence on individual functioning in our model and research. It has been argued that child temperament and parenting may interact in a transactional manner in their contributions to social and behavioral development (e.g., Collins et al., 2000; Schaffer, 2000). The transactional process needs to be explored in cultural context.

Third, our research has focused mostly on relations between temperament and peer interactions and relationships. It has been demonstrated that children and adolescents' friendships represent a unique aspect of peer experiences and may make contributions to social and psychological adjustment beyond the overall peer acceptance and rejection. It will be interesting to examine whether children's friendships differ across cultures and what role temperament and socialization play in determining the cultural variations.

Finally, our cross-cultural work has been conducted mainly in Chinese and Canadian children. It will be important to examine personal characteristics and peer relationships in other Asian and Western cultures. Moreover, because of practical difficulties, the samples of the Chinese children and adolescents were drawn from urban areas of China. Generalization of the findings to rural areas of the country should be made with caution. In short, cultural influence on peer relationships is a complex issue involving multiple personal and situational factors. Continuous exploration is essential for achieving a better understanding of the issue and the underlying processes in which different factors affect and interact with each other in development.

References

Asendorpf, J. (1990). Beyond social withdrawal: Shyness, unsociability, and peer avoidance. *Human Development, 33*, 250–259.

Asendorpf, J. (1991). Development of inhibited children's coping with unfamiliarity. *Child Development, 62*, 1460–1474.

Benedict, R. (1934). Anthropology and the abnormal. *Journal of General Psychology, 10*, 59–82.

Black, B., & Logan, A. (1995). Links between communication patterns in mother-child, father-child, and child-peer interactions and children's social status. *Child Development, 66*, 255–271.

Boivin, M., Hymel, S., & Bukowski, W. M. (1995). The roles of social withdrawal, peer rejection, and victimization by peers in predicting loneliness and depressed mood in childhood. *Development and Psychopathology, 7*, 765–785.

Bornstein, M. H. (1995). Form and function: Implications for studies of culture and human development. *Culture and Psychology, 1*(1), 123–138.

Bronfenbrenner, U. (1988). Interacting systems in human development. Research paradigms: Present and future. In N. Bolger, A. Caspi, G. Downey, & M. Moorehouse (Eds.), *Persons in context: Developmental processes* (pp. 25–49). New York: Cambridge University Press.

Bronfenbrenner, U., & Morris, P. A. (1998). The ecology of developmental processes. In W. Damon (Series Ed.) & R. M. Lerner (Vol. Ed.), *Handbook of child psychology: Vol 1. Theoretical models of human development* (pp. 993–1028). New York: Wiley.

Cai, X., & Wu, P. (1999). A study of the modernity of social concept of younger students in China. *Psychological Science (China), 22*, 148–152.

Chamberlain, P., & Patterson, G. R. (1995). Discipline and child compliance. In M. H. Bornstein (Ed.), *Handbook of parenting: Vol 4. Applied and practical parenting* (pp. 205–225). Mahwah, NJ: Lawrence Erlbaum Associates.

Chan, J., & Eysenck, S. B. G. (1981, August). *National differences in personality: Hong Kong and England.* Paper presented at the joint IACCP-ICP Asian Regional Meeting, National Taiwan University, Taipei, Taiwan.

Chao, R. K. (1994). Beyond parental control and authoritarian parenting style: Understanding Chinese parenting through the cultural notion of training. *Child Development, 65*, 1111–1119.

Chao, R. K. (1995). Chinese and European American cultural models of the self reflected in mothers' childrearing beliefs. *Ethos, 23*, 328–354.

Chen, X. (2000). Social and emotional development in Chinese children and adolescents: A contextual cross-cultural perspective. In F. Columbus (Ed.), *Advances in psychology research* (Vol. I, pp. 229–251). Huntington, NY: Nova Science Publishers.

Chen, X., Cen, G., Li, D., & He, Y. (2005). Social functioning and adjustment in Chinese children: The imprint of historical time. *Child Development, 76*, 182–195.

Chen, X., Chang, L., & He, Y. (2003). The peer group as a context: Mediating and moderating effects on the relations between academic achievement and social functioning in Chinese children. *Child Development, 74*, 710–727.

Chen, X., Chen, H., & Kaspar, V. (2001). Group social functioning and individual socioemotional and school adjustment in Chinese children. *Merrill-Palmer Quarterly, 47*, 264–299.

Chen, X., Dong, Q., & Zhou, H. (1997). Authoritative and authoritarian parenting practices and social and school adjustment. *International Journal of Behavioral Development, 20*, 855–873.

Chen, X., Hastings, P., Rubin, K. H., Chen, H., Cen, G., & Stewart, S. L. (1998). Childrearing attitudes and behavioral inhibition in Chinese and Canadian toddlers: A cross-cultural study. *Developmental Psychology, 34*, 677–686.

Chen, X., Li, D., Li, Z., Li, B., & Liu, M. (2000). Sociable and prosocial dimensions of social competence in Chinese children: Common and unique contributions to social, academic and psychological adjustment. *Developmental Psychology, 36*, 302–314.

Chen, X., Liu, M., Rubin, K. H., Cen, G., Gao, X., & Li, D. (2002). Sociability and prosocial orientation as predictors of youth adjustment: A seven-year longitudinal study in a Chinese sample. *International Journal of Behavioral Development, 26*, 128–136.

Chen, X., Rubin, K. H., & Li, B. (1995a). Social and school adjustment of shy and aggressive children in China. *Development and Psychopathology, 7*, 337–349.

Chen, X., Rubin, K. H., & Li, Z. (1995b). Social functioning and adjustment in Chinese children: A longitudinal study. *Developmental Psychology, 31*, 531–539.

Chen, X., Rubin, K. H., Li, B., & Li. Z. (1999). Adolescent outcomes of social functioning in Chinese children. *International Journal of Behavioural Development, 23*, 199–223.

Chen, X., Rubin, K. H., Liu, M., Chen, H., Wang, L., Li, D., et al. (2003). Compliance in Chinese and Canadian toddlers. *International Journal of Behavioral Development, 27*, 428–436.

Chen, X., Rubin, K. H., & Sun, Y. (1992). Social reputation and peer relationships in Chinese and Canadian children: A cross-cultural study. *Child Development, 63*, 1336–1343.

Chen, X., Wang, L., Chen, H., & Liu, M. (2002). Noncompliance and childrearing attitudes as predictors of aggressive behavior: A longitudinal study in Chinese children. *International Journal of Behavioral Development, 26*, 225–233.

Chen, X., Wu, H., Chen, H., Wang, L., & Cen, G. (2001). Parenting practices and aggressive behavior in Chinese children. *Parenting: Science and Practice, 1*, 159–183.

Cillessen, A. H., van Ijzendoorn, H. W., van Lieshout, C. F., & Hartup, W. W. (1992). Heterogeneity among peer-rejected boys: Subtypes and stabilities. *Child Development, 63*, 893–905.

Coie, J. D., Dodge, K. A., & Coppotelli, H. (1982). Dimensions of types of social status: A cross-age perspective. *Developmental Psychology, 18*, 557–560.

Coie, J. D., Lochman, J. E., Terry, R., & Hyman, C. (1992). Predicting early adolescent disorder from childhood aggression and peer rejection. *Journal of Consulting and Clinical Psychology, 60*, 783–792.

Coie, J. D., & Kupersmidt, J. (1983). A behavioral analysis of emerging social status in boys' groups. *Child Development, 54*, 1400–1416.

Collins, W. A., Maccoby, E. E., Steinberg, L., Hetherington, E. M., & Bornstein, M. H. (2000). Contemporary research on parenting. *American Psychologist, 55*, 218–232.

Crockett, L. A., & Silbereisen, R. K. (2000). *Negotiating adolescence in times of social change*. Cambridge, England: Cambridge University Press.

DeRosier, M., Kupersmidt, J., & Patterson, C. (1994). Children's academic and behavioral adjustment as a function of the chronicity and proximity of peer rejection. *Child Development, 65*, 1799–1813.

DeSouza, A., & Chen, X. (2002, July). *Social initiative and responses of shy and non-shy children in China and Canada.* Paper presented at the Biennial Conference of International Society for the Study of Behavioral Development (ISSBD), Ottawa, Canada.

Dodge, K. A., Petit, G. S., McClaskey, C. L., & Brown, M. (1986). Social competence in children. *Monographs of the Society for Research in Child Development, 51*(2, Serial No. 213).

Dodge, K. A., Schlundt, D. C., Schocken, I., & Delugach, J. D. (1983). Social competence and children's sociometric status: The role of peer group entry strategies. *Merrill-Palmer Quarterly, 29*, 309–336.

Edwards, C. P. (1995). Parenting toddlers. In M. H. Bornstein (Ed.), *Handbook of parenting: Vol 1. Children and parenting* (pp. 41–63). Mahwah, NJ: Lawrence Erlbaum Associates.

Elder, G. H., Jr. (1998). The life course and human development. In W. Damon (Series Ed.) & R. M. Lerner (Vol. Ed.), *Handbook of child psychology: Vol 1. Theoretical models of human development* (pp. 939–991). New York: Wiley.

Feng, Y. L. (1962). *The spirit of Chinese philosophy*. London: Routledge, & K. Paul.

Fox, N., Rubin, K. H., Calkins, S., Marshall, T. R., Coplan, R. J., Porges, S. W., et al. (1995). Frontal activation asymmetry and social competence at four years of age. *Child Development, 66*, 1770–1784.

Freedman, D. G., & Freedman, M. (1969). Behavioral differences between Chinese-American and American newborns. *Nature, 224*, 1227.

Furman, W., & Robbins, P. (1985). What's the point? Issues in the selection of treatment objectives. In B. H. Schneider, K. H. Rubin, & J. E. Ledingham (Eds.), *Children's peer relations: Issues in assessment and intervention* (pp. 41–54). New York: Springer-Verlag.

Hartup, W. W. (1992). Social relationships and their developmental significance. *American Psychologist, 44*, 120–126.

Hinde, R. A. (1987). *Individuals, relationships and culture*. Cambridge, England: Cambridge University press.

Hinde, R. A. (1995). Individuals and culture. In J. P. Changeux & J. Chavaillon (Eds), *Origins of the human brain* (pp. 186–199). New York: Oxford University Press.

Ho, D. Y. F. (1986). Chinese pattern of socialization: A critical review. In M. H. Bond (Ed.), *The psychology of the Chinese people* (pp. 1–37). New York: Oxford University Press.

Huang, M. (1999). A comparative study of the value outlook of Chinese adolescent students. *Journal of Southwest China Normal University (Philosophy and Social Sciences), 25*, 83–88.

Hymel, S., Rubin, K. H., Rowden, L., & LeMare, L. (1990). Children's peer relationships: Longitudinal prediction of internalizing and externalizing problems from middle to late childhood. *Child Development, 61*, 2004–2021.

Kagan, J. (1989). Temperamental contributions to social behavior. *American Psychologist, 44*, 668–674.

Kagan, J. (1998). Temperament and the reactions to unfamiliarity. *Child Development, 68*, 139–143.

Kagan, J., Kearsley, R. B., & Zelazo, P. R. (1978). *Infancy: Its place in human development*. Cambridge, MA: Harvard University Press.

Kobayashi-Winata, H., & Power, T. G. (1989). Child rearing and compliance: Japanese and American families in Houston. *Journal of Cross-Cultural Psychology, 20*, 333–356.

Kochanska, G., & Aksan, N. (1995). Mother-child mutually positive affect, the quality of child compliance to requests and prohibitions, and maternal control as correlates of early internalization. *Child Development, 66*, 236–254.

Kochanska, G., & Radke-Yarrow, M. (1992). Early childhood inhibition and the dynamics of the child's interaction with an unfamiliar peer at age five. *Child Development, 63*, 325–335.

Kopp, C. B. (1982). Antecedents of self-regulation: A developmental perspective. *Developmental Psychology, 18*, 199–214.

Kriger, S. F., & Kroes, W. H. (1972). Child-rearing attitudes of Chinese, Jewish, and Protestant mothers. *Journal of Social Psychology, 86*, 205–210.

Kuczynski, L., & Kochanska, G. (1990). Development of children's noncompliance strategies from toddlerhood to age 5. *Developmental Psychology, 26*, 398–408.

Larson, R. W. (1999). The uses of loneliness in adolescence. In K. J. Rotenberg & S. Hymel (Eds.), *Loneliness in childhood and adolescence* (pp. 244–262). New York: Cambridge University Press.

Liang, S. (1987). *The outline of Chinese culture*. Shanghai, China: Shanghai Teachers' University Press.

Lin, C. C., & Fu, V. R. (1990). A comparison of child-rearing practices among Chinese, immigrant Chinese, and Caucasian-American parents. *Child Development, 61*, 429–433.

Liu, M., Chen, X., Rubin, K. H., Zheng, S., Cui, L., Li, D., Chen, H., & Wang, Li. (in press). Autonomy- vs. connectedness-oriented parenting behaviors in Chinese and Canadian mothers. *International Journal of Behavioral Development.*

Luo, G. (1996). *Chinese traditional social and moral ideas and rules*. Beijing, China: University of Chinese People Press.

Maccoby, E. E., & Martin, C. N. (1983). Socialization in the context of the family: Parent-child interaction. In E. M. Hetherington (Ed.), *Handbook of child psychology: Vol.4. Socialization, personality and social development* (pp. 1–102). New York: Wiley.

Miyake, K., Chen, S. J., & Campos., J. J. (1985). Infant temperament, mother's mode of interactions, and attachment in Japan: An interim report. In I. Bretherton & E. Waters (Eds.), Growing points of attachment theory and research. *Monographs of the Society for Research in Child Development, 50* (1–2, Serial No. 209), 276–297.

Mizuta, I., Zahn-Waxler, C., Cole, P. M., & Hiruma, N. (1996). A cross-cultural study of preschoolers' attachment: Security and sensitivity in Japanese and US dyads. *International Journal of Behavioral Development, 19*, 141–159.

Ollendick, T. H., Ross, W. G., Weist, M. D., & Oswald, D. P. (1990). The predictive validity of teacher nominations: A five-year followup of at-risk youth. *Journal of Abnormal Child Psychology, 18*, 699–713.

Oyserman, D., Coon, H. M., & Kemmelmeier, M. (2002). Rethinking individualism and collectivism: Evaluation of theoretical assumptions and meta-analyses. *Psychological Bulletin, 128*, 3–72.

Piaget, J. (1932). *The moral judgment of the child.* Glencoe, IL: Free Press.

Putallaz, M., & Gottman, J. M. (1981). Social skills and group acceptance. In S. R. Asher & J. M. Gottman (Eds.), *The development of children's friendships* (pp. 116–149). Cambridge, England: Cambridge University Press.

Rothbart, M. K., & Bates, J. E. (1998). Temperament. In W. Damon (Ed.) & N. Eisenberg (Vol. Ed.), *Handbook of child psychology: Vol. 3. Social, emotional, and personality development* (5th ed., pp. 105–176). New York: Wiley.

Rubin, K. H. (1989). *The Play Observation Scale.* Waterloo, Canada: University of Waterloo.

Rubin, K. H., & Asendorpf, J. (1993). *Social withdrawal, inhibition, and shyness in childhood.* Hillsdale, NJ: Lawrence Erlbaum Associates.

Rubin, K. H., Bukowski, W., & Parker, J. (1998). Peer interactions, relationships, and groups. In W. Damon (Ed.) & N. Eisenberg (Vol. Ed.), *Handbook of child psychology: Vol. 3. Social, emotional, and personality development* (5th ed., pp. 619–700). New York: Wiley.

Rubin, K. H., Burgess, K. B., & Coplan, R. J. (2002). Social withdrawal and shyness. In P. K., Smith & C. H. Hart, Craig (Eds.), *Blackwell handbook of childhood social development* (pp. 330–352), Malden, MA: Blackwell.

Rubin, K. H., Chen, X., McDougall, P., Bowker, A., & McKinnon, J. (1995). The Waterloo Longitudinal Project: Predicting internalizing and externalizing problems in adolescence. *Development and Psychopathology, 7*, 751–764.

Rubin, K. H., Coplan, R. J., Fox, N. A., & Calkins, S. D. (1995). Emotionality, emotion regulation, and preschoolers' social adaptation. *Development and Psychopathology, 7*, 49–62.

Rubin, K. H., & Krasnor, L. R. (1986). Social cognitive and social behavioral perspectives on problem-solving. In M. Perlmutter (Ed.), *Minnesota Symposia on Child Psychology* (Vol. 18, pp. 1–68). Hillsdale, NJ: Lawrence Erlbaum Associates.

Rubin, K. H., Stewart, S. L., & Chen, X. (1995). The parents of aggressive and withdrawn children. In M. H. Bornstein (Ed.), *Handbook of parenting: Vol. I. How children influence parenting* (pp. 255–284). Hillsdale, NJ: Lawrence Erlbaum Associates.

Schaffer, H. R. (2000). The early experience assumption: Past, present and future. *International Journal of Behavioral Development, 24*, 5–14.

Schmidt, L. A., & Fox, N. A. (1998). The development and outcomes of childhood shyness: A multiple psychophysiologic measure approach. In R. Vasta (Ed.), *Annals of child development* (Vol. 13, pp. 13–47). London: Kingsley.

Silbereisen, R. K. (2000). German unification and adolescents' developmental timetables: Continuities and discontinuities. In L. A. Crockett, & R. K. Silbereisen (Eds), *Negotiating adolescence in times of social change.* Cambridge, England: Cambridge University Press.

Stevenson-Hinde, J., & Shouldice, A. (1993). Wariness to strangers: A behavior systems perspective revisited. In Ke. H. Rubin & J. Asendorpf (Eds.), *Social withdrawal, inhibition, and shyness in childhood* (pp. 101–116). Hillsdale, NJ: Lawrence Erlbaum Associates.

Sullivan, H. S. (1953). *The interpersonal theory of psychiatry*. New York: Norton.

Super, C. M., & Harkness, S. (1986). The developmental niche: A conceptualization at the interface of child and culture. *International Journal of Behavioral Development, 9*, 545–569.

Triandis, H. C. (1990). Cross-cultural studies of individualism and collectivism. *Nebraska Symposium on Motivation* (Vol. 37, pp. 41–133). Lincoln: University of Nebraska Press.

Whiting, B. B., & Edwards, C. P. (1988). *Children of different worlds*. Cambridge, MA: Harvard University Press.

Yang, K. S. (1986). Chinese personality and its change. In M. H. Bond (Ed.), *The psychology of the Chinese people* (pp. 106–170). New York: Oxford University Press.

Zhang, W. W. (2000). *Transforming China: Economic reform and its political implications*. New York: St. Martin's Press.

Zhou, Q, Eisenberg, N., Wang, Y., & Reiser, M. (2004). Chinese children's effortful control and dispositional anger/frustration: Relations to parenting styles and children's social functioning. *Developmental Psychology, 40*, 352–366.

7 Emotional Aspects of Peer Relations Among Children in Rural Nepal

Pamela M. Cole, Alisha R. Walker, and Mukta Sing Lama-Tamang

The quality of relationships between any two people in any culture determines and is determined by emotional factors. Attraction, rejection, attachment, conflict, trust, jealousy, and intimacy all reflect emotional dimensions of relationships. Friendships and peer interactions require emotional skill and also contribute to children's general social and emotional adjustment (Parker et al., 1995). Peer relations are thought to be unique because they are formed with persons who are close in age and developmental status and are more egalitarian than other relationships (Hartup & Moore, 1990; Ladd, 1988). Friendships are regarded as voluntary and based on a mutual decision to form a relationship (Ladd, 1988; Rubin, Bukowski, & Parker, 1998). Peers teach unique skills to each other (e.g., negotiation and conflict management), when neither partner is the designated authority. Therefore, peer relationships provide a context for behaving in ways that might not exist within the family (Hartup & Sancilio, 1986; Sullivan, 1953).

The definition of peers as nonfamilial, reciprocal relationships of choice with persons close in age requires some additional consideration due to cultural variations in what constitutes a family and a peer, and in what constitutes choice and reciprocity. In the small Himalayan kingdom of Nepal, all persons, including peers, are regarded in familial terms. Moreover, among persons of the same age, every relationship is hierarchical; even children determine and behave according to their rank relative to each other. Nepal is a collectivist society where the sense of self is defined in an interdependent manner rather than in the independent way typical in the West (Markus & Kitayama, 1991). The difference has implications for emotion regulation (Kitayama & Markus, 1994). In our work, we attribute differences in emotion regulation, between two Nepali ethnic groups and between them and U.S. children, to the way culture influences the nature of relationships. Village school children in remote villages in Nepal believe that they should either not feel angry or not act angrily with their peers, even in justified situations. Their cultural values regard anger as threatening interpersonal harmony and disrespectful of elders, even if the elder is only a few hours older.

The literature on culture and emotion includes very little work with children and less on emotions in children's peer relationships. Moreover, most cross-cultural studies compare children from two very different nations. Many elements of culture vary, and it becomes impossible to learn how or why culture influences emotional aspects of relationships. Within-society comparisons can provide a more specific examination of cultural context. In this chapter, we describe how children from two distinct ethnic groups in Nepal believe anger and shame function in peer relationships. The children, Tamang and Brahmans, are from communities that are similar in many ways. Among them, they share common societal values yet differ in how they achieve them. We examine how these differences may explain why Tamang, Brahman, and U.S. children differ in their views about communicating anger and shame to others. We begin with a brief background on Nepal and the similarities and differences between the Tamang and Brahmans. We present qualitative and quantitative evidence of how peer relations in rural Nepal differ from those described in the extant peer literature, drawing from anthropology, history, political science, psychology, religious studies, and sociology to understand how culture influences emotion.

Nepalese Society

Nepal's geography and history help situate the particular developmental niches in which Nepali children's emotions are socialized. Nepal is a collectivist society, but to say only this misses its valuable cultural diversity (Gurung, 1998). Located between India and China, Nepal's mountainous Himalayan terrain has contributed to the preservation of culturally distinct customs. Our research was conducted in the "middle hills," steep but arable ridges of up to 10,000 feet, dotted with thousands of small subsistence farming villages. The remote villages lack telephones, televisions, or motorable roads, which further isolates and maintains their cultural differences.

The Nepalese census (Central Bureau of Statistics, 2003) identified 100 groups, 44 of which were officially classified as ethnic groups. The Tamang are one of these groups, an indigenous people with their own identity, language, and customs (Gautam & Thapa-Magar, 1994; Gurung, 2003). The remaining groups are caste groups, such as the high-caste Brahmans, who are racially and culturally distinct from the Tamang. True to their collectivist orientation, the many groups have coexisted without the deep ethnic and religious conflicts seen elsewhere in the world. Tensions in this multicultural society can and do exist, but the motivation to preserve social harmony means frustration and conflict must be well managed.

The political history of Nepal explains the tensions that do exist between indigenous groups, like the Tamang, and high-caste groups, like the Brahmans. Modern Nepal was founded in 1768 by an ambitious regional king, Prithvi Narayan Shah, who joined former chiefdoms and small kingdoms into one nation. As part of his "unification" effort, Hinduism was declared the national religion, and Hindu social order was extended to all of the people of Nepal. In 1854, this goal was furthered by the *Muluki Ain*, a law that ranked every citizen, Hindu or not, by caste and made violations of caste illegal. Brahmans retained their highest caste as wearers of the sacred cord, and Tamang were classified as enslavable *matwali* (alcohol-using caste; Gurung, 2003). A single cultural framework, Hinduism, was imposed on Nepal's cultural diversity. In this way, groups who were merely different became superior or inferior. Certain behaviors that are acceptable among Buddhists are unacceptable to Hindus and were disapproved. Certain behaviors that are acceptable among Hindus are not to Buddhists, yet became the model of behavior. For example, animal sacrifice is a traditional feature of Hindu worship. Buddhism's principle of compassion proscribes killing animals. Hindus regard cows as sacred and do not kill them or eat beef. Although Buddhists eat meat, including beef, they simply do not kill animals. The placement of one set of values as superior to another, and the resulting oppression of indigenous non-Hindus, as well as Hindu low caste members, created intercultural tension and views that the majority is unfair to its peers (e.g., Cameron, 1998; Lama-Tamang, 2004). Yet, these sentiments have not been expressed in open anger. In fact, Nepali peoples have oral traditions that depict the gods of various religions as relatives.

This glimpse of life in Nepal reveals a multicultural society in which group differences are maintained by the rugged terrain and the slow rate of development, and in which the value placed on social harmony has not (yet) overridden frustrations and tensions that arise in the attempt to create a unified society. These differences begin to illustrate how culture influences the ways in which people feel and act on their feelings in their peer relationships. Nepali children learn to be competent members of their own ethnic groups as well as cooperative co-citizens in a stratified society that values harmony in relationships. This social context has clear implications for how anger and shame function within peer relationships.

Culture and Emotion

Societal values, religion, and political status are often depicted as an outer ring, a macrolevel influence, on human development (e.g., Bronfenbrenner, 1986). For them to influence early emotional development, they must penetrate local practices. Culture can be defined as shared practices, supported by beliefs about how a community should be organized and what constitutes proper conduct, which transmit meanings and values from generation to generation. From the child's vantage, macrolevel factors influence the child if they are palpable features of the developmental niche, integrated into routines and socialization practices (Super & Harkness, 1993; Weisner, 2002). Culture clearly influences how individuals communicate and behave emotionally (Mesquita & Frijda, 1992). A collectivist orientation and an interdependent sense of self require emotional behavior that supports interpersonal harmony, respect for authority, and conformity to community norms. Anger is discouraged and submission of the individual's rights and needs encouraged (Kitayama & Markus, 1994; Markus & Kitayama, 1991).

It would be simplistic, however, to assume that all collectivist groups are identical. The Tamang and Brahmans differ in the practices that have been transmitted across generations. In addition, because religion defines proper conduct and pervades everyday practices in Nepal, it is essential to understand its influence in the socialization of emotion. Furthermore, the historical and sociopolitical conditions that created a majority/minority group structure among peers also influence with whom and how one can assert dominance and who is better off remaining submissive. The specific cultural values that define appropriate conduct in each group should and do emerge in their children's beliefs about conveying emotions to others.

Anger is a motivational stance reflecting appraisal of blocked goals or injustice in matters of personal well-being and readiness to act to overcome barriers (e.g., Barrett & Campos, 1987). Anger must be managed carefully in intimate communities that place the well-being of the group above individual needs and where personal well-being is based on group well-being (Kitayama & Markus, 1994). Consequently, in Nepal, anger is not a valued emotion. Negative emotions that convey awareness of how one appears to others, however, are valued. In both languages in which we worked (Tamang and Nepali), the same word is used to connote shame, embarrassment, and shyness, but mainly shame. The appearance of shame indicates to Nepalis that a person understands that his needs do not supercede respect for others, conformity to group norms, and the interest in the well-being of the relationship or the group.

Cultural Comparison of Tamang and Brahman Children

Tamang and Brahmans have many features of their lives in common and yet they have culturally distinct ways of achieving harmony and defining competent social behavior. We focus on three differences that matter for the socialization of emotion – cultural heritage, religion, and majority/minority status. The high degree of similarity between the two ethnic groups gave us a scientific advantage in pointing more specifically to what about culture influences emotional functioning in peer relationships. We begin describing cultural similarities between Tamang and Brahman and then focus on their distinct differences.

Between-Group Cultural Similarities

As stated, Nepal is a collectivist society (Hofstede, 2001; Triandis, 1994). Although any global classification minimizes important differences among collectivist nations and the people within any nation, the characterization captures the high degree of import given to social harmony, social conformity, and respect for authority in Nepal. In rural Nepal particularly, Tamang and Brahmans share these same values. The household is the child's first experience of the collective. Tamang and Brahman village children are reared in conjoint patrilocal families. That is, the eldest male is the head of a household that includes the families of married sons and unmarried offspring. The interdependent and hierarchical nature of the household is instantiated in all discourse. Nepalis use complex, differentiated sets of kinship terms constantly. During the first six months of a child's life, caregivers begin teaching the different terms for each relationship (see Table 7.1). These same terms are later used in relationships outside of the household and the village.

These kinship terms must be used, as to use someone's first name is considered to be talking "down" to that person. Kinship terms constantly locate the self in the network of relationships. All people are referred to by different terms, depending on who is speaking to them, and those same terms are used with other same-sexed members of the household. In effect, each interaction restates hierarchical kinship status such that individuality is subordinate to the network of relationships, an example of how one develops an interdependent sense of self (Markus & Kitayama, 1991). In this way, children learn to appreciate hierarchy and relatedness early in life. This extends to interactions with peers. Every child with whom the child interacts must be referred to in kinship terms. Even children born an hour apart refer to each other as older and younger.

Table 7.1. *Main Forms Tamang and Brahman Children Use to Address Peers*

	Native Language	
Familial Relationship with Other Children	*Tamang*	*Nepali*
Children of same or younger generation		
Older sister	Nana	Didi
Younger sister	Anga	Bahini
Older brother	Jyojyo	Dai
Younger brother	Ale	Bhai
Children of older generation		
Paternal aunt	Aru	Kaki
Maternal aunt	Angi	Maiju
Paternal uncle	Agu	Kaka
Maternal uncle	Ashyang	Mama

In addition to the collective, interdependent nature of their communities, the villages were of equivalent size with all households supported by subsistence farming. They were similar in the population density of the target ethnic group, with less than 10% from other groups. Primary schools (grades one through five) had been founded within four years of each other. Infant mortality was high and access to health care limited. Literacy rates among adults were very low. Thus, the two villages were similar in practices that promoted interdependence in the sense of self, appreciation of hierarchy in relationships including peer relations, and an emphasis on a collectivist orientation that is typical of agrarian societies. These similarities heighten the chance of linking differences in communicating emotions to specific ethnic differences.

Between-Group Cultural Differences

Despite these similarities, there are important differences between the Tamang and Brahmans. They differed in three distinct ways that influence proper social behavior, including expressing anger and shame – religion, cultural practices, and majority/minority status.

Differences in Religious Values

Buddhism. Tamang practice a form of Tibetan Buddhism. Buddhism is a close relative of Hinduism. The two religions believe in the cycle of reincarnation but differ in their beliefs about the way to enlightenment and escape from the cycle. Buddhists believe moderation, tolerance, compassion, and inner peace are the way, eschewing the asceticism of Hinduism. Being reborn as a human involves a capacity for conscious control over human frailties. The human can understand that emotions are attachments to the present world (relationships, material gains) and thus a source of yearning and misery. Buddhism teaches to accept emotions as part of the human condition and to use one's mind to reappraise mortal yearnings as temporary.

How do Buddhist principles penetrate local practices? There is no direct religious education for the rural Tamang child, although a second-born son is often sent to a monastery to become a lama (monk). The formal ways that people learn Buddhist principles that affect emotional life are rites, especially funerals (*gewa*; e.g., Holmberg, 1989). For example, in talking to the bereaved, lamas exhort the bereaved that anger and grief cannot return the dead, that they interfere with passage to the next life (Cozort, 1995; Goleman, 2003), and harm one's *sem* (heart–mind, Desjarlais, 1992). Apart from exposure to these periodic rites, children mainly acquire the values of compassion, tolerance, and a peaceful mind implicitly through everyday socialization practices.

Hinduism. Brahmans are high-caste Hindus. Hinduism is based on the premise that spiritual purity is the means to escape the cycle of reincarnation. Caste is a method for ranking people in terms of their purity; maintaining caste status is crucial to the social order and spiritual advancement (Kinsley, 1993). To accomplish this, Hinduism strictly regulates individual behavior and interaction to avoid caste violations that constitute spiritual pollution. Because there are many sources of pollution in daily life (for example, water is a source of pollution if not handled properly), avoidance requires constant vigilance and self-discipline.

As within any group, there is considerable variation in self-discipline and adherence to the strict rules of behavior. Nonetheless, rural Brahman life is highly organized by these rules (e.g., Bennett, 1983; Cameron, 1998; Skinner, Pach, & Holland, 1998). Children therefore acquire the rules as part of their everyday socialization experience. In addition, boys of age receive the sacred thread, the symbol of their high caste, in a formal ceremony. Despite poverty and illiteracy, Brahman villagers in our studies had a clear identity as members of a privileged caste. They prided themselves on their orderly and disciplined way of life and judge their children by their discipline, evident in their school achievement and understanding of the way of life (Cole, Tamang, & Shrestha, in press).

In sum, Buddhist religion clearly discourages fostering and dwelling on emotions, both positive and negative, and emphasizes compassion and tolerance of others. Anger is regarded as a particularly destructive emotion, interfering with inner peace and with compassion and tolerance. No emotion has more potential to interfere with earning merit to escape the cycle of reincarnation. Hindu religion speaks less directly to specific emotions but encourages skill at self-regulation of desires. The hierarchy of the caste system also cultivates pride and superiority. Finally, it may be valuable to access anger when others threaten one's spiritual purity.

Tamang and Brahman communities have immediate concerns in addition to those of spiritual advancement in the next life. They must farm to survive, and they accomplish this in small, intimate communities that require social order to function. Tamang and Brahmans organize their social order in different ways that extend beyond religious differences.

Differences in Cultural Practices

Tamang. Tamang culture has a distinct emphasis on egalitarianism as a means of achieving social order and harmony. As an example, Tamang women share equally in decision making, are free to have wealth, and are free to leave their marriages or re-marry as widows (MacDonald, 1989; March, 2002). Egalitarianism is also evident in the practice of sharing wealth and good fortune to avoid creating status differences (Fricke, 1986). Tamang individuals experience jealousy, resentment, and selfishness, but the priority placed on maintaining interpersonal equality and harmony overrides sustaining and acting on those emotions; good feelings are derived by all when good fortunes are shared. Moreover, such generosity yields benefits in times when life is difficult. Promoting cheer and sharing resources is common practice. Tamang highly value camaraderie and cooperation. Although poor, a family always tries to extend the warmest hospitality as part of its firm interest in establishing and nurturing relationships (March, 1987).

The Tamang also tolerate deviation from these norms in the service of maintaining peaceful, harmonious relationships. Thus, they avoid direct confrontation. Even in talking about rearing children, they do not assume a high degree of interpersonal control. Children become competent "if listening" (Cole et al., in press). All of the aforementioned cultural values dictate against being angry. It is often said that anger is useless. In sum, the Tamang way of creating a social order emphasizes equality and harmony, tolerating but minimizing individual differences and avoiding the assertion of anger-based behaviors.

Brahmans. Brahman social order, based in the caste system, has been described as strict and hierarchical (e.g., Bennett, 1983; Cameron, 1998;

Skinner et al., 1998). Valuing social harmony, Brahmans believe it is rightfully achieved by behaving according to the strictures of caste. They respect those who show the highest degree of self-restraint and care in their personal and social behavior. The need for restraint and care pervades the most basic tasks, such as the preparing, carrying, and consuming of food and water, and personal hygiene. To maintain purity throughout the daily routine requires a high degree of sustained attention and inhibitory control, skills that are important to behavioral self-control. In addition, Brahmans are confident in their position, a confidence that promotes self-esteem and supports ambition to achieve but also risks arrogance and mistreatment of those perceived as lower (Cameron, 1998).

Brahman practices, compared with those of the Tamang, less obviously discourage anger. The Brahman practices foster skill at self-discipline and a sense of entitlement and ethnic pride as the high, learned caste. Anger has a place in this specific cultural framework. For example, protecting spiritual purity and achieving academic goals require disdain for sources of pollution and effort to protect the self as well as to overcome and persist at difficult tasks. Anger that disrupts social harmony, as construed by Brahmans, is managed by the skill of self-discipline.

As for shame, both Tamang and Brahmans emphasize that each person needs to know his or her place in the family and community. They value respect for authority and devalue self-assertion in most contexts. The appearance of shame in a child conveys that the child has acquired such an appreciation. In both communities where we worked, we observed caregivers asking children whether they lacked shame when the children engaged in bold, selfish, or assertive acts. When we interviewed children individually, they kept their heads lowered, their eyes averted, and their hands folded together, and were very cooperative. Shame is a valued emotion, and a common parenting practice, in many Asian societies (e.g., Fung, 1999; Miller, 1996). It implies understanding of the goals of social conformity, muting self-assertion, and respecting authority. In addition to cultural priorities that give shame a place for expression and not anger, we must also consider the influence of group differences in majority/minority status.

Differences in Majority/Minority Group Status

Because of the ethnic composition and remote locations of our villages, elementary school children have minimal exposure to other groups. Their early exposures to other adults, however, are a potential source of influence on their emotions. When adults of different status interact with each other, they convey emotions. As we know from social referencing work, a young child can detect wariness or confidence in caregivers. Children probably observe proper behavior between elders and their junior peers before they understand what is spoken or the precise nature of their relationships. Therefore, a child may also detect arrogance in a high-caste person interacting with a person of lower caste. Likewise, a child from an indigenous group may witness submissiveness in caregivers in the presence of high-caste persons. Through social learning, children acquire models of emotions in peer interactions.

Rural Nepali children meet few peers from other groups in primary school. By 2003, most villages had a primary school of grades one through five; secondary schooling includes grades six through ten (Ministry of Education and Sports, 2003). The Tamang schools in our studies had a few Magar (another indigenous group) students, and the Brahman schools had a few *dalit* (untouchable) caste students. Children in first grade were aware of the differences. A Brahman six-year-old child introduced us to a classmate, saying, "He is *Kami*" (one untouchable caste). The village children who attended secondary school walked thirty to forty-five minutes one way, where they were immersed in classes with children from other groups. They had no relationship history with these children, so rural secondary schools were the first setting in which they experienced a peer context more like that described in the extant literature. Even so, each child begins these new relationships by determining who is elder and behaving accordingly.

Our participating children attended primary school, where they gained their first concrete information about ethnic groups and castes. The primary school texts embrace Nepal's multicultural society but also communicate the high-caste as the ideal (Lama-Tamang, 2004). Textbooks then confer a sense of privilege to high-caste children and inadequacy for others. Teachers also influence children's identity in ways that affect dispositions to behave angrily or with shame. Children in the Tamang villages were taught by high-caste persons (e.g., Brahmans), who historically have had more access to higher education (Lama-Tamang, 2004). The 1990 constitution permitted teaching in native languages, but few high-caste persons speak an indigenous tongue.

In sum, one source of information about relative status among peers outside of the home is the school setting. Textbooks and teacher behavior convey to children that they are or are not like highly respected persons (teachers). Even before one has a well-developed understanding of intergroup relations, the experiences we have described can influence children's ideas about conveying anger and shame. The development of a sense of privilege or entitlement permits anger in certain situations when one's rightful privilege is thwarted and a sense of inadequacy contributes to inhibiting anger and feeling self-conscious and ashamed.

Among adults, the Tamang struggle with their ethnic identity. Their oral history recalls a Tamang kingdom and better times, but for more than 200 years they have been a politically disenfranchised indigenous people. History reveals that they were oppressed (e.g., forced into enslavement, forced to surrender land, barred from education). Minority status influences emotional life, creating self-doubt and shame, fostering resentment, and making the expression of anger, frustration, and resentment risky when one lacks social power. A submissive self-presentation gives the appearance of conforming to the social hierarchy and avoids evoking anger from higher status persons.

Brahman villagers expressed clear ethnic pride. This was striking in the face of how disadvantaged they were in terms of health care, income, and even political influence and their recognition and self-consciousness about their poverty. Yet, this did not motivate them to be ashamed as much as it motivated them to self-improve. Adults conveyed pride to and in their children, and this was evident in their emphasis on children's school achievement, even though most caregivers were uneducated. Although their children lacked shoes and good clothes, they were taught self-respect and self-discipline and adherence to age-old rituals. This identity was reinforced in the school where they were educated in their own tongue, by teachers from their own group, and through books that make high-caste Hinduism a national ideal. Thus, although shame was valued in conveying respect for elders, the Brahman village cultural context encouraged pride and self-confidence. Such a sense of self may create a context in which anger is less dangerous than it is for the minority group.

Peer Relationships and Emotions Across Three Cultures

Although the salience and texture of relationships vary across cultures, all people strive for a balance of relatedness and autonomy (Rothbaum et al., 2000). Cultural variations in the customs for achieving that balance constrain or afford what can and cannot be expressed emotionally (Kitayama & Markus, 1994). In collectivist societies, emotional behavior must maintain respect for elders, conformity to community rules, and an interest in preserving social harmony. Individuals in these societies tend to focus on the emotions, thoughts, and behaviors of others when regulating their own emotions (Eid & Diener, 2001). For adults living in collectivist societies, emotions are closely tied to their social environment and relationships with others, which is reflective of their cultural beliefs (Mesquita, 2001). Our work reveals that, for children, even within collectivist societies, specific values and practices are associated with different ways of regulating emotions.

There are too few cross-cultural studies of peer relationships. There are none in Nepal. Moreover, only one study made an effort to assess culture beyond mere citizenship in a nation, assessing the degree to which Korean students adopted Korean values (Han & Park, 1995). The literature indicates that young children's friendships are based primarily on proximity, common play activities, and physical characteristics and school-age children's friendships are based on affection and support (Furman & Bierman, 1983). Nepali children likely learn unique skills in peer interactions but their peers are treated as relatives, and social hierarchy is always considered. For example, we interviewed children about how they handle disagreements with a friend. The need for deference is evident:

> [Do you have a friend?] Sita is my friend. I like to be with her. But sometimes she makes me angry. She will say, "Do it this way. Do it that way." When she pushes her way, I have to do what she says [Then you are angry with her?] But she is my aunt. If I say aunt, then it is like she is my mother. [That means . . .?] I love her and I respect her. [11-year-old Tamang girl talking about friendship with her slightly older, 11-year-old aunt]

A child's emotional conduct in peer interactions influences the quality of those relationships and those peer relationships are also an important context for the development of emotion regulation and emotional display rules (Parker & Gottman, 1989). First, to engage in cooperative activities, such as play, children must be emotionally responsive and able to regulate their emotions. They must be able to share in the joy of play without disrupting it and modulate frustrations, disappointments, and strong urges to get their own way. Evidence based on children from Western nations indicates that those who have more experience with peers develop better social understanding, more readily recognize others' emotions, and understand the relation between beliefs and actions in others than children with less peer experience (Denham, 1998; Maguire & Dunn, 1997). Furthermore, children's regulatory skill seems to moderate the relation between emotionality and problem behaviors (Contreras et al., 2000; Lemerise & Arsenio, 2000) as well as proneness to anger and conflict with peers (Calkins et al., 1999). In Nepal, children must also exercise social skill and emotional restraint in their interactions. Although pertinent work has not been conducted in Nepal, it is reasonable to predict that children who are selfish and unable to coordinate their emotional needs with those of their peers will be less socially competent.

Second, the quality of friendship in childhood as well as the presence of a friendship relationship is directly related to a child's emotional adjustment. Children who have friends are not necessarily involved in quality friendships. Peer relationships that are comprised of a number of negative features, such as conflict, tend to be much lower in quality than those relationships that contain several positive features (Berndt, 1996). What constitutes positive and negative behaviors in relationships may differ, however, for different cultures. For example, socially inhibited behavior has been negatively associated with social adjustment for children in Western societies (Asendorpf, 1991), but for Chinese children has been positively associated with peer acceptance and school competence (Chen, Rubin, & Li, 1995). In addition, the presence of certain negative features may have a stronger effect on relationships for children from Eastern cultures. Taiwanese children have less conflict in their friendships than Canadian children, but the presence of conflict in Taiwanese friendships seems to be more detrimental to the relationship (Benjamin et al., 2001).

In Western cultures, children without any friends have inferior interpersonal skills and are lonely and dissatisfied with their social lives (Parker & Asher, 1993). Children without friends may be generally disliked by the peer group and therefore at risk for significant social and psychological problems in the future, such as school dropout, criminal activity, and psychological maladjustment (Parker & Asher, 1987). Children in rural Nepal, however, may be better protected from this particular pathway to maladjustment. Although poor relationships surely create risk for adjustment problems, the likelihood of such poor relationships is limited. Nepali children cannot openly reject or even avoid peers. All are extended family and live in close proximity. Moreover, children are socialized from an early age to be concerned for and considerate of others. One often sees a preschool-age child respond to the distress of a toddler or infant. As in many agrarian communities, young children quickly are expected to care for (e.g., carry on the back) younger children.

Empirical Evidence on Emotions in Peer Interactions

Our work focused on children's beliefs about whether anger and shame are appropriate to convey and their reasons for why they would or would not reveal them. Because our interview findings are based on self-reports of what children would feel and do in hypothetical situations, we do not assume that they reflect children's actual social behavior. Nonetheless, they convey interesting cultural variations in children's ideas of what one should do in such situations.

We initially hypothesized that children raised in a traditional Tamang village would understand that anger should not be shown to adults and possibly peers. Three features of Tamang society justified this hypothesis. First, Tamang prize interpersonal harmony and achieve it through generosity, cheerfulness, tolerance, and compassion. Second, Buddhist philosophy discourages strong emotion, particularly anger. Third, Tamang emphasize a child's being socially poised, never angry, and knowledgeable about his or her place in relation to others (Cole et al., in press). In addition, Tamang status as a political minority group could have an early influence, further deterring anger and fostering more submissive emotions.

Anger reflects a specific motivational stance toward a situation – that is, a desirable goal that can and should be achieved is blocked or thwarted (e.g., Barrett & Campos, 1987). When anger is communicated to others, it conveys assertion of the individual's own needs and desires and willingness to act powerfully or forcefully to achieve those goals. We expected Nepalese children to avoid acting in anger. In our initial study (Cole & Tamang, 1998), first-grade children were told six vignettes about situations, adapted from a procedure that had been used with young children in the United States, that evoked anger. Two stories involved peer interaction. In one, the target child was building a tower of rocks (for U.S. children, a tower of blocks) when another child intentionally knocked it down. In the second peer vignette, the target child was playing outdoors when another child hit the target child. We asked first-graders how they would feel if each event happened to them, whether they would show their feelings, and what they would do. They could point to schematic faces to indicate which emotion they felt, and they had the choices of anger, happiness, fear, or okay. We knew that these basic emotion terms were understood from previous research (Harris et al., 1987).

Tamang first-graders told us they would feel *thiken*, a word that translates into feeling okay. It should be noted that feeling okay connotes a less than ideal state in American English but is a fine, content, desirable feeling in Tamang. Brahman first-graders were significantly more likely to endorse feeling angry. When asked about revealing feelings, Tamang children said they would show how they felt – there was no reason not to show that you felt okay – but Brahman first-graders would *not* show their anger to anyone, peer or parent. Finally, asked what they would do, both groups of children said they would just be quiet and not do or say anything. Thus, the important finding was a difference between Tamang and Brahman first-graders in the endorsement of anger in challenging situations.

We pursued this finding in another study (Cole, Bruschi, & Tamang, 2002). We changed the method in three ways to broaden our ability to understand these findings. First, we added the emotion of shame because we realized that it was a more salient negative emotion in Tamang society than anger. Shame reflects a different motivational stance than anger – that is, a goal was desired or achieved that one realizes is evaluated negatively by others. When shame is communicated, it conveys recognition that one is being judged by others and ready to submit or relinquish goals. Perhaps the Tamang first-graders would endorse shame instead of saying they would be okay, if they had the choice of a more socially acceptable negative emotion. Second, we interviewed second- and fifth-graders to increase our ability to have children explain their responses more than first-graders could. Third, we included a group of rural children, also second- and fifth-graders, from the United States, to place Tamang and Brahman children's responses in the context of children who were more commonly portrayed in the mainstream literature.

We generated nine new vignettes, six of which involved difficult situations that were designed to be relevant, with very minor adaptations, to each cultural group. Some of the actors were friends and some parents. Three vignettes involved blocked or thwarted goals that might afford anger, for example, a friend or father spills tea all over the child's just completed homework, and it has to be done all over again. Three were designed to evoke others' judgment of a child, which could afford shame, for example, a friend or parents laugh at a child who has just fallen in the mud.

Although the literature suggests that children's emotional responses vary as a function of whether parents or peers are the audience (e.g., Zeman & Garber, 1996), we found no effect of the relationship status of the actor to the child. One reason for this difference, even for the U.S. children in our sample, may be that the peers and parents were the actors who caused the emotion and not simply an audience. Another possibility is that U.S. rural children may differ from the middle-class, suburban, and urban children that are typically studied in the U.S.

As can be seen in Table 7.2, we again found reluctance in Tamang children to endorse anger, regardless of vignette type. In effect, it seemed that Tamang school children might engage in secondary appraisals of situations to avoid anger. The modal responses of the children from each group to each question are presented in Table 7.2.

Notably, Tamang children did endorse shame more than U.S. or Brahman children, but some still endorsed feeling okay. Brahman and U.S. children endorsed anger and justified it on the basis of unfair or wrong behavior of the other. There was, however, a notable difference between Brahman and U.S. children about communicating anger. U.S. children felt that they would want others to know they were angry, whereas Brahman children were relatively

Table 7.2. *Children's Modal Responses Regarding Emotional Reactions to Challenging Situations*

	Children's Cultural Context		
Questions and modal answers	*Tamang*	*Brahman*	*U.S.*
How would you feel?	Ashamed/okay	Angry	Angry
Would you want others to know?	Yes	No	Yes
Why (or why not?)	My fault	Must cooperate	Can fix
What would you do?	Just stay quiet	Just stay quiet	Act to fix

uniform in saying they would not. Tamang children, who rarely endorsed anger, more typically felt they would reveal how they felt (ashamed or okay).

Moreover, the justifications that each group tended to provide reflected three distinct profiles for each cultural context. U.S. children's justifications for wanting their anger known revealed their sense of agency and instrumentality. They described the need to assert their rights and, moreover, guarantee that others would not repeat such rude or unfair mistakes. Therefore, they not only felt entitled to their anger but also felt instrumental in being able to use their anger to remedy the situation in the moment and in the future. When asked what they would do, their intended actions were neither destructive nor inappropriate. Instead, they described appropriate forms of self-assertion. For example, a common response was, "I'd tell him because then he would know how I felt and not do that again." Such a response pattern is consistent with a cultural context in which individual expression and rights are valued. Anger is acceptable as long as it is appropriately expressed.

By contrast, Brahman children, who endorsed anger as often as U.S. children, were forthright that they would not show anger. They typically explained that friends "must cooperate with each other" (*saathisanga milnuparchha*). For them, the priority was not correcting friends' behavior but maintaining their continuing commitment to a harmonious relationship with their friends. Brahman children believed it was wrong for friends to destroy their homework or laugh when they had fallen in mud but nonetheless acted in ways that showed they were still friendly and cooperative. Therefore, in their responses, there was less evidence of the instrumental value of anger in teaching others, correcting wrongs, or sticking up for oneself.

Tamang children, as mentioned, did not endorse anger but rather seemed to reappraise the situation. Those who endorsed shame in provoking situations explained that they were responsible for the problem (e.g., "It was my fault

I fell," "I shouldn't have put my homework near the tea"). Their preference for endorsing shame must be qualified by the fact that the same word also means embarrassed or shy. The important point is that all three are submissive, self-conscious emotions. Therefore, where Brahman and U.S. children would endorse anger, an emotion that readies an individual to assert the self, Tamang children opted for a submissive emotion. To maintain interpersonal harmony, they appeared to have the idea that anger was useless and that one should be willing to take personal responsibility for negative outcomes.

As shame seemed to be valued in both Brahman and Tamang communities, and because both Brahman and Tamang children's actions in these situations reflected a submissive stance ("I would just stay quiet"), why would Tamang children endorse shame when Brahmans endorsed anger? Although Buddhism discourages all emotions (and is quite consistent with the goal of being *thiken*, i.e., calmly okay), it is not the case that Hinduism as a *religion* promotes anger. It is as likely that Tamang culture, more than Brahman culture, emphasizes minimizing and tolerating individual differences and creating a sense of peace, values that are consistent with Buddhist prescriptions for inner peace and compassion. Turning the question around another way, it is also possible that aspects of the Brahman cultural context support *feeling* angry if not expressing it. Well-regulated anger can be adaptive in helping to overcome obstacles, such as persisting at studying difficult schoolwork. Anger would not lead to violations of cultural standards because it is regulated at the level of expressive control. This then would be consistent with the Brahman emphasis on self-discipline and academic achievement.

Anger may also support majority group behavior, as it reflects a willingness to dominate, whereas anger in a minority group member may create risk of retaliation. The Tamang's minority group status may contribute to a tendency to appear submissive. Untouchable caste members also try to appear duly subservient, a stance that is consistent with the emotion of shame, shyness, or embarrassment (Cameron, 1998). Looking down, dropping one's head, and appearing still or nervous are all nonverbal methods of communicating that one knows one's inferior status.

Epilogue

Our work revealed group differences in how children regulate emotions with peers and parents. Both Tamang and Brahman children agreed that one should remain quiet and not do or say anything in the types of emotion-eliciting situations we described to them. This was in stark contrast to rural U.S.

children, who described appropriate but assertive, instrumental behavior when provoked. However, the ways in which Tamang and Brahman children imagined they would reach their quiet, unobtrusive behavior involved different ways of regulating anger. Tamang children were quite reluctant to endorse anger, possibly engaging in secondary appraisals of situations that helped them avoid feeling angry. Brahman children seemed to have no need to avoid feeling angry but were clear and articulate that one should not show it to peers or parents.

We have described the similarities between these two communities, both in terms of demographic characteristics as well as shared cultural values. We have also shown that differences between the two groups might actually set the context for the two different ways of regulating anger. Shame is frequently attributed to "Eastern" peoples as a valued emotion. We showed group differences, among Asian peoples, in the endorsement of shame. Three facts are consistent with this tendency. Tamang emphasize cheerfulness, generosity, compassion, and minimizing differences. Tamang practice Buddhism, which holds that anger disturbs inner peace and relational harmony. Tamang are a minority group. Each and all of these facts may foster an avoidance of *experiencing* anger and foster a more submissive stance. Brahmans emphasize social hierarchy more than Tamang, in the interest of protecting high caste. Brahmans have pride in their ethnicity as the learned caste. Brahmans, even poor villagers, can identify with the political majority: their language, religion, customs, and superior place. These conditions might entitle Brahmans to anger, which they nonetheless learn to regulate through expressive control but have access to as needed. Their strict personal and social practices may also cultivate the self-control that supports effective expressive control of felt anger.

In sum, we hope our work illustrates the importance of a cross-cultural perspective in determining what is universal and what is variable among the different children of the world. We also hope it illustrates the value of a multidisciplinary approach that begins to take culture out of the realm of the abstract and puts it into dynamic motion as something that penetrates daily practices and reaches emotional lives. The coupling of hierarchical relationships among children of equivalent age and developmental status may account for important differences in how children relate emotionally to their peers, especially in the case of anger, compared with many U.S. children. Our work also points out the value of considering both within- and between-group contexts, both of which can influence emotional functioning and social relationships. We found that we depended on many other disciplines to understand the psychological phenomena in which we were interested. Moreover, we found that it was difficult to do this work without the expertise of members of the cultures.

Acknowledgments

The authors wish to thank the villages and towns in Nepal and the United States who participated in projects that contributed to this chapter. We also thank the women who assisted in data collection. The work could not have been done without the contributions of Carole Bruschi, Tirtha Dong, and most especially, Babu Lal Tamang. Support for this work came from the U.S. Fulbright Program and the National Science Foundation.

References

Asendorpf, J. B. (1991). Development of inhibited children's coping with unfamiliarity. *Child Development, 62*, 1460–1474.

Barrett, K. C., & Campos, J. J. (1987). Perspectives on emotional development II: A functionalist approach to emotions. In J. Osofsky (Ed.), *Handbook of infant development* (2nd ed., pp. 555–578). New York: Guilford Press.

Benjamin, W., Schneider, B., Greenman, P., & Hum, M. (2001). Conflict and childhood friendship in Taiwan and Canada. *Candadian Journal of Behavioral Science, 33*, 203–211.

Bennett, L. (1983). *Dangerous wives, sacred sisters: Social and symbolic roles of high-caste women in Nepal*. New York: Columbia University Press.

Berndt, T. J. (1996). Exploring the effects of friendship quality on social development. In W. M. Bukowski (Eds.), *The company they keep: Friendship in childhood and adolescence* (pp. 346–365). New York: Cambridge University Press.

Bronfenbrenner, U. (1986). Ecology of the family as a context for human development: Research perspectives. *Developmental Psychology, 22*, 723–742.

Calkins, S., Gill, K., Johnson, M., & Smith, C. (1999). Emotional reactivity and emotion regulation strategies as predictors of social behavior with peers during toddlerhood. *Social Development, 8*, 310–334.

Cameron, M. M. (1998). *On the edge of the ausipicious: Gender and caste in Nepal*. Chicago: University of Chicago Press.

Central Bureau of Statistics. (2003). *Population monograph of Nepal, volume 1*. Kathmandu, Nepal: His Majesty's Government.

Chen, X., Rubin, K., & Li, Z. (1995). Social functioning and adjustment in Chinese children: A longitudinal study. *Developmental Psychology, 31*, 531–539.

Cole, P. M., Bruschi, C., & Tamang, B. L. (2002). Cultural differences in children's emotional reactions to difficult situations. *Child Development, 73*, 983–996.

Cole, P. M., & Tamang, B. L. (1998). Nepali children's ideas about emotional displays in hypothetical challenges. *Developmental Psychology, 34*, 640–646.

Cole, P. M., Tamang, B. L., & Shrestha, S. (in press). Cultural socialization of young children's emotions in rural Nepal. *Child Development*.

Contreras, J. M., Kerns, K. A., Weimer, B. L., Gentzler, A. L., & Tomich, P. L. (2000). Emotion regulation as a mediator of associations between mother-child attachment and peer relationships in middle childhood. *Journal of Family Psychology, 14*, 111–124.

Cozort, D. (1995). "Cutting the roots of virtue:" Tsongkhapa on the results of anger. *Journal of Buddhist Ethics, 2,* 83–104, jbe.la.psu.edu

Denham, S. A. (1998). *Emotional development in young children.* New York: Guilford Press.

Desjarlais, R. R. (1992). *Body and emotion: The aesthetics of illness and healing in the Nepal Himalayas.* Philadelphia: University of Pennsylvania Press.

Eid, M., & Diener, E. (2001). Norms for experiencing emotions in different cultures: Inter- and intranational differences. *Journal of Personality and Social Psychology, 81*, 869–885.

Fricke, T. E. (1986). *Himalayan households: Tamang demography and domestic processes.* Ann Arbor: University of Michigan Press.

Fung, H. (1999). Becoming a moral child: The socialization of shame among young Chinese children. *Ethos, 27*, 180–209.

Furman, W., & Bierman, K. (1983). Developmental changes in young children's conceptions of friendship. *Child Development, 54*, 549–556.

Gautam, R., & Thapa-Magar, A. (1994). *Tribal ethnography of Nepal (Vols. I and II).* Delhi, India: Book Faith India.

Goleman, D. (Ed.). (2003). *Destructive emotions: How can we overcome them*? New York: Bantam Books.

Gurung, H. (1998). *Nepal: Social demography and expressions.* Kathmandu, Nepal: New Era.

Gurung, H. (2003). *Social demography of Nepal.* Kathmandu, Nepal: Himal Books.

Han, G., & Park, B. (1995). Children's choices in conflict: Application of the theory of individualism-collectivism. *Journal of Cross-Cultural Psychology, 26*, 298–313.

Harris, P. L., Olthof, T., Terwogt, M. M., & Hardman, C. E. (1987). Children's knowledge of the situations that provoke emotion. *International Journal of Behavioral Development, 10*, 319–343.

Hartup, W. W., & Moore, (1990). Early peer relations: Developmental significance and prognostic implications. *Early Childhood Research Quarterly, 5*, 1–17.

Hartup, W. W., & Sancilio, M. F. (1986). Children's friendships. In E. Schopler & G. B. Mesibov (Eds.), *Social behavior in autism* (pp. 61–80). New York: Plenum.

Hofstede, G. (2001). Culture's consequences (2nd ed.). Beverly Hills, CA: Sage.

Holmberg, D. H. (1989). *Order and paradox: Myth, ritual, and exchange among Nepal's Tamang.* Ithaca, NY: Cornell University Press.

Kinsley, D. R. (1993). *Hinduism: A cultural perspective*, 2nd edition. Upper Saddle River, NJ: Prentice Hall.

Kitayama, S., & Markus, H. R. (1994). *Emotion and culture: Empirical studies of mutual influence.* Washington, DC: American Psychological Association.

Ladd, G. (1988). Friendship patterns and peer status during early and middle childhood. *Developmental and Behavioral Pediatrics, 9*, 229–238.

Lama-Tamang, M. S. (2004). Indigenous peoples of Nepal and human rights. In *Human rights year book 2004* (pp. 121–146). Kathmandu, Nepal: Informal Sector Service Center.

Lemerise, E., & Arsenio, W. (2000). An integrated model of emotion processes and cognition in social information processing. *Child Development, 71*, 107–118.

MacDonald, A. W. (1989). Notes on language, literature and cultural identity of Tamang. *Kailash, 15*, 165–190.

Maguire, M. C., & Dunn, J. (1997). Friendships in early childhood, and social understanding. *International Journal of Behavioral Development, 21*, 669–686.

March, K. S. (1987). Hospitality, women and efficacy of beer. *Food and Foodways, 1*, 351–387.

March, K. S. (2002). *If each comes halfway: Meeting Tamang women in Nepal*. Ithaca, NY: Cornell University Press.

Markus, H., & Kitayama, S. (1991). Culture and the self: Implications for cognition, motivation, and emotion. *Psychological Review, 98*, 224–253.

Mesquita, B. (2001). Emotions in collectivist and individualist contexts. *Journal of Personality and Social Psychology, 80*, 68–74.

Mesquita, N., & Fridja, N. H. (1992). Cultural variations in emotions: A review. *Psychological Bulletin, 112*, 179–204.

Miller, P. J. (1996). Instantiating culture through discourse practices: Some personal reflections on socialization and how to study it. In R. Jessor, A. Colby, & R. A. Shweder (Eds.), *Ethnography and human development: Context and meaning in social inquiry* (pp. 183–204). Chicago: University of Chicago Press.

Ministry of Education and Sports. (2003). *Education for all 2004–2009: Core document*. Kathmandu, Nepal: His Majesty's Government.

Parker, J. G., & Asher, S. A. (1987). Peer relations and later personal adjustment: Are low-accepted children at risk? *Psychological Bulletin, 102*, 357–389.

Parker, J. G., & Asher, S. A. (1993). Friendship and friendship quality in middle childhood: Links with peer group acceptance and feelings of loneliness and social dissatisfaction. *Developmental Psychology,* 29, 611–621.

Parker, J. G., & Gottman, J. M. (1989). Social and emotional development in a relational context: Friendship interaction from early childhood to adolescence. In T. J. Berndt & G. W. Ladd (Eds.), *Peer relationships in child development* (pp. 95–131). New York: Wiley.

Parker, J. G., Rubin, K. H., Price, J. M., & DeRosier, M. E. (1995). Peer relationships, child development, and adjustment: A developmental psychopathology perspective. In D. Cicchetti & D. Cohen (Eds.), *Developmental psychopathology: Vol. 2. Risk, disorder, and adaptation* (pp. 96–161). New York: Wiley.

Regmi, M. C. (1978). *Thatched huts and stucco palaces: Peasants and landlords in nineteenth century Nepal*. New Delhi, India: Vikash.

Rothbaum, F., Pott, M., Azuma, H., Miyake, K., & Weisz, J. (2000). The development of close relationships in Japan and the United States: Paths of symbiotic harmony and generative tension. *Child Development, 71*, 1121–1142.

Rubin, K., Bukowski, W., & Parker, J. (1998). Peer interactions, relationships, and groups. In W. Damon (Ed.), *Handbook of child psychology* (vol. 4, pp. 619–700). New York: Wiley.

Skinner, D., Pach, A., & Holland, D. C. (1998). *Selves in time and place: Identities, experiences, and history in Nepal*. Lanham, MD: Rowman & Littlefield.

Sullivan, H. S. (1953). *The interpersonal theory of psychiatry*. New York: W. W. Norton.

Super, C. M., & Harkness, S. (1993). The developmental niche: A conceptualization at the interface of child and culture. In R. A. Pierce & M. A. Black (Eds.), *Life-span development: A diversity reader* (pp. 61–77). Dubuque, IA: Kendall/Hunt.

Triandis, H. C. (1994). *Culture and social behavior*. Champaign, IL: McGraw-Hill.

Weisner, T. S. (2002). Ecocultural pathways, family values, and parenting. *Parenting: Science and Practice, 2*, 325–334.

Zeman, J., & Garber, J. (1996). Display rules for anger, sadness, and pain: It depends on who is watching. *Child Development, 67*, 953–973.

8 Emotion, Emotion-Related Regulation, and Social Functioning

Nancy Eisenberg, Qing Zhou, Jeffrey Liew, Claire Champion, and Sri Untari Pidada

It is a well-established finding that children who are popular with peers tend to be prosocial and relatively appropriate in their social interactions (Rubin, Bukowski, & Parker, 1998). Thus, it is reasonable to predict that children who are liked by peers tend to be fairly well regulated. However, children who are overcontrolled – rigid and overly constrained in their behavior – may not be especially attractive to peers. In addition, the degree to which children regulate versus express their emotions may have a different significance in different cultures and, consequently, be differentially related to developmental outcomes.

In this chapter, we review conceptions of regulation/control relevant to managing emotion and its expression, discuss possible reasons for similarities and differences in the relations of emotionality and regulation to quality of children's social functioning, and summarize research from studies in three cultures outside of North America.

Emotion-Related Regulation/Control: Conceptual Distinctions

There is considerable debate regarding the definition of emotion regulation (Campos, Frankel, & Camras, 2004; Cole, Martin, & Dennis, 2004). In an attempt to include the many aspects of such regulation, Eisenberg and Spinrad (2004) defined emotion-related self-regulation as the process of influencing (i.e., initiating, avoiding, inhibiting, maintaining, or modulating) the occurrence, form, intensity, or duration of internal feeling states, emotion-related physiological and attentional processes, motivational states, and/or the behavioral concomitants of emotion in the service of accomplishing affect-related biological or social adaptation or achieving individual goals. Numerous processes can be involved in emotion-related self-regulation, such as shifting or focusing attention (e.g., shifting attention from a distressing activity or thought and focusing it on something else), cognitively reinterpreting an event, inhibiting emotion-related indicators/behaviors (e.g., facial expressions or reactive aggression), or activating behaviors that will change or deal with the situation or divert one's attention or energy (e.g., biking when upset). Systematic planning also can be viewed as an aspect of emotion-related regulation.

We have suggested that emotion-related (self-) regulation involves voluntary or effortful responding and that it is useful to differentiate it from control-related processes that do not (Eisenberg & Morris, 2002; Eisenberg & Spinrad, 2004). We do not wish to imply that regulation necessarily involves a highly conscious intention to change emotion or behavior; we mean that the cognitions, attention, or behaviors involved in regulation can be voluntarily controlled by individuals (often not at a highly conscious level) and are not solely automatic or reflexive.

We view control as a construct that partly overlaps with, but is not the same as, emotion-related regulation. Control is defined in the dictionary as inhibition; such inhibition can be voluntary or the result of processes over which the individual has relatively little control (e.g., as in the case of the highly inhibited children, who seem to have difficulty modulating their inhibition to novel, and perhaps stressful, stimuli). Similarly, behavior can be voluntarily activated and used to achieve goals or it can occur in a less voluntary manner. For example, impulsive children may be "pulled" toward rewarding or positive situations with little ability to inhibit themselves. In our view, regulation involves optimal levels of control, and neither too much impulsivity nor rigid, overly inhibited behavior.

The concept of voluntary control is reflected in Rothbart's concept of effortful control (a major dimension of temperament), defined as, "the ability to inhibit a dominant response to perform a subdominant response" (Rothbart & Bates, 1998, p. 137) or "the efficiency of executive attention, including the ability to inhibit a dominant response and/or to activate a subdominant response, to plan, and to detect errors" (Rothbart & Bates, in press). Effortful control is reflected in effortful attentional regulation, as well as in inhibitory and activational control – defined as the abilities to effortfully inhibit behavior or activate behavior as needed, even if the person does not really desire to do so (e.g., when children are ordered to cease a pleasurable activity or perform an aversive task, respectively). Effortful control likely involves executive functioning in the prefrontal cortex (Mirsky, 1996) and/or the anterior cingulate gyrus in the paleocortex – which appears to be directly related to awareness of one's planned behavior, correction of errors, and the control of thoughts and feelings (e.g., Posner & DiGirolamo, 2000; Posner & Rothbart, 1998).

The biological or temperamental systems related to a less voluntary approach or inhibition have sometimes been labeled as reactive systems involving links to emotion (Derryberry & Rothbart, 1997). In our view, they include both impulsivity or surgent approach behavior (perhaps based on reward dominance) and overly inhibited or rigid behavior as reflected in very low impulsivity and high behavioral inhibition. Pickering and Gray (1999) and others (Cacioppo, Gardner, & Berntson, 1999) have argued that approach/avoidance motivational systems related to impulsive (under-controlled) and overly inhibited behaviors are associated with subcortical systems.

One reason that the difference between effortful control and reactive control is important is that they would be expected to relate differently to the quality of children's social functioning and adjustment. Because effortful control (or regulation) is flexible and can be turned on and off as needed, it would be expected to predict high peer status, socially appropriate behavior, and adjustment. In contrast, as mentioned previously, overly inhibited behavior (i.e., reactive overcontrol), as is seen in some shy or withdrawn children (who are likely shy because of social anxiety or an inhibited reaction to novelty), is likely to be viewed less positively by peers. Moreover, children who are impulsive are likely to exhibit limited social skills, and their impulsive behavior may undermine the quality of their relationships with peers. Consistent with these arguments, in the United States, effortful control generally has been positively related to measures of social skills and popularity, and this relation tends to be especially strong for children prone to negative emotions (see Eisenberg, Fabes, Guthrie, & Reiser, 2000, for a review). Effortful control (or regulation) may be somewhat less important for predicting outcomes in children who are not prone to experience or express negative emotions because they are less likely to behave in appropriate, unregulated ways. In contrast to effortful control, impulsivity (reactive undercontrol) tends to be negatively related or unrelated to adult-reported popularity (Spinrad et al., 2004) (and ego control, which probably taps primarily high control versus impulsivity, generally has been modestly positively related; e.g., Eisenberg et al., 1997, 2000). In addition, highly inhibited children who are socially withdrawn (who are likely high in reactive control) tend to be low in popularity (see Rubin et al., 1998). Thus, the initial research, much of which has been conducted in North America, suggests that both emotion-related regulation (including effortful control) and reactive control predict children's social competence and peer status, but only high effortful control is associated with high peer status.

Emotion-Related Regulation/Control, Quality of Social Functioning, and Culture

One of the main theoretical frameworks for conceptualizing cultural differences is the distinction between individualistic and collectivistic worldviews. In cultures high on collectivism, individuals are viewed as interdependent on (rather than relatively independent of) one another; in addition, mutual obligations and common goals or values of the groups tend to be emphasized over personal goals and values. Accordingly, in collective cultures, the individual's psychological well-being is believed to depend more on the successful fulfillment of social roles and obligations and on maintaining harmonious relationships with in-group members than on the fulfillment of personal goals (Markus & Kitayama, 1991). Because of their orientation to the group, individuals with a collectivistic orientation are viewed as willing to consider group members' needs and well-being rather than solely focusing on their own needs and interests. In addition, because the experience and direct expression of certain emotions (e.g., self-focused emotions, such as anger, sadness, and fear) may disrupt group harmony and threaten the individual's connectedness with others, people in collective cultures are believed to devalue the internal experience and restrict the direct expression of such emotions (or use subtle expressions of emotion).

Oyserman, Coon, and Kemmelmeier (2002) found that the emphasis on group harmony and duty to the group seemed to be particularly important in differentiating the United States from more collectivistic cultures (especially in Asia). The emphasis on individualism/autonomy versus collectivism in cultures likely is only a matter of degree, is manifest differently in different cultures, and varies within cultures and individuals in a given culture (Greenfield, Keller, Fuligni, & Maynard, 2003; Oyserman et al., 2002). Nonetheless, the collectivistic versus individualistic distinction has been used to frame the issue of differences in norms/beliefs related to the overt expression of goals and emotions in cultures that differ in an emphasis on relatedness or maintaining group harmony.

There are other cultural differences besides the collectivism and individualism worldviews that have important implications for emotion and its regulation. In Figure 8.1, we propose a conceptual model for describing the hypothesized relations of culture, emotion regulation, and social functioning (especially in peer interaction). There are a number of reasons to expect both

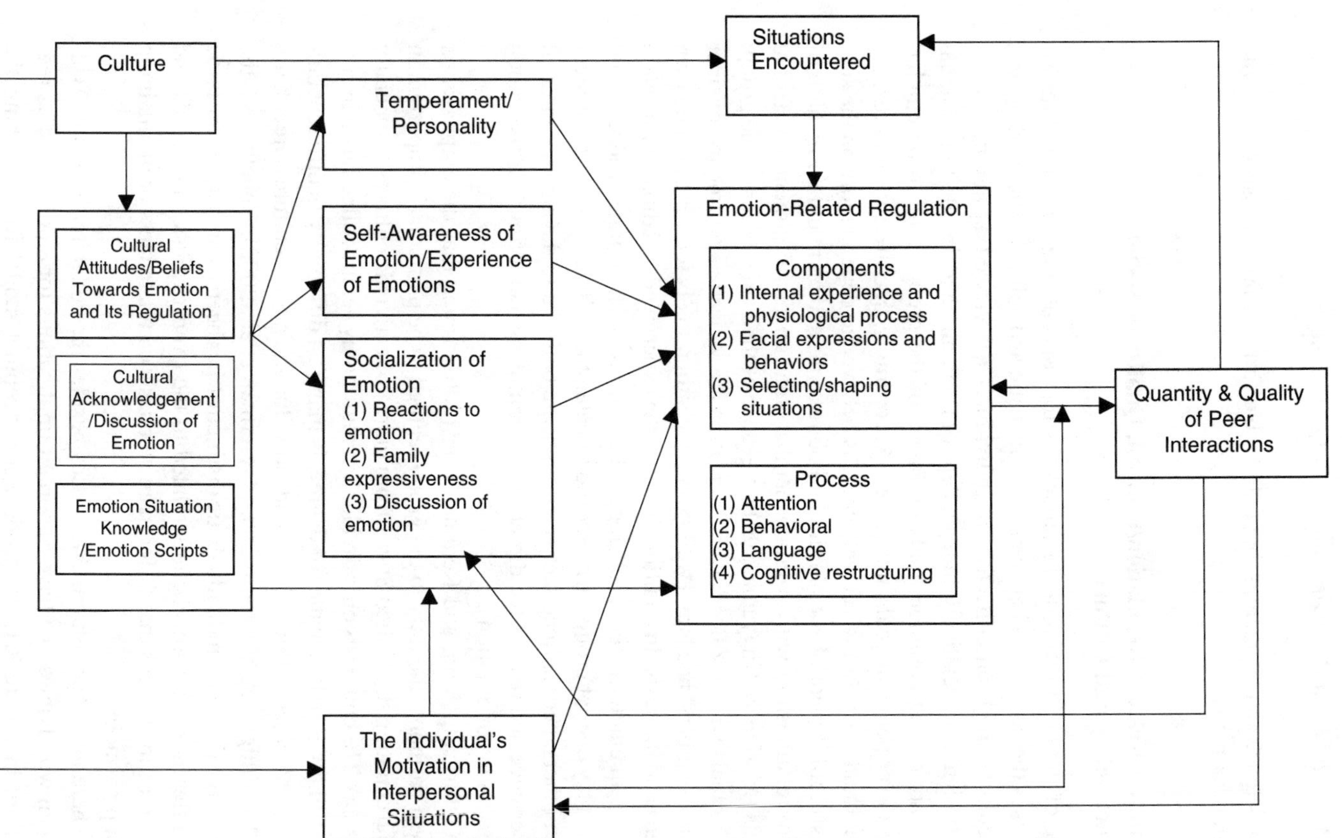

Figure 8.1. The conceptual model of culture, emotion regulation, and peer context.

similarities and differences among cultures in the pattern of relations between emotion-related regulation or control and quality of social functioning. First, cultures likely differ in their attitudes toward, and beliefs about, the experience and expression of emotion (Mesquita & Frijda, 1992; Tsai, 2004). In some cultures, such as the Inuit, for example, anger is viewed negatively in many contexts (e.g., when directed toward children; Briggs, 1998), whereas in others, the open expression of emotions (including anger) is more normative and sometimes even encouraged (Miller & Sperry, 1987; see more detailed discussion in later sections). In cultures in which specific emotions are viewed negatively, parents are likely to discourage their children from expressing them (Zahn-Waxler, Friedman, Cole, Mizuta, & Hiruma, 1996). These differences would be expected to result in cultural (and subcultural) differences in display rules regarding when, where, and how emotional or social behaviors should be expressed (e.g., Matsumoto, 1993). Second, there may be differences in the degree to which cultures acknowledge and discuss emotion (Cole & Tamang, 1998), and perhaps even in the degree to which people attempt to try to understand their own and others' emotions. Based on a literature review, Lillard (1998) argued that not only might different emotions exist in different cultures (see Menon & Shweder, 1994), but that the felt need to infer and interpret mental states probably differs across cultures. Third, it is likely that there are cultural differences in the degree to which people believe that emotions are controllable and in notions about the consequences of emotion (Lillard, 1998). For example, Lutz (1985) reported that if an Ifaluk person exhibits a jealous rage, the person who displayed possessions that invoked the rage is likely to be viewed as responsible. Fourth, the social scripts and folk psychologies (Lillard, 1998) regarding everyday situations, including which emotions are expressed in which contexts and to what degree, probably vary considerably across contexts. Such scripts might even include information on the emotional significance of events and, thereby, affect appraisals of emotion-eliciting situations (see Mesquita & Frijda, 1992). For all these reasons (and others), people in different cultures are likely to differ in their experience of emotion, as well as in the degree to which they believe it is important and possible to regulate their emotion. Moreover, such factors undoubtedly affect which emotions parents believe children can modulate and the degree to which they attempt to teach children about doing so.

It is quite possible that cultural differences in the experience and expression of emotion translate to differences in relations of peer competence to children's emotionality, emotional displays, and emotion regulation. For example, in cultures that value the suppression of emotion, the expression of intense emotions, even positive ones, might be related to lower evaluations of social competence and lower peer status. In such cultures, emotion regulation may be especially important in predicting quality of peer relationships (although emotion regulation would be expected to relate to higher peer competence in most, if not all, cultures). In contrast, in cultures that value affectively laden speech and interactions, children who are spontaneous and expressive may be popular, whereas those who are less expressive may be viewed as overly restrained and less attractive.

Despite the aforementioned reasons to expect cross-cultural differences in emotionality and emotion-related regulation and in their associations with peer competence, there also are reasons to expect some similarities in the ways in which children's emotion-related regulation/control is related to the quality of their social functioning (e.g., socially appropriate behavior and peer status). First, because effortful control involves the executive attention system, it is likely that basic, temperamentally based modes of regulation are similar in people in all cultures. Consistent with this idea, the structure of children's temperament (including their effortful control) is fairly similar in China and the United States (Ahadi, Rothbart, & Ye, 1993). Thus, we would expect skills, such as attention shifting and focusing, inhibitory control, and activational control, to be important in emotion-related regulation in all cultures. Moreover, if subcorticol systems (such as the limbic system) play a role in reactive overcontrol and undercontrol, these systems are likely to function similarly in most people. Second, in all societies, there are some situations in which people are expected to modulate (e.g., suppress, diminish, or heighten) their emotional behavior. Although these situations might differ somewhat across cultures, the ability to regulate emotion when it is culturally normative or appropriate to do so would be expected to contribute to social competence in all cultures. For example, the rules regarding social communication and group interactions that exist in all cultures (although the specifics clearly vary) require effortful control to implement. Thus, the ability to regulate emotion and emotion-related behavior would be expected to be adaptive in all cultures, despite differences in the degree to which, or the contexts in which, such regulation is expected.

Based on the aforementioned arguments, several predictions seem reasonable. First, we might expect to find differences in children's language and cognitions related to emotion that affect both emotion knowledge and regulation. Second, there may be mean differences in the degree to which individuals rely on, or are proficient at, a given aspect of emotion-related regulation. For example, as we discuss shortly, individuals from a collectivistic culture (or any group that emphasizes the interdependence of group members and maintaining harmonious relations) may exhibit higher degrees of behavioral regulation, especially in public settings, than those from an individualistic culture. Third, it is probable that there are cross-cultural differences in the relative use of various types of regulation selected by well-socialized individuals to modulate their emotion. For example, an individual from the United States may tend to use language that directly describes emotions and feelings, whereas an individual from the Chinese culture may use language that indirectly reflects feelings. In addition, masking anger may be more adaptive for individuals in the collectivist cultures, whereas the expression of tempered anger, sometimes accompanied by discussion of what caused the anger, might be deemed more appropriate in cultures that emphasize individuals' personal feelings and openness in communication. Of course, such differences may be apparent or relevant in some contexts, or in regard to some stressors or emotions, and not in others. Finally, in cultures in which emotion regulation is deemed more important, there might be a stronger relation between such regulation and quality of children's social functioning.

As already noted, we would also expect to find differences in the relations of parenting to children's emotion-related regulation in different cultures. Cultural beliefs about both the expression of emotion and child-rearing techniques would be expected to be reflected in parents' beliefs about the acceptability and effectiveness of various aspects of parenting and, consequently, in parents' choice and degree of utilization of specific parenting techniques. Similarly, the degree to which the regulation of emotion is valued in general probably affects parents' attempts to teach such regulation. Finally, cultural values and goals regarding emotionality, its regulation, and parenting techniques (e.g., causes, consequences) may affect the effectiveness of parents' attempts to use various models of parenting.

Research in China

Chinese culture (especially in the mainland China) has been found to be higher on collectivism and lower on individualism than European American culture (Oyserman et al., 2002). Thus, in China, the open expression of emotions (especially strong and negative ones) often may be seen as endangering the harmony of close interpersonal relationships, which are viewed as more important to individuals than their own psychological status. Thus, individuals in Chinese culture (compared with those in the Western culture) may tend to inhibit the direct expression of dysphoric or strong negative emotions and pay more attention to concrete interpersonal transactions or situations than to their own internal emotional experience in social interactions. In addition, they may substitute somatic complaints for complaints of emotional distress (Kleinman, 1980). Consistent with these speculations, investigators have found that Chinese infants display fewer emotional facial expressions than U.S. infants (Camras et al., 1998). In other studies, Chinese preschoolers and adults, compared with their North American peers, gave lower intensity ratings of protagonists' feeling states in emotionally charged stories than did American counterparts (Wang, 2003), and Chinese children made fewer spontaneous references to emotions in their autobiographical memories (Wang, 2004). Moreover, Chinese individuals were found to report more somatic symptoms of depression than symptoms of emotional distress (which are less culturally acceptable than the former) (Parker, Gladstone, & Chee, 2001).

In addition to the mean difference in individuals' overall degree of emotional expressiveness between Chinese and European American cultures, some researchers have hypothesized that the function and significance of emotion in social interactions in Chinese culture may differ from that in Western culture. For example, Potter (1988) theorized that in Western cultures, emotional experience is taken as a legitimizing basis for social action and that social relationships are derived from and affirmed by the experience and expression of individuals' feelings. In contrast, in Chinese culture, because social structure does not rest on emotional ties, emotions are thought of as concomitant phenomena in social life, but lacking the power to create, maintain, or change social relationships. Thus, emotional expressiveness is likely to play a less crucial role in interpersonal relationships in Chinese culture than it does in Western cultures. In support of this hypothesis, Kang et al. (2003) found that college students' emotional expressiveness was positively associated with the quality of their interpersonal relationships for European American students, but was unrelated for Chinese participants. In contrast, emotion differentiation, or the propensity to make subtle distinctions within emotional experiences, was related to higher quality relationships for Chinese (but not European American) students, which suggests that being sensitive to others' feelings may be more important for maintaining good interpersonal relationships than is expressing one's own feelings in Chinese culture.

Despite the aforementioned differences, cross-cultural similarities in emotional functioning, and its antecedents and consequences, have also been found in the literature on Chinese individuals. In general, cross-cultural differences seem most likely to be found in cross-cultural comparative studies and to be manifest as differences in either mean levels (e.g., means of expressivity) or the magnitudes of relations among constructs (e.g., the relation between parental warmth and children's emotional expressivity). In contrast, cross-cultural similarities are most likely to be noted when comparing findings from within-culture studies and when comparing similarities in the pattern (e.g., valence or direction) of relations among constructs (despite differential strength). For example, in the literature on depression, cross-cultural differences were found in the means for depressive symptoms and for the means of the antecedents or correlates of depression. Hong Kong youths reported higher depressive symptoms and hopelessness, and lower self-efficacy and cognitive distortions, than U.S. youths (Stewart et al., 2004). Further, mainland Chinese adolescents reported fewer stressful life events and less conflict with parents, and perceived their parents as warmer and more accepting than did their U.S. counterparts (Greenberger, Chen, Tally, & Dong, 2000). Nonetheless, cross-cultural similarities were found in the pattern of interrelations between depressive symptoms and their correlates. Self-efficacy, negative cognitive errors, and hopelessness showed similar patterns of associations with depressive symptoms in Hong Kong and in the United States (Stewart et al., 2004). Moreover, life events, parental warmth, conflict with parents, and peer warmth showed similar patterns of relations to adolescents' depressive symptoms in mainland China and in the United States, although the magnitude of these relations differed somewhat across cultures (Greenberger et al., 2000). These results suggest that depressed mood is a significant and maladaptive phenomenon in both cultures, although its specific manifestation, antecedents, and consequences may vary in degree across the two cultures.

There is debate regarding the adaptive meaning of children's shy and inhibited behaviors (which may reflect reactive overcontrol) in Chinese culture. Chen and colleagues (e.g., Chen, Rubin, & Li, 1995; Chen, Rubin, & Sun, 1992) found that Chinese children's shy, inhibited, and sensitive behaviors (assessed by peer nominations of being shy, sad, or having easily hurt feelings) were positively related to peer acceptance and adults' ratings of competence, whereas the opposite relations were found in Western children. Moreover, Chen et al. (1998) found that toddlers' behavioral inhibition during free play was associated with mothers' warmth and acceptance in the Chinese sample, but was associated with mothers' punishment orientation in the Canadian sample. In contrast, other researchers (Chang, 2003; Hart et al., 2000; Schwartz, Chang, & Farver, 2001) found positive associations between Chinese children's shy, socially withdrawn behaviors (assessed by peer nominations or adults' ratings of being alone, submissive, or withdrawing) and peer rejection, similar to those obtained from Western samples. Moreover, both Chinese and European American mothers reacted with negative emotions to children's socially withdrawn behaviors depicted in hypothetical vignettes (Cheah & Rubin, 2004). The seemingly "inconsistent" findings across studies may suggest that different types of shy and inhibited behaviors have different adaptive meanings in Chinese culture: reserved and sensitive behaviors help maintain interpersonal harmony and thus are socially adaptive, whereas reticent and withdrawn behaviors undermine one's connectedness with the group and thus are socially maladaptive.

However, any differences in the significance of shyness in China and the United States may be waning. In a recent study, Chen et al. (2005) examined the relations between shyness–sensitivity and Chinese children's social functioning in three cohorts (1990, 1998, and 2002). They found that, although shyness was associated with social and academic achievement in the 1990 cohort, the relations became weaker or nonsignificant in the 1998 cohort; moreover, shyness was positively associated with peer rejection, depression, and low school competence in the 2002 cohort. Chen et al. (2005) suggested that the differences in the pattern of relations across cohorts might reflect the influence of social and economic changes and the introduction of individualistic values in China over the last decade.

There has been little research on the regulation of emotional functioning in Chinese children. Similar to the research on shyness–sensitivity, an important research question is whether the adaptive functions of emotion-related regulation (e.g., attentional and inhibitory control) in children's social adjustment found in the European American culture can be generalized to the Chinese culture. In a recent study, Zhou, Eisenberg, Wang, and Reiser (2004) examined the concurrent relations of effortful control and dispositional anger/frustration to Chinese elementary school children's social functioning. Two aspects of effortful control were examined: the ability to sustain attention (i.e., attention focusing) and the ability to effortfully inhibit behavior (i.e., inhibitory control). (Attention shifting, another component of effortful control, was not reported very reliably in this sample.) Because in collectivistic societies, such as China, the ability to effortfully control one's emotions or behavioral tendencies if needed appears to be valued as a means of maintaining harmonious interpersonal relationships, higher effortful control was expected to predict higher social functioning. Similarly, because the experience and public display of anger and frustration are at odds with the maintenance of one's interdependence with the group and, when unchecked, may evoke interpersonal conflict (Markus & Kitayama, 1991), Chinese children with higher dispositional anger/frustration were expected to be lower on social functioning than their less emotional peers. However, the relations between negative emotionality (e.g., anger/frustration) and social functioning were expected to vary with a child's level of effortful control: as has been found in the United States (e.g., Belsky, Friedman, & Hsieh, 2001; Eisenberg et al., 2000; Eisenberg, Spinrad et al., 2004; Stifter, Spinrad, & Braungart-Rieker, 1999), anger/frustration was predicted to be more strongly associated with poor social functioning for children with lower (in contrast to higher) effortful control. For children who are higher in effortful control, negative emotionality may play a less important role than other factors (e.g., the internalization of norms) in their socially competent behavior.

Data on the Relations of Effortful Control and Anger/Frustration to Quality of Chinese Children's Social Functioning

The aforementioned hypotheses were tested in a sample of 425 first- and second-graders (7–10 years old) in Beijing, China. Children's effortful control and dispositional anger/frustration were assessed by parents' and teachers' reports on subscales of the Child Behavioral Questionnaire (Rothbart et al., 2001). Children's social functioning was assessed by parents' and teachers' reports of socially appropriate behavior (Harter, 1979) and externalizing problems (Lochman & Conduct Problems Prevention Research Group, 1995), as well as peer nominations of aggression and sociability/leadership (the Revised Class Play; Masten, Morison, & Pelligrini, 1985). High effortful control and low dispositional anger/frustration uniquely predicted higher quality social functioning. Moreover, an interaction was found when predicting social functioning: anger/frustration was negatively related to social functioning for children with lower effortful control but was weakly related or unrelated to social functioning for those with mean to high levels of effortful control. These results are consistent with previous findings with samples of primarily European American children, indicating that there are some similarities in the adaptive meanings of effortful control and dispositional anger/frustration in Chinese and European American cultures.

In this Chinese sample, parents' and teachers' reports of children's dispositional anger/frustration were not correlated with each other; teachers' (but not parents') reports of anger/frustration were predictive of peers' nominations of high aggression and low leadership/sociability; and the mean of teachers' ratings of children's anger/frustration was lower than that of parents. Chinese children may express anger/frustration more freely at home than at school because its display is less acceptable in public settings such as school or in front of out-group individuals (e.g., teachers or some peers) than in private settings such as home or in front of in-group individuals (e.g., family). Perhaps teachers' ratings of anger/frustration were more predictive of peers' ratings of social functioning than parents' ratings because both teachers and peers observed children's emotions and behaviors mostly at school.

Data on the Relations of Parenting to Chinese Children's Emotion-Related Regulation and Social Functioning

In the Zhou et al. (2004) study, as well as in another study, the associations of parenting with Chinese children's emotion regulation and social behavior were somewhat similar to those obtained with European American samples. Chang, Schwartz, Dodge, and McBride-Chang (2003) found that harsh parenting was associated with Chinese kindergarteners' emotional dysregulation, which in turn mediated the relation between harsh parenting and children's aggression at school. Similarly, Zhou et al. (2004) found that authoritarian parenting (i.e., low warmth and high demandingness) was related to Chinese children's relatively low effortful control and high dispositional anger/frustration, which (especially for effortful control) mediated the relation between authoritarian parenting and children's poor social functioning (i.e., low adult-reported socially appropriate behaviors and peer-nominated leadership/sociability, as well as high adult-reported externalizing problems and peer-nominated aggression). Despite the finding that Chinese parents generally are more authoritarian than their European American counterparts (e.g., Steinberg, Dornbusch, & Brown, 1992; Wu et al., 2002), it appears that the functional implications of harsh discipline or authoritarian parenting for children's emotional and social competence are similar across the two cultures.

Zhou et al. (2004) also found modest evidence for an association of authoritative parenting (i.e., high warmth and high demandingness) with Chinese children's effortful control (albeit only for parents' reports) and high-quality social functioning; moreover, children's effortful control mediated the relation of authoritative child-rearing practices to children's social competence. It is possible that parents high on authoritativeness are more open and receptive to children's dispositional emotion-related characteristics, which resulted in a modest positive relation to children's regulation and social competence.

In summary, Chinese children's effortful control generally related to their social competence in the same manner that has been found in the United States. In addition, the pattern of relations of parenting with children's regulation and social competence was similar to that found in the United States, although findings for authoritative parenting were likely less robust than those typically found in the United States.

Research in Indonesia

Relative to the United States, Indonesia, like China, has been described as highly collectivistic (Hofstede, 1991), and there is some (albeit very limited) evidence supporting this assumption (Oyserman et al., 2002). Thus, we would expect cultural attitudes, beliefs, and norms to encourage expressive and social behaviors (including facial and verbal expressions) that facilitate and promote social harmony and to discourage expressive and social behaviors that hinder or disrupt social relationships. We would also expect such cultural attitudes or beliefs to influence individuals' motivation in interpersonal situations (e.g., need or desire for affiliation), as well as the types of situations individuals seek or encounter (see Figure 8.1). In fact, social scientists tend to describe Indonesians in ways that are consistent with the qualities attributed to collectivistic individuals (e.g., Magnis-Suseno, 1997; Mulder, 1989). Specifically, maintaining close and harmonious relationships are highly valued in Indonesia, and the expression of emotion, especially negative emotion, seems to be discouraged. The Javanese in Indonesia traditionally believe that experiencing negative emotions (such as anger) could harm people's health and shorten their lives (Geertz, 1976; Wellenkamp, 1995). Furthermore, the Javanese traditionally are known as the most *halus* (i.e., maintaining composure and not revealing emotions) of all Indonesians (Heider, 1991). Similarly, the Balinese (who lived on an island neighboring the Javanese) believe in the shaping of emotional expressions and sanction actions that disrupt or decay social bonds and relationships (Wilkan, 1989).

Consistent with traditional cultural norms and beliefs about emotions and emotional expression, one of the most important display rules in Indonesia (which is also shared across many other cultures, including North American) is the control and masking of anger (Heider, 1991, p. 116). Heider (1991) reported that display rules for the masking of anger are particularly strict for the Javanese relative to other regional cultures in Indonesia. Interestingly, Heider reported that the display rule for the masking of happiness is strictly enforced by the Minangkabau (in West Sumatra, Indonesia), but was less evident in Java (unless it is so intense and draws enough attention to the self to disrupt group harmony). However, it is likely that the expression of positive emotion generally is less valued in Asian collectivistic cultures than in the United States (Tsai, 2004).

If traditional Indonesian beliefs and norms (including display rules and emotional scripts) emphasize the minimization or masking of negative emotions (such as anger) as a way to avoid disrupting relationships and harming the health of self and others, we would expect emotion-related regulation of negative (and perhaps positive) emotions to be extremely important for harmonious and successful relationships and social acceptance (including peer competence). Children's shyness (which might hinder peer relationships) and sympathy (which should facilitate peer relationships or social engagement and affiliation) are also important aspects of children's social functioning that might be linked with children's emotion-related regulation. Consequently, it is logical to expect well-regulated, relatively non-negative Indonesian children to be socially competent, well liked by peers, low in shyness (because they are not involuntarily inhibited from engaging in peer play or relationships), and sympathetic (because they could attend to rather than easily become distressed by others' emotions); as reported previously, findings in North America generally support such relations (e.g., Eisenberg et al., 2000; Eisenberg, Fabes, & Murphy, 1995; Eisenberg, Fabes, et al., 1998; see Eisenberg, Losoya, & Spinrad, 2003, for a review of literature on sympathy/empathy).

In addition, the ways parents socialize emotionality (e.g., through how they express emotions in the home) likely impact Javanese children's development of self-regulation and their social functioning (see Figure 8.1). In North America, investigators generally have found that parents' positive expressivity (including the expression of positive emotion in the family) is positively associated with children's social skills, prosocial behaviors, and adjustment (e.g., Boyum & Parke, 1995), whereas parental negative expressivity sometimes is negatively associated with children's social development (e.g., Eisenberg, Gershoff et al., 2001; see Eisenberg, Cumberland, & Spinrad, 1998; Halberstadt, Crisp, & Eaton, 1999). Given an emphasis on *halus* (i.e., maintaining composure and not revealing emotions) and display rules regarding masking anger among the Javanese, we expected similar relations between parental negative expressivity and children's emotion-related regulation and social functioning in Indonesia as in North America. However, because of the regional nature of display rules for the masking of happiness within Indonesia (e.g., by the Minangkabau in West Sumatra; Heider, 1991), we were unsure of what to predict for the relation of parental positive expressivity with children's emotion-related regulation and social functioning.

Data on the Relation of Effortful Control to Quality of Indonesian Children's Social Functioning

To empirically explore the relation of emotionality and regulation to social and peer competence (and other aspects of social functioning important to social relationships) in Indonesia, we conducted a longitudinal study (Eisenberg, Liew, & Pidada, 2001, 2004; Eisenberg, Pidada, & Liew, 2001) involving children who lived in Bandung, a center for education and technology located on the island of Java. There were 127 third-grade children in the initial assessment, 112 of whom participated in the follow-up study three years later. Children were recruited from a "private public" school in Bandung, with the majority of them growing up in middle-class families.

Parents, teachers, and peers (parents were involved in only the first assessment) provided information on children. Multiple teachers (three for Time 1 and two for Time 2) completed measures on children's negative emotionality, regulation, and social functioning (i.e., social competence, externalizing or aggressive behaviors, shyness, and sympathy) using Rothbart's Child Behavior Questionnaire (Rothbart et al., 2001), Lochman et al.'s (1995) measure of externalizing problems, and our own measures of sympathy and socially appropriate behavior (Eisenberg et al., 2000; Eisenberg, Cumberland, & Spinrad, 1998). In addition to completing similar measures as teachers, at Time 1 parents provided information on how often they expressed positive or negative emotions in the home (Halberstadt, Cassidy, Stifter, Parke, & Fox, 1995). Peers individually nominated and ranked four classmates they liked most and four they liked least in their classrooms, as well as four classmates who were most likely to show anger, aggression, and prosocial behavior.

At Time 1, third-grade children who were emotionally intense or easily angered were viewed negatively (i.e., disliked) by their peers. In contrast, children who were well regulated (in their attention, emotions, and behaviors) tended to enjoy positive peer relationships. Children who were seen as sympathetic by parents and teachers were also viewed as well regulated. In addition, although shy children were not viewed by teachers or peers as particularly inclined to negative emotion, they were seen by teachers as low on regulation and tended to be neglected (i.e., not particularly liked or disliked) by their peers (Eisenberg, Pidada et al., 2001).

Similarly, there were associations between sociometric group status (popular, rejected, average, controversial, or neglected categorical groups) and children's regulation and negative emotionality at Time 1 (third grade). Consistent with findings in North America (e.g., Coie, Dodge, & Kupersmidt, 1990), children classified as rejected were rated lower on regulation by teachers than all other groups. In addition, children classified as rejected were rated higher on negative emotionality by teachers than popular, neglected, and average-status children. Thus, consistent with cultural attitudes or beliefs of *halus* and display rules for masking anger, children who were poorly regulated and easily angered or intense in their emotions were most at risk for peer rejection.

In our follow-up assessment three years later, the general pattern of findings again suggested that children who were well regulated and low in negative emotionality were viewed by teachers as socially skilled and low in problem behavior, as well as low in shyness. For boys, high teacher-reported regulation and low negative emotionality were related to teachers' report of low shyness, high sympathy, positive peer evaluations (reports of liking and of children's prosocial behavior), and low negative peer evaluations (i.e., being disliked and starting fights). For girls, they were associated with only teacher-reported social competence and low shyness. In addition, both boys and girls designated as prone to anger by their peers tended to be evaluated negatively by peers.

Furthermore, parents' and teachers' ratings of boys' low negative emotionality and high regulation when children were in the third grade predicted peer liking or acceptance and teachers' ratings of social skills when boys were in the sixth grade. Boys' regulation or negative emotionality in the sixth grade also predicted their concurrent social functioning, even after accounting for their levels of regulation or negative emotionality in the third grade.

Finally, we examined if there were differences in children's regulation and negative emotionality for children who differed in peer sociometric group status in the sixth grade (including girls and boys). Sixth-graders who were rejected or controversial with peers were rated by peers as more readily angered than popular or neglected children. Popular and average sixth-graders were rated by teachers as more regulated three years prior (i.e., in third grade) than were rejected children. Popular boys (but not girls) were also rated by teachers as higher on social skills and sympathy than other boys, except for controversial boys (who were also high on social skills).

Unlike in the third grade, there were relatively few findings for girls in the sixth grade. One plausible explanation for this sex difference is that most girls were viewed as regulated and socially skilled enough so that there was little variability by sixth grade (there was lower variability in some measures for sixth-grade girls). Alternatively, Indonesian males traditionally might be expected to uphold display rules and emotional scripts related to polite, formal social behaviors more than females (e.g., Mulder, 1989). Thus, teachers and peers might differentiate more among boys in regard to their regulation and emotionality (including suppressing disruptive or strong negative emotions).

Data on the Relation of Parenting to Quality of Indonesian Children's Effortful Control and Social Functioning

In the initial assessment in third grade, our data supported the view that parents' expressions of hostile and abrasive negative emotions were negatively related to children's regulation, and in turn, were associated with low levels of children's social acceptance, social skills, and sympathy (see Eisenberg, Liew et al., 2001). These findings were very similar to those obtained in the United States. However, somewhat more so than in the United States, parental expression of softer negative emotions was also related to high externalizing problem behaviors and low popularity (as well as low regulation). Moreover, unlike in the United States (e.g., Eisenberg, Gershoff et al., 2001; Halberstadt et al., 1999), parents' reported expressions of positive emotions generally were unrelated to children's regulation or social functioning. The difference in the pattern of findings between North American and Indonesian parents' expressions of positive emotions with child outcomes is consistent with traditional

Indonesian attitudes and beliefs about intense emotionality; it is likely that parents' strong expressions of positive emotion are interpreted differently in Indonesia than in the United States (e.g., perhaps as unregulated; see Tsai, 2004). This pattern of findings is consistent with the notion that different cultural views on emotion and the desirability of its regulation may moderate the relations of these variables to children's peer-related competence.

France

France is a European, industrialized Western country, similar to the United States in many respects. However, because socioemotional development is not a topic of interest to many French researchers, little is known about emotion-related regulation and its correlates in France. As proposed in the model, culture is expected to influence the socialization of emotion, as well as emotion-related regulation. Nonetheless, given the similarities between the cultures of France and the United States, the relations among socialization, emotion regulation, adjustment, and social functioning were expected to be similar in the two countries.

Some cross-national differences in parenting may have implications for the development of emotion regulation. Bornstein et al. (1998) found that French mothers believe that their parenting practices have very little influence on their children's development. French mothers also reported that they rely on the child-care system heavily and, in contrast to American parents, rated themselves as having a low investment in parenting. Thus, it is possible that French mothers do not spend a lot of time teaching their children about emotions because they believe that their parenting is not very influential.

Moreover, in a review of the literature, Suizzo (2002) found that, although French parents are concerned with their children being well raised (e.g., traditional social rules, such as politeness, neatness, sharing toys, and being discrete in public, are valued), their children's individuality is also important, and they encourage social and cognitive stimulation. Suizzo further noted that French parents value affection and close relationships, but are also concerned about the self-control of emotions and do not wish for too much closeness with their children. Therefore, it is possible that control of emotion-linked behavior is more valued in France than in the United States. On the other hand, however, French families tend to be less nuclear than in North America (e.g., Canada; Claes, Lacourse, Bouchard, Luckow, & Debra, 2001); families in France tend to have strong intergenerational bonds (D'Costa, 1985). French children may therefore learn about emotions, display rules, and emotion regulation strategies from many people in different complementary ways.

To our knowledge, relevant studies of display rules, emotion knowledge and understanding, and cultural attitudes and beliefs toward emotion and emotion regulation in France are not available. However, results from two different studies on the French emotion words suggest that there are cultural differences in the prototypicality, familiarity, and frequency of emotion words (Van Goozen & Frijda, 1993; Niedenthal et al., 2004). Furthermore, Van Goozen and Frijda (1993) compared several languages on their equivalence in regard to the use of emotion words. They found of the twelve most frequently mentioned emotion words in English and French, only five words were mentioned in both languages (joy, sadness, fear, anger, and happiness). The other seven most frequently used emotion words (in the order of frequency) in French were anxiety (twice, different words in the French language), surprise, gay, disgust, crying, and laughter, whereas the other seven most frequently mentioned emotion words in English were depression, hate, love, confusion, jealousy, excitement, and boredom. These findings highlight the need for studies investigating French attitudes and beliefs on emotions, rather than studies originating from the United States involving an English-based emotion lexicon.

Data on the Relation of Parenting to Quality of French Children's Effortful or Reactive Control and Social Functioning

With a sample of 182 French high school students, the relations among parenting, regulation, impulsivity, and social functioning were investigated (Champion, 2003). Adolescents, their parents, and teachers completed questionnaires on these constructs (using mostly the same or similar measures to those used in prior studies in the United States, China, and Indonesia). Correlational analyses as well as structural equation modeling were used to analyze the data. In regard to parenting, parental expression of emotion in the family was not related to adolescents' effortful control. This finding contrasts with studies done in the United States (with elementary school-aged children; e.g., Eisenberg, Valiente et al., 2003). It is unclear if the difference in findings was the result of the age of the youth in the sample or cultural issues. However, relations similar to the ones found in the United States were found between family expressiveness/parenting and social competence. Adolescents whose families expressed more positive emotions tended to have fewer problem behaviors, whereas adolescents whose families expressed more negative emotions tended to have more problem behaviors. Unexpectedly, the relations between family expressiveness and popularity were weak. Once again, it is unclear if the findings were the result of the age of the youth in the sample or cultural issues.

Relations of Effortful and Reactive Control to French Youths' Social Competence

Although it appears that many of the relations among French students' regulation, impulsivity, and social functioning were similar to those found in the United States, it is important to consider the differences and how the French culture may influence some of these constructs and relations among them.

Although regulation was originally hypothesized to tap attention focusing, attention shifting, and inhibitory control, in this study, parents' reports of attention shifting did not load with the other two constructs. As children grow into adolescence, most of the activities that they have to attend to require attention focusing or inhibitory control, especially in France. School days in France are particularly long, with classes that start at eight in the morning and go until five or even six in the evening. Children come home and still have to focus on homework after school. In addition, the pressure from parents to be "bien élevé" (well-raised; Suizzo, 2002) stresses the importance of being able to inhibit behaviors when needed and to fit the norms. Therefore, it is possible that in France, especially as children get older, attention shifting is not as good an indicator of effortful, voluntary regulation as we have found in the United States (whereas the abilities to focus attention and to inhibit behavior when needed are good measures of regulation). However, it is also possible that it is difficult for adults to differentiate among adolescents (rather than children) who can shift attention because the range of variability may be narrow.

Consistent with findings in the United States (Eisenberg et al., 2000; Eisenberg, Spinrad et al., 2004), effortful control – that is, adolescents' abilities to focus their attention and to inhibit their behaviors when needed – was correlated with greater popularity and better adjustment. In addition, adolescents who were more impulsive tended to have fewer internalizing problems.

However, it is interesting to note that, in contrast with some United States findings and with the proposed model, impulsivity was not related to externalizing and was positively related to popularity. Although it is possible that as children grow older, their ability to use more voluntary processes such as effortful control overrides overt expressions of impulsivity (or more generally, reactive control) in most situations, it is also possible that the cultural context that surrounds French children was responsible for these findings. From the fourth author's recollection of high school in France, the popular youth were the ones who displayed more daring and challenging, and somewhat more impulsive, behaviors. It is possible that some level of impulsive behaviors is considered somewhat desirable and adaptive in France. In fact, in the French culture, one very important value is to have an "esprit de critique" (spirit of critic), which means that a valued and encouraged behavior is to criticize and express one's opinions and thoughts on everything. In high school, the fourth author remembers some professors encouraging students to go on strikes for ideas that they believed in. Adolescents who are more overtly critical and express their opinions and thoughts are likely to be the same adolescents who are spontaneous, daring, and somewhat more impulsive. Therefore, it is possible that "impulsivity" is defined differently and seen as more positive and adaptive in French culture. It would be useful to survey French citizens to assess their definition of the word "impulsive" and if it is seen as positive and desirable.

It appears that there are many commonalities in the processes and means of emotion regulation and their adaptive function in France and the United States. However, the results of this study suggest that the role of culture in the development and adaptive significance of emotion regulation need to be considered even in countries that seem very similar to the United States, including European, industrialized Western countries. Nonetheless, until studies involving North American adolescents are published, it will be unclear if the apparent differences found in this study were the result of culture or the age of the study participants.

There may be some cultural differences in friendship and peer relationships in France that could be explained by differences in emotion regulation. Most people are familiar with the stereotypes that French people are colder and ruder than Americans. However, once somebody gets to know French people, he or she would likely notice that they often are quite friendly and open to a genuine friendship. It is possible that French people inhibit their facial expressions and behaviors more than Americans, which would explain this first impression of "coldness and rudeness." This is only speculation, which highlights the pressing need for more research looking at culture and emotion regulation.

In summary, the role of the French culture in socialization, emotion-related regulation, and peer interaction is not very well understood. Although studies replicating some of the findings found in the United States are helpful in comparing the relations among these constructs, there is a pressing need for research establishing similarities or differences of these constructs themselves. In addition, it appears that researchers need to be careful when translating measures from English to French that include emotion-related constructs. Because of differences in conceptions of some emotions, there may be subtle differences in how the expression and control of emotions affect French children's peer relationships.

Conclusions and Methodological Challenges

Our findings suggest that emotion-related regulation relates in a similar manner to peer and social competence in cultures that differ considerably. Thus, some paths in our model – especially the path between emotion-related regulation and quality of peer relationships – may vary relatively little, at least in industrialized societies. Cross-cultural differences in the relations of reactive over/undercontrol (e.g., impulsivity, inhibition) to social functioning may be somewhat more likely, but may be changing as Eastern cultures are increasingly exposed to Western values and norms. In addition, there appear to be some similarities, as well as differences, across Asian/Southeast Asian cultures and the United States in parenting variables that are linked to children's regulation (and social competence). Our limited data support the tentative conclusion that there may be larger cultural differences in links of emotion-related socialization with children's regulation (and, hence, their social competence and adjustment) than in associations between children's regulation and socioemotional functioning. However, because the research we reported was conducted within a culture (although the Indonesian data were compared with findings with the same measures in the United States), it is difficult to draw firm conclusions about cross-cultural differences in model paths (see Figure 8.1). Research involving similar populations and measures conducted simultaneously in different cultures is needed to provide a stronger test of the hypothesized pathways in our model.

The study of emotion regulation with peer and social functioning in multiple cultures affords opportunities to explore how such processes operate in diverse (similar and contrasting) contexts. However, studying emotion regulation and peer or social competence in multiple cultures also raises thorny methodological issues. We highlight several methodology issues, while at the same time acknowledging the difficulty in overcoming some of them.

Before making comparisons between cultures, it would be useful to assess the meaning of emotion regulation and peer/social competence in the cultures that are being studied. This is because it is desirable to use culturally derived rather than imposed meanings to establish that the same or similar constructs are actually being compared. For example, to compare across cultures, it is helpful to establish what it means (for particular age groups or gender) to be emotionally regulated or to be socially skilled or competent with peers in the target cultures. Some relevant information on local meaning of constructs sometimes is available in the writings of anthropologists and other social scientists. Indeed, one way to establish the meanings of emotions and social behaviors includes the study of local norms and beliefs. Obviously, it is advantageous to consult local or multicultural research associates and members of the cultures being studied (including the use of focus groups with community or indigenous members) to ensure the integrity of interpretations as culturally sensitive and grounded. We suggest that it is often advantageous to study socioemotional development within cultures to determine culturally grounded meanings of constructs before comparing across cultures. Moreover, once measures are developed, statistical information on cultural equivalence, although often difficult to obtain, would be informative.

To arrive at findings and interpretations that are culturally sensitive and grounded, measures or instruments that assess emotion regulation and social competence need to be ecologically valid (including accurate translation of measures and research protocol to reflect local meanings). Moreover, because there are multiple ways that emotion regulation and social competence could be expressed or demonstrated, emotion regulation ideally should be tapped through multiple modalities (e.g., verbal, facial, behavioral, or physiological responding). Of course, difficulties in conducting research in other cultures often can preclude a multimethod approach. Nonetheless, until more research involves a multimethod, multicultural approach, we will not fully understand the role of emotion-related regulation in the development of children's socioemotional competence.

Acknowledgments

This research was supported by a grant from the National Institutes of Mental Health to Nancy Eisenberg.

References

Ahadi, S. A., Rothart, M. K., & Ye, R. (1993). Children's temperament in the US and China: Similarities and differences. *European Journal of Personality, 7*, 359–377.

Belsky, J., Friedman, S. L., & Hsieh, K. H. (2001). Testing a core emotion-regulation prediction: Does early attentional persistence moderate the effect of infant negative emotionality on later development? *Child Development, 72*(1), 123–133.

Bornstein, M., Haynes, M., Azuma, H., Galperin, C., Maital, S., Ogino, M., et al. (1998). A cross-national study of self-evaluations and attributions in parenting: Argentina, Belgium, France, Israel, Italy, Japan, and the United States. *Developmental Psychology, 34*, 662–676.

Boyum, L. A., & Parke, R. D. (1995). The role of family emotional expressiveness in the development of children's social competence. *Journal of Marriage and the Family, 57*, 593–608.

Briggs, J. L. (1998). *Inuit morality play: The emotional education of a three-year-old.* New Haven, CT: Yale University Press.

Cacioppo, J. T., Gardner, W. L., & Berntson, G. G. (1999). The affect system has parallel and integrative processing components: Form follows function. *Journal of Personality and Social Psychology, 76*, 839–855.

Campos, J. J., Frankel, C. B., & Camras, L. (2004). On the nature of emotion regulation. *Child Development, 75*(2), 377–394.

Camras, L., Oster, H., Campos, J., Campos, R., Ujiie, T., Miyake, K. et al. (1998). Production of emotional facial expressions in American, Japanese, and Chinese infants. *Developmental Psychology, 34*, 616–628.

Champion, C. (2003). *The role of socialization, control, and resiliency in French adolescents' social functioning*. Unpublished Master's thesis, Arizona State University.

Chang, L. (2003). Variable effects of children's aggression, social withdrawal, and prosocial leadership as functions of teacher beliefs and behaviors. *Child Development, 74*, 535–548.

Chang, L., Schwartz, D., Dodge, K. A., & McBride-Chang, C. (2003). Harsh parenting in relation to child emotion regulation and aggression. *Journal of Family Psychology, 17*, 598–606.

Cheah, C. S. L., & Rubin, K. H. (2004). European American and mainland Chinese mothers' responses to aggression and social withdrawal in preschoolers. *International Journal of Behavioral Development, 28*, 83–94.

Chen, X., Cen, G., Li, D., & He, Y. (2005). Social functioning and adjustment in Chinese children: The imprint of historical time. *Child Development, 76*, 182–195.

Chen, X., Hastings, P. D., Rubin, K. H., Chen, H., Cen, G., & Stewart, S. L. (1998). Child-rearing attitudes and behavioral inhibition in Chinese and Canadian toddlers: A cross-cultural study. *Developmental Psychology, 34*, 677–686.

Chen, X., Rubin, K. H., & Li, Z. (1995). Social functioning and adjustment in Chinese children: A longitudinal study. *Developmental Psychology, 31*, 531–539.

Chen, X., Rubin, K. H., & Sun, Y. (1992). Social reputation and peer relationships in Chinese and Canadian children: A cross-cultural study. *Child Development, 63*, 1336–1343.

Claes, M., Lacourse, E., Bouchard, C., & Luckow, D. (2001). Adolescents' relationships with members of the extended family and non-related adults in four countries: Canada, France, Belgium and Italy. *International Journal of Adolescence and Youth, 9*, 207–225.

Coie, J. D., Dodge, K. A., & Kupersmidt, J. B. (1990). Peer group behavior and social status. In S. R. Asher & J. D. Coie (Eds.), *Peer rejection in childhood* (pp. 17–59). Cambridge, England: Cambridge University Press.

Cole, P. M., Martin, S. E., & Dennis, T. A. (2004). Emotion regulation as a scientific construct: Methodological challenges and directions for child development research. *Child Development, 75*, 317–333.

Cole, P. M., & Tamang, B. L. (1998). Nepali children's ideas about emotional displays in hypothetical challenges. *Developmental Psychology, 34*, 640–646.

D'Costa, R. (1985). Family and generations in sociology: A review of recent research in France. *Journal of Comparative Family Studies, 16*, 319–327.

Derryberry, D., & Rothbart, M. K. (1997). Reactive and effortful processes in the organization of temperament. *Development and Psychopathology, 9*, 633–652.

Eisenberg, N., Cumberland, A., & Spinrad, T. L. (1998). Parental socialization of emotion. *Psychological Inquiry, 9*, 241–273.

Eisenberg, N., Fabes, R. A., Guthrie, I. K., & Reiser, M. (2000). Dispositional emotionality and regulation: Their role in predicting quality of social functioning. *Journal of Personality and Social Psychology, 78*, 136–157.

Eisenberg, N., Fabes, R. A., & Murphy, B. (1995). Relations of shyness and low sociability to regulation and emotionality. *Journal of Personality and Social Psychology, 68*, 505–517.

Eisenberg, N., Fabes, R. A., Shepard, S. A., Murphy, B. C., Jones, J., & Guthrie, I. K. (1998). Contemporaneous and longitudinal prediction of children's sympathy from dispositional regulation and emotionality. *Developmental Psychology, 34*, 910–924.

Eisenberg, N., Gershoff, E. T., Fabes, R. A., Shepard, S. A., Cumberland, A. J., Lososya, S. H., et al. (2001). Mothers' emotional expressivity and children's behavior problems and social competence: Mediation through children's regulation. *Developmental Psychology, 37*, 475–490.

Eisenberg, N., Guthrie, I. K., Fabes, R. A., Reiser, M., Murphy, B. C., Holgren, R., et al. (1997). The relations of regulation and emotionality to resiliency and competent social functioning in elementary school children. *Child Development, 68*, 295–311.

Eisenberg, N., Liew, J., & Pidada, S. U. (2001). The relations of parental emotional expressivity with quality of Indonesian children's social functioning. *Emotion, 1*, 116–136.

Eisenberg, N., Valiente, C., Morris, A. S., Fabes, R. A., Cumberland, A., Reiser, M., Gershoff, E. T., Shepard, S. A., & Losoya, S. (2003). Longitudinal relations among parental emotional expressivity, children's regulation, and quality of socioemotional functioning. *Developmental Psychology, 39*, 2–19.

Eisenberg, N., Liew, J., & Pidada, S. U. (2004). The longitudinal relations of regulation and emotionality to quality of Indonesian children's socioemotional functioning. *Developmental Psychology, 40*, 805–812.

Eisenberg, N., Losoya, S., & Spinrad, T. L. (2003). Affect and prosocial responding. In R. J. Davidson, K. Scherer, & H. H. Goldsmith (Eds.), *Handbook of affective science* (pp. 787–803). Oxford, England: Oxford University Press.

Eisenberg, N., & Morris, A. S. (2002). Children's emotion-related regulation. In R. Kail (Ed.), *Advances in child development and behavior* (Vol. 30; pp. 190–229). Amsterdam: Academic Press.

Eisenberg, N., Pidada, S., & Liew, J. (2001). The relations of regulation and negative emotionality to Indonesian children's social functioning. *Child Development, 72*, 1747–1763.

Eisenberg, N., & Spinrad, T. L. (2004). Emotion-related regulation: Sharpening the definition. *Child Development, 75*, 334–339.

Eisenberg, N., Spinrad, T. L., & Cumberland, A. (1998). Socialization of emotion: Reply to reviewers. *Psychological Inquiry, 9*, 317–333.

Eisenberg, N., Spinrad, T. L., Fabes, R. A., Reiser, M., Cumberland, A., Shepard, S. A., et al. (2004). The relations of effortful control and impulsivity to children's resiliency and adjustment. *Child Development, 75*, 25–46.

Geertz, C. (1976). *The religion of Java*. Chicago: University of Chicago Press.

Greenberger, E., Chen, C., Tally, S. R., & Dong, Q. (2000). Family, peer, and individual correlates of depressive symptomatology among U.S. and Chinese adolescents. *Journal of Consulting and Clinical Psychology, 2*, 209–219.

Greenfield, P. M., Keller, H., Fuligni, A., & Maynard, A. (2003). Cultural pathways through universal development. Development. *Annual Review of Psychology, 54*, 461–490.

Halberstadt, A. G., Cassidy, J., Stifter, C. A., Parke R. D., & Fox, N. A. (1995). Self-expressiveness within the family context: Psychometric support for a new measure. *Psychological Assessment, 7*, 93–103.

Halberstadt, A. G., Crisp, V. W., & Eaton, K. L. (1999). Family expressiveness: A retrospective and new directions for research. In P. Philippot, R. S. Feldman, & E. Coats (Eds.), *The social context of nonverbal behavior* (pp. 109–155). New York: Cambridge University Press.

Hart, C. H., Yang, C., Nelson, L. J., Robinson, C. C., Olsen, J. A., Nelson, D. A., et al. (2000). Peer acceptance in early childhood and subtypes of socially withdrawn behavior in China, Russia, and the United States. *International Journal of Behavioral Development, 24*, 73–81.

Harter, S. (1979). *Perceived competence scale for children: Manual.* Denver: University of Denver, Colorado.

Heider, K. G. (1991). *Landscapes of emotion.* Cambridge, UK: Cambridge University Press.

Hofstede, G. (1991). *Cultures and organizations: Software of the mind.* London: McGraw-Hill.

Kang, S., Shaver, P. R., Sue, S., Min, K., & Jing, H. (2003). Culture-specific patterns in the prediction of life satisfaction: Roles of emotion, relationship quality, and self-esteem. *Personality and Social Psychology Bulletin, 29*, 1596–1608.

Kleinman, A. (1980). *Patients and healers in the context of culture.* Berkeley: University of California Press.

Lillard, A. (1998). Ethnopsychologies: Cultural variations in theories of mind. *Psychological Bulletin, 123*, 3–32.

Lochman, J. E., & Conduct Problems Prevention Research Group. (1995). Screening of child behavior problems for prevention programs at school entry. *Journal of Consulting and Clinical Psychology, 63*, 549–559.

Lutz, C. (1985). Ethnopsychology compared to what? Explaining behavior and consciousness among the Ifaluk. In G. White & J. Kirkpatrick (Eds.), *Person, self, and experience* (pp. 35–79). Berkeley: University of California Press.

Magnis-Suseno, F. (1997). *Javanese ethics and world-view: The Javanese idea of the good life.* Jakarta: Penerbit PT Gramedia Pustake utama.

Markus, H. R., & Kitayama, S. (1991). Culture and the self: Implications for cognition, emotion, and motivation. *Psychological Review, 48*, 224–253.

Masten, A., Morison, P., & Pelligrini, D. (1985). A revised class play method of peer assessment. *Child Development, 21*, 523–533.

Matsumoto, D. (1993). Ethnic differences in affect intensity, emotional judgments, display rule attitudes, and self-reported emotional expression in an American sample. *Motivation and Emotion, 17*, 107–123.

Menon, U., & Shweder, R. A. (1994). Kali's tongue: Cultural psychology and the power of shame in Orissa, India. In S. Kitayama & H. Markus (Eds.), *Emotion and culture* (pp. 241–282). Washington, DC: American Psychological Association.

Mesquita, B., & Frijda, N. H. (1992). Cultural variations in emotions: A review. *Psychological Bulletin, 112*, 179–204.

Miller, P., & Sperry, L. L. (1987). The socialization of anger and aggression. *Merrill-Palmer Quarterly, 33*, 1–31.

Mirsky, A. F. (1996). Disorders of attention: A neuropsychological perspective. In G. R. Lyon & N. A. Krasnegor (Eds.), *Attention, memory, and executive function* (pp. 71–93). Baltimore: Brookes .

Mulder, N. (1989). *Individual and society in Java: A cultural analysis.* Yogualarta, Indonesia: Gadjah Mada University Press.

Niedenthal, P. M., Auxiette, C., Nugier, A., Dalle, N., Bonim, P., & Fayol, M. (2004). A prototype analysis of the French category "émotion." *Cognition and Emotion, 18*, 289–312.

Oyserman, D., Coon, H. M., & Kemmelmeier, M. (2002). Rethinking individualism and collectivism: Evaluation of theoretical assumptions and meta-analyses. *Psychological Bulletin, 128*(1), 3–72.

Parker, G., Gladstone, G., & Chee, K. T. (2001). Depression in the planet's largest ethnic group: The Chinese. *American Journal of Psychiatry, 158*, 857–864.

Pickering, A. D., & Gray, J. A. (1999). The neuroscience of personality. In L. Pervin & O. John (Eds.), *Handbook of personality* (pp. 277–299). San Francisco: Guilford.

Posner, M. I., & DiGirolamo, G. J. (2000). Cognitive neuroscience: Origins and promise. *Psychological Bulletin, 126*, 873–889.

Posner, M. I., & Rothbart, M. K. (1998). Attention, self-regulation, and consciousness. *Transactions of the Philosophical Society of London, B,* 1915–1927.

Potter, S. H. (1988). The cultural construction of emotion in rural Chinese social life. *Ethos, 16*(2), 181–208.

Rothbart, M. K., Ahadi, S. A., Hershey, K. L., & Fisher, P. (2001). Investigations of temperament at three to seven years: The Children's Behavior Questionnaire. *Child Development, 72*, 1394–1408.

Rothbart, M. K., & Bates, J. E. (1998). Temperament. In W. Damon (Series Ed.) & N. Eisenberg (Vol. Ed.), *Handbook of child psychology: Vol. 3. Social, emotional, and personality development* (5th ed., pp. 105–176). New York: Wiley.

Rothbart, M. K., & Bates, J. E. (in press). Temperament. In W. Damon & R. M. Lerner (Series Ed.) and N. Eisenberg (Vol. Ed.), *Handbook of Child Psychology, Vol. 3. Social, emotional, and personality development* (6th ed). New York: Wiley.

Rubin, K. H., Bukowski, W., & Parker, J. G. (1998). Peer interactions, relationships, and groups. In W. Damon (Series Ed.) & N. Eisenberg (Vol. Ed.), *Handbook of child psychology: Vol. 3. Social, emotional, and personality development* (5th ed., pp. 619–700). New York: Wiley.

Schwartz, D., Chang, L., & Farver, J. M. (2001). Correlates of victimization in Chinese children's peer groups. *Developmental Psychology, 37*, 520–532.

Spinrad, T. L., Eisenberg, N., Cumberland, A., Fabes, R. A., Valiente, C., Shepard, S. A., et al. (2004). *The relations of temperamentally based control processes to children's social competence: A longitudinal study.* Manuscript submitted for publication.

Steinberg, L., Dornbusch, S. M., & Brown, B. B. (1992). Ethnic differences in adolescent achievement: An ecological perspective. *American Psychologist, 47*, 723–729.

Stewart, S. M., Kennard, B. D., Lee, P. W. H., Hughes, C. W., Mayes, T. L., Emslie, G. J., et al. (2004). A cross-cultural investigation of cognitions and depressive symptoms in adolescents. *Journal of Abnormal Psychology, 113*, 248–257.

Stifter, C. A., Spinrad, T. L., & Braungart-Rieker, J. M. (1999). Toward a developmental model of child compliance: The role of emotion regulation in infancy. *Child Development, 70*, 21–32.

Suizzo, M. (2002). French parents' cultural models and childrearing beliefs. *International Journal of Behavioral Development, 26*, 297–307.

Tsai, J. L. (2004, May). Affect valuation: Theory, measurement, and cultural variation. Paper presented at the American Psychological Society, Chicago.

Van Goozen, S., & Frijda, N. H. (1993). Emotion words used in six European countries. *European Journal of Social Psychology, 23*, 89–95.

Wang, Q. (2003). Emotion situation knowledge in American and Chinese preschool children and adults. *Cognition and Emotion, 17*, 725–746.

Wang, Q. (2004). The emergence of cultural self-constructs: Autobiographical memory and self-description in European American and Chinese children. *Developmental Psychology, 40*, 3–15.

Wellenkamp, J. C. (1995). Everyday conceptions of distress: A case study from Toraja, Indonesia. In J. A. Russell, J. M. Fernandez-Dois, A. S. R. Manstead, & J. C. Wellenkamp (Eds.), *Everyday conceptions of emotion: An introduction to the psychology, anthropology, and linguistics of emotion. NATO ASI Seies D: Behavioural and social sciences* (Vol. 81, pp. 267–280). Dordrecht, the Netherlands: Kluwer Academic Press.

Wilkan, U. (1989). Managing the heart to brighten face and soul: Emotions in Balinese morality and health care. *American Ethologists, 16*, 294–312.

Wu, P., Robinson, C. C., Yang, C., Hart, C. H., Olsen, S. F., Porter, C. L., et al. (2002). Similarities and differences in mothers' parenting of preschoolers in China and the United States. *International Journal of Behavioral Development, 26*, 481–491.

Zahn-Waxler, C., Friedman, R. J., Cole, P. M., Mizuta, I., & Hiruma, N. (1996). Japanese and United States preschool children's responses to conflict and distress. *Child Development, 67*, 2462–2477.

Zhou, Q., Eisenberg, N., Wang, Y., & Reiser, M. (2004). Chinese children's effortful control and dispositional anger/frustration: Relations to parenting styles and children's social functioning. *Developmental Psychology, 40*, 352–366.

Commentary I

9 Temperamental and Emotional Influences on Peer Relationships

Joan Stevenson-Hinde

Following on from the book's first section concerning theoretical and methodological issues, the three chapters in this section focus on "within-individual" influences on peer relationships, as a logical prelude to the final sections concerning interactions with parents and peers. This organization reflects the levels of analysis outlined by Hinde (1987), which range from the individual to interactions, relationships, groups, and society (Fig. 9.1; further described in Chapter 6, p. 128). As indicated by the bidirectional arrows in Figure 9.1, each level influences and is influenced by sociocultural structure, with its beliefs, values, conventions, and institutions. Chen, Wang, and DeSouza's model (Chapter 6, Fig. 6.1) elaborates on this by considering specific individual characteristics in relation to their value in self-oriented versus group-oriented cultures. Particular characteristics, such as shyness–inhibition, are arranged on two main dimensions, namely social initiative and self-control. These are considered to be manifestations in the social domain of Rothbart's fundamental temperamental dimensions, namely reactivity and regulation (Rothbart & Bates, 1998).

Within Rothbart's framework, behavioral assessments include activity, duration of orienting, distress to limitations, smiling, soothability, and *fear*. Indeed, all the major theories of childhood temperament contain a dimension related to fearfulness (reviewed in Goldsmith et al., 1987), a trait recognized over many years (e.g., Kagan, 1994), in many species (Gosling & John, 1999), including other primates (Stevenson-Hinde, Stillwell-Barnes, & Zunz, 1980). In addition, fearfulness is a particularly salient individual characteristic in childhood, when increasing exploration beyond the family leads to encounters with unfamiliar people and events. Fearfulness is therefore an excellent choice for seeking relations with cultural contexts, as indeed Chen and his group have been doing over the past 15 years.

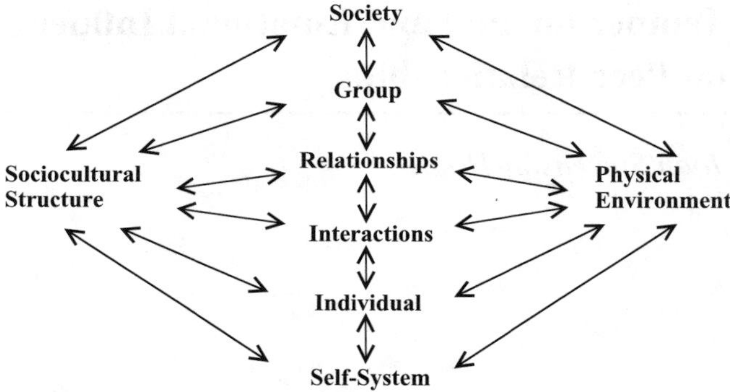

Figure 9.1. A diagram of different levels of social complexity. Each level influences and is influenced by others and by the sociocultural structure (adapted from Hinde, 1987).

Similar biological bases of fearfulness have been identified across many species, and it is reasonable to suppose that neurophysiological mechanisms of fear should operate in similar ways across different cultures. This is consistent with the view set out in Chapter 8 by Eisenberg et al. that "basic, temperamentally based modes of regulation are similar in people of all cultures.... Moreover, if subcortical systems (such as the limbic system) play a role in reactive over- and under-control, these systems are likely to function similarly in most people" (p. 176). For example, behavioral inhibition has been associated with a high and steady heart rate, elevated cortisol, and right frontal (vs. left frontal) EEG asymmetry. Current models based on research with both animals and humans focus on variation in the excitability of neural circuits in the limbic system, with the amygdala playing a central role (reviewed in Davidson & Rickman, 1999; Marshall & Stevenson-Hinde, 2001, see Fig. 3.1; Schmidt, Polak, & Spooner, 2001).

Furthermore, both twin and adoption studies indicate that individual differences in fearfulness are heritable, with genetic factors accounting for around 40 percent to 60 percent of the variance (reviewed in Schmidt et al., 2001). Molecular genetic studies identify genes that code for the regulation and transportation of neurotransmitters and relate them to complex human traits, such as novelty seeking and shyness (reviewed in Plomin & Rutter, 1998). For example, dopamine D4 receptor (DRD4) polymorphisms (long alleles) are associated with novelty seeking and related behavior. Because short alleles code for a receptor apparently more efficient in binding dopamine, "the theory is that individuals with the long-repeat DRD4 allele are dopamine deficient and seek novelty to increase dopamine release" (Plomin & Caspi, 1998,

p. 393). In addition, a polymorphism in the promoter region of the serotonin transporter gene (5-HTTLPR) has been associated with anxiety-related traits (Lesch et al., 1996). A short allele may contribute to reduced serotonin promotion and expression. Without the regulating effects of serotonin, the amygdala and hypothalamic-pituitary-adrenal system become overactive, leading to the physiological profile of fearful or anxious individuals (Schmidt et al., 2001). In brief, it seems highly likely that such basic neurobiological and genetic *mechanisms* of behavior should operate across different cultures. What could *differ* across cultures is the *threshold of activation* of such mechanisms, with bidirectional effects on behavioral development. As Chen et al. point out, further research is needed here.

Like fearful behavior, attachment behavior is also universal. Indeed, it was in a non-Western culture with multiple caregivers in Uganda that an infant's use of mother as a "secure base" was first fully appreciated and documented (Ainsworth, 1967). Bowlby postulated that both sets of behavior share a common evolutionary function: protection from harm (Bowlby, 1969/1982). The argument is that individuals who exhibited fear of the unfamiliar would have been more apt to survive and leave offspring who in turn reproduce – that is, to have increased their inclusive fitness – than those who did not. In a similar way, attachment behavior and its complement, caregiving behavior, would have been selected for during the course of evolution.

However, universality does not imply heritability. Neither a carefully conducted behavior genetic study of two samples of twins in London and Leiden (Bokhorst et al., 2003) nor a molecular genetic study with a reasonably large sample size ($N = 132$; Bakermans-Kranenburg & van IJzendoorn, 2004) found significant genetic influences on patterns of attachment. Instead, the key influence on patterns of attachment is maternal (or caregiver) styles of interaction. It is worth emphasizing in this section that early mother–child interactions are highly relevant to emotional development. In Bowlby's own words:

> What is happening during these early years is that the pattern of communication that a child adopts towards his mother comes to match the pattern of communication that she has been adopting towards him. Furthermore, from the findings stemming from the Adult Attachment Interview, it seems clear that the pattern of communication a mother adopts towards her infant and young child is modelled on the pattern characteristic of her own intra-psychic communications. Open and coherent intra-psychic communication in a mother is associated with open and coherent two-way communication with her child, and vice versa. (1991, pp. 295–296)

Thanks to the foundations built by Mary Ainsworth, a significant relation between observed maternal "sensitive responsiveness" and security of attachment has been found in many cultures, ranging from Baltimore (Ainsworth et al., 1978) to Indonesian communities (Zevalkink, 1997). Indeed, a meta-analysis of many studies, including non-Western cultures, has shown significant associations between sensitivity and security (deWolff & van IJzendoorn, 1997). Furthermore, intervention studies indicate the causal influence of maternal sensitivity in promoting security (Bakermans-Kranenburg, van IJzendoorn, & Juffer, 2003). In their review chapter, van IJzendoorn and Bakermans-Kranenburg (2004) conclude:

> In sum, the causal role of maternal sensitivity in the formation of the infant–mother attachment relationship is a strongly corroborated finding. Correlational, experimental, and cross-cultural studies have replicated the association between sensitivity and attachment numerous times, and through different measures and designs. In general, the maternal impact on the infant-mother attachment relationship has been shown to be much larger than the impact of child characteristics such as temperament. During the first few years after birth, parents are more powerful than their children in shaping the child–parent bond." (p. 208)

Thus, the phenomenon of infants becoming attached to one or more specific caregivers, with security dependent on child-rearing antecedents of sensitive responsiveness to the infant's signals appears to be universal. It is essential to appreciate that *security* concerns not all of a child's interactions with a caregiver, but only how a child interacts with the caregiver when stressed. Although based on careful observations, it is an assessment of the quality (vs. quantity) of those interactions. Therefore, it is not surprising that the coding of security involves "reading through" temperamental aspects of the child (such as fear of the unfamiliar) or personality of the mother (such as sociability).

Now if factors promoting maternal sensitivity were to vary in a systematic way across cultures, then one would expect a difference in the *distribution* of attachment patterns. Hinde and Stevenson-Hinde (1991) identified three desiderata – biological, cultural, and psychological – which, although interrelated, may differ, especially in modern industrialized societies. Thus, a pattern required for the "biological desiderata" of increasing inclusive fitness need not be the same as a pattern fitting "cultural desiderata" (e.g., in Bielefeld, where an avoidant pattern was the norm vs. in Regensburg, where a secure pattern predominated; Grossmann et al., 1988). However, it was the secure pattern that Bowlby, as a practicing psychiatrist, saw as absolutely basic for "psychological well-being," including a sense of competence even in difficult circumstances. Indeed, if the strange situation is properly carried out, it does appear that security is the norm in most cultures (van IJzendoorn & Sagi, 1999).

Concerning attachment in Asian infants, Chen et al.'s statement that "Asian infants have been found to be more fearful and insecure and display more ambivalent behaviors in the strange situation than Western infants" (p. 129) is possibly misleading. Because the temperamental construct "fearful" is conceptually distinct from the relational construct "insecure," one should be cautious about considering them as one (see, e.g., Stevenson-Hinde, 2005). One study referred to (Mizuta et al., 1996) actually found that "Japanese and US dyads did *not* [ital. mine] differ in overall levels of security and sensitivity in separation and reunion behaviours" (p. 141). Furthermore, a validated attachment coding system was not used. As Mizuta et al. themselves caution, the

> findings are in need of replication before accepting them as firmly established. The Japanese children and their mothers were temporarily living outside their own country. We do not yet know if we would find similar results in Japanese dyads living in Japan. Also, we did not use traditional methods to assess attachment organisation, making direct comparisons of our findings with those obtained from other attachment studies impossible. (1996, p. 156).

The other study Chen et al. refer to is a much-cited Japanese study by Miyake, Chen, and Campos (1985). Although they *did* find a possibly higher than expected proportion of children classified as "ambivalent," their *N* of only 25, plus their modification of the strange situation, renders their findings questionable. That is, rather than the recommended procedure of curtailing a three-minute separation episode very soon after any distress occurs (e.g., Ainsworth et al., 1978), which is routinely used even in Western samples, Miyake et al. curtailed an episode only after two minutes of distress had occurred. After such prolonged distress, most twelve-month-olds, in any culture, would be so upset that they would be difficult to soothe on reunion and therefore would fit an "ambivalent," classification. Not surprisingly with this procedure, 28 percent of infants were classified as "ambivalent," and no infants were classified as "avoidant."

Turning to China, in a strange situation study carried out in Beijing (Hu & Meng, 1996), the distributions were remarkably similar to the global ones: 68 percent secure infant–mother dyads, 16 percent avoidant, and 16 percent ambivalent. All the subjects (sixteen boys, fifteen girls) were only children, and all but one family lived with grandparents. Thus, China could provide a fertile area for research, on attachment to grandmother as well as to mother (for a comprehensive review of cross-cultural patterns, see van IJzendoorn & Sagi, 1999).

Chen's research group has shown that, compared with Western children, Chinese children tended to display more shy behavior in novel situations. Furthermore, in their early samples, shyness was associated with having mothers who were accepting and approving, and peers who were supportive and cooperative. Such positive associations with shyness continued into middle and later childhood. For example, a longitudinal study of a Chinese sample showed that shyness in early childhood predicted later sociometric status, social and academic competence, and indices of psychological well-being.

Now in both the United Kingdom and the United States, shyness (i.e., high behavioral inhibition) has been significantly associated with an insecure–ambivalent pattern of attachment (Stevenson-Hinde & Marshall, 1999; reviewed in Stevenson-Hinde, 2005). This raises the question of whether such a relation would hold in a culture that approves of shyness. Quite possibly the relation would hold. As we have seen, insecurity is associated with insensitive maternal responsiveness to infants' signals, and mothers of insecure–ambivalent children are also unpredictable. Thus, their "infants live with the constant fear of being left vulnerable and alone . . . the anxiety associated with this fear of separation lasts beyond infancy as well" (Weinfield et al., 1999, p. 78). In this way, an insecure–ambivalent pattern of attachment would promote high behavioral inhibition *relative to the cultural norm*. Furthermore, one might predict that the cultural norm for behavioral inhibition would be associated with security, because secure children do not tend to be "extreme in either the inhibited or uninhibited direction" (Calkins & Fox, 1992, p. 1469; Stevenson-Hinde & Marshall, 1999). If so, then the distribution of patterns of attachment would be similar to universal ones, as indeed shown by the Chinese attachment study (Hu & Meng, 1996) mentioned previously.

Perhaps uniquely, Chen et al.'s chapter documents changes over time within a culture. It presents a "natural experiment" on the effect of changing cultural attitudes and illustrates the need to specify exactly *when* data were collected. That is, although the aforementioned positive relations with shyness occurred in 1990, they became less in 1998 and reversed in 2002, when shyness became associated with peer rejection, school problems, and depression. These changes were associated with economic reform toward a capitalistic system and a competitive environment, valuing assertiveness rather than shyness. This neatly illustrates the importance of identifying particularly relevant characteristics of a culture in order to make clear links with behavioral development, as indeed suggested by Eisenberg et al. in their conclusions.

Chen et al. note that, unlike in individualistic Western cultures, in collectivist societies, social initiative is not so highly valued, and children are encouraged to consider others and exert self-control from a very early age. Regarding Nepal as "a collectivist society where the sense of self is defined in an interdependent manner rather than in the independent way typical in the West" (Chapter 7, p. 2), Cole, Walker, and Lama-Tamang are concerned with implications for emotion regulation, not only between West and East, but also within Nepal. They were able to identify differences between two collectivist societies in rural Nepal: the Brahmans, who are high-caste Hindus and the Tamang, who practice a form of Tibetan Buddhism and who are looked down on, reinforced by historical and sociopolitical conditions that created a majority/minority structure between these two groups. Buddhism discourages dwelling on emotions and regards anger as destructive and interfering with inner peace. But Hinduism, with its caste system, cultivates pride and superiority, so that it may be valuable to access anger when others threaten one's spiritual purity and attainment of goals.

When vignettes were read to children, emotional reactions to challenging situations differed accordingly. In both Nepalese cultures, the appearance of shame indicates an understanding that respect for others comes before one's own needs. However, both feeling shame and expressing it were endorsed more by the subordinate Tamang children than by the Brahmans (Table 7.2). With anger, the Tamang children were reluctant to endorse it and appeared to engage in secondary appraisals of situations to avoid anger. Both Brahman and U.S. children did endorse feeling angry, but unlike the U.S. children, the Brahman children did not want others to know they were angry. Thus, only in the Western culture was the overt expression of anger endorsed. Returning to Chen et al.'s circle diagram (Chapter 6, Fig. 6.1), anger could be placed in the upper left quadrant, perhaps between defiance and hostile aggression. And perhaps shame could be placed in the lower right, along with shyness.

In addition to collectivism versus individualism, Eisenberg et al. identify cultural differences in attitudes toward the expression of emotions. For example, in France, an "esprit de critique" is valued, to the extent of professors encouraging students to go on strikes for ideas that they believe in. Sadly, any such "esprit" in the United States seems to have been suffocated post-September 11th. Eisenberg et al. consider similarities and differences in relations between emotions and social functioning in children from three different cultures, China, Indonesia, and France. Their wide-ranging review is related to a conceptual model of culture, emotion regulation, and peer context (Chapter 8, Fig. 8.1). They found that "some paths in our model – especially the path between emotion-related regulation and quality of peer relationships – may vary relatively little, at least in industrialized societies" (p. **X**). Their overall conclusion is that "there may be larger cultural differences in links of emotion-related socialization with children's regulation (and, hence, their social competence and adjustment) than in associations between children's regulation and socioemotional functioning" (p. **X**). Taken together, the three chapters in this section illustrate how well-documented characteristics of different cultures may influence salient characteristics of children, with the additional suggestion that influences are bidirectional (Fig. 9.1).

References

Ainsworth, M. D. S. (1967). Infancy in Uganda: Infant care and the growth of love. Baltimore: Johns Hopkins University Press.

Ainsworth, M. D. S., Blehar, M. C., Waters, E., & Wall, S. (1978). *Patterns of attachment.* Hillsdale, NJ: Lawrence Erlbaum Associates.

Bakermans-Kranenburg, M. J., & van IJzendoorn, M. H. (2004). No association of the dopamine D4 receptor (DRD4) and -521 C/T promoter polymorphisms with infant attachment disorganization. *Attachment & Human Development, 6*, 211–218.

Bakermans-Kranenburg, M. J., van IJzendoorn, M. H., & Juffer, F. (2003). Less is more: Meta-analyses of sensitivity and attachment interventions in early childhood. *Psychological Bulletin, 129*, 195–215.

Bokhorst, C. L., Bakermans-Kranenburg, M. J., Fearon, R. M. P., van IJzendoorn, M. H., Fonagy, P., Schuengel, C. (2003). The importance of shared environment in mother-infant attachment security: A behavioral genetic study. *Child Development, 74*, 1769–1782.

Bowlby, J. (1969/1982). *Attachment and loss, Vol. I: Attachment.* London: Hogarth Press.

Bowlby, J. (1991). Postscript. In C. M. Parkes, J. Stevenson-Hinde, & P. Marris (Eds.), *Attachment across the life cycle* (pp. 293–297). London: Routledge.

Calkins, S. D., & Fox, N. A. (1992). The relations among infant temperament, security of attachment, and behavioral inhibition at twenty-four months. *Child Development, 63*, 1456–1472.

Davidson, R. J., & Rickman, M. (1999). Behavioral inhibition and the emotional circuitry of the brain. In L. A. Schmidt & J. Schulkin (Eds.), *Extreme fear, shyness, and social phobia* (pp. 67–87). Oxford, England: Oxford University Press.

DeWolff, M. S., & van IJzendoorn, M. H. (1997). Sensitivity and attachment: A meta-analysis on parental antecedents of infant attachment. *Child Development, 68*, 571–591.

Goldsmith, H. H., Buss, A. H., Plomin, R., Rothbart, M. K., Thomas, A., Chess, S., et al. (1987). Roundtable: What is temperament? *Child Development, 58*, 505–529.

Gosling, S. D., & John, O. P. (1999). Personality dimensions in nonhuman animals: A cross-species review. *Current Directions in Psychological Science, 8*, 69–75.

Grossmann, K., Fremer-Bombik, E., Rudolph, J., & Grossmann, K. E. (1988). Maternal attachment representation as related to patterns of infant-mother attachment and maternal care during the first year. In R. A. Hinde & J. Stevenson-Hinde (Eds.), *Relationships within families* (pp. 241–262). Oxford, England: Clarendon Press.

Hinde, R. A. (1987). *Individuals, relationships, and culture.* Cambridge, England: Cambridge University Press.

Hinde, R. A., & Stevenson-Hinde, J. (1991). Perspectives on attachment. In C. M. Parkes, J. Stevenson-Hinde, & P., Marris (Eds.), *Attachment across the life cycle* (pp. 52–65). London: Routledge.

Hu, P., & Meng, Z. (1996). *An examination of infant-mother attachment in China.* Poster presented at the meeting of the International Society for the Study of Behavioral Development, Québec City, Canada.

Kagan, J. (1994). *Galen's prophecy.* New York: Basic Books.

Lesch, K.-P., Bengel, D., Heils, A., Sabol, S. Z., Greenberg, B. D., Petri, S. et al. (1996). Association of anxiety-related traits with a polymorphism in the serotonin transporter gene regulatory region. *Science, 274*, 1527–1531.

Marshall, P. J., & Stevenson-Hinde, J. (2001). Behavioral inhibition: Physiological correlates. In W. R. Crozier & L. E. Alden (Eds.), *International handbook of social anxiety* (pp. 53–76). Chichester, England: Wiley.

Miyake, K., Chen, S. J., & Campos., J. J. (1985). Infant temperament, mother's mode of interactions, and attachment in Japan: An interim report. In I. Bretherton & E. Waters (Eds.), Growing points of attachment theory and research. *Monographs of the Society for Research in Child Development, 50* (1–2, Serial No. 209), 276–297.

Mizuta, I., Zahn-Waxler, C., Cole, P. M., & Hiruma, N. (1996). A cross-cultural study of preschoolers' attachments: Security and sensitivity in Japanese and US dyads. *International Journal of Behavioral Development, 19*, 141–159.

Plomin, R., & Caspi, A. (1998). DNA and personality. *European Journal of Personality, 12*, 387–407.

Plomin, R., & Rutter, M. (1998). Child development, molecular genetics, and what to do with genes once they are found. *Child Development, 69*, 1223–1242.

Rothbart, M. K., & Bates, J. E. (1998). Temperament. In W. Damon (Ed.) and N. Eisenberg (Vol. Ed.), *Handbook of child psychology: Vol. 3. Social, emotional, and personality development* (5th ed., pp. 105–176). New York: Wiley.

Schmidt, L., Polak, C. P., & Spooner, A. L. (2001). Biological and environmental contributions to childhood shyness: A diathesis-stress model. In W. R. Crozier & L. E. Alden (Eds.), *International handbook of social anxiety* (pp. 29–51). Chichester, England: Wiley.

Stevenson-Hinde, J. (2005). On the interplay between attachment, temperament, and maternal style. In K. E. Grossmann, K. Grossmann, & E. Waters (Eds.). *The power and dynamics of longitudinal attachment research.* New York: Guilford Press.

Stevenson-Hinde, J., & Marshall, P. J. (1999). Behavioral inhibition, heart period, and respiratory sinus arrhythmia: An attachment perspective. *Child Development, 70*, 805–816.

Stevenson-Hinde, J., Stillwell-Barnes, R., & Zunz, M. (1980). Subjective assessment of rhesus monkeys over four successive years. *Primates, 21*, 66–82.

van IJzendoorn, M. H., & Bakermans-Kranenburg, M. J. (2004). Maternal sensitivity and infant temperament in the formation of attachment (pp. 233–258). In G. Bremner & A. Slater (Eds.), *Theories of infant development.* London: Blackwell.

van IJzendoorn, M. H., & Sagi, A. (1999). Cross-cultural patterns of attachment: Universal and contextual dimensions. In J. Cassidy & P. Shaver (Eds.), *Handbook of attachment: Theory, research, and clinical applications* (pp. 713–734). New York: Guilford Press.

Weinfield, N. S., Sroufe, L. A., Egeland, B., & Carlson, E. A. (1999). The nature of individual differences in infant-caregiver attachment. In J. Cassidy & P. R. Shaver (Eds.), *Handbook of attachment: Theory, research, and clinical applications* (pp. 68–88). New York: Guilford Press.

Zevalkink, J. (1997). *Attachment in Indonesia: The mother-child relationship in context*. Doctoral dissertation, University of Nijmegen, Nijmegen, The Netherlands (ISBN 90-9010829-7).

PART III

Peers and Parents

10 Parenting and Peer-Group Behavior in Cultural Context

David A. Nelson, Larry J. Nelson, Craig H. Hart, Chongming Yang, and Shenghua Jin

Whether specific patterns of parenting are similarly associated with child peer group behavior in diverse cultural contexts has been a fascinating topic of inquiry. From classic anthropological studies dating back to the early twentieth century to the current interest in cross-cultural studies, knowledge concerning the question of universality and cultural variation in parenting linkages to childhood adjustment has expanded at an unprecedented rate (e.g., Harkness & Super, 2002). As the general field of parenting research has uncovered distinctions in parenting styles and practices (e.g., Darling & Steinberg, 1993; Hart, Newell, & Olsen, 2003), these concepts have increasingly been applied to other cultures as well. Furthermore, the study of peer relationships has also increased in complexity. For example, descriptions of social behavior have evolved to represent significant subtypes of childhood aggression (e.g., physical and relational) and peer withdrawal (e.g., reticence, solitary–passive, solitary–active).

In this chapter, we highlight cultural commonalities and variations in parenting and certain child peer group behaviors that have emerged from recent studies conducted in a number of cultures around the world. For example, our own collaborative work represents cultures of Adelaide, Australia; Beijing, China; Voronezh, Russia; as well as Provo, Utah, and Baton Rouge, Louisiana (United States). As a whole, these research endeavors uniquely contribute to cross-cultural developmental science. More often than not, a relatively coherent picture regarding parenting and child outcomes is emerging from numerous cultural studies.

The structure of this chapter is as follows. The first section discusses the challenges of creating measures that are adaptable to different cultures. The problem of "imposed etics" dominates this discussion. The second section deals with specific child social behaviors and their applicability across cultures. This chapter focuses on subtypes of aggression and social withdrawal, as well as sociable behavior. The third section concerns parenting styles and practices. We briefly review Western research regarding various parenting styles (e.g., authoritative, authoritarian, psychologically controlling, and oversolicitous parenting) and past research suggesting that correlates of parenting are expected to be consistently related to distinct child outcomes across cultures. Finally, the measurement of indigenous parenting practices is described as a means of enriching cultural conceptions of parenting styles and practices, and suggestive data are provided.

The final section discusses universality and cultural variation in how these parenting behaviors are linked to aggressive, withdrawn, and sociable peer group behaviors. Culturally indigenous parenting practices, when relevant, are included in this summary. Research regarding parental beliefs and perceptions regarding these child behaviors is also included to provide for a more complete understanding of why parenting styles and practices might relate to child behavior. In addition, the roles that mothers and fathers may play in influencing child behavior for various cultures will be highlighted as data permits.

Challenges of Cross-Cultural Research

Considering cross-cultural patterns of parental influence on children's social development necessarily begins with the fundamental question as to whether certain patterns of child adaptive and maladaptive behaviors are identifiable and have similar meaning across cultural contexts. In prelude to a synopsis of the research, a brief summary of the challenges of cross-cultural methodology is appropriate. In attempting to apply Western psychological constructs to other cultures, researchers begin with the assumption of *functional equivalence* of behavioral dimensions, meaning that the behaviors in question are understood to be present and of similar psychological meaning across cultures. Given this assumption, the primary methodological concern is the emic–etic problem (Berry, 1989). Emic refers to behaviors arising from a particular culture (culture-specific), whereas etic refers to behaviors that are similar across cultures (culture-universal; Bornstein, 1991). One possible pitfall of cross-cultural research is that imposed etics may result, in which Western theoretical concepts are inappropriately imposed on other cultures. To counter accusations of an imposed etic, scholars may demonstrate various levels of measurement equivalence across cultures (Triandis, 2000).

At the most fundamental level, research instruments may be described as *conceptually equivalent* if they appear to be similarly understood by individuals in each cultural setting. To assure conceptual equivalence when using rating scales, it is common practice that all items in measures of interest are forward- and back-translated by linguists who are fluent in English (given English-speaking Western culture as a starting point) as well as the language of the culture of comparison (e.g., Chinese, Russian, Italian, etc.). Feedback is also elicited from research participants regarding the appropriateness of the translated measures. Furthermore, open-ended questions may elicit responses from study participants that are consistent with the theme of a particular parent or child behavioral construct (not originating in that culture).

Beyond these basic safeguards, a more stringent standard is required to achieve *metric equivalence*, in which similar psychometric properties are obtained for two sets of data from different cultures. Some structural equation modeling (SEM) modeling techniques are particularly useful in cross-cultural comparison. For example, we have adopted multisample confirmatory factor analytic techniques that can identify invariant measures of these constructs. Full invariance of measurement (where all items of interest are deemed equivalent) across cultures is often difficult to achieve, especially when comparison involves more than two cultures. In contrast, a standard of partial invariance, wherein the majority of items are statistically shown to be invariant across cultures, may be most useful (e.g., Olsen et al., 2002; Vandenberg & Lance, 2000). One benefit of partial invariance is that items that do vary across cultures are simultaneously considered in the context of those items that are invariant. This may lead to useful hypothesizing and research regarding the cultural nuances behind a particular behavior.

Subtypes of Aggression: Cross-Cultural Evidence

Most research has examined relations between parenting and child social functioning in three broad domains: aggression, social withdrawal, and sociability. To understand these relations, it is necessary to first discuss the meaning of these behaviors in cultural context. In regard to aggression, research has expanded in conceptually significant ways in the past decade, and a number of cross-cultural studies have kept pace with these changes. The most notable contribution of recent aggression research is the identification of multiple forms of aggression. Specifically, the introduction of the construct of *relational aggression* has provided a point of contrast to physical aggression (Crick & Grotpeter, 1995). Relational aggression is defined as behavior in which the perpetrator seeks to harm others through "purposeful manipulation and damage of their peer relationships" (Crick & Grotpeter, 1995, p. 711). Similar constructs in the literature include *indirect aggression* (Feshbach, 1969; Lagerspetz, Björkqvist, & Peltonen, 1988) and *social aggression* (Cairns et al., 1989; Galen & Underwood, 1997; Xie et al., 2002).

Relational aggression includes both overt (direct) and covert (indirect) forms of relational manipulation. Overt forms include the practice of purposefully excluding or avoiding another. Covert forms may include gossip and rumor-spreading, in which the source of the aggressive behavior is difficult to detect. Relational aggression is considered by peers to be mean, hurtful behavior and is associated with negative psychosocial adjustment correlates (see Crick et al., 1999, for a review). Relational aggression is most useful in that it defines patterns of aggressive behavior that are much more common than physical aggression in the peer groups of girls.

Until the advent of relational aggression, studies typically focused exclusively on physical forms of aggression, defined as a universal characteristic of human development across cultures (Coie & Dodge, 1998). However, few studies have considered relational aggression outside of Western samples, and even studies of physical aggression have been somewhat limited in that the social meaning of such behavior in childhood (e.g., psychosocial correlates) are not well documented, especially in cultures that have only recently begun to receive empirical attention (e.g., China; see Chen, Rubin, & Li, 1995).

An increasing number of studies have identified relational or indirect forms of aggression among children in diverse cultures. In particular, studies have shown that peers, observers, and teachers are able to reliably distinguish relational forms of aggression among preschoolers in Australia (Russell et al., 2003), Russia (Hart, Nelson et al., 1998), China (e.g., Nelson, Hart, Yang, Olsen et al., in press; Nelson, Hart, & Yang, 2005; Yang et al., 2004), Japan (Isobe & Sato, 2003; Hatakeyama & Yamazaki, 2002), and the United States (Bonica et al., 2003; Crick, Casas, & Mosher, 1997; McNeilly-Choque et al., 1996; Ostrov & Keating, 2004; Ostrov et al., 2004; Sebanc, 2003). Researchers in Finland (e.g., Björkqvist, Lagerspetz, & Kaukiainen, 1992; Lagerspetz et al., 1988), Italy (Tomada & Schneider, 1997), Australia (e.g., Owens, 1996), and Indonesia (French et al., 2002) have also identified relational or indirect aggression in middle-childhood and adolescence. Relational aggression is spontaneously mentioned in descriptions of disliked peers in Indonesia, giving further credence to the idea that relational aggression is not an imposed etic, but a construct universally recognized across diverse cultures (French et al., 2002).

Beginning with playground observational work (with four- to six-year-old children) that reliably measured different forms of aggression and withdrawal (McNeilly-Choque et al., 1996; Nelson, 1996; Nelson, Robinson et al., 2005), we have developed teacher-rated and peer behavioral nomination measures. Items typical of physical and relational aggression are shown in Table 10.1 (which shows peer nomination items). Consistent with our earlier description

Table 10.1. *Items Typical of the Aggression Constructs Used in Peer Nomination Procedures*

Constructs and Representative Items
Physical Aggression
Who likes to mess up or knock down other children's things?
Who grabs toys or things from other children?
Who pushes other kids out of the way to get something they want?
Who starts fights (physical) with other children?
Relational Aggression
Who won't let some of the other kids play with them, and they even might tell other kids to go away?
Who tells other kids they cannot play unless they do what everyone wants them to do?
Who won't let some kids sit beside them because they don't like them?
Who tells some other kids not to be friends with someone?
Who won't listen to someone if they are mad at them (they may even cover their ears?)

of multisample confirmatory factor analysis, we have found that physical and relational aggression (as measured via teachers or peers) can be statistically distinguished in the United States, China, and Russia. In addition, most, if not all, items are found invariant and compose similar factor structures across these cultures (Nelson, Hart, Yang, & Jin, 2005; Nelson, Hart, & Yang, 2005).

Subtypes of Withdrawal: Cross-Cultural Evidence

Social withdrawal refers to "the consistent (across situations and time) display of all forms of solitary behavior when encountering familiar/unfamiliar peers" (Rubin, Burgess, & Coplan, 2002, p. 330). As suggested in this definition, multiple forms of withdrawn behavior have been identified. However, unlike the study of aggression in which the same constructs (e.g., relational or physical aggression) can be studied across various ages, the subtypes of withdrawal vary according to developmental periods.

In early childhood (3–7 years of age), extensive work has been done exploring subtypes of withdrawal. Although recent work has started to examine the motivational factors (i.e., social disinterest or conflicted shyness) related to the display of withdrawn behaviors (e.g., Coplan et al., 2004), most of the extant work has focused on measuring solitary–passive, solitary–active, and reticent behaviors (Coplan et al., 1994).

Solitary–passive withdrawal is characterized by the quiet exploration of objects and constructive activities while playing alone (e.g., building with blocks while alone). Reticence is defined as frequent onlooking and unoccupied behaviors in both familiar and unfamiliar social contexts (e.g., wandering aimlessly, watching other children without joining in). Solitary–active behavior is characterized by solitary–functional play (repeated sensorimotor actions with or without objects, such as swinging by oneself) or by solitary dramatic/pretend play (e.g., pretending by oneself to be an animal or a machine). Solitary–active behavior differs from reticence and solitary–passive withdrawal in that it often reflects a child who has been isolated by the peer group rather than one who withdraws from the peer group.

These three forms of withdrawal have been identified among children in various cultures. For example, using our own newly developed teacher measure derived from playground observational assessments, we compared preschoolers in China, Russia, and the United States and found evidence for statistical invariance in the measurement of these constructs (Hart, Yang et al., 2000; See Table 10.2 for items). However, even though these subtypes are recognizable and measurable in each setting, it is probable that the correlates or interpretation of such behaviors may vary across cultures. For example, in Western cultures, reticence may represent a failure to exert oneself individually, whereas in Eastern cultures, it may represent a failure to conform to collectivistic group norms.

Research shows that there are significant and differential correlates of withdrawn behavior in early childhood. Studies conducted in the United States and Canada have revealed that reticence is associated with anxious–fearful and hovering behaviors, peer rejection, dysregulated emotions, and internalizing disorders (e.g., Coplan & Rubin, 1998; Hart, DeWolf, & Burts, 1993; Hart, Yang et al., 2000; Rubin, Coplan et al., 1995). In contrast, solitary–passive behavior is considered to be fairly benign at the beginning of early childhood (age 4). Specifically, solitary–passive behavior is positively associated with competent problem solving with peers, task persistence, performance on object-oriented tasks, and emotion regulation (Coplan et al., 1994; Coplan & Rubin, 1998; Rubin, 1982; Rubin, Coplan et al., 1995). By ages 5 to 6 years, however, it begins to be linked to maladjustment in boys (Coplan et al., 2001). Finally, solitary–active behavior is *negatively* associated with adjustment (e.g., positive group interactions, perspective-taking ability, and problem-solving ability), as well as *positively* associated with social maladjustment, impulsivity, emotion dysregulation, and peer rejection (e.g, Coplan et al., 1994; Rubin, 1982; Rubin, Coplan et al., 1995).

Far fewer studies have been conducted examining the correlates and outcomes of these subtypes of withdrawal in other cultures. In regard to reticence, findings reflect a similar association with maladjustment across

Table 10.2. *Items Typical of the Social Withdrawal and Sociability Constructs Used in Teacher Ratings*

Constructs and Representative Items
Reticence
Wanders aimlessly during free play.
Appears to be doing nothing.
Stares at other children without interacting with them.
Watches other children play without joining in.
Is fearful in approaching other children
Solitary Passive
Would rather play alone.
Does artwork by self, away from others.
Does constructive activities alone (e.g., blocks, puzzles).
Reads books alone, away from others.
Plays with toys by self rather than with other children.
Solitary Active
Pretends to be something alone (fireman, doctor, airplane) without interacting.
Does pretend/dramatic play by self.
Animates toys by self (e.g., pretends an inanimate object – doll or stick – is alive).
Sociability
Likes to talk with peers.
Makes new friends easily.
Has many friends.
Peers enjoy talking with him/her.

cultures including a link with peer rejection in China and Russia (Hart, Yang et al., 2000). Studies involving other cultures have thus far failed to reveal a connection between either solitary–passive or solitary–active behavior and psychosocial adjustment in preschoolers.

During middle-childhood and adolescence, there are fewer distinctions between forms of withdrawal. Using more global definitions of withdrawal, studies have shown that it tends to be linked to indices of maladjustment in middle-childhood and adolescence across several cultures. In the United States and Canada, withdrawal has been linked to negative self-perceptions (e.g., Hymel, Bowker, & Woody, 1993), peer rejection (Hymel et al., 1993; Rubin, Chen, & Hymel, 1993), victimization (Boivin, Hymel, & Bukowski, 1995), low self-worth (Rubin, Chen et al., 1995), specific language impairment (Hart et al., 2004), and loneliness (Renshaw & Brown, 1993; Rubin, Chen et al., 1995). Similarly, childhood withdrawal has been associated with peer rejection in Cuba, Italy, Argentina, and the Netherlands (Attili, Vermigli,

& Schneider, 1997; Cillessen et al., 1992; Schaughency et al., 1992; Valdivia, Schneider, Chavez, & Chen, 2005), lower self-perceptions in Brazil, Canada, and Italy (Chen et al., 2004), loneliness in Cuba and Canada (Valdivia et al., 2005) poor test performance on individual exams (face-to-face with the teacher) in Great Britain (Crozier & Hostettler, 2003), and long-term outcomes in Sweden, such as marrying and becoming fathers later for boys and attaining lower levels of education for girls (Kerr, Lambert, & Bem, 1996).

The link between withdrawal and maladjustment is found even in China. It was long argued that shy, wary, and anxious behaviors may be linked to positive outcomes in China (e.g., Chen, Rubin, & Sun, 1992; Chen et al., 1995) because these behaviors may reflect group-dependence, sensitivity, and social restraint that may be more valued in the Chinese culture (see Chen, Liu, Li, et al., 2000; Ho, 1986, Lau, 1996). However, other aspects of social withdrawal, especially social solitude and social disinterest, are often discouraged in Chinese children because of their incompatibility with the collectivistic orientation (e.g., Cheah & Rubin, 2004; Oyserman, Coon, & Kemmelmeier, 2002). Moreover, recent research reveals that shyness–social wariness is linked to maladjustment (e.g., peer rejection, school problems, depression), as social assertiveness and competitiveness are increasingly required in today's market-oriented China (e.g., Chen et al., 2005; Schwartz, Chang, & Farver, 2001).

Sociable Peer Group Behavior

Compared with research on maladaptive forms of peer group behavior, less attention has been devoted to studying children's sociability in diverse cultural settings. Studies conducted in North America indicate that children who engage in friendly/amicable behavior and who are prosocial in their helping, sharing, and comforting behaviors are typically better adjusted to school, less aggressive and withdrawn, less prone to psychosocial problems, and better accepted by peers (e.g., Hart et al., 1997; Ladd & Profilet, 1996). Sociable behavior appears to be highly adaptable in other cultural settings as well. Our recent findings, for example, suggest that preschoolers who engage in friendly–outgoing behavior are more likely to be accepted by peers in China, Russia, and the United States (Hart, Yang et al., 2000). Similar results have been obtained in China for children and youth (Chang, 2003; Chen, Dong, & Zhou, 1997; Chen, Li et al., 2000; Chen, Liu et al., 2002). We now turn our attention to discussing parenting constructs identified across cultural settings that, as we show later, are associated with children's aggressive, withdrawn, and sociable peer group behavior in different cultures.

Culturally Relevant Parenting Constructs

A key challenge for cross-cultural studies is to identify universal human behaviors but also to be sensitive to the impact of cultural context (Cournoyer, 2000). In regard to the first part of this goal, the majority of research studies that have assessed parenting linkages with child behavior across cultures have focused on stylistic dimensions of parenting derived from Western conceptualizations. Among the most commonly studied parenting styles across cultures are dimensions of authoritarian, authoritative, and psychologically controlling parenting (e.g., Chang et al., 2004; Chen et al., 1997; Olsen et al., 2002; Russell et al., 2003). Oversolicitous parenting, especially as it relates to child social withdrawal, is also beginning to receive cross-cultural attention.

Conceptualization of parenting styles is primarily framed in reference to parental control or demandingness as well as parental warmth and acceptance (see Maccoby & Martin, 1983; Peterson & Hann, 1999). Authoritative parenting, as it is commonly defined, is a mix of appropriate behavioral control (demandingness) and parental warmth. Authoritative parenting is commonly associated with competent child and adolescent outcomes in Western samples (Hart et al., 2003; Mackey, Arnold, & Pratt, 2001; Steinberg, Darling, & Fletcher, 1995). Dimensions of authoritative parenting typically consist of such parenting strengths as connection, reasoning-oriented regulation, and autonomy granting. Authoritarian parenting, in contrast, is defined by high levels of excessive behavioral control and lower levels of acceptance. This style is epitomized by frequent engagement in physical and verbal coercion (e.g., corporal punishment, yelling), punitiveness, and restriction of autonomy. These elements may communicate parental rejection of the child and, accordingly, is more often associated with child behavioral difficulties.

In addition, psychological control is a parenting construct that is receiving increased attention in recent research, even in cross-cultural studies (e.g., studies in Russia and China; Hart, Nelson et al., 1998; Olsen et al., 2002; Yang et al., 2004). Whereas authoritarian parenting focuses on behavioral control, psychological control is composed of stylistic dimensions reflecting a parental attack on the child's developing need for psychological autonomy (Barber, 1996, 2002; Nelson & Crick, 2002). In contrast with behavioral control, which is needed in appropriate amounts (e.g., adequate parental monitoring, positive psychological reasoning strategies), psychological control at any level is deemed harmful to the child's individuation. Barber (1996) outlines the stylistic dimensions of psychological control in defining it as a form of control that

"... potentially inhibits or intrudes upon psychological development through manipulation and exploitation of the parent-child bond (e.g., love withdrawal and guilt induction), negative, affect-laden expressions and criticisms (e.g., disappointment and shame), and excessive personal control (e.g., possessiveness, protectiveness)" (p. 3297).

Finally, an oversolicitous approach to parenting is one that is both excessively warm and excessively controlling (see Rubin et al., 2003; Burgess et al., 2001). These parents are overly protective and controlling to the point of being intrusive. Although these parents may often have their children's best interests in mind (i.e., safety, learning, social interaction), the constraints that oversolicitous parents place on their children may actually limit children's opportunities to practice social skills, learn how to regulate their own emotions, and build their own cognitive constructions.

In our own work, we have found similar factor structures across cultures in terms of the dimensions of parenting styles noted earlier (e.g., connection, reasoning-oriented regulation, and autonomy granting as dimensions of authoritative parenting). Factor structures of authoritative and authoritarian parenting similar to those obtained with U.S. samples have been obtained in Australia (Russell et al., 2003), China (Porter et al., in press; Wu et al., 2002), and Russia (Hart, Nelson et al., 2000). Table 10.3 provides items reflective of parenting styles used in our own work, including items representing psychologically controlling and oversolicitous parenting. These forms of parenting are also relevant across cultures, and covered in more detail later.

Given that parental acceptance/rejection is a key feature in defining the aforementioned parenting styles, Rohner's parental acceptance–rejection theory is relevant to our discussion (PARTheory; Cournoyer, 2000; Khaleque & Rohner, 2002; Rohner 1975, 1986). This socialization theory is based on the simple hypothesis that children the world over may suffer psychologically in direct proportion to the degree they feel rejected by their parents. The universal nature of this theory is defined by an evolutionary perspective purporting the universal emotional need for positive connections to caregivers. The tenets of PARTheory have been tested in numerous studies conducted around the world, and similar results have been obtained. Accordingly, there is ample foundation for the expectation that parenting styles might be commonly associated with child maladjustment in cultures the world over. Furthermore, parenting practices, though they may be differentially emphasized across cultures, likely communicate parental acceptance or rejection and thus contribute to the overall style, or pervasive interaction climate, that is the essence of parenting styles (e.g., Darling & Steinberg, 1993; Mize & Pettit, 1997).

Table 10.3. *Items Typical of the Parenting Dimensions Used in Parental Reports*

Authoritative Dimensions and Representative Items

Warmth/Acceptance (Connection)

Gives praise when child is good.

Expresses affection by hugging, kissing, and holding child.

Tells child that we appreciate what he/she tries to accomplish.

Gives comfort and understanding when child is upset.

Shows sympathy when child is hurt or frustrated.

Aware of problems or concerns about child in school.

Encourages child to talk about his/her troubles.

Reasoning/Induction (Regulation)

Talks it over and reasons with child when misbehaving.

Encourages child to talk about consequences of behavior.

Explains the consequences of the child's behavior.

Gives the child reasons why rules should be obeyed.

Democratic Participation (Autonomy Granting)

Apologizes to child when making a mistake in parenting.

Allows child to give input into family rules.

Takes child's desires into account before asking the child to do something.

Encourages child to express himself/herself, even when disagreeing with parents.

Authoritarian Dimensions and Representative Items

Physical Coercion

Spanks when child is disobedient

Uses physical punishment as a way of disciplining child.

Slaps child when the child misbehaves.

Grabs child when he/she is being disobedient.

Guides child by physical punishment more than by reason.

Verbal Hostility

Explodes in anger towards child.

Yells or shouts when child misbehaves.

Argues with child.

Nonreasoning/Punitive

Punishes by taking privileges away with little explanation.

Punishes by putting child off with little or no justification.

When child asks why he/she has to conform, says, "Because I said so."

Psychological Control Representative Items

Becomes less friendly with our child if our child does not see things his/her way.

Makes our child feel guilty when our child does not meet our expectations.

Tells our child that we get embarrassed when he/she does not meet our expectations.

Tells our child he/she is not as good as other children.

Loses temper easily with our child.

Oversolicitous Representative Items

Readily intervenes if there is a chance that our child will fail at something.

Gets anxious when our child tries to do something new or difficult for him/her.

Feels guilty when our child does not measure up to his/her potential.

Fearful that others will not think well of my child.

Tries to control much of what our child does.

Tends to be overly involved in our child's activities

Considering Culturally Indigenous Parenting

The aforementioned results suggest that there are elements of parenting that appear to be universal in their applicability. However, in addition to testing the relevance of Western-derived parenting style dimensions for other cultures, there is also value in attempting to establish culturally indigenous parenting measures. In particular, scholars have argued that Western parenting constructs may fail to capture important features of child-rearing in other cultures (Wu et al., 2002). Accordingly, such approaches are promising in helping to illuminate cultural nuances behind what otherwise appear to be similar behaviors and outcomes.

We draw from Chinese parenting research for illustrative purposes because this is the culture where most empirical knowledge to date on indigenous practices has been accumulated. There is already a long history of research dedicated to conceptualizing what is likely unique about Chinese parenting (Chao, 1994; Chen, 1998; Fung, 1999; Ho, 1986). Much of this stems from debates over the meaning of parental control in Chinese parenting. In particular, studies find that Chinese parents tend to be more coercive, restrictive, and controlling in their parenting styles compared with North American parents (Chiu, 1987; Leung, Lau, & Lam, 1998; Porter et al., in press; Wu et al., 2002). A number of scholars have elaborated on the meaning of this cultural difference by suggesting that control strategies among traditional Chinese parents are uniquely indigenous and therefore qualitatively different from traditional conceptions of authoritarian parenting. Chao (1994, 2001; Chao & Tseng, 2002), for example, has argued that what appears to be more authoritarian parenting among Chinese parents is uniquely defined by the indigenous concept of "training" (*Guan Jiao* in Mandarin Chinese). This form of control is purported to be demonstrative of parental involvement and concern and therefore beneficial rather than destructive to child development.

Building on these previous Chinese parenting conceptualizations, as well as focus group interviews with parents, we sought to empirically identify a number of parenting practices that were reported to define indigenous elements of Chinese parenting (Wu et al., 2002; see Table 10.4 for representative items). The first element, *encouragement of modest behavior*, is consistent with emphasis of group over individual accomplishments and interests. This notion is consistent with a collectivist society that favors interpersonal harmony rather than individual goals (Chen et al., 1998). Accordingly, one would expect less endorsement of this practice in parents residing in individualist cultures such as the United States. The second dimension, *protection*, is focused on keeping young children safely nearby and, by extension, fostering

Table 10.4. *Items Representing Culturally Indigenous Chinese Parenting Practices (Wu et al., 2002)*

Directiveness
Tells our child what to do.
Demands child do things.
Scolds or criticizes when our child does not meet expectations.

Protection
Expects child to be close by when playing.
Overly worries about child getting hurt.
It is important to supervise all of our child's activities.

Shaming/Love Withdrawal
Tells child that he/she should be ashamed when misbehaving.
Tells child we get embarrassed when he/she doesn't meet our expectations.
Makes child feel guilty when our child doesn't meet our expectations.
Less friendly with our child if our child does not see things his/my way.

Encouragement of Modesty
Discourage child from expressing his/her points of view around others.
Discourage child from proudly acknowledging compliments or praise from friends or adults.
Discourage child from appearing overconfident to others about his/her abilities.
Discourage child from showing off his/her skills or knowledge to get attention.

Maternal Involvement
Mothers express love by helping children to succeed in school.
A mother's sole interest is in taking care of her children.
Children should be in the constant care of their mothers.
Mothers should do everything for their children's education.

dependency on parents for meeting the child's needs. Chinese parents are more protective than U.S. parents (Chen et al., 1998), who set a premium on independent child functioning. Third, *shaming and love withdrawal* are considered important mechanisms for socializing young children in China so that, "they are encouraged to act so as to maximize the positive esteem they are granted from others while trying to avoid incurring their disapproval" (Schoenhals, 1993, p. 192). Ho (1986) has reported that Chinese mothers engage in greater levels of "love-oriented" child-rearing, including love withdrawal to deal with child misbehavior, than their American counterparts. Shaming behavior that includes derogatory comments and threats of abandonment are consonant with the description of psychological control noted earlier (Fung, 1999; Wu et al., 2002). Fourth, *directiveness* is deemed vital for helping to correct young Chinese children's social and academic behavior in ways that promote conformity to societal expectations. This element of Chinese parenting also contrasts with the emphasis of U.S. parents on granting relatively greater autonomy to their children. Finally, *maternal care and involvement* is reflective of Chao's (1994; 2001) work, which places emphasis on Chinese mothers sacrificing significant time and energy to foster their children's academic achievement.

The primary purpose of the Wu et al. (2002) study was to empirically test whether these indigenous Chinese parenting practices might be similarly identified in both cultures (making them culture-general or culture-specific dimensions) and, if so, if they might nonetheless differ in emphasis across cultures. We expected many of these elements to be culture-general, given that parenting behaviors similar to those described earlier (e.g., maternal involvement, shaming/love withdrawal) have been identified in previous Western research. Still, these parenting dimensions may find differential application across cultures. Similarly, we sought to identify whether authoritarian and authoritative parenting styles, normally affiliated with Western parenting conceptualizations, were relevant across both cultures and might also differ across cultures.

Accordingly, Chinese mothers and American mothers were compared in their self-reported engagement in these indigenous Chinese as well as Western stylistic dimensions of parenting. Interestingly, multisample confirmatory factor analyses yielded mostly invariant factor structures for all of these dimensions of parenting across cultures, showing all indigenous Chinese parenting constructs to be empirically identifiable in the parenting of both Chinese and North American mothers. Furthermore, the indigenous constructs were relatively independent from each other as well as the authoritative and authoritarian constructs. However, with the exception of only one construct (maternal involvement), Chinese mothers reported more frequent engagement in the parenting practices considered indigenous to China. These results reinforce the notion that influence of culture is manifest in child-rearing orientations, with Chinese mothers scoring higher on most parenting dimensions considered most consistent with the collectivist foundation of their society.

As for the North American derived constructs, Chinese mothers reported lower levels of some authoritative dimensions (warmth/acceptance, autonomy granting) and higher levels of physically coercive practices that comprise an authoritarian style (cf. Porter et al., in press). The reduced emphasis on granting autonomy is expected, as it is practically the opposite of the indigenous constructs representing protection and directiveness. The contrast between lower levels of warmth and greater levels of physical coercion also appear consistent with previous research acknowledging the rather stern, straightforward approach of Chinese parents to their parental role in "training." For example, Chinese mothers rely on scolding and criticism to promote self-control in their children (Lin & Fu, 1990).

Nonetheless, Chinese mothers did not differ from American mothers in their reported levels of reasoning-oriented regulation (an authoritative practice) as well as verbal hostility and nonreasoning/punitive practices (authoritarian parenting). In this case, reasoning-oriented regulation seems consistent with the emphasis of the indigenous practices of protection and directiveness. In sum, we found both divergence and commonality in emphasis of these elements of parenting across these different cultural settings. The fact that all parenting dimensions were identified in both cultures is most significant, given that the "cultural distance" (i.e., differences in language, religion, socioeconomic conditions, political system, etc.) between the United States and China is noteworthy (see Triandis, 1994). These results also coincide with that of Chen and colleagues, who were the first to effectively document "Western" parenting styles among mainland Chinese parents (e.g., Chen et al., 1997; Chen, Liu, & Li, 2000). The next step is to examine whether these parenting constructs differentially relate to child peer-group behavior outcomes across cultures. The next section details studies of this nature.

Parenting and Child Peer-Group Behavior Across Cultures

In this section, the focus is on parenting linkages with child peer-group aggressive, withdrawn, and sociable behavior in non-Western cultures. Furthermore, we complement this emphasis with an overview of studies that describe parental beliefs and perceptions relating to these child behaviors. Unique beliefs and perceptions likely lend themselves to the patterns of more or less adaptive parenting that vary according to the individual child's levels of aggressive, withdrawn, or sociable behavior.

Parental Beliefs and Perceptions Regarding Child Aggression

Much of what parents do in seeking to socialize their children is influenced by parental beliefs and perceptions of their child's social behavior (Hart et al., 1997). It is important to understand possible cultural differences in beliefs because they provide the lens through which parenting styles and practices can be examined. If parents perceive a behavior to be harmful and yet changeable, they may respond differently than if the behavior is considered benign and unchangeable (e.g., a trait) in the culture. Similarly, given the value placed on a behavior by one's culture, parents may select a parenting approach that they believe will either reinforce or diminish a particular behavior in their children.

When it comes to parental beliefs and perceptions regarding aggressive behavior in children, relational aggression is unexplored. In contrast, a significant number of research studies demonstrate that Western parents are genuinely concerned about physically aggressive behaviors and that beliefs regarding the source of such behavior, its modifiability, and developmental course is uniquely related to physical aggression in children (see Rubin & Burgess, 2002, for a recent review). In particular, mothers of preschoolers who place great importance on social skills and believe that these skills can be taught are more likely to have socially competent children (Rubin, Mills, & Rose-Krasnor, 1989) and are more involved in promoting social competence (Mize, Pettit, & Brown, 1995). In contrast, mothers of physically aggressive children tend to see the negative behavior as an internal, unchanging attribute (Rubin et al., 1989; Coplan et al., 2002) and also believe that they have personally failed because of their own incompetence as parents (Ladd & Le Sieur, 1995), undercutting their ability to act to assist their children in pursuing more appropriate interaction with others. They are also more likely to respond to (physically) aggressive behavior than other problematic behavior (e.g., social withdrawal) with power assertive strategies (Dodge, Pettit, & Bates, 1994; Mills & Rubin, 1990). Such negative reactions to aggressive behavior are understandable, given parental reports that both Western mothers and fathers feel anger, disappointment, and embarrassment when they witness their child engaging in physically aggressive behavior (Coplan et al., 2002; Mills & Rubin, 1990, 1993; Rubin & Mills, 1990).

Unfortunately, attention to parental beliefs and perceptions regarding aggressive behavior has been primarily an empirical focus with North American parents. Few studies exist that investigate these beliefs and perceptions in other cultures, thereby creating a context for contrast and comparison. There are a couple of notable exceptions, however. For example, Schneider et al. (1997) compared the beliefs of English Canadian and Italian mothers of seven-year-old children in regard to physically aggressive and socially withdrawn behavior. Both groups of mothers reported greater emotional reactions to aggressive rather than withdrawn behavior. However, the Italian mothers' emotional reaction was relatively subdued compared with Canadian mothers, with Italian mothers reporting less anger, embarrassment, confusion, or concern in regard to aggression. Italian mothers were also more likely to attribute physical aggression to traits within the child and reported that they would endorse high levels of power assertion to curb aggressive behavior. Finally, Italian mothers were also less likely to believe that they could help children be better accepted by peers, which appears consistent with the trait-like attribution they held for aggressive behavior.

Another exception is the recent work of Cheah and Rubin (2004), who similarly examined European American and Mainland Chinese mothers' responses to physical aggression (externalizing behaviors) and social withdrawal in preschool children. Both American and Chinese mothers regarded aggressive behavior negatively, and both groups similarly believed aggression to be the result of situational forces rather than innate personality traits. Chinese mothers were, however, less likely to believe aggression to be stable or intentional. In regard to supervision, both sets of mothers reported greater control and firmness in dealing with aggression than withdrawal, and they believed that aggression required more directive action to curb it. Interestingly, Chinese mothers were twice as likely to endorse particular intervention strategies that dealt with training the child to act properly and correction through inductive reasoning. Chinese mothers consistently ascribed to the notion of *jiao-yu*, meaning to "teach [the child] the right way." This emphasis is consistent with research on Chinese parenting (Chao, 1994), which points to the importance of training.

Other cultural research findings suggest that parents in North America, China, and Russia all engage in more directive action involving the initiation and arrangement of peer contacts if their children are perceived by teachers as more aggressive or withdrawn (Hart, Yang et al., 1998). Although parental beliefs and perceptions were not directly measured in this work, these findings indicate that parents may be prone to taking remedial action that involves promoting meaningful relationships with peers when they perceive their preschool-age children to be less socially competent. Alternatively, other findings indicate less compensatory parental intervention in the face of child social incompetence, particularly when parents view difficult child behaviors as being less under their control and more difficult to socialize (Profilet & Ladd, 1994; Rubin et al., 1989). To sort out these contradictory findings, future cultural studies should take parental beliefs and perceptions into account as moderating factors when examining associations between parenting behaviors and inept child peer-group behavior.

Parenting Behaviors Linked to Child Aggression

Parental beliefs and perceptions contribute to the establishment of particular parenting styles and practices that are the focus of this chapter. Whereas few studies have assessed parental beliefs and perceptions in cultures outside North America, a much greater number have assessed connections between parenting and child outcomes. A significant number of these studies address parental correlates of child aggression. These studies have commonly tested the universality of commonly found associations in North America between negative parenting styles (i.e., authoritarian, psychological control) and child behavioral problems.

Of all the non-Western cultures in which the connection between parenting styles and child outcomes has been investigated, China has received the most empirical attention. There is good reason for this, given significant theoretical debate in the last decade over the meaning of Chinese parenting. As noted earlier, proponents of the indigenous meaning of Chinese parental control (e.g., "training,") assert that Chinese children may benignly view strict or power assertive parental control as concordant with high parental expectations (Chao & Sue, 1996). In contrast, Lau and Yeung (1996) cite evidence indicating that Chinese children, like their Western counterparts, consider controlling parenting behavior to be adverse. Hoffman (1960) long ago asserted that unqualified parental power assertion would likely evoke child hostility and opposition and, accordingly, difficulties in the child's proper internalization of control. This assertion is tested in the studies we detail here.

Some of the studies reviewed here also include attention to the significant tendency of Chinese parents to engage in psychological controlling behavior. In particular, Ho (1986) has reported that Chinese mothers are more likely than American parents to use "love-oriented" methods of discipline (e.g., love withdrawal) to deal with child misbehavior. In addition, Chinese parents engage in shaming behavior, threats of abandonment, and derogatory comments, all of which are consonant with the description of psychological control (Fung, 1999; Wu et al., 2002).

Several studies focus on the negative effect of coercive parenting in China, showing a consistent connection to children's externalizing (aggressive/disruptive) behaviors across various age groups. For example, Chen and colleagues have completed a number of studies with various age groups that find consistent connections between parenting dimensions and aggressive behavior. For example, Chen and Rubin (1994) showed that parental acceptance (as measured by Rohner's measure of parental acceptance/rejection) was negatively associated with peer and teacher ratings of aggressive behavior in Chinese fourth- and sixth-grade children. Chen et al. (1997) also found that authoritative parenting was negatively related to peer-nominated aggression in a sample of Chinese eight-year-old children. In contrast, authoritarian parenting was positively associated with aggression. Chen et al. (2001) also found similar results between parenting dimensions and observed peer-directed aggression in a sample of Chinese preschoolers. Furthermore, in a study initiated with toddlers, Chen, Wang et al. (2002) found that the child-rearing of mothers and fathers of Chinese two-year-olds was predictive of verbal and physical aggression in free-play episodes two years later. In particular, parental power assertion, for both mothers and fathers, was positively associated with aggression. In contrast, maternal induction and paternal warmth were negatively related to aggression. Finally, Chen, Liu, and Li (2000) showed that paternal warmth was negatively associated with aggressive/disruptive behavior in their young adolescents two years later. Paternal indulgence also positively predicted future aggressive/disruptive behavior.

Lei Chang and colleagues have also tested the connection between parenting styles and aggressive behavior in Chinese samples. In particular, harsh parenting on behalf of Chinese mothers and fathers was directly and indirectly (through emotional regulation) tied to child aggression in kindergarten (Chang et al., 2003). In a more recent study, Chang et al. (2004) also found harsh parenting to predict externalizing behavior in fourth-grade children in Hong Kong.

In our own work, a number of studies have identified connections between coercion as well as psychological control and aggression in Chinese preschoolers. Olsen and colleagues (2002), for example, found maternal psychological control to be linked to externalizing behaviors for Chinese boys and internalizing behavior for Chinese girls. In another study (Yang et al., 2004), we focused on connections between parental physical/verbal coercion and psychological control and aggression subtypes in Chinese preschoolers, with analyses conducted separately by parent–child dyad (both mothers and fathers were included). Using structural equation modeling to pit psychological control against coercion, we examined their associations with physical and relational aggression. Results showed that parental coercion and psychological control were associated with both forms of aggression.

Finally, Nelson, Hart, Yang, Olsen et al. (in press) used a latent sum-and-difference SEM model to assess the combined and differential contributions of Chinese mothers and fathers, in terms of their physically coercive and psychologically controlling parenting, to physical and relational aggression in preschoolers. Results showed combined parenting effects to be more prevalent than differential effects in predicting aggression. Furthermore, physical coercion predicted aggression in boys, whereas psychological control was primarily predictive of aggression in girls.

Beyond investigations in China, there are limited studies that have assessed the connection of parenting styles to child aggression in other cultures. However, a fairly consistent story is emerging among these studies. For example, our published Russian data (Hart, Nelson et al., 1998), using more traditional regression analytic approaches, reveals similar associations between teacher ratings of preschool children's physical and relational aggression and authoritative and authoritarian parenting. Specifically, findings indicate that less parental warmth and responsiveness, and more coercion and psychological control, are associated with greater levels of childhood relational and physical aggression.

Research in Australia also documents the relevance of parenting styles and their connection to child aggression in another Western culture. Russell and colleagues (2003) compared the parenting styles of U.S. and Australian mothers and fathers (of preschool-age children). The study also found, after controlling for child temperament, only in the case of fathers' parenting was there evidence of a link to aggression, with authoritarian parenting predicting children's physical aggression. This was true for both U.S. and Australian fathers.

Taken collectively, the findings from these studies stand in contrast to the idea that parenting styles may vary in effect by culture (Baumrind, 1996; Chao & Tseng, 2002; Coie & Dodge, 1998, Deater-Deckard & Dodge, 1997; Grusec, 2002). Thus, although mean-level differences may exist across cultures, the adaptive meanings of these parenting styles appear consistent across cultures (Chen, 2000). Coercive parenting, in particular, is associated with negative outcomes in children across cultures and developmental periods. However, indigenous patterns of parenting practices have not received scrutiny in this area of research and may yield important future insights into the role of culture in the development of aggression.

Parental Beliefs and Perceptions Regarding Child Withdrawal

Across several cultures, evidence is consistent in showing that parents tend to view child withdrawal negatively. Specifically, mothers in the United States and Canada tend to (a) attribute withdrawal to internal causes, such as temperament, age, or mood; (b) react to withdrawal with anxiety, concern, disappointment, and puzzlement; and (c) respond to withdrawal by focusing on the child's present feelings with the use of low-power assertion strategies, such as information seeking, planning and providing social opportunities, or ignoring the behavior (Cheah & Rubin, 2004; Rubin & Mills, 1990). In examining the beliefs of both European American mothers and Chinese mothers, Cheah and Rubin (2004) noted several important similarities and distinctions. For example, in China, mothers also tend to respond to withdrawal negatively (i.e., anxiety, puzzlement, disappointment, and anger), but compared with their European American peers, they tend to attribute it to external causes (e.g., provocation, accident). Furthermore, like European American mothers, Chinese mothers focused on changing withdrawn behavior by teaching and persuading the child to engage in social interaction and exposing the child to social situations. However, Chinese mothers said they would use these strategies with the intent to teach the child to know how to act appropriately in similar situations in the future (in contrast with European American mothers, who intended to deal with the child's needs in that moment).

Similar studies have been conducted in other cultures as well. Compared with English Canadian mothers, Italian mothers felt lower levels of guilt and concern when presented with hypothetical scenarios of withdrawal and attributed the behavior to a trait in a child that could not be changed (Schneider et al., 1997). Schneider and colleagues hypothesized that the lack of concern regarding children's peer relationships in Italy may stem from Italian families favoring a strong connection with extended family rather than peers. In another study by Cheah and Park (2005) Korean mothers reacted to scenarios of social withdrawal. These mothers reacted with negative emotions (e.g., puzzled, disappointed, anxious, and angry) to social withdrawal and favored lower-powered/indirect strategies (e.g., creating opportunities for the child to play with others to practice their skills) as ways to achieve social-centered goals (e.g., helping children to get along well with others, improving their interactions with peers, and developing their general social competence or comfort in social situations).

Parenting Behaviors Linked to Child Withdrawal

Researchers have found several important links between parenting and fearful, inhibited, and withdrawn behaviors in children in Western cultures. Most notably, emerging evidence suggests that an oversolicitous style of parenting (i.e., overly protective/controlling, intrusive behavior) is linked to children's social withdrawal. For example, Rubin, Burgess, and Hastings (2002) found that mothers of inhibited toddlers (aged two) who engaged in intrusive parenting behaviors (e.g., unsolicited intervention) had children who engaged in high amounts of reticent/wary behavior at age four. There was no relation between age-two inhibition and age-four reticence for children whose mothers were not intrusive. Similarly, Rubin et al. (1999) found that parental perceptions of child shyness/social wariness at age two predicted both mothers' and fathers' expressed lack of encouragement of independence. Indicative of European American mothers' goal to focus on the child's immediate needs (Cheah & Rubin, 2004), these studies suggest that some parents may respond to perceived wariness in their children with parental behaviors (i.e., intrusive, overprotective parenting) that actually exacerbate the problem by not allowing children opportunities to develop regulatory and coping skills to deal with their social anxieties in future social settings.

Emerging work in China is beginning to look at the linkages between parenting and withdrawal. In one of the first studies examining these associations in China using a sample of toddlers and their parents, Chen and colleagues found a positive relation between inhibition and parental acceptance and encouragement of achievement, and a negative correlation with parental control (Chen et al., 1998). Although these findings may reflect a link between "positive" parenting and inhibition, emerging evidence suggests a different picture once children enter early childhood. In our own work (Nelson, Hart, Wu et al., in press), we have begun to examine many of the indigenous practices noted earlier in the Wu et al. (2002) study (i.e., encouragement of modest behavior, protection, shaming, directiveness) that, when overemphasized, were hypothesized to be tied to children's withdrawn behaviors (i.e., reticence, solitary–passive withdrawal, solitary–active behavior). Overemphasis of protection, for example, included items such as "readily intervenes if there is a chance that our child will fail at something." Engagement in coercive behavior was also considered in this study.

In particular, we expected that parenting practices that limited children's opportunities to practice social skills and regulate their own emotions (i.e., maternal overprotection, directiveness, and coercion) or punished "wrong" behaviors (i.e., shaming and coercion) would be positively associated with socially fearful and incompetent (i.e., immature and impulsive) behaviors (i.e., reticent and solitary–active behaviors). Conversely, because parents may want to foster behaviors conducive to academic performance (i.e., solitary–passive behavior) and social acceptance (modesty – not appearing proud or overconfident), they may use shaming or modesty encouragement to motivate children to engage in these behaviors.

Chinese mothers' self-reports of indigenous parenting were correlated with teacher ratings of child behavior. Results showed that maternal directiveness was linked to reticent behavior in girls. Furthermore, maternal overprotection was positively related to solitary–passive behavior, reticence, and modesty in girls. For girls, maternal coercion was positively associated with solitary–active and reticent behavior. Finally, maternal shaming was positively related to all forms of withdrawn behaviors in boys and girls, as well as modest behavior in boys.

Taken together, these findings identify links between parenting practices and social withdrawal in China that are largely consistent with findings in Western cultures such as the United States. Collectively, the literature is beginning to show that parents tend to perceive shy, fearful behaviors as problematic in cultures that promote self-sufficiency and individualism (e.g., United States, Canada) as well as in collectivist cultures that promote group harmony (e.g., China, Korea). Furthermore, parenting that limits children's opportunities to practice social skills and regulate their own emotions tends to be linked to fearful and immature forms of withdrawal across most of the cultures that have been studied to this point.

Parental Beliefs and Perceptions Regarding Child Sociability

The cross-cultural literature on parenting and peer sociability is more limited than studies of parenting and childhood aggression and withdrawal. This is especially the case in regard to relevant parental beliefs and perceptions. Findings of Western studies support the notion that parents who empower children with the abilities to initiate, communicate, and manage their own peer relationships are more likely to have children who are more sociable with peers. However, this type of parental management appears to be more likely in cases where parents *perceive* their children as being more outgoing and sociable to begin with (Profilet & Ladd, 1994) and who *believe* more strongly that informal peer-play activities are important to children's development (Ladd & Hart, 1992). Thus, more research is necessary to understand cultural nuances in parental beliefs and the ways that parents perceive child sociability and promote childhood interactions with peers through specific parenting practices.

Parenting Behaviors Linked to Child Sociability

Research focusing on parenting practices in North America suggests that mothers who actively orchestrate peer-group experiences are more likely to have preschool children who have a larger number of playmates and more consistent play companions (Ladd & Golter, 1988). Parental peer-group initiations have also been associated with more sociable behavior with peers in preschool classrooms (Ladd & Hart, 1992) and to greater classroom peer acceptance, particularly for boys (Ladd & Golter, 1988; Ladd & Hart, 1992). Further evidence suggests that parents who verbally coach their children about how to extend invitations to play have children who initiate more of their own play dates (Ladd & Hart, 1992). Similar findings have been obtained for German grade-schoolers, with children engaging in closer, more stable friendships with peers if their parents actively arrange and stimulate peer contacts (Krappman, 1989). In our cross-cultural work, connections between parental initiation of their children's peer contacts and teacher-rated child sociability have been replicated in Voronezh, Russia, but not in other cultural samples including Beijing, China (Hart, Yang et al., 1998).

Beyond direct parenting effects on peer sociability, indirect effects, through the vehicle of parenting styles, are also notable. Although numerous North American studies have been conducted that show linkages between more authoritative and less authoritarian parenting styles and sociable child peer-group behavior (see Hart et al., 2003 for a review), few studies of this nature have been conducted in other cultural settings. One exception is a recent study by Russell et al. (2003), which examined how parenting patterns in Australia and the United States might be associated with preschoolers' sociable behavior. Consistent with arguments that parenting can have different consequences for child development depending on child characteristics, authoritarian parenting appeared to diminish sociable peer-group behavior for children who were rated lower (rather than higher) on temperamental qualities that reflect outgoing traits. In another notable study of nine and twelve-year-old children in mainland China, parental acceptance as indexed by items such as "I talk to my child in a warm and affectionate way" was associated with socially competent behavior in school (Chen & Rubin, 1994). Similar findings linking more authoritative and less authoritarian parenting with child peer group sociability have also been obtained in other Chinese samples. (e.g., Chen et al., 1997; Chen, Liu, & Li, 2000). Beyond this, little is known about how parenting styles and practices can facilitate or diminish sociable child behavior with peers in diverse cultural settings.

Conclusion

In conclusion, based on data we have reviewed, it would appear that many of the child behavioral orientations and stylistic patterns and practices of parenting that have been identified in North American cultural contexts are empirically identifiable in and are applicable to many non-Western cultural contexts. Culturally indigenous parenting practices are also worthy of study and are thus far consistent with the notion that certain practices may be more heavily emphasized in particular cultures. However, the Wu et al. (2002) study also shows that practices considered indigenous to China are also readily identifiable in the U.S. culture. This finding suggests that parents may hold much in common, even across significant cultural distances.

Furthermore, there are also significant similarities in the beliefs and perceptions of parents across cultures when it comes to the behaviors of interest here. These beliefs naturally tie in with parenting dimensions, which are consistently associated with aggression, social withdrawal, and sociability across cultures studied to date. Accordingly, as Chen (2000) has observed in regard to United States–China comparisons, findings regarding the correlates of parenting styles suggest that the adaptive meanings of parenting styles are consistent across these cultures.

As noted earlier in regard to PARTheory, parental acceptance (warmth) appears to be a defining dimension of parenting across cultures. MacDonald (1992) has also argued that warmth is a unique dimension of parenting that has evolved as a mechanism for promoting cohesive family relationships and paternal investment in child-rearing. Warmth also facilitates compliance and assimilation of adult values in child offspring. Thus, the continuum between warmth and coldness in family relationships is a "pan-human phenomenon" (p. 754). Nonetheless, patterns of warmth vary significantly within as well as across cultures and consistently correlate with more or less adaptive functioning. Accordingly, differences in mean levels of parenting behaviors across cultures warrants more detailed study, especially in regard to how these mean differences may lead to unique child outcomes or greater prevalence of particular social behaviors, relatively speaking, within cultures.

Though much good research has been completed in this domain, our impression is that cross-cultural science has yet to mature. In particular, there are several limitations of the comparative research currently assembled. Studies are often composed of limited samples and are not fully representative of the diversity that is often found within each culture that has been covered here. For example, our Chinese data represent an urban sample of well-educated parents in Beijing, China, which is hardly representative of the diversity of populations found in the whole of China (with substantial differences across cities and regions by ethnicity, socioeconomic status levels, education levels, and rural versus urban environments). Furthermore, though a significant number of non-Western cultures have yielded important data consistent with the theme of this chapter, there are still many cultures around the world that have not yet been explored. Accordingly, it is premature to state that connections between parenting and child peer-group behavior that are thus far consistent across cultures will remain so in future work. Studies may yet emerge that define elements of parenting or child social behavior that are truly unique because of cultural influences. In sum, cross-cultural comparative study of parenting and child behavior has already produced a significant number of important studies, and this field will continue to provide opportunities for significant research for decades to come.

Acknowledgments

Portions of this chapter were presented in M. Bornstein and M. L. Siedl de Moura (Chairs), *Multicultural studies of social development in early life* at the XVIIIth biennial meetings of the International Society for the Study of Behavioural Development, held in Ghent, Belgium. Funding for Brigham Young University (BYU) research reported in this chapter was provided by the College of Family, Home, and Social Sciences, the Camilla Eyring Kimball Endowment, the BYU Family Studies Center, and the Zina Young Williams Card Professorship awarded to Craig H. Hart.

References

Attili, G., Vermigli, P., & Schneider, B. (1997). Peer acceptance and friendship patterns among Italian schoolchildren within a cross-cultural perspective. *International Journal of Behavioral Development, 21*, 277–288.

Barber, B. K. (1996). Parental psychological control: Revisiting a neglected construct. *Child Development, 67*, 3296–3319.

Barber, B. K. (Ed). (2002). *Intrusive parenting: How psychological control affects children and adolescents*. Washington, DC: American Psychological Association.

Baumrind, D. (1996). The discipline controversy revisited. *Family Relations, 45*, 405–414.

Berry, J. W. (1989). Imposed etics-emics-derived etics: The operationalization of a compelling idea. *International Journal of Psychology, 24*, 721–735.

Björkqvist, K., Lagerspetz, K. M. J., & Kaukiainen, A. (1992). Do girls manipulate and boys fight? Developmental trends in regard to direct and indirect aggression. *Aggressive Behavior, 18*, 117–127.

Boivin, M., Hymel, S., & Bukowski, W. M. (1995). The roles of social withdrawal, peer rejection, and victimization by peers in predicting loneliness and depressed mood in childhood. *Development and Psychopathology, 7*, 765–785.

Bonica, C., Arnold, D. H., Fisher, P. H., Zeljo, A., & Yershova, K. (2003). Relational aggression, relational victimization, and language development in preschoolers. *Social Development, 12*, 551–562.

Bornstein, M. H. (Ed.). (1991). *Cultural approaches to parenting*. Hillsdale, NJ: Lawrence Erlbaum Associates.

Burgess, K. B., Rubin, K. H., Chea, C. S. L., & Nelson, L. J. (2001). Behavioral inhibition, social withdrawal, and parenting. In L. E. Alden & W. R. Crozier (Eds.), *International handbook of social anxiety: Concepts, research and interventions relating to the self and shyness*. (pp.137–158). New York: Wiley.

Cairns, R. B., Cairns, B. D., Neckerman, H. J., Ferguson, L. L., & Gariepy, J. L. (1989). Growth and aggression: I. Childhood to early adolescence. *Developmental Psychology, 25*, 320–330.

Chang, L. (2003). Variable effects of children's aggression, social withdrawal, and prosocial leadership as functions of teacher beliefs and behaviors. *Child Development, 74*, 535–548.

Chang, L., Lansford, J. E., Schwartz, D., & Farver, J. M. (2004). Marital quality, maternal depressed affect, harsh parenting, and child externalizing in Hong Kong Chinese families. *International Journal of Behavioral Development, 28*, 311–318.

Chang, L., Schwartz, D., Dodge, K. A., & McBride-Chang, C. (2003). Harsh parenting in relation to child emotion regulation and aggression. *Journal of Family Psychology, 17*, 598–606.

Chao, R. K. (1994). Beyond parental control and authoritarian parenting style: Understanding Chinese parenting through the cultural notion of training. *Child Development, 65*, 1111–1119.

Chao, R. K. (2001). Extending research on the consequences of parenting style for Chinese Americans and European Americans. *Child Development, 72*, 1832–1843.

Chao, R. K., & Sue, S. (1996). Chinese parental influence and their children's school success: A paradox in the literature on parenting styles. In S. Lau (Ed.), *Growing up the Chinese way* (pp. 93–120). Hong Kong: The Chinese University Press.

Chao, R. K., & Tseng, V. (2002). Parenting of Asians. In M. H. Bornstein (Ed.), *Handbook of parenting: Volume 4. Social conditions and applied parenting* (pp. 59–93). Mahwah, NJ: Lawrence Erlbaum Associates.

Cheah, C. S. L., & Park, S. (2005). *South Korean mothers' beliefs regarding aggression and social withdrawal in preschoolers*. Manuscript submitted for publication.

Cheah, C. S. L., & Rubin, K. H. (2004). European American and mainland Chinese mothers' responses to aggression and social withdrawal in preschoolers. *International Journal of Behavioral Development, 28*, 83–94.

Chen, X. (1998). The changing Chinese family: Resources, parenting practices, and children's social-emotional problems. In U. P. Gielen & A. L. Comunian (Eds.), *Family and family therapy in international perspective*. (pp. 150–167). Trieste, Italy: Edizioni LINT.

Chen, X. (2000). Growing up in a collectivistic culture: Socialization and socioemotional development in Chinese children. In U. P. Gielen & A. L. Comunian (Eds.), *International perspectives on human development* (pp. 213–232). Lengerich, Germany: Pabst Science.

Chen, X., Cen, G., Li, D., & He, Y. (2005). Social functioning and adjustment in Chinese children: The imprint of historical time. *Child Development, 76*, 182–195.

Chen, X., Dong, Q., & Zhou, H. (1997). Authoritative and authoritarian parenting practices and social and school performance in Chinese children. *International Journal of Behavioral Development, 21*, 855–873.

Chen, X., Hastings, P. D., Rubin, K. H., Chen, H., Cen, G., & Stewart, S. L. (1998). Child-rearing attitudes and behavioral inhibition in Chinese and Canadian toddlers: A cross-cultural study. *Developmental Psychology, 34*, 677–686.

Chen, X., Li, D., Li, Z., Li, B., & Liu, M. (2000). Sociable and prosocial dimensions of social competence in Chinese children: Common and unique contributions to social, academic, and psychological adjustment. *Developmental Psychology, 36*, 302–314.

Chen, X., Liu, M., & Li, D. (2000). Parental warmth, control, and indulgence and their relations to adjustment in Chinese children: A longitudinal study. *Journal of Family Psychology, 14*, 401–419.

Chen, X., Liu, M., Li, B., Cen, G., Chen, H., & Wang, L. (2000). Maternal authoritative and authoritarian attitudes and mother-child interactions and relationships in urban China. *International Journal of Behavioral Development, 24*, 119–126.

Chen, X., Liu, M., Rubin, K. H., Cen, G., Gao, Z., & Li, D. (2002). Sociability and prosocial orientation as predictors of youth adjustment: A seven-year longitudinal study in a Chinese sample. *International Journal of Behavioral Development, 26*, 128–136.

Chen, X., & Rubin, K. H. (1994). Family conditions, parental acceptance, and social competence and aggression in Chinese children. *Social Development, 3*, 269–290.

Chen, X., Rubin, K. H., & Li, B. (1995). Social and school adjustment of shy and aggressive children in China. *Development and Psychopathology, 7*, 337–349.

Chen, X., Rubin, K. H., & Sun, Y. (1992). Social reputation and peer relationships in Chinese and Canadian children: A cross-cultural study. *Child Development, 63*, 1336–1343.

Chen, X., Wang, L., Chen, H., & Liu, M. (2002). Noncompliance and child-rearing attitudes as predictors of aggressive behavior: A longitudinal study of Chinese children. *International Journal of Behavioral Development, 26*, 225–233.

Chen, X., Wu, H., Chen, H., Wang, L., & Cen, G. (2001). Parental affect, guidance, and power assertion and aggressive behavior in Chinese children. *Parenting: Science and Practice, 1*, 159–183.

Chen, X., Zappulla, C., Coco, A. L., Schneider, B., Kaspar, V., De Oliveira, A. M., et al. (2004). Self-perceptions of competence in Brazilian, Canadian, Chinese and Italian children: Relations with social and school adjustment. *International Journal of Behavioral Development, 28*, 129–138.

Chiu, L. H. (1987). Child-rearing attitudes of Chinese, Chinese-American, and Anglo-American mothers. *International Journal of Psychology, 22*, 409–419.

Cillessen, A. H., Van IJzendoorn, H. W., Van Lieshout, C. F., & Hartup, W. W. (1992). Heterogeneity among peer-rejected boys: Subtypes and stabilities. *Child Development, 63*, 893–905.

Coie, J. D., & Dodge, K. A. (1998). Aggression and antisocial behavior. In W. Damon (Series Ed.) & N. Eisenberg (Vol. Ed.), *Handbook of child psychology: Vol. 3. Social, emotional and personality development* (pp. 779–862). New York: Wiley.

Coplan, R. J., Hastings, P. D., Lagace-Seguin, D. G., & Moulton, C. E. (2002). Authoritative and authoritarian mothers' parenting goals, attributions, and emotions across different childrearing contexts. *Parenting: Science and Practice, 2*, 1–26.

Coplan, R. J., Molina, M. G., Lagace-Seguin, D. G., & Wichmann, C. (2001). When girls versus boys play alone: Gender differences in the relations between nonsocial play and adjustment in kindergarten. *Developmental Psychology, 37*, 464–474.

Coplan, R. J., Prakash, K., O'Neil, K., & Armer, M. (2004). Do you "want" to play? Distinguishing between conflicted shyness and social disinterest in early childhood. *Developmental Psychology, 40*, 244–258.

Coplan, R. J., & Rubin, K. H. (1998). Exploring and assessing nonsocial play in the preschool: The development and validation of the Preschool Play Behavior Scale. *Social Development, 7*, 72–91.

Coplan, R. J., Rubin, K. H., Fox, N. A., Calkins, S. D., & Stewart, S. L. (1994). Being alone, playing alone, and acting alone: Distinguishing among reticence and passive and active solitude in young children. *Child Development, 65*, 129–137.

Cournoyer, D. E. (2000). Universalist research: Examples drawn from the methods and findings of parental acceptance-rejection theory. In U. P. Gielen & A. L. Comunian (Eds.), *International perspectives on human development* (pp. 213–232). Lengerich, Germany: Pabst Science.

Crick, N. R., Casas, J. F., & Mosher, M. (1997). Relational and overt aggression in preschool. *Developmental Psychology, 33*, 579–588.

Crick, N. R., & Grotpeter, J. K. (1995). Relational aggression, gender, and social-psychological adjustment. *Child Development, 66*, 710–722.

Crick, N., Werner, N. E., Casas, J. F., O'Brien, K. M., Nelson, D. A., Grotpeter, J. K., et al. (1999). Childhood aggression and gender: A new look at an old problem. In D. Bernstein (Ed.), *Volume 45 of the Nebraska symposium on motivation: Gender and motivation* (pp. 75–141). Lincoln: University of Nebraska Press.

Crozier, W. R., & Hostettler, K. (2003). The influence of shyness on children's test performance. *British Journal of Educational Psychology, 73*, 317–328.

Darling, N., & Steinberg, L. (1993). Parenting style as context: An integrative model. *Psychological Bulletin, 113*, 487–496.

Deater-Deckard, K., & Dodge, K. A. (1997). Externalizing behavior problems and discipline revisited: Nonlinear effects and variation by culture, context, and gender. *Psychological Inquiry, 8*, 161–175.

Dodge, K. A., Pettit, G. S., & Bates, J. E. (1994). Socialization mediators of the relation between socioeconomic status and child conduct problems. *Child Development, 65*, 649–665.

Feshbach, N. D. (1969). Sex differences in children's modes of aggressive responses toward outsiders. *Merrill-Palmer Quarterly, 15*, 249–258.

French, D. C., Jansen, E. A., & Pidada, S. (2002). United States and Indonesian children's and adolescents' reports of relational aggression by disliked peers. *Child Development, 73*, 1143–1150.

Fung, H. (1999). Becoming a moral child: The socialization of shame among young Chinese children. *Ethos, 27*, 180–209.

Galen, B. R., & Underwood, M. K. (1997). A developmental investigation of social aggression among children. *Developmental Psychology*, *33*(4), 589–600.

Grusec, J. E. (2002). Parental socialization and the acquisition of values. In M. H. Bornstein (Ed.), *Handbook of parenting: Volume 5. Practical issues in parenting* (pp. 143–167). Mahwah, NJ: Lawrence Erlbaum Associates.

Harkness, S., & Super, C. M. (2002). Culture and parenting. In M. H. Bornstein (Ed.), *Handbook of parenting: Vol. 2. Biology and ecology of parenting* (pp. 253–280). Mahwah, NJ: Lawrence Erlbaum Associates.

Hart, C. H., DeWolf, M. D., & Burts, D. C. (1993). Parental discipline strategies and preschoolers' play behavior in playground settings. In C. H. Hart (Ed.), *Children on playgrounds: Research perspectives and applications* (pp. 271–313). Albany: State University of New York Press.

Hart, C. H., Nelson, D. A., Robinson, C. C., Olsen, S. F., & McNeilly-Choque, M. K. (1998). Overt and relational aggression in Russian nursery-school-age children: Parenting style and marital linkages. *Developmental Psychology, 34*, 687–697.

Hart, C. H., Nelson, D. A., Robinson, C. C., Olsen, S. F., & McNeilly-Choque, M. K., & McKee, T. R. (2000). Russian parenting styles and family processes: Linkages with subtypes of victimization and aggression. In K. A. Kerns, J. M. Contreras, & A. M. Neal-Barnett (Eds.), *Family and peers: Linking two social worlds* (pp. 47–84). Westport, CT: Praeger.

Hart, C. H., Newell, L. D., & Olsen, S. F. (2003). Parenting skills and social/communicative competence in childhood. In J. O. Greene & B. R. Burleson (Eds.),

Handbook of communication and social interaction skill (pp. 753–797). Mahwah, NJ: Lawrence Erlbaum Associates.

Hart, C. H., Olsen, S. F., Robinson, C. C., & Mandleco, B. L. (1997). The development of social and communicative competence in childhood: Review and a model of personal, familial, and extrafamilial processes. In B. R. Burleson (Ed.), *Communication yearbook 20* (pp. 305–373). Thousand Oaks, CA: Sage.

Hart, C. H., Yang, C., Nelson, D. A., Jin, S., Bazarskaya, N., Nelson, L. J., et al. (1998). Peer contact patterns, parenting practices, and preschoolers' social competence in China, Russia, and the United States. In P. Slee & K. Rigby (Eds.), *Children's peer relations* (pp. 3–30). London: Routledge.

Hart, C. H., Yang, C., Nelson, L. J., Robinson, C. C., Olsen, J. A., Nelson, D. A., et al. (2000). Peer acceptance in early childhood and subtypes of socially withdrawn behavior in China, Russia, and the United States. *International Journal of Behavioral Development, 24*, 73–81.

Hart, K. I., Fujiki, M., Brinton, B., & Hart, C. H. (2004). The relationship between social behavior and severity of language impairment. *Journal of Speech, Language, and Hearing Research, 47*, 647–662.

Hatakeyama, M., & Yamazaki, A. (2002). An observational study of preschooler's aggressive behavior in free play, in relation to gender and peer group status. *The Japanese Journal of Developmental Psychology, 13*(3), 252–260.

Ho, D. Y. F. (1986). Chinese pattern of socialization: A critical review. In M. H. Bond (Ed.), *The psychology of the Chinese people* (pp. 1–37). Oxford, England: Oxford University Press.

Hoffman, M. L. (1960). Power assertion by the parent and its impact on the child. *Child Development, 31*, 129–143.

Hymel, S., Bowker, A., & Woody, E. (1993). Aggressive versus withdrawn unpopular children: Variations in peer and self perceptions in multiple domains. *Child Development, 64*, 879–896.

Isobe, M., & Sato, S. (2003). Relational aggression and social skills of preschool children. *Japanese Journal of Educational Psychology, 51*, 13–21.

Kerr, M., Lambert, W. W., & Bem, D. J. (1996). Life course sequelae of childhood shyness in Sweden: Comparison with the United States. *Developmental Psychology, 32*, 1100–1105.

Khaleque, A., & Rohner, R. P. (2002). Perceived parental acceptance-rejection and psychological adjustment: A meta-analysis of cross-cultural and intracultural studies. *Journal of Marriage and Family, 64*, 54–64.

Krappman, L. (1989). Family relationships and peer relationships in middle childhood. In K. Kreppner & R. M. Lerner (Eds.), *Family systems and life-span development* (pp. 93–104). Hillsdale, NJ: Lawrence Erlbaum Associates.

Ladd, G. W., & Golter, B. (1988). Parents' management of preschoolers' peer relations: Is it related to children's social competence? *Developmental Psychology, 24*, 109–117.

Ladd, G. W., & Hart, C. H. (1992). Creating informal play opportunities: Are parents' and preschoolers' initiations related to children's competence with peers? *Developmental Psychology, 28*, 1179–1187.

Ladd, G. W., & Le Sieur, K. D. (1995). Parents and children's peer relationships. In M. H. Bornstein (Ed.), *Handbook of parenting: Vol. 4. Applied and practical parenting* (pp. 377–410). Hillsdale, NJ: Lawrence Erlbaum Associates.

Ladd, G. W., & Profilet, S. M. (1996). The Child Behavior Scale: A teacher-report measure of young children's aggressive, withdrawn, and prosocial behaviors. *Developmental Psychology, 32*, 1008–1024.

Lagerspetz, K. M. J., Björkqvist, K., & Peltonen, T. (1988). Is indirect aggression typical of females? Gender differences in aggressiveness in 11- to 12-year-old children. *Aggressive Behavior, 14*, 403–414.

Lau, S. (1996). *Growing up the Chinese way: Chinese child and adolescent development*. Hong Kong: The Chinese University Press.

Lau, S., & Yeung, P. P. W. (1996). Understanding Chinese child development: The role of culture in socialization. In S. Lau (Ed.), *Growing up the Chinese way* (pp. 29–44). Hong Kong: The Chinese University Press.

Leung, K., Lau, S., & Lam, W. (1998). Parenting styles and academic achievement: A cross-cultural study. *Merrill-Palmer Quarterly, 44*, 157–172.

Lin, C. C., & Fu, V. R. (1990). A comparison of child-rearing practices among Chinese, immigrant Chinese, Caucasian-American parents. *Child Development, 61*, 429–433.

Maccoby, E. E., & Martin, J. A. (1983). Socialization in the context of the family: Parent-child interaction. In E. M. Hetherington (Ed.) & P. H. Mussen (Series Ed.), *Handbook of child psychology* (pp. 1–102). New York: Wiley.

MacDonald, K. (1992). Warmth as a developmental construct: An evolutionary analysis. *Child Development, 63*, 753–773.

Mackey, K., Arnold, M. L., & Pratt, M. W. (2001). Adolescents' stories of decision making in more and less authoritative families: Representing the voices of parents in narrative. *Journal of Adolescent Research, 16*, 243–268.

McNeilly-Choque, M. K., Hart, C. H., Robinson, C. C., Nelson, L. J., & Olsen, S. F. (1996). Overt and relational aggression on the playground: Correspondence among different informants. *Journal of Research in Childhood Education, 11*, 47–67.

Mills, R. S. L., & Rubin, K. H. (1990). Parental beliefs about problematic social behaviors in early childhood. *Child Development, 61*, 138–151.

Mills, R. S. L., & Rubin, K. H. (1993). Socialization factors in the development of social withdrawal. In K. H. Rubin & J. B. Asendorpf (Eds.), *Social withdrawal, inhibition, and shyness in childhood* (pp. 117–148). Hillsdale, NJ: Lawrence Erlbaum Associates.

Mize, J., & Pettit, G. S. (1997). Mothers' social coaching, mother-child relationship style, and children's peer competence: Is the medium the message? *Child Development, 68*, 312–332.

Mize, J., Pettit, G. S., & Brown, G. (1995). Mothers' supervision of their children's play: Relations with beliefs, perceptions, and knowledge. *Developmental Psychology, 31*, 311–321.

Nelson, D. A., & Crick, N. R. (2002). Parental psychological control: Implications for childhood physical and relational aggression. In B. K. Barber (Ed.), *Intrusive parenting: How psychological control affects children and adolescents* (pp. 168–189). Washington, DC: American Psychological Association.

Nelson, D. A., Hart, C. H., & Yang, C. (2005). *Russian and U.S. comparative data regarding physical and relational aggression: Temperament and peer status linkages*. Manuscript in preparation.

Nelson, D. A., Hart, C. H., Yang, C., Olsen, J. A., & Jin, S. (in press). *Aversive parenting in China: Associations with child physical and relational aggression.* Child Development.

Nelson, D. A., Hart, C. H., Yang, C., & Jin S. (2005). *Aggression subtypes in U.S. and Chinese preschoolers: Cultural equivalence, statistical distinctiveness, and peer outcomes*. Manuscript submitted for publication.

Nelson, D. A., Robinson, C. C., & Hart, C. H. (2005). Relational and physical aggression of preschool-age children: Peer status linkages across informants. *Early Education & Development, 16*, 115–139.

Nelson, L. J. (1996). *Relations between sociometric status and three subtypes of withdrawn behavior in preschool children: A multi-method perspective*. Unpublished master's thesis, Brigham Young University, Provo, Utah.

Nelson, L. J., Hart, C. H., Wu, B., Yang, C., & Olsen, S. (in press). Relations between Chinese mothers' parenting practices and social withdrawal in early childhood. *International Journal of Behavioral Development*.

Olsen, S. F., Yang, C., Hart, C. H., Robinson, C. C., Wu, P., Nelson, D. A., et al. (2002). Maternal psychological control and preschool children's behavioral outcomes in China, Russia, and the United States. In B. K. Barber (Ed.), *Intrusive parenting: How psychological control affects children and adolescents* (pp. 235–262). Washington DC, American Psychological Association.

Ostrov, J. M., & Keating, C. F. (2004). Gender differences in preschool aggression during free play and structured interactions: An observational study. *Social Development, 13*, 255–277.

Ostrov, J. M., Woods, K. E., Jansen, E. A., Casas, J. F., & Crick, N. R. (2004). An observational study of delivered and received aggression, gender, and social-psychological adjustment in preschool: "This White Crayon Doesn't Work...." *Early Childhood Research Quarterly, 19*, 355–371.

Owens, L. D. (1996). Sticks and stones and sugar and spice: Girls' and boys' aggression in schools. *Australian Journal of Guidance & Counseling, 6*, 45–55.

Oyserman, D., Coon, H. M., & Kemmelmeier, M. (2002). Rethinking individualism and collectivism: Evaluation of theoretical assumptions and meta-analyses. *Psychological Bulletin, 128*, 3–72.

Peterson, G. W., & Hann, D. (1999). Socializing parents and children in families. In S. Steinmetz, M. Sussman, & G. W. Peterson (Eds.), *Handbook of marriage and the family* (rev. ed., pp. 327–370). New York: Plenum Press.

Porter, C. L., Hart, C. H., Yang, C., Robinson, C. C., Olsen, S., Zeng, Q., et al. (in press). A comparative study of child temperament and parenting in Beijing, China and the Western United States. *International Journal of Behavioral Development*.

Profilet, S. M., & Ladd, G. W. (1994). Do mothers' perceptions and concerns about preschoolers' peer competence predict their peer-management practices? *Social Development, 3*, 205–221.

Renshaw, P. D., & Brown, P. J. (1993). Loneliness in middle childhood: Concurrent and longitudinal predictors. *Child Development, 64*, 1271–1284.

Rohner, R. P. (1975). *They love me, they love me not*. New Haven, CT: HRAF Press.

Rohner, R. P. (1986). *The warmth dimension: Foundations of parental acceptance-rejection*. Thousand Oaks, CA: Sage.

Rubin, K. H. (1982). Nonsocial play in preschoolers: Necessarily evil? *Child Development, 53*, 651–657.

Rubin, K. H., Burgess, K. B. (2002). Parents of aggressive and withdrawn children. In M. H. Bornstein (Ed.), *Handbook of parenting: Vol. 1. Children and parenting (2nd ed.*; pp. 383–418). Mahwah, NJ: Lawrence Erlbaum Associates.

Rubin, K. H., Burgess, K. B., & Coplan, R. J. (2002). Social withdrawal and shyness. In P. K. Smith & C. H. Hart (Eds.), *Blackwell handbook of child social development* (pp. 330–352). Malden, MA: Blackwell Publishers.

Rubin, K. H., Burgess, K. B., & Hastings, P. D. (2002). Stability and social-behavioral consequences of toddlers' inhibited temperament and parenting behaviors. *Child Development, 73*, 483–495.

Rubin, K. H., Burgess, K. B., Kennedy, A. E., & Stewart, S. L. (2003). Social withdrawal in childhood. In R. A. Barkley & E. J. Mash (Eds.), *Child psychopathology (2nd ed.*, pp. 372–406). New York: Guilford Press.

Rubin, K. H., Chen, X., & Hymel, S. (1993). Socioemotional characteristics of withdrawn and aggressive children. *Merrill-Palmer Quarterly, 39*, 518–534.

Rubin, K. H., Chen, X., McDougall, P., Bowker, A., & McKinnon, J. (1995). The Waterloo longitudinal Project: Predicting internalizing and externalizing problems in adolescence. *Development and Psychopathology, 7*, 751–764.

Rubin, K. H., Coplan, R. J., Fox, N. A., & Calkins, S. D. (1995). Emotionality, emotion regulation, and preschoolers' social adaptation. *Development and Psychopathology, 7*, 49–62.

Rubin, K. H., & Mills, R. S. L. (1990). Maternal beliefs abut adaptive and maladaptive social behaviors in normal, aggressive, and withdrawn preschoolers. *Journal of Abnormal Child Psychology, 18*, 419–435.

Rubin, K. H., Mills, R. S. L., & Rose-Krasnor, L. (1989). Maternal beliefs and children's competence. In B. H. Schneider, G. Attili, J. Nadel, & R. P. Weissberg (Eds). *Social competence in developmental perspective* (pp. 313–331). New York: Kluwer Academic/Plenum Publishers.

Rubin, K. H., Nelson, L. J., Hastings, P., & Asendorpf, J. B. (1999). The transaction between parents' perceptions of their children's shyness and their parenting styles. *International Journal of Behavioral Development, 23*, 937–958.

Russell, A., Hart, C. H., Robinson, C. C., & Olsen, S. F. (2003). Children's sociable and aggressive behavior with peers: A comparison of the U.S. and Australia, and contributions of temperament and parenting styles. *International Journal of Behavioral Development, 27*, 74–86.

Schaughency, E. A., Vannatta, K., Langhinrichsen, J., Lally, C. M., Seely, J. (1992). Correlates of sociometric status in school children in Buenos Aires. *Journal of Abnormal Child Psychology, 20*, 317–326.

Schneider, B. H., Attili, G., Vermigli, P., & Younger, A. (1997). A comparison of middle class English-Canadian and Italian mothers' beliefs about children's peer-directed aggression and social withdrawal. *International Journal of Behavioral Development, 21*, 133–154.

Schoenhals, M. (1993). *The paradox of power in the People's Republic of China middle school*. Armonk, NY: M.E. Sharpe.

Schwartz, D., Chang, L., & Farver, J. M. (2001). Correlates of victimization in Chinese children's peer groups. *Developmental Psychology, 37*, 520–532.

Sebanc, A. M. (2003). The friendship features of preschool children: Links with prosocial behavior and aggression. *Social Development, 12*, 249–268.

Steinberg, L., Darling, N. E., & Fletcher, A. C. (1995). Authoritative parenting and adolescent adjustment: An ecological journey. In P. Moen, G. H. Elder Jr., & K. Luescher (Eds.), *Examining lives in context: Perspectives on the ecology of human development* (pp. 423–466). Washington, DC: American Psychological Association.

Tomada, G., & Schneider, B. H. (1997). Relational aggression, gender, and peer acceptance: Invariance across culture, stability over time, and concordance among informants. *Developmental Psychology, 33*, 601–609.

Triandis, H. C. (1994). *Culture and social behavior*. New York: McGraw-Hill.

Triandis, H. C. (2000). Cross-cultural versus cultural psychology: A synthesis? In U. P. Gielen & A. L. Comunian (Eds.), *International perspectives on human development* (pp. 81–95). Lengerich, Germany: Pabst Science.

Valdivia, I. A., Schneider, B. A., Chavez, K. L., & Chen, X. (2005). Social withdrawal and maladjustment in a very group-oriented society. *International Journal of Behavioral Development*, 29, 219–228.

Vandenberg, R. J., & Lance, C. E. (2000). A review and synthesis of the measurement invariance literature: Suggestions, practices, and recommendations for organizational research. *Organizational Research Methods, 3*, 4–69.

Wu, P., Robinson, C. C., Yang, C., Hart, C. H., Olsen, S. F., Porter, C. L., et al. (2002). Similarities and differences in mother's parenting of preschoolers in China and the United States. *International Journal of Behavioral Development, 26*, 481–491.

Xie, H., Swift, D. J., Cairns, B. D., & Cairns, R. B. (2002). Aggressive behaviors in social interaction and developmental adaptation: A narrative analysis of interpersonal conflicts during early adolescence. *Social Development, 11*, 205–224.

Yang, C., Hart, C. H., Nelson, D. A., Porter, C. L., Olsen, S. F., Robinson, C. C., et al. (2004). Fathering in a Beijing, Chinese sample: Associations with boys' and girls' negative emotionality and aggression. In R. D. Day & M. E. Lamb (Eds.), *Conceptualizing and measuring father involvement* (pp. 185–215). Mahwah, NJ: Lawrence Erlbaum Associates.

11 Real and Symbolic Entry of Children in the Social World of Peers and Parent–Child Interactions

Cultural and Cross-Cultural Aspects

Paul P. Goudena

In this chapter, I rely on the notions of independent and interdependent pathways to relationship formation (Greenfield et al., 2003) to put peer interaction and parenting in a cross-cultural perspective and apply the equality model and apprentice model (Keller, 2003) to analyze culture-specific parental practices with children. I then attempt to integrate the main ideas from these different theoretical models and perspectives in the chapter.

According to Greenfield et al. (2003), the analysis of independent and interdependent cultural pathways may be undertaken in a fruitful way by using three perspectives: the ecocultural, the values, and the sociohistorical approaches. The ecocultural approach focuses on the way individuals adapt to specific environmental conditions, such as a densely populated urban area or a small-scale agrarian village setting. The independent pathway is more connected with the first setting, and the interdependent pathway more with the second setting. The values approach pays special attention to the systems of beliefs and ideas that individuals – especially parents – have concerning human development and socialization goals. These "ethnotheories" are shared by members of cultural communities. People from non-Western cultures, for example, often share the cultural ideal of interdependence. Individuals should be responsible members of their communities, respect older people, and be loyal to the family. In Western industrialized societies, independence is the cultural ideal. Appreciation of individual assertiveness and high self-esteem, and giving priority to individual goals, are indices of such an orientation. The sociohistorical approach is directed at analyzing cultural activities and practices, with special interest in the learning process within these settings ("apprenticeship"). Also, the historical context of cultural practices is taken into account. For a large part, cross-cultural research carried out from the sociohistorical perspective focused on cognitive processes and cognitive development. Culture-specific interactional routines (e.g., variations in the amount of verbal and nonverbal instruction during learning) and the context-bound nature of cognitive functioning are among the topics studied.

Greenfield et al. (2003) consider relationship formation as a universal developmental task, which may be mastered in culture-specific ways. During the life course, there are different relationships, including the first (attachment) relationship of the infant with a caregiver, interaction and friendship with peers, relations with siblings, romantic partnership, and the relationship of adult children with their aged parents. Thus, parent–child and child–peer interaction, the focus of this chapter, may be situated within the larger domain of relationships. Understanding the issue of relationship formation may proceed along one of two prototypical trajectories, the independent and interdependent pathways. Such a conceptualization does not deny the fact that, within individualistic and collectivistic cultures, much variability often exists. As Greenfield et al. (2003, p. 468) point out, these "two value systems are merely ideal paradigms that get instantiated in a multiplicity of concrete and historically differentiated cultural contexts." Although Oyserman, Coon, and Kemmelmeier (2002) have recently noted several problems with the notions of individualism and collectivism, such terms remain useful in analyzing cultures at the level of the values shared by people, the ecocultural setting they live in, and the socialization practices that prevail. As Greenfield et al. (2003, p. 467) emphasize, their notions of independent and interdependent pathways are based on naturalistic observation and culture-sensitive ethnography, and not on "standardized questionnaires administered to various national groups" – on which the Oyserman, Coon, and Kemmelmeier (2002) meta-analyses and criticism were based. Consistently, I will highlight cross-cultural research based on direct or indirect reports of behaviors of children and parents.

From the perspective of culture-specific pathways, an important question is whether the findings concerning the social world of peers based on Western children are universal or particular to the independent context. According to the ecocultural point of view, the environmental conditions within which the independent pathway proceeds are in many aspects different from the settings in which children develop socially along the interdependent pathway. Konner (1975), arguing from an evolutionary perspective, has pointed out that the focus on the peer setting in Western studies cannot be considered to be representative of children's social environment in other parts of the world. According to Konner, interaction between same-aged peers is only one of the possible forms of interaction between children and the product of child-care and socialization practices in advanced industrial states. In non-Western societies, interaction within mixed-age groups is much more common, allowing for a greater variety of interactional behaviors, such as instruction and nurturance (Farver & Howes, 1988). These types of behavior are more representative of the interdependent pathway toward constructive interaction with other children.

In the next paragraph, I discuss different perspectives on the relation between parent–child interaction and child–child interaction. Then, I examine in more detail the "equality model" and the "apprentice model" of parenting, connecting them with the independent and interdependent pathways to constructive peer interaction.

Parent–Child Interactions and Children's Entry in the Social World of Peers

Both children and adults may be viewed as individuals on their way to the mastery of relationship formation in different phases of their lives. Those adolescents or adults who become a parent not only carry with them their own history of relationship formation, but also their cultural belief system or ethnotheory (Harkness & Super, 1996) about the nature of children and socialization practices. How are parent–child interactions and parental socialization practices related to children's functioning in the social world of peers? Two main positions concerning this question may be distinguished. The first position states that the quality of parent–child interactions is related to the quality of child–peer relations. Different theoretical orientations defend such a point of view. From an attachment perspective, the quality of the attachment relationship is seen as related to the child's functioning in the world of peers (e.g., LaFreniere & Sroufe, 1985). From a social learning perspective (e.g., Parke & Ladd, 1992), social skills practiced during parent–child interaction are considered to be important for later child–peer interaction. In contrast, the second main position implies a negative association or difference between parent–child and child–child interactions. An example is Piaget's (1932) emphasis on the symmetrical character of child–child interaction. Piaget contrasted this type of interaction with parent–child interaction, which he characterized as asymmetrical because the parent often has greater power in their interactions with the child. The unique symmetrical character of child–child interaction is necessary for the process of decentration, the capability of taking the viewpoint of the other. Piaget's emphasis was on cognitive development. On a more general behavioral level, Hinde (e.g., Hinde & Tamplin, 1983) studied interactions of young children with mother at home and with peers and adults at school. The researchers found hardly any parallels between children's behavior at home and in school.

It is not my intention to review in depth the different positions in the debate about the relation between parent–child and child–child interactions. I discuss certain aspects of this debate that, in my opinion, are particularly important from a cross-cultural point of view. It is important to realize that most research and theorizing about this topic are situated within the independent pathway of relationship formation. For example, Parke's (e.g., Parke et al., 1994) family–peer linkage model, according to which parents may function as instructors or managers of their children with respect to peer interaction, presupposes two rather distinct domains of family interaction and peer interaction. In a similar way, Hinde's emphasis on the differences between the interactional worlds of home and school is possible only because these two ecocultural settings exist. However, not all societies have separate schooling facilities, combined with children's participation in same-age classrooms.

Keller's (2003) conceptualization of socialization practices may be helpful for a discussion of parent–child interactions from a cross-cultural perspective. Keller (2003) proposed two models for culture-specific parental practices with infants that are also relevant to parent–child interaction with children of older ages. The "equality model of infancy" appears to reflect the types of socialization practices that are typically applied by urban middle-class families who favor independent developmental goals (such as uniqueness and autonomy). In contrast, the "apprentice model of infancy" emphasizes parental socialization activities that are more typical of rural agrarian settings in which interdependent goals (such as harmony and obligation to the family) are pursued. As Keller emphasizes, independence and interdependence are not parts of the same dimension, but represent two separate dimensions that may occur in specific mixtures and are subject to change. This point is especially relevant in multicultural societies, where immigrant families may come to value, for example, independent goals for the domain of knowledge acquisition, but retain interdependent goals for relationship formation (cf. Kagitcibasi, 1996).

Consistent with Keller's models, Russell, Pettit, and Mize (1998) have proposed a conceptual framework that incorporates both symmetrical and asymmetrical aspects of parent–child relationships. The authors point out that parent–child interactions may contain horizontal (symmetrical) qualities, just as child–peer relations do, as well as vertical qualities. Interacting with their parents, young children may learn on the horizontal plane those skills that are of great value for interaction with peers. Russell et al. (1998) are in particular referring to aspects like reciprocity and shared power. These horizontal qualities may be especially displayed in play settings and during control exchanges. According to Russell et al. (1998, p. 325), during parent–child play, the following types of interaction may be designated as an opportunity for horizontal qualities to occur: matching of affective states, turn-taking, synchronous exchanges, joint determination of the content and direction of play, and parent and child being mutually compliant during play. Clearly, these horizontal qualities fit nicely in the equality model of parenting. Russell et al. (1998) construct a connection between parent–child and child–peer relations that implies that those children who have no opportunities to be involved with their parents in activities that allow for horizontal qualities to occur are in a disadvantaged position when interacting with peers. Consider the following example given by Kagitcibasi (1996, p. 45):

> Recently, while waiting for luggage at a major European airport, I noticed a young Turkish family consisting of a father, mother, and two little boys. They were obviously living in Western Europe as an ethnic minority family of lower socioeconomic status. (...) The bigger boy was about 4 to 4 1/2 years old, and the smaller one was about 3. The bigger boy was trying hard to get his father's attention and to engage him in a conversation, as he was repeatedly telling the father some things and asking eagerly, "Isn't it so, daddy?" The father was not responding; he was not even looking at the child. The mother did not intervene or respond in any way either. She, like her husband, was looking aimlessly into space, as if the children were not there. The smaller boy, in turn, was actively searching for the attention of his older brother. After insistent repetitions, the bigger boy gave up on catching the father's attention and turned to his younger brother, and the two of them carried on.

Kagitcibasi (1996) contrasts this episode with the much greater verbal responsiveness of Western middle-class parents (especially from the United States) with their children and emphasizes cultural differences in parent–child interactions. The question I want to bring forward is: when verbal responsiveness to children is low and there is no "equality context" for interaction in certain cultures, will children then have more problems with entry in the social world of peers? In other words, does parenting according to the apprentice model put children at risk for constructive peer interactions in these societies? The vertical qualities of parent–child interactions include instruction, nurturance, demands for compliance and obedience, and a strong emphasis on conformity to social norms. When we look at the ecocultural setting in which the interdependent pathway to relationship formation outside the family progresses, in particular the mixed-age group, certain interactional aspects of the apprentice model (e.g., instruction, nurturance; cf. Farver & Howes, 1988) may be encountered. The child's experiences in vertical parent–child interactions may be useful for this type of peer interaction. However, children's interactions with peers, especially at the same age, also involve matching of affective states, turn-taking, synchronous exchanges, joint determination of the content and direction of play, and mutual compliance during play, just as Russell et al. (1998) propose for children developing on the independent pathway of learning to interact with peers. How do parent–child interactions affect different types of peer interactions?

In a study with two- to five-years-olds from the United States, Black and Logan (1995) analyzed turn-taking skills and utterance types during parent–child and child–peer play interactions in relation to children's sociometric status. They found that patterns of communication that children used in conversation with their parents were, to a large extent, similar to the communication patterns they showed when interacting with peers. Sociometric status was related to type of communication pattern, both during parent–child and during child–peer interaction. For example, parents of rejected children differed from parents of popular children with respect to question-and-answer behavior. Parents of rejected status children often responded noncontingently to their children's requests or did not respond at all. Rejected children showed the same type of communication pattern when interacting with peers. According to Black and Logan (1995, p. 267), "The question and answer behavior of parents with rejected children appears to be an interactive link to children's behavior in the peer group."

Different results were found in a recent investigation of Dutch children (Gerrits, Goudena, & Van Aken, in press). In this study, we observed and analyzed parent–child and child–peer interactions, looking for horizontal and vertical qualities, as proposed by Russell et al. (1998). Dutch seven-years-olds were videotaped while interacting in a play setting with their mother, their father, and a peer, respectively. Horizontal and vertical qualities were found in both parent–child and child–peer interactions, suggesting that features of adult–child interaction are present in children's social world of peers (cf. Corsaro, 1985). It turned out that, with respect to horizontal qualities, parent–child interaction was most characterized by mutual responsiveness and child–peer interaction by balance of control, shared positive emotions, and simultaneous play. Interestingly, however, showing shared positive emotions in parent–child interactions was not related to peer preference. Moreover, consistency between the parent–child and child–peer contexts was low. The results indicate that dyads with the same child displayed different behaviors in different interaction contexts. The lack of relations between peer status and behavioral characteristics of parent–child interactions and the lack of consistency between different interaction contexts seem to suggest that the social worlds of the family and peers are relatively autonomous, at least for seven-years-olds in the Dutch culture; there may not be strong causal linkage between these two worlds. It is difficult to conclude why the Black and Logan (1995) and the Gerrits et al. (in press) studies did not produce the same results concerning this causal linkage issue. Two important differences between the two studies that may be relevant in this respect are the different ages of the participants (mean ages, 42 and 86 months, respectively) and the type of system used for coding interactions. In the Black and Logan study, mainly utterance type and type of turn were scored, whereas in the Gerrits et al. study, coding of emotional expression, type of play behavior, and dyadic categories constituted the basis for analysis. Obviously, more empirical research is needed to shed light on the possibly shifting relations between the social worlds of family and peers, as children develop from early to middle childhood. The Gerrits et al. results are largely consistent with the findings on the relations between parent–child attachment and child–peer interactions. A meta-analysis by Schneider, Atkinson, and Tardif (2001) reports small to moderate effects of child–mother attachment on peer interactions. As the authors note, the small overall effect size is not in line with a strong causal claim of attachment theory, but is more "consistent with the notion that attachment is only one among many influences on peer relations" (Schneider et al., 2001, p. 93).

A possible conclusion one may draw from these studies is that different styles of parent–child interactions across cultures (e.g., those in the Turkish family and the U.S. family noticed by Kagitcibasi, 1996) may have limited effects on children's competence in the peer context. However, the lack of a strong causal role of parental practices in children's peer relations does not necessarily imply, in my opinion, that these two social worlds of childhood are not related in a meaningful way. Peer culture is based on both a reproduction of adult values and behaviors and active contributions of children themselves (Corsaro, 1985). From such a perspective, parents may still play an important role, but their influences may be filtered and reconstructed by children during their interactions with peers. Therefore, it is possible to detect the contributions of culture-specific socialization goals and values to peer interactions. We have explored this possibility in a study with Andalusian and Dutch children.

In collaboration with Spanish colleagues, I studied peer interaction in a society with a collectivistic orientation (south of Spain: Andalusia) and in an individualistic society (The Netherlands). The focus was on play behavior and on conflict resolution (Goudena & Sánchez, 1996; Martínez Lozano, 2003; Sánchez Medina, Martínez Lozano, & Goudena, 2001). We expected that, through the socialization process, social interactions between children would in part reflect the adult social world, as proposed by Corsaro (1985). Thus, in the Andalusian collectivistic culture, we expected children to function more often as part of a (large) group than in the Dutch individualistic culture. We observed free-play behavior of five-year-old children in a school setting during leisure time. Because we did not conceive of culture as one cohesive structural organization without internal differentiation (cf. Oyserman, Coon et al., 2002; Valsiner, 1988), both the Andalusian and the Dutch sample consisted of an urban and a rural subgroup.

The results of the study (Goudena & Sánchez, 1996) confirmed our expectations concerning the differences between Andalusian and Dutch children. Andalusian children engaged more in peer conversation than Dutch children. Also, Andalusian children showed a stronger social orientation in their behaviors, whereas the Dutch children were more directed toward movements and objects (e.g., functional and constructive play). Much more often than Dutch children, Andalusian children functioned in large (i.e., more than four children) groups than Dutch children. Dutch children participated more in dyads and small groups. Interestingly, for some variables (e.g., peer conversation), an interaction effect between culture and gender was found. For example, Andalusian girls engaged more in peer conversation than Andalusian boys, whereas for Dutch girls and boys, this was the same. Finally, the Andalusian urban group resembled the Dutch urban and rural group in many respects. Thus, the Andalusian rural group contributed much to the observed differences between cultures.

In a later study with different participants, we tried to capture more the dynamics of social interaction (Martínez Lozano, 2003; Sánchez Medina, et al., 2001). The focus was on interpersonal conflicts between five-years-old children from the two cultures. A distinction was made between conflict issue (control of object or place, control of play, or control of behavior), conflict strategy (verbal or nonverbal, directive or nondirective), and conflict outcome (compromise, submission, or physical or social rupture). We found that Andalusian children started a conflict more often than Dutch children to control play or nonplay behavior. For Dutch children, the most important issue to start a conflict was control of object or place. Control of object or place has to do with competition and individuation, and control of play and nonplay behavior with the coordination of communality in a social group. The results with respect to strategy use also confirmed our expectations. Andalusian children used more often nondirective tactics during conflicts than Dutch children. The latter used more directive tactics. The Andalusian social interaction setting apparently privileges more a nondirective negotiation style than the Dutch interaction setting. The type of resolution that ended conflicts had a clear relation to the culture. As one would expect, Dutch children used social or physical rupture endings much more often than Andalusian children, who preferred submissive endings of conflicts. Along general lines, these results show clear differences between the two cultures with respect to conflict issue, conflict strategy, and conflict resolution.

The following two examples were taken from Sánchez Medina et al. (2001, pp. 157–158). The first episode takes place within a Dutch rural setting. Two boys are playing together. The target child (Arjan: A) is one of the participants of the study who is being followed for a fixed period of time:

1. A and Martijn (M) are making a road in the sand. With the aid of a container, M marks the limits of the road.
2. A walks to M.
3. A: May I use it?
4. M: What?
5. A: May I use it?
6. M: 'No!!!'
7. A walks away from M. (p. 157)

In this episode, the conflict issue is control of an object. After the refusal of M (line 6) to give the object to A, the conflict ends with a physical rupture: A walks away.

The second episode takes place within an Andalusian urban setting. Two girls are playing together. Maria (M) is the target child.

1. M and Ana Cecilia (AC) are deciding whether to play a game of Sleeping Beauty or Snow White.
2. AC: I want to play Snow White.
3. M: Well, you play, not me.
4. M lets go of AC and leaves upset
5. AC goes after her.
6. AC: Well, alright Maria (again takes her by the hand).
7. M: Do you want to play a game of Clowns?
8. AC: No, I don't feel like it.
9. M begins to act silly, imitating a clown, and then they both end up laughing. (p. 158)

In the second episode, the conflict issue is control of behavior (what to play). After M's refusal to play Snow White (line 3), M leaves but AC follows her and verbally and nonverbally (line 6) restores the contact and tries to negotiate. The conflict ends with a compromise.

Theorists and researchers have argued that cultural differences exist in communication and conflict resolution (see Oyserman, Coon et al., 2002; Triandis, 1990, for reviews). Our studies with young children show that even five-years-olds may have appropriated culture-specific social dynamics of the adult world and display culturally endorsed interaction styles in the peer world.

A confusing finding from our studies is that there is a stronger similarity between social behaviors prevalent within the independent pathway to relationship formation and the socialization practices of parents guided by the equality model of parenting than between social behaviors – in particular between peers – typical of the interdependent pathway and parenting behaviors according to the apprentice model. For example, in the conflict episode from a collectivistic setting given earlier, the aspects of restoration of contact, negotiation, and compromise are not at the heart of the apprentice model of parenting, which is characterized by obedience and vertical transmission of values (cf. Keller, 2003).

To pursue this issue further, it may be interesting to discuss findings from an African collectivistic culture: the Gusii people from Kenya (LeVine et al., 1994). LeVine et al. use the term "respect and obedience model" to indicate the rules according to which the Gusii parents interact with their children. The content of this model largely coincides with the apprentice model of parenting: Gusii parents expect their children to be easily manageable (i.e., by being obedient), to participate in domestic activities, to show respect to their parents and other people who are older, and to conform to the social rules of the community. Children are rarely praised or involved in a question–answer sequence with the parent. Interestingly, LeVine et al. contrast the consequences of parenting according to this model with the American middle-class perspective: "(...) failure to prepare the child for schooling through the early development of language skills, self-confidence, and assertiveness, and an excessive emphasis on compliance to authority instead of equality and independence – thus leaving the child without the skills and virtues thought to be needed in the modern world" (LeVine et al., 1994, pp. 264–265). However, as LeVine et al. point out, at the level of practice, a different appreciation may emerge:

> Respect and obedience are long-term goals of Gusii socialization, only partly attained during the preschool years and only partly in the context of the mother-child relationship. Lessons learned with the mother in early childhood are elaborated and redefined in the sibling group and the initiation ceremonies of later childhood and in relationships with older adults during adolescence and young adulthood, both before and during marriage. (p. 265)

Thus, an important task for the Gusii mother is to provide a context for optimal development of her children. The mother may also, of course, interact directly with her children in accordance with the apprentice model of parenting. But older siblings, other children, and other adults are also important socialization agents. Respect and obedience are important aspects of socialization, but certainly not the only ones. Guided participation by other children and adults also plays an important role. Moreover, many children, as LeVine et al. (1994, p. 266) put it, evaded parental authority and had social experiences "not covered, or authorized, by the model." Thus, a picture of children's social development emerges, in which parent–child interaction certainly plays a socializing role, but in which other socializing agents (older siblings, other children, and adults) are at least as important. Specific social skills relevant for peer interaction (e.g., "horizontal qualities"; Russell et al., 1998) do not seem to be learned during parent–child interaction, but, apparently, there is enough "free social learning space" in other interaction settings to progress adequately along the interdependent pathway toward mastery of relationship formation.

Such a social learning space was analyzed in more detail within another collectivistic culture (China) by Chen, Chen, and Kaspar (2001). As the authors point out, informal peer groups, formed on a voluntary basis, are not considered to be in accordance with collectivistic principles. Nonetheless, these informal peer groups do exist. Chen et al. investigated groups with children, with ages ranging from nine to fourteen years. Consistent with findings from research in Western and individualistic cultures, they found that peer sociability was positively related to indices of socioemotional (e.g., social preference) and school adjustment. Moreover, it was found that shyness–sensitivity was positively related to peer acceptance, corroborating results from earlier studies conducted in China. Different from the negative valuing of shyness–sensitivity in individualistic cultures, in China such behavior is valued positively. In line with findings from Western studies, child overt aggression was related to adjustment problems. A picture of Chinese children's social interactions emerges that seems to be similar in many aspects to Western peer groups. However, in China the appreciation and consequences of shyness–sensitivity are fundamentally different from individualistic valuations of these behaviors. Interestingly, Chen et al. (2001) found that social functioning of group peers within the informal peer group had "(...) unique contributions to individual social and school adjustment and adjustment problems, over and above the child's self social functioning" (p. 264). These groups appear to "(...) constitute an important socialization force that contributes, independently and/or in interaction with adults' influences to socioemotional and cognitive development" (p. 292).

From such findings, a picture of the interdependent pathway to relationship formation emerges in which not only parent–child interactions are important, but also other long-lasting social settings. Informal peer groups, in particular, may provide children with opportunities to practice, among other things, the horizontal interaction qualities described by Russell et al. (1998). With regard to the question how parenting according to the apprentice model may contribute to children's social competence, particularly competent social functioning in the peer group, a possible answer is as follows. What children learn from apprentice model-parenting are the rules and social behaviors that are relevant for interaction with people who deserve respect and expect obedience. The specific social tactics of peer interactions are learned outside the home, for example, in informal peer groups, or in groups consisting of both peers and younger and older children. Compared with children developing along the independent pathway, children following the interdependent pathway are confronted with a stronger separation between the parental/adult world and the world of peers, at least with respect to vertical and horizontal aspects of relationships. With respect to values (e.g., adherence to group norms, loyalty to the family), these different social worlds may resemble each other very much (cf. Corsaro, 1985).

Symbolic Entry of Children in the Social World Outside the Family

In Western and perhaps many other societies, prosocial behaviors, such as cooperativeness, rule-following, and helpfulness, as well as the skills of turn-taking and interpersonal sensitivity, are important ingredients of adequate interpersonal functioning, particularly in the peer group. From the point of view of the child, the most important question is: Do I really *feel* that I am participating in that social world outside my family? Put differently, do children answer in the affirmative when asked whether they think to be really worthwhile compared with others, do they have positive views of themselves, and do they perceive significant others, such as parents, as a source of help when encountering difficulties in that strange world outside the family? In the Western research tradition, these questions have been studied with concepts such as internal working model (Bowlby, 1969; Bretherton, 1991), self-representations (Harter, 2003), and perceived security (Kerns, Klepac, & Cole, 1996). I put these conceptualizations under the label of "symbolic entry in the social world."

In a recent cross-cultural study (Chen et al., 2004), relations between self-perceptions of competence and social and school adjustment were investigated. Children (ages ranged from ten to sixteen years) from Brazil, Canada, China, and Italy participated in this project, permitting a view of possible cultural differences in the associations between self-perceptions of competence and social adjustment. Canada may be thought of as an individualistic culture and China as a collectivistic culture. As Chen et al. (2004) indicate, Brazil and Italy may be considered to be cultures in which mixtures of values (such as the importance of relational bonds and individual autonomy) are present. Across cultures, it turned out that "sociability-competence and academic achievement were positively associated with self-perceptions of scholastic competence and general self-worth" (Chen et al., 2004, p. 135). With respect to social adjustment, two important findings stand out. First, in all four cultures, aggressive children – notwithstanding their difficulties in social and school adjustment – "did not report negative self-perceptions of social and scholastic competence and self-worth" (Chen et al., 2004, p. 136). Apparently, the often-noted overestimation of self-competence of aggressive children is not only present in Western countries. Second, with the exception of China, shyness–sensitivity was negatively associated with self-perceptions of social competence. Chinese children perceive their own social competence according to Chinese values prevalent in the Chinese culture. In China, shy and inhibited behavior is considered to be an index of maturity and adequate social participation. For example, Chinese mothers have a warm and accepting attitude toward their behaviorally inhibited toddlers, whereas Canadian mothers tend to act negatively toward their inhibited children (Chen et al., 1998).

The aforementioned findings show the importance of studying the relations between self-perceptions, parenting behaviors, and social functioning in the peer group from a cross-cultural perspective. Discussing parental practices of the African Gusii people, LeVine et al. (1994) point out that the fact that Gusii children do not receive any praise or positive support from their mothers or other adults would imply, from a Western perspective, that Gusii children are at risk for severe emotional problems. However, LeVine et al. did not find in their longitudinal study that these children "suffer from glaring mental deficits or psychiatric abnormalities" (1994, p. 273). Such findings challenge the usual notions of emotional development.

From a cross-cultural point of view, the situation becomes more complicated when we try to take into account the fact that the self is experienced in different ways in individualistic and collectivistic societies (see, for example, Kagitcibasi, 1996, for a discussion of culture and self). Consequently, we should be cautious in the use of conceptual structures that have their origin in research on the independent developmental pathway. For example, the notion of self-perceived competence (Harter, 1999) and the corresponding measurement instrument presuppose children's ability to look at their competencies (e.g., in the domains of social acceptance and physical appearance) from a distance and to compare their standing on these domains with those of other children. As Markus, Mullally, and Kitayama (1997, p. 23) noted:

> Most American children seem quickly to develop habits of identifying positive features of their own behavior, come to believe they are better than their peers, and each develop an identity or "self" in a way that is attribute-based. They are often in situations in which they are required to compare themselves with others, and they are encouraged to feel good when they have reason to believe that they have some attributes that distinguish them from others in a positive manner.

As the authors point out, the European American attribute-based self is not a universally existent and appreciated phenomenon, but is seen as immature and undesirable in, for example, Japan. In societies where interdependency and a strong sense of participation in the community are important, the self is more seen and experienced as part of a greater whole. Some theorists of Japanese selves go even so far as to refer to the self as "indeterminate, multiple, and moving, and all of these characterizations are consistent with the absence of a constant or fixed 'I' or 'you'" (Markus et al., 1997, p. 27).

Pursuing this line of thought, one may conclude that the conceptualization and measurement instruments used to capture the experience and perception of self and aspects of self should be carefully scrutinized for its application in societies where interdependency is the prevalent mode of interaction. Both the experience of cultural participation and the experience of social rejection may be heavily influenced by culture-specific factors.

Concluding Remarks

How are parent–child interactions and parental socialization practices related to children's functioning in the social world of peers? I have discussed this issue from a developmental point of view, using the notions of independent and interdependent pathway to relationship formation and the notions of equality model and apprentice model of parenting. It seems that children developing along the interdependent pathway encounter a stronger separation between the parent/adult social world and the social world of peers, in particular, with respect to vertical and horizontal aspects of relationships. Horizontal aspects of social interaction may be learned outside the family in, for example, informal peer groups. Nonetheless, empirical research until now does not produce clear answers to questions about the relations between parent–child interactions and children's social functioning outside the family. To what extent the cultural system that endorses vertical parent–child interactions is beneficial or harmful for children to learn social skills in the peer context will also be an interesting question.

It might be more fruitful to consider parent–child interactions as *one* of the social situations in which children develop (cf. Lerner et al., 2002) and to direct our research attention also to other specific interactional settings, such as same-age and mixed-age groups, subgroups of same-age groups within mixed-age groups, close friendship relations, and hierarchical relations outside the family. By examining children's development along the independent or interdependent pathway against a more varied social and institutional background, a more complete and accurate picture of children's social functioning may be obtained. It may also be more productive to investigate both individualistic and collectivistic aspects of social functioning. For example, both the independent and interdependent pathways may consist of learning cooperative *and* competitive behavioral routines. How, and in what proportions, these different routines are displayed may depend on the specific ecocultural conditions and the corresponding values concerning social interactions in a specific culture (cf. Oyserman, Kemmelmeier et al., 2002).

Acknowledgments

I thank the editors for their suggestions for revision.

References

Black, B., & Logan, A. (1995). Links between communication patterns in mother-child, father-child, and child-peer interactions and children's social status. *Child Development, 66*, 255–271.

Bowlby, J. (1969). *Attachment and loss: Vol. 1. Attachment*. London: Penguin.

Bretherton, I. (1991). Pouring old wine into new bottles: The social self as internal working model. In M. R. Gunnar & L. A. Sroufe (Eds.), *Self-processes and development, Minnesota Symposium on Child Psychology, 23*, 1–41. Hillsdale, NJ: Lawrence Erlbaum Associates.

Chen, X., Chen, H., & Kaspar, V. (2001). Group social functioning and individual socioemotional and school adjustment in Chinese children. *Merrill-Palmer Quarterly, 47*, 264–299.

Chen, X., Hastings, P. D., Rubin, K. H., Chen, H., Cen, G., & Stewart, S. L. (1998). Child-rearing attitudes and behavioral inhibition in Chinese and Canadian toddlers: A cross-cultural study. *Developmental Psychology, 34*, 677–686.

Chen, X., Zappulla, C., Lo Coco, A., Schneider, B., Kaspar, V., De Oliveira, A. M., et al. (2004). Self-perceptions of competence in Brazilian, Canadian, Chinese and Italian children: Relations with social and school adjustment. *International Journal of Behavioral Development, 28*, 129–138.

Corsaro, W. A. (1985). *Friendship and peer culture in the early years*. Norwood, NJ: Ablex.

Farver, J. A. M., & Howes, C. (1988). Cross-cultural differences in social interaction: A comparison of American and Indonesian children. *Journal of Cross-Cultural Psychology, 19*, 203–215.

Gerrits, M. H., Goudena, P. P., & Van Aken, M. A. G. (in press). Child-parent and child-peer interaction: Observational similarities and differences at age seven. *Infant and Child Development*.

Goudena, P. P., & Sánchez, J. A. (1996). Peer interaction in Andalusia and Holland: A comparative study. *Infancia y Aprendizaje, 75*, 49–58.

Greenfield, P. M., Keller, H., Fuligni, A., & Maynard, A. (2003). Cultural pathways through universal development. *Annual Review of Psychology, 54*, 461–490.

Harkness, S., & Super, C. M. (Eds.) (1996). *Parents' cultural belief systems*. New York: Guilford.

Harter, S. (1999). *The construction of the self: A developmental perspective*. New York: Guilford.

Harter, S. (2003). The development of self-representations during childhood and adolescence. In J. P. Tangney & M. R. Leary (Eds.), *Handbook of self and identity* (pp. 610–642). New York: Guilford.

Hinde, R. A., & Tamplin, A. (1983). Relations between mother-child interaction and behaviour in preschool. *British Journal of Developmental Psychology, 1*, 231–257.

Kagitcibasi, C. (1996). *Family and human development across cultures: A view from the other side*. Mahwah, NJ: Lawrence Erlbaum Associates.

Keller, H. (2003). Socialization for competence: Cultural models of infancy. *Human Development, 46*, 288–311.

Kerns, K. A., Klepac, L., & Cole, A. (1996). Peer relationships and preadolescents' perceptions of security in the child-mother relationship. *Developmental Psychology, 32*, 457–466.

Konner, M. (1975). Relations among infants and juveniles in comparative perspective. In M. Lewis & L. A. Rosenblum (Eds.), *Friendship and peer relations* (pp. 99–129). New York: Wiley.

LaFreniere, P. J., & Sroufe, L. A. (1985). Profiles of peer competence in the preschool: Interrelations between measures, influences of social ecology, and relation to attachment history. *Developmental Psychology, 21*, 56–69.

Lerner, R. M., Rothbaum, F., Boulos, S., & Castellino, D. R. (2002). Developmental systems perspective on parenting. In M. Bornstein (Ed.), *Handbook on parenting* (Vol. 2, 2nd ed., pp. 315–344). Mahwah, NJ: Lawrence Erlbaum Associates.

LeVine, R. A., Dixon, S., LeVine, S., Richman, A., Leiderman, P. H., Keefer, C. H., et al. (1994). *Child care and culture: Lessons from Africa*. Cambridge, England: Cambridge University Press.

Markus, H. R., Mullally, P. R., & Kitayama, S. (1997). Selfways: Diversity in modes of cultural participation. In U. Neisser & D. A. Jopling (Eds.), *The conceptual self in context: Culture, experience, self-understanding* (pp. 13–61). Cambridge, England: Cambridge University Press.

Martínez Lozano, V. (2003). *Cultura, socialización e interacción entre iguales: Un estudio del conflicto en preescolares andaluces y holandeses* (Culture, socialization, and peer interaction: A study of conflicts in Andalusian and Dutch preschoolers). Unpublished doctoral dissertation, Sevilla, Spain: Universidad Pablo de Olavide.

Oyserman, D., Coon, H. M., & Kemmelmeier, M. (2002). Rethinking individualism and collectivism: Evaluation of theoretical assumptions and meta-analyses. *Psychological Bulletin, 128*, 3–72.

Oyserman, D., Kemmelmeier, M., & Coon, H. M. (2002). Cultural psychology, a new look: Reply to Bond (2002), Fiske (2002), Kitayama (2002), and Miller (2002). *Psychological Bulletin, 128*, 110–117.

Parke, R. D., & Ladd, G. W. (1992). *Family-peer relationships: Modes of linkage*. Hillsdale, NJ: Lawrence Erlbaum Associates.

Parke, R. D., Burks, V. M., Carson, J. L, Neville, B., & Boyum, L. A. (1994). Family-peer relationships: A tripartite model. In R. D. Parke & S. G. Kellam (Eds.), *Exploring family relationships with other social contexts* (pp. 115–146). Hillsdale, NJ: Lawrence Erlbaum Associates.

Piaget, J. (1932). *The moral judgment of the child*. London: Routledge & Kegan Paul.

Russell, A., Pettit, G., & Mize, J. (1998). Horizontal qualities in parent-child relationships: Parallels with and possible consequences for children's peer relationships. *Developmental Review, 18*, 313–352.

Sánchez Medina, J. A., Martínez Lozano, V., & Goudena, P. P. (2001). Conflict management in preschoolers: A cross-cultural perspective. *International Journal of Early Years Education, 9*, 153–160.

Schneider, B. H., Atkinson, L., & Tardif, C. (2001). Child-parent attachment and children's peer relations: A quantitative review. *Developmental Psychology, 37*, 86–100.

Triandis, H. C. (1990). Cross-cultural studies of individualism and collectivism. In J. J. Berman (Ed.), *Cross-cultural perspectives: The Nebraska Symposium on Motivation 1989* (pp. 41–134). Lincoln: University of Nebraska Press.

Valsiner, J. (1988). Ontogeny of co-construction of culture within socially organized environmental settings. In J. Valsiner (Ed.), *Child development within culturally structured environments* (pp. 283–297). Norwood, NJ: Ablex.

12 Culture, Family Contexts, and Children's Coping Strategies in Peer Interactions

Yiyuan Xu, Jo Ann M. Farver, Lei Chang, Lidong Yu, and Zengxiu Zhang

In most cultures, the family setting provides children with an initial set of experiences that will allow them to become productive adults, express their individual differences, form and maintain social contacts with others, and learn how to cope with daily hassles and major life stressors. Predominant beliefs or "parental ethnotheories" (Harkness & Super, 1996) about what is desired and appropriate child behavior guide parents' particular approaches to socialization. Therefore, regularities within settings, customs, and parents' belief systems organize children's developmental experiences and provide the information from which children construct the rules of their culture (Super & Harkness, 1986; Whiting, 1980). Depending on the cultural context, socialization involves activities in which children are steered away from certain behaviors and are strongly encouraged to engage in others. When upset with their peers, children may yell, hit someone, cry, seek help from others, or keep their feelings to themselves. Over time and with experience, children learn to cope with peer conflict using strategies that are normative within their peer group and adaptive to the goals and beliefs of their cultural community.

At present, we know very little about sociocultural settings in which children encounter stress and develop specific coping strategies. In this chapter, we draw on data from our ongoing studies of Chinese children's socioemotional functioning with their peers to begin to address this gap in the research literature. We begin by outlining a theoretical framework of stress and coping and discuss how it can be applied to the study of Chinese children's coping strategies. Next, we examine two factors that may influence children's coping, the family, and their temperament. Finally, we present a biocultural model to explore how aspects of the broad sociocultural context, family functioning, and children's temperamental differences contribute to how children cope with interpersonal stressors.

A Framework for Examining Stress and Coping in Cultural Settings

Peer conflict is inevitable and represents a continual source of stress for most children. School-age children often report being excluded from peer play groups, being teased, or pushed around by other others. Consequently, children must learn how to approach and manage potentially stressful situations in ways that are both personally satisfying and produce favorable outcomes. Children's appraisals of and responses to peer-related stressors are referred to as coping strategies in peer interactions. In the research literature, coping has been defined as "conscious volitional efforts to regulate emotion, cognition, behavior, physiology, and the environment in response to stressful events or circumstances" (Compas et al., 2001, p. 88). In a model proposed by Weisz and colleagues (Band & Weisz, 1988; McCarty et al., 1996; Rothbaum, Weisz, & Snyder, 1982; Weisz, Rothbaum, & Blackburn, 1984a), children's coping strategies can be categorized into three broad types: primary control strategies that involve direct attempts to change aspects of a situation to reduce the source of the stress (e.g., problem solving), secondary control strategies that involve changing oneself to fit the situation, (e.g., support seeking), and relinquished control strategies where no attempt is made to either modify or adjust to the situation, (i.e., doing nothing). Depending on the nature of their negative peer encounters, children are likely to use a primary or secondary control strategy, a combination of both, or they may elect not to respond at all. According to Band and Weisz (1988), children's choice of coping strategy also depends on how much control they have over a particular situation. A primary control strategy, such as telling peers to stop teasing or name calling, would be most effective when children feel they have some degree of control over the altercation. On the other hand, secondary control strategies, such as talking to others to gain support and encouragement or avoiding thoughts about the problem, would be effective when primary control strategies fail, are impossible to enact, or the situation is perceived to be uncontrollable.

Children's sense of control over events in their immediate environment and their corresponding coping strategy vary as a function of how their wider culture approaches or views control-expectancies. Broadly speaking, there is some evidence to suggest that Asian populations, in general, feel less in control of their lives than do their Western counterparts (Nisbett, 2003), and rather than attempting to control situations, Asians are more likely than Westerners to adjust to them (Morling, Kitayama, & Miyamoto, 2002). Surveys have also shown that, for Western individuals, feeling in control of one's life or events is far more important for their mental health than it is for Asian populations; for Asians, their perceived well-being is enhanced by being part of a group whose members might aid in providing control (Sastry & Ross, 1998). Thus, the distinctive value systems found in Asian and Western cultures may foster a preference for some coping strategies over others.

There is also abundant research that illustrates how Asian and Western cultures have different norms for self-expression and views about the self, others, and the interdependence of the two, which are likely to influence their coping mechanisms. For example, Markus and Kitayama (1991) found that Asian groups tended to emphasize the relatedness and interdependence among individuals or the "we," and Western populations tended to focus on the individuated self or the "I." The Eastern interdependent view of the self is generally expressed in a collectivistic orientation characterized by being attentive to others' needs, attempting to "read" others' minds, and maintaining harmonious shared experiences. In contrast, the Western independent view of the self is generally expressed in an individualistic orientation, where attending to the self, individuality, self-assertion, and "saying" what is on one's mind is encouraged. Therefore, it was not surprising that Weisz et al. (1984a, 1984b) found that North Americans were more likely to use primary (i.e., changing the environment) rather than secondary control coping strategies (i.e., changing the self), whereas the reverse was true for many East Asian populations. In cultural communities where individuals are taught from an early age to align themselves with their group and to maintain harmonious interactions with other members, secondary control strategies may be the norm. On the other hand, in settings where individuals are encouraged to make existing realities fit their own wishes, and self-fulfillment, self-reliance, and independent thinking are valued human attributes, primary control strategies may be the most common way to respond to interpersonal stress.

In linking these lines of research together, a general pattern begins to emerge for how children's coping strategies vary as a function of their local sociocultural setting. However, existing models of coping behavior have been developed by Western researchers, and these may not be totally consistent with non-Western value systems. Morling and Fiske (1999) argue that viewing secondary coping strategies as efforts to "change the self" also reflects an independent construal of the self. In primary and secondary control coping, individuals' stable desires are the focus, and the goal is to bring the environment into closer alignment with their preferences. When such attempts are impossible, individuals employ compensatory secondary control strategies to restore their self-esteem and sense of individual agency. For example, in American culture, if a child is teased by peers, he may first cope with the stress using a primary coping strategy, such as approaching the peer and asking him to stop. But if he knows that this peer is powerful and has many accomplices, he may cry to elicit empathy or comfort from others (a secondary coping strategy). Either way, the child initially uses or thinks of using a primary control strategy, then he either pursues it or manages its loss.

It is also likely that individuals in East Asian cultures use strategies other than the three discussed here. One possibility is *ren* (in Mandarin) (Huang, 2002), which can be roughly translated as forbearance. *Ren* may not be apparent in Western settings, but it is a common behavior pattern in the Chinese context. *Ren* is derived from the Confucian notion of dialecticism, wherein changing the world and changing the self are inseparable and sometimes equivalent. The Chinese notion of *ren* considers backing off in response to a challenging situation as not much different from moving forward, and under some circumstances, it is more desirable than moving forward (*yi tui wei jin* in Mandarin). In response to stress in peer interactions, many Chinese children may choose *ren* as a coping strategy to refrain from arguing or confronting others. However, *ren* does not mean avoiding trouble, but instead it represents a direct attempt to elicit respect or reciprocated *ren* behavior from one's peers. *Ren* rests on the notion that reciprocated *ren* is necessary for maintaining the stability of the status hierarchy and is linked to the fulfillment of one's social role. Thus, as a coping behavior, *ren* serves to maintain harmonious peer relations and is consistent with a collectivistic orientation and an interdependent sense of self.

In summary, when confronted with peer conflict, the likelihood that children will use one type of coping strategy over another is related to the degree to which their cultural community emphasizes a relational or aggregate mode. Children who use coping strategies that are closely aligned with prevailing cultural values, expectations, and peer group norms are likely to be the most successful in dealing with peer-related stress, to experience satisfying peer relationships, and to manifest overall positive developmental outcomes. However, how children acquire coping strategies remains an open question. In the next section, we consider this question.

Factors Associated With Children's Coping Strategies in Peer Interactions

The Family Environment

Compas (1998) suggested that the family context plays an important role in how children cope with stress. This proposition is consistent with Parke and Ladd's (1992) view that children's experiences in the home transfer to social exchanges with their peers. In general, much of children's socialization occurs through parental modeling. Children observe how their parents respond to stressful situations and, later, when coping with their own peer-related conflicts, they practice, validate, and incorporate their parent's methods into their own repertoire (Kliewer & Lewis, 1995). Parents also directly train their children about how to interpret stressful events and what strategies are appropriate responses to particular situations. In either case, parents' passive modeling or active coaching involves the transmission of values and goals to their children, and their coping strategies are a direct reflection of these efforts. For example, by socializing children to behave autonomously, North American families may inadvertently encourage their children to take a more active approach in resolving peer confrontations, whereas Asian families may encourage their children to develop coping strategies, such as *ren,* which is consistent with their cultural norms. Take Mainland China as an example. Mainland China has experienced dramatic changes in the last two decades, and whether traditional values are still applicable to parenting behaviors is uncertain. Nevertheless, the degree to which mothers adhere to Chinese values can be expected to shape how children interpret a stressful situation and their choice of coping strategy. Children that are reared in traditional Chinese families where parents strongly adhere to a Confucian or Taoist value system are more likely to view peer relations and to use coping strategies that are attuned to these beliefs. On the other hand, Chinese mothers who have considerable exposure to Western views of child-rearing may encourage their children to be independent and self-reliant and to use coping strategies that further personal, rather than group-oriented goals. Accordingly, less traditional Chinese children may believe that changing the environment is a more effective coping strategy than changing themselves, and they may be more inclined to use direct problem-solving strategies.

Clearly, the quality of family life, in terms of how connected family members feel to one another, is also likely to influence how parents socialize their children and convey their ideas about effective appraisals and responses to interpersonal stressors. The degree of family cohesion, or the emotional bond that exists between children and their parents (Olson, Sprenkle, & Russell, 1979), creates an atmosphere that is either supportive or conflictual, which has a direct bearing on children's socioemotional functioning. Children who have supportive home environments and perceive the relationship with their parents to be positive tend to be more socially competent (Hoelter & Harper, 1987; Olson et al., 1979), whereas children whose home environments are perceived as conflictual and negative often manifest behavioral problems and low self-esteem (Burt, Cohen, & Bjorck, 1988; Olson et al., 1979). Cohesive family environments help children develop a sense of security, acceptance, and control over potentially stressful situations. Thus, as mentioned earlier, when children perceive they have some control or degree of choice about how to respond to stressful peer encounters, they may be more likely to use primary control strategies, such as direct problem solving. Studies of North American children and adolescents have reported that high family cohesion was positively associated with the use of active, approach, and problem-solving strategies (Kliewer & Lewis, 1995), whereas low family cohesion was associated with emotional ventilation and passive avoidant coping strategies (Hanson et al., 1989; Stern & Zevon, 1990).

At the same time, a family is embedded in a wider cultural milieu, which consists of values and norms for children's behavior. In all cultures, parents want their children to be adaptive to their environment. Parents' goals for their children's development, the means by which they accomplish those goals, and their view of what is culturally desirable behavior will be conveyed to their children in the course of daily interaction. Accordingly, based on the values that are thought to characterize Chinese culture, we would expect to find a positive relation between family cohesion and the coping strategy *ren* or secondary coping strategies. However, as discussed earlier, Mainland China continues to experience dramatic societal transitions that will inevitably produce changes in the traditional value system and human behavior. At present, there are no studies that have directly examined the relation between characteristics of the family and children's coping strategies.

Children's Temperament

How children cope with stress is also attenuated, to some extent, by their temperament (Compas et al., 2001). Temperament is defined as a biologically based source of individual difference, which is present early in life, relatively stable over time, and consistent across contexts (Rothbart & Bates, 1998). The two basic aspects of temperament are reactive and regulatory. The reactive aspects, which include positive and negative affectivity, may contribute to how children cope with peer-related stress. Children who are high in negative affectivity also tend to have a low threshold of autonomic and emotional arousal in stressful situations. Therefore, they are likely to use secondary and relinquished control strategies because they often perceive themselves as unable to control or change aspects of their environments. In contrast, children who are high in positive affectivity may chose to act more directly in response to stressful peer encounters by using primary strategies, such as problem solving and social support seeking. The regulatory aspects of temperament include attention regulation (i.e., attention focusing/shifting) and effortful control. In contrast to negative/positive affectivity, which largely involves passive or involuntary actions, the regulatory aspects of temperament, especially effortful control, involve voluntary actions that serve to modulate actions and emotions when an individual has no desire to do so (Kochanska, Murray, & Harlan, 2000; Rothbart & Bates, 1998; Reed, Pien, & Rothbart, 1984). To some degree, individual differences in self-regulation may reduce children's capacity for conscious volitional efforts that are integral to being able to cope. Thus, because of insufficient modulation of their emotional arousal, children who lack self-regulation may use problem-focused aggression instead of direct problem-solving strategies to respond to peer-related stressors.

At the same time, children's self-regulation, and in particular, effortful control, may be mediated by their culture (Chen, 2000). For example, North American children who have strong attention regulation and effortful control over reactivity may be more likely to use problem-solving strategies that reflect the predominant values of their culture: assertiveness and independence. On the other hand, similarly self-regulated Chinese children may choose *ren* as a coping strategy in response to the same stressful situation, a strategy that is compatible with Chinese patterns of socialization. Depending on the setting, children's lack of or insufficiently developed self-regulatory functions may be associated with their incompetent or ineffective coping strategies, whereas the reverse would be expected for children who have high self-regulation. Thus, to some extent, although sociocultural contextual demands define the limit of what are desirable and normal responses to stressful events, individual differences in children's temperament help to further explain within-cultural variations in children's coping strategies in a probabilistic sense. That is, some children's biological predispositions may exert considerable influence on their behavior and their choice of coping strategy in peer interactions.

A Biocultural Model

Research on stress and coping has relied heavily on models of the appraisal and coping process. Based on Lazarus and Folkman's (1984) model, coping is considered to be a process where individuals cognitively appraise the demands of stressful situations and use available resources to manage the relation between the self and the environment. Researchers have recognized the importance of social contexts where children encounter stress and develop specific coping strategies (Compas et al., 2001; Berg, Meegan, & Deviney, 1998). However, few have proposed a theoretical model to accommodate the

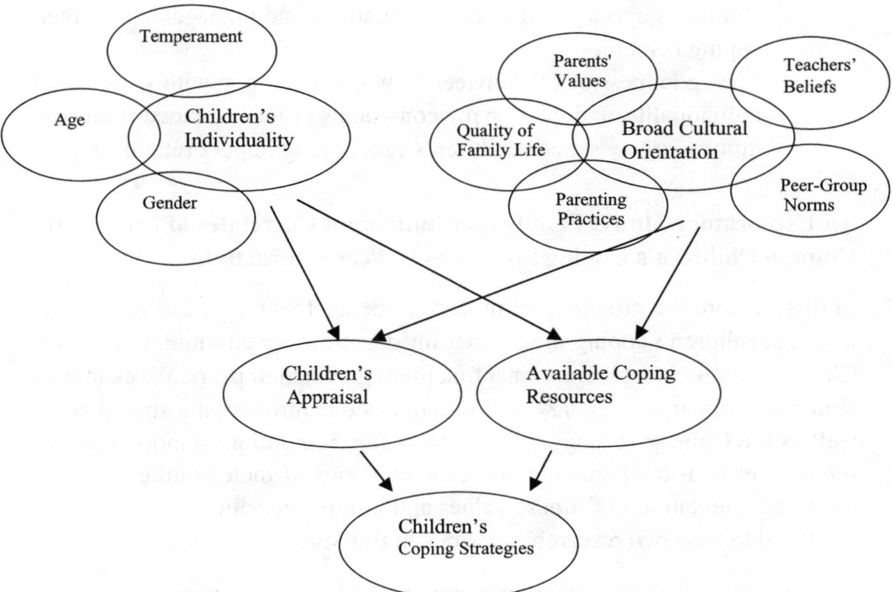

Figure 12.1. A Biocultural model of children's coping strategies in peer interactions.

"developmental niche," which provides a range of options and limitations in children's repertoire of coping strategies.

Thus, to begin to understand how culture and children's individual temperament contribute to how they cope with interpersonal stressors, we present a biocultural model. As shown in Figure 12.1, we propose:

1. How children cope with stress depends on their appraisal of a stressful situation and how they manage their available coping resources (Lazarus & Folkman, 1984).
2. Children's available coping resources and their appraisal of stressful situations are shaped by the conditions of their community, which includes but is not limited to, the broad orientation (collectivism vs. individualism); parents' socialization goals, values, and beliefs; qualities of family life (cohesion among family members); teachers' beliefs and attitudes; peer group norms; and children's individuality, such as temperament, age, and gender.
3. Local sociocultural conditions and children's individuality influence their coping strategies in the peer group through the mediation of

children's appraisal of stressful situations and management of their coping resources.

4. The "goodness of fit" between how children cope with stress, their individuality, and the varying constraints of local sociocultural conditions largely shapes children's functioning in peer relationships.

An Exploratory Study: Family and Individual Correlates of Mainland Chinese Children's Coping Strategies in Peer Interactions

In this section, we provide preliminary evidence to support our biocultural model of children's coping strategies using data from our continuing studies of Chinese children's socioemotional functioning with their peers. We examined children's primary, secondary, and relinquished control coping strategies, as well as the Chinese strategy referred to as *ren*, in relation to individual differences in their temperament and characteristics of their families, such as mothers' orientation to Chinese values and family cohesion.

We addressed two research questions in this study:

1. Are different coping strategies related to children's peer relationships?
2. How does mothers' orientation to Chinese values, family cohesion, and children's temperament influence how children cope with stressful peer experiences?

We expected that the degree to which mothers adhere to Chinese values, the cohesiveness of the family, and children's temperamental reactivity and self-regulation would influence children's coping strategies. Specifically, when controlling for children's age, gender, and temperament, mothers' adherence to Chinese values was expected to be associated with children's use of *ren* or secondary control coping strategies in resolving peer conflicts. No hypotheses were made regarding the relation between family cohesion and children's coping strategies.

Mainland China: A Diversifying Cultural Context

Overall, Chinese culture continues to maintain an interdependent orientation. At the core of the Chinese value system are Confucianism and Taoism, which guide social relations and underscore the importance of harmony and social obligations. As Ryan (1985) observed, a basic tenet of Taoism is the refutation of self-assertion and actions that further individuals' goals at the expense of the group. Similarly, Confucianism involves the perfection of interpersonal skills with an emphasis on an obligation to the family, the group, and community (Munro, 1985). Together, Confucianism and Taoism provide a philosophical basis and structure for individuals' social behavior, which reflects the needs, expectations, and anticipated reactions of others.

However, Mainland China is also rapidly changing, and the ever-expanding suburban areas of cities like Beijing and Shanghai are becoming increasingly Westernized. It has been proposed that, over the past 20 years or so, the traditional Chinese value system has collapsed in response to the dramatic changes produced by the Cultural Revolution, recent industrialization, modernization, and the associated stratification of Chinese society (Chang et al., 2003). In addition, the one-child policy has contributed to changes in parenting practices and has produced a "child-centered" rather than an "age-centered" society. Recent studies of Chinese only-children have shown that they are more aggressive or externalizing (Tao et al., 1999) and are more self-centered and individualistic (Rosenberg & Jing, 1996) than are non-only children.

At the same time, about 70 percent of China's population resides in rural areas and in smaller cities, where the influence of imported values and beliefs is not as prominent as in the urban areas. During recent informal interviews with Mainland Chinese parents who live in a nonmetropolitan area, we found that, in line with the traditional kinship structure, many parents continue to prefer male over female children (despite heavy government training), children persist in being emotionally dependent on their parents, Chinese school environments remain orderly and authoritarian, and the ideal Chinese child is still described as one who is academically competent and achievement oriented, has high moral character, and is prosocial, group-oriented, and modest. Thus, the diversification of contemporary Mainland Chinese society has produced substantial within-cultural variation in basic values and beliefs. Obviously, it is erroneous to assume that all Chinese people uphold or have abandoned the traditional values drawn from Confucian and Taoist doctrines to the same extent, without measuring individual's orientation to Chinese values.

In the current study, individual variations in Chinese values were directly assessed in a sample of Mainland Chinese mothers who were recruited from a middle-sized Chinese city. Located in Eastern China, Zhenjiang is a manufacturing and commercial center and is one of the hub cities on the Yangtze River. With a population of about one million, Zhenjiang is considered to be more representative of a Chinese city than are the mega-metropolitan areas of Beijing or Shanghai. In Zhenjiang, residents have similar levels of education and income as other Chinese cities of comparable size, and there has been less contact with the Western popular media and entertainment. Therefore, this city provided a unique opportunity to examine how variations in Chinese parents' value systems may influence children's socialization, and in particular, how children cope with stress in peer interactions.

Description of the Study

We studied 191 fourth- and fifth-graders recruited from an elementary school in Zhenjiang, P. R. China. The families were from varied socioeconomic backgrounds: 59 percent of the parents were semiskilled workers, such as taxi drivers, construction or manufacturing workers, company clerks, and service providers; 31 percent were professional workers, government officials, or business administrators; 11 percent were doctors, professors, or engineers; 5 percent were unskilled workers, such as food service workers, machine operators, and laborers; and 4 percent were unemployed.

Children's coping strategies were measured using teachers' ratings. Following a strategy adopted in Eisenberg et al. (1998), we developed three vignettes that describe hypothetical social stressors that children across varied cultural communities might typically experience during peer interactions. These were: a child is teased by peers about a new item of clothing; while waiting in line, a child is bumped by a peer who tries to take his or her place; and a child is left out of his or her favorite game by peers. Teachers were asked to rate how each child in their classrooms would most likely respond to or cope with these situations using eight possible coping strategies derived from the research literature: (a) direct problem solving (e.g., taking action to change the problem or fix the situation); (b) problem-focused aggression (e.g., resolving the problem using aggression); (c) problem-focused avoidance (e.g., avoiding the situation or staying away from the troublemaker); (d) support seeking (e.g., talking to peers or teachers to get help); (e) emotion-focused crying (e.g., crying to elicit comfort); (f) emotion-focused aggression (e.g., releasing pent-up feelings, kicking a wall or desk after being embarrassed); (g) does nothing (e.g., giving up or making no effort to deal with the situation); and (h) *ren* (e.g., refraining from arguing or confronting peers).

To measure children's perceived family cohesion with their mothers and fathers, they were group administered the cohesion subscale of the Family and Cohesion Evaluation Scales II (FACE II; Olson et al., 1979). Mothers' orientation to Chinese values was assessed using the Asian Values Scale (AVS; Kim, Atkinson, & Yang, 1999). The AVS is based on Confucian beliefs about socialization goals and societal virtues. The AVS consists of six subscales: conformity to norms, family recognition through achievement, emotional self-control, collectivism, humility, and filial piety. Because of the modest sample size and moderate to high correlations among the six Chinese value subscales, mothers' orientation to Chinese values was aggregated to form a single variable, which was used in the subsequent analyses.

Children's temperamental reactivity and self-regulation were assessed using both mothers' and teachers' ratings on the Early Adolescent Temperament Questionnaire-Parent (EATQ-P) report form (Capaldi & Rothbart, 1992; Ellis, & Rothbart, 2001; Xu et al., 2004) and on the revised Positive and Negative Affect Schedule (PANAS) (Watson, Clark, & Tellegen, 1988; Eisenberg et al., 1998). Finally, children were asked to nominate up to three peers in their class whom they like the most and three peers whom they like the least. The number of nominations each child received was standardized within class. A peer nominated social preference score was generated from the standardized difference between the liked most and liked least scores.

The results showed within-cultural variations in Chinese children's use of coping strategies. Primary, secondary, and relinquished control strategies, as well as the Chinese way of *ren* were apparent in the teachers' ratings of children's responses to the three stressful peer situations. An exploratory factor analysis revealed that children's coping strategies consisted of six clusters: direct problem solving, disengagement (problem-focused avoidance/doing nothing), aggressive (problem-focused aggression/emotion-focused aggression), support seeking, emotion-focused crying, and *ren.* These findings provided some preliminary evidence that *ren* was distinguishable from coping strategies identified in prior studies carried out with North American children.

Ren differs from the other types of coping in several ways. Consistent with an emphasis on social harmony and a group orientation, the Chinese way of *ren* involves a pattern of behavior based on a philosophy or worldview that is not necessarily shared by Western culture, and it is not encompassed in the three common coping strategies previously described. When Chinese children use the *ren* strategy in response to peer animosity, they refrain from arguing or confronting their peers, but they are not avoiding or running away from the situation which would be the case in problem-focused avoidance. Children who use *ren* to cope with a stressful situation, generally yield to others' opinions or desires while adjusting their own feelings and behavior. This pattern of response typically fixes the problem or removes the source of conflict because the children who are involved respect their peer's propriety and tolerance. *Ren* cannot be classified into either primary or secondary control coping. *Ren* is also different from problem-focused avoidance or relinquished control coping, both of which have been linked to learned helplessness, or deficits in self-efficacy (Weisz et al., 1984a).

The correlational analyses showed that different types of coping strategies were associated with children's social preference in varying ways. Children's social preference as rated by their teachers and peers was positively associated with direct problem-solving and support-seeking strategies, and negatively associated with aggressive strategies. The Chinese strategy *ren* was positively correlated only with peers' nominations of social preference. These results suggest that Chinese children use multiple strategies in coping with peer conflicts. Not surprising, aggressive strategies, which are considered immature and disruptive in most settings, were negatively associated with peers' nominations of children's social preference.

To examine how mothers' orientation to Chinese values, family cohesion, and children's temperament were related to their coping strategies, a series of hierarchical regression analyses were conducted. The different types of coping strategies were treated as criterion variables. In each regression analysis, children's age and gender were entered in the first step, followed by children's temperament in the second step, and mothers' orientation to Chinese values and children's perceived family cohesion in the third step. Consistent with our expectations, the results showed that mothers' orientation to Chinese values was positively associated with children's use of *ren* and negatively associated with aggressive coping strategies. However, mothers' adherence to Chinese values was not associated with children's use of direct problem solving, which suggests that primary control coping may not be as highly valued by traditional Chinese families as one might expect. On the other hand, children's use of direct problem-solving strategies was related to their family cohesion. These results could be interpreted in light of research on the quality of family life and children's outcomes. That is, family cohesion may promote children's sense of control over interpersonal stressors, which in turn encourages their use of direct problem solving, regardless of their mothers' value orientation.

We also found that children's self-regulation positively predicted *ren* and direct problem-solving strategies and negatively predicted aggressive strategies. These results are consistent with the significant relations found for *ren* and direct problem solving and child outcomes. Both strategies were associated with children's peer acceptance, pointing to the diversity of potentially effective coping strategies in contemporary Chinese peer groups. Children's range of choice in coping responses may be a reflection of the recent changes in Mainland China, which have shifted how some Chinese parents socialize their children to behave with their peers. Overall, the results provided some preliminary support for our biocultural model: mothers' orientation to traditional values, family cohesion, and children's temperament contributed to how Chinese children cope with stress in peer interactions.

Conclusions and Future Directions

The biocultural model illustrated in Figure 12.1 presents an initial step toward understanding non-Western children's coping strategies in peer settings. Children's peer relationships, coping strategies, and the expression of their individual temperamental qualities are all part of an interrelated developmental process, which is mediated by the cultural context in which they occur. However, because our chapter was largely exploratory, further studies are needed to fully test the model proposed here. For example, parents' value orientation and family cohesion may influence children's choice of coping strategies through the mediation of children's appraisal of peer stressors and access to coping resources, such as friendship. Potential mediating factors in children's appraisal and coping resources deserve additional research attention.

In the study discussed here, we examined only a few variables of interest as illustrated in Figure 12.1. Recent North American and Chinese findings have suggested that children's use of particular coping strategies may be influenced by their peer-group experiences in school and in neighborhood settings (Bowker et al., 2000; Chang, 2003, 2004; Chang et al., 2004; Chen, Chang, & He, 2003). Thus, studies of peer-group norms and teachers' values and beliefs should be addressed in studies with other cultural communities.

Disentangling the relation between children's coping strategies and their behavioral predispositions also deserves additional research attention. Children who experience the most difficulty in regulating negative emotional behavior may also have trouble learning to negotiate with peers and coping with conflict in the peer group. Moreover, the effects of different coping strategies on child outcomes, such as peer acceptance, rejection, and overall psychological adjustment, would contribute to our understanding of how children develop social competence within the peer group.

Our intention was not to culturally stereotype Asian or Western populations, as we acknowledge that there is much variation within any cultural group. Our efforts to directly measure within-group variation in mothers' orientation to Chinese traditional values represents an initial effort to "unpackage" the individualistic/collectivistic dimensions. More research integrating multiple aspects of across- and within-culture variations in children's coping strategies in peer interactions is needed.

Future studies using a multi-informant approach to assess children's coping strategies are also needed. Although teachers are a good source of information about children's behavior in school settings, information gleaned from children themselves would serve to cross-validate teachers' views and provide a "child's-eye view" of their coping efforts. Observations of children's behavior during peer-related conflict would compliment children's self-reports and teachers' ratings. A greater range of internal coping strategies could be examined, such as cognitive avoidance and pure cognition. Perhaps additional coping strategies, such as *ren* mentioned in this chapter, could be tested. Our investigation of *ren* as a Chinese way of coping was largely speculative and warrants further study, not only within the Chinese setting but with other cultural groups. A logical next step would be to examine open-ended interviews with Chinese children and to conduct a confirmatory factor analysis of the various terms associated with *ren*.

Finally, we only explored how fourth- and fifth-graders cope with social stress associated with peer animosity. Previous research suggests that how children cope with stress may be a function of their age. Therefore, future studies that take a developmental perspective are clearly warranted.

References

Azuma, H. (1984). Secondary control as a heterogeneous category. *American Psychologist, 9*, 970–971.

Band, E., & Weisz, J. (1988). How to feel better when it feels bad: Children's perspectives on coping with everyday stress. *Developmental Psychology, 24*, 247–253.

Berg, C. A., Meegan, S. P., & Deviney, F. P. (1998). A social-contextual model of coping with everyday problems across the lifespan. *International Journal of Behavioral Development, 22*, 239–261.

Bowker, A., Bukowski, W. M., Hymel, S., & Sippola, L. K. (2000). Coping with daily hassles in the peer group during early adolescence: Variations as a function of peer experience. *Journal of Research on Adolescence, 10*, 211–243.

Burt, C. E., Cohen, L. H., & Bjorck, J. P. (1988). Perceived family environment as a moderator of young adolescents' life stress adjustment. *American Journal of Community Psychology, 16*, 101–122.

Capaldi, D. M., & Rothbart, M. K. (1992). Development and validation of an early adolescent temperament measure. *Journal of Early Adolescence, 12*, 153–173.

Chang, L. (2003). Variable effects of children's aggression, social withdrawal, and prosocial leadership as functions of teacher beliefs and behaviors. *Child Development, 74*, 535–548.

Chang, L. (2004). The role of classroom norms in contextualizing the relations of children's social behaviors to peer acceptance. *Developmental Psychology, 40*, 691–702.

Chang, L., Liu, H. Wen, Z., Fung, K. Y., Wang, Y., & Xu, Y. (2004). Mediating teacher liking and moderating authoritative teaching on Chinese adolescents' perceptions of antisocial and prosocial behaviors. *Journal of Educational Psychology, 96*, 369–380.

Chang, L., Schwartz, D., Dodge, K. A., & McBride-Chang, C. (2003). Harsh parenting in relation to child emotion regulation and aggression. *Journal of Family Psychology, 17*, 598–606.

Chen, X. (2000). Social and emotional development in Chinese children and adolescents: A contextual cross-cultural perspective. In F. Columbus (Ed.), *Advances in psychology research* (Vol. 1, pp. 229–251). Huntington, NY: Nova Science.

Chen, X., Chang, L., & He, Y. (2003). The peer groups as a context: Mediating and moderating effects on relations between academic achievement and social functioning in Chinese children. *Child Development, 74*, 710–727.

Compas, B. E. (1987). Coping with stress during childhood and adolescence. *Psychological Bulletin, 101*, 393–403.

Compas, B. E. (1998). An agenda for coping research and theory: Basic and applied developmental issues. *International Journal of Behavioral Development, 22*, 231–237.

Compas, B. E., Connor-Smith, J. K., Salzman, H., Thomsen, A. H., & Wadworth, M. E. (2001). Coping with stress during childhood and adolescence: Problems, progress, and potential in theory and research. *Psychology Bulletin, 127*, 87–127.

Eisenberg, N., Shepard, S. A., Fabes, R. A., Murphy, B. C., & Guthrie, I. K. (1998). Shyness and children's emotionality, regulation, and coping: Contemporaneous, longitudinal, and across-context relations. *Child Development, 69*, 767–790.

Ellis, L., & Rothbart, M. (2001, April). *Revision of the Early Adolescent Temperament Questionnaire*. Paper presented at the Biennial Meeting of the Society for Research in Child Development, Minneapolis, MN.

Hanson, C. L., Cigrang, J. A., Harris, M. A., Carle, D. L., Relyea, G., & Burghen, G. A. (1989). Coping styles in youths with insulin-dependent diabetes mellitus. *Journal of Consulting and Clinical Psychology, 57*, 644–651.

Harkness, S., & Super, C. M. (1996). *Parents' cultural belief systems*. New York: Guilford.

Hoelter, J., & Harper, L. (1987). Structural and interpersonal family influences on adolescent self-conception. *Journal of Marriage and the Family, 46*, 129–139.

Huang, L. (2002). "Ren" or not "ren"? Between the critique of modernity and indigenous notion of "ren." In C. Yeh (Ed.), *From modernity to indigenization* (pp. 111–135). Taiwan, Taipe: Yuanliu.

Kim, B. S. K., Atkinson, D. R., & Yang, P. H. (1999). The Asian Values Scale: Development, factor analysis, validation, and reliability. *Journal of Counseling Psychology, 46*, 342–352.

Kliewer, W., & Lewis, H. (1995). Family influences on coping processes in children and adolescents with Sickle Cell Disease. *Journal of Pediatric Psychology, 20*, 511–525.

Kochanska, G., Murray, K. T., & Harlan, E. T. (2000). Effortful control in early childhood: Continuity and change, antecedents, and implications for social development. *Developmental Psychology, 36*, 220–232.

Lazarus, R. S., & Folkman, S. (1984). *Stress, appraisal, and coping*. New York: Springer.

Markus H. R., & Kitayama, S. (1991). Culture and the self: Implications for cognition, emotion, and motivation. *Psychological Review, 98*, 224–253.

McCarty, C. A., Weisz, J. R., Wanitromanee, K., Eastman, K. L., Suwanlert, S., Chaiyasit, W., et al. (1999). Culture, coping, and context: Primary, secondary control among Thai and American Youth. *Journal of Child Psychology and Psychiatry and Allied Disciplines, 40*, 809–818.

Morling, B., & Fiske, S. (1999). Defining and measuring harmony control. *Journal of Research in Personality, 33*, 379–414.

Morling, B., Kitayama, S., & Miyamoto, Y. (2002). Cultural practices emphasize influence in the United States and adjustment in Japan. *Personality and Social Psychology Bulletin, 28*, 311–323.

Munro, D. J. (1985). *Individualism and holism: Studies in Confucian and Taoist values*. Ann Arbor: Center for Chinese Studies, University of Michigan.

Nisbett, R. E. (2003). *The geography of thought: How Asians and Westerners think differently . . . and why*. New York: Free Press.

Olson, D. H., Sprenkle, D. H., & Russell, C. S. (1979). Circumplex model of marital and family systems, I: Cohesion and adaptability dimensions, family types, and clinical applications. *Family Process, 18*, 3–27.

Parke, R. D., & Ladd, G. W. (1992). *Family-peer relationships: Modes of linkage*. Hillsdale, NJ: Lawrence Erlbaum Associates.

Reed, M. A., Pien, D. P., & Rothbart, M. K. (1984). Inhibitory self-control in preschool children. *Merrill-Palmer Quarterly, 30*, 131–147.

Rosenberg, B. G., & Jing, Q. (1996). A revolution in family life: The political and social structural impact of China's one child policy. *Journal of Social Issues, 52*, 51–69.

Rothbart, M. K., & Bates, J. E. (1998). Temperament. In Damon, W., & Eisenberg, N. (Eds). *Handbook of child psychology: Vol. 3. Social, emotional, and personality development* (5th ed, pp. 105–176). New York: Wiley.

Rothbaum, F., Weisz, J. R., & Snyder, S. S. (1982). Changing the world and changing the self: A two-process model of perceived control. *Journal of Personality and Social Psychology, 42*, 5–37.

Ryan, A. S. (1985). Cultural factors in casework with Chinese-Americans. *Social Casework, 66*, 333–340.

Sastry, J., & Ross, C. E. (1998). Asian ethnicity and the sense of personal control. *Social Psychology Quarterly, 61*, 101–120.

Stern, M., & Zevon, M. A. (1990). Stress, coping, and family environment. *Journal of Adolescent Research, 5*, 290–305.

Super, C. M., & Harkness, S. (1986). The developmental niche: A conceptualization at the interface of child and culture. *International Journal of Behavioral Development, 9*, 545–569.

Tao, G., Qiu, J., Li, B., Zeng, W., Xu, J., & Goebert, D. (1999). A longitudinal study of psychological development of only and non-only children and families: A 10-year follow-up study in Nanjing. *Chinese Mental Health Journal, 13*, 210–212.

Watson, D., Clark, L. A., & Tellegen, A. (1988). Development and validation of brief measures of positive and negative affect: The PANAS scales. *Journal of Personality and Social Psychology, 54*, 1063–1070.

Weisz, J. R., Rothbaum, F. M., & Blackburn, T. C. (1984a). Standing out and standing in: The psychology of control in America and Japan. *American Psychologist, 9*, 955–969.

Weisz, J. R., Rothbaum, F. M., & Blackburn, T. C. (1984b). Swapping recipes for control. *American Psychologist, 39*, 974–975.

Whiting, B. B. (1980). Culture and social behavior: A model for the development of social behavior. *Ethos, 8*, 95–116.

Xu, Y., Farver, J. M., Yu, L., Zhang, Z., & Cai, B. (2004, July). *Validation of the Early Adolescent Temperament Questionnaire (EATQ) with Mainland Chinese adolescents*. Poster presented at the Biennial Meetings of the International Society for the Study of Behavioral Development, Ghent, Belgium.

PART IV

Peer Interactions and Social Behaviors

13 The Cultural Organization of Yucatec Mayan Children's Social Interactions

Suzanne Gaskins

Most studies of social interactions with peers, including studies of friendship, assume that the basic rules and values about children's interaction in European American culture are universally shared by all cultures around the world – for example, parental goals for children's social interaction, concepts of friendship, and patterns of interacting with other children. Ethnographic studies of other cultures strongly suggest that this is not a reasonable assumption to make. Rules about social interaction in general and the nature of friendship in particular vary widely from one culture to the next. Thus, the culturally structured goals for the socialization of children and the daily activities of children also differ (e.g., Whiting & Edwards, 1988). Under these conditions, children's social behavior, including their interaction with other children, will differ widely by culture. This chapter illustrates such variation through a case study of Yucatec Mayan children growing up in their traditional village in Mexico. These children spend most of their time interacting with family members, including their siblings and other children who are their close relatives. Friendships and other significant peer relationships outside of this family circle are rare. This chapter examines how the literature on friendship and peer interactions is relevant for interpreting these children's experiences as well as how this case study is relevant for reevaluating current theories about children's social interactions.

Activity theory is the theoretical perspective that underlies this study. Although little of the research on friendship and peer interaction is currently framed by activity theory, it provides a model of how everyday experiences (that are claimed to be important in this domain) come to shape development. Activity theory, which grows out of Vygotsky's social/historical theory of development (Vygotsky, 1934/1987, 1978), emphasizes the importance of activities as the appropriate unit of analysis for study (Leont'ev, 1979; Luria, 1976). They also stress that those activities must be interpreted in terms of the particular contexts in which they occur, an argument made also by Bronfenbrenner (1979). This approach of studying the individual in activity in context has been widely applied to the study of cognitive development in children (e.g., Gauvain, 2000; Rogoff, 1990) but has been less frequently used in the study of social development. It is in harmony with approaches in other social science fields that situate human behavior and communication in "practice" (Bourdieu, 1977). Although some researchers from this tradition limit their consideration of context to the immediate context of behavior, much of the socializing power of participation in everyday activity in context comes from the consistency of patterns of daily activity over time, and that consistency is built on shared beliefs, understandings, and practices – in other words, culture. It is this more cultural interpretation of activity theory that forms the basis this chapter.

Although little research on friendship and peer interactions relies on the broader sociocultural perspective of activity theory, there is a general acceptance that context is important. Some who have studied social interaction with peers and friends have recognized its explanatory power of describing and analyzing "peer culture" (e.g., Corsaro, 1985). Others, although they do not explicitly adopt this perspective, recognize that patterns of peer interactions are operating in a particular school or other setting where social interaction is being studied. But most scholars studying friendship and peer interaction have failed to recognize the fundamental influence of culture in organizing the activities and contexts involved in social interaction. The goal of this chapter is to demonstrate some of the serious consequences of this omission.

Why Peer Interaction Needs to Be Studied as a Culturally Specific Construct

Because everyday activities and contexts are culturally structured and widely variable, theorists who see these activities and contexts as contributing to developmental outcomes must study other cultures to substantiate any universal claims. Moreover, European American culture and those most closely related to it are not normative groups representing the species; in most comparative studies, they are, in fact, the most unusual from a comparative perspective (Richman et al., 1988; Whiting, 1963). Because research on friends and peers relies heavily on everyday activities and contexts to predict and interpret development, the focus needs to be turned to how friends and peers function in other cultures rather than primarily focusing on fine-tuning theoretical distinctions among European American children in laboratory studies.

Some peer researchers have made this point (Schneider, 1998; Tietjen, 1994), but it is only slowly coming to have an effect on research.

There are a few existing studies from other cultures that suggest consideration of cultural contexts will be productive. Tietjen (1989) argues that social support in general is a culturally relative concept and that supportive interactions must be studied in "ecological" perspective and provides data comparing Sweden and Papua New Guinea that demonstrates substantial cultural differences. This research supports the position that children's socialization into social support systems occurs in a culturally specific "developmental niche" (Super & Harkness, 1986). Krappman (1996), who focuses on friendship in particular, argues that even though it is found "across all, or at least most societies," it is "manifested in a rich variety of ways depending on the cultural system" (p. 19). Recent research on friendship and peer interaction supports this claim. For instance, Chen and colleagues report that shy, sensitive behaviors were positively correlated with peer acceptance and competence for Chinese children, although they were negatively correlated for Canadian children (Chen, 1992; Chen, Rubin, & Li, 1995). DeRosier and Kupersmitdt (1991) found that compared with children in the United States, fourth- and sixth-grade children in Costa Rica had social support networks that were far more positive overall, and friends were much less central than family members. Similarly, French et al. (2001) report that Indonesian children rank family members higher on companionship and satisfaction as social support than U.S. children, and friends were ranked lower (even though friends were seen as the primary source of intimacy for children in both cultures). Even comparison across first-world countries demonstrates important differences. For example, friendships tend to be more stable in Italy than in Canada (Schneider et al., 1997).

There is even more research on differences across ethnic groups in the United States (e.g., Howes & Wu, 1990; Kupersmidt et al., 1995; Zakriski & Coie, 1996). Unfortunately, such comparisons often fall prey to misleading presumptions about the inherent positive value of the majority norms and the inherent "risk" involved in the minority norms. Such a "deficit" model of comparison, in which deviations from the majority norm are evaluated only by what is "missing" rather than considering what is present but different, does nothing to enlighten us about the potential diversity in children's friendships and peer relations. But when comparisons across ethnic groups are made with a more neutral set of assumptions, they can be enlightening. For instance, Kovacs and colleagues found that African American children had more friends overall and more friends of the opposite sex than did European American children, and they argue that this may be a result of being socialized to develop larger networks or it may be the result of larger extended families with closer ties (Kovacs, Parker, & Hoffman, 1996).

However, because the available information on friendship and peer relations in other cultures is still very limited (Hartup, 1999), there is clearly a need to explore this in varied cultures. Further, doing research in other countries, among modernized subpopulations in big cities, is not the same as studying intact cultural groups that represent more distinct alternatives to the predictable social organization of Western cultures. In particular, there is a need to study cultures in which there are significant differences from the European American family structure and social patterns of interaction that dominate in most of the currently available data. The most important contrasts would be provided by data from a variety of agricultural peasant societies and hunter–gatherer societies where maximal variation in social patterns exist. This work must be supported by ethnographic accounts of social interaction, socialization, and everyday activities in the cultures studied that can provide an understanding of the cultural context of children's social interactions.

The Cultural Specificity of Children's Interactions: The Case of the Yucatec Maya

In what follows, the nature of children's interaction in one agricultural peasant group, the Yucatec Maya of Mexico, is analyzed. Yucatec Mayan children growing up in traditional villages spend most of their time in interaction with extended family members (including children who are siblings, cousins, aunts, uncles, nieces, and nephews), not with friends or other same-age peers. Their experience provides a useful contrast to existing data on friendship and other peer interactions, both because they experience an everyday world that is in stark contrast to the everyday world of European American children and because children in many peasant groups similarly experience a world in which they interact primarily with family members (Whiting, 1963).

There are three important developmental questions for this cultural analysis: (a) Do children in a peasant culture like the Yucatec Maya, compared with European American children, have different social experiences early in life that prepare them differently for interactions with peers? (b) Are there important differences in the characteristics of social interaction with friends (and other peers) and with siblings? and (c) Do such differences in everyday social interactions lead to different developmental outcomes? To answer these questions, children's everyday activities must first be situated in an ethnographic description of the culture to address a number of relevant background issues. These include the characteristics of the adult social world and their parental ethnotheories of children's learning and socialization. Then, Mayan children's behavior will be described, including their patterns of social interaction: activities children participate in; who serves as playmates, models, mirrors, and guides; what social skills are practiced and how; and who provides social acceptance, companionship, and intimacy. This case study will then be used to answer the three aforementioned developmental questions to evaluate the generalizability of our knowledge about children's social interactions.

A Brief Ethnographic Overview of the Yucatec Maya

The Yucatec Maya Indians of Mexico are peasant farmers who traditionally have grown primarily corn and beans. In the last twenty years, this work has been augmented by efforts to earn cash, both inside and outside of the village (Gaskins, 2003). Since colonial times, the Yucatec Maya have lived in small villages near natural water sources (called *cenotes* in Spanish, sink holes in the limestone shell that forms the peninsula) and have had their farm lands surround the village. One such traditional village, with about 1,400 inhabitants, is the location of the ethnographic research that is presented here.

The present analysis is based on ethnographic fieldwork conducted in this village spanning more than twenty-five years. This fieldwork was conducted during two long field stays (of twenty-one months and twelve months) and almost annual shorter stays (of one to three months' duration). Over the years, approximately six years of total time has been spent living in the village. The central focus of the fieldwork has been children and their families. Many households have been observed, both informally (that is, when I have been invited as a guest) and formally (that is, when I have solicited their participation to be part of focused studies on children's general allocation of time, children's activities and socialization during the first eighteen months, and children's play). Approximately forty households have been formally studied. In addition to extensive observation of everyday activities and participation in informal conversations about topics relevant to this research, more structured interviews and experimental tasks have been conducted to obtain structured information about parents' beliefs and values and children's cognitive understandings. All fieldwork has been conducted in Yucatec Maya, the everyday language of the home and the only language of many women and children.

Within the village, economic and social units consist of nuclear or extended families who live in compounds within the village. Compounds are walled yards, typically fifty by fifty meters square. Four of these compounds make up a square "city block," and these are distributed around a town center. By preference, when adult children move away from their parents' compounds, they move nearby (if there is available land), so extended families tend to be geographically close and often are adjacent, even when they are not living within the same compound. Within each compound, there are one to three single-room houses, with walls of vertical poles and roofs of either thatch (preferred) or oil-permeated cardboard (cheaper and more readily available). Nuclear families may have only one house they use for both sleeping, cooking, and eating. Extended families might have separate sleep houses for each nuclear family and one house for the extended family that is dedicated to food preparation and other common activities. Much of the daily activity in the compound takes place in the yard directly outside the houses. Because the walls of the houses are porous (that is, it is easy to both be seen and be heard through them) and the doors are always open, the boundaries between inside and outside are not distinct. The compound as a whole, more than the individual structures built in it, serves as "home."

Men and their older sons do the heavy work involved in the traditional annual cycle of slash-and-burn farming, which includes felling trees, burning, planting, weeding, and harvesting. This work takes them away from the village on a regular, but not daily, basis, often from early morning until late afternoon. Today, men who participate in the broader market economy are also absent when they leave the village (sometimes for the day, sometimes for weeks at a time) to earn money through wage labor available in the tourist zone that is in and around Cancun, Mexico. Women and their older daughters (and smaller children of both sexes) often help in the lighter agricultural chores, especially planting and harvesting secondary crops. Most of the time, however, they stay in the compound and help with domestic chores, such as child care, preparing corn and other crops for cooking, cooking (over a wood fire on the floor), washing clothes, house and yard maintenance, attending to domestic animals and commercial crops in the compound, and mending and embroidering clothes. They also engage in chores that keep them within or close to the village, including collecting firewood, shopping, and running errands. Men and older boys, when they are home, can participate in some of these chores as well. The family works together as a single economic unit, with somewhat distinct and complementary roles for men and women, and children are legitimate participants to the extent their understanding and skill level allow (Gaskins, 2003).

Yucatec Maya Adults' Social Lives

Friendship has been defined as having a number of characteristics for European Americans, including being voluntary, private, intimate, reciprocal, negotiated, companionable, and outside of family (e.g., Corsaro, 1985; Hartup, 1999; Krappmann, 1996; Youniss, 1980). These characteristics provide a useful backdrop for the following description of the social interactions of Yucatec Mayan adults. The purpose of describing adult Mayan social lives is to provide a contrast to the social lives of European American adults to demonstrate that the developmental end goal for children in the two cultures differs significantly.

For the Mayans, family members have a virtual monopoly on Yucatec adults' social interactions, whether this is measured in time spent with companions in daily life or at special events, the level of intimacy or reciprocity, or any number of other ways. Most adults live within sight and sound of many other adult family members. These are the people with whom food is eaten, help is sought, gossip is exchanged, and daily joys and sorrows are shared. For men, this is usually their parents, siblings, uncles, and cousins. For women, because they typically join the husband's family once they marry, it is usually their in-laws. These social roles are filled to a lesser degree by the women's relatives, depending on how close they live and how well they get along. Special events also primarily involve family members. When work requires a large number of people (such as building a house, celebrating a developmental milestone of a child's life, or conducting traditional religious ceremonies focused on the family), the workers who are invited to share the labor and the food are almost always family members. These opportunities, which occur somewhat frequently, provide an opportunity for family reunions, where relatives who live in other towns come home, and groups of women and men have many hours to visit while they work.

Reflecting this social reality, the Yucatec Maya language has many words for family members and family relationships. There are individual words for specific relatives (e.g., "older brother," "older sister," "younger sibling," "father," "mother"). There is also a general term used for relatives, *laak'*, which is vague in its scope of reference. Its most narrow meaning is "siblings of any age," but it is often expanded to include "cousins," and this can include (as in English) both first cousins and more distant ones. Its most general sense is "other," so when it is possessed, it becomes "one's others" and can refer to all of one's relatives. In contrast, there is no specific word for "friend" in Yucatec Maya; occasionally *laak'* is used to refer to a close friend, but this is really a metaphor, implying that the friend is as close as a relative (similar to the urban African American "go for brother"; Liebow, 1968). Most commonly, when such a relationship is invoked, the Spanish word *amigo* is used, but with a Mayan accent applied (*áamigo*). Yucatec Mayan dictionaries provide three other words for "friend" that are in limited regional use within the Yucatan peninsula: *uts* (which more generally means "good"), *etail* (which has a root that means "with" – see following discussion – it probably means something like "inherent companion"), and *núup* (which has the sense of "twin" or "similarity"), but none of these are in wide use in the village discussed here. Often, one's relationship to someone who is not a relative is expressed as someone with whom one shares an activity or a characteristic: *éet-xok* (with + study = fellow student) or *éet-xib* (with + male = fellow man) (Acadamia de la Lengua Maya de Yucatán, 2003; Bricker, Po'ot Yah, & Dzul de Po'ot, 1998).

The centrality of family relationships in defining social interaction is reflected in the first question posed when I have a visitor come to the village: *máax tech*, or "who is this person to you?" In a sense, the villagers do not want (or do not know how) to engage with my visitor until they understand our relationship. The expected answer is that the person is some kin relation to me – my sister, my daughter, my aunt. The strength of this expectation is seen when any other answer, like "my friend," is echoed back to me as, "Oh, *just* your friend," accompanied by an obvious waning of interest.

The social world of a young woman changes radically at marriage. She leaves her parents' home and moves to her in-laws' home. She is expected not to visit her own family for a period of time to make a "clean break." She may or may not know her new husband very well, but she is certainly not used to the new world of women with whom she must now work and socialize. Some young women take a year or longer to begin to feel at home. They are often initially very shy and withdrawn. They spend a lot of time alone or with just their husband, talk only when necessary, eat very little, and try to do chores under the direction of the mother-in-law as well as possible to avoid comment or sanction. Eventually, the women from her husband's family who begin as strangers become her primary support system for going through illness, childbirth, marital difficulties, child-rearing, economic crises, and so forth. Her own mother, sisters, cousins, and wives of brothers become secondary, so that even if they live in the same small village, she may not see them for months or even years at a time.

In addition to blood kin and kin through marriage, the Yucatec Maya also participate in a system of fictive kinship, called in Spanish *compadrazgo*, found throughout Mesoamerica (Foster, 1953; Redfield & Villa Rojas, 1934). For each child, there are several events that require the services of godparents (called *páadrinos*, borrowed from Spanish): a traditional Maya infant ceremony called *hetzmek*, the infant's church baptism, first communion, graduation from school (preschool, elementary school, and if completed, secondary school), and marriage. When people accept the obligation of being godparent to the child, they also become *compadres* (co-parents) to the parents, and the parents accept a relationship of gratitude and obligation to them. *Compadres* are required to show respect (as demonstrated through formal greetings) but they are also entitled to seek support and favors that otherwise would be inappropriate.

In theory, this *compadrazgo* system provides adults with a wide range of friends outside of the family. If one couple has ten children, there is a theoretical possibility of seventy new social bonds beyond kin to be cemented – not to mention those additional ones that would come when the couple agreed to serve as godparent to others. But in practice, most godparents are chosen from within the family. Grandparents of the child are usually chosen for the most important godparent relationship (baptism) and siblings and cousins are often chosen for the more minor ones. Sometimes, a relative who is more distant is chosen in an intentional move to strengthen a bond that does not receive daily support. Thus, for example, a couple might choose the wife's sister who married into another town (and her husband) to be the *hetzmek* or marriage godparents. For graduation godparents (which is seen as accepting a smaller obligation) and sometimes for marriage godparents (which is a significantly larger one), people from outside the family may be chosen. When this happens, it is almost always a teacher or some other high-status acquaintance, often someone who lives in a larger town nearby. Rather than produce a new personal friend, this choice of a person of higher status produces a new opportunity for access to resources, whether it be loans of money, use of a house in town, advice from a more knowledgeable person, or increased social status.

Compared with the social system experienced by most European Americans that includes not only family but also coworkers, neighbors, and personal friends, having family being the primary daily interlocutors and social support system is compact and straightforward. Beyond acquaintances (of whom there are many, because in a small village almost everyone knows everyone else), there is essentially a large but closed set of people with whom individuals interact closely. Within this set, interaction is organized primarily by relationship, generation, and gender, but age is also an important factor for children. Daily living patterns, personal compatibility, and mutual interests also influence the pleasure found in the company of others and the intimacy of relationships.

Someone who has lived only in a relatively large community, one in which it is possible to be both anonymous to the many and intimate with only a few, may find it difficult to imagine what it feels like to live in a face-to-face world like a small village. Everyone knows a lot about everyone else – what they did yesterday and what they did thirty years ago when they were a child. Gossip is common and often causes trouble. Everyone knows and has a lot in common with almost everyone else. In many such peasant communities, people make limited distinctions between acquaintances and friends. Moreover, they expect that people do not choose their primary interactional partners but rather accept those that are given by the social structure of their community. In the case of the Yucatec Maya, relatives are the primary social partners.

Yucatec Maya experience a very full and diverse social world, even though it is limited to relatives. Two married adults with small children usually have four parents, perhaps a dozen siblings (who are married with children), at least some of their eight grandparents still alive, and several dozen aunts and uncles (who are also married with children and perhaps grandchildren) – plus perhaps a few more *padrinos* (their own fictive parents) and *compadres* (fictive parents for their children). Limiting one's primary social interaction to relatives hardly seems isolating where there are dozens or perhaps even hundreds of them.

With large family networks, people may feel the need to find ways to reduce the number of close relationships, not expand them. There are many examples of how persons in the village limit the range of obligations to family members. People can offer financial, material, or labor help to a relative in need, but it is not expected, and people can ask for specific help, but it is not automatically forthcoming. Not every family member will be invited to every social event. Even adult children with aging parents have no formal obligation to support them, unless they are still living in the same household. Such gifts as food or medicine that are given to the elders are considered unsolicited, and children vary widely in how much support they offer to their parents.

Because of this minimal obligation, interactions among Mayan relatives are sometimes more similar to interactions among European American friends than might be expected. Food exchange among relatives is quite common, but, like the food given to parents, the giving is nominally voluntary. It is expected, however, that the favor will be returned under similar circumstances. Exchange of labor for large projects (e.g., house building), borrowing of tools and other expensive objects, and the loaning of money are all done in the spirit of reciprocity, even between brothers. When the reciprocity is broken, it is the source of much argument and strong feelings of ill will. But most of the time, favors are readily granted because those granting the favor recognize that they will need help in the future, and the closed set of a person's relatives is the only place to go to ask for it.

In sum, for adult Yucatecan Mayans living in a traditional village, relatives provide primary companionship (in daily activities and at special events), support (including emotional, practical, and economic) when necessary, and advice and information. Family relationships represent the only intimate relationships in the culture. Most family relationships among adults are reciprocal. They are often continuously negotiated – sometimes more successfully than others. While acknowledging that these relationships themselves are not voluntary – one cannot choose family members – there is an element of choice in the amount of time and other resources you spend on family members, especially for those family members who live in a separate compound. Nevertheless, the sense of inalienable connectedness and the moral responsibilities that accompany kinship are never far from the surface; justifications of behavior are often given in terms of family ties – "I did that because he is my relative."

Socialization Beliefs and Practices

This world in which family members are the primary social companions is the one that Yucatec Mayan children observe, participate in, and are being socialized for. Parents' expectations for children's behavior in daily interactions reflect the social fact that they live in a world of family members. In addition, there are other more general beliefs that influence the cultural structure of everyday activities of Mayan children, and in turn the social opportunities they are presented with.

In general, Yucatec Mayan parents and other caregivers are very caring, very attentive, but very busy with other work. Work is seen as the primary organizing principle for the daily activity of the household (Gaskins, 1999). Children's development is thought to be primarily a process of unfolding or maturation, and parents do not see their role as maximizing developmental potential. Rather, there is a matter-of-fact assessment and acceptance of children for who they are and how they act (Gaskins, 1996). Development is not seen as requiring the construction of a special world of childhood; rather, it is seen as occurring within the world of ongoing work and other family activities. In this world, the general expectation is that children will make accommodations to the needs of the family unit rather than vice versa.

Children are also accepted as independent agents in the household, unless they get in the way of the work that needs to be done, cause trouble to others, or damage belongings (Gaskins, 1999). Adults show a great deal of respect for the children's desires and priorities. Children, even as young as age five, have considerable freedom to select activities and move about. It is not uncommon for mothers to send children of this age out on errands all over town, and if they don't return promptly, there is little concern (unless, of course, they were told to come right back). It is assumed that they have found something they want to do and will return when they are done. In one case, quite a while after a five-year-old boy left the compound on an errand, his grandmother and aunt realized that he had never returned. They spent some time speculating where he might be, decided he had probably gone to his uncle's house to see the new baby pigs, and with this plausible explanation, they spent no more time worrying about him. Nor did they scold him when he finally returned (from, it turned out, visiting the piglets).

Children are also allowed to make serious decisions about their lives, particularly when these decisions do not have serious consequences. Three-year-olds decide if they want to go to preschool or not (often having to argue with their parents in either case). One five-year-old, whose parents divorced and left the village to earn money, was allowed to decide with which grandparent he wanted to live, essentially being allowed to determine his own child custody. When asked why children are allowed to make these decisions, people shrug their shoulders and point out that the children will go where they want anyway on a daily basis, so why try to make them do something against their wishes?

There are two domains where parents work actively to socialize their children. First, socialization aims to develop the skills and motivation needed to do adult work competently (Gaskins, 1999). This socialization begins as soon as the child can understand and execute simple commands and increases over time. Children welcome this guidance, as they recognize the importance of work and want to become legitimate participants in the ongoing household activity (Gaskins, 2000). They volunteer to do chores and show great pride when they are allowed to do something that uses newly gained skills. Parents request participation from the child to the extent that they judge the child competent. Rather than encouraging the child to participate in activities that are beyond the child's ability and then providing the help needed to accomplish them (as suggested by Vygotsky's (1978) concept of the zone of proximal development), they permit participation only to the extent that the child is actually able to do the task. Thus, children may be allowed to participate in smaller tasks, or minor subroutines of larger tasks, before being able to do more complicated tasks (Gaskins, 1999). As their skills increase, so do the interactional contexts in which they may participate.

Second, socialization aims to help children learn proper patterns of social interaction and display these patterns appropriately. The most basic principle here is showing proper respect for older family members and proper responsibility for younger family members (Gaskins & Lucy, 1986). This principle defines a person's interaction with every member of the household as well as other family members who live outside the compound. For instance, children are expected at a minimum to greet parents, grandparents, and *padrinos* with a "good morning," "good afternoon," or "good evening" each time this greeting has not been given for that portion of the day. Thus, children greet their mothers on waking; they greet others in this category if they are present or at any other time during the morning when they see them. From noon until sundown, children must greet all of these people again on first contact, either promptly at noon if they are together or when they are next seen. And the courtesy is repeated again in the evening. Adults follow this same pattern, greeting their own parents, grandparents, *padrinos*, and *compadres* (and high-status outsiders) throughout the day. Thus, woven into the daily fabric of interaction is a regular public display of social hierarchy.

Children, from the time that they are very young, are also regularly reminded of their position relative to each of their siblings. Children are scolded for not listening to their older siblings and for not taking care of or being generous with their younger ones. By the time a child goes to primary school at age six or seven, it is unacceptable in the eyes of their parents for them to fail to treat an older sibling with respect or a younger sibling with nurturance. Older children are told to fulfill the desires of the younger for no other reason than the little ones are "poor things" and "your younger sibling." At the same time, they are given the authority to order them to do things, and it is expected that they will be obeyed. Older siblings (even by age four) recognize and exercise their authority; they tell their younger siblings what to do and what not to do and appeal to an older family members to help them assert their authority when their younger sibling fails to respond to their orders. They know that if they do not, they will be judged as having failed in their duty as older sibling and will be held responsible for the behavior of younger siblings. At times, this sense of responsibility leads them to defend their younger siblings against their own parents. For instance, a five-year-old girl was seen arguing with her very angry mother that her three-year-old sibling did not deserve to be punished because he could not understand what he had done wrong. She did this because of her already well established sense of responsibility for looking out for her brother's welfare, despite the fact that she was in danger of redirecting her mother's considerable anger toward herself.

The Everyday Social Life of Yucatec Mayan Children

After the first two or three years of life, children spend much of their time either participating in the work of the household or in watching the activity of others (Gaskins, 2000). The percentage of their day spent in these two activities increases as children get older. They also spend some of their time in play with other children. Whereas children under the age of two spend much of their time within sight of their mother or other adult caretaker, children older than two become "yard children" and join the other children in activity spaces that are often beyond the immediate supervision of adults. Children's activities usually occur inside or directly outside the compound, and they almost always involve multiaged groups of close relatives. Younger children's participation in the joint activities is at first somewhat marginal, but they gradually become more interested in and more competent at playing in the multiaged group of children. For older children, play becomes intertwined with child care of the younger participants, and this fact allows children to spend time in play, even as the expectations for their contribution toward the work of the household increase. Even within the play context, the authority and responsibility of older siblings is never suspended.

When engaged in work activities or observation of other people, children are likely to interact with both adult and child relatives. If the task is difficult, adults typically supervise or direct the work. But if the task is within the children's abilities, they may work alone or with other children beyond direct adult supervision. Thus, children might engage with siblings or cousins in chores such as shopping, selling food door-to-door, processing food items, harvesting yard crops, or collecting firewood in the nearby forest. Younger children might choose to watch older children as they work (or as they play) without trying to join in. And in play, all children who live in a yard together have the right to enter into any play that is ongoing, even when their entry forces the other children to make significant adjustments in their play. Thus, regardless of the activity, children spend their time each day in the company of their siblings and other close relatives.

All activities the children engage in must take multiaged skills and interests into account. In work, this means that older children who are supervising younger ones must be able to judge, as their parents do, what skills their younger siblings have mastered and how they can successfully participate in the work at hand. In play, older children must be able to find ways for the younger children to participate. In pretend play, for example, marginal roles are typically assigned to younger children. In games with rules, the rules are modified to reflect the younger children's lack of skill, and older children are quick to lay aside their own interests in service of helping the younger ones participate. For example, in a game of stickball, a younger child will be allowed to put the ball on the ground and hit it rather than having to swing at a pitched ball. Even the pitcher on the other team will tell the child when he should run to another base and when he is safer to stay on the first base reached. In a game of marbles, an older brother might honestly advise a younger one which marble is easiest to attack, even if that marble belongs to that same older brother. The older siblings take more pleasure in the successful execution of the game (across skill levels) than in winning. Selfishly, this stance makes sense because they have no choice as to whether or not their younger siblings join in; the only chance they have to play at all is to make the necessary accommodations that allow the pretense or the game to proceed. Added to this is a sincere pleasure in supporting the younger siblings.

For ten months of the year, children also go to school. In this village, there is a preschool (for children three to five years of age), a primary school (with six grades) and a secondary school (with three grades). Each grade in the primary school has a single classroom with about thirty children with one teacher. Within the classroom itself, much of the time is spent in writing or in reciting lessons in unison, and there are few opportunities for social interaction. The time walking to and from school and during the thirty-minute morning recess does not provide as much peer interaction as might be expected. Many children walk to and from school alone. Others walk with their siblings or neighbors, who are often cousins or other relations. It is unusual for any child to have a regular walking companion who is also not part of daily life in the compound. During recess, children have several options of what to do. There is usually a game, like baseball, being supervised by a teacher. Here, even though many children play together, there is little opportunity for talking. There is also food that is sold as snacks. Most children choose to buy something to eat, standing (and pushing) in line for up to half of their recess period. Once they have a snack, they tend to form small clusters of two to three children and find a corner to eat and talk. Again, these children are usually relatives who are close in age. When children have finished eating, they usually stay together talking, walk around, or play informal games. Although children are certainly exposed to a wider range of children at school through shared activities, both in the classroom and out, this exposure does not lead to friendships as they as these are typically defined for European American children. The majority of companionship in the schoolyard is still organized by family ties; conversely, peers from school are rarely talked about at home or become play partners or companions outside of school.

With this pattern of daily social interaction being limited primarily to siblings and other close relatives, children are constantly asked to practice and improve a number of social skills. By age four, children usually find themselves somewhere in the middle of the compound's child hierarchy and are therefore required to practice the full set of skills, some toward those children who are older and some towards those children who are younger. All interactions are with people they know intimately, and there is rarely a time in any day that does not involve observation or interaction with someone. But this intimacy does not come with privacy. A subset of children may not exclude from an activity any sibling who chooses to join in (except on the grounds of incompetence for participating in work). The children's interactions, although not intended or experienced as unkind, are direct and even blunt, colored by knowledge of personal character and past mistakes. There is motivation to maximize positive behavior and to restrain negative behavior because the children interacted with today are the only possible social partners of tomorrow. Children argue and fight but reconcile easily. They are given great leeway to negotiate among themselves with little interference from adults, but the negotiations are not between equals, and the basis for legitimacy of demands is not reciprocity but the rights inherent in the children's relative social standing to one another.

When children are acting as older siblings, they are required to take into account the needs, abilities, and emotions of someone else. They must be able to put their own desires second to those of others. They practice the arts of cajoling, distracting, asserting authority, serving as ombudsman and judge, and directing. They have the pleasure of receiving the trust, affection, cooperation, and dependency of someone who needs them. They recognize their own competencies and power compared with those they take care of. They learn the rules they have been taught more completely as they try to teach them to others. They bear real responsibilities with direct consequences for people they love. And they know that their efforts at child care are a true contribution to the work of the compound and are thereby valued by the adults who are important to them.

When children are acting as younger siblings, they are required to articulate their point of view persuasively and to judge what demands are reasonable and how best to be heard (who to communicate with, when, where, and how). They must decide when it will be effective to persist in expressing their views and when it is better to stop. They also must decide when they can get away with ignoring the suggestions and commands of others and when they cannot. They must know the system well enough to judge when their older siblings,' assertive behavior is justified by their dominant position in the social hierarchy and when it might be overturned by an appeal to higher authorities. They take pleasure in being cared for, in spending time with and having special privileged relationships with caregiver siblings, and in being allowed to participate in their older siblings' activities as more legitimate participants as their competence increases.

Comparing European American and Yucatec Mayan Children's Social Worlds

The previous description of Yucatec Mayan children provides an opportunity to compare their social world with that of European American children. The three questions posed earlier about cultural variation in three central developmental issues in the literature on friendship and peer interaction can now be addressed through a consideration of how the precursors, characteristics, and developmental outcomes of interactions with other children are shaped differently by each group's daily experiences in their culturally organized worlds.

Differences in Early Social Experiences

Do children in a peasant culture like the Yucatec Maya, compared to European American children, have different social experiences early in life that prepare them differently for interactions with peers? For European American children, it is thought that social skills develop first in early attachment relationships, through practice within the family structure, and from early experiences with peers that are heavily mediated by parents. In addition, the personality characteristics of an individual child (e.g., being shy vs. outgoing) are seen as important. Finally, as children's friendships become more complex, they learn new skills that transfer to other interactional contexts (e.g., social problem-solving skills might first be learned in close friendships).

Yucatec Mayan children undoubtedly also learn social skills in their early attachment relationships; but some of their primary attachments are to child caregivers, who may be the same children that become playmates later. At the same time, those child caregivers are never acting as independent child social partners, but always as caregivers, often modeling their behaviors on those they see used by adult caregivers. Thus, the line between attachment figures (who are often children) and peers (who are often the same children) is less clearly demarcated in their world. Likewise, there is a less clear-cut distinction between their early social experiences within the family and those that come later with peers, because their social world remains primarily within the family. Parents do not mediate these experiences; rather, older siblings are given the responsibility to socialize younger siblings into the social world of children. There is little opportunity for generalization of skills to new partners, except as a younger sibling comes to take on the role of older sibling when younger children are added to the family. Although personality characteristics are undoubtedly important for the Yucatec Maya, there tends to be a strong acceptance of children as they are, no matter what characteristics they bring to their daily social interactions (reflecting a more general cultural value of acceptance of personal character).

In sum, although the source of social skills may be similar in both cultures, the application of those skills to peer interaction is quite different. European American children experience a discontinuity in social partners that requires them to learn skills through interactions in one social world (adult–child within the family) and then apply them to interactions in another (child–child with peers), whereas Yucatec Maya experience a continuity in social partners with whom they practice their increasing skills over time (Benedict, 1938).

Differences in Social Interaction With Friends and Siblings

Are there important differences in the characteristics of social interaction with friends (and other peers) and with siblings? A partial list of important characteristics that have been claimed by researchers to define the friendships of European American children includes voluntary association, companionship, reciprocity between equals, negotiation, intimacy, emotional bond, privacy, same-age peers (with similar competencies), similarities of experience and interest, independent of family, and contrast with adult–child relationships (Corsaro, 1985; Hartup, 1999; Krappman, 1996; Youniss, 1980). Yucatec Mayan children have some of these characteristics present in their interactions among siblings, but not others. As described in the ethnographic section of this chapter, there is companionship, negotiation, intimacy, emotional bond, similarity of experiences and interests, and contrast with adult–child relationships. There is no voluntary association, no reciprocity between equals, no privacy, no similarity of competencies, and obviously, no independence from family. With half of the characteristics of friendship shared between European American friends and Yucatec Mayan siblings, it becomes clearer why it has been difficult to demonstrate the unique contribution of friendship to development. The Yucatec Maya case demonstrates that at least some of the characteristics of European American friends overlap with other kinds of relationships under certain conditions. To the extent that these overlapping characteristics are in fact contributing to the effect of friendship on children's development, other social relationships have the potential to provide similar experiences as friendship. Friendships, then, can be reconceptualized as a culturally specific form of providing children with close daily social interaction with other children rather than a unique, and presumed universal, social construct. Some of the characteristics of friendship can be seen as general ones that are shared with other forms of child social interaction, whereas others can be seen as specific to friendship and thereby not necessarily generalizable across cultures.

Differences in Developmental Outcomes

Do such differences in everyday social interactions lead to different developmental outcomes? The question about developmental outcomes of friendship can be posed either in terms of what is gained by having friends/successful peer relationships or in terms of what is lost by not having friends/peer isolation or rejection. Research on European American children examines individual variation across children. Although it has been difficult to show that there are unique developmental outcomes to having friends, it has been somewhat easier to show that children without friends or who experience rejection are at a social disadvantage. Even here, though, it has been difficult to demonstrate a causal relationship (Hartup, 1996).

If friendship is a unique relationship with important developmental consequences, then Yucatan Mayan children become a convenient "natural experiment," providing a group of children who grow up without friends. European American and Mayan children could be compared on social skills, self-esteem, or other variables. Given that Yucatec Mayan children all develop into socially competent adults, it is unlikely that large group differences would be found that were independent of cultural differences in socialization goals. It would appear, at least at some general level, that their social development is not disadvantaged because of the lack of friends.

An alternative is to accept that there is enough overlap in the two social experiences (granting that friendship is not a unique kind of childhood social interaction) to expect similar outcomes on social development outcome variables. The question would then become whether individual variation among the Yucatec Maya, in terms of having or not having significant social relations with other children, produce similar results as those found for European American children. This turns out to be infeasible, because there is little variation among the Maya. Every child grows up having a network of siblings and cousins who serve as primary social partners; within this network, all children are accepted (even those who are difficult to get along with!) and are full participants for their age. Some children grow up in larger or more integrated families than others, but virtually all children have the daily companionship of multiple siblings (or cousins). From a Mayan perspective, the social isolation and rejection that many European American children face, and that has been studied in such detail, would be seen as unnatural, unhealthy, and unhappy. Such a realization refocuses the question from being one of whether the Yucatec Mayan children are somehow deficient because they have no friends into being one of whether the European American culture is less than optimal for supporting all children's social and emotional growth.

Unpacking the Concept of Friendship

Hartup (1999) claims that one question stands out above all others motivating research over the last thirty years: "What contributions are made by interactions and relationships between children to the growth and development of children as individuals, to their capacities to relate to others, regulate their actions, and work out effective adaptations?" (p. 109). This question seems to be a reasonable one, one that could be profitably asked about not only children who have a lot of peer interaction outside the family, but also children who interact primarily with children who are relatives. But he then goes on to say, "Most investigators believe that the unique benefits of peer experience stem from the developmental equivalence of the participants and the egalitarian nature of their interaction" (p. 109). Note that his intention is to contrast peer experience with adult–child interaction, but in doing so, he also implicitly suggests that peer interactions that occur between children who have an equal and egalitarian relationship are particularly important. These particular benefits may not apply to sibling interaction, because siblings are not the same age and their relationship is not defined as "among equals." Finally, in concluding the same paragraph, he writes, "Children's relations with other children are thus structured differently from relations with adults both cognitively and behaviorally" (p. 109). As with the first quotation, this one also appears relevant to sibling interaction; in fact, it is a point made by researchers who focus on sibling interaction (Zukow-Goldring, 2002).

This example illustrates that when the literature on friendship and peer interaction focuses on the contrast between adults and children, much of it applies to same-aged peers and friends as well as to siblings. In all cultures, differing social competencies exist between adults and children; the point of development is to close that gap (Bruner, 1972). But peer relations researchers often make two unwarranted and perhaps unintended assumptions when they lump together the adult versus child claims with more specific claims about friendship. These researchers stress the importance of interaction between friends and other same-aged peers. The relationships among same-aged peers are presumed to be particularly important as opportunities for acquiring and practicing social skills, information about the self and about the world, intimacy and emotional support, and a chance to negotiate the management of close relationships (e.g., Hartup, 1992). The Yucatec Mayan case study demonstrates that this assumption does not hold up across cultures, and that Mayan children get many (but not all) of the same things from their interactions with siblings that European American children get from friends. This raises the issue that the assumption may be unwarranted for many European American children, as well, who have siblings and other relatives with whom they interact on a regular basis in many of the ways that friends interact (Dunn, 1999, 2002). If and how siblings also fill the role of friends for European American children – and how such friendships differ from nonsibling friendships – is often ignored in research on friendship because it focuses on relationships between children outside the home.

Researchers in the peer relations area also appear to assume that the conditions for children's social interactions are the same everywhere – in particular, as seen in Hartup (1999), that friendship is between same-aged children. For the Yucatec Mayan children, their primary social interactions with other children are with persons who differ from them in age. In many other cultures, as well, friendships are not restricted to children of the same age nor are they voluntary. For instance, among a hunter–gatherer group, the !Kung bushmen, Konner (1981) reports that groups of same-age children do not exist, because the tribes are small and therefore all children interact with each other; further, he argues this is true in hunter–gatherer societies in general. Even many European American children interact with children who are older or younger (see French, 1987, for a review of the literature on how relative age effects children's social interactions).

The perspective gained by looking at a second cultural group helps us recognize that this assumption – that friends will be the same age and have similar levels of abilities – comes from culturally specific European American norms about children's interactions that grow out of cultural ideas and practices. It limits our understanding of the effects of friendship by focusing research on same-aged peers and ignoring other conditions under which friendship can occur. This assumption occurs in part as an artifact of cultural institutions that are age-graded, such as schools, where friendship and peer interaction are largely studied. But it also stems, in part, from Piaget's theoretical claim (1965) that children of about the same age (and therefore at about the same level of conceptual development) can provide an important impetus for questioning faulty conclusions about events in the world and thereby serve as a prod for cognitive development.

Undoubtedly, peers who are working at about the same level bring specific affordances to the interaction. But children who interact with peers who are older or younger do not necessarily gain less from such peer interactions, but rather gain something different (French, 1987). Vygotsky's theory of development suggests that children have much to gain in social understanding from friends and other social partners who are older and therefore more competent. In contrast to Piaget's theory, Vygotsky suggests children learn things first on the interpersonal level through interaction with *more competent others*, including older children, and then come to master these skills independently on the intrapersonal level (Vygotsky, 1934/1987, 1978). Even in situations where the older child is not specifically focused on helping the younger, the younger child must work harder to "keep up" with the older child's abilities and can profit from having a more competent model to imitate. One example of research that supports the argument that older friends could be advantageous to development is the work by Perner, Ruffman, and Leekam (1994), who found that children with older siblings achieve a theory of mind earlier than children who do not have older siblings.

There may also be much to be gained from friends who are younger. For example, during interaction across competence levels, older children are required to take the perspective of the younger to help scaffold the shared tasks (Wood, Bruner, & Ross, 1976); this may also cause the older children to reflect on their own understanding as they compare it with that of the younger children. In general, taking care of someone younger is likely to be an act that sharpens one's understanding of self and enhances self-esteem. The power of such behavior can be seen in Harlow's classic studies of the healing power of social interaction with younger, more dependent partners (1969). He found that monkeys that had been raised in isolation (and, by lacking in socialization experiences with a caregiver, also lacked social skills with peers) could improve their social skills significantly as adolescents if allowed to spend time with younger monkeys. Furman, Rahe, and Hartup (1979) found a similar phenomenon with shy nursery school children who decreased in shyness after spending time in a classroom with younger children.

It seems quite plausible that most of these age-related characteristics would be found in all cases of multiage social interaction, whether it takes place primarily in the family context between siblings (where it is the norm), or between classmates in a school that has multiaged classrooms, between two friends outside of school who are different ages, or even two friends of the same age who have different levels of competency for a shared activity. As in the Mayan case, in some contexts, European American children are given regular opportunities to be both an older and a younger child in everyday interactions. Just as the general comparison between adult–child and child–child interactions demonstrates differences that generalize across different kinds of child–child interactions, so it might be expected that the generalization would hold when comparing characteristics of interaction with a child of the same age (or skill level), an older child, or a younger child. If so, once the assumption that all interactions are between children of the same age is questioned, other differences between sibling and friend can be investigated that are currently blurred by the relative age differences that often come with (but are not inherent to) those two statuses.

Hartup (1996) and Aboud and Mendelson (1996) have argued that if the explanatory power of friendship is going to be realized to its fullest, then friendship cannot remain a unified concept but must be broken down into components. They have offered as candidates for useful components the type of friends a child has and quality of the friendship (i.e., positive or negative). Depending on these components, friendship may have a unique, an advantageous, or a disadvantageous effect on developmental outcomes. Their analysis is an important step in unpacking the concept of friendship.

But, in fact, there is much to be said for taking *all* the criteria that have been used traditionally to identify the undifferentiated concept of "friendship" and explore each, in particular, the contribution each makes to an individual's development. Thus, not only would it be useful to study primary social interactions between children of different ages, but also to compare variation of other characteristics of friendship, for example, interactions that occur inside and outside the family, as well as comparing those that are and are not voluntary, private, or reciprocal. Studying different cultures is a helpful way to do this because there is great variation in the form of social interaction patterns experienced by children. The case study presented here, for instance, found none of those characteristics in Yucatec Mayan children's everyday relationships with other children, even though other characteristics, such as companionship, negotiation, intimacy, emotional bond, similarity of experiences and interests, and contrast with adult–child relationships were present.

Such comparative work not only provides new data, but it can prompt many types of questions that might otherwise remain unasked. For example, what does the voluntary nature of a friendship contribute toward development, and what changes if the friendship becomes "inalienable" (Cohen, 1966), as it can through fictive kinship? What does intimacy contribute, and what is lost in those instances when friendship does not imply intimacy (e.g., in the case of

Italian American teenagers described by Gans, 1962)? What do reciprocal and negotiated relationships contribute; do close friends move beyond reciprocity and negotiation, and if so, how does the influence of friendship change? And do friends outside the family contribute to development uniquely, or is their contribution similar to that of siblings or cousins who are particularly close?

The value of looking at friendship and peer interactions in children in other cultures thus goes beyond "seeing how others live." Although it is fascinating to consider the scope of variation in social interaction provided for our species through different patterns of cultural learning, it serves an additional purpose of allowing European American researchers to recognize that the patterns they study within their own culture are also culturally structured and need to be understood not as "natural" but as contributing to specific goals we have for our children's development and socialization. If they fail to recognize this, they will fail to understand the full complexity of children's social worlds.

References

Aboud, F. E., & Mendelson, M. J. (1996). Determinants of friendship selection and quality: Developmental perspectives. In W. M. Bukowski, A. F. Newcomb, & W. W. Hartup (Eds.), *The company they keep: Friendship in childhood and adolescence* (pp. 87–114). Cambridge, England: Cambridge University Press.

Acadamia de la Lengua Maya deYucatán. (2003). *Diccionario Maya popular*. Merida, Mexico: Compañía Editorial de la Penísula.

Benedict, R. (1938). Continuities and discontinuities in cultural conditioning. *Psychiatry, 1*(2), 161–167.

Bourdieu, P. (1977). *Outline of a theory of practice*. Cambridge, England: Cambridge University Press.

Bricker, V., Po'ot Yah, E., & Dzul de Po'ot, O. (1998). *A dictionary of the Maya language as spoken in Hocabá, Yucatán*. Salt Lake City: University of Utah Press.

Bronfenbrenner, U. (1979). *The ecology of human development*. Cambridge, MA, Harvard University Press.

Bruner, J. (1972). The nature and uses of immaturity. *American Psychologist, 27*, 688–704.

Chen, X. (1992). Social reputation and peer relationships in Chinese and Canadian children: A cross-cultural study. *Child Development, 63*, 1336–1343.

Chen, X., K. Rubin, H., & Li. Z. (1995). Social functioning and adjustment in Chinese children: A longitudinal study. *Developmental Psychology, 31*, 531–539.

Cohen, Y. A. (1966). Patterns of friendship. In Y. A. Cohen (Ed.), *Social structure and personality* (pp. 351–386). New York: Holt, Reinhart, & Winston.

Corsaro, W. A. (1985). *Friendship and peer culture in the early years*. Norwood, NJ: Ablex.

DeRosier, M. E., & Kupersmidt, J. B. (1991). Costa Rican children's perceptions of their social networks. *Developmental Psychology, 27*, 656–662.

Dunn, J. (1999). Siblings, friends, and the development of social understanding. In W. A. Collins & B. Lauresen (Eds.), *Relationships as developmental contexts* (pp. 263–279). Mahwah, NJ: Lawrence Erlbaum Associates.

Dunn, J. (2002). Sibling relationships. In P. K. Smith & C. H. Hart (Eds.), *Blackwell handbook of childhood social development* (pp. 223–237). Malden, MA: Blackwell.

Foster, G. M. (1953). Confradía and compadrazgo in Spain and Spanish America. *Southwest Journal of Anthropology*, *9*(1), 1–28.

French, D. C. (1987). Children's social interaction with older, younger, and same-age peers. *Journal of Social and Personal Relationships*, *4*, 63–86.

French, D. C., Rianasari, M., Pidada, S., Nelwan, P., & Buhrmester, D. (2001). Social support of Indonesian and U.S. children and adolescents by family members and friends. *Merrill-Palmer Quarter*, *47*(3), 377–394.

Furman, W., Rahe, D., & Hartup, W. W. (1979). Rehabilitation of socially-withdrawn preschool children through mixed-age and same-age socialization. *Child Development, 50*, 915–922.

Gans, H. J. (1962). *The urban villagers: Group and class in the life of Italian-Americans*. New York: Free Press.

Gaskins, S. (1996). How Mayan parental theories come into play. In S. Harkness & C. M. Super (Eds.), *Parents' cultural belief systems: Their origins, expressions, and consequences* (pp. 345–363). New York: Guilford.

Gaskins, S. (1999). Children's daily lives in a Mayan village: A case study of culturally constructed roles and activities. In A. Göncü (Ed.), *Children's engagement in the world: Sociocultural perspectives* (pp. 25–61). New York: Cambridge University Press.

Gaskins, S. (2000). Children's daily activities in a Mayan village: A culturally grounded description. *Journal of Cross Cultural Research*, *34*(4), 375–389.

Gaskins, S. (2003). From corn to cash: Change and continuity within Mayan families. *Ethos*, *31*(2), 248–273.

Gaskins, S., & Lucy, J. A. (1986, December). *Passing the buck: Responsibility and blame in the Yucatec Maya.* Paper presented at the American Anthropological Association, Philadelphia.

Gauvain, M. (2000). *The social context of cognitive development*. New York: Guilford Press.

Harlow, H. F. (1969). Age-mate or peer affectional system. In D. S. Lehrman, R. A. Hinde, & E. Shaw (Eds.), *Advances in the study of behavior* (Vol. 2, pp. 333–383). New York: Academic Press.

Hartup, W. W. (1992). Friendships and their developmental significance. In H. McGurk (Ed.), *Childhood social development* (pp. 175–205). Gove, England: Earlbaum.

Hartup, W. W. (1996). The company they keep: Friendships and their developmental significance. *Child Development*, *67*, 1–13.

Hartup, W. W. (1999). Peer experience and its developmental significance. In M. Bennett (Ed.), *Developmental psychology: Achievements and prospects* (pp. 106–125). Philadelphia: Psychology Press.

Howes, C., & Wu, F. (1990). Peer interactions and friendships in an ethnically diverse school setting. *Child Development*, *61*, 537–41.

Konner, M. J. (1981). Evolution of human behavior development. In R. H. Munroe, R. L. Munroe, & B. B. Whiting (Eds.), *Handbook of cross-cultural human development* (pp. 3–51). New York: Garland STPM Press.

Kovacs, D. M., Parker, J. G. & Hoffman, L. W. (1996). Behavioral, affective, and social correlates of involvement in cross-sex friendship in elementary school. *Child Development, 67*, 2269–2286.

Krappman, L. (1996). Amicitia, drujba, shin-yu, philia, Freundschaft, friendship: On the cultural diversity of a human relationship. In W. M. Bukowski, A. F. Newcomb and W. W. Hartup (eds.), *The Company They Keep: Friendship in Childhood and Adolescence* (pp. 19–40). Cambridge, England: Cambridge University Press.

Kupersmidt, J. B., Griesler, P. C., DeRosier, M. E., Patterson, C. J., & Davis, P. W. (1995). Childhood aggression and peer relations in the context of family and neighborhood factors. *Child Development, 66*, 360–375.

Leont'ev, A. N. (1979). The problem of activity in psychology. In J. Wertsch (Ed.), *The concept of activity in Soviet psychology* (pp. 37–71). Armonk, NY: M. E. Sharp.

Liebow, E. (1968). *Tally's corner*. Boston, MA: Little, Brown.

Luria, A. R. (1976). *Cognitive development: Its social and cultural foundations.* Cambridge, MA: Harvard University Press.

Perner, J., Ruffman, T., & Leekam, S. R. (1994). Theory of mind is contagious: You catch it from your sibs. *Child Development, 65*, 1228–1238.

Piaget, J. (1965). *The moral judgment of the child*. New York: Free Press.

Redfield, R., & Villa Rojas, A. (1934). *Chan Kom: A Maya village*. Chicago: University of Chicago Press.

Richman, A. L., LeVine, R. A., New, R. S., & Howrigan, G. A. (1988). Maternal behavior to infants in five cultures. *New Directions for Child Development, 40*, 81–97.

Rogoff, B. (1990). *Apprenticeship in thinking: Cognitive development in social context.* New York: Oxford University Press.

Schneider, B. H. (1998). Cross-cultural comparison in research on the social and emotional adjustment of children and adolescents. *Developmental Psychology, 34*(4), 793–797.

Schneider, B. H., Fonzi, A., Tani, F., & Tomado, G. (1997). A cross-cultural exploration of the stability of children's friendship and the predictors of their continuation. *Social Development, 6*, 322–339.

Super, C. M., & Harkness, S. (1986). The developmental niche: A conceptualization at the interface of child and culture. *International Journal of Behavioral Development, 9*, 545–569.

Tietjen, A. M. (1989). The ecology of children's social support networks. In D. Belle (Ed.), *Children's social networks and social supports* (pp. 37–69). Oxford, England: Wiley.

Tietjen, A. M. (1994). Supportive interactions in cultural context. In F. Nestmann & K. Hurrelmann (Eds.), *Social networks and social support in childhood and adolescence* (pp. 395–407). Oxford, England: Walter De Gruyter.

Vygotsky, L. S. (1934/1987). *Thinking and speech*. New York: Plenum Press.

Vygotsky, L. S. (1978). *Mind in society: The development of higher psychological processes*. Cambridge, MA: Harvard University Press.

Whiting, B. B. (Ed.). (1963). *Six cultures: Studies of child rearing*. New York: Wiley.

Whiting, B. B., & Edwards, C. P. (1988). *Children of different worlds*. Cambridge, MA: Harvard University Press.

Wood, D., Bruner, J. & Ross, G. (1976). The role of tutoring in problem solving. *Journal of Child Psychology and Psychiatry*, *17*, 89–100.

Youniss, J. (1980). *Parents and peers in social development: A Sullivan-Piaget perspective*. Chicago: University of Chicago Press.

Zakriski, A. L., & Coie, J. D. (1996). A comparison of aggressive-rejected and nonaggressive-rejected children's interpretations of self-directed and other-directed rejection. *Child Development*, *67*(3), 1048–1070.

Zukow-Goldring, P. (2002). Sibling caregiving. In M. H. Bornstein (Ed.), *Handbook of parenting* (Vol. 3, pp. 256–286). Hillsdale, NJ: Lawrence Erlbaum Associates.

14 Cross-Cultural Differences in Competition Among Children and Adolescents

Barry H. Schneider, Maria del Pilar Soteras de Toro, Sharon Woodburn, Marta Fulop, Consuelo Cervino, Seth Bernstein, and Monica Sandor

The nature and levels of competition in which children and adolescents engage have important social and educational consequences and may be linked to their social competence and interpersonal relations. In the social-psychological literature, competition is typically viewed as producing negative outcomes at both the individual and group levels (e.g., Sparkes, 1991; Thomas, 1978; Walster, Walster, & Berscheid, 1978). Competition, as either a goal or behavior, is frequently portrayed as detrimental to group cohesion and as negatively affecting friendships and other relations. However, it is often viewed, with some reluctance, as also necessary for individual achievement and success (e.g., Domino, 1992, 2000; Thomas, 1978). Cooperation, on the other hand, is described as necessary for the maintenance of friendships and for the successful attainment of group goals (e.g., Foster, 1984; Gelb & Jacobsen, 1988; Thomas, 1978). In some cultures, however, competition is considered by some to be an essential part of a child's development and necessary for the acquisition of a variety of social skills (LeTendre, 1996; Richard et al., 2002).

This chapter begins with a selective examination of contemporary definitions of competition. Recently, more complex views of competition and cooperation have emerged that consider the terms as existing on a variety of levels that are context-specific, interwoven with cognitive and biological factors, and culturally mediated. These definitions will be introduced later and may eventually help revise the image of competition as either totally evil or healthy and also add nuance to the characterization of cultures as either competitive or noncompetitive. We follow with some remarks about how current limitations to the vocabulary used to describe cultures hamstrings cross-cultural research on competition. The next section is a review of the cross-culture literature on competition among children and adolescents. Although much work has been done in this area, the true extent of knowledge about cultural differences in competition is still quite limited because of the methodological limitations of the studies, as will be explained. We then present the results of a four-nation study based on a multidimensional conceptualization of competition. This study complements many existing studies quite well, although its questionnaire methodology is not without shortcomings. Finally, we speculate on directions for future research.

Definitions of Competition

There has been a shift in the literature away from conceptualizing competition as a unidimensional entity towards a definition that encompasses the myriad of cognitive and contextual complexities of the phenomenon (Richard et al., 2002). Shwalb, Shwalb, and Murata (1989) highlight the motivational aspects of competition in arguing that individualistic acts do not necessarily constitute competitive acts. This is because there are instances in which a participant whose behaviour appears to be competitive might be more interested in individual accomplishment than in rivalry. Richard et al. (2002) describe how either competitive or cooperative structures can be inferred from the same behaviors that occur as children play with a ball. A game such as tennis involves articulated rules that predetermine a mutually exclusive outcome, where one player wins at the expense of the other. This would traditionally be considered a competitive situation, whereas a context involving children tossing a ball to one another with the goal of improving skill sets would be considered cooperative. However, the motivational states of the participants may diverge from the intended or expected outcomes of the imposed game structure (Richard et al., 2002). In the first instance, the participants in the tennis match may have personal goals and attitudes that are more consistent with a cooperative structure, such as illustrating the tennis proficiency of members of their country or ethnic group. A converse situation might occur in which one participant might use a cooperative setting for competitive purposes, such as impressing a parent or coach with one's ball-tossing ability, even if no one is keeping score (Richard et al., 2002).

Van Avermaet (1996) proposes an outcome continuum to help conceptualize a particular event in terms of competition or cooperation. Where the outcomes are the same for the participants, for example, in a situation where two players could both win a game or contest, the behavior would be considered cooperative. If the outcomes are inherently mutually exclusive in a situation, the event is considered competitive. Charlesworth (1996) and other evolutionary biologists believe that competition or cooperation can be inferred from resource allocation. Situations involving an unequal sharing of a resource involve competition by definition, even if cooperative strategies were required to mediate the allocation of resources. Such unequal sharing might occur, for example, if two children have to decide which of them can take home a model airplane they enjoyed building together. Thus, the model airplane constitutes a limited resource at the end of the exchange. In their view, cooperation only occurs when there is a collaborative effort between individuals to acquire equal amounts of a shared resource.

Ryckman et al. (1997) have argued that the aforementioned definitions emerge from a unidimensional view of competition that perpetuates the perception that competition can be only totally healthy or totally unhealthy. Their multidimensional model describes two types of competition: *hypercompetitive* and *personal development*. Hypercompetitive competition refers to competing to be considered better than others, whereas personal development competition refers to a personal desire to succeed at a particular activity. Variations of these terms exist: Griffon-Pierson (1990) distinguishes between *interpersonal* and *goal* competition, whereas Tassi and Schneider (1997) distinguish between *other-referenced* and *task-oriented* competition. It should be noted that some theorists (Kohn, 1992; Sherif, 1976) dispute the notion that competition can be applied to instances of competing against oneself, arguing that competitive behavior is always referenced to another person or group.

Studies by Tassi and Schneider have shown that school peers have very different impressions of classmates who compete for different reasons. Tassi and Schneider (1997) distinguished between other-referenced competition (i.e., competing to be proven superior to others), which was deemed as having negative consequences, and task-oriented competition (i.e., competing to do well at something), which was seen as having positive outcomes. That original study was limited because of the problem of shared method variance – both the competitive behaviors and social acceptance by peers were measured primarily by reports from peers. This was remedied in more recent work in which they examined these hypotheses using new, multidimensional peer- and teacher-rating scales, which demonstrated very satisfactory psychometric properties. Participants were 215 nine- and ten-year-old pupils from the province of Florence, Italy. Data from both the peer- and teacher-rating scales revealed that task-oriented competition was linked significantly to social acceptance. On the other hand, hypercompetitive competition was related to social rejection and aggression when it was motivated by the desire to be proven superior to others. We suspect that these findings have something to do with the core values of Italian society in which individual initiative is quite acceptable in general (the exception is in the family domain, where

Italy is probably more traditional; Fonzi et al., 1997; Schwartz and Ros, 1995). Similar data are needed to determine whether the conclusions generalize to the peer cultures of other family-oriented societies.

In any case, the emergence of multidimensional models of competition adds complexity to the task of comparing levels of competition in different cultures. It is very conceivable that a given culture might be characterized, for example, by high levels of personal-development competition but low levels of hypercompetitiveness, or vice versa.

Understanding Both Between-Culture Differences and the Social Forces Operating Within Cultures

As detailed later in this chapter, numerous studies have shown differences among cultures in levels of competition among children (e.g., Domino, 1992; Kagan & Madsen, 1971). The differences are not surprising given the broad range of socialization factors that are culturally specific. However, there have also been some instances in the literature where certain expected cultural differences were not mirrored in research findings. These exceptions could be expected, if only because of a trend in the literature to reduce cultural categorization to a question of individualism versus collectivism instead of a more accurate, fluid representation of the value systems operating within a given culture. Previous research is also based on a highly simplistic conceptualization of competition.

Recent researchers (e.g., Ryckman et al., 1997) have discussed the need to go beyond simplistic cross-national comparisons in research and to articulate the process by which children from different cultures either internalize the value systems around them or coordinate them with their own internal cognitive and affective mechanisms. Researchers are keenly aware that, in most cultures, societal values and norms are transmitted in relationships with family and peers. Researchers have attended relatively little to other modes of socialization, such as the mass media. With a greater understanding of these processes, new research could sketch child-rearing strategies that would optimize desirable personal qualities and behaviors (Ryckman et al., 1997). In our view, this may mean optimizing children's competence at competing at times, in places, and in ways that will enhance both their achievements and their adjustment, while at the same time socializing them to refrain from competing at the wrong times, in the wrong places, and in the wrong ways. This chapter reviews and critiques the current body of literature on cross-cultural differences in competition among children and adolescents after first outlining the attempts to define competition and examining why cultures might differ in the levels of competition and in the consequences of competing for individuals.

The interpretation of existing data on cultural differences in competitive behavior is somewhat limited because the studies are mostly based on notions of culture and of the socializing forces that operate within cultures that are excessively simple and inconsistent with contemporary advances in theory-building. Research hypotheses are typically developed by attempting to match the competitive or cooperative behaviors of individuals with a particular societal value system. For example, it is often postulated that children living in a society that promotes individualistic values might be more competitive than children living in a society in which collectivistic values predominate (e.g., Domino, 1992). This is logical because, as already introduced, competition entails by definition striving, at least to some extent, to secure a limited resource for oneself as an individual and, consequently, denying it to other members of the collective unit.

In our view, this approach oversimplifies the value systems operating in various cultures because it betrays the complexity and the uniqueness of individual cultures and groups. The examination of cross-cultural differences in competition must be based on an understanding of the specific relationship between the individuals and the society in question. This investigation would involve both an attempt to describe a particular culture in terms of value systems and social organization as well as articulation of the process by which these systems interact with individuals and groups living in the society. With regard to cross-cultural differences in competition, the questions can be narrowed to:

1. What is the nature of the value systems (note plural) being transmitted in a culture?
2. Whom are they originating from and how are they being transmitted?
3. How do children process the messages they are receiving?
4. How do they live these values in their primary interactions with family and peers?

The discussion that follows will begin with the nature and complexity of the value systems that might exist in a particular culture and then progresses to an examination of how these value systems might interact at the individual and group levels to produce unique manifestations of competitive behaviors and attitudes among children and adolescents of different cultures.

Debated since the 1930s and still unresolved is the question of how extensively competition is rooted in the biological programming of the human species. Is competition a necessary evil, an unnecessary evil, or not necessarily evil? Freud attributed hostility to a destruction instinct, neurotic egocentricity to a narcissistic libido, an obsession with money to an anal libido, and acquisitiveness to orality. All of these are features of hypercompetitiveness. We think it wrong to ignore totally the inherent aspects of human nature and to attribute competitive behaviors totally to the socialization patterns of families and cultures. Nevertheless, anthropological research has shown that cultures tend to differ greatly in social behaviors, such as competition. The relationship between an individual and society, instead of being necessarily a clash between instinct and culture, as Freud envisioned, could be symbiotic or antagonistic. An example is the genesis of what Horney (1937) described as *hypercompetitiveness*, which she defined as the need by individuals to compete and win at any cost as a means of maintaining or enhancing feelings of self-worth, with manifestations of aggressiveness, exploitation, and derogation of others depending on context. She viewed these exaggerated personality traits as developing from living in an individualistic society that fostered extreme individualistic values that she viewed as detrimental to personality development. Sampson (1977, 1988) referred to this form of cultural ethos as *self-contained individualism*, which promotes a segregation of self and other such that an individual adhering to this form of individualism would not feel any degree of dependence or responsibility toward other members of the society and would not require others for the completion of their lives.

In the literature, the dichotomy of individualism and collectivism is presented as macrosystems of organization from which a myriad of subcategories follow. Schwartz (1992) contrasts the two forms in terms of goals or objectives: Individuals in individualistic cultures pursue self-centered goals, whereas individuals in collectivistic cultures seek group goals. He lists the general value types that an individualistic culture might be expected to produce as power, hedonism, stimulation, achievement, and self-direction, whereas collectivistic cultures would produce values such as conformity, tradition, security, universalism, security, and benevolence. Of particular relevance to this chapter is the finding that concern for autonomy can coexist in a society with concern for group harmony. In fact, this pattern is predominant in most Western European countries (e.g., Schwartz & Ros, 1995). Accordingly, children and adolescents in those countries have to prepare for a society in which competition is not clearly normative and consistent with the prevailing value structure, nor entirely alien to the structure of the society. We believe that sorting this out may in fact be quite healthy for them. Equally healthy is learning to make distinctions between domains of society where competition may and may not be appropriate. This potentially beneficial challenge applies particularly to children in many Asian nations, where collectivistic values apply to relationships with friends and family members but where individualistic values are increasingly evident in the domains of education and work (Kim et al., 1994).

Thus, although the theoretical division between individualism and collectivism is of some use, some of the shortcomings in the previous research on cross-cultural differences in competition evolve from the notion that cultures are far too complex to be labeled with such a simple dichotomy. It is more useful to conceptualize cultures as fluid hybrids operating along a continuum with individualism and collectivism at the poles. Although Horney (1937) emphasized the negative impact of extreme individualism on the psyche, Sampson (1988) theorized that internalized conceptualizations of self and other did not have to be segregated and labeled this ensembled individualism. Drawing on critical relational theory, Sampson postulated that the self is inexorably entwined with others, such that individuals are constituted by and in relation to the people around them. Ryckman and Hamel (1992) draw comparisons between ensembled individualism and personal development competitiveness, which they define as an attitude in which the primary goal of competition is facilitating personal growth rather than winning. Therefore, implicit in the definition of ensembled competition is the assumption that the other individuals provide a means to attain goals that would not otherwise be possible when pursued alone or through subjugation of others. In this model, individuals conceive of themselves as free and independent and desiring of pleasure and success, but only if achieved in conjunction with others. Ryckman and Hamel found little difference in terms of individualism/collectivism between participants identified as hypercompetitive and as engaging in personal-development competition. However, the two groups of research participants with different competitive styles were quite distinct in the value they placed on power and its avoidance, and also in terms of their valuing of cooperation. Thus, in attempting to predict competitive behavior from values, it is important to consider a wide range of values, not just individualism versus collectivism.

The mechanisms by which cultural values are transmitted to and interpreted by individual members of a culture are complex and multitiered. Any theory that revolves around one level of socialization is contingent on the interactions operating above and below the selected factor. This is also the site where developmental trends interact with social forces. Elucidating why children of different cultures might display different levels of competition requires not only an understanding of the specific value systems operating in a particular culture, but also an investigation of how these systems might differentially affect cognitive development in the individual (Knight, Bernal, & Carlo, 1995). Carlo et al. (2001) suggest that cognitive development affects the rate of acquisition and complexity of value-based behaviors, whereas socialization informs the particular nature of the behaviors in question. Some cross-cultural researchers (Haidt, Koller, & Dias, 1993; Miller & Bersoff, 1992; Wainryb & Turiel, 1995) have characterized the issue as one of between-group factors, such as individualism and collectivism, versus within-group factors, such as cognitive development, family child-rearing practices, peer interactions, and gender. They have argued that value-based psychological outcomes are more influenced by within-group variables than between-groups variables, whereas we would suggest that cognitive development must always occur in a social medium, and thus the two are inexorably linked. At any rate, the social and cognitive locations where values are negotiated must be considered in any attempt to understand cultural differences.

One primary socializing factor is child-rearing and the nature of the value messages children receive from parents. Knight, Cota, and Bernal (1993) conducted research that they interpret as evidence that family socialization influences ethnic identity, which in turn informs performance on resource-allocation tasks. Domino (1992) explains the repeated finding that Chinese children display more cooperation than American children in a social values task by suggesting that Chinese child-rearing methods feature cooperation, conformity, and good behavior. He also postulates that the emphasis in Chinese storytelling on nature and on the spiritual world differs from the American emphasis on cause-and-effect rationality. These values are clearly linked to societal ideology. Hareven (1987) remarks that the Confucian ideology that underlies Chinese values views the family unit as a microcosm of society. Similarly, Alcock (1974) applies Weber's (1904) thesis to competition, arguing that the *Protestant Ethic* has helped facilitate a culture of dominance-based competition in Western youth. Horney (1937) felt that the relationship between society and family could also be inductive: Parents who create a trusting and caring environment raise children who appreciate others and tend toward cooperation. Some researchers have found that participation of children in the family's economy and chores at home correlates with cooperative behavior (Madsen, 1967; Whiting & Whiting, 1975). On a community level, Madsen (1967) has also suggested that children raised in rural areas tend to be less competitive than those raised in urban subcultures, reflecting inherent differences between city and country dwellers in the degree of interdependence with other community members.

Schools are the locus for the interactions between children and their peer groups. Much of the theoretical discussion in the psychological literature about how peer interactions may reflect, mediate, or precipitate cultural differences in competition has centered about the interaction of cognitive development and socialization forces. Some theorists and researchers have suggested that the Piagetian stage of *decentration* is instrumental in the development, or lack thereof, of prosocial behaviors, which are generally considered to include cooperative behaviors. Piaget (1951) stated that children develop the capacity to relate to perspectives other than their own through repeated interactions with peers. Studies by Hollos (1980) have shown that children living in cultures where ample opportunity is available for verbal and social interaction with peers are less competitive than those who socialize primarily with immediate family. Domino and Hannah (1987) and Shwalb et al. (1989) have researched the Japanese school system and its emphasis on addressing and assessing groups rather than individuals, although this does not seem to entail any reduction of competition. They note that the value that Japanese schools place on cooperation overrides what they claim is a developmental trend toward increased competitiveness as children age. Research conducted in several cultures regarding this age-related trend are inconclusive (e.g., Graves and Graves, 1984; Handel, 1989; Madsen, 1971). Some have argued that children learn to more adeptly apply competitive or cooperative strategies to the contextual demands of a particular task as they increase their capacities for social perspectivism (essentially, the ability to understand different perspectives on a social situation; (Kagan & Madsen, 1971; Shwalb et al. 1989). In any case, it is clear that social factors, especially school culture and the nature of children's interactions with peers, can, among other effects, influence the course of these developmental trends that relate to the proclivity to competitive behavior in any culture.

In summary, it is evident that a simple reduction to individualistic versus collectivistic, despite the value of that distinction, is not sufficient to explain why children and adolescents from different cultures exhibit variation in competitive behaviors and goals. They differ because of complex interactions between the different types and continuums of value systems operating at various sublevels and because of the interactions these systems have with within-group and individual factors.

Literature Review

The bulk of the experimental research performed on cross-cultural differences in competition was conducted in the 1970s. Reflecting the levels of theory and method of the times, virtually all the research focused on the unidimensional conception of competition as measured by children's behavioral responses to laboratory-based resource allocation measures or dyadic games. Most, but not all, of the experiments were comparisons of Anglo Americans with another cultural or ethnic group. We offer Table 14.1 as a summary of this body of research with the intent of portraying limitations and only the most tentative of conclusions, as dictated by the dated and methodologically monotonous nature of the database.

As shown in the table, many of the experimental contexts in the literature consist of variations of Madsen's (1967) Cooperation Board. The Cooperation Board is 18 inches × 18 inches (45 cm × 45 cm), over which two pieces of string intersect, forming an "X" with the point of intersection over the center of the board. Holding the string together at the point of intersection is a pen holder and a pen. Each diagonal piece of string threads through eyelets positioned at the corners of the board, where the children are stationed. The children can alternately pull or release the strings toward or away from themselves, but only a combination of actions can send the pen in a direction other than from a direct line from the center toward one of the corners. In the cooperative group-reward condition, four numbered target circles are drawn in between the corners near the border of the board, and the children have to pass the pen, in order, through each of the circles as many times as possible in one- or two-minute trials. In the cooperative individual-reward condition, the children's names are each assigned to a specific circle, and crossing a particular circle results in a reward to that specific player. There is also a competitive set, where named circles were drawn in the path of the direct line from center to corner. In this condition, children can pull the string directly toward themselves to obtain an individual reward. Other children can resist the pull by tugging on the string and setting the pen off course. Another of the more common techniques for measuring competition involves what is referred to as the Social Values Task, or Social Behavior Scale. In this variation of the Prisoner's Dilemma game, dyadic groups of children make token allocation choices by choosing between two outcomes on a series of game cards. The options usually permit considerations of equality, relative gain, individualism, and rivalry (minimizing the outcome of the other).

Madsen's (1967) pioneering study examined the performances of three subsets of Mexican culture: urban middle class, urban poor, and rural. The subjects were boys and girls in the second grade; the urban sample came from the public school in the city of Puebla, the urban poor sample came from a private church-operated school, and the rural sample consisted of all of the second-grade children in the small town of Texoloc. All groups cooperated under the group-reward condition, but only the rural group continued cooperating under the individual-reward condition. The urban poor

Table 14.1. *Major Published Cross-Cultural Studies of Competition Amongst Children and Youth*

Author (year)	Countries or Cultures Compared	Measure of Competition	Sample Size	Age Range	Culture Found More Competitive	Comments/Criticisms
Avellar and Kagan (1976)	Anglo American and Mexican-American	Choice cards that allowed rivalrous or nonrivalrous choices	112	5–9 years	Anglo American	Sample from a lower SES area than the Kagan and Madsen (1972a) study
Concha, Garcia, and Perez (1975)	Anglo American and Cuban-American	Madsen Cooperation Board	96	10–17	Cuban-Americans	no SES control. Authors believe effect due to acculturation
Domino (1992)	Chinese and American	Social Values Task – card game with choices of cooperation, individualism, competition	152	10–12	Chinese more cooperative; Americans more individualistic	Samples from one city in each country, perhaps not equivalent nor representative of the respective cultures (see Kagan & Madsen, 1972b)
Domino (2000)	Chinese and American	Open-ended story completion; Social Values Task	160	10–13	Chinese more cooperative; Americans more individualistic	Author questions the validity of the tasks for Chinese children
Hollos (1980)	Farm areas and village in Hungary	Three tasks to measure perspective-taking, and Communication; Madsen Cooperation Board	48	6–8	Village children performed better on perspectivism, role-taking and communication tasks. Farm children less competitive	
Kagan, Madsen (1971)	Mexican, Mexican-American, and Anglo American	Board game with instructions manipulated by experimenter	320	4–9	Mexicans most cooperative in every condition, Americans most competitive	One of the first studies to refer to competitive behaviour as non-adaptive
Kagan, Madsen (1972a)	Anglo American and Mexican (rural)	Social Values Task	96	8–10	Mexican	

(*continued*)

Table 14.1 (*continued*)

Author (year)	Countries or Cultures Compared	Measure of Competition	Sample Size	Age Range	Culture Found More Competitive	Comments/Criticisms
Kagan, Madsen (1972b)	Anglo American and Mexican	Cooperation Box – Children had to open a box with a hinged lid with spring latches; Board game	160	7–10	Mexican	Samples may not be representative of cultures
Knight, Kagan (1977a)	Anglo American (low and high-SES subsamples), Mexican-American	Social Values Task	197	5–9	Anglo Americans	Introduced broader scale to distinguish between competitiveness and individualism
Knight, Kagan (1977b)	Anglo American, 1st to 3rd generation Mexican-American	Social Values Task	143	9–11 (approx. – U.S. grades 4–6)	Third-generation Mexican-Americans	
Madsen (1967)	Urban Mexican (middle-class, poor), Rural Mexican	Candy, sharing scenario; drawing task; Madsen Cooperation Board	Not reported	8–10	Rural	Urban poor sample consisted only of girls (reasons not specified)
Madsen (1971)	Rural Mexican, Anglo American	Madsen Marble Pull – Marble placed in block in middle of a string leading to each player.	112	4–11	Rural Mexican	
Madsen, Shapira (1970)	Urban Afro-American, Anglo American, Mexican-American, and Mexican village	Madsen Cooperation Board	144	7–9	Afro-American and Mexican-American both higher than Mexican village	
Madsen, Shapira (1977)	US, West Germany, Israeli Kibbutz, Urban Israeli	Madsen Marble Pull	224	7–9	All other samples more competitive than kibbutz children	
Madsen, Yi (1975)	Urban and Rural South Korean	Madsen Cooperation Board; Madsen Marble Pull; Circle Matrix Board	256	8–9	Urban	In this and other studies, differences in competitive responding vary according to the instructions given
McClintock and Nuttin, Jr. (1969)	United States and Belgium	Electronic game based on resource allocation matrix	328	7–12 (approx.)	No significant differences	Boys only

(*continued*)

Table 14.1 (*continued*)

Author (year)	Countries or Cultures Compared	Measure of Competition	Sample Size	Age Range	Culture Found More Competitive	Comments/Criticisms
Miller, Thomas (1972)	Blackfoot Indian and Urban Canadian	Madsen Cooperation Board	96	7–10	Aboriginals	
Munroe and Munroe (1977)	East African and American	Circle Matrix Board	94	5–10	Americans	Very wide age range
Richmond, Weiner (1973)	Rural Euro-American, Rural Afro-American randomly assigned to "Black-Black, Mixed, White-Black" groups	Madsen Cooperation Board	216	7–8	Afro-Americans more cooperative; Mixed groups were in between, and Euro-Americans were most competitive	Sample not representative of population, Participants probably knew each other (sample came from one rural school)
Shapira, Madsen (1969)	Kibbutz and urban Israelis	Madsen Cooperation Board	80	6–10	Urban	Kibbutz children grew up together; Urban sample from a summer camp where children had known each other for three weeks.
Shapira, Madsen (1974)	Kibbutz and urban Israelis	Madsen Cooperation Board; Social Values Task	620	8–11	Urban (some results not statistically significant)	
Sommerlad, Bellingham (1972)	Australian-European, Aboriginal	Madsen Cooperation Board	96	12–15	Aboriginal group more cooperative; Aboriginal students in academic stream more competitive than aboriginals in the applied stream	Older sample than most of the other studies
Sparkes (1991)	Anglo American and Chinese (Taiwanese)	Modified Madsen Marble-Pull game	160	3–4	Taiwanese	Much younger sample than most
Thomas (1978)	Pacific Islands (Cook Islands, Western Samoa, Fiji) and New Zealand	Madsen Cooperation Board; Activity Preference Selections	96	11–14	Cook Islands	
Toda, Shinotsuka, McClintock, Stech (1978)	Anglo American, Japanese, Belgian, Greek, Mexican-American	Maximizing Difference Game (see McClintock and Nuttin Jr., 1969)	814	7–12 (approx.)	Japanese	Cultural differences far more evident at lower ages; Most participants were male

group fell somewhere in between the performance of the rural group and urban middle-class group. In the competitive condition, the urban middle-class group averaged significantly more competitive responses than the other two groups. Madsen anecdotally reported that the rural and urban poor groups seemed to shun direct conflict, whereas the middle-class group sought it out. He partly explained the differences by suggesting that procurement of food and subsistence materials creates cooperative behavior conditions, whereas those who live in comfort are free to pursue more competitive goals within a capitalistic structure. Socioeconomic distinctions thus would interact with cultural factors to produce the observed behaviors.

Most of the studies involving Anglo Americans, Mexican Americans, urban Mexicans, and rural Mexicans show a fairly consistent replication of the trend outlined earlier (Avellar & Kagan, 1976; Kagan & Madsen, 1971, 1972a, 1972b; Knight & Kagan, 1977a, 1977b; Madsen, 1971; Madsen & Shapira, 1970): Mexican children are less competitive and more cooperative than Mexican American children, who are less competitive and more cooperative than Anglo American children. In many of these studies, Anglo American children tend to compete in ways that deny rewards to others but also result in a net loss of reward to themselves, leading some of the authors (e.g., Madsen, 1971) to refer to this type of behavior as *nonadaptive* or *irrational*. The terms can also apply to a cooperative response that results in a general lowering of reward outcomes, as in Kagan and Madsen's (1972b) comparison of Anglo American and Mexican children. In that study, the Mexican children avoided conflict, even when doing so meant an unbalanced outcome with less reward for themselves. The cultural embeddedness of the patterns seen in the aforementioned American and Mexican comparative studies were further supported by Knight and Kagan's study (1977b), in which third-generation Mexican Americans were found to be more competitive than their second-generation Mexican American peers. The results of these studies have led the authors involved to suggest the relationships between value systems and competitive behavior discussed in the previous section.

The outcomes of studies involving comparisons of American and Chinese children are not quite as consistent. Domino (1992, 2000), using both story completions and social values tasks like those used by Kagan and Madsen (1971), has shown that Chinese children choose strategies that result in equality and group enhancement, whereas American children take the opposite tack and exhibit behaviors consistent with individualism and competition. Domino's results were not supported by Sparkes (1991), who compared Anglo Americans with a Taiwanese sample. Taiwanese children playing a marble-pull game exhibited more competitive responses than the Anglo American sample. Although there are a myriad of possible explanations for the differing results, one methodological issue in comparing the two is the markedly different age range used in each study. Sparkes sampled three- and four-year-olds, whereas Domino sampled ten- to twelve-year-olds. This discrepancy-highlights one of the difficulties in performing a macroanalysis of cross-cultural studies in competition, especially considering the fact that studies have indicated conflicting results with respect to age and levels of competition. Nevertheless, it must also be remembered that a capitalist market economy has operated in Taiwan for several generations but not in China at the time most of the data in the studies listed were collected, making comparison difficult.

Certain studies, including the bulk of the Anglo American/Mexican comparisons, suggest an increase in established tendencies with age. For example, in Knight and Kagan (1977a), Anglo American children appear to become more competitive with age, whereas Mexican Americans became slightly more prosocial. However, other studies (eg., Handel, 1989; Stingle & Cook, 1985), have shown the opposite developmental trend in Anglo American children.

Moving beyond comparisons involving Mexican and Chinese children, we note that studies comparing Anglo American children with children of other cultures have yielded conflicting results (Concha, Garcia, & Perez, 1975; Madsen & Shapira, 1977; McClintock & Nuttin, 1969; Munroe & Monroe, 1977; Toda et al., 1978). Whereas some (Madsen & Shapira, 1977; Munroe & Monroe, 1977) replicate the results of the Anglo American/Mexican comparison studies, indicating that Americans are more competitive than members of the other culture, others offer different findings. Toda et al. (1978) used a Maximizing Difference Game to distinguish between the competitive and cooperative play preferences of Anglo American, Japanese, Belgian, Greek, and Mexican American children. The game was based on Kagan's design of the forced-resource allocation model explained earlier, wherein dyads make allocation choices based on rivalrous or nonrivalrous choices. Toda et al. used an animated version with several procedural modifications. The younger Belgian boys (the study involved mostly boys) were less competitive than the other groups, although by early adolescence, the gap narrowed almost completely. The younger samples within the remaining national groups displayed varied levels of competition in their responses, but by the sixth grade (age approximately twelve years) all of the samples displayed relatively high levels of competitive choices. Interestingly, the authors chose to compare their results with those of Mead's (1937) qualitative study of "primitive" cultures in the South Pacific. They note that their sample of children from industrialized nations did not display the same variations in competitive motivation that Mead's samples did.

A few researchers have conducted comparative studies involving aboriginal populations (Hollos, 1980; Madsen & Yi, 1975; Miller & Thomas, 1972; Shapira & Madsen, 1969, 1974; Sommerlad & Bellingham, 1972; Thomas, 1978; Yackley & Lambert, 1971). Miller and Thomas (1972) found that a Blackfoot Indian group was more cooperative than the urban Canadian sample under the individual response conditions of the Madsen Cooperation Board. Similarly, Sommerlad and Bellingham (1972) reported that an Australian aboriginal sample was more cooperative than an Australian European sample, also with the Cooperation Board. The same study revealed that Aboriginal students in the academic stream of the Australian school system were more competitive than the Aboriginal students in the applied stream, indicating that the school context may provide some of the basis for the behaviors. Thomas (1978) noted the same phenomenon in his comparison of Pacific Island children, whose responses on the Cooperation Board were, in his view, mediated by the relative Westernization of the culture in question. Cook Islands children displayed responses very similar to New Zealand children. Thomas postulated that the differences occurred because the educational and social models of the Cook Islands were systematically designed to reflect Western norms, whereas the other Pacific Islands nations studied, Western Samoa and Fiji, had thus far minimized such Westernization.

Critics of experimental research on cross-cultural differences in competition and cooperation (e.g., Faucheux, 1976; Smith & Bond, 1998) have pointed out that high levels of cultural bias may confound both the results and the authors' interpretations of them. Within a broader critique of the direction of social psychology at the time, Faucheux (1976) deconstructs two McClintock and McNeel (1966a, 1966b) experiments carried out in the 1960s that used the Maximizing Difference Game. He effectively demonstrates how the initial interpretation of the study in question, that Belgian children are more competitive than American children, can be reversed by considering some of the ethnocentric assumptions used in the interpretation of the data. This leads to a point generated by Faucheux, and reiterated by Smith and Bond (1998), that the empirical examination of competition and cooperation consists of a supposed measurement procedure that is imposed cross-culturally without consideration of whether the meaning of these structures might differ in other cultures. This potentially leads to situations where participants in a study might respond for reasons that are fundamentally different from how an experimenter might interpret them. In Faucheux's view, the methodological trends in social psychology at the time led to experimental designs that were language-free to examine what was purportedly a universal form of social behavior, gaming. In the closer look at the McClintock and McNeel studies (1966a, 1966b), Faucheux examined the language of the participants carefully and was able to arrive at a conclusion opposite to the original one. Smith and Bond (1998) suggested that, instead of labeling a cultural group as competitive or cooperative, a better approach might be to manipulate the contextual situations that elicit different responses in each group. Such studies might integrate designs that allow participants to articulate how they were interpreting a particular situation to develop a more complete understanding of the behavior.

Sampling issues also compromise the usefulness of the studies. Most of the experimental research was conducted with samples that may not be fully representative of the cultures under study. For example, most of the studies by Madsen, Kagan, and associates (e.g. Kagan & Madsen, 1971; Madsen, 1971; Madsen & Shapira, 1970) were conducted with samples from the same Mexican rural region and from the Los Angeles area. Other potential confounding variables include nonequivalence in terms of levels of familiarity (Toda et al., 1978), especially in the rural and kibbutz samples, where the children knew each other on a far more intimate level than the children assembled from various city schools in order to constitute the urban sample. It is probably unrealistic to expect that researchers sample broadly from multiple cultures. Nevertheless, even if it is impossible to obtain two or more subsamples within each culture, it would be helpful to see more research reports containing at least a justification of the single samples within each culture, providing at least a reassurance that the sample is not *a*typical.

More generally, experimental games have become increasingly suspect in general, although, as Pruitt and Kimmel (1977) remarked, there is some virtue in studying real-life behavior, even under simulated conditions, instead of relying on marks that can be made all too easily on questionnaires. Pruitt and Kimmel argue that experimental games do not really simulate the conditions under which people have to make value decisions. Furthermore, even if gaming behavior is evident in most or all cultures, the particular games used are often not very involving or enjoyable. Some more engaging games have appeared in the literature since the 1970s (Fonzi et al., 1997; Hartup et al., 1993), but the concern remains valid because the fast-paced electronic games now available to children in many cultures have raised the ante in recent years.

How do the data obtained from direct observation of a simulated situation correlate with information that might be obtained from children's self-reports or reports by parents and teachers? The studies from the heyday of experimental-game research in the 1970s do not provide any answers.

However, more recently, Schneider and Udvari, in an unpublished study of competition within sixty-five dyads of twelve- and thirteen-year-old friends in a suburb of Toronto, used both direct observation of the friends interacting in a laboratory-analogue situation and ratings by both friends of the competition in their relationships. In small seminar rooms at their schools, the dyads of friends took part in a drawing task developed by Butler (1996, 1998). The participants were given drawing materials and instructed to work separately on making the best picture they could. The experimenters recorded the numbers of glances at the friend's work. They also asked the children to comment on the reasons they looked at their friend's drawings. Schneider and Udvari computed correlations between these data and the friends' ratings of several dimensions of competition in their relationship. Of the twenty resulting correlation coefficients between four different dimensions of competition and five scales derived from the direct observations and follow-up questions, only one achieved statistical significance ($r = .21$), no more than would be expected by chance! This does not mean that either or both of the measures are invalid, but that scores on measures of competition are likely to depend greatly on the social context and the method used.

The limitations of the experimental method for studying competition eventually precipitated in a shift toward more qualitative methods of examining the complexities of competitive behavior (e.g., LeTendre, 1996; Shwalb, Shwalb, & Murata, 1991). Unfortunately, none of these studies are of particular relevance to the theme of this chapter and volume because they did not involve cross-cultural comparisons and were not conducted with school-aged children. Thus, there is a critical need for new research to make explicit the extent of cross-cultural differences in competition between children and in the consequences of competition in different cultures. The "gold standard" in methodology would probably involve observing competition directly, in real life, where and when it happens, and understanding the meaning of the competitive behavior in the cultures being studied. This could involve either quantitative or qualitative methodology, or some combination of the two. Unfortunately, there is hardly a trace of research using this gold standard in the current literature.

In addition to the conceptual and methodological improvements we have already alluded to, we note that most of the data are quite old. The social forces inhibiting children from competing, or compelling them to do so, have changed dramatically in the past few decades in many countries, including the Latin American and East Asian countries, where the classic studies took place. Therefore, recent data are needed to portray the realities of competition in those societies today.

A Four-Nation Study of Multiple Dimensions of Competition

In an attempt to address some of the shortcomings in previous cross-cultural studies with regard to methodology and theoretical conceptions of competition, Schneider et al. (2005) conducted a study in which they compared Canadian, Cuban, Costa Rican, and Spanish early adolescents on multiple dimensions of competition and basic social values. Their study constitutes an improvement over its predecessors because it involved multiple dimensions of competition and multiple cultures. Their questionnaire method is perhaps best considered a useful complement or alternative to the many previous studies in which laboratory-analogue situations were the cornerstone of the methodology, although the questionnaire method has other methodological shortcomings. Questionnaires are, of course, not without their limitations. Questionnaires are not equally familiar in all cultures; precise translation of items and perfect item equivalence are very difficult to achieve (Van de Vijver & Leung, 1997).

Like children in the majority culture of the United States, English Canadians are raised under a belief system that emphasizes and legitimizes personal autonomy (Schwartz & Ros, 1995). Lipset (e.g., 1986) maintained that the value orientations of English Canadians are less individualistic than those of U.S. respondents of the majority culture. However, subsequent studies have failed to confirm that assertion (e.g., Baer, Grabb, & Johnston, 1993).

Spanish society is sometimes classified as falling between the poles of individualism and collectivism. In this sense, it follows somewhat the Western European value pattern identified by Schwartz and Ros (1995) in which the value placed on individual autonomy is balanced by a simultaneous valuing of group harmony. Another way of understanding the place of Spain on the continuum of individualism/collectivism is to consider the reference point: Spain is typically considered more collectivistic than Northern Europe but less collectivistic than most of Latin America, Africa, and Asia. It is very commonly held that Spanish society has become increasingly individualistic in the past few decades of urbanization, modernization, and industrialization; although some sources from as early as 50 years ago describe Spaniards as individualistic (Fischer, Manstead, & Mosquera, 1999; Gourveiea, de Albuquerque, Clemente, & Espinosa, 2002; Gourveiea, Clemente, & Espinosa, 2003; Marias, 1947).

Latin Americans are known to have values very different from those of North Americans. In Cuba, the collectivism of Latin American society is compounded by the collectivistic political ideology. Hofstede (1980) noted that a "capitalist market economy fosters individualism and in turn depends upon it (p. 233)" whereas "various socialist types of economic order foster collectivism and in turn depend upon it, although to varying degrees (p. 233)." Aguirre (1984) described the ways in which Cuban collective ideology is translated into daily instances of collective behaviors that permeate social encounters. Outside observers of this society are impressed by the degree to which Cubans depend on their families and friends for both emotional support and everyday practical assistance (e.g., Griffiths & Griffiths, 1979; Moses, 2000).

Like Cubans, Costa Ricans are known to place high value on cooperation with fellow members of their communities and extended families (Biesanz et al., 1982). Such collectivism is especially evident when joint effort is needed to achieve a common goal, such as preserving democracy or achieving universal literacy. However, in other respects, the collectivism of Costa Ricans is balanced by a phenomenon known commonly as "enmontanamiento" (shutting oneself behind a mountain barrier), meaning that they, individualistically, are basically concerned about their own welfare and that of their families (Biesanz et al., 1982; Láscaris, 1975). Although the issue of competition is not discussed directly in sociological accounts of the Costa Ricans, our impression is that cutthroat competition to achieve one's own goals at the expense of others would threaten the general concern for harmony. It is also our impression that the Costa Rican school system is characterized by far fewer contests and awards than either the Cuban or Canadian. Pride in Costa Rica and its achievements is very evident in the Costa Rican school system (Biesanz et al., 1982), but there is not a comprehensive character-education system based on national ideas and emphasizing cooperation in all aspects of life, as prevails in Cuban schools. Daily living conditions in Costa Rica seem to provide no great impetus for competition. Unlike Cubans, most Costa Ricans experience few daily shortages in the economic sphere. Higher education is available to far more Costa Ricans than Cubans, with small private universities springing up in Costa Rica in recent years, complementing two major public universities and sharply reducing competition for admission. Laments about what critics call the "quantitative revolution" (Biesanz et al., 1982) at all levels of Costa Rican schooling emphasize the low level of performance demanded of students. In summary, the very different cultures of Cuba, Costa Rica, and Central Canada provide a valuable opportunity to compare individualistic and collectivistic societies with different social norms regarding competition and cooperation and different limitations on the resources available to individuals.

It was imperative that we consider the combined effects of culture and gender as well as cultural differences in this particular study. Competitive behavior, however hostile, may be more acceptable for boys and men in some cultures than for girls and women in the same cultures. In cultures that are classified as "masculine" (Hofstede, 1980), there are sharp gender role distinctions. Among the distinctions that characterize the masculine Latin societies is the provision of autonomy and tolerance for aggression among males only and the legitimization for males only of actively seeking out resources that are limited (Schneider, 1971).

The participants were 390 seventh-grade Canadian students (approximate age range, twelve to thirteen years) from two urban centers (Toronto and Montreal), a similar number of seventh-graders from Heredia, Costa Rica (part of the San Jose metropolitan area), 200 seventh-graders from Santiago de Cuba, and 140 seventh-graders from Valencia, Spain. We developed Likert-type questions about competition based on pilot interviews. We interspersed these questions with the items of Friendship Qualities Scale, an established measure of the quality of friendships, including closeness, conflict, help, and security. Example items included "(friend's name) and I often compare our school marks to see who did better, and he (she) gets upset if I do better in our tests or assignments" (Hypercompetiveness), and "(friend's name) and I often play sports or games against each other; we see who's better, but we don't really care who wins (Non-hostile social comparison).

To understand the basic social goals and values that might explain cross-national differences in competitive behavior, we used two parallel twenty-one–item self-report scales developed by Duda and Nicholls (1992). Each domain-specific version (i.e., for academics and sport activities) of the scale consists of four factors: Task Orientation (e.g., "I feel really successful when I keep practicing hard"); Ego Orientation (e.g., "I feel really successful when I can do better than my friends"); Cooperation (e.g., "I feel really successful when my friends and I help each other do our best"); and Work Avoidance (e.g., "I feel really successful when I don't have to try"). The Work Avoidance scale, which is peripheral to the purposes of this study, was eliminated because of the low alpha.

Some of the major cross-cultural differences are depicted in Figures 14.1 and 14.2. As shown, there was much more hypercompetitiveness in the friendships of the Spanish and Canadian samples than in the two Latin American samples, whereas all three of the countries were relatively equal in nonhostile social comparison. Paralleling these differences in competitive behavior were differences in basic social goals. Canadian and Spanish participants endorsed goals involving ego orientation significantly more often than did Cubans and Costa Ricans. Cubans were, however, the most task oriented of the four samples, followed by Canada and Spain (significantly lower than Cubans), with Costa Ricans significantly lower than the other three. In terms of cooperative

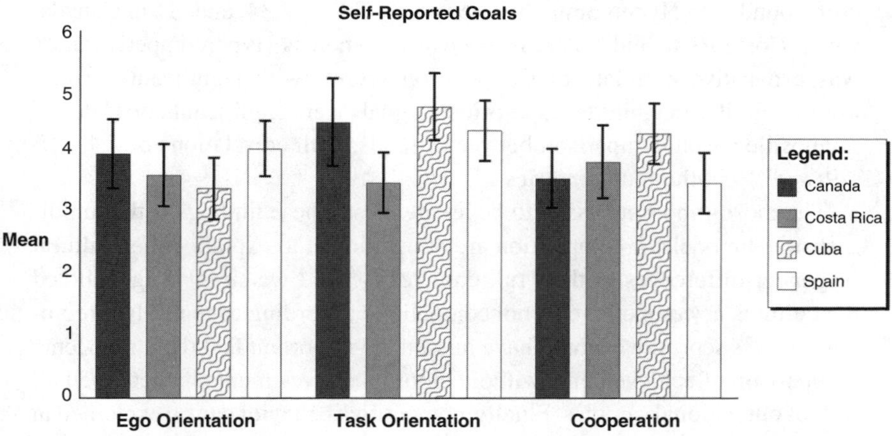

Figure 14.1. Cross-national differences in social goals.

goals, the scores from each of the four countries, as depicted in Figure 14.1, were significantly different from each other.

There were also significant gender differences, more pronounced in some of the countries than others. Boys' Hypercompetitiveness scores were significantly higher than those of girls in all countries. In terms of nonhostile social comparison between friends, however, the only significant gender differences were in Costa Rica, where girls' scores were very much lower ($p < .001$) than those of boys. (see Figure 14.2)

Our expectation that competitive behavior would correlate with basic social goals was very clearly confirmed. In all four countries, ego-oriented goals

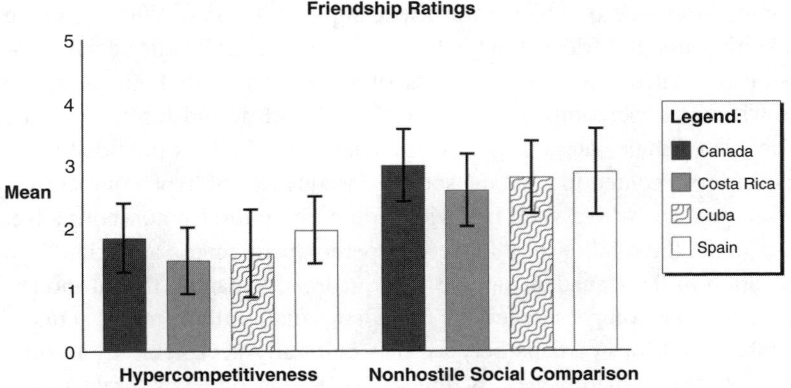

Figure 14.2. Cross-national differences in competition between friends.

corresponded to Hypercompetitiveness (r = .34, .39, .34, and .21 in Canada, Cuba, Costa Rica, and Spain, respectively), whereas Hypercompetitiveness was a negative correlate of Cooperation scores, with significant correlations of similar magnitude. Task-oriented goals were significant correlates of nonhostile social comparison between friends, with correlations of .24, .27, .29, and .19 in the four countries.

The most important lesson to be learned from these findings is that unidimensional models of competition are not sufficient to explain either cultural or gender differences in their full complexity. Had we simply pigeonholed the cultures as competitive or noncompetitive according to their Hypercompetitiveness scores, we would have missed the important fact that "innocent" comparison of achievements without emotional investment characterized all four of our national samples. Finally, competitive behavior can be explained in part by, and may be rooted in, basic social goals at the levels of the individual and of the culture.

We hypothesized that hypercompetitiveness would predict conflict between friends and the eventual dissolution of their friendships in the two Latin American samples, where hostile competition to advance individual interests is inconsistent with the prevailing group-oriented structure of society. Data on the quality and stability of the friendships are available from Canada, Cuba, and Costa Rica; a fuller report appears in Schneider et al. (2005). Whereas hypercompetitiveness was predicted to be associated with a lack of closeness and stability between friends, it was hypothesized that nonhostile competition would enhance companionship, especially in Canada and Spain, where individuals are freer than in Latin America to chose to spend time together after school hours. Enjoyment of competition was expected to facilitate friendship stability, especially among males, whereas avoidance of competition would enhance the friendships of females. With regard to competitiveness and friendship quality and stability, nonhostile social comparison correlated with the closeness of male friends in Latin America only, whereas hypercompetitiveness correlated with friendship termination in Canadian females and the Latin American samples. This provided some support for our contention that the social consequences of hypercompetitiveness are greatest where such behavior would be culturally non-normative. Interestingly, the relationship between hypercompetitiveness and friendship termination in the Canadian sample was quadratic, meaning that at moderate levels, hypercompetitiveness in Canadian youth culture might actually facilitate friendship, perhaps because it is culturally acceptable to a point, whereas hypercompetitiveness at higher levels constitutes a threat to the friendship bond. The authors caution that the data provide only a single age level and are also not comprehensive in terms of the sampling of the world's cultures.

Future Research Needs

In summary, most of the research on cross-cultural differences in competition was conducted in the 1970s and was based on unidimensional constructions of competition. The simplistic distinction between competitive and noncompetitive was usually measured by analogue games that may not truly reflect the participants' mental representations of competition. Current incarnations of the research in this field have focused on multidimensional constructs of competition and make use of measures that may better reflect competition in real life.

Challenges for future research in this area include developing representative sampling methods that allow for measures of dynamic, heterogeneous populations and refining the validity of the measurement techniques for gauging different forms of competition. With a clearer understanding of how competition affects friendship and peer relations, parents, teachers, and recreation leaders in different cultures can develop strategies that can optimize children's competence at competing in ways – and only in ways – that enhance their social adjustment and their overall well-being within specific cultural contexts. Such flexibility would better prepare children for an adult world in which cultures are in constant evolution and in constant contact with each other.

References

Aguirre, B. E. (1984). The conventionalization of collective behavior in Cuba. *American Journal of Sociology, 90*, 541–566.

Alcock, J. E. (1974). Cooperation, competition, and the effects of time pressure in Canada and India. *Journal of Conflict Resolution, 18*, 171–197.

Avellar, J., & Kagan, S. (1976). Development of competitive behaviors in Anglo-American and Mexican-American children. *Psychological Reports, 39*, 191–198.

Baer, D., Grabb, E., & Johnston, W. A. (1993). National character, regional culture, and the values of Canadians and Americans. *Canadian Review of Sociology and Anthropology, 30*, 13–36.

Biesanz, R., Biesanz, K. Z., & Biesanz, M. H. (1982). The Costa Ricans. Prospect Heights, IL: Waveland Press.

Butler, R. (1996). Effects of age and achievement goals on children's motives for attending to peers' work. *British Journal of Developmental Psychology, 14*, 1–18.

Butler, R. (1998). Age trends in the use of social and temporal comparison for self-evaluation: Examination of a novel developmental hypothesis. *Child Development, 69*, 1054–1073.

Carlo, G., Roesch, S. C., Knight, G. P., & Koller, S. H. (2001). Between- or within-culture culture variation? Culture group as a moderator of the relations between individual differences and resource allocation preferences. *Applied Developmental Psychology, 22*, 559–579.

Charlesworth, W. R. (1996). Cooperation and competition: Contributions to an evolutionary and developmental model. *International Journal of Behavioral Development, 19*, 25–39.

Concha, P., Garcia, L., & Perez, A. (1975). Cooperation versus competition: A comparison of Anglo-American and Cuban-American youngsters in Miami. *The Journal of Social Psychology, 95*, 273–274.

Domino, G. (1992). Cooperation and competition in Chinese and American children. *Journal of Cross-Cultural Psychology, 23*, 456–467.

Domino, G. (2000). Social values: A comparison of Chinese and American children. In A. L. Comunian, & U. P. Gielen (Eds.), *International perspectives on human development* (pp. 358–378). Eichengrund Germany: Past Science Publishers.

Domino, G., & Hannah, M. T. (1987). A comparative analysis of social values of Chinese and American children. *Journal of Cross-Cultural Psychology, 18*, 58–77.

Duda, J. L., & Nicholls, J. G. (1992). Dimensions of achievement motivation in schoolwork and sport. *Journal of Educational Psychology, 84*, 290–299.

Faucheux, C. (1976). Cross-cultural research in experimental social psychology. *European Journal of Social Psychology, 6*, 269–322.

Fischer, A. H., Manstead, A. R., & Mosquera, P. M. R. (1999). The role of honour-related vs. individualistic values in conceptualizing pride, shame, and anger: Spanish and Dutch cultural prototypes. *Cognition and Emotion, 13*, 149–179.

Fonzi, S., Schneider, B. H., Tani, F., & Tomada, G. (1997). Predicting children's friendship status from their dyadic interaction in structured situations of potential conflict. *Child Development, 68*, 496–506.

Foster, W. K. (1984). Cooperation in the game and sport structure of children: One dimension of psychosocial development. *Education, 105*, 201–205.

Gelb, R., & Jacobsen, J. L. (1988). Popular and unpopular children's interaction during cooperative and competitive peer group activities. *Journal of Abnormal Child Psychology, 16*, 247–261.

Gourveiea, V. V., Clemente, M., & Espinosa, P. (2003). The horizontal and vertical attributes of individualism and collectivism in a Spanish population. *Journal of Social Psychology, 143*, 43–63.

Gourveiea, V. V., de Albuquerque, J. D., Clemente, M., & Espinosa, P. (2002). Human values and social identities: A study in two collectivistic cultures. *International Journal of Psychology, 37*, 333–342.

Graves, N. B., & Graves, T. D. (1984). Preferences for cooperative, competitive and individualistic learning. *Cooperative Learning, 5*(3–4), 19–20.

Griffin-Pierson, S. (1990). The Competitiveness Questionnaire: A measure of two components of competitiveness. *Measurement and Evaluation in Counseling and Development, 23*, 108–115.

Griffiths, J., & Griffiths, P. (1979). *Cuba: The second decade*. London: Writers and Readers Publishing.

Hartup, W. W., French, D. C., Laursen, B., Johnston, M. K., & Ogawa, J. R. (1993). Conflict and friendship relations in middle childhood: Behavior in a closed-field situation. *Child Development, 64*, 445–454.

Haidt, J., Koller, S. H., & Dias, M. G. (1993). Affect, culture, and morality, or is it wrong to eat your dog? *Journal of Personality and Social Psychology, 65*, 613–628.

Hareven, T. K. (1987). Reflections on family research in the People's Republic of China. *Social Research, 54*, 663–689.

Handel, S. J. (1989). Children's competitive behavior: A challenging alternative. *Current Psychological Research and Reviews, 8*, 120–129.

Hofstede, G. (1980). *Culture's consequences: International differences in work-related values*. Beverly Hills, CA: Sage.

Hollos, M. (1980). The development of competitive, cooperative and role-taking behaviors. *Ethos, 8*, 3–23.

Horney, K. (1937). *The neurotic personality of our time*. New York: Norton.

Kagan, S., & Madsen, M. C. (1971). Cooperation and competition of Mexican, Mexican-American, and Anglo-American children of two ages under four instructional sets. *Developmental Psychology, 5*, 32–39.

Kagan, S., & Madsen, M. C. (1972a). Experimental analyses of cooperation and competition of Anglo-American and Mexican children. *Developmental Psychology, 6*, 49–59.

Kagan, S., & Madsen, M. C. (1972b). Rivalry in Anglo-American and Mexican children of two ages. *Journal of Personality and Social Psychology, 24*, 214–220.

Kim, U., Triandis, H. C., Kagitcibasi, C., Choi, C., & Yoon, G. (1994). *Individualism and collectivism: Theory, methods, and applications*. Thousand Oaks, CA: Sage.

Knight, G. P., Bernal, M. E., & Carlo, G. (1995). Socialization and development of cooperative, competitive and individualistic behaviors among Mexican-American children. In E. E. Garcia & B. M. McLaughlin (Eds.), *Meeting the challenge of linguistic and cultural diversity in early childhood*. New York: Teachers College Press.

Knight, G. P., Cota., M. K., & Bernal, M. E. (1993). The socialization of cooperative, competitive, and individualistic preferences among Mexican-American children: the mediating role of ethnic identity. *Hispanic Journal of Behavioral Sciences, 15*, 291–309.

Knight, G. P., & Kagan, S. (1977a). Acculturation of prosocial and competitive behaviors among second- and third-generation of Mexican-American children. *Journal of Cross-Cultural Psychology, 8*, 273–284.

Knight, G. P., & Kagan, S. (1977b). Development of prosocial and competitive behaviors in Anglo-American and Mexican-American children. *Child Development, 48*, 1385–1394.

Kohn, A. (1992). *No contest: The case against competition*. New York: Houghton Mifflin.

Láscaris, C. (1975). *El Costarricense* [The Costa Rican]. San Jose: EDUCA.

LeTendre, G. (1996). Youth and schooling in Japan: Competition with peers. *Berkeley Journal of Sociology, 41*, 103–136.

Lipset, S. D. (1986). Historical traditions and national characteristics: A comparative analysis of Canada and the United States. *Canadian Journal of Sociology, 11*, 113–155.

Madsen, M. C. (1967). Developmental and cross-cultural differences in the cooperative and competitive behavior of young children. *Psychological Reports, 20*, 1307–1320.

Madsen, M. C. (1971). Developmental and cross-cultural differences in the cooperative and competitive behavior of young children. *Journal of Cross-Cultural Psychology, 2*, 365–371.

Madsen, M. C., & Shapira, A. (1970). Cooperative and competitive behavior of urban Afro-American, Anglo-American, Mexican-American, and Mexican village children. *Developmental Psychology, 3*, 16–20.

Madsen, M. C., & Shapira, A. (1977). Cooperation and challenge in four cultures. *The Journal of Social Psychology, 102*, 189–195.

Madsen, M. C., & Yi, S. (1975). Cooperation and competition of urban and rural children in the Republic of South Korea. *International Journey of Psychology, 10*, 269–274.

Marias, J. (1947). Sobre una psicologia del espanol [About the psychology of the Spaniards]. *Revista de Psicologia General y Aplicada, 2*, 487–498.

McClintock, C. G., & McNeel, S. (1966a). Cross cultural comparisons of interpersonal motives. *Sociometry, 29*, 406–427.

McClintock, C. G., & Mcneel, S. (1966b). Reward and score feedback as determinants of cooperative and competitive game behavior. *Journal of Personality and Social Psychology*, 1966, 606–613.

McClintock, C. G., & Nuttin, J. M. (1969). Development of competitive game behavior in children across two cultures. *Journal of Experimental Social Psychology, 5*, 203–218.

Mead, M. (1937). *Cooperation and competition among primitive peoples*. New York: McGraw-Hill.

Miller, J. G., & Bersoff, D. M. (1992). Culture and moral judgment: How are conflicts between justice and friendship resolved. *Journal of Personality and Social Psychology, 62*, 541–554.

Miller, R., & Thomas, R. (1972). Cooperation and competition among Blackfoot Indian and urban Canadian children. *Child Development, 43*, 1104–1110.

Moses, C. (2000). Real life in Castro's Cuba, Wilmington, DE: Scholarly Resources.

Munroe, R. L., & Munroe, R. H. (1977). Cooperation and competition among East African and American children. *The Journal of Social Psychology, 101*, 145–146.

Piaget, J. (1951). Pensée égocentrique et pensée sociocentrique. *Cahiers Internationaux de Sociologie, 10*, 34–49.

Pruitt, D. G., & Kimmel, M. J. (1977). Twenty years of experimental gaming: Critique, synthesis, and suggestions for the future. *Annual Review of Psychology, 28*, 363–392.

Richard, J. F., Fonzi, A., Tani, F., Tassi, F., Tomada, G., & Schneider, B. H. (2002). Cooperation and competition. In P. K. Smith & C. H. Hart (Eds.), *Handbook of childhood social development* (pp. 515–532). Oxford, England: Blackwell.

Ryckman, R. M., & Hamel, J. (1992). Female adolescents' motives related to involvement in organized team sports. *International Journal of Sports Psychology, 23*, 147–160.

Ryckman, R. M., Libby, C. R., van den Borne, B., Gold, J. A., & Lindner, M. A. (1997). Values of hypercompetitive and personal development competitive individuals. *Journal of Personality Assessment, 69*, 271–283.

Sampson, E. E. (1977). Psychology and the American ideal. *Journal of Personality and Social Psychology, 35*, 767–782.

Sampson, E. E. (1988). The debate on individualism: Indigenous psychologies of the individual and their role in personal and societal functioning. *American Psychologist, 43*, 15–22.

Schneider, B. H., Woodburn, S., Soteras-de Toro, M., & Udvari, S. (2005). Cultural and gender differences in the implications of competition for early adolescent friendship, *Merrill-Palmer Quarterly, 51*, 163–191.

Schneider, J. (1971). On vigilance and virgins: Honour, shame and access to resources in Mediterranean societies. *Ethnology, 10*, 1–23.

Schwartz, S. H. (1992). Universals in the content and structure of values: Theoretical and empirical tests in 20 countries. In M. Zanna (Ed.), *Advances in experimental social psychology* (Vol. 25, pp. 1–65). New York: Academic Press.

Schwartz, S. H., & Ros, M. (1995). Value priorities in Western European nations: A cross-cultural perspective. In G. BenShakhar & A. Lieblich (Eds.), *Studies in psychology: A volume in honor of Sonny Kugelmas*. Jerusalem: Magnes.

Shapira, A., & Madsen, M. C. (1969). Cooperative and competitive behavior of Kibbutz and urban children in Israel. *Child Development, 40*, 609–617.

Shapira, A., & Madsen, M. C.. Between- and within-group cooperation and competition among kibbutz and non-kibbutz children. *Developmental Psychology, 10*, 140–145.

Sherif, C. W. (1976). The social context of competition. In D. Landers (Ed.), *Social problems in athletics* (pp. 18–36). Urbana, IL: University of Illinois Press.

Shwalb, D. W., Shwalb, B. J, & Murata, K. (1989). Cooperation, competition, individualism and interpersonalism in Japanese fifth and eighth grade boys. *International Journal of Psychology, 24*, 617–630.

Shwalb, D., Shwalb, B. J., & Murata, K. (1991). Individualistic striving and group dynamics of fifth- and eighth-grade Japanese boys. *Journal of Cross-Cultural Psychology, 22*, 347–361.

Smith, P. B., & Bond, M. H. (1998). *Social psychology across cultures*. London: Prentice-Hall Europe.

Sommerlad, E. A., & Bellingham, W. P. (1972). Cooperation-competition: A comparison of Australian European and Aboriginal school children. *Journal of Cross-Cultural Psychology, 3*, 149–157.

Sparkes, K. K. (1991). Cooperative and competitive behavior in dyadic game-playing: A comparison of Anglo-American and Chinese Children. *Early Child Development and Care, 68*, 37–47.

Stingle, S., & Cook, H. (1985). Age and sex differences in the cooperative and noncooperative behavior of pairs of American children. *Journal of Psychology, 119*, 335–345.

Tassi, F., & Schneider, B. H., (1997). Task-oriented versus other-referenced competition. *Journal of Applied Social Psychology, 27*, 1557–1580.

Toda, M., Shinotsuka, H., McClintock, C. G., & Stech, F. J. (1978). Development of competitive behavior as a function of culture, age, and social composition. *Journal of Personality and Social Psychology, 36*, 825–839.

Thomas, D. R. (1978). Cooperation and competition among children in the Pacific Islands and the New Zealand: The school as an agent of social change. *Journal of Research and Development in Education, 12*, 88–96.

Van Avermaet, E. (1996). Cooperation and competition. In A. S. R. Manstead & M. Hewstone (Eds.), *The Blackwell encyclopedia of social psychology* (pp. 136–141). Cambridge, MA: Blackwell.

Van de Vijver, F., & Leung, K. (1997). *Methods and data analysis for cross-cultural research*. Thousand Oaks, CA: Sage.

Wainryb, C., & Turiel, E. (1995). Diversity in social development: between or within cultures. In M. Killen & D. Hart (Eds.), *Morality in everyday lives* (pp. 283–313). New York: Cambridge University Press.

Walster, E., Walster, G., & Berscheid, E. (1978). *Equity: Theory and Research*. Boston: Allyn & Bacon.

Weber, M. (1904). *The Protestant ethic and the spirit of capitalism*. New York: Scribner's.

Whitting, B. B., & Whitting, J. (1975). *Children of six cultures*. Cambridge, MA: Harvard University Press.

Yackley, A., & Lambert, W. E. (1971). Inter-ethnic group competition and levels of aspiration. *Canadian Journal of Behavioral Science, 3*, 135–147.

15 Ethnic Peer Victimization and Psychological Well-Being Among Early Adolescents

Maykel Verkuyten

Peer interactions and the development of peer relationships are among the most central issues in children's lives. Peer relationships have been studied from a developmental and environmental perspective. For example, friendships differ in form, content, and meaning, depending on age (see Durkin, 1995). Peer relationships and friendships also differ depending on cultural and social characteristics and circumstances. These cultural and social factors can be conceptualized and examined in different ways, including in terms of ethnicity.

Ethnic preferences and cross-ethnic relations have been studied using measures such as ratings of the number of friends and their ethnic backgrounds. Cross-ethnic relations and friendships are found to be relatively uncommon, increasingly so with age (see Schneider et al., 1997, for a review). This has been found in various countries (e.g., Aboud, Mendelson, & Purdy, 2003; Clark & Ayers, 1992), including the Netherlands (e.g., Dors, 1987; Teunissen, 1988). Two major explanations are being put forward for this uncommonness.

First, there can be real cultural differences, making it less likely that cross-ethnic relationships develop. From a cross-cultural perspective, friendship patterns can be studied in relation to cultural adjustment among ethnic minorities and migrants as well as the cultural meanings of friendship and the norms and values guiding friendship behavior (e.g., Argyle et al., 1986; Wheeler, Reis, & Bond, 1989). For example, ethnic majority and minority groups often differ in their endorsement of collectivist cultural values. And in one of our studies, we found that the endorsement of these values is related to greater sensitivity to friends, to having more intimate relationships with fewer friends, and to endorsing rules with third parties more (Verkuyten & Masson, 1996). Thus, cultural differences may be one of the factors that explain why cross-ethnic relations and friendships are relatively uncommon.

Second, these relationships may be rather uncommon because of perceived cultural features. Ethnicity is most often thought of as culture that is transmitted across generations, and perceived ethnocultural characteristics can underlie peer relations in at least two ways. One is that friendship choices are typically claimed to be based on personal characteristics and that culture is seen as shaping personality (e.g., Saharso, 1992). In one of our studies, a Turkish early adolescent explained his preference for Turkish peers by saying, "When you see a Turkish peer, you have the feeling that he will think the same as you do, that he is like you because he has the same culture." Culture is presented here as a mold that determines people's personality and self. People are inevitably marked by their culture, which makes them similar to others in their ethnic group and different from peers of other cultural groups. Hence, a discourse about enculturation can be used to explain cultural determination and preferences for peers of the same ethnic group.

The other way in which perceived cultural differences can underlie peer relations is that these perceptions can form the basis of negative stereotypes and discriminatory practices. In continental Europe, the emphasis in understanding group differences is on ethnicity and culture rather than on race. For example, in the Netherlands, the terms "race's," "racial group," or "Whites and Blacks" are not often used. The distinction between ethnically Dutch and non-Dutch is typically made in terms cultural beliefs and practices and, as will be discussed, perceived cultural differences underlie patterns of ethnic victimization and exclusion.

This chapter focuses on ethnic peer victimization among early adolescents. In many Western countries, there is growing concern about prejudiced attitudes and discriminatory behavior among children, both in schools and in neighborhoods. Peer victimization based on one's ethnocultural group membership contributes to the problems and conflicts of ethnic minority children around the world. It affects children's social adjustment and self-feelings. Studies by Harter (1999), for example, have shown that (dis)approval from peers, such as classmates, is far more predictive of self-esteem than is (dis)approval from one's close friends. And in their sociometer perspective on the self, Leary and Baumeister (2000) have argued and shown that self-feelings function to monitor the degree to which a person is being excluded by others. Ethnic victimization is painful and can result in various negative outcomes.

There are, however, relatively few studies on ethnic victimization and its relations to social adjustment and well-being among children. The research to date has been predominantly carried out among African Americans and focuses on race. Clearly, there is a need for examining different ethnic groups and in other countries. In their research among African Americans, Wong, Eccles, and Sameroff (2003, p. 1227) concluded that we need to "examine how different types of ethnic devaluation affect adolescents of different ethnic groups in diverse geographic settings." It is obvious that the particular national context has an influence on the ethnic groups considered, the ideas and questions asked, and the research conducted. This is true for any national context, including the United States, where most developmental findings are produced.

In this chapter, our empirical research on ethnic peer victimization among early adolescents (aged: nine to twelve years) living in the Netherlands is discussed. This research focuses on the meaning of ethnic victimization and its effect on peer relations and psychological well-being. To obtain a better understanding of the precise role of peer victimization based on one's ethnic group membership, peer victimization that is related to individual characteristics is also considered. Children can be called names, excluded, ridiculed, and harassed because of their group membership, such as because they are a Turk or Muslim. Peer victimization, however, may also stem from individual social deficits of the victimized, for example, the child acts or dresses "strangely" or stutters. Before discussing our research, it is useful to first describe the Dutch situation. The first section presents empirical results on the extent of ethnic victimization in the Netherlands and the role of multicultural education. In the next section, the role of being a target of ethnic victimization for the development of attitudes toward cross-ethnic peer relations is examined. In the last section, the relationship between ethnic victimization and self-esteem will be discussed.

The Dutch Context

It was not until the late 1960s that Dutch industry started recruiting migrant labor on a large scale. Most of these migrant workers were Turkish and Moroccan men who were either single or had left their families behind in their home country. In the mid-1970s, a process of family reunification began, as first the Turks and later the Moroccans were joined by their wives and children. At the same time, large numbers of Dutch nationals from Suriname settled in the Netherlands. In the 1990s, many refugees and asylum seekers who had fled countries such as Iraq, Iran, Sudan, Ghana, Somalia, and Ethiopia sought refuge in the Netherlands.

In 2002, there were approximately 1.5 million immigrants residing in the Netherlands (10% of total population). The Turks formed the largest single group (320,000), followed by the Surinamese (309,000), the Moroccans

(273,000), and the Antilleans (117,000). More than half of these ethnic minorities live in the four largest cities, and many neighborhoods, in these cities show the majority of their population to be members of ethnic minorities. In these neighborhoods, there are large concentrations of immigrants; the immigrant population itself is ethnically heterogeneous, and these groups live together with Dutch people. There are, however, areas with a large concentration of (particular) ethnic minority groups, and there are, for example, many Islamic primary schools attended only by Muslims.

The position of most ethnic minority groups is worse than that of the ethnic Dutch in terms of housing, schooling, and employment. For example, studies indicate that ethnic-minority-group children consistently perform less well in school. It is the Moroccans and the Turks who have the poorest academic results, regardless of how academic performance is defined (e.g. Tesser, Van Dugteren, & Merens, 1996). Furthermore, these two Islamic groups are at the bottom of the ethnic hierarchy, or put differently, they are the least accepted by the Dutch (Hagendoorn, 1995). In our studies, we have focused predominantly on the Turkish, Moroccan, and Surinamese groups.

Experiences With Ethnic Name-Calling and Social Exclusion

In some contexts, children from the majority group can feel they are a target of ethnic victimization. However, the frequency, severity, and meaning is apt to be quite different than that of ethnic minorities. Ethnographic research in primary schools has provided important insights into the subtle and complex nature of victimization and discrimination in children's lives (e.g., Connolly, 1998; Holmes, 1995; Troyna & Hatcher, 1992; Van Ausdale & Feagin, 1996). The dynamics of ethnic victimization are examined in detail among different ethnic groups and in relation to the characteristics of particular settings. However, these studies provide no information on the extent of ethnic victimization among children. This kind of victimization may be common or not, and incidence of ethnic victimization may depend on the characteristics of schools.

In one study, we asked eighty ethnically Dutch early adolescents to write down anonymously whether they would like to be friends with a Moroccan child and an asylum seeker of their own age (Verkuyten & Steenhuis, 2005). Forty-four percent of the children wrote that they did not want to be friends with a Moroccan child, and 53 percent did not want to be friends with an asylum seeker. Around a third of the participants said "yes" to this question, and the rest indicated that they perhaps wanted to be friends. There was a significant positive association between the two questions (.61, $p < .01$), but there were also some children who said "yes" to one group and "no" to the other. We also asked the children to explain their answers. The children declining friendship predominantly pointed to stereotypical trait attributes of the cultural "other" describing them as being aggressive, quarreling, arrogant, and criminals. Cultural characteristics that make peer interactions more difficult were also mentioned, such as speaking another language, having different traditions, wearing different clothes such as a headscarf, and coming from a different culture in general (e.g., "It is very strange all those different children, sometimes you do not know what they mean or do"). Cultural differences were put forward as self-evident and acceptable reasons for not wanting to have cross-ethnic friendships.

The children responding favorably to friendships indicated that the "others" were nice, funny, and interesting or that they were just like themselves and other children and that culture did not matter. Furthermore, some children with a positive attitude explicitly denied that, for them, ethnicity is important for friendships but that *other* children do not like ethnic minorities. They wrote, for example, that "many Dutch children behave nasty towards foreigners only because they have a different culture or wear a headscarf."

We examined these negative reactions to minority groups more extensively by focusing on the extent to which children themselves feel a victim of ethnic name-calling and social exclusion. Among others, Olweus' (1993) questionnaire, that was devised to assess bullying among children in Sweden and Norway, has been modified and used widely for research in different countries. Because the modified versions typically do not include questions on ethnic victimization, however, little is known about this form of victimization.

Several questionnaire studies, particularly in the United Kingdom, have focussed more explicitly on the degree and frequency of experiences with peer victimization among ethnic minority and majority group children. For example, Eslea and Mukhtar (2000) assessed 243 children and found that ethnic victimization was widespread among Hindu, Indian Muslim and Pakistani children, and that all three groups suffered equally. Furthermore, Moran et al. (1993) compared thirty-three matched pairs of White and Asian children. They found no difference in the overall incidence of victimization, nor did they find differences in or specific types of victimization except for ethnic name-calling, which was reported more frequently by Asian children (see also Boulton, 1995).

These examples are rather small-scale studies, making it difficult to assess the incidence and frequency of ethnic victimization. Smith and Shu (2000) studied a larger sample of 2,308 primary and secondary school pupils in

England. One question was on ethnic name-calling, which was experienced by 14 percent of the sample. However, 90 percent of the pupils were White, and ethnic differences were not examined in this study. Siann et al. (1994) studied a sample of 1,139 secondary school pupils. Compared with White pupils, ethnic minorities believed more often that ethnic minority pupils are victimized more than their majority counterparts. However, no information about personal experiences was gathered. Hanish and Guerra (2000), in a sample of 1,956 U.S. children, found that Hispanic children faced lower levels of peer victimization than did either African American or White children. Another example comes from Simons et al.'s (2002) study on 867 African American early adolescents. Of the children, 76 percent reported that someone had insulted them because they were African American, 46 percent indicated that they had experienced racial slurs, and 33 percent reported that they had been excluded from an activity.

In the Netherlands, we examined the prevalence of ethnic name-calling and social exclusion by peers in different studies (Verkuyten & Thijs, 2000). In one study, among 865 primary school children from 26 schools, we found no difference in the overall frequency of victimization. However, for ethnic name-calling, a clear significant difference was found. In total, 40 percent of the Turkish children reported no experiences with ethnic name-calling, 52 percent reported some incidents, and 7 percent indicated frequent experiences. For the Dutch children, the rates were 77 percent, 21 percent, and 2 percent, respectively. In a second study among 490 pupils in nineteen primary schools, similar differences between Turkish and Dutch children were found.

We (Verkuyten & Thijs, 2002) conducted another large-scale study in eighty-two primary schools across the Netherlands and tried to address two issues on which previous surveys have provided little information (see, for example, Hanish & Guerra, 2000). First, because ethnic victimization is predominantly based on perceived cultural differences, it is particularly important to consider the role of multicultural education. This will be discussed in a following section. Second, we examined the prevalence of ethnic victimization among Dutch, Surinamese, Moroccan, and Turkish children.

Experiences With Ethnic Victimization

In the existing research, there is a tendency to treat ethnic minorities as a homogeneous group that contrasts with the majority group (Eslea & Mukhtar, 2000); that is, a distinction between White and non-White or between majority and minority group predominates. This approach ignores the many visible

Table 15.1. *Percentages for Personal Experiences With Ethnic Name Calling and Social Exclusion for Four Ethnic Groups and in Two Situations*

	DUTCH (N = 1641)	TURKISH (N = 612)	MOROCCAN (N = 463)	SURINAMESE (N = 135)
Personal experiences				
Ethnic name calling in school				
Never	79%	58%	65%	66%
Occasional	19%	35%	29%	28%
Frequent	2%	7%	6%	6%
Ethnic name calling in neighborhood				
Never	74%	53%	63%	67%
Occasional	24%	42%	33%	28%
Frequent	2%	5%	3%	5%
Ethnic exclusion in school				
Never	81%	74%	73%	70%
Occasional	11%	14%	15%	19%
Frequent	8%	12%	12%	11%
Ethnic exclusion in neighborhood				
Never	80%	72%	73%	72%
Occasional	15%	17%	17%	16%
Frequent	5%	11%	10%	12%

Source: From Verkuyten & Thijs, 2002, Table 15.1, Copyright 2002 by Taylor & Francis Ltd.

and cultural differences between ethnic groups that may affect the experiences of ethnic minority group children. Verkuyten and Kinket (2000), for example, found that Dutch children showed different preferences for contact with peers of different ethnic minority groups. Turkish children were least liked, followed by Moroccans, and the Surinamese were more accepted, a pattern of preferences that also has been found among Dutch adolescents and adults (see Hagendoorn, 1995). Hence, it is, for example, likely that Turkish children are particularly confronted with ethnic victimization. Table 15.1 presents the results for personal experiences with ethnic name-calling and ethnic exclusion in school and in the neighborhood.

Four clear results emerged. First, in agreement with studies on victimization in general (e.g., Glover et al., 2000; Smith & Shu, 2000), being a frequent or regular victim of ethnic name-calling (highest percentage is seven) and ethnic exclusion (highest percentage is twelve) is relatively exceptional. Second, the results show that Turkish, Moroccan, and Surinamese children are more likely to become victims of ethnic name-calling and social exclusion than Dutch children. One out of five Dutch children, for example, reported having experienced ethnic name-calling, whereas this was the case for at least one out of three ethnic minority group children. Hence, a clear difference between Dutch children on the one hand and ethnic minority group children on the other was found. Furthermore, Turkish children, more often than Moroccan and Surinamese children, indicated that they had experienced ethnic name-calling.

Third, the percentages for ethnic name-calling were higher than those for ethnic exclusion. Incidents of name-calling were more common than social exclusion, which is found in many other studies on victimization (e.g., Borg, 1999; Smith & Shu, 2000). Hence, for all groups, being the victim of ethnic name-calling was more common or more noticed than experiencing ethnic exclusion.

Fourth, it was also found that there were no differences between the situation at school and the direct neighborhood. That is, an approximately equal number of children reported experiences with ethnic name-calling and ethnic exclusion in both situations. Furthermore, the correlation between the questions on both situations was high (> 0.58).

Multicultural Education

In many countries, curricula aimed at combating racism and discrimination and promoting positive group relations have been proposed and implemented. Since 1985, Dutch primary schools have been legally obliged to implement a multicultural curriculum that tries to foster understanding and appreciation of cultural diversity, to promote positive interethnic interactions, and to combat racism and discrimination. Although schools differ considerably in how they carry out such multicultural curricula, a shared assumption is that multicultural education is effective in children's awareness of cultural differences as well as ethnic prejudice and discrimination.

Little is known about the effectiveness of multicultural initiatives in reducing ethnic victimization (Banks, 1995; Bigler, 1999). Additionally, this kind of victimization may not only depend on curricula and materials used but probably also on the way teachers actually deal with cultural diversity and negative peer interactions. What may be particularly important is the extent to which a teacher is perceived to act on ethnic name-calling and exclusion.

Furthermore, most of the existing studies have serious conceptual and methodological problems (see Schofield, 1991; Schofield & Eurich-Fulcer, 2001). For example, there are several studies that formulate more general conclusions and policy implications for schooling, based on findings from just four or five schools. It is, however, difficult to draw more general conclusions about multicultural education on the basis of research comparing only a few schools. Apart from the extent and form of multicultural education, there are always many other school characteristics that may explain the differences found, such as the level of ethnic segregation. To avoid such problems, a whole array of schools should be studied. Furthermore, individual and school characteristics should be taken into account simultaneously by using multilevel analysis (e.g., Simons et al., 2002).

In our nationwide study, the multilevel analyses showed that experiences with ethnic victimization were not only determined by individual characteristics, but also independently by classroom settings and structures. This means that children in the same class were more similar to each other regarding experiences with victimization than they were to children in different school classes. Subsequently we examined the effects of multiculturalism while controlling statistically for the percentage of majority group pupils and the level of ethnic heterogeneity in the class.

We found that children reported being victimized more if they reported *more* time was spent on multicultural issues. This suggests that multicultural education may lead to a higher awareness of ethnic victimization and that children learn to label and interpret negative forms of behavior in terms of prejudice and discrimination (Bigler, 1999; Verkuyten & Thijs, 2000). Another finding in support of this interpretation was that the effect for multicultural education was limited to Dutch children (see also Verkuyten, 2003a). Ethnic minority children did not report being victimized more when enjoying a higher level of multicultural education. For the Dutch children, bringing cultural differences and racism to their attention may have a sensitizing effect leading to greater vigilance. In contrast, ethnic minority group children are probably well aware of the existence of racism and discrimination in the first place, which would explain why their level of awareness would remain unaffected.

Finally, in all ethnic groups, fewer children reported experiences with ethnic victimization when they believed that they could tell their teacher about it and that the teacher would react. This result suggests that actual practices and informal contacts affect ethnic name-calling and ethnic exclusion more directly than do more formal aspects of multicultural education, such as the curriculum and material used. The extent to which the teacher is perceived to act on ethnic name-calling and ethnic exclusion seems particularly important.

Ethnic Victimization and Intergroup Attitudes

It is quite likely that being teased, excluded, or called names because of one's cultural group membership affects children's evaluative reactions toward other ethnic groups. Personal experiences with ethnic victimization may lead to a less favorable attitude toward other ethnic groups, making the development of cross-ethnic relationships and friendships even more unlikely.

Existing research has largely ignored, however, the role of children's negative experiences in understanding ethnic attitudes. Research on the contact hypothesis has typically focused on the social conditions under which positive contact may reduce prejudice (Allport, 1954; Brown, 1995). Aboud and Fenwick (1999) found that when peers make their ethnic beliefs explicit they can exert considerable influence. Particularly the direct expression of positive beliefs was found to reduce prejudicial attitudes. The role of negative contact is less clear because it has not been examined empirically.

Ethnic group attitudes can be examined as a function of personal experiences with ethnic name-calling and social exclusion. These forms of behavior are public expressions of prejudice and frequent sources of conflict and may affect children's attitudes. We investigated this issue in two studies among Turkish and Dutch early adolescents. The results of these studies clearly indicate the importance of addressing children's own experiences for understanding their ethnic attitudes and thereby for the development of cross-ethnic relations and friendships.

We focused on the relationship between experiences with being a victim of ethnic name-calling and exclusion and ethnic group attitudes (Verkuyten, 2002). Among both the Turkish and Dutch early adolescents, ethnic victimization was negatively related to the evaluation of the other ethnic group. In both studies, more experience with being a target of ethnic victimization was associated with a less positive evaluation of peers of the other ethnic group. In addition, in the first study, there was no relation with the evaluation of one's own ethnic group. However, in the second study and for the Turkish early adolescents, a significant negative association was found between experiencing ethnic victimization and the evaluation of the one's own ethnic group. Turkish children facing more ethnic victimization had a less positive attitude toward peers of their own group. The devaluation communicated in name-calling and social exclusion because of their ethnic group membership seems to give rise to a distancing from one's own ethnic group.

Hence, these results indicate that the expression of negative beliefs in the form of name-calling and social exclusion increases the victim's negative attitude toward the other ethnic group, making cross-ethnic peer relations more unlikely. In addition, for minority group children, it can lead to a less positive evaluation of one's own ethnic group, which might mean that this group becomes less attractive for identification and support. However, other studies have shown that perceived discrimination can also lead to a more strong orientation on and identification with one's ethnic group (see Schmitt & Branscombe, 2002).

Ethnic Victimization and Self-Esteem

Victimization experiences based on individual social deficits of children can lead to the internalization of problems of high self-blame and low self-esteem (see Deater-Deckard, 2001). These psychological effects are problematic in themselves and also affect the extent and nature of peer relations and friendships. It is likely that perceived *ethnic* victimization also negatively affects psychological well-being and feelings of self-worth.

There is extensive empirical support for the relationship between perceived discrimination and self-feelings among late adolescents and adults in different countries, such as the United States (e.g. Kessler, Mickelson, & Williams, 1999), Canada (e.g., Noh et al., 1999), Finland (e.g., Liebkind & Jasinskaja-Lahti, 2000), and the Netherlands (e.g., Koomen & Fränkel, 1992). There are a few studies among young adolescents. Fisher, Wallace, and Fenton (2000), for example, showed that perceived peer discrimination was significantly associated with psychological distress and low global self-worth among adolescents (thirteen to nineteen years of age) from a variety of racial and ethnic backgrounds attending an urban public school in the United States. Rumbaut (1995) studied a sample of more than 5,000 fourteen- to fifteen-year-old immigrant adolescents in southern California and Florida. He found that perceived discrimination elevated depressive symptoms and that anticipated discrimination on the labor market was significantly associated with decreased global self-worth. And in one of our studies, we found a negative relationship between perceived discrimination by peers and global self-worth among a similar age group of Turkish and Moroccan youth in the Netherlands (Verkuyten, 1998).

Studies among early adolescents are even more scarce. One example is a study conducted by Szalacha et al. (2003) among Puerto Rican children. The authors found that perceiving discrimination and worrying about discrimination were negatively associated with self-esteem and positively with depression and stress. Similar results were found by Wong et al. (2003) and by Simons et al. (2002) in their studies of African American children.

In our studies, we have tried to improve our understanding of the relationship between ethnic victimization and self-esteem in two ways. In the next section, we discuss the social psychological distinction between the personal and the group level of behavior and identity (Sherif, 1966; Tajfel &

Turner, 1986). We then discuss the developmental literature on risk factors (e.g., Lewis & Feiting, 1998; Werner, 1993; Wong et al., 2003).

Ethnic and Personal Victimization

Children may victimize one another in different ways, in various contexts, and on the basis of different criteria. Victimization may, for example, focus on individual behavior or on social category membership. Tajfel (1978) has proposed a continuum of behavior going from interpersonal to intergroup behavior (see also Sherif, 1966). The former is characterized as being based on personal relationships and individual characteristics. The latter occurs when the interaction is shaped by membership in social groups. Both forms of behavior are ideal types, with all social situations falling somewhere in between, but the relative emphasis can differ considerably.

Interpersonal relations do not have to correspond with intergroup relations. Choices for particular others as best friends do not have to imply a positive attitude toward the ethnic group of one's friend. A Dutch child can consider Ahmed a best friend but can dislike Turks as a group. This distinction can be important for understanding ethnic victimization. In conditions of ethnic victimization, children are called names, excluded, shunned, or treated unfairly because they belong to a particular ethnocultural group and not because they are short or tall, moody, act "weird" or stutter. Hence, ethnic victimization is an instance of intergroup behavior that involves children in a particular way. It has a strong internal component because something about oneself as a member of a cultural group is at stake. This kind of victimization is an attack on and negative response to something about the self that is often central and difficult to change. One implication of the distinction between personal and group levels of behavior is that it is likely that being treated negatively on the basis of one's ethnic identity has a negative influence on the self-evaluation of this identity and not necessarily on the evaluation of one's personal self.

Ethnicity has received relatively little attention among peer victimization researchers. Typically, the focus has been on personal victimization (based on individual social deficits) rather than on ethnic victimization (based on ethnic group membership; see Deater-Deckard, 2001; Hawker & Boulton, 2000, for reviews). In contrast, studies on ethnic victimization have not considered other forms of victimization. However, the distinction between personal and ethnic victimization may be useful for understanding the precise role of the latter for psychological well-being.

We examined this issue in our large-scale national study among Dutch, Turkish, Moroccan, and Surinamese children (Verkuyten & Thijs, 2005). In this study, questions regarding both ethnic victimization and personal victimization were asked. Using structural equation analysis it was first examined whether the early adolescents distinguished between personal victimization and ethnic victimization, as well as between perceptions of name-calling and social exclusion from play.

A good fit for a four-factor solution was found in which a distinction between personal and ethnic victimization and name-calling versus social exclusion emerged. The four-factor solution was adequate for all four ethnic groups, but additional analyses also showed some group differences. For example, the latent factors of personal and ethnic victimization were more strongly associated among the Turkish and Moroccan participants than they were for the Dutch and Surinamese. Hence, for the former two groups, ethnic victimization was more closely related to personal victimization. One possible interpretation of this is that ethnic identity is a psychologically more central or important part of the Turkish and Moroccan early adolescents' self (see Verkuyten & Thijs, 2005). This could explain why members of these groups tend to make less of a distinction between personal and ethnic victimization.

Another interpretation is that, for the Turks and Moroccans, experiences with personal and ethnic victimization are perhaps more strongly intertwined. These two groups are the least accepted in the Netherlands and may face a higher level of uncertainty about whether the negative reactions of others are indicators of something about themselves as an individual or as an ethnic group member. Compared with other groups, the chance of negative treatment is higher and situations of personal victimization may be harder to differentiate from ethnic group membership cues than for members of other ethnic groups.

A second aim of this study was to examine the relationship between ethnic victimization and self-esteem. In doing so, we made a distinction between ethnic self-esteem and feelings of global self-worth. Multifaceted or hierarchical models of the self place global self-worth at the apex, and other self-evaluations, such as academic, social, and ethnic self-esteem, as sources for global self-worth (e.g., Byrne & Shavelson, 1996; Harter, 1999; Hoelter, 1986; Rosenberg, 1979). Self-evaluations are considered to be dependent on specific experiences and actual behavior. Hence, these models propose that the intermediate level in the hierarchy – in our case, ethnic self-esteem – has a mediating role in linking ethnic victimization to feelings of global self-worth. For example, a child may generally have a rather negative view about herself because she has a negative attitude toward her ethnic identity, and she has this attitude because she experiences ethnic victimization. With ethnic victimization, a part of the self is implicated. Therefore, it is likely that being treated negatively on the basis of one's ethnic identity has a negative influence on the self-evaluation of this identity and thereby on global self-worth.

Our results provided clear, supporting evidence for this idea. For all four groups, personal victimization was related negatively to global self-worth but not to ethnic self-esteem. Furthermore, for all groups, ethnic self-esteem was found to mediate the relationship between perceived ethnic victimization and feelings of global self-worth. Hence, ethnic victimization is related to global self-worth because it affects the evaluation of ethnic identity, which is part of the individual's self-concept. This result helps us to understand exactly how ethnic victimization affects global self-worth.

The results also showed that name-calling had a stronger and more consistent negative effect on global self-worth than social exclusion from play. A possible reason is that situations of teasing and name-calling are explicit and public expressions of negativity. In general, these forms of peer victimization are less ambiguous than being excluded from play activities, which often is easier to justify. For example, children can argue that every child is free to choose with whom he or she wants to play and therefore has a right to choose his or her playmates (see Verkuyten et al., 1997). Peer exclusion has also been found to be justified by appealing to effective group functioning (Killen & Stangor, 2001). Hence, when peers make their evaluations and beliefs explicit, they can exert considerable influence. Thus, it seems important to examine factors such as the clarity and intensity of the victimization as well as possible attributions and justifications.

In another study, we further examined the usefulness of the distinction between the personal and the group levels (Verkuyten & Thijs, 2001). We again made a distinction between ethnic and personal victimization and examined ethnic self-esteem and personal self-esteem as predictors of self-reported peer victimization. Following social identity theory (Tajfel & Turner, 1986), self-reported victimization was expected to be related to self-esteem at the same level of abstraction. Hence, it was predicted that personal self-esteem and not ethnic self-esteem would be negatively related to self-reported personal victimization. On the other hand, ethnic self-esteem, and not personal self-esteem, was expected to be negatively related to ethnic victimization. These predictions were tested in an experimental questionnaire study among 106 Turkish children in which we elicited self-reports on experiences with either personal or ethnic victimization. As expected, it was found that personal self-esteem negatively predicted personal victimization but not ethnic victimization, and ethnic self-esteem tended to predict reports of ethnic victimization but not personal victimization.

We also examined the causal effects of both personal and ethnic victimization by assessing momentary self-feelings directly after self-reported peer victimization. It was expected that peer victimization had a negative effect on momentary self-feelings, independently of the level of personal and ethnic self-esteem. Furthermore, to examine the possible different effects of personal and ethnic victimization, a between-subjects design was used with two conditions. For one group of Turkish children, experiences with personal victimization were elicited, whereas for the other group, ethnic victimization was made salient. We explored whether personal and ethnic victimization differed in their negative effect on momentary self-feelings. In contrast with personal victimization, ethnic victimization is more specific for ethnic minority children than for children of the majority group. Hence, compared with personal victimization, ethnic victimization may be more strongly related to negative self-feelings. The results showed that peer victimization had a negative causal effect on momentary self-feelings independent of the level of personal and ethnic self-esteem. In addition, peer victimization based on ethnic group membership had a somewhat stronger negative effect on self-feelings than victimization based on individual social deficits.

Social and Cultural Threats and Sources

Ethnic peer victimization is a risk factor or threat to the psychological development of children. This form of victimization conveys to children that they are different and devalued because of their cultural group membership and because they are not part of the peer group. However, there are many other developmental risks that can negatively affect healthy development. In addition, there are also sources or protective factors in children's lives. These factors may counteract or buffer the effects of threats and serve as sources for psychological well-being. Hence, to get a clear understanding about the effect of ethnic victimization on self-esteem, it is important to examine other threats as well as sources of feelings of self-worth. In addition, it seems important to examine threats and sources that may be particularly relevant for ethnic minority group children.

In an analysis of the responses of 1,070 Turkish and Moroccan early adolescents, we examined ethnic victimization as well as intergenerational discrepancies in attitudes toward Dutch cultural practices as potential threats to self-esteem (Verkuyten, 2003b). The Turks and Moroccans stem from more traditional collectivist cultures but are living in the Netherlands, which is an individualistic western European country. This situation may lead to conflicting cultural demands affecting self-esteem. By focusing on both the perception of ethnic victimization and perceived intergenerational cultural discrepancies, we tried to examine the relative importance of these two aversive conditions to global self-worth.

In addition, we examined whether ethnic identification and values concerning family integrity make a positive contribution to self-esteem. Different theories of ethnic identity suggest that a healthy identification with one's ethnic group is a source of positive self-esteem and a psychological buffer against discrimination (e.g., Cross, 1991; Schmitt & Branscombe, 2002). Feeling a strong connection and relatedness to one's ethnic group can play a key role in self-esteem development and in managing ethnic victimization. In addition, family harmony and integrity are most predictive for self-esteem, at least through adolescence (Harter, 1999). The importance of family integrity may be particularly strong in collectivist cultures that emphasize the interconnected nature of the self, group solidarity, and sharing and stable relationships (e.g., Triandis, 1994; Triandis, McCusker, & Hui, 1990). Family integrity is probably one of the most meaningful dimensions for children, and its importance has been highlighted in cross-cultural work and in relation to acculturation processes and immigrant experiences (Kagitcibasi, 1990; Lay, et al., 1998). Hence, we examined family integrity values, in addition to ethnic identity, as a potential source of global self-worth.

The threats and sources of self-esteem were examined in relation to positive and negative self-esteem. There is an ongoing debate about whether global self-esteem is a unidimensional construct or whether it consists of a positive self-concept dimension (contentment with self) and a negative self-concept dimension (depreciation or dissatisfaction with self; see Verkuyten, 2003b). For example, several studies have asserted that the well-known Rosenberg Self-esteem Scale is unidimensional (e.g., Hensley & Roberts, 1976; Marsh, 1996), whereas other researchers have revealed both a positive and negative factor of this scale (e.g., Bachman & O'Malley, 1986; Owens, 1993, 1994), which has also been found in cross-cultural research (Farruggia et al., 2004). The analysis in our study showed that a positive and negative dimension existed and that both dimensions shared only a limited amount of variance (4%).

The results for the threat factors indicated that perceived ethnic victimization by peers was independently related to positive and negative self-esteem. Victimization decreased positive self-esteem and enhanced negative self-esteem. In addition, perceived parent-child discrepancies in the attitude toward Dutch cultural practices were also related to self-esteem. A stronger discrepancy was associated with reduced positive self-esteem and enhanced negative self-esteem. Immigrant early adolescents often adapt faster than their parents to the values and practices of the dominant society. This dissonant acculturation (Portes, 1997) may lead to conflicts over cultural values and practices, particularly because the collectivist norms of respect for elders and obedience to parents make parent–child discrepancies less acceptable (e.g., Phinney, Ong, & Madden, 2000; Szapocznik, & Kurtenis, 1993). These conflicts can lead to greater dissatisfaction (Rosenthal, Ranieri, & Klimidis, 1996) and can negatively affect feelings of self-worth.

Considering the potential sources of self-esteem, ethnic identification turned out to be related only to positive and not to negative self-esteem. Thus, a strong ethnic identity contributed to enhanced positive global self-esteem but did not result in improved negative self-esteem or reduced self-depreciation. This suggests that ethnic identification does not protect self-esteem but rather serves as a source for self-worth.

In addition, family integrity as an important aspect of collectivism was found to be related to positive self-esteem supporting the idea that family support and involvement is central for the development of feelings of self-worth. Family integrity, however, was also related to negative self-esteem. Participants who valued family integrity more had *higher* negative self-esteem. Thus, family integrity contributed to enhanced positive as well as negative self-esteem. Hence, family integrity seems to be not only a source but also a burden for self-esteem. A possible reason is that, for ethnic minority children, the endorsement of family integrity involves not just family support and involvement but also cultural discrepancies and conflicts. Collectivist values that Turks and Moroccans endorse at home differ from the values of the individualistic Dutch. This may lead to conflicting demands and feelings of confusion, resulting in enhanced negative self-esteem.

The pattern of results for sources and threats also suggests that there is an asymmetry of positive and negative events for the development of self-esteem (Leary & Baumeister, 2000; Rozin & Royzman, 2001). In general, favorable events are pleasant and have an impact on positive feelings in particular. Negative events and experiences, however, are much rarer and typically have a more generalized emotional effect. Leary and Baumeister (2000), for example, found self-esteem to be lowered more by social exclusion than it was enhanced by inclusion. People are sensitive to threats to the self, as these are typically more exceptional and have a more generalized aversive effect on both positive and negative self-feelings. In contrast, favorable events are considered less diagnostic than negative ones and are thought to predominantly affect positive feelings. Our findings partially support this asymmetry because victimization and cultural conflict affected both positive and negative self-esteem adversely, whereas ethnic identity as a source of self-esteem was only related to positive self-esteem.

Conclusions

The relation between culture and peer relations can take many different forms and can be approached from various perspectives. An important and obvious one is to examine differences in the cultural meanings of friendship and the cultural norms and values guiding peer relations (see Schneider et al., 1997; Verkuyten & Masson, 1996). These kinds of cultural differences can explain why cross-ethnic peer relations and friendships are relatively uncommon. However, there is also the danger here of implicitly adopting the essentialist and reified notion of cultures related to specific ethnic groups. Most anthropologists argue against equating ethnicity and culture, as this involves the "culturalization" of ethnicity and consequently the downplaying of social and material circumstances.

Furthermore, such an equation obscures the interactive, reflexive, and conflicting character of cultures. Cultures are interactive because norms and practices are adjusted and (re)confirmed in daily life. Children are not merely passive carriers of culture, they are also involved in the continuous construction of new meanings related to their daily social interactions (Corsaro & Eder, 1990). Additionally, cultures have numerous rules, convictions, and values permitting divergent and conflicting interpretations. Often, cultural meanings are not self-evident, but are objects of debate and negotiation. There are ongoing changes in which cultural characteristics are used, mixed, and transformed in relation to the circumstances in which children live.

Cultural differences can also in another way explain why cross-ethnic relations and friendships are relatively uncommon. Culture can be seen as molding individual personalities, and friendships are typically claimed to be based on who the other is as a person. Perceived cultural differences can also form the basis of negative stereotypes and discriminatory practices that affect peer relations. European studies on "new racism" have shown that the idea of inherent cultural differences is used to exclude and abnormalize ethnic minority groups (e.g., Barker, 1981; Wieviorka, 1995). Perceived cultural beliefs and practices also underlie processes of peer victimization among children. Ethnic differences are typically understood in cultural terms, and children are called names or excluded socially because of their ethnocultural background.

In our program of research among early adolescents from different ethnic groups living in The Netherlands, we focused on ethnic victimization, and its relationship to group attitudes and psychological well-being. Ethnic minority group children face more ethnic victimization, and this form of victimization is related to a more negative attitude toward peers from other ethnic groups and to lower self-esteem. These results indicate that cross-ethnic peer interactions and peer relationships cannot be fully understood without taking (negative) social conditions into account. Perceived cultural characteristics underlie stereotypes and prejudices and therefore imply social status differences. However, studies that take social and cultural explanations into account simultaneously are scarce. Typically, research on cross-ethnic relations focuses either on negative social circumstances and minority status or on cultural characteristics and acculturation changes. However, for understanding these peer relationships, it seems important to consider both kinds of factors together. For example, ethnic victimization can be examined as an important condition for acculturation (Berry, 1990) and cultural differences can affect the perception and interpretation of ethnic victimization and discrimination (Ogbu, 1993). Furthermore, as discussed and as suggested by the developmental literature on risks factors, cultural values can buffer or compensate for the negative effects of ethnic victimization (e.g. Werner, 1993; Wong et al., 2003).

A further issue raised by this chapter is the relationship between developmental and social processes. The chapter has focused on perceived cultural differences and negative social circumstances. This focus corresponds to social psychologists' tendency to emphasize the realities of current conditions. However, peer interactions and peer relationships as well as ethnic attitudes differ in form, content, and meaning, depending on age (Ruble et al., 2004). Developmentalists aim to describe and explain changes over time in children's abilities, knowledge and behavior. For example, developmental models expect a close relationship between ethnic identity and perceived ethnic victimization in late adolescence (e.g., Cross, 1991; Phinney, 1989), whereas negative experiences with prejudice and victimization are not considered critical developmental factors in early adolescence. Peer interactions and peer relationships are dependent on opportunities, social stereotypes, norms and values, and many other social and cultural factors, but they also depend on children's growing ability to make sense of social and cultural differences, to simultaneously attend to two or more different perspectives, and to perceive peers in individualized terms. Hence, for explaining peer interactions and peer relationships, it seems important to integrate developmental and social psychological perspectives. Bronfenbrenner's (1979) ecological theory is one example of such integration; genetic social psychology (e.g., Emler & Ohana, 1993) and developmental social psychology (Durkin, 1995) are two others.

To conclude, ethnicity is an important factor in the choice of children's peer relations and friendships. Cultural factors affect children's perceptions, expectations and values, and the ethnocultural background can convey to children that they are different and devalued. Ethnic victimization stimulates group processes of segregation and conflict, leads to more negative evaluations of other ethnic groups, and threatens the healthy development of children. These outcomes make the development of cross-ethnic relationships and friendships problematic and unlikely. Many societies and local settings are ethnically diverse, and this will only increase in the near future. Hence, future work involving a wide range of contexts, ethnic groups, and methods is needed to provide further understanding about the experiences of children of different ages and the way in which these affect cross-ethnic interactions and peer relations, and children's development more generally.

References

Aboud, F. E., & Fenwick, V. (1999). Exploring and evaluating school-based interventions to reduce prejudice. *Journal of Social Issues, 55*, 767–786.

Aboud, F. E., Mendelson, M. J., & Purdy, K. T. (2003). Cross-race peer relations and friendship quality. *International Journal of Behavioral Development, 27*, 165–173.

Allport, G. W. (1954). *The nature of prejudice*. Cambridge, MA: Addison-Wesley.

Argyle, M., Henderson, M., Bond, M., Izuka, Y., & Contarello, A. (1986). Cross-cultural variations in relationship rules. *International Journal of Psychology, 21*, 287–315.

Bachman, J. G., & O'Malley, P. M. (1986). Self-concepts, self-esteem, and educational experiences: The frog pond revisited (again). *Journal of Personality and Social Psychology, 50*, 35–46.

Banks, J. A. (1995). Multicultural education: Its effects on students' racial and gender role attitudes. In J. A. Banks & C. M. Banks (Eds.), *Handbook of research on multicultural education*, (pp. 617–627). New York: MacMillan.

Barker, M. (1981). *The new racism*. London: Junction Books.

Berry, J. W. (1990). Psychology of acculturation. In Berman, J. J. (Ed.), *Nebraska Symposium on Motivation, 1989: vol. 37. Cross-Cultural Perspectives* (pp. 201–233). Lincoln: Nebraska University Press.

Bigler, R. S. (1999). The use of multicultural curricula and materials to counter racism in children. *Journal of Social Issues, 55*, 687–705.

Borg, M. G. (1999). The extent and nature of bullying among primary and secondary school children. *Educational Research, 41*, 137–153.

Boulton, M. J. (1995). Patterns of bully/victim problems in mixed race groups of children. *Social Development, 4*, 277–293.

Bronfenbrenner, U. (1979). *The ecology of human development: Experiments by nature and design*. Cambridge, MA: Harvard University Press.

Brown, R. (1995). *Prejudice: Its social psychology*. Oxford, England: Blackwell.

Byrne, B. M., & Shavelson, R. J. (1996). On the structure of social self-concept in pre-, early, and late adolescents: A test of Shavelson, Hubner, and Stanton (1976) model. *Journal of Personality and Social Psychology, 70*, 599–613.

Clark, M. L., & Ayers, M. (1992). Friendship similarity during early adolescence: Gender and racial patterns. *The Journal of Psychology, 126*, 393–405.

Connolly, P. (1998). *Racism, gender identities and young children*, London: Routledge.

Corsaro, W. A., & Eder, D. (1990). Children's peer cultures. *Annual Review of Sociology, 16*, 197–220.

Cross, W. E. (1991). *Shades of Black: Diversity in African-American identity*. Philadelphia: Temple University Press.

Deater-Deckard, K. (2001). Annotation: Recent research examining the role of peer relationships in the development of psychopathology. *Journal of Child Psychology and Psychiatry, 42*, 565–579.

Dors, H. G. (1987). *Vriendschap en sociale relaties in multi-etnische samengestelde schoolklassen (Friendship and social relations in multi-ethnic schools)*. Lisse, The Netherlands: Swets & Zeitlinger.

Durkin, K. (1995). *Developmental social psychology: From infancy to old age*. Oxford, England: Blackwell.

Emler, N., & Ohana, J. (1993). Studying social representations in children. In G. M. Breakwell & D. V. Canter (Eds.), *Empirical approaches to social representations* (pp. 63–89). Oxford, England: Clarendon.

Eslea, M., & Mukhtar, K. (2000). Bullying and racism among Asian schoolchildren in Britain. *Educational Research, 42*, 207–217

Farruggia, S. P., Chen, C., Greenberger, E., Dmitrieva, J., & Macek, P. (2004). Adolescent self-esteem in cross-cultural perspective: Testing measurement equivalence and a mediation model. *Journal of Cross-Cultural Psychology, 35*, 719–733.

Fisher, C. B., Wallace, S. A., & Fenton, R. E. (2000). Discrimination distress during adolescence. *Journal of Youth and Adolescence, 29*, 679–695.

Glover, D., Gough, G., Johnson, M., & Cartwright, N. (2000). Bullying in 25 secondary schools: incidence, impact and intervention. *Educational Research, 42*, 141–156.

Hagendoorn, L. (1995). Intergroup biases in multiple group systems: The perception of ethnic hierarchies. In W. Stroebe & M. Hewstone (Eds.), *European Review of Social Psychology* (pp. 199–228). Chichester, England: Wiley.

Hanish, L. D., & Guerra, N. G. (2000). The roles of ethnicity and school context in predicting children's victimization by peers. *American Journal of Community Psychology, 28*, 201–223.

Harter, S. (1999). *The construction of the self: A developmental perspective*. New York: Guilford Press.

Hawker, D. S. J., & Boulton, M. J. (2000). Twenty years' research on peer victimization and psychosocial maladjustment: A meta-analytic review of cross-sectional studies. *Journal of Child Psychology and Psychiatry, 41*, 441–455.

Hensley, W. E., & Roberts, M. K. (1976). Dimensions of Rosenberg's self-esteem scale. *Psychological Reports, 38*, 583–584.

Hoelter, J. W. (1986). The relationship between specific and global evaluations of self: A comparison of several models. *Social Psychology Quarterly, 49*, 129–141.

Holmes, R. M. (1995). *How young children perceive race*, Thousand Oaks, CA: Sage.

Kagitcibasi, C. (1990). Family and socialization in cross-cultural perspective: a model of change. In Berman, J. (ed.), *Nebraska Symposium on Motivation, 1989* (pp. 135–200). Lincoln: Nebraska University Press.

Kessler, R. C., Mickelson, K. D., & Williams, D. R. (1999). The prevalence, distribution, and mental health correlates of perceived discrimination in the United States. *Journal of Health and Social Behavior, 40*, 208–230.

Killen, M., & Stangor, C. (2001). Children's reasoning about inclusion and exclusion in gender and race peer group contexts. *Child Development, 72*, 174–186.

Koomen, W., & Fränkel, E. G. (1992). Effects of experienced discrimination and different forms of relative deprivation among Surinamese, a Dutch ethnic minority group. *Journal of Community and Applied Social Psychology, 2*, 63–71.

Lay, C., Fairlie, P., Jackson, S., Ricci, T., Eisenberg, J., Sato, T., Teeäär, A., & Melamud, A. (1998). Domain-specific allocentrism-idiocentrism: A measure of family connectedness. *Journal of Cross-Cultural Psychology, 29*, 434–460.

Leary, M. R., & Baumeister, R. F. (2000). The nature and function of self-esteem: Sociometer theory. In M. Zanna (Ed.), *Advances in Experimental Social Psychology* (Vol. 32, pp. 1–61). San Diego, CA: Academic Press.

Lewis, M., & Feiting, C. (Eds.)(1998). *Families, risks, and competence*. Mahwah, NJ: Lawrence Erlbaum Associates.

Liebkind, K., & Jasinskaja-Lahti, I. (2000). The influence of experiences of discrimination of psychological stress: A comparison of seven immigrant groups. *Journal of Community and Applied Social Psychology, 10*, 1–16.

Marsh, H. W. (1996). Positive and negative global self-esteem: A substantively meaningful distinction or artifactors? *Journal of Personality and Social Psychology, 70*, 810–819.

Moran, S., Smith, P. K., Thompson, D., & Whitney, I. (1993). Ethnic differences in experiences of bullying: Asian and White children. *British Journal of Educational Psychology, 63*, 431–440.

Noh, S., Beiser, M., Kaspar, V., Hou, F., & Rummens, J. (1999). Perceived racial discrimination, depression and coping: A study of southeast Asian refugees in Canada. *Journal of Health and Social Behavior, 40*, 193–207.

Ogbu, J. (1993). Differences in cultural frame of reference. *International Journal of Behavioral Development, 16*, 483–506.

Olweus, D. (1993). *Bullying at school: What we know and what we can do*. Oxford, England: Blackwell.

Owens, T. J. (1993). Accentuate the positive and the negative: Rethinking the use of self-esteem, self-deprecation, and self-confidence. *Social Psychology Quarterly, 56*, 288–299.

Owens, T. J. (1994). Two dimensions of self-esteem: Reciprocal effects on positive self-worth and self-deprecation on adolescent problems. *American Sociological Review, 59*, 391–407.

Phinney, J. S. (1989). Stages of ethnic identity in minority group adolescents. *Journal of Early Adolescence, 9*, 34–49.

Phinney, J. S., Ong, A., & Madden, T. (2000). Cultural values and intergenerational value discrepancies in immigrant and non-immigrant families. *Child Development, 71*, 528–539.

Portes, A. (1997). Immigration theory for a new century: Some problems and opportunities. *International Migration Review, 31*, 799–825.

Rosenberg, M. (1979). *Conceiving the self.* New York: Basic Books.

Rosenthal, D., Ranieri, N., & Klimidis, S. (1996). Vietnamese adolescents in Australia: relationships between perceptions of self and parental values, intergenerational conflict, and gender dissatisfaction. *International Journal of Psychology, 31*, 81–91.

Rozin, P., & Royzman, E. B. (2001). Negativity bias, negativity dominance, and contagion. *Persononality and Social Psychology Review, 5*, 296–320.

Ruble, D. N., Alvarez, J., Bachman, M., Cameron, J., Fuligni, A., Garcia Coll, C. et al. (2004). The development of a sense of "we": The emergence and implications of children's collective identity. In M. Bennett & F. Sani, F. (Eds.), *The development of the social self* (pp. 29–76). London: Psychology Press.

Rumbaut, R. G. (1995). The crucible within: Ethnic identity, self-esteem, and segmented assimilation among children of immigrants. *International Migration Review*, 28, 748–794.

Saharso, S. (1992). *Jan en Alleman: Etnische jeugd over etnische identiteit, discriminatie en vriendschap (Ethnic youth on ethnic identity, discrimination and friendship).* Utrecht, The Netherlands: Van Arkel.

Schmitt, M. T., & Branscombe, N. R. (2002). The meaning and consequences of perceived discrimination in disadvantaged and privileged social groups. In W. Stroebe & M. Hewstone (Eds.), *European review of social psychology* (Vol. 12, pp. 167–199). Chichester, England: Wiley.

Schneider, B. H., Smith, A., Poisson, S. E., & Kwan, A. B. (1997). Cultural dimensions of children's peer relations. In S. Duck (Ed.), *Handbook of personal relationships* (2nd ed., pp. 121–146). Chichester, England: Wiley.

Schofield, J. W. (1991). School desegregation and intergroup relations: A review of the literature. In G. Grant (Ed.), *Review of research in education* (Vol. 17, pp. 335–399). Washington, DC: American Educational Research Association.

Schofield, J. W., & Eurich-Fulcer, R. (2001). When and how school desegregation improves intergroup relations. In R. Brown & S. L. Gaertner (Eds.), *Blackwell handbook of social psychology: Intergroup processes* (pp. 475–494). Oxford, England: Blackwell.

Sherif, M. (1966). *Group conflict and co-operation: Their social psychology.* Londodn: Routledge and Kegan Paul.

Siann, G., Callaghan, M., Glissov, P., Lockhart, R., & Rawson, L. (1994). Who gets bullied? The effect of school, gender and ethnic group. *Educational Research, 36*, 123–134.

Simons, R. L., Murry, V., McLoyd, V., Lin, K-H., Cutrona, C., & Conger, R. D. (2002). Discrimination, crime, ethnic identity, and parenting as correlates of depressive symptoms among African American children: A multilevel analysis. *Development and Psychopathology, 14*, 371–393.

Smith, P. K., & Shu S. (2000). What good schools can do about bullying: Findings from a survey in English schools after a decade of research and action. *Childhood, 7*, 193–212.

Szalacha, L. A., Erkut, S., Garciá Coll, C., Alarcón, O., Fields, J. P., & Ceder, I. (2003). Discrimination and Puerto Rican children's and adolescents' mental health. *Cultural Diversity and Ethnic Minority Psychology, 9*, 141–155.

Szapocznik, J., & Kurtenis, W. (1993). Family psychology and cultural diversity. *American Psychologist, 28*, 400–407.

Tajfel, H. (1978). Interindividual behaviour and intergroup behaviour. In H. Tajfel (Ed.), *Differentiation between groups* (pp. 27–60). London: Academic Press.

Tajfel, H., & Turner, J. (1986). The social identity theory of intergroup behavior. In S. Worchel & W. Austin (Eds.), *Psychology of intergroup relations* (pp. 7–24). Chicago: Nelson-Hall.

Tesser, P. T. M., Van Dugteren, F. A., & Merens, A. (1996). *Rapportage Minderheden 1996: Bevolking, arbeid, onderwijs en huisvesting*. Rijswijk, The Netherlands: Sociaal Cultureel Planbureau.

Teunissen, J. (1988). *Etnische relaties in het basisonderwijs (Ethnic relations in primary education)*. Wageningen, The Netherlands: RUU.

Triandis, H. C. (1994). Theoretical and methodological approaches to the study of collectivism and individualism. In U. Kim, H. C. Triandis, C., Kagitcibasi, & G. Yoon (Eds.), *Individualism and collectivism* (pp. 41–51). London: Sage.

Triandis, H. C., McCusker, C., & Hui, C. H. (1990). Multimethod probes of individualism and collectivism. *Journal of Personality and Social Psychology, 59*, 1006–1020.

Troyna, B., & Hatcher, R. (1992). *Racism in children's lives: A study of mainly White primary schools*. London: Routledge.

Van Ausdale, D., & Feagin, J. (1996). Using racial and ethnic concepts: The critical case of very young children. *American Sociological Review, 61*, 779–793.

Verkuyten, M. (1998). Perceived discrimination and self-esteem among ethnic minority adolescents. *The Journal of Social Psychology, 138*, 479–493.

Verkuyten, M. (2002). Ethnic attitudes among minority and majority children: The role of ethnic identification, peer group victimization and parents. *Social Development, 11*, 558–570.

Verkuyten, M. (2003a). Ethnic in-group bias among minority and majority early adolescents: The perception of negative peer behaviour. *British Journal of Developmental Psychology, 21*, 543–564.

Verkuyten, M. (2003b). Positive and negative self-esteem among ethnic minority early adolescents: Social and cultural sources and threats. *Journal of Youth and Adolescence, 32*, 267–277.

Verkuyten, M., & Kinket, B. (2000). Social distances in a multiethnic society: The ethnic hierarchy among Dutch preadolescents. *Social Psychology Quarterly, 63*, 76–85.

Verkuyten, M., Kinlet, B., & van der Wielen, C. (1997). Preadolescents' understanding of ethnic discrimination. *Journal of Genetic Psychology, 158*, 97–112.

Verkuyten, M., & Masson, K. (1996). Culture and gender differences in the perception of friendship by adolescents. *International Journal of Psychology, 31*, 207–217.

Verkuyten, M., & Steenhuis, A. (2005). Early adolescents' understanding and reasoning about asylum seeker peers and friendships. *Journal of Applied Developmental Psychology* (in print).

Verkuyten, M., & Thijs, J. (2000). *Leren (en) waarderen: Discriminatie, zelfbeeld, relaties en leerprestaties in 'witte' en 'zwarte' bassisscholen* (Learning and evaluating: Discrimination, self-concept, relations and educational achievements in 'white' and 'black' primary schools.) Amsterdam: Thela Thesis.

Verkuyten, M., & Thijs, J. (2001). Peer victimization and self-esteem of ethnic minority group children. *Journal of Community and Applied Social Psychology, 11*, 227–234.

Verkuyten, M., & Thijs, J. (2002). Racist victimization among children in the Netherlands: The effect of ethnic group and school. *Ethnic and Racial Studies, 25*, 310–331.

Verkuyten, M., & Thijs, J. (2005). Ethnic discrimination and global self-worth in early adolescence: The mediating role of ethnic self-esteem. *International Journal of Behavioral Development.*

Werner, E. E. (1993). Protective factors and individual resilience. In S. J. Meisels & J. Shonkoff (Eds.), *Handbook of early childhood intervention* (pp. 78–96). New York: Cambridge University Press.

Wheeler, L., Reis, H. T., & Bond, M. H. (1989). Collectivism-individualism in everyday social life: The middle kingdom and the melting pot. *Journal of Personality and Social Psychology, 57*, 79–86.

Whitney, I., & Smith, P. K. (1993). A survey of the nature and extent of bully/victim problems in junior/middle and secondary schools. *Educational Research, 35*, 2–25.

Wieviorka, M. (1995). *The arena of racism*. London: Sage.

Wong, C. A., Eccles, J. S., & Sameroff, A. (2003). The influence of ethnic discrimination and ethnic identification on African American adolescents' school and socioemotional adjustment. *Journal of Personality, 71*, 1197–1232.

Commentary II

16 On Hand-Holding, Spit, and the "Big Tickets"

A Commentary on Research from a Cultural Perspective

Kenneth H. Rubin

To begin with, I would like to commend the editors of this volume for bringing culture to bear on the topic of child and adolescent development. From a personal perspective, culture did not become part-and-parcel of my research life until I was fortunate enough to have been invited by Harold Stevenson to attend an International Society for the Study of Behavioral Development (ISSBD) Workshop in Beijing in 1987. Participating in that workshop were senior scholars from the People's Republic of China and a group of senior scholars from Western countries. The two groups exchanged reports of their research and views about developmental processes. In separate sessions, the senior Western social scientists offered lectures to a group of younger Chinese Developmental Scientists.

Among the many wonderful memories I have of this workshop, two stand out. First, whilst interacting with the younger scholars, I asked members of the group to tell me about their research. Much of the ongoing research appeared to be attempts to replicate the work of Western scientists. But when I asked the young scientists what they were finding, an almost uniform response was: "We must be doing something *wrong*. We are not replicating the published findings!"

Second, the visiting scientists were taken on a tour of a new children's hospital in Beijing. As we passed through the hospital's library, I was impressed by the many contemporary books and journals on psychology that lined the shelves. What was remarkable was the relative absence of any such literature in Chinese script! Given my interests in both normal and typical development and the development of psychopathology, it struck me that the young Chinese students I had met with earlier may be assuming that developmental normalcy and abnormalcy are defined by that which they were reading in books and journals appearing on bookshelves, such as those in the children's hospital. On brief reflection, I experienced a true "eureka" incident. It seemed to me that the young Chinese scholars who were reporting that they must be doing something wrong in their work were, in fact, conducting their research in entirely appropriate ways and reporting entirely appropriate findings – for Chinese children and their parents! At that moment, I clearly understood the significance of culture in the study of child development.

The essays in the "parenting" and "peer interactions" sections I have read for this commentary are exemplary because, like my "eureka" moment, the authors have recognized the significance of cultural diversity and the distinction between culture-specific behaviors and meanings and culture-universal behaviors and meanings. From their work and that of others, we come to understand that cultures impart meanings to given individual characteristics, behaviors, and relationships. In some cases, the meanings associated with given behaviors appear to be universal, or almost universal; in other cases, the meanings are very much culturally defined.

Domain Theory and Cultural Universals

To some extent, the study of the cross-cultural universality, or of cross-cultural diversity in the meanings of social behavior, share a kinship with research on the topic of the domain theory of morality (Killen et al., 2001; Nucci, Killen, & Smetana, 1996). According to this line of research, the *moral domain* comprises issues about justice (e.g., fairness), others' welfare (e.g., victimization), and rights. These moral issues are generalizable across cultures and appear to be unalterable. The *social-conventional domain* comprises regularities designed to ensure the smooth functioning of particular social groups and cultures (e.g., customs, values). These concepts do not apply across cultures and are viewed as context-specific and adjustable. Thus, from the perspective of domain theorists, behaviors, characteristics, trends, values, and opinions that comprise the social conventional domain are socially or "culturally" driven; in the case of the moral domain, the meaning or acceptance of a given behavior or characteristic is likely to be universally shared.

Nelson and colleagues argue that aggression is viewed as uniformly unacceptable. In this regard, aggression would be part-and-parcel of the moral domain. Regardless of form (e.g., physical or relational aggression) or function (instrumental versus harmful goals), these authors suggest that aggression is unacceptable in both collectivistic and individualistic cultures and groups. And it is unacceptable whether the peer group is homogeneous or heterogeneous in terms of participant age or sex.

But is aggression universally unacceptable? At the moral level, one might argue that aggression is universally viewed as abhorrent. But within each society, there are likely to be subgroups that view aggression through a social-conventional lens. A good example derives from the work on deviancy training and delinquency carried out in North America and Western Europe. In this research, investigators find that children who deviate from the norm (typically insofar as their aggressive behavior is concerned) find social support within peer networks of like-behaved counterparts (e.g., Dishion et al., 1996). It is in such groups that popularity and group acceptance are determined by behavior that is generally viewed as dysfunctional. In these cases, it is not the aggressive child or adolescent who is considered an "outsider" and who suffers from peer rejection; rather, the entire peer group or network is viewed in a negative manner by the larger society, which views aggression from the lens of the moral domain. Thus far, researchers have not examined whether such subgroup norms exist in cultures other than those found in "Western" countries. It would be a good idea to do so.

At the "face" level, there do seem to be obvious exceptions to the almost universal rule that aggression is unacceptable to peers and parents alike. For example, if the motivation for hostility is viewed by prominent members of the culture as well earned and if the targets of aggression are viewed by the society as enemies, rejection of hostility may be replaced by admiration. In short, aggression and hostility may not be cross-culturally abhorred, unless, of course, it is directed at particular members of the aggressor's *in-group* of significant others (e.g., family members, familiar peers). For some reason, the research of developmental scientists has yet to direct itself to such issues. It should – and it should do so from cultural and cross-cultural perspectives.

"Big-Ticket" Constructs and Everyday Behavior

Most current efforts to study social behavioral or social relationship phenomena from a cross-cultural perspective tend to focus on "big-ticket" items. When attempting to determine whether a social behavior is culturally acceptable, the spotlight is on such constructs as aggression (and more recently, social withdrawal). When attempting to determine whether or not a behavior is "acceptable" in the peer group, researchers tend to use measures assessing popularity (or peer acceptance). When attempting to determine how such big-ticket behaviors develop, we turn to such Western-defined constructs as authoritative or authoritarian parenting. In so doing, we often neglect, reject, or otherwise miss out on very interesting cultural nuances that have significant bearing on child and parent behavior.

It seems very clear that behavior viewed as socially conventional and acceptable in some cultures is viewed as ignominious in others. One might posit that children who demonstrate socially conventional behavior will be well liked by their peers and well socialized by their parents. Those who defy social convention are likely rejected (and correspondingly, poorly socialized by their parents). But what do these socially conventional behaviors actually look like? I would argue that most such behaviors do not comprise big-ticket constructs and thus are ignored by traditionally trained social developmentalists. For example, in some societies, it is viewed as acceptable to spit in public; the rationale offered is that one must not retain in one's body phlegm or unhealthy substances. In other societies, spitting in public is viewed as repulsive, impolite, and likely to elicit the scorn of peers and adults.

In China, spitting on the streets *had* been viewed as rather normative; yet, when the SARS epidemic arose, the Chinese government mandated a change in this social convention and began handing out "spit bags" to the citizens (heavy fines are also now the norm for public spitting in many of China's urban areas). Young women promoting the 2008 Olympics have been seen to hand out "spit bags" with the following note: "Spitting on the ground is dangerous to your health, and spit contains infectious diseases. But with one small bag in your hands, your health will always be invincible."

Within an instant, that which was viewed as healthy and acceptable behavior for the individual was viewed as unhealthy for the collective. The socially conventional ideal had changed almost over night. Yet no one has bothered to study the phenomenon! From a purely Western perspective, why bother? After all, we're discussing spit! But from the perspective of a scholar who is interested in the significance of changing cultural norms in rapidly developing societies, the phenomenon could be extremely interesting. A reasonable question to ask might be whether such changes in social conventions are accompanied by changes in the acceptability of persons who maintain the status quo! Might the once acceptable person become rejected? Might the perceived motivation for the behavior change from personal hygiene to an act of defiance against the collective? Obviously, these are not topics that Western researchers investigate; we tend to be consumed by the study of the big-ticket variables (e.g., aggressive behavior, competition, victimization, or authoritarian parenting).

Here is another example of social convention that may determine a person's acceptance within a given culture. In some cultures, it is acceptable for young adolescents to involve themselves in romantic relationships and to demonstrate the existence of such affectionate relationships with public displays or symbols of affection (holding hands; exchanging rings). In other cultures, it is the parent who decides the identity of their offspring's romantic partners (Keller, 2004). Public displays of intimacy have long been forbidden in many cultures. For example, in China, the public display of anger or affection is traditionally frowned on. But again, as with spitting, perceptions of the acceptability of public demonstrations of affection are changing rapidly; teenagers in China are no longer hesitating to hold hands in public. The social conventional "rules" are rapidly changing, yet we know little about how such changes came to be and how they affect the peer status of those who deviate from long-held traditional behaviors. Parental reactions to such changes are also unknown.

Needless to say, few "mainstream" Western social developmental and clinical psychologists spend time examining social conventional differences in the acceptance or rejection of public spitting or demonstrations of affection; instead, as I noted above, they opt to focus on the big-ticket constructs of aggressive (physical, relational) or prosocial (helping, sharing, caring) behavior and inevitably reach conclusions pertaining to cross-cultural universals or differences. Those who study parenting also focus on the "bigger" pictures – whether parenting operates on vertical or horizontal planes, whether the cultural focus is on independence or interdependence (or some combination of the various dimensions), or whether authoritative and authoritarian parenting exists in all countries and cultures. By focusing on such constructs, one inevitably must ask big-ticket questions. For example, if parents choose a vertical framework or an apprenticeship model for their relationships with their children, will that affect the quality of peer interactions and relationships? Or if parents are punitive, will their children be aggressive in the peer group? These questions are certainly worth asking. But somehow, I believe that the typical "Western" researcher studying development from a cross-cultural perspective ends up missing some rather interesting and significant phenomena.

Perhaps then, it is time for Western psychologists to stop exporting big-ticket story lines and invest their time and energy in better understanding the construct of social convention in non-Western cultures of interest. Allow me to offer a few reasonable questions about a big-ticket item that may comprise many little-ticket variables:

1. What defines *social competence* in Western, Eastern, Northern, and Southern cultures? Can one identify the many components that define socially competence? Does the definition of competent behavior differ at different developmental stages? Do the components that define socially competent behavior differ at these developmental stages? To address these questions from a cultural perspective, simply asking parents, teachers, and peers would be a good start. One might learn, for example, that bowing as a sign of respect is an important

component of social greeting in some cultures; shaking hands on greeting (touching) may be significant in some cultures and unacceptable in others; hugging on greeting may be the norm in some cultures and forbidden in others. I have yet to read a manuscript on such little-ticket, yet potentially significant, behaviors in any developmental journal.

2. How do parents go about socializing the various components of social competence in these cultures?
3. How do peers react to children and adolescents who fail to conform to the cultural norms vis-à-vis the conventionally defined components of social competence?
4. How do these peer reactions affect the child *intrapersonally*?
5. How do these peer reactions affect the child's possibilities of establishing close relationships with others?

One can ask the same process-oriented questions with regard to emotional competence and of course to social and emotional incompetence.

An excellent example can be taken from the chapter by Xu et al., who introduce the construct, *ren*. According to Xu and colleagues, "When Chinese children use the strategy *ren* in response to peer animosity, they refrain from arguing or confronting their peers, but they are not avoiding or running away from the situation, which would be the case in problem-focused avoidance." One would not know about *ren* if one was a Westerner arriving in China with a firm, inflexible lock on the measures to be used to study predetermined big-ticket constructs, such as social competence/incompetence or adjustment/maladjustment. Given that *ren* is part-and-parcel of Chinese culture, it makes sense to ask the aforementioned process-oriented questions: How does *ren* develop? Does temperament matter? How about parenting? What is its display associated with? What happens to children who fail to display *ren*? Might the origins, correlates, and consequences of displaying or not displaying *ren* differ across cultures?

Another example is *hyo* or filial piety. *Hyo* (孝 in Chinese; 효 in Korean) is considered the essential element that shapes parent–child relationships and parenting throughout much of Asia (Chung et al., 1997). *Hyo* is defined as a relationship based on mutual responsibilities, in which "parents love their children" and "children serve and respect their parents with sincerity" (Kim, in press). From *Confucianism*, *Hyo* mandates that parents must be affectionate with their children and their children must respect and be devoted to them. In *Buddhism*, *hyo* defines parents' infinite love and children's "payback" for that love (Kim, in press).

I would guess that not many Western psychologists know of *hyo*. We tend to be consumed by the study of another parent–child relationship construct – *secure attachment*. Just as researchers have examined the causes, correlates, and developmental consequences of secure and insecure attachment relationships, one might very well consider these factors insofar as they relate to *hyo*. In fact, ignoring this parent–child relationship construct in Eastern cultures may preclude an understanding of how extrafamilial relationships (with peers) develop, what these relationships may look like, and what the defining provisions of friendship might be. In short, it is time for Western researchers to ask their Eastern counterparts what it is that matters to them! The continued importing of big-ticket Western constructs and measures requires a significant note of caution. In this regard, Gaskins' approach to the study of Yucatec Mayan children is exemplary in that it allows us to understand unique cultural beliefs and the everyday social lives of children in that particular society.

Some Final Remarks

In summary, I have suggested that researchers truly interested in making cross-cultural comparisons should begin focusing on constructs other than the traditional big-tickets items. Culturally defined socially conventional behaviors and relationships should be identified, given that they probably have some significant bearing on children's lives at home and in the peer group. In this regard, it might not be a bad idea to begin simply by asking parents about their parenting goals and the strategies they suggest as most productive to meet these goals. What do they believe to be important for their children to know or for their children to demonstrate at each of several developmental periods (infancy, toddlerhood, early childhood, middle childhood, early adolescence, etc.)? In the world of social and emotional development, one might ask such questions as: When should children be able to share or to willingly and spontaneously help others? When should children learn to comply with the wishes of a parent? A teacher? A friend? When should children be able to resolve their interpersonal conflicts with siblings or peers? When should children be able to develop friendships with others? These questions beg asking parents (and children) for the cultural meanings of altruism, friendship, social competence, and victimization.

One might also ask children of different ages to define friendship or to consider what it is that will gain them the respect of their peers. Unlike the primary goal of popularity that consumes many American children, the respect of peers may be far more important in other cultures. And if *hyo* is the relationship goal for Asian parents and their children, perhaps a peer analogue of *hyo* is the primary relationship goal for Asian children with their age-mates.

Lastly, there now appear to be links established between the behaviors studied in contemporary cross-cultural research and neurophysiology. Take, for example, the related constructs of behavioral inhibition and social reticence (constructs associated conceptually and empirically with the big-ticket construct, social withdrawal). Western toddlers are less inhibited than their Eastern age-mates (e.g., Chen et al., 1998; Rubin et al., 2005). In Western cultures, inhibited toddlers and preschoolers are viewed as extremely shy and fearful; their parents are overprotective (e.g., Rubin et al., 1997). In Eastern cultures, such behaviors may be interpreted by parents as the demonstration of reservedness and quiescence; parents of inhibited Chinese toddlers demonstrate acceptance (e.g., Chen et al., 1998).

Perhaps most interestingly, inhibited and reticent Western children demonstrate relatively lower activity in the left frontal cortex; when heart rate is recorded, interbeat intervals are shorter than is the case for noninhibited or reticent children (e.g., Fox et al., 2001; Rubin et al., 1997). These data provide evidence that unique patterns of brain electrical activity may reflect increasing arousal of particular brain centers involved in the expression of fear and anxiety (LeDoux, 1989). For example, preschoolers exhibiting relatively lower left frontal asymmetry are more likely to withdraw from mild stress. Preschoolers exhibiting the opposite pattern of activation are more likely to approach. These patterns of frontal activation reflect a dispositional characteristic underlying behavioral responses to the environment. Similarly, *vagal tone* is an index of respiratory sinus arrhythmia that assesses the functional status or efficiency of the nervous system (Porges & Byrne, 1992) and marks both general reactivity and the ability to regulate one's level of arousal. In the context of a neurobiological model of behavioral inhibition, high inhibition should be associated with low vagal tone and low heart period variability. Indeed, researchers have found concurrent associations between low heart period (high heart rate) and increased behavioral inhibition as assessed in infancy and childhood (Anderson, Bohlin, & Hagekall, 1999; Kagan et al., 1984).

If inhibited or reticent behavior actually "means" something different in different cultures, should it not be the case that the physiological concomitants should differ as well? If being reticent and reserved represents cultural normalcy, then brain and heart activity should appear "normal." Given the growing amount of work on cultural meanings of normalcy, it appears timely for researchers to begin studying brain–behavior connections. All of which is to say that the three chapters I read have provided us with a welcome initial foray into the study of peers and parenting from a cross-cultural perspective. But we do have a long way to go.

Acknowledgments

The writing of this commentary was supported by National Institute of Mental Health grant # MH58116 to Kenneth H. Rubin.

References

Anderson, K, Bohlin, G., & Hagekall, B. (1999). Early temperament and stranger wariness as predictors of social inhibition in 2 year olds. *British Journal of Developmental Psychology, 17*, 421–434.

Chen, X., Hastings, P. D., Rubin, K. H., Chen, H., Cen, G., & Stewart, S. L. (1998). Child-rearing practices and behavioral inhibition in Chinese and Canadian toddlers: A cross-cultural study. *Developmental Psychology, 34*, 677–686.

Chung, O. K., Kim, K. W., Yoon, C. H., Yoo, G. H., Choi, Y. H., Choi, K. S., et al. (1997). Perception of parental filial piety and child-rearing behavior. *Korean Journal of Child Studies, 18*(1), 81–107.

Dishion, T. J., Spracklen, K. M., Andrews, D., & Patterson, G. (1996). Deviancy training in male adolescents friendships. *Behavior Therapy, 27*(3), 373–390.

Fox, N. A., Henderson, H. A., Rubin, K. H., Calkins, S. D., & Schmidt, L. A. (2001). Stability and instability of behavioral inhibition and exuberance: Psychophysiological and behavioral factors influencing change and continuity across the first four years of life. *Child Development, 72*, 1–21.

Kagan, J., Reznick, J. S., Clarke, C., Snidman, N., & Garcia-Coll, C. (1984). Behavioral inhibition to the unfamiliar. *Child Development, 55*, 2212–2225.

Keller, M. (2004). A cross cultural perspective on friendship research. *Newsletter of the International Society for the Study of Behavioral Development, 28*, 10–14.

Killen, M., Pisacane, K., Lee-Kim, J., & Ardila-Rey, A. (2001). Fairness or stereotypes?: Young children's priorities when evaluating group exclusion and inclusion. *Developmental Psychology, 37*, 587–596.

Kim, K. W. (in press). "Hyo (효)" and parenting in Korea. In K. H. Rubin & O. B. Chung (Eds.), *Parental beliefs, parenting, and child development in cross-cultural perspective*. London: Psychology Press.

LeDoux, J. (1989). Cognitive-emotional interactions in the brain. *Cognition and Emotion, 4*, 267–274.

Nucci, L. P., Killen, M., & Smetana, J. G. (1996). Autonomy and the personal: Negotiation and social reciprocity in adult-child exchanges. *New Directions for Child Development,* San Francisco: Jossey-Bass.

Porges, S. W. (1995). Cardiac vagal tone: A physiological index of stress. *Neuroscience and Biobehavioral Reviews, 19*, 225–233.

Porges, S. W., & Byrne, E. A. (1992). Research methods for measurement of heart rate and respiration. *Biological Psychology, 34*, 93–130.

Rubin, K. H., Hastings, P. D., Stewart, S., Henderson, H. A., & Chen, X. (1997). The consistency and concomitants of inhibition: Some of the children, all of the time. *Child Development, 68*, 467–483.

Rubin, K. H., Hemphill, S. A., Chen, X., Hastings, P., Sanson, A., LoCoco, A., et al. (2005). Parenting beliefs and behaviors: Initial findings from the International Consortium for the Study of Social and Emotional Development (ICSSED). In K. H. Rubin & O. B. Chung (Eds.), *Parental beliefs, parenting, and child development in cross-cultural perspective*. London: Psychology Press.

PART V

Friendships

17 Friendships of Indonesian, South Korean, and U.S. Youth

Exclusivity, Intimacy, Enhancement of Worth, and Conflict

Doran C. French, Okhwa Lee, and Sri Untari Pidada

Friendships, although generally conceptualized as voluntary associations between individuals, invariably occur within a cultural context. McCall (1988) argued that friendships are institutionalized, and that individuals are guided by cultural blueprints, which may specify persons who can and cannot be friends, the types of interactions that friends expected to have, and the emotional connectedness that friends are typically experience (see Bigelow, Tesson, & Lewko 1996, for a similar analysis). Participants in the friendship as well as others observing this friendship may experience tension if the friendship deviates from these blueprints. Unfortunately little attention has been devoted to understanding the cultural context within which friendships exist in part because anthropologists have paid limited attention to this subject (Bell & Coleman, 1999).

In this chapter, we review our research on the friendships of Indonesian, Korean, and U.S. youth in an effort to understand cultural variation in these relationships. We begin with a discussion of friendship in Indonesia, Korea, and the United States, followed by a brief review of some of the methodological underpinning of our work. We then focus on understanding cultural differences in the structure of friendship by exploring friendship exclusivity, which is the extent to which close friendship groups are open to inclusion of others. In the next section, we present our work on the characteristics of relationships across cultures, specifically focusing on provisions (i.e., intimacy and enhancement of worth), longevity, and conflict. The chapter concludes with a discussion of some of the implications of our research for theories about cultural variation in friendship.

Friendships of South Korea, Indonesian, and U.S. Youth

South Korea

Conceptions of friendship in South Korea are influenced by Confucianism, which identifies friendship as one of five basic relationships necessary for a stable society (Kim, 1996) and outlines a set of obligations appropriate to this relationship. The extreme intimacy of this relationship between both friends and family members is captured by the word "cheong," a concept closely related to the Japanese concept of "amae." This refers to the melding of identities of individual participants into a new collective unit and incorporates elements of unconditional acceptance, trust, and intimacy. Cheong typically develops slowly between persons with an extensive shared history (Choi, Kim, & Choi, 1993).

It appears that Korean friendships are high in exclusivity because of the extreme intimacy of relationships between in-group members. Gudykunst, Yoon, and Nishida (1987) found that the communications of Korean students with in-group members were more personal and effortless than those of U.S. students. Brandt (1974) observed Korean and U.S. skiers at a resort in Korea and noted that, in contrast to the relatively fluid social interchanges of the U.S. skiers, Korean skiers appeared more likely to stay within their defined groups. These findings, in conjunction with discussions with Korean psychologists, suggest that Korean friendships are exclusive and that Korean youth are likely to interact with small groups of close friends.

Indonesia

Indonesian and U.S. children have approximately the same number of reciprocal friendships (French et al., 2003), and college students in these countries identify approximately the same number of close friends (French, Bae et al., in press). Many of the features of middle-class urban Indonesian children's friendships appear similar to those of U.S. children (French et al., 2003). Indonesian children develop friendships with peers who resemble them, they obtain companionship and intimacy from friends, and children with friends exhibit greater social competence and adjustment than those without friends.

Both anthropological and empirical data suggest that Indonesians may be less focused on developing close specific friendships and instead are more strongly focused on integration into the community and social network. A major feature of Indonesian social life involves maintaining personal harmony with others in the larger community, a concept captured by the term "rukun" (Magnis-Suseno, 1997). Indonesian adults reported that maintaining harmonious group relationships was more important than developing specific friendships (Noesjirwan, 1978). Norms of engaging and maintaining polite interactions with strangers and acquaintances (Noesjirwan, 1977) may also serve to increase social interactions between individuals and others in their community.

The relative de-emphasis of specific friends was illustrated by Jay's (1969) ethnographic report that few specific friendships were evident in a Javanese village. Urban adolescents have friends, although their peer interaction primarily occurs within large mixed-sex groups rather than dyads (Koentjaraningrat, 1985). Mulder (1996) argued that lasting friendships are rare and not particularly desired. Thus, we expected the friendships of Indonesian youth to be less exclusive and less close than those of Korean and U.S. youth.

United States

Friendships are also extremely important for persons in the United States, particularly among children, adolescents, and older individuals (Brown, 1990). These relationships are typically private and without public recognition (Brain, 1976). The label "friend" is used to describe a wide variety of relationships, ranging from casual acquaintances to individuals who are as close and sometimes closer than family members (Hays, 1988). Considerable variation exists in the extent to which individuals have friends and their degree of closeness with these individuals (Rubin, 1985).

We expected the friendship interactions of U.S. youth to be less exclusive that those of Korean youth. This hypothesis was based on the Triandis et al. (1988) suggestions that persons in individualistic cultures, such as the United States, are sociable and move freely across multiple social groups, as well as the suggestion that U.S. individualists are less likely than collectivists to restrict interaction to those with whom they are intimate. Furthermore, the variability in closeness of persons identified as friends led us to expect that friendship groups might include persons who are very close as well as others who are not. In contrast to our prediction that U.S. youth would be less exclusive than Korean youth, we were uncertain whether U.S. and Indonesian youth would differ on this dimension.

Methodology

Prior to reviewing specific findings, we will provide an overview of some of the methodological issues that have emerged in our studies of friendship in Indonesia, South Korea, and the United States and some of the approaches that we have used to address these. There are serious methodological issues in cross-cultural research (Vijver & Leung, 1997), and there is little consensus about how to resolve these. Among the most pressing issues are the need to incorporate multimethod and multiagent assessment strategies, the importance of including qualitative as well as quantitative approaches, and the difficulty of generalizing from research samples to larger populations.

Multimethod and Multiagent Assessment

Patterson, Reid, and Dishion (1992) have argued that problems of error associated with both measurement type and source of information are ubiquitous in studies of social development. This problem is even more pronounced in cross-cultural research in which complexities of response bias, translation issues, problems of equivalence of item meaning, and difficulty understanding local meanings are added (e.g., Rogoff, 2003; Vijver & Leung, 1997).

Patterson et al. (1992) advocated using multiple methods and multiple reporting agents, and assessing concordance across methods and agents. French, Setiono, and Eddy (1999) argued that a similar strategy should be used in cross-cultural research, and we have pursued this within the limits of our resources, employing teacher ratings and peer reports, as well as questionnaire, interview, and daily diary methods of assessment.

We are particularly skeptical of relying exclusively on questionnaire measures derived from single sources for two reasons. First, cross-cultural comparisons of rating scales invariably involve issues of response biases (e.g., Chen, Lee, & Stevenson, 1995). These effects can be quite large (Smith, 2001), and we have evidence of response bias in our own work. Second, there are concerns about the extent to which scores have the same meaning across cultures. This is most dramatically illustrated by the work of Weisz et al. (1995), who found that Thai children were rated higher than U.S. children by teachers, whereas direct observations revealed that U.S. children, in fact, exhibited higher rates of classroom problem behavior than Thai children.

Qualitative and Quantitative Assessment

We have attempted to understand friendship and culture by collecting quantitative information and making explicit comparisons across cultures. At the same time, however, we are very skeptical of cross-cultural work in which questionnaires or other measures are given to participants from different countries and the results interpreted without reference to the context of the culture, a process identified in the cross-cultural literature as "imposed etic" (Berry, 1989).

We have attempted to provide participants with the opportunity to describe social phenomena, for example, friendships or conflicts, in their own words. Our study of friendship began with an interview study in which children in Indonesia and the United States described peers that they liked. These descriptions were coded with a deductively derived system only after we found that content analyses of the descriptions yielded similar findings across the two cultures. The value of this approach is illustrated in our recent study of children's conflict in the United States and Indonesia (French, Pidada, Denoma et al., 2005). Content analyses of open-ended descriptions led us to understand processes that would have been missed had we used only structured assessment methods.

We need, however, to go much further in our efforts to understand local meanings by using more qualitative assessment methods. In particular, we would like to make greater use of interviews, linguistic analyses (e.g., Fitch, 1998), and experience sampling methods (e.g., Larson, 1989).

Generalization Within and Across Cultures

One of the major difficulties of doing studies in different cultures is making assumptions that the small samples being studied are typical of larger populations. Our work in Indonesia has been conducted in Bandung, a city of about 2 million people located on the island of Java, and our samples have primarily included persons of Javanese and Sundanese ethnicity. We do not know the extent to which our findings can be generalized to other populations in Indonesia. Similarly, our U.S. studies have been conducted in public schools and a small university in central Illinois, whereas our studies of Korean youth have been conducted in a major university in Seoul and in public schools in a medium-sized South Korean provincial city. We do not know the extent to which our results from these groups are representative of persons in the populations of these countries.

Comparison of differences in the friendships of United States, Indonesian, and Korean youth are complicated by the difficulty of assessing the contribution of social class. It is particularly difficult to compare persons in developing countries, such as Indonesia, with those in more economically advantaged countries, such as South Korea and the United States, because selection of participants who are equivalent on one dimension (e.g., occupational prestige, income, or relative within-culture economic status) invariably produces gross inequalities on other dimensions. At the same time, it is necessary to address this issue because social class effects may be strong and pervasive. Social class has been shown to be related to socialization in both the United

States (e.g., McLoyd, 1998) and Indonesia (Zevalkink, 1997), collectivism in Indonesia (Marshall, 1997), and friendship reasoning in the United States (Selman, 1980).

To date, we have addressed the issue of social class by selecting samples of children and adolescents from schools serving middle-class populations and by selecting college students from selective universities. Indonesian middle-class families share many common features with middle-class U.S. and Korean families. Children in these families typically complete high school and frequently college. Parents are most often employed in business or professional occupations, and they have similar access to economic resources, such as home ownership and automobiles.

Nevertheless, we recognize that this is only a partial answer to addressing complex issues of social class. In future work, it will be important to assess the amount of variance explainable by social class within cultures under study as a way of estimating the extent to which social class variation may explain between-country variation.

Exclusivity of Friendships

The concept of exclusivity is similar to that of boundary permeability in family systems theories (Minuchin, 1985) and refers to the extent to which friendship systems allow inclusion of others who are not close friends. Waldrop and Halverson (1975) provided a classic discussion of this issue in conjunction with their study of individual differences in intensivity/extensivity. They found that girls exhibited more friendship intensity than boys and that sociability was associated with intensivity for girls and extensivity for boys.

Suggestions that friendship exclusivity might vary across cultures comes from the work of Triandis et al. (1988), who hypothesized that persons in collectivist cultures tend to limit interaction to a narrow group of individuals whom they know well. In contrast, those in individualistic cultures are more likely to interact with many different persons and easily connect with a wide range of individuals whom they incorporate into their friendship circles. This reasoning led us to explore the possibility that cultural variability in friendship exclusivity might be partially explained by the individualism and collectivism dimensions.

Based on our understanding of friendships in Indonesia, South Korea, and the United States, we expected Korean friendships to be more exclusive than those of Indonesian youth; U.S. youth were expected to fall between these extremes. Following, we will present evidence in support of this position derived from three sources. First, we report preferences for exclusivity in the friendships of both college students and adolescents derived from a self-report scale. Second, we evaluated reactions to violations of exclusivity norms in college students and adolescents. Finally, we assessed diary reports of the social interactions of college students to assess the extent to which interactions with close friends were exclusive.

In two studies, we analyzed college students' ratings of the exclusivity of their friendships using a scale that was modified from a measure developed by Parker (1997). In both studies (French, Bae et al., in press; French, Lee, & Pidada, 2004), Korean college students expressed greater preference for exclusive interaction with friends than either U.S. or Indonesian students, effects that were large in magnitude in both studies. In neither study did Indonesian or U.S. students differ on this dimension. Across studies, women rated their friendships as more exclusive than did men.

French, Lee, and Pidada (2004) compared the ratings of the reciprocal friendships of Indonesian and U.S. seventh-grade students. Consistent with the findings noted earlier, Korean adolescents rated their friendships as more exclusive than Indonesian youth, effects that were also large in magnitude. In contrast to the findings from the study of college students, no gender effects emerged. We have not yet assessed the U.S. sample.

In the next set of analyses, we assessed reactions to violations of exclusivity. Participants were presented with a series of scenarios that described violations of exclusivity norms. For example, participants were asked: "Pretend that you have a small group of friends that you often spend time with. One day, your best friend brings another person to the group, a person that none of the rest of you knows." Participants responded by appraising the extent to which they viewed this as a norm violation and the extent to which they would experience anger if such behavior occurred.

We expected Korean students to react more strongly than either Indonesian or U.S. students to violations of friendship exclusivity. These hypotheses were born out in studies with both college students and adolescents. Korean college students (French, Lee et al., 2004) reacted more strongly to exclusivity violations than either U.S. ($d = .82$) or Indonesian ($d = .69$) students. Female students reacted more strongly to violations than male students, although this effect was small ($d = .26$). Similar differences emerged in the comparison of Korean and Indonesian seventh-grade students (French, Pidada, & Lee, 2004). Korean adolescents exhibited stronger reactions to exclusivity violations than Indonesian students ($d = .67$), but in contrast to the college student analyses, no gender differences emerged.

Finally, we analyzed friendship exclusivity from the daily diary reports of the social interactions of college students in the United States, Indonesia, and

South Korea (French, Bae, et al., in press). In this study, students completed assessment of all social interactions that lasted longer than ten minutes over a two-week period using a variation of the Rochester Interaction Record (RIR) (Reis & Wheeler, 1991). Students listed the identity of all persons involved in each interaction using initials or nicknames, and consequently it was possible to discern the relationship between participants and each individual with whom they interacted using data from a social network inventory. From these reports, we developed an exclusivity index, which was the percentage of close friend interactions that included only close friends. As expected, Korean students exhibited the highest percentage of exclusive friend interactions (78%) and Indonesian students the least (51%), an effect that was large in magnitude ($d = 1.05$). U.S. students fell between these two extremes (62%) and differed significantly from both Korean ($d = .62$) and Indonesian students ($d = .46$).

Potentially relevant to the question of exclusivity is the size of friend groups because exclusive groups are likely to be smaller than less exclusive groups. Evidence consistent with this hypothesis came from the diary analyses of interactions. The mean number of participants in Korean close-friend interactions was 2.71, a group size that was significantly smaller than that of Indonesian (3.58) or U.S. (3.29) groups. U.S. and Indonesian students did not differ from each other.

Thus, across studies and methods, consistent evidence emerged suggesting that South Korean students preferred and exhibited exclusive friendship interactions to a greater extent than Indonesian students. Across studies, relatively few differences emerged between U.S. and Indonesian students, the exception being the results from the diary assessment of exclusivity.

Friendship Characteristics: Provisions, Longevity, and Conflict

In this section, we focus on characteristics of the friendships of Indonesian, Korean, and U.S. youth. We first review our work pertaining to two relationship provisions, that is, intimate disclosure and enhancement of worth. Then, we turn to longevity of friendships and conflict.

Friendship Provisions

The theoretical perspective on friendship provisions comes from the work of Weiss (1974), who developed a taxonomy of social provisions that individuals seek in their relationship with others, including reliable alliance, enhancement of worth, intimacy, affection, companionship, nurturance, and instrumental help. Other researchers (e.g., Berndt & Perry, 1986; Parker & Asher, 1993;

Bukowski, Boivan, & Hoza, 1994) have arrived at somewhat similar taxonomies, but no firm consensus regarding the specific provisions that underlie friendship presently exists (Furman, 1996).

Empirical efforts to establish the discriminate validity of friendship dimensions has been relatively disappointing. At present, there is little evidence that the more narrow-band scales tap more than the general positive and negative dimensions of relationships (Furman, 1996).

Our reading of the anthropological reports from Indonesia, as well as our own observations and pilot work, led us to believe that the cross-cultural comparison of intimacy and enhancement of worth would be particularly interesting. Although recognizing the lack of discriminate validity of narrow-band friendship quality scales, we chose to assess these aspects of relationships. Cross-cultural work likely affords greater variation in friendship dimensions than within-country studies, and thus the value of discriminating separate dimensions of friendship may emerge through such study.

Intimate Disclosure. We anticipated that cultural differences in the salience of specific friendships would be reflected in friendship intimacy. Based on our prior discussion, we hypothesized that friendships of Indonesian youth would be somewhat lower in intimacy than those of South Korean and U.S. youth. We have some evidence, although it is inconsistent, that supports these hypotheses.

One set of analyses focused on ratings of intimate disclosure provided by college students in our revised version of the Friendship Quality Questionaire (FQQ). French, Bae et al. (2004) found that U.S. and Korean students rated their friendships higher in intimacy than Indonesian students ($d = .58, .51$, respectively). In contrast, French, Lee et al. (2004) found no differences between students in the three countries. In both studies, women reported more intimacy than men ($d = .43, .60$, respectively).

In two other studies, we assessed children's perceptions of the intimacy of their friendships. French, Pidada, and Victor (2005) found that eleven- and fourteen-year-old U.S. students rated their friends using the FQQ higher in intimacy than Indonesian students ($d = .42$). In contrast, however, no differences between U.S., and Indonesian children emerged in the comparison of references to intimacy in open-ended descriptions of friendships. In a second study, French, Pidada, and Lee (2004) found that Korean seventh-grade students rated reciprocal friends higher in intimacy than Indonesian students ($d = .52$).

We obtained additional assessments of intimacy in children and adolescents from ratings obtained using the Network of Relationships Inventory (NRI;

Furman & Buhrmester, 1985). One advantage of this measure over the other assessment procedures used was that participants rated intimacy of family members (i.e., mothers, fathers, and siblings) in addition to intimacy with friends. We suspect that this provided participants with an anchor to appraise their level of friendship intimacy in relation to intimacy in other relationships. French et al. (2001) found that U.S. students rated their intimacy with friends higher than Indonesian students, an effect that was attributable to the greater intimacy of U.S. than of Indonesian girls. French, Pidada et al. (2004) found that Korean seventh-grade adolescents rated the intimacy of their reciprocal friends higher than Indonesian students, an effect that was small in magnitude ($d = .28$). Girls rated their friendships higher in intimate disclosure than boys ($d = .64$). U.S. data are not yet available.

Finally, we assessed the disclosure of self and others during college students's interactions with close friends by analyzing the diary reports. For RIR each interaction, students rated the extent to which they and their companions engaged in self-disclosure. Korean students reported more disclosure with friends than either U.S. or Indonesian students ($d = .122, 1.15$), whereas U.S. and Indonesian students did not differ from each other.

Thus, although our results are inconsistent, it appears that most of these findings point toward lower intimacy among friends in Indonesia than in either Korea or the United States. Some exceptions to this, however, have emerged, and thus our conclusions must be somewhat tentative.

The interpretation of the intimacy scores is complicated by the possible effect of response sets. Some investigators (Chen et al., 1995; Hui & Triandis, 1989) have found that U.S. and Asian populations differ in the extent to which they use extreme points on rating scales. We have seen evidence of this in some of our studies (e.g., French, Bae et al., in press; French, Pidada, & Victor, 2005), but not others. When evidence of this response set has emerged, we have used the procedure outlined by Bond (1988) of standardizing each item score by using the mean and standard deviation of each individual's responses. Thus, item scores reflect the relative positioning of each friendship dimension relative to those of the other dimensions for each individual. When this method was used, the significant difference between U.S. and Indonesian children disappeared in the two studies in which significant response effects had been found. The use of this procedure had no effect on the results from any of the other studies.

The confusion regarding cultural differences in intimacy across cultures is likely to be present as long as we and other researchers are forced to rely on global ratings of intimacy. Our use of intimacy ratings of interaction episodes in the French, Bae et al. (in press) study provides a partial remedy to this problem. Although based on self-report, participants rated the disclosure of specific interactions rather than providing global ratings. Disclosure scores were the composite of ratings of multiple interactions. The information obtained by these measures, however, may differ in important ways from the more global ratings obtained from the FQQ and NRI. Diary methods likely provide information about typical disclosure processes, whereas global ratings likely assess the extent to which peak levels of intimacy occur across multiple interactions. It may be possible to connect this to the exclusivity dimension discussed earlier. One would expect friendships in which friends interact very frequently in groups that include only close friends to be intimate much of the time. In contrast, less exclusive friendships might engage in intimate disclosure only during those times in which only close friends are present. Diary and experience sampling methods may provide useful and complementary approaches for obtaining information about culture and disclosure processes.

Enhancement of Worth. The theoretical discussion of enhancement of worth as a dimension of friendship dates from the work of Sullivan (1953), who highlighted the role of same-sex friends during childhood and adolescence as validators of personal worth and promoters of self-esteem. We suspect that the importance of this aspect of friendship might vary across cultures.

Kitayama et al. (1997) argue that the search for self-enhancement is more prominent among European Americans than it is for persons in Japan and other countries that hold interdependent views of the self. Fiske et al. (1998) suggested that, in many independent cultures, praise is common and situations are constructed to promote self-esteem. Tietjen (1989) argued that promotion of self-esteem was more important in individualistic than collectivist cultures. Consistent with these hypotheses, Chen et al. (2004) found enhancement of worth to be a more salient aspect of Canadian than Chinese children's friendships.

Within Javanese and other ethnic groups in Indonesia, it is considered important to control egoism, which is viewed as disruptive of social harmony (Magnis-Suseno, 1997). Persons are expected to refrain from acting in accord with self-interest and instead attend to the needs of others. Self-respect is seen as residing in the positive views of others rather than self-appraisal (Mulder, 1992). Whereas U.S. parents view the promotion of self-respect in children as one of their most important child-rearing goals, Indonesian parents view this as among the least important (McDonald, 2003).

The promotion of self-esteem appears to be a major emphasis within North American populations and permeates multiple aspects of society, including education (Damon, 1995). The focus on self-esteem is illustrated by the listing of more that 2,500 titles in the catalog of the Amazon Internet bookstore focused on self-esteem, many of which are devoted to increasing this in self or others.

We explored the provisions of validation of self in the friendships of children, adolescents, and college students. The scale assessing this provision was developed from the modified version of the FQQ, and consequently our findings are subject to the previously noted difficulties of assessing cultural differences from questionnaire results. Nevertheless, our results are consistent in the findings that Indonesian youth rate this aspect of relationships as less salient than either U.S. or Korean youth.

In two studies previously discussed, we have explored enhancement of worth in the friendship of college students. In French, Bae et al. (in press), U.S. and Korean students rated enhancement of worth higher than Indonesian students ($d = .99, .94$, respectively). Similarly, French, Lee et al. (2004) found that U.S. students rated enhancement of worth as a more salient aspect of their friendships than did Indonesian youth ($d = .29$), although no differences emerged between Korean students and those in the other two countries.

Similar differences in enhancement of worth within the friendships of Indonesian, Korean, and U.S. friendships emerged from the study of children and adolescents. French, Pidada, and Victor (2005) found that U.S. eleven- and fourteen-year-old students rated their friendships higher on this provision than Indonesian students ($d = .1.27$), whereas French, Pidada et al. (2004) found that Korean students rated their reciprocated friendships higher in enhancement of worth than did Indonesian thirteen-year-old adolescents ($d = .37$).

The findings regarding the relative importance of enhancement of worth in U.S. and Indonesian youth are consistent with our hypotheses. It is interesting to speculate on the failure to find lower levels of enhancement of self in Korean relative to U.S. students in light of the suggestions by Kitayama et al. (1997) and Fiske et al. (1998) that the focus on self-esteem is somewhat diminished in interdependent cultures. We suspect that a focus on enhancement of worth in Korean friendships may be in part explained by the extreme importance of "face" in Korea, and the role of friends in maintaining this (Lim & Choi, 1996).

Further research on enhancement of worth in the friendships of youth in different cultures might profitably focus on how this is manifested in the context of daily interaction. Perhaps persons select others as friends who provide this enhancement. Alternatively, individuals may selectively reinforce their friends to provide them with greater enhancement in a process similar to that outlined by Dishion et al. (1996) with respect to deviancy training.

Longevity of Friendships

Based on the anthropological literature, we hypothesized that there would be differences in the longevity of friendships in Korea, Indonesia, and the United States. Korean friendships were expected to be particularly long lasting. It is common for persons in Korea to establish highly intimate friendships during their school years and to continue to maintain these throughout their life-span. In contrast, we expected friendships in Indonesia to be lower in longevity than either friendships in the United States or South Korea. We based this hypothesis on the anthropological and empirical work suggesting the primacy of social network involvement over the development of intense dyadic relationships (Noesjirwan, 1978). It is also a general presumption, evidenced from both informant reports and common expressions, that friendship is based on regular companionship. When individuals separate from each other, it is presumed that their friendship dissolves, to be reestablished when contact resumes. No predictions were made about the relative longevity of Korean and U.S. friendships.

Results from two of our studies provided evidence that the friendships of Korean and U.S. college students are longer in duration than those of Indonesian students. French, Bae et al. (in press) analyzed reports of the length of association between the participant and his or her closest friends (both the same and opposite sex) as reported on a social network inventory. Korean students reported knowing their closest friends for a longer time ($M = 4.78$ years) than Indonesian students ($M = 2.93$ years), whereas U.S. students knew their friends significantly longer than Indonesian students, but did not significantly differ from Korean college students ($M = 3.96$ years). Similar findings emerged from the French, Lee et al. (2004) study. Korean and U.S. college students reported knowing their single closest same-sex friend for longer periods (6.54, 6.06 years, respectively) than did Indonesian students (4.12 years).

Conflict

In addition to the more positive features of intimacy and enhancement of worth, conflict is also an important part of friendship. Most conflict occurs within close relationships, such as friendships, and the success of these relationships may be more a function of successful resolution rather than avoidance of conflicts. We have been particularly interested in exploring conflict because this is undoubtably embedded within a cultural context (Leung & Wu, 1990; Markus & Lin, 1999).

Many anthropologists have reported that minimal overt conflict is exhibited by Javanese, Sundanese, and other cultural groups in Indonesia (Koentjaraningrat, 1985). A central feature of Javanese society is the need to maintain harmony in face-to-face interaction and to avoid conflict, a concept captured by the word "rukun" (Magnis-Suseno, 1997). Persons are expected to be indirect rather than direct in action and words, and conflict and unpleasant interactions are minimized by avoiding certain people and refraining from topics that are potentially conflictual. If a conflict arises, common strategies to manage this include displaying indifference or politeness (Mulder, 1992) or by disengaging from either the issue or the protagonist (Magnis-Suseno, 1997).

In contrast, conflict among U.S. European American populations is often viewed as inevitable and reflective of the continual struggle between desires for integration and autonomy (Rothbaum et al., 2000). When conflicts arise, the most preferred resolution strategy is to address these directly and to respond with assertive negotiated solutions (Markus & Lin, 1999).

We have assessed conflict in three ways. First, we have assessed conflict in the reports of friendships using the modified version of the FQQ. Second, we have assessed conflict among friends and other relationship targets using the NRI. Finally, we have explored reports that children provided about their conflicts with peers, including friends.

Inconsistent patterns of friendship conflict emerged from our assessment of conflict as assessed by the modified version of the FQQ. In neither of our two studies of the friendships of U.S., Indonesian, and Korean college students did country or sex differences emerge (French, Bae et al., in press; French, Lee et al., 2004). In contrast, French, Pidada, and Victor (2005) found that eleven- and fourteen-year-old U.S. adolescents rated their friendships as more conflictual than Indonesian adolescents ($d = .31$) and French, Pidada et al. (2004) found that Korean adolescents rated their reciprocal friendships as higher in conflict than Indonesian youth ($d = .67$).

Findings from the analysis of the NRI revealed that Indonesian adolescents reported lower levels of conflict with friends than either U.S. or Korean youth. In French et al. (2001), Indonesian adolescents reported lower levels of conflict with friends than U.S. adolescents ($d = .54$), and in French, Pidada et al. (2004), Indonesian adolescents reported lower levels of conflict than Korean adolescents ($d = .49$).

Indonesian adolescents thus rated their friendships as lower in conflict than either U.S. or Korean youth, effects that emerged both from the FQQ and NRI analyses. These results are consistent with the anthropological information suggesting that conflict is likely to be minimized within Indonesian close relationships. The reliance on rating scales, however, may introduce the possibility that these results are attributable to response sets or culturally specific interpretations of the severity of conflict, and thus research using different methods is needed.

Cultural differences in conflict within friendships may emerge in the way that this is addressed rather than its frequency and severity. To explore this question, nine- to eleven-year-old children in the United States and Indonesia reported the details of conflicts that they experienced with peers, including the initiation, behavior during the conflict episode, and the resolution (French, Pidada, Denoma et al., 2005). Most of the conflicts occurred with friends (68%). Considerable similarity emerged between the described conflicts of U.S. and Indonesian children. Across countries, conflicts were typically short, amicably settled, and did not involve aggression.

We had hypothesized that differences between Indonesian and U.S. children would emerge in the type of strategies used during conflict and the manner in which conflicts were resolved. We thus anticipated that Indonesian children would use disengagement more frequently than U.S. children, a finding that emerged from our analyses. Similarly, we anticipated that U.S. children would more frequently use negotiation, results that also emerged.

The most interesting question focused on culturally specific links between strategies and social competence. Consistent with expectations that disengagement is considered an appropriate method of addressing conflict in Indonesia, engagement in disengagement was positively associated with teacher ratings of social preference and negatively associated with teacher ratings of aggression, findings opposite from those that emerged in the United States. These findings illustrate a method of addressing cultural differences by assessing within-culture associations of behavior with social competence that avoids some of the difficulties discussed earlier that are inherent in making direct cross-cultural comparisons. We hope to make more use of this strategy in our future research.

Implications

In this section, we discuss the implications of thinking about systematic differences in cultures between the emphasis on specific friendships and group integration. We first address the implications of this for theories of culture and friendship. We then discuss suggestions for future research.

Theories of Culture and Friendship

Triandis et al. (1988) and Reis, Collins, and Berscheid (2000) have attempted to explain cultural variation in friendship using the constructs of individualism and collectivism. The argument has been made that collectivists interact with a small number of in-group members with whom they share long lasting and highly intimate relationships. In contrast, individualists tend to develop relatively fluid and nonintimate relationships with persons in a variety of groups.

Questionnaire results and anthropological observations provide consistent evidence that persons in both South Korea and Indonesia are high in collectivism (e.g., Marshall, 1997; Yoon & Choi, 1994). Thus, to the extent that friendship variation is explained by the individualism and collectivism dimensions, we would expect that parameters of friendship exhibited by Korean and Indonesian youth to be similar to each other and dissimilar from the friendships of U.S. youth. The findings from the studies reviewed here are inconsistent with this position, with Indonesian and Korean students differing from each other on this dimension in ways that are difficult to explain from the Triandis et al. (1988) position.

Based on the Triandis et al. (1988) hypothesis, we would expect Indonesian and Korean students to be more exclusive in their interactions than U.S. students. This finding was directly contradicted by our results in which significant differences were consistently found between Korean and Indonesian youth. Rather than being dissimilar from both Korean and Indonesian youth, U.S. youth fell between the extremes of these two groups.

Other evidence from the French, Bae et al. (in press) study also contradicts the Triandis et al. (1988) hypothesis that collectivists interact with a small group of individuals that they know well. From diary reports of two weeks of interaction, we found that Indonesian college students engaged in interactions lasting at least ten minutes with almost twice as many different people as either Korean or U.S. children, an effect that was very large in magnitude. In addition, Indonesian students exhibited more interactions per day than either Korean or U.S. students. U.S. and Korean students did not differ from each other on either of these variables.

Triandis et al. (1988) also suggest that friendships of persons in collectivist cultures are closer and more intimate than those in individualistic cultures. Again, our findings directly refute these arguments. First, we could expect close friendships to last longer than less close friendships, and we might expect that Korean and Indonesian friendships last longer than those of U.S. students. In contrast to these expectations, in two studies (French, Bae et al. in press; French, Lee et al., 2004), we found that Indonesian college students reported knowing their close friends for shorter periods than either Korean or U.S. students. Second, we could expect that Korean and Indonesian youth would exhibit greater intimacy in their friendships than U.S. youth. This again is contradicted by our findings. In most of our analyses, Indonesian youth reported lower levels of intimacy with friends than either U.S. or Korean youth, and in no analysis did they report higher levels of intimacy than U.S. youth. This provides further evidence against the Triandis et al. position.

We believe that the findings reported here points toward the need to refine the Triandis et al. (1988) position with respect to friendship and collectivism. At a minimum, it appears necessary to expand models of collectivism and friendship to include one in which individuals seek wide integration within a peer network, but attach somewhat less importance to establishing extremely close and intimate specific friendships. This pattern may be somewhat common in societies in which the in-group extends beyond kin and immediate friends to a larger group and there are strong economic, ideological, or social bonds between group members. Within such communal groups, specific close friendships may be seen as potentially disruptive to the larger community.

The Israeli kibbutz societies are probably the most extensively studied communal group (see Sharabany, this volume). Within these societies, researchers have reported a focus on extensivity of interactions in conjunction with a de-emphasis of close relationships between individuals (Josselson et al., 1977). Bettelheim (1969) and Josselson et al. (1997) suggested that developing extremely close relationships with specific persons was seen as a rejection of others in the larger group and a potential source of jealousy and conflict. Rabin and Beit-Hallahmi (1982) found that kibbutz-reared adults preferred developing numerous but less intense relationships with others in preference to developing highly close relationships with specific persons, findings that closely parallel those of Noesjirwan's (1978) regarding Indonesian friendships.

Unfortunately, limited theoretical foundations exist for understanding culture and friendships. Future research might profitably focus on uncovering prototypical patterns of friendship within cultures. In addition to the patterns discussed previously, other are likely. For example, Gaskins (this volume) argues that the Yucatec Maya of Mexico have extensive involvement with family members, but have limited involvement with friends. Based on the arguments of Cohen (2002), there are probably only a limited number of stable patterns that are likely to exist.

Directions for Further Research

This chapter concludes with a brief discussion of three issues pertinent to the topic of friendship and culture. These include the importance of looking at friendship across the life-span, addressing the extreme within-culture variability of patterns of friendship, and finally the need to expand the range of methods that are used to explore friendship and culture.

Developmental Patterns of Friendship

The importance and nature of friendship likely varies across the life-span (Brown, 1990). In the studies we have done to date, we have assessed friendship during adolescence and during college years, times when friendship is likely to be particularly salient, at least for U.S. participants. Friendship, however, may vary at different points in the life-span, and the relative importance of friendship across cultures may vary depending on the developmental period in which it is assessed. For example, friendships in Korea appear to be very important across the life-span. Considerable socializing occurs with same-sex friends, and in many cases, adult relationships had been established during adolescence or young adulthood. The extent to which friendship is similar or different from adult friendship patterns seen in the United States and other countries is unknown but needs exploration.

Within-Culture Variation

Although the focus of this chapter is on between-country differences in friendship, it would be neglectful to ignore the considerable within-culture variability. Within the context of moral development, Wainryb and Turieal (1995) argue that the focus on broad cultural differences ignores the considerable within-culture variability. In our data, we have seen considerable variability within the United States, Indonesia, and South Korea on all friendship dimensions that we have assessed. In part, our success in understanding variability across cultures is dependent on researchers' ability to understand friendship within cultures. As noted in this volume, it is important to understand how friendship is similar and different among various U.S. subpopulations (see chapters by Way and Azmitia et al., this volume). Additional steps might include developing theories of friendship, understanding the specific qualities that underlie friendship, understanding the relation between friendship and popularity, and finally understanding the developmental course of friendship.

Methodology

Further progress in understanding culture and friendship will likely be dependent on the expansion of methodologies to explore this. Unfortunately, we and others have relied extensively on self-report methods, some of the limitations of which we have discussed and illustrated in our results. Although we believe that enhanced sophistication of our methodologies using procedures such as those advocated by Card and Little (this volume) will be helpful, we argue that progress will be limited until we can move beyond self-report information obtained using questionnaires, rating scales, and interviews. Unfortunately, our ability to do this is limited.

One possibility is to make more use of observational methods. Perhaps the procedures used by Corsaro (this volume) may profitably be used to explore differences across cultures. To date, however, most observational research has been done within cultures, and the opportunity to use it to make cross-cultural comparisons is limited. This difficulty arises in part because observed behavior is strongly affected by context, and this is seldom similar across cultures. Furthermore, the interactions of children and adolescents with their friends typically occur in settings that are difficult for observers to enter, and if they do, it is difficult for observers to appreciate the meaning of the behavior they are observing. Nevertheless, there may be an opportunity to make observations within somewhat standardized contexts that may make comparison across cultures possible.

Another promising approach is to use methods such as experience sampling (used by Larson, 1989) to understand the role of friendships in the lives of children within different cultures. Perhaps researchers can profitably begin by asking questions that require relatively low levels of inference and abstraction. These might include questions about (a) how much time students in different cultures spend with peers, (b) what activities they perform with peers, (c) what the gender composition of peer groups is, and (d) what thoughts and emotions youth experience when they are with peers and friends. As part of this focus on the structural aspects of friendships, we might begin to develop a better understanding of intensivity and extensivity of friendships, a topic that may be an important parameter of cross-cultural variation in friendship. The review by Brown, Larson, and Saraswathi (2002) illustrates how little researchers know about these basic structural features of peer interaction in different societies.

Finally, our approach to understanding culture and friendship has focused on assessing the characteristics of specific friendships. We believe that the characteristics of individual relationships are likely consistent with the prototypical models that persons within cultures hold for these relationships. For example, persons in different cultures likely have different expectations about the extent to which intimacy is displayed within friendships. These beliefs likely guide their selection of persons to be friends who meet these expectations as well as processes of selectively shaping the behavior of friends to correspond to these expectations. At the same time, these expectations likely affect the assessment of intimacy. Thus, individuals might report high amounts of intimacy in their friendships in part because they expect that friendships exhibit these characteristics. The research on the characteristics of friendships might profitably be complemented by studies that directly assess the cognitive models that individuals in different cultures hold for these relationships. Promising approaches include the attempts to understand friendship rules (Bigelow et al., 1996), linguistic analyses of relationship terms (Fitch, 1998), as well as the application of multidimensional scaling to understand the meanings of friendship labels in different cultures (Maeda & Ritchie, 2003).

References

Adams, R. G., & Allan, G. (1998). *Placing friendship in context*. Cambridge, England: Cambridge University Press.

Bell S., & Coleman, S. (1999). The anthropology of friendship: Enduring themes and future possibilities. In S. Bell & S. Coleman (Eds.), *The anthropology of friendship* (pp. 1–19). Oxford, England: Berg.

Berndt, T. J., & Perry, T. B. (1986). Children's perceptions of friendships as supportive relationships. *Developmental Psychology, 22*, 640–648.

Berry, J. (1989). Imposed etics-emics-derived etics: The operalization of a compelling idea. *International Journal of Psychology, 24*, 721–735.

Bettelheim, B. (1969). *The children of the dream: Communal child-rearing and its implications for society*. New York: Macmillan.

Bigelow, B. J., Tesson, G., & Lewko, J. H. (1996). *Learning the rules: The anatomy of children's relationships*. New York: Guilford.

Bond, M. H. (1988). Findings universal dimensions of individual variation in multicultural studies of values: The Rokeach and Chinese value surveys. *Journal of Personality and Social Psychology, 55*, 1009–10015.

Brain, R. (1976). *Friends and lovers*. New York: Basic Books.

Brandt, V. S. R. (1974). Skiing cross-culturally. *Current Anthropology, 15*, 64–74.

Brown, B. B. (1990). A life-span approach to friendship: Age related dimensions of an ageless relationship. In H. Z. Lopata & D. R. Maines (Eds.), *Friendship in context*. (pp. 23–50). Greenwich, CT: JAI Press.

Brown, B. B., Larson, R. W., & Saraswathi, T. S. (2002). *The world's youth: Adolescence in eight regions of the globe*. New York: Cambridge

Bukowski, W. M., Boivan, M., & Hoza, B. (1994). Measuring friendship quality during pre- and early adolescence: The development and psychometric properties of the Friendship Qualities Scale. *Journal of Social and Personal Relationships, 11*, 471–484.

Bukowski, W. M., & Hoza, B. (1989). Popularity and friendship: Issues in theory, measurement, and outcome. In T. J. Berndt & G. W. Ladd (Eds.), *Peer relations in child development* (pp. 15–45). New York: Wiley.

Bukowski, W. M., Hoza, B., & Newcomb, A. F. (1994). Using rating scale and nomination techniques to measure friendship and popularity. *Journal of Social and Personal Relationships, 11*, 485–488.

Bukowski, W. M., Pizzamiglio, M. T., Newcomb, A. F., & Hoza, B. (1996). Popularity as an affordance for friendship: The link between group and dyadic experience. *Social Development, 5*, 189–202.

Chen, X., Kaspar, V., Zhang, Y., Wang. L., & Zheng, S. (2004). Peer relationships among Chinese and North American boys: A cross-cultural perspective. In N. Way & J. Chu (Eds.), *Adolescent boys: Exploring diverse cultures of boyhood.* (pp. 197–218). New York: New York University Press.

Chen, C., Lee, S. Y., & Stevenson, H. W. (1995). Response styles and cross-cultural comparisons of rating scales among East Asian and North American students. *Psychological Science, 6*, 170–175.

Choi, S. C., Kim, U., & Choi, S. H. (1993). Indigenous analysis of collective representations: A Korean perspective. In U. Kim & J. W. Berry (Eds.), *Indigenous psychologies: Research and experience in cultural context* (pp. 193–210). Newbury Park, CA: Sage.

Cohen, D. (2002). Cultural variation: Considerations and implications. *Psychological Bulletin, 127*, 451–471.

Damon, W. (1995). *Greater expectations: Overcoming the culture of indulgence in America's homes and schools*. New York: Free Press.

Dishion, T. J., Spacklen, K. M., Andrews, D. W., & Patterson, G. R. (1996). Deviancy training in male adolescent friendships. *Behavior Therapy, 27*, 373–390.

Fiske, A. P., Kitayama, S., Markus, H. R., & Nisbett, R. E. (1998). The cultural matrix of social psychology. In D. T. Gilbert, S. T. Fiske, & L. Gardner (Eds.), *The handbook of social psychology* (Vol. 2, pp. 915–980). New York: Wiley.

Fitch, K. L. (1998). *Speaking relationally: Culture, communication, and interpersonal connection*. New York: Guilford.

French, D. C., Bae, A., Pidada, S., & Lee, O. (in press). Friendships of Indonesian, S. Korean and U.S. College Students. *Personal Relationships*.

French, D. C., Jansen, E. A., Riansari, M., & Setiono, K. (2003). Friendships of Indonesian children: Adjustment of children who differ in friendship presence and similarity between mutual friends. *Social Development, 12*, 606–621.

French, D. C., Lee, O., & Pidada, S. (2004). *College student friendships: S. Korea, Indonesia, and the United States*. Manuscript in preparation.

French, D. C., Pidada, S., Denoma, J., Lawton, A., & McDonald, K. (2005). Reported Peer Conflicts of Children in the United States and Indonesia. *Social Development, 17*, 458–472.

French, D. C., Pidada, S., & Lee, O. (2004). Friendships of Indonesian and Korean adolescents. Manuscript in preparation.

French, D. C., Pidada, S., & Victor, A. (2005). Friendships of Indonesian and United States youth. *International Journal for Behavioral Development, 29*, 304–313.

French, D. C., Riansari, M., Pidada, S., Nelwan, P., & Buhrmester, D. (2001). Social support of Indonesian and U. S. children and adolescents by family members and friends. *Merrill-Palmer Quarterly, 47*, 377–394.

French, D. C., Setiono, K., & Eddy, J. M. (1999). Bootstrapping through the cultural comparison minefield: Childhood social status and friendships in the United States and Indonesia. In W. A. Collins & B. Laursen (Eds.), *Relationships as developmental contexts: Minnesota Symposium of Child Psychology* (Vol. 30, pp. 109–131). Hillsdale, NJ: Lawrence Erlbaum Associates.

Furman, W. (1996). The measurement of friendship perceptions: Conceptual and methodological issues. In W. M. Bukowski, A. F. Newcomb, & W. W. Hartup (Eds.), *The company they keep: Friendship in childhood and adolescence* (pp. 41–65). Cambridge, England: Cambridge University Press.

Furman, W., & Buhrmester, D. (1985). Children's perceptions of the personal relationships in their social networks. *Developmental Psychology, 21*, 1016–1024.

Gottman, J. M., & Parker, J. G. (1986). *Conversations of friends: Speculations on affective development*. Cambridge, England: Cambridge University Press.

Gudykunst, W. B., Yoon, Y., & Nishida, T. (1987). The influence of individualism-collectivism on perceptions of communication in ingroup and outgroup relationships. *Communication Monographs, 54*, 295–306.

Hartup, W. W. (1992). Conflict and friendship relations. In C. U. Shantz & W. W. Hartup (Eds.), *Conflict in child and adolescent development* (pp. 186–215). Cambridge, England: Cambridge University Press.

Hays, R. B. (1988). Friendship. In S. W. Duck (Ed.), *Handbook of personal relationships* (pp. 391–408). New York: Wiley.

Heine, S. J., Lehman, D. R., Markus, H. R., & Kitayama, S. (1999). Is there a universal need for positive self-regard? *Psychological Review, 106*, 766–794.

Hofsteade, G. (1991). *Culture and organizations: Software of the mind*. London: McGraw Hill.

Hui, C. H., & Triandis, H. C. (1989). Effects of culture and response format on extreme response style. *Journal of Cross-Cultural Psychology, 20*, 296–309.

Jay, R. R. (1969). *Javanese villagers: Social relations in rural Modjokuto*. Boston: MIT Press.

Josselson, R., Lieblich, A., Sharabany, R., & Wiseman, H. (1997). *Conversation as method: Analyzing the relational world of people who were raised communally*. Thousand Oaks, CA: Sage.

Kim, K. (1996). The reproduction of Confucian culture in contemporary Korea: An anthropological study. In Wei-Ming, T. (Ed.), *Confucian traditions in east Asian modernity: Moral education and economic culture in Japan and the four mini-dragons*. (pp. 202–227) Cambridge, MA: Harvard University Press.

Kitayama, S., Markus, H., Matsumoto, H., & Norasakkunkit, V. (1997). Individual and collective processes in the construction of the self: Self-enhancement in the United States and self-criticism in Japan. *Journal of Personality and Social Psychology, 72*, 1245–1267.

Koentjaraningrat (1985). *Javanese Culture*. New York: Oxford University Press.

Larson, R. (1989). Beeping children and adolescents: A method for studying time use and daily experience. *Journal of Youth and Adolescence, 18*, 511–530.

Leung, K., & Wu, P. G. (1990). Dispute processing: Across-cultural analysis. In R. W. Brislin (Ed.), *Applied cross-cultural psychology* (pp. 209–231). Newbury Park, CA: Sage.

Lim, T. S., & Choi, S. H. (1996). Interpersonal relationships in Korea. In W. B. Gudykunst, S. Ting-Toomey, & T. Nishida (Eds.), *Communication in personal relationships across cultures* (pp. 122–136). Thousand Oaks, CA: Sage.

Maeda, E., & Ritchie, L. D. (2003). The concept of *shinyuu* in Japan: A replication and comparison of Cole and Bradac's study on U. S. friendships. *Journal of Personal and Social Relationships, 20*, 579–598,

Magnis-Suseno, F. (1997). *Javanese ethics and world-view: The Javanese idea of the good life*. Jakarta, Indonesia: Gramedia Pustaka Utama.

Markus, H. R., & Lin, L. R. (1999). Conflictways: Cultural diversity in the meanings and practices of conflict. In D. A. Prentice & D. T. Miller (Eds.), *Cultural divides: Understanding and overcoming group conflict* (pp. 302–333). New York: Russell Sage Foundation.

Marshall, R. (1997). Variances in levels of individualism across two cultures and three social classes. *Journal of Cross-Cultural Psychology, 28*, 490–495.

McCall, G. J. (1988). The organizational life cycle of relationships. In S. Duck (Ed.), *Handbook of personal relationships: Theory, research, and interventions* (pp. 467–486). New York: Wiley.

McDonald, K. (2003). *Cultural scripts of parental intervention into young children's conflicts*. Unpublished undergraduate thesis, Illinois Wesleyan University, Bloomington.

McLoyd, V. (1998). Socioeconomic disadvantage and child development. *American Psychologist, 53*, 185–204.

Minuchin, P. (1985). Families and individual development: Provocations from the field of family therapy. *Child Development, 56*, 289–302.

Mulder, N. (1992). *Individual and society in Java: A cultural analysis*. Yogyakarta, Indonesia: Gadjah Mada University Press.

Mulder, N. (1996). Southeast Asia: Religion, everyday life, cultural change. Chiang Mai, Thailand: Silkworm.

Noesjirwan, J. (1977). Contrasting cultural patterns of interpersonal closeness in doctors' waiting rooms in Sydney and Jakarta. *Journal of Cross-Cultural Psychology, 8*, 357–368.

Noesjirwan, J. (1978). A rule-based analysis of cultural differences in social behavior: Indonesia and Australia. *International Journal of Psychology, 13*, 305–316.

Ogbu, J. U. (1981). The origins of human competence: A cultural-ecological perspective. *Child Development, 52*, 413–429.

Parker, J. G. (1997). *The friendship attribute Q-sort*. Unpublished manuscript, Pennsylvania State University, PA: University Park.

Parker, J. G., & Asher, S. R. (1993). Friendship and friendship quality in middle childhood: Links with peer group acceptance and feelings of loneliness and social dissatisfaction. *Developmental Psychology, 29*, 611–621.

Patterson, G. R., Reid, J. B., & Dishion, T. J (1992). *Antisocial boys*. Eugene, OR: Castalia.

Rabin, A. I., & Beit-Hallahmi, B. (1982). *Twenty years later: Kibbutz children grow up*. New York: Springer.

Reis, H. T., Collins, W. A., & Berscheid, E. (2000). The relationship context of human behavior and development. *Psychological Bulletin, 126*, 844–872.

Reis, H. T., & Wheeler, L. (1991). Studying social interaction with the Rochester Interaction Record. *Advances in Experimental Social Psychology, 24*, 269–318.

Rogoff, B. (2003). *The cultural nature of human development*. Oxford, England: Oxford University Press.

Rothbaum, F., Pott, M., Azuma, H., Miyake, K., & Weisz, J. (2000). The development of close relationships in Japan and the United States: Paths of symbiotic harmony and generative tension. *Child Development, 71*, 1121–1142.

Rubin, L. B. (1985). *Just friends: The role of friendship in our lives*. New York: Harper and Row.

Selman, R. L. (1980). *The growth of interpersonal understanding*. New York: Academic Press.

Smith, P. B. (2001). Cross-cultural social influence. In D. Matsumoto (Ed.), *The handbook of culture and psychology* (pp. 361–374). New York: Oxford University Press.

Sullivan, H. S. (1953). *The interpersonal theory of psychiatry*. New York: Norton.

Tietjen, A. M. (1989). The ecology of children's social support networks. In D. Belle (Ed.), *Children's social support networks and social supports* (pp. 37–69). New York: Wiley.

Triandis, H. C. (1995). *Individualism and collectivism*. Boulder, CO: Westview.

Triandis, H. C., Bontempo, R., Villareal, M. J., Asai, M., & Lucca, N. (1988). Individualism and collectivism: Cross-cultural perspectives on self-ingroup relationships. *Journal of Personality and Social Psychology, 54*, 323–333.

Vijver, F. J. R., & Leung, K. L. (1997). *Methods and data analysis for cross-cultural research*. Thousand Oaks, CA: Sage.

Yoon, G., & Choi, S. C. (1994). *Psychology of the Korean people: Collectivism and individualism*. Seoul, South Korea: Dong-A Publishing.

Wainryb, C., & Turiel, E. (1995). Diversity in social development: Between or within cultures? In M. Killen & D. Hart (Eds.), *Morality in everyday life: Developmental perspectives*. Cambridge, England: Cambridge University Press.

Waldrop, M. F., & Halverson, C. F. (1975). Intensive and extensive peer behavior: Longitudinal and cross-sectional analyses. *Child Development, 46*, 19–26.

Weiss, R. S. (1974). The provisions of social relationships. In Z. Rubin (Ed.), *Doing unto others* (pp. 17–26). Englewood Cliffs, NJ: Prentice Hall.

Weisz, J. R., Chaiyasit, W., Weiss, B., Eastman, K. L., & Jackson, E. W. (1995). A multi-modal study of problem behavior among Thai and American children at school: Teacher reports versus direct observation. *Child Development, 66*, 402–415.

Zevalkink, J. (1997). *Attachment in Indonesia: The mother-child relationship in context*. Unpublished doctoral dissertation, University of Nijmegen, The Netherlands.

18 The Cultural Practice of Close Friendships Among Urban Adolescents in the United States

Niobe Way

The study of culture and human development is an increasingly popular area of research in the social sciences. Typically focusing on family-related topics such as child-rearing beliefs and practices, research on culture and human development has investigated the ways in which adult members of different cultural communities make meaning of their worlds and how these meanings shape child development (e.g., Harkness & Super, 2002; Harwood, Miller, & Irizarry, 1995). Despite this recent increase in research, however, there remain numerous gaps in our understanding of these complex processes. One of the most obvious gaps relates to the ways in which culture shapes the development of friendships among adolescents. Studies of culture and human development have rarely compared how friendships, for example, are experienced by adolescents in diverse cultural communities or how friendships themselves are cultural practices within such communities. Although the study of peer cultures has been the topic of numerous sociological studies over the past two decades (see Adler & Adler, 1997; Corsaro & Eder, 1990), an understanding of how dyadic friendships in particular are shaped by and shape the cultural communities in which they exist and are themselves a form of cultural practice has not yet been attained.

Researchers, particularly in the American context, have tended to conceptualize friendships as a universal rather than a culturally situated set of relationships. This universal conceptualization is evident in the large body of research on the friendships of American, middle-class, White youth and the almost nonexistent body of research on the friendships of those who are not American, middle-class, and White. The implicit and explicit assumption in the research on the American, middle class, White youth is that the findings derived from these youth generalize to all youth, and thus there is little reason to explore the friendships of other groups. Yet, the few research projects that have explored other groups besides the American, White, middle-class have consistently found friendship patterns that differ from this group (Chen et al., 2004; DuBois & Hirsch, 1990; Hamm, 1994; Way, 2004). For example, research on White youth has consistently found gender differences in levels of support in close friendships among adolescents, whereas research with African American youth has rarely found such gender differences (e.g., DuBois & Hirsch, 1990; Jones & Costin, 1997; Way & Chen, 2000). Such findings draw attention to the importance of researchers examining the cultural contexts in which friendships are embedded.

Moving to a model of friendships that underscores the cultural nature of friendships raises new questions. How do adolescents from different cultural communities experience or practice friendships? How are these experiences or practices of friendships a reflection of the communities from which they come? How are communities shaped by the practice of friendships? As a developmental researcher committed to understanding how culture and human development intersect, my goal over the past fifteen years has been to explore the development of friendships among urban low-socioeconomic status, ethnic minority youth from the United States. I have been interested in understanding how such youth experience their friendships, how these experiences change over time from early to late adolescence, and how their experiences are a reflection of the multiple cultural communities of which they are a part (e.g., American, Chinese, boys, girls, urban). The focus of this chapter is on the central findings of my research.

The Cultural Practice of Friendships

A critical question in studies of culture and development is the definition of culture. As many have argued (see Rogoff & Angelillo, 2002), culture is not the equivalent of a social category, such as race, ethnicity, socioeconomic status, gender, or nationality. Culture describes beliefs, attitudes, and practices in a dynamic community or context that reflect the historical moment – it is an active process rather than a category that is inherent in the person. A cultural community is "composed of generations of people in coordination with each other over time, with some common and continuing organization, values, understanding, history, and practices that transcend the particular individuals. At the same time, individuals and their generational cohorts change community traditions, with changing times and conditions" (Rogoff & Angelillo, 2002, p. 222). In other words, cultural communities are both continuous over time and responsive to the historical moment. Social categories, such as race, ethnicity, or gender, are not in and of themselves culture (i.e., the category itself does not provide the meaning of culture), yet they often constitute a core part of what it means to be from a particular cultural community or context.

Within cultural communities such as the Chinese American community in New York City, for example, there are a wide variety of beliefs, attitudes, and behaviors, but there is also an enduring set of beliefs, attitudes, and behaviors related to being Chinese, American, and from New York City that bring the people who are part of these cultural communities together. Furthermore, it is through relationships within and across these cultural communities that these beliefs, values, and behaviors are "practiced." Thus, friendships are a type of cultural practice in so much as it is through these relationships that adolescents, for example, "practice" their peer-related beliefs, values, and behaviors that are a reflection of their cultural communities. However, this reflection is not a passive one but an active one, in which adolescents are responding to, resisting, or transforming the beliefs, values, and behaviors that are typical of their cultural communities. By conceptualizing friendships as a cultural practice with which adolescents are fully engaged, the ways in which these relationships are embedded in cultural communities are underscored.

Theoretical and Empirical Background

Theories of friendships indicate that friendships provide particular benefits to adolescents, such as companionship and a sense of intimacy, self-worth, and validation, and that each of these benefits or "provisions" (see Weiss, 1974) influences the other (Hamm and Faircloth, 2004; Sullivan, 1953). Intimacy, for example, enhances an adolescent's sense of self worth and provides a feeling of mutual validation between friends (Sullivan, 1953). In addition, the extent to which these relational provisions are experienced depends on development, with children's friendships providing companionship and adolescent friendships providing intimacy and emotional support as well as companionship (Aboud & Mendelson, 1996; Buhrmester & Furman, 1987; Hartup, 1993). Most research on friendships draws from this theoretical model and focuses on, for example, the extent to which particular provisions or components of friendships (e.g., support, intimacy) are evident during different developmental periods or across gender or, more recently, across ethnicity, or how these provisions are associated with various indicators of adjustment (Brown & Klute, 2003; Bukowski, Newcomb, & Hartup, 1996; Furman & Buhrmester, 1985; Savin-Williams & Berndt, 1990).

A common finding from this body of research, one that has dominated the conversation about friendships for over a decade, is that adolescent girls are more likely than boys to experience intimate self-disclosure and emotional support in their friendships, whereas adolescent boys are more likely than girls to have "activity-oriented" friendships (Belle, 1989; Buhrmester

& Furman, 1987; Savin-Williams & Berndt, 1990). Yet the research that supports this claim, as well as most research on adolescent friendships, has been limited by its focus on White, middle-class adolescents and its almost exclusive use of survey methodology. The focus on White, middle-class adolescents has resulted in theories of friendships that may or may not reflect the realities of adolescents from different cultural communities and contexts. The focus on survey methodology has furthermore limited our ability to understand how the meaning of friendships may vary within and across cultural communities.

Underscoring the importance of examining friendships in context, friendship research with African American and White adolescents has found that the gender difference in intimate self-disclosure so commonly found among White adolescents is not evident among African American adolescents. For example, Jones, Costin, and Ricard (1994) found that African American males were more likely to reveal their personal thoughts and feelings to male friends than were European American males. Furthermore, European American adolescents were the only ones who revealed significant gender differences in levels of self-disclosure in their friendships. Similarly, DuBois and Hirsch (1990) found, in their study of African American and White junior high school children, that White girls reported having significantly more supportive friendships than White boys. No gender difference in friendship support, however, was detected among the African American students. They also found that African American boys were more likely to have intimate conversations with their best friends than were White boys, whereas no differences were found between African American and White girls. In our survey-based research with low-income, African American, Latino, and Asian American adolescents, gender differences in support from friends were evident only among the Latino adolescents and not among the African American or Asian American adolescents (Way & Chen, 2000). In a study of peer culture among African American, urban youth, Goodwin (1990) found less gender segregation than has been commonly reported by researchers studying peer culture among White youth. These studies not only underscore the dangers of generalizing about friendships based on data derived from White adolescents, but also raise questions about how cultural communities shape the meaning of friendship, intimacy, and support.

The Relationships Among Peers (R. A. P.) Studies

In response to the need to understand friendship development among adolescents from diverse communities, I have been conducting a series of longitudinal, qualitative, and quantitative studies over the past fifteen years (The R. A. P. studies) of boys and girls from poor and working-class urban environments in the northeastern part of the United States (Way, 1995, 1998; Way & Chen, 2000; Way & Pahl, 1999, 2001). My questions have addressed the following three questions: (a) how do African American, Latino, and Asian American adolescents from low-income, urban families experience or practice closeness in their nonfamilial friendships?; (b) how do these experiences or practices change from middle to late adolescence?; and (c) how is the experience or practice of close friendships a reflection of the adolescents' cultural communities?

Methodology

My longitudinal studies have included approximately 350 adolescents who have been interviewed each year for a three- to five-year period. The ethnic composition of each study included African American, Puerto Rican, and Dominican youth. Two of my four studies also included Asian Americans who primarily identified themselves as Chinese American. All of the youth in my studies came from poor or working-class families and attended neighborhood schools that are struggling to keep their doors open in the midst of the chaos and dysfunction that permeate the buildings.

The adolescents in my studies were interviewed by me, one of my colleagues, or a graduate student at a local university. The interviewers were ethnically diverse and came from various socioeconomic backgrounds. Often, they had had extensive experience working as counselors or teachers in urban settings. Most of the interviewers participated in intensive interviewer training sessions that lasted two to three months and focused on improving listening skills and interviewing skills in general. The adolescents were often interviewed by the same interviewer each year for three- to five-years to create a safe space for the participants and thus enhance, to the greatest degree possible, the quality of the interview.

The semistructured interviews in each study were typically one-to-one interviews that lasted two hours. The interview protocol (similar across all of the four studies) focused on how adolescents described their beliefs, values, and behaviors regarding friendships, what made them feel close to their best friendships, what they valued about their friendships, and how they saw their friendships changing over time. Although each interview included a standard set of questions, follow-up questions were open-ended to capture the adolescents' own ways of describing their relationships. All interviews were audiotaped and transcribed.

The data analysis of the interview transcripts included two techniques: "narrative summaries" (Miller, 1988) and a variation of a data analytic technique called the "listening guide" (Brown & Gilligan, 1992). The intent of the narrative summaries is to condense the stories told by each participant while retaining the essence of the stories being told by the adolescents (see Miller, 1991). In the analyses presented in this chapter, my research team and I created brief summaries of each discussion of friendship in each interview. Each narrative summary was read independently by the data analysts who looked for themes in the summaries (e.g., distrusting peers). Reading for themes involved highlighting each passage, sentence, or word in the transcription that suggested the particular theme being traced. This process of highlighting helps to create a trail of evidence for the themes one is following. My technique of listening for themes is based on the listening guide (Brown & Gilligan, 1992), which encourages the listener to pay close attention to the form (i.e., how the story was told) and content of the interview and to follow one's own process of interpretation. A theme retained for further analysis had to be identified as such by at least three of the four data analysts independently in any one year of the study. Once themes were generated and agreed on, each data analyst returned to the original interviews and noted in what year in the project and where in the interview itself these themes emerged. They also took note of how the themes changed over time. Both narrative summaries and the listening guide encourage the listener to attend closely to the voices of the adolescents and to attune to the relational elements of the research process (see Way, 1998 for a more thorough discussion of these data analytic techniques).

Our thematic analysis of the interviews of the adolescents indicated that the practice of close friendships among urban adolescents involved both metathemes – themes that were evident across most or all of the adolescents in the study – and gender and ethnic-specific themes. A metatheme, for example, was that trust formed the root of closeness with friends – it was the reason the adolescents felt close to their friends. Furthermore, like the root of a tree that extends in many directions, there were multiple ways of experiencing trust and closeness. The experience of trust and closeness involved: (a) sharing secrets, (b) sharing money, (c) protecting each other from harm, (d) receiving and providing assistance with daily tasks, and (e) bringing their friends into the fold of their families. The interview data also suggested that the practice of friendships was shaped by the multiple cultural communities in which the adolescents were apart. In the following pages, I describe these meta and gender and ethnic specific themes and the ways in which they may reflect the values and beliefs of the adolescents' communities.

The Practice of Closeness

Sharing secrets

As predicted from the theoretical and research literature, the vast majority of the adolescent girls and boys spoke with great passion and conviction about their ability to share "everything" with their close friends. When asked what makes her feel close to her best friend, Amanda said, "She keeps everything a secret, whatever I tell her." Maria said her best friend knows her "like the back of her hands. . . . I can talk to her about anything, like if I call her, I'm hysterically crying or something just happened or whatever, . . . and maybe she'll be doing something, she'll stop doing that to come and talk to me and to help me." Brian said in response to a similar question, "I tell [my best friends] anything about me and I know they won't tell anybody else unless I tell them to." A key part of Justin's friendship is the mutuality, "He could just tell me anything and I could tell him anything." When asked to define a best friend, Justin said, "Like I always know everything about him. . . . We always chill, like we don't hide secrets from each other." When asked to explain why he feels close to his friends, Malcolm said, "If I'm having problems at home, they'll like counsel me, I just trust them with anything, like deep secrets, anything."

To find out whether friends could be trusted with "deep secrets," girls in particular often put their friends through "trust tests," which involved providing confidential information and seeing "if it gets out." When Gabriele was asked how an "acquaintance" becomes a friend, she responded:

> G: I give them a test. I start them off with something personal and I see if they tell somebody. That just tells me which level I will put them in. Like my best friend, I told her like family problems and stuff, she never told nobody.
> I: How does one go from the friend level to the best friend level?
> G: There's another test there too. See I tell 'em something personal but not that personal. I will say something that I don't want my aunt to know and then I see if they tell her, and if they don't tell her, they go to the next level.

Trust tests appeared to help girls decide who was trustworthy among their seemingly untrustworthy peers.

Sharing secrets was one of the primary ways in which the adolescents trusted and felt close to their friends. In contrast to previous research with White middle class adolescents (e.g., Belle, 1989), there were no gender differences in the emphasis on shared secrets. Although trust tests were more common among the girls than the boys, boys were as likely as girls to indicate that they felt close to their friends because they could trust their friends with their "deep[est] secrets." There were, however, age differences in the content of "shared secrets." Secrets during the first year of the study often included revealing who someone has a crush on or how someone did on an academic test, whereas by the fourth year, shared secrets focused more on conflicts in romantic relationships or with family at home. As the adolescents grew older, the content of their secrets became seemingly more complex.

Sharing Money

Like a mantra, the adolescents, particularly the boys, indicated that they trusted their close friends to share their secrets and their money. Knowing that a friend will hold their money and not spend it or steal it was an important way in which adolescents trusted and felt close to their friends. When Randall was asked "In what ways do you trust your friends?" he responded "I trust them to hold my money . . . if I lend them money, they'll pay me back." When Nathan was asked how his best friend is different from his friends who are less close, he said:

> I could leave any amount of money with him. He gave me money, I give him money. If I need something, he gives it to me, I give it to him [if he needs something].
> I: Can you tell me about a time that you trusted your best friend?
> N: [On Friday] he asked me if he could borrow fifty dollars and he gave it back to me by Monday. He gave me back seventy-five, he was like, thanks for lending it to him. He gave me back extra.

When asked about a recent time that she trusted her best friend, Nicole said, "We went shopping and I put money in her pocket, but I forgot about how much I had given her. And then she gave me the right amount back." Mark claimed that the ways he knows he can trust his friend is that if "I give them a stack of money to hold, they wouldn't be like 'oh well I lost it.' . . . They would like keep it in a safe spot and wouldn't tell anybody that they are holding that money for me." When Mike was asked why he feels close to his best friends, he said, "If I lend them money, I usually don't have to ask them for the money, usually get it back, I don't even have to ask for it." In addition to knowing that friends would pay them back, the adolescents emphasized their willingness to loan money to their friends.

Not only were there gender differences in this theme, with the boys more likely than the girls to emphasize the importance of shared money, there were also age differences. As the adolescents grew older, they became less likely to emphasize the importance of sharing money in discussions of their close friends. As the adolescent grew cognitively and relationally more sophisticated, their definition and experience of closeness became more emotionally and less materially based. This pattern is supported by our quantitative-based research that indicated a sharp increase over time in boys' reports of intimate self-disclosure in their male friendships from middle to late adolescence (Way & Greene, in press).

Protection from Harm

Another way that the adolescent boys experienced trust and closeness with their friends was through the protection of each other in fights. The boys repeatedly discussed the importance of knowing that their friends will protect them in fights and that they will, in turn, protect their friends. When Raphael was asked by his interviewer "What could you trust with your friends?" he said, "Let's just say I had a big fight, I got beat up, I had like five guys against me, they'll come and they'll help me out." When Akil was asked why he trusts his best friend, he said, "You get into a fight with somebody else, [my best friend] will tell me to calm down, chill . . . like when someone jumps me, he will help me." He also said he feels close to his friend because he knows that he would protect him in a fight.

Armondo discussed how his bond with his friends was enhanced through their mutual protection. He described a time when he and his three male friends were confronted by another group of boys who wanted to fight them. He explained to his interviewer how it was up to him to protect his friends: "And I'm behind my friend . . . if something happened to him where it was like he couldn't react fast enough and I was behind him, it would have been up to me to . . . protect him and help him out." Had he not protected his friend, Armondo said he would have been isolated by his friends: "If something had happened and I didn't do anything, I'm just standing like a big dummy, you know, I mean, none of them would ever want to hang out with me again."

Protecting each other was not only about "backing each other up" in fights, but also about helping each other calm down, thus preventing a fight. Chris, a Puerto Rican student who was sixteen at the time of the interview, emphasized how his best friend Scott helped him stay out of trouble. For him, this was a crucial aspect of why they were best friends:

> I: Why do you think your friendship with Scott is better than with other friends?
> C: Well with him when I'm in an argument with somebody that disrespected me and he just comes out and backs me up and says, "Yo, Chris, don't deal with that. Yo, let's just go on." you know, 'cause I could snap.

Another way the boys protected each other was by showing concern about harmful behaviors, such as smoking, selling drugs, and cutting class. Jorge, a fourteen-year-old Dominican boy, told his interviewer that his best friend was like a little brother to him. However, Jorge was trying to change his friend's behavior.

> I: What do you not like about this friendship?
> J: That he smokes weed and that he sells drugs, Well, I'm trying to change him. He's trying to stop 'cause I told him. I be talking to him and he's trying to get off drugs and smoke.

The stories of mutual protection between boys and their friends were striking in their vulnerability. They did not emphasize, as one might expect based on stereotypes of boys, their own protection of their friends. They provided stories of both being protected by and of protecting their friends, suggesting a level of comfort in the interdependency of their friendships.

The theme of protection from harm was evident during each year of the interviews; however, the type of protection provided or received shifted over time. Protection from harm primarily involved physical fights ("having each other's back") during the first few years of the study; during late adolescence, it expanded to include protecting each other from emotional harm as well. Boys, such as Chris, spoke about trying to soften the effect on their friends of being "disrespected" or betrayed by their peers. The change over time in the theme of mutual protection suggested that friendships among the boys became more emotionally nuanced over time.

Providing and Receiving Help

Providing and receiving help from friends was another important component of adolescents' experiences of trust and closeness with their friends. This theme was heard during each year of the interview and did not vary in form or content over time. For example, Markia explained why her best friend is her best friend:

> She helps me out like when I need her to babysit. I could call her and if I need her to watch the baby for a minute, two, she'll take him for the

> whole day.... She helps me out with him. She's like "Well if you ever need something just tell me, just say 'I'm low on pampers,'' she will come through with a box of pampers, you know even if I don't need anything, she'll still bring it. You know I love her for that.

Although Markia's situation was atypical among the girls in my studies, the equation of assistance with love was not. Adolescents spoke about the deep connection they experienced with their friends as a result of the assistance provided by them.

The emphasis on mutual assistance in friendships did not vary by gender or age. Ethnic differences, however, were suggested in the type of tasks with which friends helped each other. For the Asian American adolescents exclusively, helping with homework was an important part of the ways in which they felt close with their friends. When Sam, a Chinese American adolescent, was asked what he likes about his best friends, he indicated that he likes that he and his friends help each other with homework assignments and tests and these experiences make him feel close to his friends. He also indicated that he likes that he can share his most intimate secrets with his best friends, and he trusts them to "hold his money." His experience of closeness resonates with the other adolescents in the sample who do not share his ethnic heritage, but his discussion of helping with homework makes his responses stand apart from his non-Asian peers. These findings draw attention to the fact that the Asian American adolescents (like their non-Asian peers) are a part of multiple cultural communities, including a community of adolescents, of urban youth, and of Asian American families.

The Family-Friend Connection

A theme expressed exclusively among the African American and Latino adolescents interviewed was that friends were close because they knew each other's families. Anthony's aunt (who is his primary caretaker) used to babysit Pedro, who is his best friend. His other best friend's mom is the best friend of his aunt. The mother of Minda's best friend is the best friend of her mother. Michael said about his best friend, "Since we were real small I have known his whole family, he knows everybody in my house, we just walk over to his crib, open his fridge without asking or something, that's how long we've know each other." Ken said he is close with his best friend's family and that is a large part of what makes the friendship "special." When asked to define a best friend, Ken said, "Like I always know everything about him, I'm close with his family, he is close to my family." Farouk said when asked what makes him close to his best friend, "Um basically 'cause he knows my family, he knows my sisters, my mom, my dad. I know his mom, his dad, we know where we each other live." Armondo said, "If you know somebody's parents, then you know how far the trust can be stretched."

Best friends, who were rarely related by blood, were often referred to as brothers, sisters, or cousins. The African American and Latino adolescents incorporated their nonfamilial friendships into their family by considering their friends to be "fictive kin" (Stack, 1974). The integration of family and friends appeared to be both a way of being close with their friends as well as a context in which their close friendships were embedded. Making friends into fictive kin may create a safe space in which close friendships can thrive.

The Context of Distrust

The adolescents in my studies described a world in which friendships are not only possible but are key relationships in their lives. Their friendships are often the relationships about which they feel most passionate and for which they will go to great lengths to maintain over time. Yet these intimate friendships exist within a context of peers who will "try to take over you and take you for everything you've got and step on you." In response to a question about the other students in the school, Anthony said, "I don't trust [them], I trust me, myself, and I. That's the way I am. I trust nobody." Although across all the years of the study, he had a male best friend in whom he confided and to whom he felt close, his perceptions of his peers involved much mistrust. Richard said about his male peers, "Can't trust anybody nowadays. They are trying to scam you, or scheme, or talk about you." Richard admited that although he has never directly experienced these types of betrayals from his male peers, he "know[s] what most of [them] are like."

During the first- and second-year interviews, distrust seemed to be a cliché that the adolescents perpetuated among themselves but that did not truly represent their feelings about their peers. Yet, by the third- and fourth-year interviews, the adolescents' feelings of distrust seemed more genuine, as they described specific friends who betrayed them and thus led them to trust no one. Although stories of love and affection for close friends were still evident in these latter-year interviews, stories of betrayal and distrust began to dominate the interviews. The adolescents, particularly the boys, increasingly believed that there were fewer options for close same-sex friendships than when they were younger (see Way, 1998).

These distrustful beliefs about peers stemmed not only from actual experiences of betrayal and deceit but also from messages from parents or other family members. Ken said in his freshman year, "Can't trust nobody. That's what my mother always used to say." He claimed again in his sophomore year, "Can't trust everybody . . . basically my mother always told me, 'You gotta watch out who you hang out with.' After talking at length about her best friend and the trust she had with her, Anna said, "I think that since my mother always puts in my brain, like, don't trust anybody. Like that always stays in the back of my mind and I feel that I can't trust [my friends] – like I can't trust anybody because you never know when they are gonna turn on you." Consistent with theory and research on "social trust" that suggests that adults from disadvantaged and oppressed communities are often distrustful of others who are not from their communities (Smith, 1997; Uslaner, 2002), our data indicated that families of the adolescents often warned the adolescents about the dangers of trusting others, particularly those who were not part of their families.

Although both girls and boys reported distrusting their peers, there were gender differences regarding who they reported distrusting. Girls were more likely to indicate that their distrust was primarily, if not exclusively, of their female peers, whereas boys were more likely to indicate that they trusted neither boys nor girls. Girls, in fact, often spoke about how they could trust boys more than girls and seemed, at times, to idealize their friendships with boys. When asked to compare her male friendships with her female friendships, Monique said, "Well in a way I think I'm closer to guy friends than girls 'cause girls stab you in your back and you can't really talk to them that much because they spread rumors around about you." Anna said, "I prefer hanging out with guys because I think they won't talk about you . . . I only tell my best [female] friend like secrets and stuff but with boys it's like a friendship. Like we all go in groups to the movies and we hang out." Elizabeth said in her freshmen year:

> To me I feel more comfortable with the guys than the girls because the girls are like always talking about other girls. This girl did this, this girl did that. . . . The girls might talk about one certain girl that they can't stand or something and I might know her.

Elizabeth continued this theme in her sophomore-year interview:

> I get along with boys more because girls . . . like they are fake. . . . You're not yourself, it's like you're trying to be somebody you're not. You think you're too good for anybody. . . . A lot of girls are jealous 'cause of some stupid reason and they want to go and get all up in your face and they want to fight you and I don't want to go through that. So I'll just stay hanging out with the guys.

Mara said in her junior year:

> M: I find it easier to talk to guys... it's easier 'cause they don't talk much or sometimes you don't want people to give opinions or judge, you just want to tell someone and they always listen... you just have someone to tell and then they might give you advice. I find it easier to talk to guys...
>
> I: And who are your friends who are guys?
>
> M: Roger... we're not that close anymore and right now he asks me for homework and I don't talk to him much. Other guys are basically the same we don't really talk.
>
> I: But you find it easier to talk to guys?
>
> M: Yeah much easier. Girls are jealous. I hate jealousy.

The striking aspect of these narratives was that in the same breath that girls spoke about trusting boys more than girls, they spoke about their close relationships with their best *girl* friends and their lack of intimate communication with boys. Similar to the theme of distrust of peers, the girls appeared to maintain clichés or cultural scripts (see Tolman, 2002) about other girls, but these clichés or scripts did not appear to prevent them from maintaining close, intimate female friendships. Additionally, as is evident from Mara's comments, an idealization of boys did not typically result in close male friendships.

The theme of distrust of peers was pervasive among the adolescents and suggested that the cultural cliché that girls, in particular, are untrustworthy is rampant among urban adolescents. Yet, the striking element of these stories of distrust was that they were embedded in stories of close and trusting, nonfamilial, same-sex friendships. This pattern suggests a type of "relational resilience" (Way, 2004) in which adolescents continue to maintain healthy and supportive nonfamilial friendships despite the seemingly strong pressures from home (e.g., parents and siblings) and school (e.g., peers and teachers) to distrust others, particularly nonfamilial peers. This relational resilience was evident throughout the four years of the study, but particularly during late adolescence when adolescents reported both strong feelings of distrust of others and high levels of trust and closeness in their same-sex, nonfamilial friendships.

Friendships in Cultural Context

My research studies suggest that the practice of friendships among ethnically diverse, low-income, urban youth in the United States involves a multidimensional experience of trust, becomes more emotionally laden and complex over time, is embedded in a context of distrust of peers, and deteriorates over time with respect to perceptions of peers in general. Each theme reflects, in varying degrees, the adolescents' cultural communities. For the remainder of this chapter, I discuss the ways in which these themes may reflect the context in which they exist.

One of the most common themes heard in our studies was the importance of shared secrets in close friendships. The vast majority of boys and girls spoke about being able to or wanting to be able to share their secrets with their best friends. This emphasis among the boys and girls on intimate self-disclosure stands in stark contrast to the research on friendships with White, middle-class adolescents that suggests that girls are more likely than boys to value and have intimate self-disclosure in their friendships.

The lack of gender differences in my studies may be the result of high levels of intimacy in the friendships of ethnic minority boys, levels of intimacy that have been found to be higher than what has been reported by White adolescent boys (see DuBois & Hirsch, 1990; Jones et al., 1994). These high levels of intimacy may diminish the likelihood of gender differences among ethnic minority youth. The extent to which adolescents have intimate friendships is likely a reflection, at least in part, of the values and beliefs in their cultural communities. The boys in my studies are immersed in communities that value interdependency (Chao, 2000; Fuligni, Tseng, & Lam, 1999; Hines & Boyd-Franklin, 1990; Townsend, 1998) and are made acutely aware of the need for mutually supportive relationships. These value systems may increase the likelihood of self-disclosure and intimacy between friends, among both boys and girls. Although nonfamilial friendships may not be encouraged by family members (as is the case in my research), the relational skills acquired as a result of an interdependent value system may extend to relationships outside of the family.

In addition to sharing secrets, another important component of close friendships, particularly among the boys, was the ability to "share money." Adolescents from all of the ethnic groups in my studies indicated that being able to loan and borrow money is a critical aspect of why they trust their best friends. This theme has not been noted with middle-class adolescents. Like shared secrets, the emphasis on shared money is likely a response to the context in which the adolescents live. Communities in which money and material items are not as readily available as in more affluent communities may lead the members of the former communities to place more value on the ability to exchange this commodity than the latter communities. It is not clear, however, why the theme of shared money was more evident in the boys' interviews than in the girls or why the theme was less evident as the adolescent grew older. Loaning or borrowing money may be another way, in addition to physical protection in fights, for boys to feel protected or to protect friends, and protecting friends may be particularly important in urban, low-income communities. This reliance, however, on material proof of their friends' support may become less necessary as boys and girls enter late adolescence and focus more on the emotional elements of their friendships. These findings underscore the importance of considering the immediate cultural context (i.e., the urban, low-income community) in the stories of friendships but also the intersection of the cultural and developmental contexts.

Receiving and providing protection from physical and emotional harm was another important component of close friendships for the boys. The importance of protection in the friendships of children and adolescents has been noted previously (Azmitia, Kamprath, & Linnet, 1996), and is typically considered more important in boys' friendships than in girls' friendships (see Youniss & Smollar, 1985). The importance of protection in the friendships of urban adolescent boys, in particular, has also been discussed by other researchers (e.g., Cunningham, 2004). Yet the ways in which these boys' experience of protection is shaped by the cultural context in which it occurs is rarely discussed. *Providing* "protection" is consistent with conventions of mainstream masculinity; thus, in some ways, it was not surprising that we detected this theme in interviews of the adolescent boys. The boys' emphasis on *receiving* protection from their friends, however, is often associated with the needs and desires of girls and women (Kimmel, 2004); thus, it was surprising that so many of the boys underscored both providing and receiving protection from their friends. In contrast to the image of the autonomous and "skill-oriented" boy evident in much of the theory and research on adolescent boys, the boys in my studies strongly valued their *mutually dependent* relationships with their male friends.

Similar to the findings regarding shared secrets, the emphasis on mutual dependency in the friendships of urban, ethnic minority adolescent boys may reflect the interdependent or relationally oriented communities from which these boys came. African American, Latino, and Asian American and low-income communities may produce adolescent boys who are more likely to articulate the importance of/or, perhaps, truly value interdependent relationships than boys raised in more autonomy focused European American and middle-class communities. These findings suggest ways in which the values and beliefs in communities may shape the social and emotional development of adolescents.

My interview data also suggest that providing and receiving help with daily tasks enhances feelings of trust and closeness among friends. The importance of providing instrumental aid has been noted throughout the friendship research (see Savin-Williams & Berndt, 1990). Although this theme was evident for all of the adolescents in my studies, the content of this help appeared to vary by ethnicity. The Asian American youth were the only adolescents who emphasized homework assistance as one of the primary ways in which they connected with their friends. This pattern underscores the importance of examining the content of a particular pattern because it may be precisely in the content where variation across cultural communities may be found. Had I only examined the frequency of providing and receiving assistance (e.g., through survey methods) I would not have detected ethnic differences across adolescents. By looking at the content of this pattern, however, I was able to detect cultural nuance among the adolescents.

Strikingly, the Asian American youth also indicated that "shared secrets" and "shared money" were important in their close friendships. The differences and similarities between the Asian American youth and the African American or Latino youth point to the ways in which youth are simultaneously immersed in various cultural communities based on their age, ethnicity, gender, urban location, and low-income status. Some of these communities are shared (e.g., youth, urban location, and low-income status) among all of the adolescents in my studies and others are not (e.g., gender or ethnicity/race).

The fifth and final theme related to the experience of trust and closeness was the integration of family and friends. Nonfamilial friends became family members among the African American and Latino youth because their family members knew these nonfamilial friends. The theme of fictive kinship in African American communities has been written about extensively (Hines & Boyd-Franklin, 1990; Stack, 1974; Townsend, 1998). What has been rarely explored, however, is why fictive kinships may flourish in certain cultural communities and not others. Why, for example, is this blending of family and nonfamilial friends only evident among the African American and Latino youth and not the Asian American youth? The absence of this theme among the Asian Americans in my studies may be due to multiple factors, including the employment patterns of the low-income Asian American parents, which often consisted of factory or restaurant jobs, that left little time for the parents to be at home with their children or to "get to know" their children's friends. In addition, the Asian American youth in my studies were more likely than their African American and Latino peers to report being discouraged by their parents from spending time with their friends outside of school (unless they were doing their homework). This discouragement may decrease the opportunities to blend friends with family. Like the theme of helping with daily tasks, it is the absence and presence of a particular theme such as "fictive kinship" that helps to elucidate the context of this theme.

Strikingly, the close friendships of the adolescents in my studies were embedded in a context of distrust of peers. Although most of the adolescents had close and intimate friendships, they typically described their peers as untrustworthy and deceitful and their negative feelings grew in intensity over time. Reasons for this mistrust may lie with the experiences of racism and harassment that haunt the daily lives of urban, low-income, ethnic minority youth (see Rosenbloom & Way, 2004). Feelings of distrust may also emanate from the urban school context in which principals, teachers, and students distrust one another in a low-resource environment where stress levels are high and rewards are few (Epstein, 1983). Much has been written about the ways in which contexts with few resources and high levels of discrimination, stress, and anxiety often produce low levels of social trust among adults (Smith, 1997). The same processes that are evident among adults may also be true of adolescents.

Yet, what was remarkable about this pattern of distrust was that it did not prevent close, trusting nonfamilial friendships from flourishing. The adolescents seemed resilient in their ability to maintain friendships in the midst of numerous messages from family members and peers discouraging nonfamilial friendships and their own feelings of distrust. It may be that the pattern of fictive kinship in African American and Latino communities allows adolescents to cross the barrier of mistrust between familial and non-familial relationships and maintain close, nonfamilial friendships. A cultural norm such as fictive kinship may provide adolescents with strategies of resistance to another norm, such as that "you can't trust anyone" who is not a family member. These findings suggest that adolescents are not only recipients of cultural norms but are also active participants in their own development who are accommodating these cultural norms to meet their needs and desires (e.g., to have close relationships with nonfamilial friends).

The interview data also suggested that both girls and boys perceive boys to be more trustworthy than girls. This finding is most likely a product, at least in part, of gender-based stereotypes. One of the most pervasive stereotypes of girls in American culture, particularly adolescent girls, is that they are "catty," "mean," and will betray others (Horn, 2004; Underwood, 2003). The girls and boys in my studies have absorbed the implicit but not necessarily explicit assumption of the stereotype of the "mean girl," which suggests that boys are more trustworthy than girls. Yet, what is striking about my findings is that the adolescent girls continue to maintain close friendships with girls and do not maintain close, nonromantic friendships, for the most part, with boys. These findings reveal, once again, the ways in which adolescents (the girls in this particular case) are shaped by cultural norms and also resist cultural norms. The girls' ability to hold on to their close friendships with other girls despite the tremendous pressures to distrust girls and to trust boys more than girls speaks to the ways in which girls are active agents in their own socialization.

Finally, findings with respect to changes over time suggest that just as cultural contexts influence the practice of friendships, so too does the developmental context. For example, as adolescents grew older, they experienced more emotionally complex friendships and they also grew more wary and cautious of their peers over time. The increase over time in both trust and distrust suggests that the development of friendships for the adolescents involves gains and losses – gains in emotional complexity and intimacy in friendships and losses of faith in peers in general. It is likely that the gains are the result of, at least in part, cognitive maturity during adolescence. The reasons for the losses, however, are less clear. An increase in cognitive maturity may correspond with a harsher, and perhaps more realistic, view of the world. In addition, as urban, low-income, ethnic minority adolescents grow older, they may experience more discrimination (see Rosenbloom & Way, 2004) and these experiences may significantly decrease their trust in others. These findings underscore the importance of examining both the cultural and developmental contexts of adolescents.

My studies over the past fifteen years have sought to understand the practice of friendships among urban, low-income adolescents. Some of the themes evident in the my studies are evident across different cultural contexts, including the context of the White, American, middle-class (e.g., the importance of shared secrets among girls, the importance of protection among boys, the importance of giving and receiving assistance for boys and girls), whereas others appear to be themes that are unique to urban low-income adolescents (e.g., the importance of shared money). Furthermore, there were similarities and differences among the urban adolescents in my studies. These similarities and differences underscore the importance of exploring the cultural context of friendships and the ways in which adolescents are a part of multiple cultural communities or contexts simultaneously.

My research with urban youth raises numerous questions for future research including the ways in which cultural communities, in addition to those examined in my studies shape and are shaped by the practice of friendships among adolescents. For example how might the practice of friendships look different for those who attend small schools that focus on the students' social, emotional, and academic development than for those who attend large schools that focus primarily on the students' academic development? These types of investigations are important for furthering our understanding of how and in what ways friendships are culturally bound. To advance our knowledge of how culture and human development are intimately linked, we need to apply a cultural lens to the study of relationships. Conceptualizing and examining adolescent friendships, in particular, as a form of cultural practice is an important step toward this larger goal.

Acknowledgments

Thank you to the National Science Foundation, the National Institute of Mental Health, and the William T. Grant Foundation for their financial support of my studies on friendships among urban adolescents. Thank you as well to the graduate students who have assisted me in my research, particularly Kerstin Pahl, Susan Rosenbloom, Rachel Gingold, Geena Kuriakose, Joanna Sattin, and Esther Marron. Parts of this chapter have been previously published (Way, 2004; Way et al., 2005).

References

Aboud, F., & Mendelson, M. (1996). Determinants of friendship selection and quality: Developmental perspectives. In W. Bukowski & A. Newcomb (Eds.), *The company they keep: Friendship in childhood and adolescences*. Cambridge studies in social and emotional development (pp. 87–112). New York: Cambridge University Press.

Adler, P., & Adler, P. (1997). *Peer power: Preadolescent culture and identity*. New Brunswick, NJ: Rutgers University Press.

Azmitia, M., Kamprath, N., & Linnet, J. (1996). Intimacy and conflict: The dynamics of boys' and girls' friendships during middle childhood and early adolescence. In L. Meyer, H. Park, M. Genot-Scheyer, I. Schwarz, & B. Harry (Eds.), *Making friends: The influences of culture and development* (pp. 225–241). Baltimore: Brookes.

Belle, D. (1989). Gender differences in children's social networks and supports. In D. Belle (Ed.), *Children's social networks and social supports* (pp. 173–188). New York: Wiley.

Brown, B., & Klute, C. (2003). Friendships, cliques, and crowds. In G. Adams & M. Berzonsky (Eds.), *Blackwell handbook of adolescence* (pp. 330–348). Malden, MA: Blackwell.

Brown, C., & Gilligan, C. (1992). *Meeting at the Crossroads*. Cambridge: Harvard University Press.

Buhrmester, D., & Furman, W. (1987). The development of companionship and intimacy. *Child Development*, *58*, 1101–1113.

Bukowski, W. M., Newcomb, A. F., & Hartup, W. (Eds.) (1996). *The company they keep: Friendship in childhood and adolescence*. Cambridge, England: Cambridge University Press.

Chao, R. (2000). Cultural explanations for the role of parenting in the school success of Asian American children. In R. Taylor & M. Wang (Eds.), *Resilience across contexts: Family, work, culture, and community* (pp. 333–363). Mahwah, NJ: Lawrence Erlbaum Associates.

Chen, X., Kaspar, V., Zhang, Y., Wang. L., & Zheng, S. (2004). Peer relationships among Chinese and North American boys: A cross-cultural perspective. In N. Way & J. Chu (Eds.), *Adolescent boys in context* (pp. 197–218). New York: New York University Press.

Corsaro, W., & Eder, D. (1990). Children's peer cultures. *Annual Review of Sociology, 16*, 197–220.

Cunningham, M., & Menier, L. (2004). The influence of peer experience, an bravado attitude, among African American males. In N. Way & J. Chu (Eds.), Adolescent Boys Explory Diverse cultures of boyhood. New York: New York University Press.

DuBois, D. L., & Hirsch, B. J. (1990). School and neighborhood friendship patterns of blacks and whites in early adolescence. *Child Development, 61*, 524–536.

Epstein, J. (1989). The selection of friend, changes across the grades & in different school environments. In I. Berdut & G. Ladid (Eds.). *Peer relationships in child development*. Oxford, England: John Wiley & Sons.

Fuligni, A., Tseng, V., & Lam, M. (1999). Attitudes toward family obligations among American adolescents with Asian, Latin American, and European backgrounds. *Child Development, 70*, 1030–1044.

Furman, W., & Buhrmester, D. (1985). Children's perceptions of the personal relationships in their social networks. *Developmental Psychology, 21*, 1016–1024.

Goodwin, M. (1990) *He-said-she said: Talk as social organization among Black children*. Bloomington: Indiana University Press.

Hamm, J. (1994). Negotiating the maze: Adolescents' cross-ethnic peer relations in ethnically diverse schools. In L. Meyer, H. Park, M. Genot-Scheyer, I. Schwarz, & B. Harry (Eds.), *Making friends: The influences of culture and development* (pp. 225–241). Baltimore: Brookes.

Hamm. J., & Faircloth, B. (2004). The role of friendship in adolescents' sense of school belonging. In N. Way & J. Hamm (Eds.), *The experience of close friendships among adolescents*. Thousand Oaks, CA: Sage.

Harkness, S., & Super, C. (2002) Culture and parenting. In M. Bornsetin (Ed.), *Handbook of parenting* (pp. 253–280). Mahwah, NJ: Lawrence Erlbaum Associates.

Hartup, W. (1993). Adolescents and their friends. In B. Larsen (Ed.), *Close friendships in adolescence* (pp. 3–22). San Francisco: Jossey-Bass.

Harwood, R., Miller, J., & Irizarry (1995) *Culture and attachment: Perceptions of the child in context*. New York: Guilford Press.

Hines, P., & Boyd-Franklin, N. (1990). Black families. In M. McGoldric, J. McPearce, & J. Giordano (Eds.), *Ethnicity in family therapy* (pp. 84–107). New York: Guilford Press.

Horn, S. (2004) Mean girls or cultural stereotypes? Essay review of social aggresssioin among girls by Marion Underwood. *Human Development, 47*, 314–320.

Jones, D. C., & Costin, S. E. (1997, April). *The friendships of African-American and European-American adolescents: An examination of gender and ethnic differences.*

Paper presented at the Society for Research on Child Development, Washington, DC.

Jones, D. C., Costin, S. E., & Ricard, R. J. (1994, February). *Ethnic and sex differences in best-friendship characteristics among African American, Mexican American, and European American adolescents*. Poster session presented at the meeting of the Society for Research on Adolescents, San Diego, CA.

Rogoff, B., & Angelillo, C. (2002). How can we study cultural aspects of human development? *Human Development*, *45*, 211–226.

Rosenbloom, S., & Way, N. (2004). Experiences of discrimination among African American, Asian American, and Latino Adolescents in an urban high school. *Journal of Youth and Society*.

Savin-Williams, R. C., & Berndt, T. J. (1990). Friendship and peer relations. In S. Feldman & G. R. Elliot (Eds.), *At the threshold: The developing adolescent*. (pp. 227–307). Cambridge, MA: Harvard University Press.

Smith, T. (1997). Factors related to misanthropy in contemporary American society. *Social Science Research*, *26*, 170–196.

Stack, C. (1974). *All our kin: Strategies for survival in a black community*. New York: Harper and Row.

Sullivan, H. S. (1953). *The interpersonal theory of psychiatry*. New York: Norton.

Tolman, D. (2002). *Dilemmas of desire: Teenage girls talk about sexuality*. Cambridge, MA: Harvard University Press.

Townsend, B. L. (1998). Social friendships and networks among African American children and youth. In L. Meyer, H. Park, M. Genot-Scheyer, I. Schwarz, & B. Harry (Eds.), *Making friends: The influences of culture and development* (pp. 225–241). Baltimore: Brookes.

Underwood, M. (2003). *Social aggression among girls*. New York: Guilford Press.

Uslaner, E. M. (2002). *The moral foundations of trust*. Cambridge, England: Cambridge University Press.

Way, N. (1995). "Can't you hear the strength and courage that I have?": Listening to urban adolescent girls speak about their relationships with peers and parents. *The Psychology of Women Quarterly, 19*, 107–128.

Way, N. (1998). *Everyday courage: The lives and stories of urban teenagers*. New York: New York University Press.

Way, N. (2004). Intimacy, Desire, & Dishust in the Friendship of Adolescent Boys. In N. Way & J. Chu (Eds.). *Adolescent Boys: Exploring diverse culture of boyhood*. New York: New York University Press.

Way, N. (2005). Friendship, among African American, Latino, & Asian American adolescents. In N. Way & J. Hamm (Eds.). *The experience of close friendships among adolescents*. New Directions for Child and Adolescent Development N. 17. San Francisco, CA: Jassey-Boss.

Way, N., & Chen, L. (2000). The characteristics, quality, and correlates of friendships among African American, Latino, and Asian American Adolescents. *Journal of Adolescent Research*, *15*, 274–301.

Way, N., & Greene, M. (In press). Changes in perceived friendship quality Jossey-Bass San Francisco from early to late adolescense. *Journal of Research on Adolescense*.

Way, N., & Pahl, K. (1999). Friendship patterns among urban adolescents boys: A qualitative account. In M. Kopala & L. Suzuki (Eds), *Using Qualitative methods in psychology* (pp. 145–162). Thousand Oaks, CA: Sage.

Way, N., & Pahl, K. (2001). Individual & contextual predictors of friendship quality among ethnic minority, low-income adolescents. *Journal of Research on Adolescence, 11*, 325–349.

Weiss, R. S. (1974). The provisions of social relationships. In Z. Rubin (Ed.), *Doing unto others* (pp. 17–26). Englewood Cliffs, NJ: Prentice Hall.

Youniss, J., & Smollar, J. (1985). *Adolescent relations with mothers, fathers, and friends.* Chicago: University of Chicago Press.

19 Latino-Heritage Adolescents' Friendships

Margarita Azmitia, Angela Ittel, and Charlotte Brenk

In the last few decades, culture has taken center stage in developmental psychology. Increased attention to culture has led to lively debates not only about the meanings and nuances of culture, but also about the meanings and nuances of ethnicity, gender, class, and other aspects of culture that play a role in development. Two of the issues under debate that have influenced our research on Latino-heritage adolescents' friendships are (a) whether and how universal and culture-specific developmental processes and outcomes can be identified and (b) how these potential universal and culture-specific processes and outcomes can be explained and integrated in developmental theory and research. In this chapter, we focus on ethnicity and how this aspect of culture contextualizes the friendships of Latino-heritage adolescents living in the United States.

Identifying, describing, and explaining between and within ethnic group similarities and variations in developmental processes and outcomes has been challenging because culture and ethnicity are fuzzy, contextual, and fluid constructs (Betancourt & Lopez, 1993; Gjerde, 2004; Phinney & Landin, 1998). Yet, we want to use our research to draw some conclusions and build theories that contain some general statements about these between- and within-cultural similarities and variations. In attempting to attain these goals, we have tried to avoid falling prey to using culture or ethnicity as empty, overgeneralizing, stereotyping concepts that lead us to construct developmental stories and theories that apply to no one in the cultural communities we are studying. We have also considered that the "story" may vary, depending on the domain of development we are investigating, with some domains showing more between- and within-ethnic-group similarities and variations than other domains.

Over the last 15 years, we have interviewed and surveyed adolescents about their ideas about friendship, their friendship experiences, and their views about how these friendship ideas and experiences intersect with their ideas and experiences in other relationship contexts, in particular, family and school, and their goals for the future. We have also assessed the association between adolescents' friendship ideas and experiences and their academic performance and mental health.

Our chapter has three parts. We first briefly review theory and research on the cultural context of development, paying special attention to ethnicity. We then present a brief description of the history and characteristics of Latinos living in the United States and the factors that contribute to shared values, concerns, goals, and practices, as well as the heterogeneity of this ethnic group. These two sections set the stage for the heart of our chapter, theory and research on Latino-heritage adolescents' friendships. In this third section, we address both similarities and differences in Latino-heritage adolescents' friendships and those of other adolescents living in the United States. Our primary contrast group is middle-class European-heritage adolescents because they have been the primary participants in research on adolescents' friendships and therefore served as the foundation of developmental theories of the characteristics, processes, and significance of these relationships.

Culture and Adolescent Development

Developmental psychologists have long called for theories and studies of adolescents' development that highlight both universal characteristics that cut across cultures and contexts as well as the unique particularities that derive from adolescents' cultural, historical, and social positioning (e.g., Cooper, 1999; Fisher, Jackson, & Villarruel, 1998; Galambos & Leadbeater, 2000; Edwards et al., this volume, Szapocznik & Kurtines, 1993, Way, this volume). One of the challenges we face as we design, carry out, and interpret research that answers their call is that the theoretical constructs that are currently available to address similarities and differences in cultural orientations and socialization practices and goals are themselves contested to the point that some scholars have questioned their utility. A case in point concerns the *individualism (independence)* and *collectivism (interdependence)* framework (Markus & Kitayama, 1991; Triandis, 1995) that has often been used to contrast the values, beliefs, relationships, and practices of European-heritage versus other ethnic-heritage groups in the United States and between the United States and other countries. As Gjerde (2004), Greenfield (1994), Killen (1997), and many others have argued, much of the research that has been carried out within the theoretical umbrella of this framework not only stereotypes cultures, but also conceptualizes them as static.

There are also important methodological concerns about research within the individualism–collectivism framework. In a recent meta-analyses of this research, Oyserman, Coon, and Kemmelmeier (2002) concluded that differences in the ways that individualism and collectivism have been operationalized and measured not only make it difficult to compare across studies, but have also weakened the empirical base for the claim of between-culture differences in the values, beliefs, concerns, goals, and practices associated with individualism and collectivism. In their conclusion, Oyserman et al. propose that researchers who use this framework to inform their work should also be more careful about specifying how values and beliefs about individualism and collectivism are expressed in cultural communities' everyday practices and consider the historical and contextual situatedness of these constructs. In our research, we have tried to follow their suggestions.

Gjerde (personal communication, October 14, 2002) has argued that even when researchers try to ensure the cross-cultural equivalence of their measures of interdependence and interdependence or of whatever other theoretical model they are employing, they can never be completely sure that the participants from different cultural communities define the constructs that are being studied in the same way, for example, that Latino- and European-heritage adolescents have similar conceptualizations of friendship intimacy. We would propose, however, that this argument can be made about any study that involves more than one participant, regardless of their cultural origin. Indeed, this is one of the arguments that has been advanced by researchers who favor a hermaneutic over a positivist approach to psychological research. As Tappan and Brown (1991) argued, however, an extreme hermaneutic perspective is of limited utility to developmental psychology because it would lead to developmental stories that are as numerous as the number of participants in our research. Certainly, each participant has his or her own unique story, but commonalities in the human experience ensure that there are also many shared elements in these developmental stories.

Despite growing awareness of its limitations, the collectivism (interdependence)–individualism(individualism) framework continues to be widely used in theoretical and empirical work on a variety of developmental domains, including adolescents' friendships and peer relationships. In our view, this framework continues to dominate, at least in part, because critiques and alternative proposals have seldom been accompanied by a concrete research agenda that allows us to move between descriptions of particular communities and developmental processes to address issues of generalization and broader theoretical concerns. More importantly, the collectivism–individualism framework continues to be used because with some caution, it *can* be useful for framing and interpreting research on adolescents' frameworks. For example, French et al. (2001) showed that, with careful attention to the operationalization and cross-cultural validation of scales that measure interdependent and independent orientations to friendship processes, this framework was useful for characterizing similarities and differences in the friendships of U.S. (relatively more individualistic) and Indonesian (relatively more collectivistic) children and early adolescents.

In our own research, we have investigated how *familism*, a construct that has been used to characterize Latino-heritage families' interdependent orientation (Sabogal Marin et al., 1987), is reflected in Latino adolescents' family and peer relationships and educational pathways. However, like Greenfield (1994) and many others, we assume that all cultural communities have values, concerns, goals, and practices that reflect independence *and* interdependence. Indeed, as Grotevant and Cooper (1986) proposed, an important relational task of adolescence is to learn to coordinate individuality and connectedness to others, a coordination captured by their concept of *individuation*. Nevertheless, we recognize that, although individuation may be universal, the particular versions of individuality and connectedness socialized and practiced by different cultural communities may vary depending on the relationship, domain, and context as well as the overall cultural beliefs and practices concerning independence and interdependence endorsed by the members of particular cultural communities at particular historical times and developmental periods (see also Fuligni, 1998).

Culturally shared and unique beliefs and practices about individuality and connectedness were evident in our study of the moral and educational goals of low-income Latino- and European-heritage families living in two small cities in central California (Azmitia et al., 1996). We found that, although both groups of families shared similar educational and moral goals, the ways in which they practiced and socialized these goals varied in ways that reflected differences in their relative emphasis on individuality and connectedness. For example, as a group low-income European-heritage parents were more likely than low-income Latino-heritage parents to view their adolescent children's academic performance as reflecting primarily their children's intelligence and study habits and only secondarily the parents' role in supporting their children's academic activities. In contrast, as a group, Latino-heritage parents viewed their children's academic performance as equally reflective of their children's abilities and behaviors and the family's emphasis and involvement in their schooling. Indeed, several parents remarked that their children's grades and behavior at school reflected on the whole family (Azmitia et al., 1996; Cooper et al., 1994).

Reese et al. (1995) have suggested that Latino-heritage families view their children's performance at school as reflective of their parenting because they conceptualize a person's education, *educación*, as including academic performance and the moral values and behaviors that are learned in their family. When their children move into adolescence and begin to want to spend more time with their friends, parents begin to worry that their children's friends may undermine their families' values. Thus, it is not surprising that Latino-heritage parents try to restrict their adolescent children's access to friends. Several of the Mexican-heritage families who participated in our longitudinal study of the role of family, friends, and school in adolescents' transition to junior high school indicated that if their children developed friendships they disapproved of or began straying from the good path of life, *el buen camino de la vida*, they would send them to Mexico to live with relatives. This potential strategy was less common in the interviews of Central American-heritage parents, perhaps because their countries did not border California (and thus, it would be much harder to send a child to live with relatives) and perhaps because many were refugees from the political strife and violence that has long plagued many Central American nations and motivated Central American families to come to the United States.

Before proceeding with further discussion of Latino-heritage families and their adolescent children's friendships, to help readers contextualize our points, we will briefly describe the four studies that provide the basis for this chapter. For the last 15 years, we have carried out studies of the role of family, peers, and school contexts in ethnically diverse children and adolescents' developmental and academic trajectories. Four of these studies were the primary sources for the present chapter. The first study, carried out in collaboration with Catherine Cooper, investigated the roles of family, peers, and school in Latino- and European-heritage adolescents' transition from elementary school to junior high school. Some of the Latino-heritage adolescents who participated in this study were members of a local academic outreach program. Through Catherine Cooper's partnership with that program, we were able to follow them through high school (Azmitia & Cooper, 1996, 2002). The second study, carried out in collaboration with Kate McLean, Erica Hoy, and Kim Radmacher, was a cross-sectional study of the roles of family, peers, and the school in ethnically diverse adolescents' transition and adjustment to junior high school and college (McLean, 2003; Radmacher & Azmitia, 2004; Reis et al., 2005). The third study, a collaboration with Catherine Cooper, Jacquelyn Jackson, Edward Lopez, Nora Dunbar, and Gabriela Chavira, involved a cross-sectional and longitudinal follow-up of Latino- and African-heritage adolescents participating in academic outreach programs and their pathways to higher education (Cooper et al., 1998; 2002). The fourth study, currently in progress, is a longitudinal study of the roles of adolescents' family, peers, school context, identity, and mental health in ethnically diverse adolescents' transition and adjustment to college (Azmitia et al., in progress).

All four studies combine quantitative analyses of surveys and interview responses, with qualitative analyses of the corpus of data generated by particular adolescents and, in the case of the first study, their parents. This multimethod approach allows us to avoid overinterpreting the between-ethnic-group differences that have emerged from inferential statistical analyses employing analysis of variance, *t* tests, or chi-square tests. As noted by Matsumoto, Grissom, and Dinnel (2001), emphasizing between-cultural-group differences can obscure large within-group variations (see also Way, this volume). In our study of early adolescent Latino- and European-heritage adolescents' transition to junior high school, this multimethod approach revealed, for example, that although as a group Latino-heritage early adolescents had statistically significantly higher scores than European-heritage early adolescents on a measure of friends' discouragement of academic performance, this between-ethnic-group difference was the result of Latino-heritage boys' significantly higher friend academic discouragement scores (i.e., the ethnicity x gender interaction was statistically significant). However, in-depth analyses of the interviews of Latino early adolescent boys with high scores of academic discouragement by friends revealed that not all of their friends discouraged their school work and that, for some boys, it was their own disengagement from school that led them to seek out similarly minded friends, a finding that is consistent with the selective association process of peer influence (Berndt, 1996).

Culturally informed theory and research on adolescent development also needs to address issues concerning the level of analysis. As Neill Korobov (personal communication, October 11, 2004) noted, if one uses a sufficiently broad lens to study different cultural communities, such as asking research participants about their values and beliefs about individualism and collectivism, one is more likely to find differences than if one asks about and observes specific cultural practices indicative of these values and beliefs. For example, although Mexican-, Filipino-, and Chinese-heritage adolescents are more likely than European-heritage adolescents to endorse the belief that adolescents should obey and respect their elders, in practice, only immigrant adolescents from these cultural communities exhibit less parent–adolescent conflict than European-heritage adolescents, a behavioral practice that indexes this belief (Fuligni, 1998).

Another reason for within-cultural community differences in beliefs and practices is that individuals often vary in their endorsement, prioritization, and execution of these beliefs and practices (Gjerde, 2004; Goodnow, 1992). For example, while as a group Mexican-heritage parents expect their adolescent children to help with chores because chores signal family interdependence and obligation, some Mexican-heritage families prioritize chores and other family obligations over school tasks and other relatively more individualistic activities (Valdés, 1996) while others prioritize school tasks over chores such that when their children are busy with school tasks, they do the chores themselves (Azmitia et al., 1996). Similarly, although as a group the Latino-heritage families who have participated in our research share the concern that peers will derail their children's progress along the good (*vis-à-vis* morality, education) path of life, they differ in the degree to which they restrict their adolescents' access to friends (Azmitia & Brown, 2002).

Globalization and immigration further complicate theory and research on Latino-heritage adolescents' friendships and peer relationships because they promote the cultural exchange that now has become more the rule than the exception. That is, in the United States, members of particular cultural communities frequently come into contact with the values, beliefs, and practices of other cultural communities (Szapocznik & Kurtines, 1993). As they construct their identities, adolescents, in particular, experience other cultures through sampling various modes of media (Arnett, 2002) or, for immigrants, joining the schools and peer cultures of their new communities. Thus, over time, immigrant adolescents may come to share many of the values, beliefs, concerns, and practices of their host communities (Fuligni, 1998; Phinney, Ong, & Madden, 2000).

Research has consistently shown that participants' generation of immigration plays an important role in between- and within-cultural differences in Latino-heritage adolescents' values, attitudes, and behaviors. Numerous studies have shown that within three generations, despite retaining an allegiance to their home culture, Latino-heritage adolescents exhibit a predominant orientation to American culture, even in values, attitudes, and behaviors that are often used to characterize Latinos, such as family interdependence or *familism* (Fuligni, 1998; Perez & Padilla, 2000). Research specifically focused on peer relationships and processes has also revealed this generational pattern. Umana-Taylor and Bámaca-Gomez (2003) found, for example, that by the third generation, Mexican-heritage adolescents' degree of resistance to peer pressure mirrored the patterns obtained in research with European-heritage adolescents. Thus, rather than assuming that we will find large between-cultural differences in the friendships of Latino- and European-heritage adolescents, we must first ask: Differences in what? And for which adolescents? And for which periods of adolescent development? Then we must try to tell a more complicated story that not only informs theory, but productively directs future research. That is, to borrow Whiting's (1976) term, we must *unpackage* Latino peer culture.

The three questions we posed above as a first step toward unpackaging Latino peer cultures stem from our view, shared by many developmental psychologists, that ethnicity and ethnic group membership should not be reified. As Phinney (1996) noted, although ethnic categories have helped us discuss and study the cultural context of development, they are arbitrary and fluid and located in particular historical time, communities, situational contexts, and individuals. That is, ethnic categories are "social constructions rather than natural entities that are simply 'out there' in the world" (Waters & Eschbach, 1995, p. 421).

The salience of ethnicity in adolescents' identities also varies across historical time, communities, situational contexts, and individuals. For example, adolescents' awareness of ethnicity varies depending on whether they are the majority or minority in a particular context, for example, school, and whether other aspects of identity (e.g., gender, social class) are more salient. Thus, as Uba (1994), Yeh and Hwang (2000), and Hurtado and Gurin (2004) have shown, ethnic identity development does not only involve individuals' consciousness of their ethnic origins – their knowledge of their ethnic group's customs, beliefs, and behavioral norms – and their adoption and expression of this knowledge in their everyday lives, but also the unconscious or conscious inhibition of ethnic schemas in favor of other identities (e.g., gender, social class) in particular contexts or periods of adolescents' lives. Before discussing whether and how ethnicity contextualizes Latino-heritage adolescents' friendships, we provide a historical context for our work by briefly reviewing the history and characteristics of Latinos living in the United States.

History and Characteristics of Latinos Living in the United States

Latinos are comprised of various cultural and ethnic subgroups and are the largest ethnic minority group in the United States. Because of historical reasons, however, up until recently, most research on ethnic variations in adolescents' friendships had been focused on European- and African-heritage adolescents. As attention to Latino-heritage youth has increased, researchers have become aware of the heterogeneity of groups that are classified as Latino. There are four primary sources of this heterogeneity: (1) *country of origin*, with Latinos including individuals of Mexican-, Central

American-, Cuban-, Dominican-, Puerto Rican-, and South American-heritage; (2) *generation of immigration*, with immigrants showing different endorsement of values and behavioral practices than subsequent generations; (3) *socioeconomic status (SES),* which plays a role in the segment of U.S. society that Latino subgroups come into contact with and thus, leads to SES differences in conceptualizations of what it means to be Latino and what it means to be American (e.g., living in inner-city south-central Los Angeles presents a different image of American culture than living in Hollywood, a much wealthier, safer, and ethnically homogenous section of Los Angeles); and (4) *geographical location*, which plays a role in the density of Latinos relative to other ethnic groups as well as in the nature of the community. For example, being Mexican may result in different patterns of acculturation and assimilation in the West, in which Mexican-heritage families have long been the largest ethnic minority group, than the Midwest, where Mexican-heritage families are an increasing presence. Also, Latino parents and adolescents face different challenges and have different resources in an agricultural community than in a large urban center.

Latino adolescents' self-labels are one indication of variations in their identification with the values, beliefs, concerns, attributions, and behavioral practices associated with being Latino. For example, the label Chicano identifies U.S.-born Mexican-descent adolescents who are part of a movement that began in the 1970s which sees ethnicity as a source of pride and whose members seek to return to their Aztec roots. On average, adolescents who label themselves as Mexican American feel more positive about assimilating to American culture than adolescents who self-label themselves as Chicano or Chicana (Hurtado & Gurin, 2004).

Adolescents' self-labels can change as a result of experiences that prompt identity work. For example, in our longitudinal study of Latino-heritage adolescents' transition to college (Azmitia et al., in progress), we have found that some adolescents who self-identified as Mexican American when they were interviewed in the fall of their first year of college self-identified as Chicano in the interviews that took place in the spring quarter of that first year and the spring quarter of their sophomore year. One such participant attributed her identity transformation to the powerful, enlightening experiences she had in her Introduction to Feminism course (one of the most popular courses in our campus). She noted that this course had opened her eyes to the historical experiences of Latinas in the United States, and she wanted to learn more about her roots and the ways that she could effect positive social change in her cultural and home community. She added that her new self-definition had caused friction between her and some of her friends, who she viewed as being in denial about their downtrodden status in the United States, and her family, who worried that her views about Latinos and Latinas would limit her chances of finding a husband. This example not only illustrates developmental changes in ethnic identity over time, but also the intersection of ethnicity with other domains of identity, and in this case, gender and relationships.

Increasingly, scholars have argued for the need to move beyond considering ethnicity in isolation toward considering its intersection with other dimensions of social identity, such as gender and social class. Although the emphasis on the intersectionality of social identities is fairly new in developmental psychology, it has a long theoretical and empirical history in sociology, feminism, and social psychology (Hurtado & Gurin, 2004; Bettie, 2002; Willis, 1977; Stewart & McDermott, 2004). As Bettie and Willis showed, some of the between-ethnic-group differences adolescents' peer relationships and friendships may be located in social class and not ethnicity. For example, Willis' classic study of working-class adolescent boys in Great Britain revealed that these boys' disengagement from school reflected their view that school discriminated against them and that, even if they graduated from high school, their social class would limit their career opportunities. Similar peer pressures for choosing vocational tracks or devaluing or disengaging from school have been observed for low-income Latino-, African-, and European-heritage adolescents living in the United States (Delgado-Gaitán, 1986; Eckert, 1989; Fordham & Ogbu, 1986). Although these findings highlight the importance of considering social class in studies of between- and within-ethnic similarities and differences in adolescents' peer relationships, attention to social class should not replace attention to ethnicity. For Latino-heritage adolescents and other adolescents of color, ethnicity and social class are intertwined because others make attributions about them based on the color of their skin or other physical attributes. In our study of the transition to college, for example, several middle- and upper-class Latino- and African-heritage adolescents said that university staff, professors, classmates, and friends usually automatically assumed that they came from poor, inner-city, or rural backgrounds, and low-income European-heritage adolescents have often remarked that others usually assume that they are middle class (see also Bettie, 2002).

U.S. Latino Adolescents' Friendships

Research on Latino-heritage adolescents' friendships has largely focused on three topics: (1) the coordination and developmental significance of relationships with family and friends, (2) the role of friends in educational and deviant pathways, and (3) the qualities of Latino-heritage adolescents' friendships relative to the qualities that have been used to characterize European-heritage adolescents' friendships. In what follows, we draw on our own and others' research to review the findings, identify gaps in the literature, and propose future directions for research.

The Intersection Between Family and Friendships

Family interdependence, or *familism*, is considered one of the defining features of Latino families and a characteristic they share with other ethnic minority families (Harrison et al., 1990; Cooper et al., 1993; Fuligni, 1998). The construct of familism includes values, attitudes, and behaviors that denote and privilege family obligations and cohesion over individual goals (Azmitia & Brown, 2002; Sabogal et al., 1987). Like their European-heritage counterparts, Latino-heritage adolescents view family and friends as central relationships in their lives (Azmitia & Cooper, 2002), but consistent with familism, some Latino adolescents, and in particular immigrants, view their family as more important than their friends and name parents, siblings, and cousins as their primary sources of emotional support and academic and future-oriented guidance.[1] The centrality of family for immigrant adolescents may be partly due to their parents' restrictions on their time with peers. (Cooper et al., 1998; Reese et al., 1998). For other Latino-heritage adolescents and young adults, and especially second- or third-generation Latinos, friends increase in salience over the course of adolescence and into young adulthood. In some domains, such as social support, these adolescent and young adult Latinos list more friends than family members as resources, a pattern that also in evident for European- and African-heritage adolescents (Levitt, Guacci-Franco, & Levitt, 1993; Levitt, Weber, & Guacci, 1993).

Although second- and third-generation Latino-heritage adolescents and young adults resemble European- and African-heritage adolescents and young adults in the composition of their social support networks, they may differ in the mental health correlates of their perceived support from family and friends. In our cross-sectional study of ethnically diverse early and late adolescents' relationships with family, friends, and teachers and their adjustment to junior high school or college, we found that perceived absence of family support was more highly correlated with depression for Latino-, African-, and Asian-heritage adolescents than for European-heritage adolescents. In contrast, although the differences were not statistically significant, the correlations between perceived absence of friend support and depression were larger for European-heritage than for Latino-, African-, or Asian-heritage adolescents (Reis et al., 2005). Although the sample was too small to carry out quantitative analyses of whether adolescents' generation of immigration qualified these results, the preliminary results from our qualitative analyses of the interviews suggest that perceived absence of family support, although rare, was particularly detrimental to immigrant or first-generation ethnic minority adolescents' mental health.

Taken together, the results of the studies we have reviewed thus far support the conclusion that whether or not studies yield between-ethnic-group differences in the salience and implications of emotional support provided to adolescents and young adults' by their family and friends depends, at least in part, on participants' generation of immigration. Nevertheless, the findings of our studies suggest that even immigrants who endorse familistic values and behaviors consider friends as major sources of emotional support and guidance (Azmitia & Cooper, 2002; Azmitia et al., in progress). Indeed, for immigrant adolescents, friends may be especially important for adaptation to the United States because the stresses of immigration can take a toll on families and reduce the support and guidance parents provide (Suárez-Orozco & Todorova, in press). Moreover, more acculturated Latino-heritage friends or their European-heritage friends or classmates may serve as "school culture brokers" for adolescents from families in which parents are unfamiliar with the U.S. school system or adolescents who have exceeded their families' educational level (Gándara, 1995; Stanton-Salazar, 2001). Thus, rather than viewing family and friends as being in competition, it may be best to view them as complementary and focus on how adolescents derive resources from these two important relationship networks (see also Youniss & Smollar, 1985).

In a collaboration with Catherine Cooper, we have used her Bridging Multiple Worlds Model (Cooper et al., 1998; Cooper et al., 2002) to investigate intersections, complementarities, and conflicts between ethnic minority adolescents' family and friend networks. Cooper's model builds on Phelan, Davidson, and Yu's (1991) Students' Multiple Worlds Model, which characterizes the ease with which adolescents move between their family, peer, and school "worlds" or contexts. Phelan et al. proposed that some adolescents move easily between these worlds because they perceive the values and expectations, norms, and behavioral practices in these three worlds as similar or at least compatible. However, other adolescents experience these worlds as incompatible or in competition and thus may chose one world and disengage from the others, struggle to make them fit, or feel marginalized from some or all three worlds. As Phelan et al. showed, adolescents' perception of the fit between their worlds is associated with their engagement in school and their mental health.

Our work builds on Phelan et al.'s (1991) model by considering whether ethnic minority males' and females' conceptualization of the fit between their worlds varies over the course of adolescence and into adulthood. We have also investigated whether the developmental variations we have observed are associated with adolescents' and young adults' identity development and performance in school. Cooper (1999) uses the "bridging" metaphor to emphasize that worlds and relationships can serve as positive bridges to competent adolescence and adulthood. However, like Phelan and colleagues, she proposes that these worlds and the people that inhabit them can set up barriers and challenges that impede development in general and the pursuit of positive identity and academic pathways in particular.

In our longitudinal studies of early, middle, and late Mexican- and Central American-heritage adolescents' transition to junior high school or college, we found that siblings can bridge family and peer worlds and peers can bridge the family and school worlds. We address the role of peers as bridges between families and schools in the next section and focus our present discussion on siblings. Our analyses of the longitudinal interviews revealed that for some Latino-heritage adolescents and especially girls whose access to friends was restricted by parents, siblings, and cousins became best friends, thus blurring the distinction between the family and peer worlds. Moreover, older siblings' academic success opened doors for accessing peers for younger siblings; it was not unusual for younger siblings to attend the same academic outreach program their older siblings had attended. At these academic outreach programs, the boys and girls developed friendships with other Latino-heritage adolescents. (Azmitia & Cooper, 2002; Gills & Azmitia, in press). Also, during their interviews, many of the college students remarked that they were committed to helping their younger siblings attend college and that attaining this goal would require convincing their parents to allow a younger sibling, often a sister, to leave home (Cooper et al., 1998; Gills & Azmitia, in press). Moreover, Latino-heritage college students were more likely than the other ethnic minority participants to state that their siblings had played a central role in their pathways to college (Gills & Azmitia, in press).

Although siblings can function as bridges between the family and peer worlds for Latino-heritage adolescents, they can also act as barriers. In our study of the transition to junior high school, we found that Latino-heritage older siblings, and especially late adolescent boys, were more likely than Latino-heritage early adolescents to experience school difficulties and engage in behaviors that parents disapproved of. The older siblings' difficulties often led parents to restrict the younger siblings' access to friends and participation in extracurricular activities and, in some cases, to the older sibling, to prevent them from following in the same bad path. In their interviews, the early adolescents themselves often remarked that they were modeling their lives to be different from that of their older siblings and were choosing their friends carefully so that they would not make the same mistakes, such as dropping out of school, using and abusing drugs and alcohol, getting pregnant, or becoming incarcerated, (Azmitia & Brown, 2002; Azmitia et al., 1997).

Taken together, our results suggest that researchers can benefit from considering the role of siblings in Latino-heritage adolescents' family and peer relationships and their developmental and educational pathways. For Latino-heritage adolescents, siblings may bridge family and peer relationships and the family and school worlds. These bridges, however, can be either positive or negative. Many of the parents that we have interviewed have said that early adolescence represents a crossroad in which their children's choice of friends and identification or de-identification with siblings can play a pivotal role in Latino-heritage adolescent boys' and girls' choice of positive or negative developmental and academic pathways and association with peers that complement or conflict with parental values and goals.

The Role of Friendships in Latino-Heritage Adolescents' Educational Pathways

Most research on Latino-heritage adolescents has focused on their educational pathways because Latinos have the highest rates of educational failure of any ethnic group in the United States. Moreover, in some states, such as California, they will soon constitute the largest school-age population (Larson & Rumberger, 1995). Although this research initially focused on school failure, more recently, researchers have focused on the successes – Latino-heritage adolescents who excel in school and, by attending higher education, increase the possibility that they will escape their families' cycle of poverty (Azmitia & Cooper, 2002; Gándara, 1995).

In our longitudinal studies of the transition to junior high school and college of academically successful and unsuccessful Mexican- and Central American-heritage adolescents, we have investigated whether and how these students' personal characteristics, the resources and challenges they derive from their family, peer, and school worlds, and the strategies they use to navigate these three worlds are associated with their educational pathways and mental health. We have focused on adolescents because of the centrality of friendships for adolescent development and the widespread view that friends discourage ethnic minority adolescents from succeeding in school because they view this success as "selling out" to a majority institution that discriminates against them (see, for example, Delgado-Gaitán, 1986; Fordham & Ogbu, 1986; Hymel et al., 1996; Willis, 1977).

Our interviews, surveys, and focus groups have revealed that although some Latino-heritage adolescents, especially boys, experienced their friends as discouraging school success, the majority indicated that their friends viewed schooling positively and supported and encouraged their academic aspirations. Often, these adolescents' academic success was a source of pride for their less academically successful circle of friends. Academic outreach programs, which provide academic support and activities that help students from ethnic and socioeconomic backgrounds that are underrepresented in higher education to develop and sustain college identities, provide spaces to meet and develop friendships with other adolescents who share their academic competencies and aspirations (Azmitia & Cooper, 2002; Cooper et al., 1998; 2002). The subgroup of the participants in our studies who are involved in academic outreach programs often view themselves as having at least two peer groups, their friends at school or their home communities and their friends at the academic outreach program. Indeed, these friends often play a key role in students remaining in the program from high school through college, when other competing peer activities often make adolescents ambivalent about devoting so much of their after-school, weekend, and summer hours to the program.

We have also found that, over the course of junior high and high school, boys are less likely than girls to remain in the academic outreach program than girls. The adolescents' interviews suggest that this gender difference in Latino-heritage adolescents' sustained participation in outreach programs occurs, at least in part, because, although Latino-heritage parents are more likely to restrict girls' than boys' access to friends, they often relax this restriction when the their daughters see their friends at the outreach program. Thus, for girls, the outreach program provides a context for friendship that is not typically available to them (Azmitia & Cooper, 2002; Cooper et al., 1998; Cooper et al., 1995). An additional factor that may play a role in this gender difference in Latino-heritage adolescents' sustained participation in academic outreach programs is that boys may be more likely than girls to see sports as an equally or more viable pathway to college. Despite Title IX, a federal law that attempts to increase girls' access to sports and athletic scholarships, most high schools and universities still devote more resources to male than female sports teams.

Taken together, our findings are consistent with the current emphasis on peers as sources of educational "capital." Latino-heritage parents often hold high educational aspirations for their children and, indeed, have often emigrated to the United States so that their children can get a better education (Cooper et al., 1994). Their lack of experience with the U.S. educational system, however, makes it difficult for these parents to provide the educational guidance their children need to attain these goals. Stanton-Salazar (2001) has suggested that schools should harness U.S.-born academically successful peers as resources for Latino-heritage immigrant students. Indeed, in her landmark study of educationally successful Latinos, Gándara (1995) found that Latino students often attributed their success to friendships with academically successful European-heritage peers. Forming friendships, or at least academic partnerships, with European-heritage peers may also be an important source of emotional support for Latino adolescents in advanced classes or premier universities because Latino students are typically underrepresented in these contexts and thus can feel isolated. As Granovetter (1974) and Gándara (1995) have argued, these "weak ties" may play a crucial role in low-income adolescents' educational and social mobility because they allow them to develop an understanding of and connections with the middle class and its institutions.

It is important to note, however, that even when their friends support their academic success, some Latino-heritage adolescents often worry that participation in different academic activities (e.g., advanced vs. remedial classes; academic outreach programs and college) will strain their friendships. Our focus groups with the Latino-heritage adolescents who participated in our longitudinal studies of the transition to junior high school and college and our interviews with the staff of the academic outreach programs revealed that in high school Latino-heritage adolescents, especially boys, often opt out of advanced classes or stop attending academic outreach programs because they feel that these academic endeavors distance them from their friends (Cooper et al., 1998; Azmitia & Cooper, 2002). Concerns about distancing from friends were also evident in the interviews of Latino-heritage college students who are participating in our ongoing longitudinal study of the transition to college. Over the course of the study, our Latino-heritage participants, and especially those who were the only members of their hometown circle of friends to attend college, have increasingly felt that their friends do not understand their university experiences. When we interviewed them at the end of their sophomore year, many of these Latino-heritage students no longer included friends from home in their circle of close friends. Although the absence of hometown friends in sophomore students' interviews obtained for all the ethnic groups that were participating in the study, Latino- and African-heritage participants expressed more regret and ambivalence about their distancing from high school friends than European- and Asian-heritage participants (Azmitia et al., in press).

Taken together, the findings from our longitudinal studies of the transition to junior high school and college suggest that friends can either support or discourage Latino-heritage adolescents' educational success and that a closer look at factors that mediate these positive and negative peer influences on academics is warranted. It is important to point out, however, that these positive and negative peer influences are not unique to Latino-heritage students and may reflect the intersection of ethnicity and social class in adolescents' educational pathways. Clearly, more research on the intersection of ethnicity, gender, and social class is needed to understand more deeply culture-specific and universal processes in friends' influence on Latino-heritage adolescents' educational and career pathways. Our review of extant research suggests that this understanding would also benefit from a more nuanced consideration of Latino-heritage adolescents' friendships. For example, most researchers do not differentiate between close friends and acquaintances and between friends at school and friends in the neighborhood (but see Way, this volume). Given the extensive research that has linked friendship quality and developmental and mental health outcomes for European-heritage adolescents, we feel that attention to variations in the quality of Latino-heritage adolescents' friendships and their developmental implications is long overdue. In what follows, we review the small but growing literature on the qualities of Latino-heritage adolescents' friendships and their developmental significance.

The Quality of Latino-Heritage Adolescents' Friendships

Only a handful of studies have addressed the question of whether theories about the qualities of adolescents' friendships, primarily constructed from work with European-heritage middle-class adolescents, adequately characterize Latino-heritage adolescents' friendships. The findings of these studies have been mixed, with some showing cross-ethnic similarities and others revealing cross-ethnic differences.

As noted earlier, studies that focus on friends' provision of emotional support and instrumental help generally reveal few between-ethnic-group differences. For example, Azmitia and Cooper (2002) found that Mexican- and European-heritage adolescents did not differ in their reliance on friends for emotional support and academic help, and Levitt et al. (1993) found similar patterns of friend support and importance in the social convoys of Latino- and European-heritage adolescents and young adults. Finally, Way and Robinson (2003) found similar associations between friend support and the psychological adjustment of African-, Latino-, and Asian-heritage adolescents. Although the preliminary analyses of our cross-sectional study of the transitions to junior high school and college (Reis et al., 2005) revealed that the perceived absence of friend support may have higher costs for the mental health of European-heritage than Latino-, African-, or Asian-heritage adolescents, the preliminary nature of these findings requires that we wait until we finish analyzing the data before putting too much stock in this result.

Studies that focus on intimacy, trust, loyalty, and companionship have yielded some between-ethnic-group differences in these qualities of adolescents' friendships, but the results vary as to whether Latino-heritage adolescents' friendships are found to be higher or lower in quality than those of other ethnic minority and ethnic majority adolescents. A handful of studies have shown that Latino-heritage adolescents' friendships may provide more intimacy and closeness than the friendships of other ethnic-minority adolescents. For example, Way and colleagues (Way, this volume; Way et al., 2001) found that Latino-heritage adolescents, especially girls, were more likely to self-report their friendships as ideal – offering high levels of affection, loyalty, intimacy, and satisfaction, moderate levels of companionship, and low levels of antagonism and conflict – than Asian-heritage adolescents, who were more likely to report their friendships as disengaged – offering low levels of affection, loyalty, companionship, intimacy, antagonism, conflict, and satisfaction (see also Goodwin & Lee, 1994). Way (this volume) suggested that Latino-heritage adolescents' intimate friendships may be an expression of endorsement of collective/interdependent values, beliefs, and practices. Way's suggestion is consistent with developmental theory and research on family-peer links showing that children and adolescents transport relationship orientations and practices that they learn in the family to their relationships with friends (Cooper & Cooper, 1992; Dishion, 1990).

If a collectivist/interdependent orientation promotes intimacy in friendships, then it is important to explain why Asian-heritage adolescents, also known for their collective/interdependent orientation, do not exhibit similar levels of intimacy in their friendships. Perhaps, as Way (this volume) suggested, this between-ethnic-group difference occurred because as a group, Asian-heritage parents place more restrictions on their children's access to friends than Latino-heritage parents. Thus, Asian-heritage adolescents, and especially girls, may not have many opportunities to develop intimate, "ideal" friendships. Research that examines within-ethnic-group variations in the association between parents' restriction of adolescents' friendships, adolescents' endorsement of interdependent/collectivist beliefs and practices, and the qualities of adolescents friendships would help test Way's suggestion and also contribute to resolving the debate over whether and how the collectivism/individualism framework is useful for describing between- and within-ethnic-group similarities and differences in adolescents' friendship practices and their developmental significance.

If the collectivism/individualism framework is to be useful for characterizing adolescents' friendships, it must also explain the findings of studies that have revealed that ethnic minority adolescents, including Latinos, report lower levels of friendship quality than their European-heritage counterparts. As mentioned earlier, the context of the study – neighborhood or school – and the confounding of social class and ethnicity in some of these studies may help reconcile these differences in the findings. For example, in their school-based study, Kuperminc et al. (2004) found that Latino- and African-heritage adolescents obtained lower friendship quality scores than European-heritage adolescents, but the researchers acknowledged that the confounding of social class and ethnicity in their study prevented them from drawing strong conclusions about between-ethnic differences in friendships. Still, consistent with Kuperminc et al.'s findings, Way and Chen (2000) reported that the Latino-, African-, and Asian-heritage low-income students they studied primarily located their close friendship networks in their neighborhood, not their school. As Cooper et al. (1993), Kuperminc et al. (2004), and Way and Chen (2000) have suggested, these findings underscore the need to study ethnic minority adolescents' nonschool friendships.

After reviewing the available literature, we feel that the question of whether the quality of Latino-heritage adolescents' friendships differs from that of other ethnic minority or ethnic majority adolescents cannot be answered at present, given the frequent confounding of social class and ethnicity. The research does show, however, that Latino-heritage adolescents use similar qualities as those used by European-heritage adolescents when they describe their friends. Therefore, it appears that our extant theories can be used as a starting point in characterizing the qualities of Latino-heritage adolescents' friendships and the association between these qualities and Latino-heritage adolescents' adjustment and mental health. We have found Way and colleagues' research (Way, this volume; Way & Chen, 2000; Way et al., 2001) especially helpful in drawing this conclusion because their qualitative, open-ended approach allows adolescents' own conceptualizations of friendships to emerge. When researchers, ourselves included, use surveys to assess friendship qualities, they are already imposing their theoretical framework on their respondents. Therefore, it becomes impossible to assess potential ethnic group variations in adolescents' friendship theories.

Research on the association between friendship qualities and adolescents' developmental outcomes also supports the conclusion that current theories of adolescents' friendships provide a useful starting point for studying Latino-heritage adolescents' developmental outcomes. Studies have revealed, for example, similarities across ethnic groups in the associations between friendship quality and school and psychological adjustment as well as engagement in delinquency and other antisocial activities and behaviors (Henry, Tolan, & Gorman-Smith, 2001; Kuperminc et al., 2004; Way et al., 2001; Way & Robinson, 2003). Nevertheless, as Kuperminc et al. suggest, there is some suggestion that poor-quality peer relationships affect low-income adolescents more negatively than middle-class adolescents because low-income adolescents are more likely than middle-income adolescents to experience stress from other relationships and contexts in their lives. Thus, further research on within-group variation in the association between friendship quality and adolescents' developmental outcomes is needed. Ideally, this research would also examine whether the findings generalize over the various contexts of adolescents' lives.

Conclusions and Future Directions for Research

Our chapter illustrated some of the findings and complexities of studying Latino-heritage adolescents' friendships and their developmental significance. We join others (e.g., Gjerde, 2004; McLoyd, 2004; Phinney, 1996; Wainryb, 2004; Way & Hamm, 2005) in calling for research that addresses the ways in which adolescents and their families interpret and perceive their experiences across the microecological and macroecological contexts of their lives and for methodological plurality in this endeavor. As mentioned, theoretical debates need to be accompanied by concrete research agendas and empirical work that describe and explain the rich, fluid, cultural context of adolescent development as well as how beliefs and attitudes are linked to specific behavioral practices and changes in these practices over time. Rather than assuming that we will find large between-culture differences in the peer relations of Latino- and European-American adolescents, we must first ask: Differences in what? And for which adolescents? And for which periods of adolescent development?

In addition, we need quantitative and qualitative research on the intersectionality of adolescents' social identities as they relate to their friendship experiences and theories about Latino-heritage adolescents' friendships that capture the significance of their heterogeneity in country of origin, generation of immigration, social class, and geographical location in the United States. To date, the research on Latino-heritage adolescents has largely been focused on low-income adolescents living in urban centers in the West or East Coasts of the United States. Thus, the familial and friendship experiences of middle- or upper-class Latinos are understudied. The opposite is the case for European-heritage adolescents. We have a wealth of information on the friendships of middle- and upper-class European-heritage adolescents, the typical participants in developmental studies, but have very little information on the friendships of low-income, working-class European-heritage adolescents. A good place to start would be by becoming familiar with the work of sociologists and anthropologists, who have long made class a central focus of their research. Interdisciplinary research and cross-fertilization would strengthen our developmental theories, productively contribute to debates about the role of culture and its various manifestations in adolescent development in general and friendships in particular, and in general, move our field forward so that we begin to capture the fluidity and contextual nature of adolescents' friendships and lives. A more realistic portrait of ethnically and socioeconomically diverse adolescents' friendships would also be useful toward developing policies that improve adolescents' experiences at school and the larger society. Given that so many ethnic minority and low-income adolescents live in poverty, more informed policies would result in a brighter, more hopeful future for them and our society.

Acknowledgments

We thank the adolescents and their families for participating in our research and our undergraduate and graduate student research collaborators for helping gather and code the data. The research reported in this chapter was supported by grants to the first author and Catherine R. Cooper from the U.S. Department of Education's Office of Educational Research and Improvement and the UC-LMRI, and grants to the first author from UC-ACCORD, UC-LMRI, and the Committee on Research and the Social Sciences Division of the University of California.

Notes

1 Although Youniss and Smollar (1985) also found that the European-heritage adolescents who participated in their study relied on their parents more than their friends for educational and career guidance, these adolescents priviledged friends over family for emotional support or at least relied on them equally.

References

Arnett, J. J. (2002). The psychology of globalization. *American Psychologist, 57*, 774–783.

Azmitia, M., & Brown, J. R. (2002). Latino immigrant parents' beliefs about the "path of life" of their adolescent children. In J. Contreras, A. Neal-Barnett, & K. Kerns

(Eds.), *Latino children and families in the United States: Current research and future directions* (pp. 77–101). Westport, CT: Praeger.

Azmitia, M., & Cooper, C. R. (1996). *Navigating and negotiating home, school, peer, and community linkages in adolescence*. Santa Cruz, CA: US. Center for Research on Education, Diversity, and Excellence.

Azmitia, M., & Cooper, C. R. (2002). Good or bad? Peer influences on Latino and European American adolescents' pathways through school. *Journal of Education for Students Placed at Risk, 6*, 45–71.

Azmitia, M., Cooper, C. R., García, E. E., & Dunbar, N. (1996). The ecology of family guidance in low-income Mexican-American and European-American families. *Social Development, 5*, 1–23.

Azmitia, M., Lopez, E., Cooper, C. R., Rivera, L., & Dunbar, N. (1997, April). *Are Mexican-descent adolescents mentors for their younger siblings?* Paper presented at the biennial meetings of the Society for Research in Child Development, Washington, DC.

Bettie, J. (2002). Exceptions to the rule. Upwardly mobile White and Mexican American high school girls. *Gender and Society, 16*, 403–422.

Berndt, T. J. (1996). Transitions in friendship and friends' influence. In J. A. Graber, J. Brooks-Gunn, & A. C. Petersen (Eds.), *Transitions through adolescence: Interpersonal domains and context* (pp. 57–84). Mahway, NJ: Lawrence Erlbaum Associates.

Betancourt, H., & López, S. R. (1993). The study of culture, ethnicity, and race in American psychology. *American Psychologist, 48*, 629–637.

Cooper, C. R. (1999). Multiple selves, multiple worlds: Cultural perspectives on individuality and connectedness in adolescent development. In A. S. Masten (Ed.), *Cultural processes in child development. The Minnesota Symposia on Child Psychology, Vol 29* (pp. 25–57). Mahwah, NJ: Lawrence Erlbaum Associates.

Cooper, C. R., Azmitia, M., García, E. E., Ittel, A., Lopez, E., & Martinez-Chavez, R. (1994). Aspirations of low-income Mexican-American and European-American parents for their children and adolescents. In F. Villarruel & R. Lerner (Eds.), *Environments for socialization and learning: New directions for child development*. San Francisco: Jossey Bass.

Cooper, C., R., Baker, H., Polichar, D., & Welsch, M. (1993). Values and communication in Chinese, Filipino, European, Mexican, and Vietnamese American adolescents with their families and friends. *New Directions for Child Development, 62*, 73–89.

Cooper, C. R., & Cooper, R. G., Jr. (1992). Links between adolescents' relationships with their parents and peers. Models, evidence, and mechanisms. In R. D. Parke & G. W. Ladd (Eds.), *Family-peer relationships: Models of linkage* (pp. 135–158). Hillsdale, NJ: Lawrence Erlbaum Associates.

Cooper, C. R., Cooper, R. G. Jr., Azmitia, M., Chavira, G., & Gullat, Y. (2002). Bridging multiple worlds: How African American and Latino youth in academic outreach programs navigate math pathways to college. *Applied Developmental Science, 6*, 73–87.

Cooper, C. R., Jackson, J. F., Azmitia, M., & Lopez, E. M. (1998). Multiple selves, multiple worlds. Ethnically sensitive research on identity, relationships, and opportunity structures in adolescence. In V. McLoyd & L. Steinberg (Eds.), *Conceptual and methodological issues in the study of minority adolescents and their families* (pp. 111–126). Hillsdale, NJ: Lawrence Erlbaum Associates.

Cooper, C. R., Jackson, J. F., Azmitia, M., Lopez, E. M., & Dunbar, N. (1995). Bridging students multiple worlds: African American and Latino youth in academic research programs. In R. F. Macías & R. G. Ramos (Eds.), *Changing schools for changing students: Research anthology on language minorities* (pp. 245–268). Santa Barbara, CA: UC Linguistic Minority Institute.

Delgado-Gaitán, C. (1986). Adolescent peer influence and differential school performance. *Journal of Adolescent Research, 1*, 103–114.

Dishion, T. (1990). The family ecology of boys' peer relationships in middle childhood. *Child Development, 65*, 876–892.

Eckert, P. (1989). *Jocks and burnouts: Social categories and identity in the high school.* New York: Teachers College Press.

Edwards, C. P., De Guzman, M. R. T., Brown, J., & Kumru, A. (this volume). Children's social behaviors and peer interactions. In X. Chen, D. French, & B. Schneider (Eds.), *Peer relations in cultural context*. New York: Cambridge University Press.

Fisher, C. B., Jackson, J. F., & Villarruel, F. A. (1998). The study of African American and Latin American children and youth. In W. Damon (Series Ed.) & R. Lerner (Vol. Ed.), *Handbook of child psychology: Vol 1. Theoretical models of human development* (pp. 865–937). New York: Wiley.

Fordham, S., & Ogbu, J. U. (1986). Black students' school success: Coping with the "burden of acting White." *Urban Review, 18*, 176–206.

French, D., Rinasari, M., Pidadi, S., Newlan, P., & Buhrmester, D. (2001). Social support of Indonesian and U.S. children and adolescents by family members and friends. *Merrill Palmer Quarterly, 47*, 377–394.

Fuligni, A. J. (1998). Authority, autonomy, and parent-adolescent conflict and cohesion: A study of adolescents from Mexican, Chinese, Filipino, and European backgrounds. *Developmental Psychology, 34*, 782–792.

Galambos, N. L., & Leadbeater, B. J. (2000). Trends in adolescent research for the new millennium. *International Journal of Behavioral Development, 24*, 289–294.

Gándara, P. (1995). *Over the ivy walls: The educational mobility of low-income Chicanos*. Albany: State University of New York Press.

Gjerde, P. F. (2004). Culture, power, and experience: Toward a person-centered cultural psychology. *Human Development, 47*, 138–157.

Goodnow, J. J. (1992). Parents' ideas, children's ideas: Correspondence and divergence. In I. E. Sigel & A. V. McGillicudy-DeLisi (Eds.), *Parental belief systems: The psychological consequences for children* (2nd ed.; pp. 293–317). Hillsdale, NJ: Lawrence Erlbaum Associates.

Goodwin, R., & Lee, I. (1994). Taboo topics among Chinese and English friends: A cross-cultural comparison. *Journal of Cross-Cultural Psychology, 25*, 325–338.

Granovetter, M. S. (1973). The strength of weak ties. *American Journal of Sociology, 78*, 1360–1380.

Greenfield, P. M. (1994). Preface. In P. M. Greenfield & R. R. Cocking (Eds.), *Cross-cultural roots of minority child development* (pp. ix–xvii). Hillsdale, NJ: Lawrence Erlbaum Associates.

Grotevant, H. D., & Cooper, C. R. (1986). Individuation in family relationships: A perspective on individual difference in the development of identity and role-taking skill in adolescence. *Human Development, 29*, 81–100.

Harrison, A. O., Wilson, M. N., Pine, C. J., Chan, S. Q., & Buriel, R. (1990). Family ecologies of ethnic minority children. *Child Development, 61*, 347–363.

Henry, D. B., Tolan, P. H., & Gorman-Smith, D. (2001). Longitudinal family and peer group effects on violence and nonviolent delinquency. *Journal of Clinical Child Psychology, 30*, 172–186.

Hurtado, A., & Gurin, P. (2004). *Chicano/a identity in a changing U.S. society. Quién soy? Quienes somos?* Tucson: The University of Arizona Press.

Hymel, S., Comfort, C., Schonert-Reichl, K., & McDougall, P. (1996). Academic failure and school dropout: The influence of peers. In J. Juvonen & K. Wentzel (Eds.), *Social motivation: Understanding children's school adjustment* (pp. 313–345). New York: Cambridge University Press.

Killen, M. (1997). Commentary: Culture, self, and development: Are cultural templates useful or stereotypic? *Developmental Review, 17*, 239–249.

Kuperminc, G. P., Blatt, S. J., Shahar, G., Henrich, C., & Leadbeater, B. J. (2004). Cultural equivalence and cultural variance in longitudinal associations of young adolescent self-definition and interpersonal relatedness to psychological and school adjustment. *Journal of Youth and Adolescence, 33*, 13–30.

Larson, K., & Rumberger, R. (1995). Doubling school success in highest-risk Latino youth: Results from a middle-school intervention study. In R. F. Macías & R. G. García-Ramos (Eds.), *Changing schools for changing families: An anthology of research on language minorities, schools, and society* (pp. 157–180). Santa Barbara: University of California Language Minority Research Institute.

Levitt, M. J., Guacci-Franco, N., & Levitt, J. L. (1993). Convoys of social support in childhood and early adolescence: Structure and function. *Developmental Psychology, 29*, 811–818.

Levitt, M. J., Weber, R. A., & Guacci, N. (1993). Convoys of social support: An intergenerational analysis. *Psychology and Aging, 8*, 323–326.

Markus, H. R., & Kitayama, S. (1991). Culture and self: Implications for cognition, emotion, and motivation. *Psychological Review, 98*, 224–253.

Matsumoto, D., Grissom, R. J., & Dinnel, D. L. (2001). Do between-culture differences really mean that people are different? *Journal of Cross Cultural Psychology, 32*, 478–490.

McLean, K. C. (2003, April). *Friendship dissolution in the transition to junior high and college*. Paper presented at the biennial meeting of the Society for Research in Child Development, Tampa, FL.

McLoyd, V. C. (2004). Linking race and ethnicity to culture: Steps along the road from inference to hypothesis testing. *Human Development, 47*, 186–191.

Oyserman, D., Coon, H. M., & Kemmelmeir, M. (2002). Rethinking individualism and collectivism: Evaluation of theoretical assumptions and meta-analysis. *Psychological Bulletin, 128*, 3–72.

Perez, W., & Padilla, A. M. (2000). Cultural orientation across three generations of Hispanic adolescents. *Hispanic Journal of Behavioral Sciences, 22*, 390–398.

Phelan, P., Davidson, A. L., & Yu, H. C. (1991). Students' multiple worlds: Navigating the borders of family, peer, and school cultures. In P. Phelan & A. L. Davidson (Eds.), *Cultural diversity: Implications for education* (pp. 52–88). New York: Teachers College Press.

Phinney, J. S. (1996). When we talk about American ethnic groups, what do we mean? *American Psychologist, 52*, 918–927.

Phinney, J. S., & Landin, J. (1998). Research paradigms for studying ethnic minority families within and across groups. In V. C. McLoyd & L. Steinberg (Eds.), *Studying minority adolescents: Conceptual, methodological, and theoretical issues* (pp. 89–109). Mahwah, NJ: Lawrence Erlbaum Associates.

Phinney, J. S., Ong, A., & Madden, T. (2000). Cultural values and intergenerational value discrepancies in immigrant and nonimmigrant families. *Child Development, 71*, 528–539.

Radmacher, K., & Azmitia, M. (2004). *Are there gendered pathways to intimacy in early adolescents' and emerging adults' friendships?* Unpublished manuscript, University of California at Santa Cruz.

Reese, L., Balzano, S., Gallimore, R., & Goldenberg, C. (1995). The concept of *educación*: Latino family values and American schooling. *International Journal of Educational Research, 23*, 51–81.

Reese, L., Kroesen, K., Ryan, G., & Gallimore, R. (1998, May). *Exploring Latino adolescents' worlds through multiple methods*. Paper presented at the annual meeting of the UC-Linguistic Minority Research Institute Santacruz, California.

Reis, O., Azmitia, M., Radmacher, K., Gills, J., Syed, M., & Tonyan, H. A. (2005). *Patterns of social support from family, friends, and teachers and ethnically diverse adolescents' mental health during developmental and school transitions*. Unpublished manuscript, University of California at Santa Cruz.

Sabogal, F., Marin, G., Otero-Sabogal, R., Marin, B., & Perez-Stable, E. (1987). Hispanic familism and acculturation: What changes and what doesn't? *Hispanic Journal of Behavioral Sciences, 9*, 397–412.

Stanton-Salazar, R. D. (2001). *Manufacturing hope and despair: The school and kin support networks of U.S. Mexican youth*. New York: Teachers College Press.

Stewart. A., & McDermott, C. (2004). Gender in psychology. *American Review of Psychology, 55*, 519–544.

Suárez-Orozco, C., & Todorova, I. L. G. (in press). Understanding the social worlds of immigrant youth. *New Directions for Youth Development: Theory, Practice, and Research.*

Szapocznic, J., & Kurtines, W. M. (1993). Family psychology and cultural diversity: Opportunities for theory, research, and application. *American Psychologist, 48*, 400–4007.

Tappan, M., & Brown, L. M. (1991). Hermeneutics and developmental psychology: Towards an ethnic of interpretation. In W. M. Kurtines, M. Azmitia, & G. Gewirtz (Eds.), *The role of values in psychology and human development* (pp. 105–130). Oxford, England: Wiley.

Triandis, H. C. (1995). *Individualism and collectivism*. Boulder, CO: Westview Press.

Uba, L. (1994). *Asian Americans: Personality patterns, identity, and mental health*. New York: Guilford.

Umana-Taylor, A. J., & Bámaca-Gomez, M. Y. (2003). Generational differences in resistance to peer pressure among Mexian-Origin adolescents. *Youth and Society, 35*, 183–203.

Valdés, G. (1996). *Con respeto: Bridging the distances between culturally diverse families and schools: An ethnographic portrait*. New York: Teachers' College Press.

Wainryb, C. (2004). The study of diversity in human development. Culture, urgency, and perils. *Human Development, 47*, 131–137.

Waters, M., & Eschbach, K. (1995). Immigration and ethnic and racial inequality in the United States. *Annual Review of Sociology, 21*, 419–446.

Way, N. (this volume). The cultural practice of close friendships among urban adolescents in the United States. In X. Chen, D. French, & B. Schneider (Eds.), *Peer relationships in cultural context*. New York: Cambridge University Press.

Way, N., & Chen, L. (2000). Close and general friendships among African American, Latino, and Asian American adolescents from low-income families. *Journal of Adolescent Research, 15*, 274–301.

Way, N., Cowal, K., Gingold, R., Pahl, K., & Bissessar, N. (2001). Friendship patterns among African American, Asian American, and Latino adolescents from low-income families. *Journal of Social and Personal Relationships, 18*, 29–53.

Way, N., & Hamm, J. (2005). *New directions for child and adolescent development: Using qualitative methods to investigate friendship processes*. San Francisco, Jossey Bass.

Way, N., & Robinson, M. G. (2003). A longitudinal study of the effects of family, friends, and school experiences on the psychological adjustment of ethnic minority, low-SES adolescents. *Journal of Adolescent Research, 18*, 324–346.

Whiting, B. (1976). The problem of the packaged variable. In K. Riegel & J. Meacham (Eds.), *The developing individual in a changing world* (pp. 303–309). Chicago: Aldine.

Willis, P. (1977). *Learning to labour: How working class kids get working class jobs*. Westmead, England: Saxon House.

Yeh, C. J., & Hwang, M. Y. (2000). Interdependence in ethnic identity and self: Implications for theory and practice. *Journal of Counseling and Development, 78*, 420–429.

Youniss, J., & Smollar, J. (1985). *Adolescents' relations with mothers, fathers, and friends*. Chicago: University of Chicago Press.

20 The Cultural Context of Children and Adolescents

Peer Relationships and Intimate Friendships Among Arab and Jewish Children in Israel

Ruth Sharabany

The aim of this chapter is to identify unique features of intimate friendship and peer relationships in two cultures within Israel. It is assumed that both groups share core collectivistic characteristics, including a strong sense of belonging to their community, priority of the community over the individual in terms of interest and decision making, duty to the community, and norms of getting along with members of their community (Oyserman, Coon, & Kemmelmeir, 2002; Triandis, 1995). Generally, the Israeli Arab society is a collectivistic and traditional society that is moving toward modernity and thus adopting more individualistic features. The kibbutz society is perhaps an extreme example of a collectivistic society, composed of communes, with shared ownership of their properties and commitments to collective decision making about individuals (therefore, we use the terms communal to describe it). Today the kibbutz is moving rapidly toward privatization, letting go of its communal structure, but retaining its collectivistic features. These two societies are both minorities in a country where urban Jewish society and a Western economy predominate. We describe the two cultures within Israel, their similarities and differences, looking for possible common features (Sharabany & Schneider, 2004). The central premise considered in this chapter is that, based on two Israeli cultures, it seems likely that in some collectivistic societies dyadic friendship with a specific person, such as a best friend, may be characterized by reduced intimacy (French, 2004). This is seemingly in contrast to having friendship groups, or peer groups, which show close relationships and exclusivity as in-group.

The chapter opens with some reflection on the nature of intimacy. Included in this theoretical introduction is a suggestion about why it is reasonable to expect cultural differences in the intimacy of close relationships. The theoretical introduction is followed by detailed descriptions of the two minority cultures. Then, the research on close relationships in Israeli Arab and kibbutz culture is discussed, followed by some reasons why simple comparisons between Arabs and kibbutzim may be misleading. The chapter concludes with an appraisal of what has been achieved and what research is needed to provide a more complete understanding of cultural differences in dyadic intimacy.

Intimate Friendship

The attainment of intimate friendship during childhood and adolescence constitutes an important developmental milestone. Intimacy has been referred to as a developmental task, central during adolescence (Erikson, 1959; Shulman et al., 1997), as a strong predictor of overall psychosocial adjustment (e.g., Erber & Erber, 2001; Newcomb & Bagwell, 1995) and as an aspect of development that evolves throughout life (Prager 1995; Sharabany, 1994a). The notion of intimacy has often been applied to the relationship with a best friend, who is a peer one has chosen and who reciprocates the choice, forming a relationship characterized by mutual emotional investment.

Intimacy can be seen as a multifaceted construct composed of various aspects that varies in quality and quantity as well as target throughout the process of development (Sharabany, 1974; Sharabany, 1994a). Intimacy can be categorized as including the following components: (1) *frankness and spontaneity*, involving self disclosure, and honest feedback; (2) *sensitivity and knowing*, including a sense of empathy that can vary in its verbal and nonverbal manifestation; (3) *attachment,* a dimension of closeness and bonding; (4) *exclusiveness*, which identifies the unique qualities present in the specific relationships and not in others, and a sense of preference for that person over others; (5) *giving and sharing*, including the sharing of material goods, as well as listening to each other; (6) *imposition*, indicating a degree of readiness to require and accept the friend's help, which may imply comfort with being needy or in debt to the friend; (7) *common activities*, spending time and doing things together, a basic component of intimate relations; and (8) *trust and loyalty*, which constitute a core ingredient of the relationship, providing the assurance that the friend will be on one's side and provide support. The multidimensionality of intimacy allows wide cultural variations to emerge in contrast to frequent definition of intimacy in terms of a single dimension, such as self-disclosure (Sharabany, 1994b). For example, intimacy may exist in the deep knowledge about a friend rather than talking (second dimension). Intimacy may be seen in the sense of bonding (third dimension) and spending time together (seventh dimension). This concept of intimate friendship and its measure has been useful in several countries, including Canada (Sicard,

1994), Hong Kong (Chou, 2000), Israel (Mayseless, Wiseman, & Hai, 1998; Sharabany 2001; Shechtman et al., 2002), Italy (Tani & Maggino, 2003), Portugal (Cordeiro, 2005), Spain (Sanchez-Queija & Oliva, 2003), and the United States (e.g., Jones & Dembo, 1989)

Cultural Dimensions of Friendships

Triandis (1995) emphasizes the distinction between collectivistic and individualistic value orientations. A *collectivistic* orientation stresses the importance of harmony in interactions, obedience, and conformity as well as consideration for relationships in decision making. *Collectivism* may be initially defined as a social pattern consisting of closely linked individuals who see themselves as parts of one or more collectives (family, coworkers, tribe, nation); are primarily motivated by the norms of, and duties imposed by, those collectives; are willing to give priority to the goals of these collectives over their own personal goals; and emphasize their connectedness to members of these collectives. By contrast, an *individualistic* orientation values personal achievement, competition, and self-improvement. Conflict and acknowledgment of differences appear to be more acceptable within individualistic societies. A preliminary definition of *individualism* is "a social pattern that consists of loosely lined individuals who view themselves as independent of collectives; are primarily motivated by their own pretences, need, rights, and the contracts they have established with others; and emphasize rational analyses of the advantages and disadvantages to associating with others" (Triandis, 1995, p. 2).

Other features of culture that may influence close relationships are the psychological orientation toward extended family as well as the modernity and complexity of the society. Uleman et al. (2000) measured individualism and collectivism in various close relationship groups. They found that the distinction between kin and non-kin orientation accounted for greater variance than the dimensions of individualism and collectivism. Their analysis showed that individuals could be simultaneously interdependent (collectivistic) with regard to one set of relationships and independent (individualistic) with regard to another set of relationships.

It is generally assumed that individualism is more prevalent in industrialized Western societies, whereas collectivism is more common in traditional societies. Based on the meta-analysis of studies of individualism and collectivism, Oyserman et al. (2002) conclude that it is better to undertake a comprehensive reassessment of individualism and collectivism within a culture rather than make a priori assumptions based on generalizations and previous studies. This contention has substantial methodological implications.

The map of collectivism–individualism is complex and does not always yield the expected differences between societies assumed to be collectivistic or individualistic (Ben-Shaul, Sharabany, & Kurman, 2004). The complexities inherent in describing and categorizing cultures pertain particularly to the cultures discussed in this chapter, as detailed in the next two sections.

The Arab Society in Israel

The Arabs living in Israel account for approximately 20% of the population. They are not a homogeneous group, as they differ on multiple dimensions, including religious affiliation and their degree of involvement in the majority culture (Sagy, Orr, & Bar-On, 1999). The context also differs for Arabs living in villages and those living in an urban environment (Daeem, 1993). By serving in the Israeli army, Druze and Bedouin come into close contact with Jews, yet they are still very traditional and live in closed societies (Turiel & Wainryb, 1998). In addition, the Bedouin are Arab Muslim nomads that traditionally raised camels, goats, or sheep and changed their tent sites seasonally in a constant search for grazing areas and water. Their nomadic lifestyle was a central feature of their identity. Today, there are approximately 40,000 Bedouin living in Israel's southern deserts. The Bedouins are undergoing extreme changes in their life circumstances. Most central is their transition from a nomadic lifestyle to living in small towns. These changes are occurring in part because of government policy and in part because of their exposure to modern society arising from service in the Israeli army. These groups, however, strive to maintain their tribal organization and traditional lifestyle. Many of the Arab groups are similar in their involvement in extended family networks, shared traditions and customs, use of a common language, and the presence of vertical authoritarian relationship patterns that are based on age and gender (Al-Haj, 1989; Dwairy, 2004; Joseph, 1999). With few exceptions, Arab children study in separate schools, use Arabic as their primary language, and live in homogeneously populated villages or informally homogeneous city neighborhoods.

Collectivistic Features of Israeli Arab Society

Berscheid (1994) stressed the importance of delineating both the type of relationship and the cultural norms in which individuals are embedded. In a study comparing Jewish Israeli and Palestinian Arab high school students, Sagy et al. (2001) found that both groups were more collectivistic than individualistic. However, their findings confirmed that the Palestinian students from

Judea scored higher than their Jewish Israeli counterparts on items emphasizing in-group orientation. Palestinian Arabs may be different from the Arabs living in Israel. However, some claim that Arab children are socialized to dependency, such as on their family (Barakat, 1993). Joseph (1999) provides a vivid portrait of Arab culture derived from the study of narratives. She describes the Arab society as patriarchal, highly socially connected, with kin being the primary members of social networks. Moreover, definitions of the self within the Arab society are based on social roles, with the most salient being hierarchy by gender and age. The collectivistic characteristics of the society indicate that relationships are valued and are expected to provide interdependence and closeness. However, these relationships and closeness are based on roles (such as kin) and not so much on voluntary relationships that are independent of roles.

One of the most detailed studies of the core values of Israeli Arabs assessed the three religious subgroups of Israeli Arabs: Muslim, Christian, and Druze (Florian, Mikulincer, & Weller, 1993). The sample included rural and urban adolescents from the eleventh grade. This study also included two subgroups of the Jewish population: Jews of European and of Middle Eastern descent. The complexity and multidimensionality of cross-cultural differences in family dynamics is highlighted by the finding that the individuals of Middle Eastern descent had a modern view of their family's adaptability, although they also showed a level of collectivism and traditionalism in their view on their family's cohesion (Florian et al., 1993). The Muslim group was reported as being most homogeneous and traditional in family orientation, as well as collectivistic. Christian and Druze groups reported a more modern perception of their family, seeing it as high in adaptability and modernization. The authors of the study see the Druze as having close contact with the Jewish Western majority by serving in the army, whereas the Christians also have contact with the West through religious leaders and pastors from Europe. Similar differences among the three religious subgroups of Arabs have been found among university students (Ben Shaul et al., 2004).

Ecological Variations Within the Arab Culture

There are substantial within-group differences about Arabs in Israel. Ecological differences within the culture have been found to have an effect on peer exposure, interdependence, size of the peer group, and delegation of authority. This point, although often stated in cross-cultural studies, cannot be overemphasized. Daeem (1993) found, for example, that Arab girls from rural areas described their inability to leave home and the sanctions of their parents. Their descriptions differed from those of Arab urban adolescent women and Jewish urban girls, who both expected the support of their family in leaving home.

Elbedour, Shulman, and Kedem (1997) suggest that because socioeconomic features of their Bedouin sample have not been measured or identified, there exists the possibility that observed ethnic differences may stem from urban/rural or from socioeconomic variations between samples. The Bedouin may also differ from both rural and urban Israeli Arabs. Abu-Saad (1999) investigated the effect of the environment and culture on the relationships and self-esteem of adolescents in a large sample of eleventh-and twelfth-grade Israeli Arabs, sixteen to eighteen years old. They assessed the connections between peer relations, family relations, and self-esteem. Arab adolescents from both cities and villages reported higher self-esteem than did Bedouins (Abu-Saad, 1999). These results suggest that the Bedouin culture is different from other Arab communities with regard to close relationships. We may speculate that their steep move toward modernization or their having a tight collectivistic community affects their perception of self and their relationships with close others.

General Background of the Jewish Society

According to Sagy et al. (1999), not only does Jewish religious ethos preach collectivism and solidarity, but Israeli society started out with a highly collectivist focus. Since the 1960s, however, Israel has been adopting an increasingly individualistic orientation. The majority of Jewish Israeli citizens constitute an in-group defined by nationality and religion. Large differences in power, income, and prestige, as well as exposure to mass media and international communication throughout the 1990s, have increased this trend.

Variations Within the Jewish Group

There are various ways to identify special groups and cultures within Israel's Jewish majority. One such division is by ethnic groups. Researchers have explored differences between the various Jewish ethnic groups and the relationships between these groups in the school setting (Klein & Eshel 1980). The two major groups are the so-called "Eastern" (or "Mizrahi," or "Sephardi") group, defined as mostly from Islamic countries and the Middle East, and the "Western" or "Ashkenazi" group, defined mostly as originating from European and Anglo countries (e.g., Shouval et al., 1984). These two groups (themselves internally heterogeneous) were stable and long established. The Eastern or Sephardi Jews have been more traditional and generally experienced economic and social disadvantage in Israel. Waves of immigration have brought about social change and have altered the distribution, relative numbers, and social map of these groups. There has been an official policy of "integration" of various socioeconomic groups of students. More recently, Jewish society has been trying to integrate waves of immigrants from Ethiopia and Russia, and researchers have investigated peer relationships among different ethnic groups within the schools (Eshel, Sharabany, & Bar-Sade 2003).

Ecological Features of the Israeli Kibbutz

Kibbutzim are collective settlements in rural areas and account for only a small minority of the Jewish population. The kibbutz has been undergoing sweeping changes. These changes are not uniform, and there are differences among kibbutzim in all the dimensions that used to characterize them (Leviatan, 2002). Central changes include economic upheavals leading to increased privatization, which is in opposition to the collectivistic ideology that has been the traditional core of the kibbutz movement. According to Leviatan (2002) privatization has ranged from the establishment of personal control and management of an individual's budget within the context of a collectivistic structure, to total privatization where kibbutz members are paid according to their work or keep their salaries earned outside the kibbutz. Historically, these societies were structured on the basis of principles of equality according to their unique needs and potential, on intensive collaboration, unconditional solidarity, cooperation and fraternity. In addition, there was a commitment to the individual attempts to satisfy the needs and to enable realization of the potential of each individual member. An overarching philosophy of the kibbutz society is an ideology that shies away from any hierarchy based on any parameter.

The kibbutzim had survived a long phase of initial hardship during prestatehood and during the early periods of Israel, when they were very important in developing agriculture and functioning as key defensive border settlements. During a second historical phase, the kibbutzim experienced economic prosperity, playing a major role in the economy, politics, and security of Israel. They evolved into an upper middle class, as defined by economic and cultural criteria, while maintaining their formal collective structure and ideology. During the late 1980s and 1990s, the economic hardship in Israel strongly affected the economy of the kibbutzim and marked the start of great changes. Many aspects of competition and differential rewards and hierarchies evolved and crept informally and gradually into the socioeconomic structures of the kibbutz (Leviatan, 2002). According to Leviatan the kibbutz had to give up a few of its "shiboleth" collectivistic features. Equal pay for all jobs was replaced with differential salary and rewards according to contribution. Direct democracy, in which all members gathered and voted on most issues, was replaced with power-limited or powerless committees. Thus, the principle of allocating resources according to the needs of members was diminished.

Although careful analysis supports the model that the crisis of ideology, values, and norms in the kibbutz was the main carrier of the change and that economic crisis was only secondary (Palgi, 2002), it is hard to separate the transformations from the economic and political macroprocesses in Israel. For reasons beyond the scope of this chapter, this change also paralleled other great upheavals in the world related to collectivistic ideologies, such as the "glasnost" in the Soviet Union. These changes in macrosystems (Bronfenbrenner, 2005) also had parallel processes involving the socialization system of the kibbutz and directly affecting the lives of families and of children in their contact with peers in the mesosystem (e.g., abandoning the communal sleeping arrangements of children in children's houses; Bronfenbrenner, 2005). Polls of kibbutz members about the changes and current state of the kibbutz showed decline in the degree that members felt they could influence processes in their own kibbutz. Thoughts about leaving the kibbutz were relatively common, signaling a continuous state of crisis or at least immense changes (Palgi & Orchan, 2003). One of the hallmarks of the change from collectivistic values and lifestyle was the gradual shift over the last 15 years away from the use of collectivistic sleeping arrangements of children, to sleeping in the parents' home.

The Israeli kibbutz is a small rural cooperative community where property is jointly owned and many responsibilities are shared. One of the most salient of those responsibilities is collectivistic child care (Sharabany & Wiseman 1993, 1998). Children are raised in groups in special children's houses within the kibbutz. They spend most of their day time with a small group of peers with whom they remain continuously from birth until adolescence, supervised by designated adults, visiting their parents' apartment daily (Sagi-Schwarz & Aviezer, in press) until the '90s they also spent their nights in children houses. Kibbutz philosophy values children's intense involvement with peers and non-family caregivers as a way to enhance the socialization to collective life, crossing family boundaries. Raising children in children's houses was a unique experiment, which was started by a combination of hardship endured by pioneers as well as a collectivistic ideology. This was viewed as an interesting natural laboratory to study various questions about socialization of children (Bronfenbrenner, 1970). One set of studies focused on attachment relationships, with findings suggesting that a large percentage of toddlers who experienced collective sleeping arrangements developed insecure attachment to their parents (Aviezer et al., 1994; Toren, 2001). The sequel of these attachment histories continues to be followed in longitudinal studies; the findings of one such study are discussed in the next section (Weiss, 2004).

Friendship Patterns of Jews and Arabs in Israel

A recent study (Ben-Shaul et al., 2004) compared the closeness of friends and family members to Arab and Jewish young adult women in the north of Israel. Intimacy between these women and their mother, their father, a sibling, and a same-sex friend were assessed. The Muslim women in this population reported similar levels of intimacy between themselves and their friends and siblings. In contrast, Jewish women reported more intimacy with friends than with siblings, which is consistent with the expectations that non-kin voluntary relationships would acquire greater significance in the more individualistic Jewish society. Women from both cultures expressed similar views regarding their relationships with their mothers as most intimate and with their fathers as least intimate. These relative patterns of intimacy are similar to those that emerged from a study of attachment patterns of Israeli women raised in kibbutzim (Edry, 1995). Women who were raised on the kibbutz in collective sleeping arrangements with their peers and women who were raised on the kibbutz in their family were asked about degree of attachment to their father, their mother, a sibling, and a best friend. The hierarchy of attachment figures, as reported by participants in this study, ranked the mother figure highest, followed by friends and siblings, with the fathers ranking lowest. Women who were raised in the family and not in children's houses rated their siblings as closer than did women who were raised in separate children's houses and separated from their siblings during the night.

These findings thus reveal consistencies and similarities in the degree of closeness to family members and friends. Differences in ecology, whether vast cultural differences, such as between Jewish and Arab women, or relatively smaller but profound in terms of the family, such as collectivistic sleeping of children versus sleeping in the family house, are associated with differences in the status of the friend in the hierarchy of closeness.

Overlap of Kin and Friends in Rural Settings

We found an unusually high percentage of reciprocated friendship dyads in the sample of Arab students, which also included students from rural villages

(Hertz-Lazarowitz, Nasser-Mazzawi, & Sharabany, in preparation). One possible interpretation is that there are significant overlaps of their school, immediate community, and kin environments, similar to the findings of studies on children's friendships in Italy (Schneider et al., 2000).

Mazzawi's (2001) study is one of the rare studies that examine friendship among Arabs. Two-hundred and sixty students (171 Christians and 86 Muslims) from the seventh and eighth grades (aged twelve to fourteen years) of two Christian private schools in Nazareth – a mostly Arab populated town in Northern Israel – participated in the study. Students completed a friendship questionnaire and the Friendship Quality Scale (Bukowski, Biovin, & Hoza, 1994), as adapted by Scharf and Hertz-Lazarowitz (2003). A measure of intimacy toward peers as a group was adapted by Hertz-Lazarowitz, Rosenberg, and Guttman (1989), based on Sharabany's (1974) intimacy scale. In addition, students self-reported on their psychosocial adaptation. Friendships with best friends were related to psychosocial adjustment. Compared with boys, girls were more secure, closer, and more helpful to their best friends, as well as to their peers.

Scharf and Hertz-Lazarowitz (2003) used the Friendship Qualities Scale (Bukowski et al., 1994) to assess the degree of intimacy between best friends and the peer relations of two Arab and Jewish groups. An impressively large sample of fifty-six mixed classrooms from fourteen schools was assessed. Jewish students reported greater emotional closeness and lower levels of conflict with their best friends, as measured by security and closeness, than did Arab students. The two groups did not differ on the instrumental dimensions of companionship and help.

Congruent with the assumption that Arab society is more collectivistic than Jewish society, the authors reported that among fourth- and fifth-graders (nine to eleven years old), Arab students rated their peer group as more intimate than Jewish students rated theirs (Scharf & Hertz-Lazarowitz, 2003). Arab students compared to Jewish students rated their friendships with classmate peers significantly higher on two composite dimensions (companionship and help; security and closeness), while they did not differ in their assessment of conflict. This finding is important to remember when we discuss the possibility that some collectivistic societies encourage closeness to community, particularly to in group, while discouraging the specific person intimacy and exclusivity (French, Lee, & Padida, this volume).

Elbedour, Shulman, and Kedem (1997) compared a sample of seventh-, ninth-, and eleventh-grade Bedouin children from a town and a village in southern Israel and a Jewish sample from the same grades from Tel Aviv area public schools, using middle- and lower-middle-class samples from both groups. Comparisons were made using several scales: Emotional closeness, control (of the relationship by the friend), conformity, balanced relatedness (acceptance of differences between self and friend), respect, and self-disclosure to the friend.

The two samples were similar in the degree of self-disclosure, which also remained stable across age. Elbedour et al. (1997) reported that, overall, the Bedouin sample scored higher than the Jewish sample on four dimensions: conformity, control, closeness, and respect. Developmental differences also emerged. In the Jewish sample, there were age differences on four of the dimensions: Balanced relatedness and respect increased, with age whereas control and similarity decreased with age. In the Bedouin sample, there was also an increase in respect and decrease in control and emotional closeness. The authors suggested that the collectivistic context might be less conducive to exclusive intimacy and best friendship. To interpret their findings, the authors argue that perhaps it is the commitment to the community and later to the family that reduces the sense of exclusive friendship among the Bedouin adolescents (Elbedour et al., 1997).

The greater emphasis on closeness to the group as opposed to closeness to the individual is also evident in other cultures. In their classic study of college students, Wheeler, Reis, and Bond (1989) compared the United States (assumed to be individualistic) and Hong Kong (assumed to be collectivistic). The diary reports of two weeks, using the Rochester Interaction Record, revealed that the Hong Kong students reported a higher percentage of group and task interactions and greater self-disclosure. This is consistent with prediction of preference for the in-group and for collaboration in collectivistic societies. In comparison, the individualistic group had twice as many interactions, and they were much shorter than those observed in the collectivistic one. Wheeler et al. (1989) suggest that individuals in collectivistic cultures are generally close and warm with their in-group and group of friends. Moreover, they suggest that persons in individualistic cultures have many superficial interactions with members of various groups. Relevant to our theme, the authors do not report about intimacy with a specific person; rather, they report mean number of interaction length and number of partners. Thus, the distinction between closeness to a group of friends and intimacy to a specific person was not made. Their general conclusion may mask selective intimate interactions. Closeness with members of one's in-group and intimacy with a specific person, such as a best friend, are not sufficiently differentiated in cross-cultural research, but they are discussed in the work of French et al. (this volume). Based on our research, it is possible that in individualistic cultures, persons may be very intimate with selected specific persons. Indeed,

Chen and Rubin (1992) found that Chinese children were group-oriented but less close to their best friends than were Canadian children who were more dyadically oriented.

Friendship, Gender, and Collectivistic Culture

Findings that girls and women have more intimate friendships than boys and men have emerged from studies in both individualistic Western societies and traditional collectivistic societies (Chou, 2000; Jones & Dembo, 1989). Only rare exceptions of this generalization have been found (Reis, 1998). We examine here sex differences in same-sex intimate friendships in two cultures: the communal kibbutz, and Arabs in Israel. The kibbutz has a strong ideology of equality of the sexes, whereas the Arab society is highly traditional, and gender is a basis for hierarchical social order.

There are consistent findings that children and adolescents in cities in the north of Israel show gender differences in their intimate friendships, with girls reporting higher intimacy (Sharabany, Gershoni, & Hofman, 1981). When reports of kibbutz children from the fifth and six grade (aged ten to twelve years) were compared with reports of children from the city, it was found in both the kibbutzim and in the cities that girls had closer and more intimate friendships (Sharabany, 1974), paralleling friendships in the United States (Jones & Dembo, 1989) and other cultures (e.g., Portugal: Pinto & Neto, 2003). Thus, in the modern collectivistic society, the gender difference is maintained.

A feature of traditional Arab culture in Israel is the presence of an extended family system, clearly defined traditional social roles, and a vertical authority structure (Dwairy, 1997, 1998, 2004). Gender role differences are also prominent. Women and children are controlled by men, and everyone is dominated by persons senior to them in terms of age. Work and career choices, as well as partner choice, are regulated by family expectations. Women are expected to respect the honor of the family – to wear modest clothes, display unassuming behavior, and bear male children (Budman, Lipson, & Meleis, 1992). Differential gender-role socialization enhances gender differences (Patai, 1973), which become more pronounced and significant in adulthood (Florian & Har-Even, 1984). For example, Florian et al. (1993) reported that Israeli Arab boys are more traditional than girls. Several studies report gender differences, with girls' friendships being generally more intimate than boys' (e.g., Elbedour et al., 1997; Scharf & Hertz-Lazarowitz, 2003).

These gender differences were replicated in the Arab samples from the northern part of Israel (Hertz-Lazarowitz, Nasser-Mazzawi, & Sharabany, in preparation). Based on the Friendship Quality Scale (Bukowski et al., 1994), girls reported being closer, more secure, and more helpful toward their best friends and peers than did boys. Thus, it seems that, in the very different collective societies, gender differences in intimate friendship are maintained in the direction that girls' friendships are more intimate.

Exclusive Dyadic Intimacy in Kibbutzim

Bettelheim (1969) spent time on a kibbutz and interviewed the members in depth, using a psychoanalytic framework. He argued that the expression of personal closeness is inhibited in the communal kibbutz setting. He stressed the difference between the relationship with the group on the one hand and the intimacy of the very personal closeness of expressing individual feelings that is inhibited in the communal setting.

> True intimacy finds no fertile soil to grow on in the kibbutz . . . a society that neither shows nor approves, nor provides opportunities for strong private emotions, as powered by a sense of the two or three of us against all the rest. [They] can be kind or playful with each other, or *devoted to death* [italics added] but they cannot show personal feelings. (Bettelheim, 1969, p. 260)

At the time he wrote this, Bettelheim's conclusions (1969) were highly criticized by several kibbutz educators and by psychologists. They argued that he misunderstood the kibbutz culture, viewing it from the perspective of an outsider and basing his conclusions on observations and interviews in a single kibbutz (e.g., Bronfenbrenner, 1970). Since the publication of Bettelheim's study, there have been many studies supporting the claim of lower dyadic intimacy (see reviews in Josselson et al., 1997; Weiss, 2004).

To address the difficulties with prior research on friendships in kibbutzim, which relied too extensively on single cases and reports by observers, Sharabany (1974) assessed a broad sample of 389 kibbutz-reared fifth- and sixth-grade children and 503 city-reared children from the same grade levels. The kibbutz children were drawn from nineteen kibbutzim of different sizes from different regions of Israel and representing different political movements. The children rated the degree of intimacy of their best friendship, using eight dimensions of intimacy (see previous section on intimacy). To asses the possibility that children from communal settings tend to describe less intimate friendship with their best friends but treat their peers in a similar way, children rated their intimacy with another same-sex peer, based on their list of "kids-I-go-around with." Compared with city children, kibbutz children rated their degree of intimacy of their friendship lower on seven of eight dimensions, except for spending time and doing things together. Findings that kibbutz children rated the dimension of doing things together higher than in the city render validity to their reports since they do spend more time together. However, there was no support for the possibility that they treat their friends similarly to peers, as children in both groups rated intimacy with friends higher than with other peers. So far, I described the reduced intimate friendships in the kibbutz, where children were raised in children's houses, spent most of the days with their peer groups, and slept away from their parents. In a smaller number of kibbutzim, children slept in their parent's houses but still spent most of their days with a peer group. Similar results have been reported in a study comparing kibbutz children with communal sleeping arrangements to those with family sleeping arrangements (Arnon, 1978). Thus, it appears that a major reason for the reduction of closeness to a selected friend in the communal upbringing of the children is the intense, age-homogeneous groups in separate children's houses.

An Explicitly Recognized Social Norm: Preference for the In-Group at the Expense of the Dyad

Parental values play a significant role in channeling the social interactions of their children. According to Schneider (1998), middle-class American parents place less emphasis on compliance, politeness, and respect, while valuing self-reliance and assertive behavior and worrying about aggression and withdrawal behaviors. The Jewish population in Israel, with its Western culture, shares particularly the latter values.

What is the attitude of parents regarding dyadic intimate relationships? In a comparison of adults from the kibbutz with those from another small rural setting (Moshav) similar in socioeconomic status, kibbutz adults reported that they preferred a larger number of friends with superficial connections to a few in-depth friendships. Fewer reported having a best friend, and those who did rated their friendship as less intimate (Beit-Hallahmi et al., 1982).

The values of two collective societies are revealed through the general responses of children to experimental manipulations in the study by Shouval et al. (1975). The responses to dilemmas of 400 Israeli children and 353 Soviet Union children were assessed. Peer pressure was experimentally manipulated to make one behave in a peer-driven mischievous way as opposed to socially acceptable, normative behavior. Israeli kibbutz children and Soviet children reacted to the dilemmas differently when exposure to parent or peers was expected and when they expected their responses to be confidential. Threat of social exposure had a greater effect on the collectively oriented groups of the kibbutz and of Soviet origin, compared with the effect on children who grew up at home in cities.

There is some evidence that norms may change when the context changes, overriding kibbutz-city differences in interactions among peers. Kibbutz children who leave the kibbutz as young adults and live in the city are as intimate in their dyadic friendships as those raised in the city (Wiseman & Lieblich 1989).

The following sociological perspective underscores the role of norms in regulating even the voluntary friendship relationships:

> Individual relationships ... are developed and managed by reference to socially and economically sustained models of what these relationships should be like.... Though there may be a greater degree of choice in friendships than in many other relationships, these ties are still patterned by contextual and situational factors lying outside the direct control of those involved. (Alan, 1993, pp. 3, 5)

There is a powerful influence of the community when the community is small and tightly knit, whether it is mainly traditional, built from extended families, or very modern and infused with individualistic implicit messages. The homogeneity of the small community pressures individuals to get along, reduce conflict, and thus conform. Conflict and exposure are threats to an individual's adjustment to the community and breed cooperation as well as conformity. Thus, ecologically similar settings breed similar adaptation strategies: less preference for the individual other, less confiding, and more getting along.

Possible Reasons for Reduced Dyadic Intimate Friendship and Exclusiveness in These Collectivistic Societies

There are several reasons for reduced intimacy with best friends in children raised in a communal setting, where there is formal communal sharing of most property, income, and services (see discussion in Sharabany, 1974 and Sharabany & Wiseman, 1998). First, perhaps children raised in the communal environment do not invest as much in close friendships because their sense of closeness and security is satisfied by the general context, the community (the experience of overall security, not based on a single factor, is called "being held" in Josselson et al., 1997). Because there are other aspects of closeness present, preference for a specific person is not sought. Second, the reduced privacy of the individual, inherent in the collectivistic lifestyle, may drive children to reduced intimacy in dyadic relationships in an effort to keep privacy and identity (Sharabany & Wiseman, 1993, 1998). Third, the exclusivity of the best friend dyad presents a threat to the smooth social functioning of the peer group, because any preferential relationship is a threat to the group as a whole. Fourth, perhaps based on the aforementioned reasons, there is a norm sanctioning a wider circle of sociability, availability, and cooperation at the expense of the deeper closer dyadic relationships. This norm is documented in a study comparing kibbutz adults to individuals living in a similar, but noncommunal, rural community, the "Moshav." Kibbutz adults expressed preference for a wider circle of friends with "shallower" relationships over having fewer but "deeper" friendships (Beit-Hallahmi et al., 1982).

We would like to stress the consistency in the finding that, in collectivistic societies, whether traditional or modern, being sociable and having harmonious helping relationships with the peer group may be different from having exclusive dyadic relationships. The latter are not sanctioned by values and norms and perhaps even are discouraged by implicit norm. Together, these findings underscore the different quality of peer and group of friends versus best-friend relationships in individualistic and collectivistic environments. This conclusion is based on the limited cases described here and would need to be replicated in a number of societies to withstand such general claim. There is a long way to go to map more specifically the features of a given society directly related to these values and practices.

Friendships Among Kibbutz Children and Among Arab Children: Can the Two Cultures Be Compared?

A common thread of reduced dyadic intimacy and considerable peer group orientation is found in several cultures regarded as collectivistic. Israeli Arab society and the kibbutz are both collectivistic, but in vastly different ways. At the dyadic friendship level, they do share some features. As "macro" social and cultural settings for children's friendships, however, Arab society and the kibbutz are quite different. Kibbutz members have been considered to be among the leading elite of Israeli society. Israeli Arabs, on the other hand, are a minority living separately in villages and, to a smaller extent, in ethnically mixed cities. Although both groups may enjoy aspects of being collectivistic in their orientation, they are also very dissimilar, as Arab society is based on tradition and family. By contrast, kibbutz values were founded on an ideology of social utopia, with an initial ideology of reducing the role and significance of the family system so that greater equality can be created among its members (ironically, a process that over some 80 years evolved in the opposite direction, as within each large kibbutz, clans formed over the years). Founders of Israel's kibbutzim were mostly from the European middle class. These ideologically secular young people, influenced by communist and socialist doctrines, opposed family dominance and actively supported equality between the sexes. The power of the family and kin was diminished, and the community sharing of daily routines and social activities were emphasized. This was most dramatically illustrated by the collective raising of children in special children's houses within the kibbutz.

The culture and values of most kibbutzim were secular, socialist, or communist, valuing equality and direct democracy, in sharp contrast to the traditional hierarchical values of age and gender, which are core values in traditional Arab society. Israeli Arab society, although in a transition of its own, is based on strong and consistent traditions. All these parameters refer to the grand overall picture, the macro level (Bronfenbrenner, 2005). There are vast individual differences within both societies, based on additional parameters, such as religious affiliation, degree of religiosity, and rural or urban residence. Perhaps the most common feature is the state of transition within both societies. For Arabs, it is from tradition to modernity and Western culture; for the kibbutz, it is from communal structure to a market economy.

Having spelled out the vast difference between these two groups, Arab and kibbutz-raised children, the common features found in regard to dyadic intimate friendship and to expressions of closeness with the peer group perhaps make a compelling argument. In some collectivistic cultures, close friendships with an in-group seem to be practiced, whereas dyadic intimacy, especially exclusiveness, is less so.

The Relationship to the Peer Group in the Kibbutz

Cooperating, Avoiding Conflict, and Conforming

Although kibbutz children live in a highly communal society, there is no explicit norm of harmony, and they do not explicitly declare closeness to the peers as a group. Moreover, they do not refrain from disclosing their negative emotions, once asked about them. In contrast, de facto, when their behavior is measured using observations and experiments (rather than self-reports), they show social skills in their behavior in a group from kindergarten age (Levi-Shiff & Hoffman, 1985), and they behave more cooperatively, sharing, reducing competition, and so forth (Shapira & Madsen, 1974). In that respect, they are just like their Italian peers when faced with a situation that may produce conflict with a friend, and they display behavioral skills of avoiding the conflict (Schneider et al., 2000).

In certain situations where there is potential for cooperation, help, and exchange, kibbutz children share more with their peer group than city children do. In a study comparing cooperative interactions of kibbutz and city children in Israel, it was found that the number of cooperative exchanges was double among the kibbutz students (Hertz-Lazarowitz et al., 1989). Even when the situation is constructed to elicit competition among members of the group, kibbutz children transformed it into one of cooperation (Shapira & Madsen, 1974).

This picture of highly cooperative behavior in the communal kibbutz concurs with collectivistic societies where connectedness and reciprocity among in-group members who are related in a network that well defines responsibilities and obligations, are highly important (Rhee, Uleman, & Lee, 1996). However, these interactions are within the group or group of friends but are not dyadic.

Negative Emotions and Criticism

The peer group in the kibbutz is very special. The members of the small peer group are more like circumstantial siblings. The group of about four to eight children is together from almost birth to adolescence. In contrast, they see their biological siblings just for few hours a day. They live together in the children's house, study together, spend their leisure time together, and eat together. Thus, the peer group interaction in the communal kibbutz is more intense than that of other children. Several studies of children in communal kibbutz revealed the expressed negative emotions toward the peer group.

Kibbutz children who had experienced communal sleeping arrangements described their peer group with more negative emotions than did city-reared children. These negative emotions were similar to those used by siblings to describe each other (Regev, Beit-Hallahmi, & Sharabany, 1980). Similar descriptions of the peer group emerged from a study of a large number of fifth- and sixth-grade kibbutzim children who saw their peer group as controlling and delivering sanctions (Devereux et al., 1974; Sharabany, 1982).

Negative Interactions With Peers

Members of the small peer group who had been raised together were close and devoted to each other, but their friendships were not as intimate as in the urban setting, where children had a more open selection of peers (Sharabany, 1982). Moreover, the great physical proximity may breed more negative interactions among the kibbutz peers, perhaps in a way similar to siblings (Devereux et al., 1974; Regev, Beit-Hallahmi, & Sharabany, 1980). In terms of their interactions with peers, kibbutz children did not express closeness to peers (depending on the particular dimension reported) compared with city children (Sharabany, 1980). When kibbutz children and city children described their relationships with several significant others, peers in the kibbutz were not described as supportive, but instead as disciplining and overseeing (Devereux et al., 1974).

A comparison of a small sample of two- and- a- half-year-old kibbutz toddlers with a similar group in the city showed that kibbutz children practiced more distant behaviors, exhibited less warmth and more verbal aggression, and spent more time alone, although they were more skillful in group activities (Levy-Shiff & Hoffman, 1985). Indeed, a recent study investigating adults from kibbutzim all over the country reveals that those raised in communal sleeping houses describe their peer group from their childhood as one creating great identification with the group, while exerting more pressure and sanctions, and being more restrictive as a group as well as overprotective (Weiss, 2004).

Summary

The aim of the present chapter was to examine dyadic intimate friendships within two cultures in Israel: Arabs and kibbutz. Both differ in many features, but they are both collectivist societies. Various defining aspects of the concepts of collectivistic versus individualistic societies were described. In the Arab society, the collectivistic features are those of a traditional society where extended families live in proximity and interdependence, social roles are defined by gender and age, and the collective monitors one's behavior. The kibbutz society is a very modern, Western society consisting of middle-class families, but there are communes in the society in which property, education of children, and most of daily life affairs are shared and decided collectively. The dyadic intimate friendships of kibbutz children are documented to report less intimate friendships and less exclusivity compared with city children. The peer group in the kibbutz is very intense, and children show great skills at getting along, avoiding competition, helping and sharing. Kibbutz children also describe the peer group in negative emotions and negative terms. Various reasons for the lowered intimacy and less exclusivity in the dyadic relationship of kibbutz children were offered. It seems that collectivistic context in this culture does encourage social closeness by way of cooperation, while moderating and discouraging exclusive dyadic friendships. The intensive nature of the ecology that characterizes the kibbutz, combined with freedom to express criticism, produces differences in the experience of the peer group compared with the collectivistic circumstances existing in the Arab society. Among Arab children, like the case of kibbutz children, the same lower dyadic intimacy is observed compared with Jewish children from the city. However, the peer group among Arab children is considered closer than it is for Jewish children from the city. It is in accord with observations from other studies, which indicate that whereas some cultures value specific and intense dyadic friendships, others emphasize acceptance and integration in a social group (French, 2004; French et al., this volume)

Conclusions, a Model, and Further Research

Individualism and collectivism are two constructs that are often used and are very helpful in trying to sum a collection of features that characterize cultures. However, we are well aware that there are different views as to what their core features are and that meta-analysis shows inconsistencies in mapping these two dimensions onto countries (Kagitçibasi, 1994; Oyserman, Kemmelmeier, & Coon 2002). I hope that by describing each of the two societies in detail, the reader is able to reach a somewhat individual conclusion about the match, or mismatch, of labeling both Israeli Arab and Israeli kibbutz collectivistic societies.

In Israel, we can see complex ways of defining cultures, which on the one hand differ vastly and on the other hand share collectivistic features. Ecological features make a great difference in their relevance to intimate friendship, relationships with peers, and the coordination of these two social relationships. A contribution of the present chapter is that I described a possible pattern that emerges beyond these vast differences.

Further study would benefit from interdisciplinary perspectives by giving voice to sociological and anthropological studies that may also yield a more differentiated picture of relevant ecological parameters. The context of rural versus urban regions, of religion, social class, and ethnicity reveals different patterns of intimate friendship. The few studies that do exist about special groups do not identify how each of these components interacts with another (Schneider, 1998).

Further assessment of the effect of situational variability (such as a cooperative learning teaching system or intergroup contacts), how it contributes to changes in the intimate friendship level of a given cultural group, and the degree of exposure to other values that are outside the in-group would have implications for interventions.

Cross-cultural investigations in psychology enable us to extract the contextual from the individual or the dyadic. It has the potential to flush out the fact that features we assume are universal are in fact the product of the specific values of a given society, particularly because our research tends to be Western centered. In contrast, features that we assume are very private and idiosyncratic may reflect implicit values and norms of a particular culture.

Studies by Chen and colleagues (Chen, 2004) provide a useful model for examining the social behavior of children from different cultures. They assess parental norms and expectations, in this case, the preference of Chinese parents for shy children and that of Canadian parents for assertive outgoing children. They assess how common each type of behavior is and find cultural differences confirming the prevalence of normative behavior. Finally, they assess the adaptability of each behavior within its culture and the lack of adaptability of non-normative behavior. This sequence of cross-cultural studies assessed the norms of the society and the reported view of the parents, observed the behavior in a natural setting, and finally evaluated the role of the identified behavior. A similar strategy may be used in the study of children's friendship in Israeli Arab and Kibbutz settings and other contexts.

We are considering the Israeli Jewish kibbutz as a natural historical laboratory. It is a Western and European culture in all respects, "horizontally" egalitarian, but collectivistic in its ideology, economy, child-rearing, and education systems. A complex picture emerges in terms of close relationships. We focused herein on the nature of intimacy with a best friend kibbutz children, we found reduced expressions of intimacy with their best friends in (Arnon, 1978; Sharabany, 1974; Weiss, 2004) and negative aspects of their relationships with peers, such as negative sanctions and great controlling by the peer group (Devereux et al., 1974; Regev et al., 1980; Sharabany, 1982). It seems to be an implicit norm that sanctions criticism (contrasting with the norm of "harmony" that may be prevalent in other traditional collective cultures such as in China). In contrast, when their behavior is observed, children in these collective settings get along by avoiding explicit competition, cleverly transforming it into cooperation (Shapira & Madsen, 1974). When they are given an opportunity, they engage in sharing and cooperating more than city children do (Hertz-Lazarowitz et al., 1989). The observed help, competition avoidance, and cooperative relationships among peers are in contrast to the negative view of the peer group in the kibbutz by children (Sharabany, 1982). When adults were asked in a study to look back on their childhood and reflect on their childhood experience, they described a complex picture of warmth as well as resentment, with large individual differences (Weiss, 2004). Few emphasize their kibbutz peer group as using sanctions, expecting exclusiveness of the group, being overprotective, and exerting pressure on its members, whereas others stress their attachment to the group, as well as enjoying the peer group, which was special to them (Weiss, 2004).

The conclusion from the review of the two groups of Arabs and kibbutz children lead to the hypothesis that, perhaps in collective societies, the social context provides social interaction and support, and closeness to family or to a group of friends. However, dyadic intimacy with a specific friend is less needed and may even be discouraged (Sharabany, 1974). In addition, notwithstanding the positive aspects of collectivistic life, there also may be implicit norms and informal negative sanctions for specific dyadic intimate friendships, particularly for preferring exclusive dyadic relationships that have the implication of excluding the rest of the collectivistic group.

References

Abu-Saad, I. (1999). Self-esteem among Arab adolescents in Israel. *Journal of Social Psychology, 139*(4), 479–486.

Alan, G. (1993). Social structure and relationships. In S. Duck (Ed.), *Social context and relationships* (pp. 1–25). In S. Duck (Series Ed.), Understanding relationships processes (Vol. 3). London: Sage.

Al-Haj, M. (1989). Social research on family lifestyles among Arabs in Israel. *Journal of Comparative Family Studies, 20*, 175–195.

Arnon, A. (1978). Emotional expression and intimate friendship toward significant others in kibbutz with familial and communal sleeping arrangements of preadolescents. Unpublished master's thesis, University of Haifa, Israel.

Aviezer, O., Van Ijzendoorn, M., Sagi, A., & Schuenegel, C. (1994). Children of the dream revisited: Seventy years of collective early child care in Israeli kibbutzim. *Psychological Bulletin, 116*, 99–116.

Barakat, H. (1993). *The Arab world: Society, culture and state*. Berkeley: University of California Press.

Beit-Hallahmi, B., Sharabany, R., Dana-Engelstein, N., Rabin, A. I., & Regev, E. (1982). Patterns of interpersonal attachment: Sociability, friendship and marriage. In A. I. Rabin & B. Beit-Hallahmi (Eds.), *Twenty years later: Kibbutz children grow up*. New York: Springer.

Ben Shaul, T., Sharabany, R., & Kurman, J. (2004, July). *Intimacy in close relationships as a function of three autonomy concepts and culture: Arab and Jewish women*. Paper presented at the Biennial Meeting of the International Society for the Study of Behavioral Development, Gent, Belgium.

Berscheid, E. (1994). Interpersonal relationships. *Annual Review of Psychology, 45*, 79–129.

Bettelheim, B. (1969). *Children of the dream: Communal child-rearing and its implications for society*. New York: Macmillan.

Bronfenbrenner, U. (1970). Dream of the kibbutz. *Saturday Review*, September 20, pp. 72–85

Bronfenbrenner, U. (2005). In U. Bronfenbrenner (Ed.), *Making human being human: Bio-ecological perspectives on human development* (pp. 106–173). Thousand Oaks, CA: Sage.

Budman, C. L., Lipson, J. G., & Meleis, A. I. (1992). The cultural consultant in mental health care: The case of an Arab adolescent. *American Journal of Orthopsychiatry, 62*(3), 359–370.

Bukowski, W. M., Hoza, B., & Biovin, M. (1994). Measuring friendship quality during pre- and early adolescence: The development and psychometric properties of the Friendship Qualities Scale. *Journal of Social and Personal Relationships, 11*, 471–484.

Chen, X. (2004, July). *Social functioning and adjustment in Chinese children: The imprint of historic time*. Paper presented at the Biennial Meeting of the International Society for the Study of Behavioral Development, Gent, Belgium.

Chen, X., & Rubin, K. H. (1992). Correlates of peer acceptance in a Chinese sample of six-year olds. *International Journal of Behavioral Development, 15*, 259–273.

Chou, K. L. (2000). Intimacy and psychosocial adjustment in Hong Kong Chinese adolescents. *Journal of Genetic Psychology, 161*(2), 141–151.

Cordeiro, R. (2005) Physical appearance and intimate friendship in adolescence: A study using a Portugese college student sample. *Social Behavior and Personality, 33*(1), 89–94.

Daeem, R. (1993). Attitudes and emotions in the separation-individuation process of adolescent girls as a function of culture and attachment. Unpublished master's thesis, University of Haifa, Israel.

Devereux, E. Shuval, R. Rodgers, R. R., & Kav-Venaki, S. (1974). Socialization practices of parents, teachers, and peers in Israel: The kibbutz versus the city. *Child Development, 45*(2), 269–281.

Dwairy, M. (1997). Addressing the repressed needs of the Arabic client. *Cultural Diversity and Mental Health, 3*(1), 1–12.

Dwairy, M. (1998). *Cross-cultural counseling: The Arab-Palestinian case*. New York: Haworth Press.

Dwairy, M. (2004). Culturally sensitive education: Adapting self oriented assertiveness training to collective minorities. In: R. Hertz-Lazarowitz, T. Zelniker, C. White Stephan, & W. G. Stephan (Eds.) Arab-Jewish Coexistence Programs. *Journal of Social Issues, 60*(2), 423–436.

Edry, G. (1995). Attachment patterns and perception of relationship with parents and peers in kibbutz women from different sleeping arrangements. Unpublished master's thesis. University of Haifa, Israel.

Elbedour, S., Shulman, S., & Kedem, P. (1997). Adolescent intimacy: A cross cultural study. *Journal of Cross Cultural Psychology, 28*(1), 5–22.

Erber, R., & Erber, M. W. (2001). *Intimate relationships: Issues, theories, and research*. Boston: Allyn & Bacon.

Erikson, E. H. (1959). *Identity and the life cycle*. New York: Norton

Eshel, Y., Sharabany, R., &, Bar-Sade E. (2003). Reciprocated and unreciprocated dyadic peer preferences and academic achievement of Israeli and immigrant students: A longitudinal study. *Journal of Social Psychology, 143*(6), 746–762.

Florian, V., & Har-Even, D. (1984). Cultural patterns in the choice of leisure time activity frameworks: A study of Jewish and Arab youth in Israel. *Journal of Leisure Research, 16*, 330–337.

Florian, V., Mikulincer, M., & Weller, A. (1993). Does culture affect perceived family dynamics? A comparison of Arab and Jewish adolescents in Israel. *Journal of Comparative Family Studies, 24*(2), 189–202.

French, C. D. (2004). Commentary: The cultural context of friendships. *International Society for the Study of Behavioral Development Newsletter, 46*(2), 1–4.

French, C. D., Lee, O., & Pidada, S. (this volume). Friendships of Indonesians, S. Korean and United States youth: Exclusivity, intimacy, enhancement of worth and conflict.

Hertz-Lazarowitz, R., Fuchs, I., Sharabany, R., & Eisenberg, N. (1989). Students' interactive and non-interactive behaviors in the classroom: A comparison between two types of classrooms in the city and the kibbutz in Israel. *Contemporary Educational Psychology, 14*, 22–32.

Hertz–Lazarowitz, R., Nasser-Mazzawi, R., & Sharabany, R. (in preparation). Friendship, prosocial reasoning and psychosocial adaptation during early adolescence. University of Haifa, Israel.

Hertz-Lazarowitz, R., Rosenberg, M., & Guttman, J. (1989). Children of divorce and their intimate relationships with parents and peers. *Youth and Society, 21*, 85–104.

Jones, G. P., & Dembo, M. H. (1989). Age and sex role differences in intimate friendships during childhood and adolescence. *Merrill Palmer Quarterly, 35*, 445–462.

Joseph, S. (Ed.). (1999). Theories and dynamics of gender self and identity in Arab families. In S. Joseph (Ed.), *Intimate selving in Arab families: Gender, self, and identity*. New York: Syracuse University Press.

Josselson, R., Leiblich, A., Sharabany, R., & Wiseman, H. (1997). *Conversation as a method: Analyzing the relational world of people who were raised communally.* Thousand Oaks, CA: Sage.

Kagitçibasi, Ç. (1994). A critical appraisal of individualism and collectivism: Towards a new formulation. In U. Kim, H. C. Triandis, C. Kagitçibasi, S-C. Choi & G. Yoon (Eds.), *Individualism and collectivism: Theory, method and applications* (pp. 52–65). Thousand Oaks, CA: Sage.

Klein, Z., & Eshel, Y. (1980). *Integrating Jerusalem schools.* New York: Academic Press.

Leviatan, U. (2002, December). Is it the end of utopia? The Israeli kibbutz at the 21st century. *The Institute for the Study and Research of the Kibbutz and the Cooperative Idea*, University of Haifa, 88.

Levy-Shiff, R., & Hoffman M. A. (1985). Social behavior of urban and kibbutz preschool children in Israel. *Developmental Psychology, 21*(6), 1204–1205.

Mayseless, M., Wiseman H., & Hai, I. (1998) Adolescents' relationships with father mother and same gender friend. *Journal of Adolescent Research, 13*, 101–128.

Mazzawi, R. (2001). *Friendship and prosocial reasoning as two factors that affect psychosocial adaptation in early adolescence.* Unpublished master's thesis, University of Haifa, Israel.

Newcomb, A. F., & Bagwell, C. L. (1995). Children's friendship relations: A meta analytical review. *Psychological Bulletin, 117*, 306–347.

Oyserman, D., Coon, H., & Kemmelmeier, M. (2002). Rethinking individualism and collectivism: Evaluation of theoretical assumptions and meta-analyses. *Psychological Bulletin, 128*(1), 3–72

Oyserman, D., Kemmelmeier, M., & Coon, H. (2002). Cultural psychology: A new look. *Psychological Bulletin, 128*, 110–117.

Palgi, M. (2002, Febuary). Organizational change and ideology: The case of the kibbutz. *The Institute for the Study and Research of the Kibbutz and the Cooperative Idea.* University of Haifa, 87.

Palgi, M., & Orchan, E. (2003, June). Opinion pole in kibbutzim 2003 and presentation of changes in attitudes during 14 years, *The Institute for the Study and Research of the Kibbutz and the Cooperative Idea.* University of Haifa 182.

Patai, R. (1973). *The Arab mind.* New York: Scribner's.

Pinto, M. da C., & Neto, F. (2003). Intimidade nas relacoes de amizade em alunos do ensino secundario. *Revista Portuguesa de Pedagogia, 37*(1), 157–176.

Prager, K. J. (1995). *The psychology of intimacy.* New York: Guilford.

Reis, H. T. (1998). Gender differences in intimacy and related behaviors: Context and process. In D. J., Canary & K. Dindia (Eds.), *Sex differences and similarities in communication: Critical essays and empirical investigations of sex and gender in interaction* (pp. 203–231). Mahwah, NJ: Lawrence Erlbaum Associates.

Regev, E., Beit-Hallahmi, B., & Sharabany, R. (1980). Affective expression in kibbutz-communal, kibbutz-familial, and city-raised children in Israel. *Child Development, 51*, 232–237.

Rhee, E., Uleman, J. S., & Lee, H. K. (1996). Variations in collectivism and individualism by in-groups and culture: Confirmatory factor analyses. *Journal of Personality and Social Psychology, 71*(5), 1037–1054.

Sagi-Schwarz, A., & Aviezer, O. (in press). Correlates of attachment to multiple care-givers in the Haifa Longitudinal Study: Kibbutz children from birth to emerging adulthood. In K. Grossman, K. Grossman, & E. Waters (Eds.), *Attachment from infancy to adulthood: The major longitudinal studies.* New York: Guilford Press.

Sagy, S., Orr, E., & Bar-On, D. (1999). Individualism and collectivism in Israeli society: Comparing religious and secular high-school students. *Human Relations, 52*(3), 327–348.

Sagy, S., Orr, E., Bar-On, D., & Awwad E. (2001). Individualism and collectivism in two conflicted societies: Comparing Israeli-Jewish and Palestinian-Arab high school students. *Youth & Society, 33*(1), 3–20.

Sanchez-Queija I. & Oliva, A. (2003). Attachment to parents and peer relationships during adolescence. *Revista de Psicologia Social, 28* (1), 71–86.

Scharf, M., & Herz-Lazarowitz, R. (2003). Social networks in the school context: Effects of culture and gender. *Journal of Social and Personal Relationships, 20*(6), 843–858.

Schneider, B. H. (1998). Cross cultural comparison as doorkeeper in research on the social emotional adjustment of children and adolescents. *Developmental Psychology, 34*(4), 793–797.

Schneider, B., Fonzi, A., Tomada, G., & Tani, F. (2000). A cross national comparison of children's behavior with their friends in situations of potential conflict. *Journal of Cross Cultural Psychology, 3*(2), 259–266.

Schneider, B., Smith, A., Poisson, S. E., & Kwan, A. B. (2000). Connecting children's peer relations with the surrounding cultural context. In R. S. L. Mills & S. Duck (Eds.), *The developmental psychology of personal relationships* (pp. 175–198). West Sussex, England: Wiley.

Shapira, A., & Madsen, M. C. (1974). Between and within group cooperation and competition among kibbutz and non kibbutz children. *Developmental Psychology, 10*, 140–145.

Sharabany, R. (1974). *Intimate friendship among kibbutz and city children and its measurement*. Unpublished doctoral dissertation, Cornell University, Ithaca, New York.

Sharabany, R. (1982) Comradeship: Peer group relations among pre adolescents in kibbutz vs. city. *Personality and Social Psychology Bulletin, 8*, 302–309.

Sharabany, R. (1994a). Continuities in the development of intimate friendships: Object relations, interpersonal relations and attachment perspectives. In R. Erber & R. Gilmour (Eds.), *Theoretical frameworks for personal relationships*. Hillsdale, NJ: Lawrence Erlbaum Associates.

Sharabany, R. (1994b) Intimate friendship scale: Conceptual underpinnings, psychometric properties and construct validity. *Journal of Social and Personal Relationships, 11*, 449–469.

Sharabany, R. (2001). Intimacy in preadolescence: Issues in linking parents and peers, theory, culture, and findings. In K. A. Kerns, J. M. Contreras, & A. M. Neal-Barnett (Eds.), *Family and peers: Linking two social worlds*. Westport, CT: Praeger.

Sharabany, R, Gershoni, R., & Hofman, J. (1981). Girl-friend, boy-friend: age and sex differences in intimate friendship. *Developmental Psychology, 17*(6), 800–808.

Sharabany, R., & Schneider, B. H. (2004). On the study of friendship in childhood and adolescence: A view from the bridge (s). *International Society for the Study of Behavioral Development Newsletter, 46*(2), 1–4.

Sharabany, R., & Wiseman, H. (1993). Close relationships in adolescence – The case of the Kibbutz. *Journal of Youth and Adolescence, 22*, 671–695.

Sharabany, R., & Wiseman, H. (1998). Adolescence with peers: Intimate friendship and emotional expression in the kibbutz. In Y. Dar (Ed.), *Socialization in a changing kibbutz: Sociological and psychological perspectives*. Hebrew University, Jerusalem: Magnes.

Shechtman, Z., Freidman, Y., Kashti, Y., & Sharabany, R. (2002). Group counseling to enhance adolescents' close friendships, *International Journal of Group Psychotherapy, 52*, 537–553.

Shouval, R., Kav-Venaki, S., Bronfenbrenner, U., Devereux, E. C., & Kiely, L. (1975). Anomalous reactions to social pressure of Israeli and Soviet children raised in family vs. collective settings. *Journal of Personality and Social Psychology, 32*(3), 477–489.

Shouval, R., Shouval, E., Kav-Venaki, R., & Sharabany, R. (1984). Ethnic and cultural variations in children's independence by ordinal position and gender. *Individual Psychology, 40*, 3–21.

Shulman, S., Laursen, B., Kalman, Z., & Karpovsky, S. (1997). Adolescent intimacy: Revisited. *Journal of Youth and Adolescence, 26*, 597–617.

Sicard, L. (1994). La relations arec les parents et les amis et le development de l'autonomie a l' adolescence. *Dai, 56–11B*, 1247, Universitye de Montreal, Canada.

Tani, F., & Maggino, F. (2003). The dimensions of intimate friendship: A scale for life span. *Eta-evolutiva, 75*(1), 104–114.

Toren, O. (2001). *The differentiation level and object representations of communal-sleeping girls and their mothers*. Unpublished master's thesis, The Hebrew University of Jerusalem, Israel.

Triandis, H. C. (1995). *Individualism and collectivism*. Boulder, CO: Westview.

Turiel, E., & Wainryb, C. (1998) Concepts of freedoms and rights in a traditional, hierarchically organized society. *British Journal of Developmental Psychology, 16*(3), 375–395.

Uleman, J. S., Rhee, E., Bardoliwalla, N., Semin, G., & Toyama, M. (2000). The relational self: Closeness to in-groups depends on who they are, culture, and the type of closeness. *Asian Journal of Social Psychology, 3*, 1–17.

Weiss, L. Y. (2004). *The importance of the peer group on the development of adult attachment style*. Unpublished doctoral dissertation, Northampton. Smith College, Northampton, Mass., USA.

Wheeler, L., Reis, H. T., & Bond, M. H. (1989) Collectivism individualism in everyday social life: The middle kingdom and the melting pot. *Journal of Personality and Social Psychology, 57*(1), 79–86.

Wiseman, H., & Lieblich, A. (1989, July). *Intimacy and loneliness in the transition to adulthood*. Paper presented at the Annual Meeting of the Israeli Psychological Association, Haifa, Israel.

Commentary III

21 Peers and Culture

Details, Local Knowledge, and Essentials

William M. Bukowski and Ryan Adams

This commentary on the chapters in the friendship section by French, Lee, and Pidada; Azmitia, Ittel, and Brenk; Way, and Sharabany is organized around three questions: (a) how does one evaluate studies of culture, friendship, and peer relationships; (b) what can studies of cultural differences tell us about friendship and peer relationships; and (c) what can studies of friendship and peer relationships tell us about culture. Aside from the specific conclusions or substance of these chapters, these questions serve as an ever-present backdrop for our thinking about them. At the risk of repeating a basic premise underlying this volume, an irony of theory and research on peer relationships is the apparent assumption that peer relationships contribute to development in pretty much the same way in all places. This assumption is ironic in light of the frequent assumption that the significance and functions of the peer system are influenced by other aspects of the social and personal context. According to this assumption, the effects of peer relations will vary across children. If the effects of peer experiences are not "fixed," even in a particular place, then why should we expect that they would not vary across places and cultures? The chapters that make up this section struggle with the question of how peer relationships intersect with cultural conditions.

Previously, it was proposed that there are at least three approaches to the study of peers and culture (Bukowski & Sippola, 1998). According to one approach, known as the *details* model, the basic processes and features of peer relationships are presumed to be largely the same across cultures. This approach allows for the possibility that the particular manifestations of some features of the peer system may vary from one place to another and may look different in different places. But it claims that the associations between features of the peer system will be the same from one place to another. For example, expressions of helpfulness and aggression may vary across places, but this approach assumes that each of these phenomena would be as strongly related to popularity in one place as it is in another. In this way, the "equations" that are developed in one culture to describe and explain the characteristics and processes of peer relations should be applied easily and successfully in another cultural context. In other words, peer relations are the same everywhere except for the details.

The second approach, described by Bukowski and Sippola (1998), was called the *local knowledge* model. Loosely based on the ideas of Clifford Geertz (1983), this model claims that developmental goals and objectives vary across cultures. As a result, the value or developmental significance of particular forms of experience will vary also. This variability will be a direct result of variations in the "needs" or the demands that a particular culture presents. Consider the differences between cultures that emphasize either collectivistic or individualistic goals. Whereas in a collectivist culture, a cooperative and helpful child might be favored by peers and a self-involved child might be shunned, in an individualistic culture, a self-oriented child who places individual achievement over group involvement would be at least tolerated by peers if not approved by them. Consider also a culture that places a great deal of emphasis on kinship. Under these circumstances, the role of peers in children's lives may have considerably less significance than in other places. According to the local knowledge approach, the extent to which findings observed in one culture will be seen elsewhere will vary as a function of differences in the developmental needs or demands that each presents.

The third model described by Bukowski and Sippola (1998) claims that, in some cases, the differences between cultures might be so vast or profound that the functioning and features of the peer system in both places cannot be reconciled. According to this *essentialist* approach, the meanings, needs, and functions that cultures ascribe to peer relations concepts or goals that organize peer interaction are culturally specific. As a result, applying ideas and findings observed in one culture to understand peer relations in another society is misguided. This approach implies that the peer relations needed to be studied in a culture-by-culture manner. In each place, one would need to reconsider what children do with each other, why they do it, how these experiences fit in with their other social activities, and how they contribute to development. The essentialist approach means that, each time, a researcher needs to start anew with a fresh, open, and informed eye.

Use of each of these approaches can be seen in the four chapters in this section. The themes that comprise the essentialist position can, in part, be seen in the chapter written by French and colleagues. They ultimately adopted a nuanced local knowledge approach to the study of friendship and culture. Nevertheless, they proposed that the best way to begin an inquiry of this sort is to take an essentialist perspective. That is, they wanted to first see how peer experiences fit into a particular cultural context. Using anthropological accounts and cultural analyses, they assessed how people in a culture thought about, or constructed, the concept of friendship and how they ascribed characteristics to it. Their efforts were as much about understanding the social forces within a culture as they were about the social construction of friendship. Their particular interest was the characteristics that youth ascribe to friendships, especially the features that are related to the intensity of friendships. By considering differences between the experiences of friendships of youth from three cultures (i.e., Korea, Indonesia, and the United States) rather than just two, French and colleagues were able to provide a richer and more thorough assessment of the cultural sources of variability in friendship features. Also, by using multiple forms of assessment, they were able to provide a very textured assessment of friendship within context. The strength of their study was their reluctance to fall back on simple ideas and to point out where well-known or standard ideas about how we should study culture should be reconsidered. Their reasoned criticisms of the overreliance on ideas about individualism and interdependence are especially important.

The projects French and colleagues discuss are important and successful studies of peer relations in at least two ways. First, they show the importance of using multiple methods of assessment, particularly the combination of qualitative and qualitative approaches. Second, they show the value of using multiple contexts for purposes of comparison. In regard to what the projects tell us about peer relations, they show that many of the basic constructs regarding peer experience can be transported from one place to another but that their importance and developmental significance will vary. With respect to what the studies tell us about culture, French and colleagues are clear in their conclusion that the reliance on a limited set of basic dimensions, such as interdependence, is inadequate. Perhaps most importantly, they show that basic aspects of peer relations, such as intensity and extensivity, can be used as dimensions to distinguish one cultural context from another.

Whereas French and his colleagues were interested in the features that youth ascribed to friendship, Way was interested in the processes of friendship. She explored this in three ways. First, she provided a new look at the association between two well-known "features" of friendship, specifically, sharing and trust. Second, she considered the role of friendship as a form of protection and help. Third, she pointed to the importance of seeing the fit between family and friends. In regard to sharing and trust, the findings from her studies showed that these phenomena are not simply correlated features of friendship but that sharing is a process that is antecedent to trust. Consistent with a details approach, Way showed that the manifestations of sharing vary across cultural groups. In some cases, the sharing of money is critical. Regardless of its manifestations, however, sharing was seen as a critical determinant of trust for adolescents, regardless of their cultural background. Protection, an understudied feature of peer relations, is another feature that probably fits with the details approach. It implies that the ways that friends protect each other will differ across contexts. The findings, however, support a local knowledge approach in the sense that the need for protection might be stronger in some contexts than others. Accordingly the significance ascribed to protection appears to vary as well. Similar conclusions are reached for the place of help in friendship.

Way's chapter has a powerful message for persons who study peer relations. The constructs we use may be somewhat consistent across contexts, but the manifestations of these constructs and their significance will vary. Also, researchers need to recognize that the features of friendship can be related to each other in functional ways instead of being seen as mere correlates of each other. The chapter also has a clear message about culture. Aside from the broad dimensions that are often used to distinguish cultures from each other, cultures have unique textures that place particular demands and constraints on experience. Knowing how peers fit into the resolution of these demands tells us how a culture works.

The local knowledge approach is seen also in Sharabany's chapter on the effects of culture on peer relationships and intimate friendships. Sharabany examines individualism and collectivism in various Arab and Jewish cultures in Israel by exploring the premise that because collectivistic cultures are group oriented, individuals will be less likely to differentiate how much they invest in specific friendships in collectivistic cultures than in individualistic cultures. Because those in collectivistic cultures focus their attention across the group rather than on a small number of friends, the levels of intimacy in friendships should be lower for those in collectivistic cultures than in individualistic cultures.

In her review of the research on this topic, Sharabany begins by providing the reader with some background information on Arab and Jewish society in Israel by describing two types of collectivistic cultures, Arab culture and kibbutz culture. Both cultures are collectivist, but there are many differences between these cultures apart from religion. Arab culture is a hierarchical, patriarchal society with strong social roles based on age and social networks that are comprised of mostly kin, whereas the kibbutz culture is based on equality and cooperation among all members, and social networks are not dominated kinships. Interestingly, results for most studies on friendships are quite similar across each of these two groups despite these cultural differences, with both of these collectivist cultures having lower intimacy than the more individualistic urban Jewish culture.

Although Sharabany uses a general framework that compares minority Arab collectivist cultures, minority Jewish kibbutz collectivist cultures, and majority urban Jewish individualist cultures to explore cultural differences in intimacy, she does not generalize that there is a simple Arab/Jewish dichotomy or minority/majority dichotomy. Instead, the focus is across many types of Arab groups, such as Palestinian and Bedouin, and Jewish groups, such as Sefardi and Ashkenazi. Differentiating across various dimensions of culture and finding very similar results within the various collectivist cultures provides insights into understanding collectivistic cultures in general. Alternatively, this same feature provides insights to understanding friendships in general. Gender differences in intimacy (i.e., females reported higher rates of intimacy than males) and differences in intimacy between friends versus other peers (i.e., participants reported higher rates of intimacy with friends than with other peers) were shown in both collectivist and individualist cultures. Overall, the insights for culture and friendships that are provided by an approach that uses various types of collectivist and individualist cultures is evidence for the value of this approach.

Azmitia and collegues examined adolescent friendships in Latino youth by reviewing their own and others' quantitative and qualitative research. Instead of relying on the collectivism/individualism dichotomy, this review primarily focused on the culture of Latinos living in the United States and how characteristics of this group are important to understanding adolescent friendships. At the core of this culture is the family. In this way, the actions of individuals within the family are a result of and a reflection on the family group. Often, parents in this culture view friends as possible impediments to the road of success, especially for girls and those children whose siblings have had previous difficulties in school or were involved in delinquent acts. On the other hand friends can also work as "bridges" from the family to the school context. Often, it is through friends that Latino students, who are at a higher risk for academic failure than other ethnic groups, find academic success. Friends can provide guidance as well as support in school for these adolescents, whose parents are often unfamiliar with the educational system, but friends can also keep adolescents from advancing in school when their friends disapprove of academic success. This chapter provides insight into friendships that might be missed in other studies of children of the majority culture by describing the characteristics of Latino friendship and in explaining the various ways that friendships are used in this culture. Overall, the strength of this chapter lies not only in the detailed descriptions of Latino friendships, but also in its focus on how to think about and study culture and adolescent development.

Research on peer relationships is moving in several directions in an effort to understand the variability in the ways that peers play a role in children's lives and in their development. The success of research on this topic depends on several critical ingredients, including ideas, methods, open mindedness, and reflection about the big questions. It also depends on the willingness of thoughtful researchers to think carefully about their questions and their data. The authors of the chapters have been able to deal with these challenges in ways that will help and inspire future research.

Acknowledgments

Work on this essay was supported by a grant to the first author from the Social Sciences and Humanities Research Council of Canada.

References

Bukowski, W. M., & Sippola, L. K. (1998). Diversity and the social mind: Goals, constructs, culture, and development. *Developmental Psychology, 34*, 742–746.

Geertz, C. (1983). *Local knowledge: Further essays in interpretive anthropology*. New York: Basic Books.

Conclusion

22 Peer Relationships in Cultural Perspective
Methodological Reflections

Barry H. Schneider, Doran C. French, and Xinyin Chen

In this concluding chapter, we reflect on some of the challenges confronting researchers who seek to understand peer relationships within a cultural context. We focus specifically on some of the methodological issues that have been raised in the chapters and implications of these issues for future study. The chapters in this volume illustrate some of the methodological advances in the study of culture and social behavior, as well as the methodological pluralism that characterizes the field. In the following sections, we will discuss: (a) the assessment of cultural influence using between-group comparisons, (b) cultural psychology, and (c) developmental perspectives.

Equivalence and Biases in Cross-Cultural Comparisons

Many of the methodological discussions focusing on culture have addressed the difficulty of making valid inferences from comparisons of multiple cultures. A basic assumption underlying the work in the field is that the variation in the social or psychological functioning of individuals in different settings may indicate the causal influence of culture on individuals. Perhaps foremost among the issues discussed in the methodological literature in cross-cultural psychology is the need to systematically sample cultures on theoretical grounds so that the cultural groups represent variations in the theoretically relevant cultural dimension.

Although some advocates of theory-based sampling of cultures, such Van den Vijver and Leung (1997), recognize the value of two-culture comparisons when researchers have a compelling theoretical reason for comparing the two cultures, any two cultures are likely to vary on so many dimensions that it is difficult to isolate the elements that are responsible for differences between groups (Jahoda & Krewer, 1997). For this reason, some researchers (e.g., Campbell & Narroll, 1972) argue that at least three cultures must be included. Multiculture analyses provide a useful alternative. For example, Bergeron and Schneider (2005) used cross-national differences on dimensions of cultural-level values to predict effect sizes of cross-national differences in aggression for 185 comparisons between pairs of cultures from a total of thirty-six studies. They found that cultures characterized by collectivistic values, high moral discipline, high level of egalitarian commitment, low uncertainty avoidance, and the presence of Confucian values showed lower levels of aggression than their counterparts. Although the advantages of multiculture studies are obvious, practical constraints on resources, difficulties establishing collaboration across multiple nations, and problems maintaining equivalence in sampling and procedure are likely to be a substantial burden for many researchers. As we discuss later, understanding the cultures under study is critical for cross-cultural research, and it is difficult for researchers to acquire such expertise in multiple cultures.

It is important in cross-cultural comparison to ensure that the sample selected from a country is representative of the larger population. This is a formidable task in cross-cultural work, just as it is in domestic research, in which it is common to generalize the results from samples in a single university or city to the larger population, which consists of diverse groups. Given practical constraints, researchers are often limited to selecting samples they assume are somewhat representative of the general population. Under such circumstances, it is essential that researchers describe their samples with as much detail as possible.

A second concern is the difficulty ensuring that data from the different cultures are equivalent except for the "culture" variable (e.g., Gudykunst, Ting-Toomey, & Chua, 1988). Samples that are representative of the general populations in different cultures are rarely equivalent. For example, because nations differ in socioeconomic conditions or education resources, random sampling is likely to lead to the lack of equivalence on these variables. Selecting samples that match on these variables may cause biases on some other, mostly unknown, dimensions, and thus cause potentially serious problems. These difficulties are also present in within-culture studies of different groups, particularly those of different ethnic groups. McLoyd (1990), for example, has documented the serious consequences of failing to control for social class differences when comparing Black and White U.S. populations. Similarly, participants from rural areas in many societies do not share the core values of city dwellers (Bethlehem, 1975). A useful strategy is to select random samples in different cultures and collect as much background information as possible, so some statistical controls may be conducted in later analyses (e.g., controlling socioeconomic status or education levels as covariates) if necessary.

Concerns of equivalence also apply to measurement. Many cross-cultural peer relationship researchers rely on questionnaires, including peer evaluations, teacher ratings, parental reports, and child self-reports. It is nearly impossible to attain totally accurate translation of the items themselves because of the problems inherent in translating virtually anything. According to an Italian proverb, *traduttore traditore*, or "the translator is a traitor" (Metzger, 1976). The translation of this proverb illustrates some of the difficulties. Because these two words differ in only one vowel sound, the proverb has an element of rhyme and alliteration in English but not in other languages. More serious problems arise in translating words used to describe personality and feeling states. For example, the contention that there are five broad dimensions of the human personality is thought by some to be linked to the way the items of personality scales sound to native listeners of American English. The nonequivalence of the terminology may result in a failure to fully replicate the five-factor structure in other languages (di Blas, Forzi, & Peabody, 2000).

Ways of dealing with obstacles in translation have been proposed, including using back-translations (van de Vijver & Leung, 1997). When multiple items are used, inaccuracy in the translation of specific terms or items is less of a concern because it is unlikely to have systematic effects on the results; the aggregate scores may "filter" out the "noises" or random errors. The problem becomes even less serious if the multimethod–multi-informant technique is used (French, Lee, & Pidada, this volume). Obviously, regardless of the specific technique, it is important to conduct rigorous psychometric examinations of the measures, such as internal consistencies, factor structure, and cross-cultural equivalence, at both the measurement and construct levels (Card & Little, this volume). Nevertheless, it is possible for data from different countries to be identical in appearance and psychometric qualities, but to have totally different emotional valence. This was pointed out by Chen and colleagues in their comparison of the attitudes of peers and parents in China and Canada toward children who are shy, anxious, and withdrawn (Chen, Rubin, & Sun 1992). At the time the data were collected, the Chinese participants felt that shyness was a positive attribute, whereas Canadian participants viewed this as negative.

Additional threats to equivalence of measurement come from cultural differences in response biases and rating reference groups. Persons in different cultures may display different response styles in answering questions (e.g., Chen, Lee, & Stevenson, 1995; Leung & Bond, 1989). For example, Chen et al. (1995) found that Asian children and adults tended to choose the midpoints on a scale, whereas North American individuals were likely to use extreme values, an effect that also emerged in French et al. (this volume). The issue of the "reference-group" effect is more challenging. Peng, Nisbett, and Wong (1997) suggest that people from different cultural groups may use different referents in their self-reports. Individuals typically evaluate themselves in comparison with others within the same culture, rather than with members of other cultures, when they provide ratings. Similar processes occur when teachers, parents, and peers evaluate children. Accordingly, cross-cultural comparisons are confounded by reference-group effects. This is most dramatically illustrated by the findings of Weisz et al. (1995) that, although teachers provided higher behavior problem ratings to Thai than American students, trained observers found that Thai students displayed fewer behavioral problems than American students.

The act of providing data to a researcher must be understood within a cultural framework (Cole, 1996). One fundamental difference is the extent to which respondents are familiar and at ease with the research methods. Many North Americans are bombarded with questionnaires, whereas members of developing cultures might find the research process unfamiliar and mystifying. There also may be cultural differences in the willingness to reveal personal information to others. For example, the maintenance of one's reputation may be particularly important in some East Asian cultures (Ting-Toomey, 1988). Authority figures in some cultures are feared or distrusted, and thus individuals might have concerns about what school or health officials will do with the information provided. Finally, cultural differences might exist in the willingness of participants to share information about the family.

In many comparisons of data from two or more countries, the data represent very unequal proportions of the investment of research resources. Research on human behavior in North America and Western Europe overshadows research in the same fields in developing countries. Therefore, studies originating in the developing world are very few in number and often very different from studies conducted in countries where behavioral science is more familiar. Hence, research agendas may be driven by the concerns of Western researchers.

Many cross-cultural researchers (e.g., Oyserman, Coon, & Kemmelmeier, 2002; Triandis, 1990) advocate direct assessments of culture as a strategy to overcome some of the difficulties in cross-cultural comparisons. A number of cultural measures concerning collectivism–individualism (Hofstede, 1980), idiocentrism–allocentrism (Triandis, 1989), independence-interdependence self-construals (Markus & Kitayama, 1991; Singelis, 1994), and cultural values (e.g., Schwartz & Sagiv, 1995) have been developed to measure cultural orientations. However, Oyserman et al. (2002) suggest that the aggregated scores of self-reports are largely ineffective in differentiating societies, even between the representative collectivistic and individualistic societies, such as China and the United States. When used for within-culture individual-level analysis, the data based on individual self-reports also have limited value in revealing cultural processes beyond "personality traits."

Cultural Psychology: An Alternative to Causal Thinking in Studying the Workings of Culture

As introduced earlier, the assumption behind the call for systematic, theory-based sampling of cultures is that the central objective of cross-cultural psychology is to demonstrate that culture is, essentially, the *cause* of the behavior being studied. Culture is, thus, treated as "an independent variable" (Jahoda & Krewer, 1997, p. 28). Jahoda and Krewer argue for an alternative approach in which intensive understanding of a single culture is sought. Several examples of the use of this approach are present in this volume, as illustrated by the work of Azmitia, Ittel, and Brenk; Corsaro; and Gaskins.

Sinha (1997) discusses the movement toward "indigenizing psychology" as a countercurrent to the uncritical importation of Western psychology into other cultures. Such importation includes the classical cause-and-effect thinking that underlies mainstream Western psychology. In its extreme form, indigenization eschews the comparison of different cultures altogether. Many theorists within the "indigenization movement," however, advocate judiciously using theoretical and methodological precepts from outside the culture to the extent that they are useful to understanding the "indigenous" culture.

It should be noted that research that offers an in-depth exploration of important and distinct features of a single culture or a small number of cultures draws heavily on the methods of anthropology. The chapters by Cole et al. and Gaskins provide examples of this approach.

The Contribution of Developmental Psychology to the Study of Culture

Valsiner and Lawrence, (1997) aptly remarked that cross-cultural psychology has not been developmental in its approach, whereas developmental psychology has not been culturally inclusive. Not surprisingly, the most compelling lesson from the core theories of human development is to consider developmental differences in the phenomena under study. Developmentalists emphasize the importance of studying individuals at different ages and exploring the continuity and discontinuity from one developmental period to another.

Thus, it is possible that similar developmental sequences exist across cultures, but that timing of experiencing the sequences varies. For example, in a classic study of the development of cognitive tempo, Salkind, Kojima, and Zelniker (1978) found a progression from impulsive to reflective response styles in American, Japanese, and Israeli children ranging from five to twelve years of age. However, Japanese children reached the optimal level of reflection at age eight, two years before their American and Israeli counterparts. These developmental differences might be hidden were a cross-cultural comparison of children of a similar age group conducted. A cross-sectional or longitudinal design featuring multiple cultures would be needed, for example, to test a contention by Sameoff and Haith (1996) that the crucial challenge of the period between five and seven years of age varies by culture. In Western societies, that age range offers the essential challenge of adjusting to school, whereas in some non-Western societies, the crucial challenge of that period is to adapt to the responsibilities of participating in the rearing of younger children and other emerging community responsibilities.

A second focus of developmental psychologists has been to test the extent to which general theories of development are widely generalizable or whether these need to be modified to explain development in different cultures. This point was made explicitly by Schneider (1998), who argued that cross-cultural studies are necessary to evaluate the appropriateness of developmental theories. For example, considerable research has assessed cross-cultural generalizability of Kohlberg's seminal stage model of moral development, a key element of which is the hypothesis that moral thinking proceeds developmentally across a series of stages that occur in an invariant order across cultures (e.g., Edwards, 1994). An important byproduct of that debate has been the recognition of a variety of systems of rationality that are shaped by culture (e.g., Shweder, 1993) and the recognition by many that Kohlberg's theory, especially as it applies to thinking at the higher stages, may be more specific to middle-class Western culture than earlier writings suggested (Turiel, 1998).

An additional example of the effort to establish generalizable theories comes from the study of emotional development. Developmental psychologists who study emotions have also embarked on at least as many searches for cross-cultural similarities as studies designed to establish and explicate cross-cultural differences. As reviewed by Saarni, Mumme, and Campos (1998), considerable research energy has been invested in attempts to demonstrate universality in children's recognition of facial expressions. This has been extended to explorations of elicitation of expressions of anger and fear. It is only in recent years that scholars of emotional development have begun to look intensively for differences among cultures as they reflect the climate of the surrounding culture and patterns of child-rearing (Saarni et al., 1998). Thus, in both the moral and emotional development areas, scholars have initially sought to assess universal patterns of development, but are now increasingly seeking to understand how this development occurs in culturally specific forms.

Another major focus of developmental psychologists has been to understand how cultural processes are implicated throughout development. Developmental researchers have a long tradition exploring how development occurs within a cultural context and how children come to adopt the values and beliefs and exhibit the behavior associated with a culture (e.g., Whiting, 1941). The work of Rogoff (2003), for example, clearly indicates the processes by which children move from unskilled to skilled members of the society.

Many researchers have called for investigation of "cultural processes" beyond cross-cultural similarities and differences (e.g., Garcia-Coll, 2005). We have also argued that it is important to understand the "meanings" of social behaviors in different cultures (Chen et al., 2005; Chen, French, & Schneider, this volume). We believe that a powerful strategy to gain in-depth understanding of the cultural processes and functional meanings of the behaviors is to investigate developmental origins, antecedents, concomitants, and outcomes, as well as developmental patterns. Aside from the benefits of clarifying the ways in which culture and development interact as causal forces, developmental research can offer the important additional advantage of enabling researchers to determine whether their findings remain stable, even when the core features of societies may change. The chapter by Chen, Wang, and DeSouza on the way Chinese children and adults regard childhood shyness illustrates the return on the investment inherent in longitudinal methods.

Methodological Decisions of the Chapter Authors

A glance back at the chapters in this volume reveals that the authors approached their study of cultural influences on peer relationships from different perspectives. Whereas some started with an interest in studying a particular aspect of cultural processes and then tested the ideas with samples in relevant cultures, others were driven by attempts to understand the extent to which findings from the peer relationship literature were generalizable across different populations. Most notable was that much of the research was grounded in attempts to understand features of the cultures under study. Such understanding often emerged from work with local researchers to develop a shared knowledge of the similarities and differences between cultures. This should not be dismissed as "convenience sampling" but instead can be seen as a reflection of the need to understand the features of the culture prior to undertaking research. To put it another way, most of the researchers in this volume have rejected the notion of strictly using an imposed etic, in which instruments from one culture are applied to another without understanding the cultural context in which the phenomena exist.

We now turn to some of the methodological issues addressed by the authors of these chapters. The lessons that could be learned from these methodological sources are not entirely consistent, meaning that researchers must make informed choices. Other choices are imposed by the limits of the resources available for a given study. Most fundamentally, the methodological and epistemological options differ in terms of whether or not one should embark on cross-cultural research with a predetermined hypothesis in mind or a broad interest in exploring diverse developmental patterns in cultural contexts. That decision may have implications for the choice of both culture and method. It may be useful to note that one needs not necessarily decide whether to consider using qualitative and quantitative methods because many influential studies in this and other fields involve a mixture of the two.

Another common feature across the chapters is the careful, painstaking description of the interplay of socializing forces at work within the culture or cultures being studied. Whereas this description of the culture was not usually the main objective of the chapter, it is often the driving force behind the hypotheses. This depth of knowledge of the culture is one feature of many of the chapters that differentiates this research from the casual, convenient, and atheoretical cross-cultural comparisons that predominated in early cross-cultural studies. Some of the authors provide details of the ways in which they became familiar with the cultures they worked with, such as the focus group interviews on parents' socialization practices described in the chapter by Nelson et al. and the preliminary interviews regarding friendship described by French et al.

Although the classic dichotomy between individualism and collectivism was rarely the main theoretical focus of the research reported here, the framework was discussed in many of the chapters. In some cases, such discussion reflects the influence of this framework in the cross-cultural literature. In other cases, the dimensions of individualism and collectivism are particularly applicable for explaining the differences that emerged. Nevertheless, differences along other dimensions were noted. For example, many of the authors discussed cross-cultural variations in relations with authority figures (e.g., Chen et al., Cole et al., Eisenberg et al., Xu et al.), differences in gender role socialization (e.g., Azmitia, Ittel, & Brenk; Corsaro; Edwards et al.; Schneider et al.; Sharabany; Way), variation in emotional expression (Eisenberg et al., Cole et al.), the impact of cultural change (Chen et al., Xu et al.), cultural norms for dealing with conflict (French et al., Goudena, Xu et al.), and the delineation of family and peer group socialization (Schneider et al.).

Armed with knowledge of the cultures involved and connected with the people needed to help define and implement the research, the chapter authors opted to use a variety of methods of peer relations research, some of which were fairly traditional, to test explicit hypotheses. In doing so, they put themselves in a good position to convince peer relations scholars of the validity of their findings. At the same time, they helped the field of peer research to avoid constructing its theoretical building blocks out of primarily North American data (Schneider, 1998). They are to be congratulated for following, in most cases, the methodologists' admonition to use multiple methods and to tap multiple sources of information. These methods included sociometrics (Eisenberg et al., Schneider et al., Sharabany, Xu et al., Verkuyten), peer and adult evaluations (Chen et al., Eisenberg et al., Nelson et al., Xu et al.), interviews (Azmitia et al., Cole et al., French et al., Goudena, Nelson et al., Sharabany, Way), and direct observations of behavior (Chen et al., Corsaro, Edwards et al., Gaskins, Goudena). Thus, the concerns noted earlier in this chapter about the use of self-report rating scales in different cultures, despite the economy and psychometric validity they bring, have not gone unheeded.

A Look Toward the Future

Our cross-cultural journey appears to have led us to an unarticulated set of methodological values (values seem to be a more fitting term than standards), which emphasize, first of all, studying cultures that the researchers know very well. We expect that researchers will continue to conceptualize cultures in a complex and multifaceted way when contemplating future studies. As a culture is explored in multidimensional detail, the psychological issues important to its members and to social scientists around the world come to light. As this process unfolds, researchers will surely continue to move beyond the limits of simple dimensional systems, (e.g., individualism/collectivism) and instead understand the unique ways that peer relationships exist within different cultural systems.

Hopefully, future studies will reflect even greater attention on some of the methodological considerations that have not been fully considered by researchers at this point. One of these is the need to move beyond the conceptualization of culture as a hermetically sealed unit independent of other cultures. Massive immigration and globalization have resulted in unprecedented contact among the world's cultures. As a result, many of the planet's citizens may be wrestling with problems inherent in reconciling divergent values that emerge from exposure to different cultures. Veroff and Goldenberger (1995) argue that this needs to be incorporated into the design of cross-cultural research. On a somewhat similar vein, many researchers argue for the systematic study of cultural change, some of which has been discussed in this volume. Given the many political upheavals that have occurred within our lifetimes, it is important for researchers to embrace a time perspective that can encompass not only the comprehensive measurement of culture at a single point in time but also the changes that many, if not most, cultures can undergo within a generation.

Two other important perspectives merit greater interest in future studies of children's relationships with their peers – the relationship perspective and the developmental perspective. The fact that we are studying individuals in relationship systems is reflected somewhat in the popularity of sociometric methods, which have remained in use for the past eighty years. Nevertheless, because the focus of the field has drifted toward the study of more intimate relationships at the dyadic and network levels (French et al., this volume; Schneider et al., this volume; Way, this volume), more attention needs to be paid to the analysis of dyadic and peer group data. The chapter by Card and Little (this volume) provides some suggestions regarding methodological approaches to do this. But researchers as well need to understand relationships as these exist within a cultural context. Such study might include investigations of the initiation, processes, and dissolution of these relationships. Findings reported in the chapter by French et al. on differences between the United States, Indonesia, and South Korea in the longevity of relationships illustrates some of richness of these areas of exploration.

Finally, the methodological lessons of developmental science need to become more central in the design of cross-cultural studies of children's peer relations. Indeed, several chapters in this book are based on longitudinal research (Chen et al., Corsaro, Eisenberg et al., Way). The authors of those chapters are able to capture the influences of culture in dynamic interaction with the influences of human development, contributing substantially to knowledge about both cultural influence and developmental change. One of the most formidable challenges faced by researchers who will continue the cross-cultural investigation of children's relationships with other children will be to replace a static perspective with a dynamic one, studying the constant changes in societies as well as the individuals within them, not to mention the developmental changes in the relationships in which these individuals participate.

References

Bergeron, N., & Schneider, B. H. (2005). Explaining cross-national differences in aggression: A quantitative synthesis. *Aggressive Behavior, 31*, 116–137.

Bethlehem, D. W. (1975). The effect of Westernization on cooperative behavior in Central Africa. *International Journal of Psychology, 10*, 219–224.

Campbell, D. T., & Narroll, R. (1972). The mutual methodological relevance of anthropology and psychology. In F. L. K. Hsu (Ed.), *Psychological anthropology* (pp. 435–468). Cambridge, England: Schenkman.

Chen, C., Lee, S. Y., & Stevenson, H. W. (1995). Response style and cross-cultural comparisons of rating scales among East Asian and North American students. *Psychological Science, 6*, 170–175.

Chen, X., Cen, G., Li, D., & He, Y. (2005). Social functioning and adjustment in Chinese children: The imprint of historical time. *Child Development, 76*, 182–195.

Chen, X., Rubin, K., & Sun, Y. (1992). Social reputation and peer relationships in Chinese and Canadian children: A cross-cultural study. *Child Development, 63*, 1336–1343.

Cole, M. (1996). *Cultural psychology: A once and future discipline*. Cambridge, MA: Harvard University Press.

Di Blas, L., Forzi, M., & Peabody, D. (2000). Evaluative and descriptive dimensions from Italian personality factors. *European Journal of Personality, 14*, 279–290.

Edwards, C. P. (1994). Cross-cultural research on Kohlberg's stages: The basis for consensus. In B. Puka (Ed.), *New research in moral development* (Vol. 5; pp. 373–384). New York: Garland.

Garcia-Coll, C. (2005). Editorial. *Developmental Psychology, 41*, 299–300.

Gudykunst, W. B., Ting-Toomey, S., & Chua, E. (1988). *Culture and interpersonal communication*. Newbury Park, CA: Sage.

Hofstede, G. (1980). *Culture's consequences: International differences in work-related values*. Beverly Hills, CA: Sage.

Jahoda, G., & Krewer, B. (1997). History of cross-cultural and cultural psychology. In J. W. Berry, P. R. Dasen, & T. S. Sawaswathi (Eds.), *Handbook of cross-cultural psychology* (Vol. 1, pp. 1–41). Needham Heights, MA: Allyn & Bacon.

Leung, K., & Bond, M. H. (1989). On the empirical identification of dimensions for cross-cultural comparisons. *Journal of Cross-Cultural Psychology, 23*, 498–509.

Markus, H. R., & Kitayama, S. (1991). Culture and the self: Implications for cognition, emotion, and motivation. *Psychological Review, 98*, 224–253.

Metzger, B. M. (1976). Trials of the translator. *Theology Today, 33*, 96–100.

McLoyd, V. C. (1990). The impact of economic hardship on Black families and children: Psychological distress, parenting, and socioemotional development. *Child Development, 61*, 311–346.

Oyserman, D., Coon, H. M., & Kemmelmeier, M. (2002). Rethinking individualism and collectivism: Evaluation of theoretical assumptions and meta-analyses. *Psychological Bulletin, 128*, 3–72.

Peng, K., Nisbett, R. E., & Wong, N. Y. (1997). Validity problems comparing values across cultures and possible solutions. *Psychological Methods, 2*, 329–344.

Rogoff, B. (2003). *The cultural nature of human development*. Oxford, England: Oxford University Press.

Saarni, C., Mumme, D. L., & Campos, J. J. (1998). Emotional development: Action, communication, and understanding. In W. Damon (Series Ed.) & N. Eisenberg (Vol. Ed.). *Handbook of child psychology* (Vol. 3, pp. 237–309). New York: Wiley.

Salkind, N. J., Kojima, H., & Zelniker, T. (1978). Cognitive tempo in American, Japanese, and Israeli children. *Child Development, 49*, 1024–1027.

Sameroff, A. J., & Haith, M. (Eds.). (1996). *The five to seven year shift: The age of reason and responsibility*. Chicago: University of Chicago Press.

Schneider, B. H. (1998). Cross-cultural comparison as doorkeeper in research on the social and emotional adjustment of children and adolescents. *Developmental Psychology, 34*, 793–797.

Schwartz, S. H., & Sagiv, L. (1995). Identifying culture-specifics in the content and structure of values. *Journal of Cross-Cultural Psychology, 26*, 92–116.

Shweder, R. A. (1993). The cultural psychology of the emotions. In M. Lewis & J. M. Haviland (Eds.), *Handbook of emotions* (pp. 417–434). New York: Guilford.

Singelis, T. M. (1994). The measurement of independent and interdependent self-construals. *Personality and Social Psychology Bulletin, 20*, 580–591.

Sinha, D. (1997). Indigenizing psychology. In J. W. Berry, P. R. Dasen, & T. S. Sawaswathi (Eds.), *Handbook of cross-cultural psychology* (Vol. 1, pp. 129–169). Needham Heights, MA: Allyn & Bacon.

Ting-Toomey, S. (1988). A face-negotiation theory. In Y. Kim & W. Gudykunst (Eds.), *Theory in interpersonal communication*. Newbury Park, CA: Sage.

Triandis, H. C. (1989). The self and social behavior in differing cultural contexts. *Psychological Review, 96*, 506–520.

Triandis, H. C. (1990). Cross-cultural studies of individualism and collectivism. In J. J. Berman, (Ed.), *Nebraska Symposium on Motivation, 1989: Cross-cultural perspectives* (pp. 41–133). Lincoln: University of Nebraska Press.

Turiel, E. (1998). The development of morality. In W. Damon (Series Ed.) & N. Eisenberg (Vol. Ed.), *Handbook of child psychology* (Vol. 3; pp. 863–932). New York: Wiley.

Valsiner, J., & Lawrence, J. A. (1997). Human development in culture across the lifespan. In J. W. Berry, P. R. Dasen, & T. S. Sawaswathi (Eds.), *Handbook of cross-cultural psychology* (Vol. 2, pp. 69–106). Needham Heights, MA: Allyn & Bacon.

Van de Vijver, F., & Leung, K. (1997). Methods and data analysis of comparative research. In J. W. Berry, P. R. Dasen, & T. S. Sawaswathi (Eds.), *Handbook of cross-cultural psychology* (Vol. 1, pp. 257–300). Needham Heights, MA: Allyn & Bacon.

Veroff, J. B., & Goldenberger, N. R. (1995). What's in a name? The case for intercultural psychology. In N. R. Goldenberger & J. B. Veroff (Eds.), *Culture and psychology* (pp. 1–22). New York: New York University Press.

Weisz, J. R., Chaiyasit, W., Weiss, B., Eastman, K. L., & Jackson, E. E. (1995). A multimethod study of problem behavior among Thai and American children in school: Teacher reports versus direct observations. *Child Development, 66*, 402–415.

Whiting, J. W. (1941). *Becoming a Kwoma: Teaching and learning in a New Guinea tribe*. New Haven, CT: Yale University Press.

Author Index

Subject Index